W9-AXQ-350

PSYCHOLOGICAL CONSULTATION AND COLLABORATION

INTRODUCTION TO THEORY AND PRACTICE

SIXTH EDITION

DUANE BROWN

University of North Carolina, Chapel Hill

WALTER B. PRYZWANSKY

University of North Carolina, Chapel Hill

ANN C. SCHULTE

North Carolina State University

PEARSON

Boston ■ New York ■ San Francisco
Mexico City ■ Montreal ■ Toronto ■ London ■ Madrid ■ Munich ■ Paris
Hong Kong ■ Singapore ■ Tokyo ■ Cape Town ■ Sydney

Executive Editor: Virginia Lanigan
Series Editorial Assistant: Scott Blaszak
Marketing Manager: Kris Ellis-Levy
Editorial-Production Service: Chestnut Hill Enterprises, Inc.
Manufacturing Buyer: Andrew Turso
Electronic Composition: Omegatype Typography, Inc.
Cover Administrator: Kristina Mose-Libon

For related titles and support materials, visit our online catalog at www.ablongman.com

Copyright © 2006, 2001, 1998, 1995, 1991, 1987 by Pearson Education, Inc.

All rights reserved. No part of the material protected by this copyright notice may be reproduced or utilized in any form or by any means, electronic or mechanical, including photocopying, recording, or by any information storage and retrieval system, without the written permission of the copyright owner.

To obtain permission(s) to use material from this work, please submit a written request to Allyn and Bacon, Permissions Department, 75 Arlington Street, Boston, MA 02116, or fax your request to 617-848-7320.

Between the time Website information is gathered and then published, it is not unusual for some sites to have closed. Also, the transcription of URLs can result in unintended typographical errors. The publisher would appreciate notification where these errors occur so that they may be corrected in subsequent editions. Thank you.

Library of Congress Cataloging-in-Publication Data
Brown, Duane.
    Psychological consultation and collaboration : introduction to theory and practice /
Duane Brown, Walter B. Pryzwansky, Ann C. Schulte.—6th ed.
        p.   cm.
    Rev. ed. of: Psychological consultation. 5th ed. © 2001.
    Includes bibliographical references and indexes.
    ISBN 0-205-41179-7 (alk. paper)
    1. Psychological consultation.   I. Pryzwansky, Walter B., 1939–   II. Schulte, Ann C.,
    1955–   III. Brown, Duane. Psychological consultation.   IV. Title.
BF637.C56B76 2005
158'.3—dc22

                                                                      2005002705

Printed in the United States of America
10   9   8   7   6   5   4   3   2   09   08   07   06

To
Caroline, Elizabeth, and Jason Keefer
William P. Erchul
and to
David and Scott Pryzwansky

CONTENTS

PREFACE

This sixth edition of *Psychological Consultation and Collaboration* is a milestone that few books reach. In 1987, when the first edition was published, we hoped that our work would reach a receptive audience and that hoped-for outcome has been realized. Since the publication of the first edition, interest in consultation has grown among almost all professional groups. Courses have been added and expanded in professional training programs, questions about consultation have been included in state licensing examinations, and role statements for many helping professionals now prominently feature consultation. Some journals such as the *Journal of Educational and Psychological Consultation* focus almost all of their attention on research and commentary about consultation, and many others regularly include articles about consultation. Clearly, many professionals and professional groups have embraced consultation as a viable helping and problem-solving strategy, but issues concerning consultation abound.

Cross-cultural consultation is one of the relatively new concerns for consultants. Most consultants realize that the Eurocentric models they have used since the 1970s are fraught with problems when used with Asian Americans, African Americans, Hispanic Americans, and American Indians. However, neither theory nor research provides clear guidelines for practice at this juncture. Nevertheless, we expanded our discussion of cross-cultural consultation in this issue by drawing on the extant literature and authoritative opinion. We believe that the beginning point for becoming a cross-cultural consultant is to develop a full understanding of one's own culture, including its strengths and weaknesses, and how the acculturation process has influenced the consultant's values and worldviews. Throughout this edition we remind the reader of his or her obligation to be knowledgeable about other cultures, culturally empathic, and skilled in cross-cultural interactions.

Collaboration and consultation have much in common, but at this time interest in collaboration as an alternative to consultation is growing rapidly, hence the name change for this edition. Consultants have long sought to make the consultation process more collaborative in all phases except intervention implementation. Now many consultants and others believe that they must take the final step, that is, collaborate in the implementation and evaluation of the intervention. This does not suggest that consultation is no longer useful, but in those cases in which it is necessary to ensure that the intervention be implemented as it was designed, collaboration may be the only viable approach. Moreover, when the task at hand is large, such as is the case with organizational reengineering, collaboration seems to be a more viable intervention than consultation when the multiplicity of factors involved is considered. Accordingly, we have placed a great deal of emphasis on collaboration in this edition.

Some issues are relatively new, while others have persisted throughout the history of consultation. One such issue is the matter of hierarchy in the consulting relationship. We address this issue just as we have in past editions. However, we take a definitive stand on the issue, particularly in Chapter 3, which outlines a behavioral–eclectic model of consultation and collaboration. Admittedly, we hedge on the issues in other places, particularly when the consultation involves consultees from cultures that are either matriarchal or patriarchal.

Although some would disagree, we do not accept the idea that there is a single best way to conduct consultation. As we have in the past, we have included chapters on the major approaches to consultation. We have also included chapters on the consulting process, the impact of consultant/collaborator and consultee characteristics on the processes, consulting with parents and consulting and collaborating with teachers, and evaluating the consulting/collaboration processes. Ethical and legal issues confronting consultants and a chapter dealing with trends and issues round out the sixth edition.

We are most appreciative of the informal support and feedback we have received from our friends and colleagues on earlier editions, and we invite additional comments regarding this edition. We are also indebted to the following reviewers who took their time either to provide extensive reviews or to answer questions about earlier editions and needs for changes: Colette L. Ingraham, San Diego State University; Raylene B. Statz, University of Mary Hardin-Baylor; Michael B. Salzman, University of Hawaii at Manoa. We hope that the changes made to this edition reflect their concerns and mirror their constructive feedback.

Duane Brown
Walter B. Pryzwansky
Ann C. Schulte

CHAPTER 1

INTRODUCTION TO CONSULTATION
ORATION

roduce, define, and differentiate
ther and from other intervention
orkers such as counselors, psy-

ion, and other interventions

laboration will be presented.
ons will be presented.

School counselors, school psychologists, school social workers, and other human services workers increasingly view collaboration as a viable alternative to consultation. Although collaboration and consultation have many common elements, there are important differences that will be identified and discussed in this section. This discussion will begin by looking at the definitions of *consultation* and *collaboration* with an emphasis on identifying points of convergence and divergence between the two processes. After the definitions of *consultation* and *collaboration* have been clarified, a brief history of the two processes will be presented. The final sections of this chapter will be devoted to some conjecture about the future of consultation and collaboration and an overview of the remainder of the book.

Defining Consultation and Collaboration

Over twenty years ago Mannino and Shore (1985, 1986) indicated that confusion existed regarding the definition of *consultation* and that the lack of definitional clarity was restricting its advancement. Gallessich (1982) and Conoley (1981b) had earlier made similar observations with the former pointing to cases in which consultation and training had been equated and the latter noting that advocacy and consultation were depicted as complementary processes. The differences among processes such as supervision, teaching, training, advocacy, and consultation will be explored later in this chapter, along with another definitional issue. In 1983 Idol-Maestas and her associates (Idol, Paolucci-Whitcomb, & Nevin, 1986; Idol-Maestas, 1983) introduced the term *collaborative consultation* and in doing so confounded the meaning of the two concepts in many people's minds, a confound that has not been clarified completely. More recently Reyes and Jason (1993) and West and Idol (1993) suggested that collaborative consultation is, in fact, a new model of consultation. Schulte and Osborne (1993) took exception to this claim, partially on the basis that historically consultation has been viewed as an in-direct service delivery model and their view that collaboration is a direct approach to delivering services to students. Some of the differences and similarities between consultation and collabora-tion will be taken up at this time, including the is-sue of consultation being an indirect service delivery model and collaboration being a direct approach to service delivery.

In 2003 Schulte and Osborne reviewed the definitions of *consultation* and *collaboration* in an attempt to clarify the two terms. They point out that some of the people who developed models of consultation (e.g., Bergan, 1977; Caplan, 1970; Dinkmeyer & Carlson, 1973) used the word *col-laborative* to denote the nature of the relationship between the consultant and the consultee. Schulte and Osborne also note that the term *collaborative relationship,* when used in conjunction with the consultation process, may have several connota-tions ranging from a relationship among equals to providing opportunities for the consultee to have input into the process. Based on Schulte and Os-borne's review, most but not all (e.g., Bergan, 1977; Erchul & Martens, 1997) authorities per-ceive the relationship between consultants and consultees in client-centered consultation as col-laborative in nature. Our view, like that of most other consultants, is that client–centered consulta-tion is an indirect service delivery model in which consultant and consultee develop strategies for aiding individuals, groups, or systems. Our view of the relationship will be discussed later.

Caplan (1970; Caplan & Caplan, 1993, 1999) may have been the first to differentiate between consultation and collaboration, but he provided few details about the differences between the two interventions. Pryzwansky (1974, 1977) provided detailed descriptions of the two processes. Both Caplan and Pryzwansky identify the major differ-ence between consultation and collaboration, which is that in consultation the consultee takes re-sponsibility for the implementation of the inter-vention and in collaboration the implementation of the intervention is a shared responsibility. To make this point somewhat differently, consultants work with consultees to assess the problem, set goals, and design interventions. Most consultants, with the exception of mental health consultants who only work with professionals (Caplan, 1970), also assume responsibility for teaching the intervention to the consultee and may share some of the respon-sibility for evaluating the outcomes of consultation. Collaborators work together from the beginning to the end, from problem identification to evaluation. According to Schulte and Osborne, Caplan and Pryzwansky concluded that collaboration might be a model of service delivery that is more acceptable when collaborators/consultants are internal to the organization. Current developments suggest that they may be correct.

Consultation and collaboration can be distin-guished from one another based on who delivers the intervention, but the matter of responsibility to the client is not resolved. Internal consultants such as school psychologists and school counselors must accept some of the responsibility for out-comes of consultation because of their ethical ob-ligations to clients and their contractual obligation to their school districts. It is well known by veteran consultants that the interventions designed by con-sultants and consultees are infrequently delivered as designed. Schulte and Osborne (2003) suggest that consultants have reacted to consultees' non-compliance by making the relationship more col-laborative. Taking the next step and adopting a collaborative approach to service delivery seems like a logical step toward compliance manage-ment. Moreover, legal guidelines embedded in the pending amendments to IDEA, the federal legisla-tion that governs the work of professionals who work with exceptional students, and professional guidelines relating to achievement and closing the achievement gap promulgated by the American School Counselor Association, seem likely to stimulate additional use of collaboration as a means of insuring the integrity of the intervention delivery process.

Consultation and collaboration are fundamen-tally different processes, but it is important to note that they are similar in many respects. Homan (2004) suggests that for collaboration to be effective collaborators must communicate clearly, trust each other, establish clear roles and agreements, monitor and evaluate, and provide for recognition of the collaborators. Steffy and Lindle (1994) and Fiedler (2000) make similar observations. Open, clear communication, relationships based on respect and trust, and clarity of roles are also important if the consultation process is to be successful. So, too, is the ability to monitor each step in the process and to evaluate both the process and outcomes of consultation. The human processes required in successful consultation and collaboration seem to be equivalent for the most part. Moreover, both consultation and collaboration are goal-oriented, thus collaborators and consultants and consultees need to subscribe to the same goals (Homan, 2004).

Perhaps the most significant similarity between collaboration and consultation is that they are both problem-solving processes, although the problem-solving processes engaged in by consultants and collaborators seem to vary to a considerable extent. The problem-solving model followed by consultants is typically portrayed as a six- or seven-step process including preentry for external consultants, relationship development, assessment of client or client system and consultee, goal setting, strategy or intervention selection, implementation, and evaluation. Rubin (2002) outlines a twelve-stage problem-solving process for collaboration. Although Rubin does not address the issue of who initiates the collaborative process directly, he seems to assume that collaboration is initiated by a person or persons who perceive that a problem exists and become actively engaged in identifying the best strategy to resolve the problem. The first step (1) that a collaborator or collaborators should take is determining whether collaboration is the best intervention to ameliorate the problem at hand. Professionals who practice consultation and involve themselves in collaborative problem solving typically have many problem-solving strategies. Caplan (1970) suggested that in-service training might be substituted for consultation if a number of consultees have knowledge or skills deficits. Supervision and advocacy may also be appropriate interventions.

However, if collaboration is the best intervention, the person or persons initiating the collaborative process should continue by: (2) developing a potential list of collaborators; (3) assessing the suitability of potential collaborators; (4) developing a recruitment strategy and recruiting collaborators; (5) developing roles and rules for the collaborators; (6) designing an action plan; (7) developing short-term objectives and interventions that will lead to success; (8) building bonds between and among partners; (9) celebrating success; (10) continuing to assess and build bonds among the collaborators; (11) being accountable by evaluating goal achievement; and (12) revisiting and renewing the mission of the collaborators. We would make at least one alteration in the collaboration sequence that Rubin suggests, that being that building bonds between collaborators should probably precede roles and rules development. Collaborative efforts typically involve teams that coalesce around a shared vision of the need for change (Keys, Bemak, Carpenter, & King-Sear, 1998; Rowley, Sink, & MacDonald, 2002). If these teams are to be successful, relationship development must come early in the process (Steffy & Lindle, 1994). Clearly the collaborative process that Rubin (2002) envisions is different in a number of important ways than the consultation process. Many of these differences relate to recruiting and energizing the collaborators.

Collaboration may be more suitable as a systems change strategy than consultation when the change agent is internal to the organization (Caplan, 1970; Pryzwansky, 1974, 1977). Consider the barriers faced by a school psychologist, school counselor, or school social worker who wishes to change the zero tolerance of drugs, fighting, and weapons at school because he or she documents that it alienates students from school and increases the likelihood of dropping out of school. That individual could consult with top-level administrators and the school board, but it seems likely that a collaborative effort that involves other stakeholders is more likely to be successful. External consultants are chosen by organizations to solve specific problems, and organizational consultants such as Schein (1969, 1989) have detailed models of systemic change that they can draw on. Internal consultants often identify existing problems, but they have the chore of convincing the organizational leaders that a problem exists and stimulating them to act. It seems likely that a team of collaborators will be more likely to convince members of the power structure that problems exist and that they have the collective expertise to deal with the concerns that have been identified than will an internal consultant.

Homan (2004), Fiedler (2002), Rubin (2002), Steffy and Lindle (1994), and Whitaker and Moses (1994) envision the goals of collaboration in somewhat grander terms than those that are typically assumed by internal consultants. These authors suggest that collaboration is a viable means of reforming schools via systemic change and/or systemic change in the community. One current approach to school reform, Total Quality Education (e.g., English & Hill, 1994), based on Total Quality Management (Deming, 1993), emphasizes the importance of collaboration in the reform process. Deming, who is credited with introducing the quality control approaches to Japan that revolutionized their manufacturing processes, emphasized both collaboration and systems thinking in all phases of management and educational processes. Deming believed that 85 percent of a worker's effectiveness is attributable to the worker's system and 15 percent to his or her skills. Other developments such as collaborative approaches to leadership in schools (Owens, 2004) and the 1997 and 2004 Amendments to IDEA, which emphasize team approaches to assessment and intervention of students with disabilities, have also increased interest in collaboration (Center for Effective Collaboration and Practice, 1998).

Collaboration appears to be well suited to change aimed at reorienting the practices of a school or community, but its utilization is not limited to large-scale problem-solving efforts. As Pryzwansky noted over three decades ago, collaboration can and often does occur in classroom settings, which, according to Bronfenbrenner (1979), is a system within the broader system of the school, when special education teachers and the regular classroom teachers collaborate to plan and deliver the educational experiences needed by exceptional children. Additionally, the American School Counselor Association (ASCA, 2003) has endorsed collaboration as a basic tool in the reorientation of school counseling programs so that they focus on enhancing educational achievement and in the design of comprehensive, K–12 school counseling programs. Reorienting the school counseling program and/or reshaping the nature of the program require systemic changes that focus on rather small aspects of the educational enterprise. ASCA's endorsement of collaboration as a basic strategy in program change is based on the extensive work of Gysbers and Henderson (2000) who designed a detailed, collaborative approach to renovating school counseling programs.

CONSULTATION DEFINED

Caplan (1970) set forth one of the most integrated definitions of *consultation* when he formulated his mental health consultation model. He stipulates that consultation involves a voluntary, nonhierarchical relationship between two professionals who are often of different occupational groups (e.g., psychologists and psychiatric nurses) and is initiated by the consultee for the purpose of solving a work-related problem. The goals of consultation, according to Caplan, are two-fold: to improve the consultee's functioning with a client, which may be an individual, a group, or an organization, and to develop the consultee's skills to the point that she or he will be able to cope with similar problems independently in the future. Caplan also stipulates that (1) typically the consultant comes from outside the consultee's organization, (2) consultation should not focus on the consultee's personal problems, and (3) the consultee has primary responsibility for implementing any solutions that evolve from the consultation process.

Although many consultants find Caplan's definition too restrictive (Heller, 1985; Meyers et al., 1979; Pryzwansky, 1974; Randolph, 1985), some of his ideas have become widely accepted, such as the triadic nature of the consultant–consultee–

client interaction and the collegial nature of the consultant–client relationship (Conoley & Conoley, 1991; Dinkmeyer & Carlson, 1973; Erchul & Martens, 1997; Gallessich, 1982; Keller, 1981; Fuqua & Kurpius, 1993; Meyers et al., 1979; Reynolds, Gutkin, Elliot, & Witt, 1984).

Two aspects of Caplan's definition have received a great amount of criticism: the external locus of the consultant and the sole responsibility of the consultee for implementing solutions generated in the process. Most current authorities on consultation agree that the consultant may belong to the same organization as the consultee (be internal versus external) and may continue to work with the consultee while he or she carries out the plans developed in consultation (e.g., Bergan, 1977; Dinkmeyer & Carlson, 1973; Fuqua & Kurpius, 1993; Gallessich, 1982; Lippitt & Lippitt, 1986; Meyers, et al., 1979; Randolph, 1985). School counselors, school psychologists, clinical and counseling psychologists, social workers, and psychiatric nurses regularly consult within their own organization as well as with members of other organizations and provide guidance, support, and assistance to consultees during the implementation of a strategy that grows out of consultation.

Another facet of Caplan's definition that has drawn a great deal of opposition is that consultation can only take place between two professionals. It should be recalled that Caplan's approach was developed in response to a certain set of conditions (i.e., the flood of refugee children that overwhelmed professionals in post–World War II Israel) that influenced his consultation model. Consultants working under different circumstances have reached different conclusions. Lippitt and Lippitt (1986) depict the consultation process as one that occurs between a consultant and a wide variety of individuals and systems, including families, voters' organizations, communities, political parties, and so forth. Heller (1985) echoes this sentiment in part when he describes consultation as one means of empowering disenfranchised social groups. Brown, Wyne, Blackburn, and Powell (1979) and Snapp and Davidson (1982) also reflect a portion of the Lippitt and Lippitt (1986) perspective when they indicate that students may be consultees.

The implicit question embedded in Caplan's (1970) view and those of Lippitt and Lippitt (1986) and others is, What is the essence of consultation? Is it an independent help-giving process that can be differentiated on its own merit from other helping processes? Or does the nature of the role-players determine when consultation occurs? Certainly many consultants in addition to Caplan (e.g., Conoley & Conoley, 1991; Gallessich, 1982; Meyers et al., 1979; Parsons & Meyers, 1984) appear to opt for the latter definition. The strength of the position that holds that consultation must occur between two professionals is that it adds precision to the definition. The weakness of this position is that it precludes the use of consultation services with parents, teachers' aides, line supervisors, nonprofessional members of community groups, students, or the groups to which they belong. (Jane Close Conoley has changed her earlier view somewhat, now holding that it is the process that makes consultation unique, not the parties involved.)

A final area of controversy regarding a definition of *consultation* is related to the one just discussed. If one accepts the idea of consultation with a family (Brown, et al., 1979; Lippitt & Lippitt, 1986; Sheridan, 1993), is the focus a work-related problem? Similarly, if one accepts Heller's (1985) ideas about working with community groups to help them assert their political muscle, is the focus a work-related problem? In the strict Caplanian sense, the answer to both of these questions is "no." However, most consultants would agree that the focus of consultation is upon all vital processes engaged in by consultees, including communication, their use of technology, their sources of information and resources, the way information and resources are transformed to achieve goals, and the products produced (Katz & Kahn, 1978; Werner & Tyler, 1993). As an example, consultation with a community group would focus upon the work of that group, broadly conceived. Consultation with a parent might focus on the information he or she has about child rearing, how that information is used, and the result (his or her children's behavior).

It is clearly the position here that Caplan's (1970) definition unduly restricts the utilization of consultation for many. It is equally the case that Caplan's definition is a viable one for the consultant who expects to practice the mental health model he set forth. There are no right and wrong definitions of *consultation* until one begins to consider the assumptions that underpin the process. However, a broader definition of *consultation* has been adopted by the authors that is more in keeping with that of Lippitt and Lippitt (1986) and that corresponds more closely to the assumptions we make about consultation in the pages that follow.

Human service consultation is defined as a voluntary problem-solving process that can be initiated and terminated by either the consultant or consultee. It is engaged primarily for the purpose of assisting consultees to develop attitudes and skills that will enable them to function more effectively with a client, which can be an individual, group, or organization for which they have responsibility. Thus, the goals of the process are two-fold: enhancing services to third parties and improving the ability of consultees to function in areas of concern to them.

The consultation relationship is an egalitarian one and in its most productive form is characterized by openness, warmth, genuineness, and empathy, since authentic communication is essential to the success of the enterprise. Even though the parameters of the consulting relationship in many ways parallel those associated with a therapeutic relationship, including the confidentiality of the communication, consultation does not focus on the psychological problems of consultees directly. The consultant may, however, point to psychological deficits of consultees that restrict their ability to deal with certain problems and suggest courses of actions to deal with them.

During consultation, the consultant may assume various roles. In crisis situations, consultants may shift temporarily to an expert mode, diagnose the problem, and prescribe solutions. At other times, the consultant may simply function as a process observer and help consultees to develop awareness of processes that are impairing their functioning in a subsystem or system. Generally speaking, however, collaboration between the consultant and consultee at each phase of the consultation process is encouraged, with the guiding principle being that consultees are to assume as much responsibility for the process as their current status permits. The consultant's functioning in the expert role for long periods of time is particularly deleterious to the consultee since it all but precludes her or him from developing the skills needed to gain independence from the consultant. Functioning in the process observation mode can be an effective means of facilitating consultee growth, but a more intense and active collaboration is more likely to achieve the long-term goals of consultation.

Finally, consultation may be delivered equally well by internal or external sources, depending to some degree on the nature of the problem, the consultee, and the environmental variables. The essence of this definition is summarized in the following list:

1. Initiated by either consultee or consultant.
2. Relationship characterized by authentic communication.
3. Consultees may be professionals or nonprofessionals.
4. Provides direct services to consultees, assisting them to develop coping skills that ultimately make them independent of consultant.
5. Is triadic in that it provides indirect services to third parties (clients).
6. Types of problems considered are work related when the concept of work is broadly conceived.
7. Consultant's role varies with consultee's needs.
8. Locus of consultant may be internal or external.
9. All communication between consultant and consultee is confidential.

Consultation Contrasted to Other Helping Relationships

In order to clearly differentiate between consultation and other helping services, it may be useful to contrast consultation with advice giving, advocacy, supervision, therapy/counseling, teaching, and organizational development. Organizational development (OD) involves a series of processes including training, action research, and consultation that are utilized by a change agent to enhance the functioning of an organization (Lippitt & Lippitt, 1986; Smith & Corse, 1986). The organizational development specialist may choose from any of these strategies depending upon the needs of the organization. However, an OD specialist who enters an organization as a consultant may employ action research such as surveys of employee perceptions of problems and proposed solutions to those problems. Similarly, training may be used as one of a vast assortment of interventions in the consulting process (Lippitt & Lippitt, 1986). Consulting, then, is one of the roles that an OD specialist may assume, although it is interrelated to a large degree with training and action research.

"Teaching is a process of imparting, in a planned systematic way, a specified body of information" (Conoley & Conoley, 1991, p. 4). As noted in the foregoing paragraph, teaching (training) is a tool that consultants employ in the consultation process, usually as a part of an intervention strategy, although it could very well be used in other stages of consultation. Teaching in the traditional sense is often a formal, didactic situation and is rarely collaborative. Much of the so-called teaching that occurs in consultation, however, is more informal and involves various forms of modeling rather than lecturettes and homework (Conoley & Conoley, 1991).

Human resource consultants increasingly find themselves in a role that stands in stark contrast to consultation: advocacy. Consultants work directly with consultees to enhance their ability to provide services to their clients. Advocates act on behalf of the disenfranchised and less powerful in our society to help them gain access to resources and services that are rightfully theirs. For example, rehabilitation psychologists may contact employers and ask them to bring their workplaces into compliance with the legal requirements set forth in the Americans with Disabilities Act. Social work-

ers may contact social welfare agencies on behalf of their non-English-speaking clients to ascertain that communication to them is in their native language, and special educators may act to ensure that the plans set forth in individualized education plans for learning-disabled students are followed. Consultation and advocacy are very different processes, but both may be employed by mental health professionals and others in their efforts to empower the people they serve (Conoley, 1981a, b).

Consulting and advocacy are separate processes. Consultants enter into implicit or explicit contracts to work with consultees to solve various types of problems. What happens when consultation fails? In many instances the consultant has fulfilled his or her contractual obligations and the process is at an end. However, there are times when legal obligations and moral and ethical imperatives require the consultant to become an advocate for the client. Consider the school psychologist or special educator who consults with a teacher who is hesitant to adopt the best instructional strategies for an emotionally disturbed student. In all likelihood the first step in securing services for the student would be to contact the parents because of the legal process outlined in IDEA. However, should parents not exercise their rights and advocate on behalf of the child, it is incumbent on the psychologist or special educator to represent the student to the principal or other decision makers who can correct the situation. Similarly, school counselors who consult with principals who refuse to change policies that retard the development of students, such as repressive disciplinary policies or institutional racism, are morally obligated to advocate for the students in the school.

Therapy/counseling is a direct relationship in which the aim is to alter the behavior of the person (client) receiving the service. Like consulting, it is usually predicated upon the assumption that a human relationship characterized by genuineness and trust is necessary for success. Also, like consultation, the goal of therapy/counseling is to produce an independent client. However, the direct nature of the service clearly differentiates it from consultation, as do the depth and intensity of the client-therapist relationship and the fact that there is usually a direct focus on the client's defenses. Mental health consultation, which will be discussed in Chapter Two, most closely parallels therapy and counseling because of Caplan's focus on addressing consultee perceptions and distortions that are interfering with his or her functioning (Conoley & Conoley, 1991).

Supervision also has some similarities with consultation as well as some important differences. Perhaps the most important differences lie in the nature of the relationship. Supervisors are clearly the experts in most supervisory relationships and are often authority figures as well because their evaluations lead to grades, raises, promotions, and so forth. This contrasts with the democratic relationship presupposed here and advocated by most consultants with the exception of Caplan's (1970) client-centered model of mental health consultation. Although supervisors aim to increase the functioning of supervisees, the evaluative nature of the relationship makes it difficult, if not impossible, to establish a totally nonthreatening relationship (Caplan, 1970; Conoley & Conoley, 1991; Gallessich, 1982).

Advice giving is probably the process most often confused with consultation. As Gallessich (1982) points out, when we use the term *consultation* colloquially, we are for the most part referring to seeking or giving advice. However, a number of implicit and explicit aspects of the advice process distinguishes it from consultation. First, one person assumes an expert role. Second, there is no explicit intention to develop expertise in the person receiving the advice. Thus, when a similar situation arises in the future, the recipient in all likelihood will have to return to the source of the advice. Third, no particular type of relationship is assumed to exist between the advice giver and receiver, although it is certainly one of expert to novice.

OTHER ISSUES

As we have already seen, many differences arise when consultation is defined. A number of conflicting issues exist in other aspects of consultation

as well. A few of the more important ones will be discussed briefly at this point.

Terminology

Three chief actors have been identified in relationship to the human services consultation process: consultant, consultee, and client. The consultant, working directly with the consultee, provides indirect services to a third party, a client. This terminology is for the most part in keeping with that employed traditionally by consultants working in human service agencies. However, a vast body of literature exists that focuses upon consulting in business and industry. In this literature (e.g., Lippitt, 1982; Lippitt & Lippitt, 1986; Steele, 1975) the client is the person with whom the consultant actually works. No rationale for this discrepancy appears in the professional literature. It could be conjectured that because much of the organizational consultation literature was developed by external consultants who consulted for pay, businesses were viewed as clients, or those who pay for services. In a practical sense, this distinction is unimportant and does not serve as a barrier to the literature, as long as the reader is aware that it exists.

Lack of True Theories

Gallessich (1982) critiqued the major approaches to consultation, which she termed clinical, mental health, behavioral, and organizational. The clinical model, sometimes termed the medical or expert service model, grew out of the medical tradition where physicians who possessed more expertise were asked to assist in diagnosing the problems being experienced by other physicians' patients. Gallessich suggests that this model has no cohesive theoretical base. Similarly, she holds that the mental health consultation model (Caplan, 1970), the behavioral model (Bergan, 1977; Russell, 1978), and the organizational consultation model (Lippitt & Lippitt, 1986; Meyers, 1978; Schein, 1969; Steele, 1975) suffer from the same malady: no integrated theoretical base.

Gallessich (1982) contends that the lack of good models has created a crisis in consultation

---

Student Learning Exercise 1.1

Label each of the following based on what you have learned in this chapter.

1. Imparting information

2. Dyadic, hierarchical consulting process

3. Empowering others by assuming their cause

4. Triadic helping process assumed to be nonhierarchical

5. Helping process involving evaluation and skill development

6. Everyone involved in the intervention process

7. Triadic process assumed to be hierarchical

8. Dyadic helping process assumed to require therapeutic relationship

9. Cross-cultural consultation requires this

10. High level of self-control valued by—

11. Groups most likely to tell you how they feel

12. Groups that are *least* likely to be future-oriented if unacculturated.

13. Would not welcome a firm handshake

14. Suspicious of people who do not make direct eye contact

15. Place the group ahead of the individual

---

1. Teaching 2. Expert or doctor–patient model 3. Advocacy. 4. Consultation (specifically client-centered consultation) 5. Supervision 6. Corroboration 7. Collaboration 8. Counseling or therapy 9. Cultural competence or cultural empathy 10. Asian Americans and American Indians 11. European Americans, Hispanic Americans, African Americans, Hispanic Americans 12. American Indians, Hispanic Americans 13. Asian Americans, Hispanic Americans, Native Americans 14. European Americans, Asian Americans 15. Hispanic American groups, most American Indian tribes

---

because techniques are not linked to conceptual or empirical foundations. The result, she believes, is that consultants do not use a coherent approach to focus their practice. She fears and draws support from numerous others (e.g., Bardon, 1985; Bowen, 1977; Glaser, 1981) that the lack of conceptual models will result in harmful consultation processes because atheoretical approaches may not allow for clear role descriptions that are needed by the consultant and consultee. Gallessich also believes that consultation without a clear conceptual

base may be technique-ridden and may not provide the consultant with adequate boundary parameters. As a result, the consultant may inadvertently stray into areas that are "off limits."

While Gallessich's (1982) concerns about the status of conceptual models of consultation appear to have some legitimacy, there is certainly some room for disagreement with such a bleak picture. Dinkmeyer and Carlson (1973) set forth a consultation model based upon the individual psychology of Alfred Adler; Bergan (1977) articulated a carefully conceived approach to consultation anchored primarily in operant learning theory. A third model, Brown and Schulte (1987), which grew out of the tenets of social learning theory (Bandura, 1977a, b), will be presented in Chapter Three. Recently, Fuqua and Kurpius (1993), Brack, Jones, Smith, White, and Brack (1993), Rockwood (1993), and Ross (1993) have discussed more than a half-dozen models of organizational consultation, and Martens (1993) has clarified the original behavioral model set forth by Bergan. It is undoubtedly the case that each of the current models of consultation is open to criticism, but the field has no shortage of models and theories.

Dimensions of Collaboration at the Systems Level

Collaboration can be dyadic, for example, when a special education resource teacher works with a regular classroom teacher to design and deliver curricular materials for the disabled students in the class. However, collaboration often involves teams or groups, defined here as any collaborating group with more than two people (Homan, 2004). Collaborating dyads or teams can have limited objectives, such as those developed by the resource teacher and the regular classroom teacher, or they can have goals that entail reengineering the entire enterprise, whether it is a school, school district, university, or business. From some perspectives (e.g., Bronfenbrenner, 1979), any intervention is a systemic intervention and, to a certain extent, we agree with this perspective. However, in this discussion we take a more circumscribed view of a *system,* which we define as an entity that has clearly differentiated subsystems.

Collaborative teams may establish either formal or informal agreements (Whitaker & Moses, 1994), but regardless of the nature of the agreement they co-labor on two levels to achieve a common goal. These twin foci are the task to be accomplished and the relationships among team members and the people affected by the problem-solving strategy. Collaboration begins with aligning peo-

ple's goals and actions to accomplish the task at hand, according to Rubin (2002). He goes on to suggest that collaboration may involve short-term or long-term problem-solving alliances. Short-term collaboration typically focuses on solving an immediate problem, while long-term alliances are more likely to be focused on systemic change. Rubin suggests that, when collaboration is used as a long-term system change strategy, it is a tool of the *change agent,* a term that seems to be preferred by many, instead of consultant or collaborator (Havelock & Zlotolow, 1995). Rubin goes on to indicate that systemic change requires changing the people in the system and that this can only be accomplished by managing relationships with them.

Change agents who initiate collaborative efforts at the system level form teams, the members of which assume roles that may change from time to time (Homan, 2004). Leaders are core participants and would include the change agent. Other team members would include workers who are active throughout the problem-solving process, occasional collaborators who move in and out of the team, one-time collaborators, advisors who provide technical assistance to the team, and general supporters of the team who are nonparticipants but who lend moral support to the team. Homan indicates that assisters and one-time participants typically overestimate their interest in or the time required to participate in the project at hand and drop out as a result. People who drop out should be retained in the communication network, as should advisors who are often one-time or short-term participants in the change effort. Nonparticipants who are inactive, but who are willing to identify themselves as supporters of the change effort or who write an occasional letter of support, should also be included in the communication network.

Steffy and Lindle (1994) identify some of the functions of the people on the collaborative team. Leaders prepare for and facilitate the meetings of the group including making process observations about the group's meetings, clarifying issues, and identifying the positive and negative aspects of the meetings. They may also keep minutes of the meeting and work to ensure that all stakeholders are kept in the communication loop.

Creating a viable collaborative team begins at the point at which the change agent begins the process of recruiting team members. This is done by establishing that the collaborative team involves a relationship of equals involving mutual respect and collegiality. When the collaborative team is an interagency group, assurances that each agency will retain its autonomy is in order from the outset. Importantly, the skills needed to function as a part of a collaborative team may require some type of training for members (Whitaker & Moses, 1994).

Collaboration is a complex process with many elements. We have adopted the following definition of *collaboration* for this book: Collaboration may be a formal process in which the roles and resources of the people and agencies involved are rather carefully set forth in the form of contracts. It may also be an informal process in which the roles and relationships of collaborators evolve as the conditions change. Collaboration may be a short-term problem-solving process or a long-term systemically oriented change process engaged in by two or more collaborators. Effective collaboration requires collaborators to view themselves as full partners and that they work to establish relationships based on respect and trust. Collaborators work to align the goals of their units or agencies and then pool the human and financial resources of their agencies to focus on the problem at hand. Change agents who conclude that collaboration is the change process of choice identify, recruit, and train collaborators. Once this step is concluded, the collaborative process continues with the use of databased approaches to describe and assess the nature of the problem, design strategies to resolve the problem, implement those strategies, and evaluate the outcomes. Continued monitoring and evaluation of the intervention follows.

What Collaboration Is Not

In the section dedicated to defining *consultation,* a number of processes that are sometime errone-

ously viewed as consultation were identified and defined, establishing that collaboration is not equivalent to consultation. However, a term that could easily be seen as similar to, or the same as, collaboration is *cooperation.* Cooperation is more of a superficial arrangement than is collaboration (Whitaker & Moses, 1994). Collaboration requires pooling resources. Cooperation does not. Collaboration requires work on shared goals. Cooperation may not require that cooperating agencies have the same goals. For example, schools may cooperate with social agencies by making referrals or providing background information, but they may be unaware of the agencies' goals or the strategies that are being used to achieve those goals. In fact, some agencies purposely erect barriers to protect themselves from incursions from outsiders. Collaboration requires that subsystems within organizations or agencies in the community (suprasystem) work together to set common goals, pool human and financial resources, and craft strategies that will resolve a defined problem. Internal collaboration requires that the boundaries between and among groups be lowered and that territoriality as it relates to the problem to be solved be eliminated. Similarly, collaboration between two agencies requires action that moves both agencies toward aligning their goals and seeking ways to work together to achieve them.

Earlier we discussed how the use of the term *collaborative consultation* might have caused confusion regarding the understanding of the two processes. We pointed out that, even though numerous aspects of consultation require collaboration, they are not the same. More recently, collaboration has been used in conjunction with another term, *advocacy.* In Fiedler's (2000) discussion of collaboration, he outlines the process of advocacy-oriented collaboration, which suggests that collaborators may engage in advocacy, an assumption that we believe is accurate. As we noted earlier, advocacy is a process in which a person or group speaks on behalf of another person or group in order to bring about change (Anderson, Chitwood, & Hayden, 1997). Therefore, an advocate is someone who takes up the cause of another person or group

(Alper, Schloss, & Schloss, 1994). Advocacy is a problem-solving process, as Hines (1987) suggests, and so is collaboration, but there are at some important differences between advocacy and collaboration. An individual may assume the role of advocate. Collaboration requires at least two people to participate. Advocates represent people. Collaborators work in conjunction with people. Advocacy grows out of a legal and/or moral imperative. Collaboration may grow out of a moral or legal imperative, but it may also be the result of a routine desire to reform current practices to make them more effective. As Fiedler suggests, collaborators may become advocates for the disenfranchised, the abused, or for people who cannot act on their own behalf. However, not all collaboration is advocacy oriented. Collaborators may choose advocacy as a strategy, but it seems unlikely that most collaboration will involve advocacy.

History of Consultation and Collaboration

Consultation and collaboration share historical roots to some degree, but for the most part they stem from different backgrounds. The earliest form of consultation can be traced to the clinical model exemplified by the doctor–patient relationship practiced in the thirteenth century (Gallessich, 1982). This clinical or expert model was practiced widely by the middle of the nineteenth century and continues in vogue in the medical community to the present time. In this approach an attending physician requests that a physician who has a higher level of knowledge regarding a specific malady examine his or her patient and render a diagnosis, often in the form of a written report. Patients are passive participants in this triadic model of doctor, expert, and patient. They present themselves for examination, the referring doctor receives the diagnosis, and medication or other treatment is prescribed. The referring physician is also somewhat passive, but he or she does identify the patient's health problem, at least in general terms, and arranges for the referral. The attending physician or the physician to whom the patient is referred may provide the treat-

ment depending on a host of factors, including the patient's wishes. Tharp and Wetzel (1969) used an expert model of consultation to train what they termed *mediators* to deliver services based on behavioral psychology. Erchul (1987) and his associates (Erchul & Chewning, 1990; Erchul & Martens, 1997) still subscribe to a consultation model based on a hierarchical relationship in which the consultant's intent is to control the nature of the intervention by controlling the nature of the consultation interview and by systematically reinforcing behavior that is aligned with the consultant's goals. However, the expert approach to consulting has declined in popularity because of the advancement of other approaches to consulting, the aversion of many human services consultants to the authoritarian philosophy underpinning the model, and the belief that the model fosters resistance to implementation of solutions generated by consultants and consultees (Schulte & Osborne, 2003).

Client-centered consultation, a term proposed by Caplan in his classic book, *The Theory and Practice of Mental Health Consultation* (1970), has its roots in education, psychology, and psychiatry, and accords both the consultee and the client a more active role in the consultation process. Caplan posited that it was necessary for the relationship between the consultant and consultee to be nonhierarchical, a relationship between equals. However, Schulte and Osborne (2003) report that Caplan did not totally eschew the authoritarian model because he believed that the consultant might have to override the wishes of the consultee from time to time in order to ensure that the consultant's views were represented in the intervention.

Organizational consultation is a triadic model of consultation that is historically linked to Kurt Lewin's (1951) field theory, and more recently, to systems theory (Bertalanffy, 1962). Elements of Lewin's field theory and his emphasis on action research as well as systems theory can also be found in the literature regarding collaboration (e.g., Havelock & Zlotolow, 1995; Rubin, 2002). Both organizational development consultation and collaboration are humanistic, based on the assumption that co-equal relationships during the change process are necessary for success. Deming's (1993) Total Quality Management approach to quality control has had a profound impact on management and leadership theory and ideas about organizational change in business and education and has increased the value associated with collaboration in the process. Deming, who died in 2003, espoused four basic concepts that included setting long-term goals, eliminating fear, jealousy, revenge, and anger from the management and change process, eliminating practices that undermine self-confidence, and fostering all opportunities to give people pride in their work and the improvements that take place. Additionally, he outlined a 14-step improvement process that will be examined in detail in Chapter 5

The perspectives of social workers and others have also influenced the evolution of our ideas about consultation and collaboration. Homan (2004), who is a social worker, emphases using systems theory as the basis for understanding the workings of the community and collaboration as the primary intervention to bring about community change. Steffy & Lindle (2004), both of whom are educational administrators, also stress the importance of identifying and integrating the systems in the community, using collaborative strategies. Fiedler (2000), a special educator, expresses a similar view. Consultation and collaboration are evolving and will continue to do so into the foreseeable future. Table 1.1 contains a series of milestones in the evolution of both consultation and collaboration.

Cultural Assumptions of Consultation and Consultation

Throughout this book we will consider cultural issues as they relate to consultation and collaboration. The issue of cross-cultural consultation is not new (e.g., Gibbs, 1980), but the discussion of cultural issues as well as issues such as gender has intensified (Brown, 2001; Celano & Kaslow, 2000;

Duncan, 1995; Duncan & Pryzwansky, 1993; Dustin & Ehly, 1992; Harris, 1993; Lopez, 2000; Sheridan & Henning-Stout, 1994). In an increasingly diverse society, consultants and collaborators may find that some consultees and collaborators prefer one model of consultation to another or may accept collaboration more readily than consultation.

Approximately a quarter-century ago, Pinto (1981) suggested that for consultants to be effective they must become what he termed *culturally empathic*. More recently, Cross-Bazron, Dennis, and Isaacs (1989) and Davis (1997) used the term *cultural competence* to describe the same phenomenon. Cultural empathy or cultural competence is the ability to understand the unique perspective of people from other cultures, assimilate cultural knowledge about an individual or group, and develop specific policies and practices to increase the quality of the consultation provided. As Pinto (1981) and King, Sims, and Osher (n.d.) suggest, culturally competent consultants or collaborators must value diversity, be aware of their own cultural heritage and its values, be aware that cross-cultural interaction results in different dynamics than when people of the same culture interact, and be able to alter their consultation paradigm in a manner that produces positive outcomes.

Altarriba and Bauer (1998) and Brown (2001) suggest that one way to operationalize what Pinto (1981) termed a *client-centered adaptive consulting style* is to first be sensitive to the communication style and cultural values of the consultee and to tailor the interview and problem-solving process to these variables. Srebalus and Brown (2001) indicate that critical aspects of nonverbal communication such as eye contact, handshakes, use of interpersonal space, and facial expressions may differ depending on the culture of the individual. Verbal styles also vary among cultural groups. A summary of some of these similarities and differences can be seen in Table 1.2.

A summary of the traditional values, that is, the values of unacculturated groups and individuals, can be seen in Table 1.3. The values listed there are based on a taxonomy developed by Kluckhorn

TABLE 1.1   Critical Events in the History of Consultation and Collaboration

Early 13th Century	Clinical model of consultation used by physicians
1920s	Lightmer Witmer, a psychologist, consults with school personnel to improve the education of children with disabilities.
1951	Lewin publishes his field theory.
1962	Bertalanffy publishes *General System Theory,* which outlines the theory he had been discussing since the mid-1940s.
1967	Tharp and Wetzel publish *Behavior modification in the natural environment,* which outlines a model of consultation that involves training moderators to deliver behavioral interventions.
1969	Schein publishes *Process Consultation: It's Role in Organizational Development,* which draws upon field theory and humanistic psychology to set forth a model of organizational consultation.
1970	Caplan publishes *The Theory and practice of mental health consultation,* which identifies four models of consultation including client-centered approaches. He also identified collaboration as distinct from consultation.
1970	Bennis publishes *Beyond Bureaucracy,* which applies systems thinking to understanding organization and outlines his process model of consultation.
1972	Altrocchi identified collaboration as distinct from consultation.
1973	Dinkmeyer and Carlson publish *Consulting: Facilitating Human Potential and Change Processes,* which sets forth a model based on Adlerian psychology.
1974, 1977	Pryzwansky suggests that collaboration is a different model of service delivery in that it involves direct delivery of services to students.
1975	Mannino and Shore publish *Effecting change through consultation,* which is one of the early organizational development consultation publications. It appeared in an edited book, *The Practice of Mental Health Consultation.*
1977	Bergan publishes *Behavioral Consultation,* which is based primarily on operant learning principles. His model, along with Caplan's, become the most influential models of consultation in education.
1978	Katz and Kahn publish, *The Social Psychology of Organizations,* which is one of the earliest applications of systems theory to organizations.
1979	Meyers, Parsons and Martin reconceptualize mental health consultation to make it more applicable in school settings.
1987	Brown and Schulte set forth a model of consultation based on Albert Bandura's social learning theory.
1987	Erchul publishes the first in a series of articles examining the nature of the collaborative relations in consultation. He concludes that the relationship should be hierarchical.
1993	Deming publishes *The New Economics for Industry, Government and Education,* in which he sets forth the idea that Total Quality Management (TQM), which is based on systems theory and using collaborative approaches, is the preferred approach to systems management and change.
1994	Corwin Press publishes a series of 12 books for educational administrators that highlight Total Quality Education, which draws on W. Edwards Deming TQM and emphasizes the importance of collaboration.
1997	Erchul and Martens publish *School Consultation: Conceptual and Empirical Bases of Practice,* which, among other things reaffirms the importance of the hierarchical relationship in behavioral consultation.
1999	Gutkin and Erchul debate the research finding regarding collaborative and non-collaborative approaches in consultation in the *Journal of School Psychology.*
2003	The American School Counselor Association endorses the importance of collaboration in the work of school counselors suggesting the collaboration is one of the themes that should underpin all that they do.

TABLE 1.2 Nonverbal Communication Styles among U.S. Cultural Groups

	PREFERRED STYLE IN HELPING	IMPLICATIONS
EUROPEAN AMERICANS		
Eye Contact	Maintain eye contact during conversations at least three-quarters of the time	Eye contact is a sign of respect Lack of eye contact may be interpreted as dishonesty
Interpersonal Space	Prefer 36–42 inches of interaction space	Closer interaction space may be seen as invasion of personal space; farther away may be equated to withdrawal
Nods; Facial Expressions	Smiles and head nods indicate interest	Failure to smile or nod head seen as a sign of disinterest
Handshake	Firm	"Weak fish" handshake may be interpreted as lack of enthusiasm or a weak personality
AMERICAN INDIANS		
Eye contact	Indirect	Direct eye contact may be viewed as disrespectful
Interpersonal Space	Respectful distance initially; later much closer distances are okay	Initially, close interpersonal distances may be viewed as invasion of personal space
Nods; Facial Expressions	Few smiles and head nods	Until client knows helper, smiles and head nods may be seen as a lack of self-control or foolishness
Handshake	Soft and pliable	Firm handshake may be viewed as aggression
AFRICAN AMERICAN		
Eye Contact	May look away when helper is speaking; can show disrespect in same manner	Lack of eye contact is seen as disrespectful
Interpersonal Space	36–42 inches preferred	More tolerant of closer distances than European Americans
Nods; Facial Expression	Expressive; nods and facial expressions common	Prefer helper to smile and exhibit warmth
Handshake	Firm; males may use brother's handshake	May misinterpret weak handshake as lack of enthusiasm
HISPANICS		
Eye Contact	Indirect eye contact, at least initially	Uncomfortable with eye contact; sign of intimacy
Interpersonal Space	24–36 inches with no barriers	Larger distances and barriers may be interpreted as aloofness
Nods; Facial Expressions	Initially reserved; smiles and head nod may occur frequently later	Lack of smiles may be seen as lack of interest or enthusiasm
Handshake	Firm for males; soft and pliable for unacculturated females	For males, weak handshake may be viewed as lack of enthusiasm
ASIAN AMERICANS		
Eye contact	Indirect	Direct eye contact may be seen as aggression or sign of unwanted affection
Interpersonal Space	Prefer respectful distance, 36 to 42 inches okay	May interpret closer interactions as aggression or unwanted affection
Nods; Facial Expressions	Few smiles, head nods may be used to signal respect	Smiles from client may convey negative feelings such as embarrassment
Handshake	Soft and pliable	Firm handshake may be viewed as aggression

Source: Srebalus, D. J., & Brown D. (2001). *Guide to the helping professions.* Boston: Allyn & Bacon (pp. 60–61). By permission of the publisher.

TABLE 1.3 Stylistic Differences in Verbal Communication among Cultural Groups in the United States

GROUP	SELF-DISCLOSURE	LOUDNESS	RAPIDITY	INTERRUPTIONS	PAUSES	DIRECTNESS
European American	acceptable; content oriented	moderate	moderate	acceptable	yes; may make uncomfortable	direct; task oriented
American Indian	unacceptable; loss of control	soft	slow; controlled	unacceptable	yes; comfortable	indirect
Hispanics	acceptable	moderate	varies	unacceptable	comfortable	indirect
African Americans	acceptable; expressive	moderate initially	moderate	acceptable	yes; may make uncomfortable	indirect initially
Asian Americans	unacceptable; sign of weakness	soft	slow	unacceptable	yes; comfortable	indirect

Source: Srebalus, D. J., & Brown, D. (2001). *Guide to the helping professions.* Boston: Allyn & Bacon (p. 61). By permission of the publisher.

and Strodtbeck (1961) and include the importance placed on self-control, time orientation, activity (dealing with problems that arise), social relationships, and relationship of human beings to nature. The traditional values of Eurocentric culture predispose individuals to value the individual more than the group, act for the benefit of the individual when problems arise, be only moderately concerned about disclosing one's thoughts and feelings, and be future oriented. Many African Americans have adopted Eurocentric values, but they may have a collateral social value instead of independence and an orientation to the present instead of the future. For those who do, the norms of the group are more important than promoting one's self. The values profile of American Indians is difficult to construct because of tribal variations. However, many unacculturated American Indians are disinclined to disclose their thoughts and feelings, tend to place the concerns of the group ahead of those of the individual, have a time orientation that is more related to natural events than it is to clocks and calendars, and believe that problems need not precipitate activity. Action-taking is most likely to occur on behalf of others as opposed to being self-serving. Asian Americans are also concerned about maintaining self-control and may be very reluctant to disclose thoughts and feelings. They are more likely to be concerned about traditions and try to use what has happened in the past to build for the future. They

are inclined to act when problems arise and often see social relationships hierarchically. Consultants may be deferred to in spite of efforts to establish egalitarian relationships. Hispanic Americans are likely to have a collateral social value, particularly as it relates to the family; thus, adhering to the norms of the group is more important than advancing one's self. Many of the subgroups of Hispanics have a present-time orientation (what is happening now is more important than what happens in the future), self-control of thoughts and feelings is only moderately important, and a being activity value. Individuals with a being activity orientation believe that activity is undertaken for the purpose of enhancing the family or group.

It is probably no surprise that Dr. W. Edwards Deming's (1993) Total Quality Management (TQM) system was rejected in this country and embraced by the Japanese when the cultural values of our country are contrasted with those of Japan. Deming stressed the importance of collaboration in the workplace, a concept that is consistent with the Japanese collateral social value and quite alien to the independence social value that dominates the Eurocentric culture of the United States Deming stresses that managers must drive out fear, break down bureaucratic barriers, and end competitive relationships. Japanese managers who live in a society that subscribes to the importance of avoiding embarrassing situations that will result in individuals losing face, clearly saw Deming's ideas as attractive, so attractive that they adopted and implemented his ideas much more quickly than he expected. It was not until the Japanese began to produce products that far exceeded the quality of products produced in the United States that managers in this country began to pay attention to TQM.

Cultural groups vary in terms of the way they perceive leadership, parenting, and education. Further, they have very different ideas about self-expression, self, control, time, and their relationship to nature. Consultants and collaborators must become aware of their own values and how these values influence their behavior and the assumptions that they act on (Brown, 2001). Moreover, they must understand the value structures of other people and include them in their consideration of how best to approach the process of consultation and collaboration including the design of intervention. One can only imagine how Deming's ideas about quality control would have been received in Japan if they had been rooted in the competitive values of Western European culture.

Interventions Utilized by Human Resource Workers

Figure 1.1 is a conceptual model of the functioning of human services professionals and educators. It draws on the earlier work of Morrill, Oetting, and Hurst, 1974) as well as Brown and his associates (1979). However, the model presented in Figure 1.1 extends and redefines to some degree the thinking of both groups. The model retains the four targets of intervention posed by Brown and associates—individuals, groups, organizations, and communities. It also retains the three purposes of intervention posed by Morrill et al., which were remediation, prevention, and development. To be more congruent with current mental health terminology, these have been renamed in the current model to primary, secondary, and tertiary mental health prevention.

Primary prevention is proactive in that it aims at enhancing the mental health of an unidentified group that is assumed to have positive mental health. Primary prevention programs may be aimed at individuals (e.g., enhancing coping skills), groups (enhancing communication patterns), organizations (improving decision making), and communities (developing mechanisms to increase community input into governance).

Secondary prevention involves the identification and treatment of problems before they have serious consequences in the life of an individual, group, organization, or community. Early identification and remediation of learning difficulties of children is a secondary prevention activity. So are preventive programs aimed at juveniles who have committed minor crimes, job enrichment programs designed to increase worker morale, and community-based programs aimed at improving housing conditions.

Tertiary prevention programs attempt to reduce the impact of debilitating mental health problems. Consultation with the mother of a self-destructive child falls into this category as does consulting with the staff of a mental health agency confronted with numerous adults who have eating disorders. Consultation with organizations where high stress and the often related symptoms of high blood pressure, heart disease, and psychosomatic ailments are common would be a tertiary prevention activity if the focus was on those already disabled. So would consultation in the community that focused on drug addicts or alcoholics.

Intervention methods in the current model have been refined somewhat from those offered previously. Direct interventions involve face-to-face contact with target groups. Training interventions, including teaching and supervision, are direct activities that may be used with varying sizes of groups for any of the three purposes. Counseling and therapy are direct interventions employed with individuals or small groups as secondary or tertiary prevention methods. Collaboration is also a direct intervention that may be used with any of the target groups.

Consultation is an indirect service engaged in with a consultee or consultees to pursue the primary, secondary, or tertiary prevention of mental health problems with any of the four target groups.

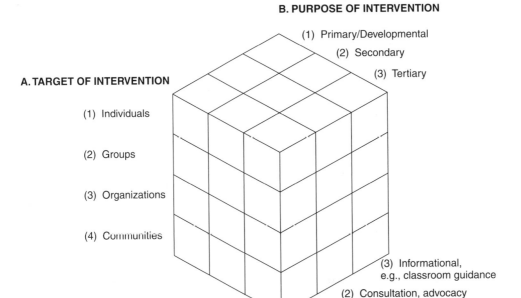

B. PURPOSE OF INTERVENTION

(1) Primary/Developmental

(2) Secondary

(3) Tertiary

A. TARGET OF INTERVENTION

(1) Individuals

(2) Groups

(3) Organizations

(4) Communities

(3) Informational,
e.g., classroom guidance

(2) Consultation, advocacy

(1) Direct, e.g., collaboration

C. METHOD OF INTERVENTION

FIGURE 1.1   Reconceptualization of Purposes and Targets of Interventions Used by Counselors, Psychologists, Social Workers, and Other Human Resource Workers

In this model, consultation is not restricted to a collaborative approach but may include a variety of approaches.

Informational approaches are also indirect, but differ from consultation in that no consultee is involved. Interventions of this type attempt to influence a target group through a number of informational activities including the use of media (Morrill et al., 1974). However, informational approaches are not restricted to the use of computers, newspapers, television, or radio, but also include brochures, books, and other printed materials that focus upon the various target groups for the purposes of preventing and/or treating mental health problems.

Which intervention method should one choose? The obvious bias of the authors is that consultation is the preferred intervention in many instances. However, a variety of factors enter into this choice including—but not limited to—the setting in which one works, the skills of the professional, the expectations of colleagues, the nature of the presenting problem, time available, and availability of the client. A rule of thumb for selecting an intervention method *should be* the one that has the greatest likelihood of achieving the intended goal at the least cost. As we shall see, consultation provides a viable alternative to direct service and informational approaches in many instances.

THE PERSPECTIVE OF THIS BOOK

A review of the professional literature from a variety of applied fields within the social sciences reveals a remarkable theoretical convergence in thinking. This convergence is upon systems theory and its applications to understanding organizations, family therapy, education, transpersonal counseling, community functioning, and so forth.

Whether one considers the simple formulation of Lewin (1951), $B = f (P \times E)$ (e.g., behavior is a function of a person/environment interaction), Bandura's (1977a) reciprocal determinism, or the interpretation of organizational functioning using systems theory by Katz and Kahn (1978), it is almost impossible to escape the conclusion that an interrelatedness exists among individuals and the small groups to which they belong, and both in turn to larger, more complex social structures such as organizations, communities, and cultures. The conclusion that interrelatedness exists, and the obvious corollary that understanding individuals or groups requires an understanding of the individual, the groups to which they belong, and the processes by which they interact, is a basic premise of this book. Other points of view will be presented as well because not all consultants have incorporated systems theory into their thinking.

A corollary to the premise of interrelatedness is that consultants cannot afford to think in old-fashioned, linear terms when they consider problems. Causation cannot be attributed to a single source. And just as problems have multiple causes, there are numerous pathways to solutions. Maybe more important, solutions designed to alleviate an identified problem in a given area may in turn produce negative consequences in another area. For example, school personnel, recognizing that student achievement was lagging, instituted tough academic programs only to find that dropping out of school increased. Similarly, businesses that have attempted to achieve production goals by utilizing improved technology have found that the potential gains are more than offset by increases in human problems. Thus, we have come full circle to our original premise. Linear thinking must give way to a type of multivariate logic that presupposes multiple causation and solutions and concerns itself with the interrelatedness among individuals, groups, and organizations.

THE REMAINDER OF THE BOOK

The four chapters that immediately follow will be devoted to outlining the major models of consulta-

tion. Chapter Two will deal with Caplanian ideas about consultation; his four approaches (Caplan, 1970) to consultation will be presented. Chapter Three will cover an eclectic behavioral model of consultation. Chapter Four includes a model of consultation based on the work of Alfred Adler. Chapter Five provides an overview of systems theory and a model of organizational consultation: organizational development.

Process variables in will be examined in Chapter Six, which also provides an overview of the consultation process including a description of the stages through which consultation passes and an examination of the techniques employed at each stage. Chapter Seven includes a discussion of the skills and characteristics needed to be an effective consultant. Chapter Eight addresses a thus far largely unexplored but critical factor in the consultation process, the consultee. Chapters Nine and Ten present ways to gather data in consultation to guide practice and evaluate effectiveness. Chapter Eleven will focus on consultation with teachers and parents.

The last section of the book will deal with some of the issues in consultation. Chapter Twelve will present a number of ethical principles that can guide the consultation effort and address certain legal pitfalls that may confront the consultant. Chapter Thirteen will be devoted to a variety of issues including consultant–consultee similarity in consultation, research needs, and consultation versus other interventions such as psychotherapy.

SUMMARY

Several major issues in collaboration and consultation were addressed in this chapter, not the least of which are the definitions of the two interventions. Consultation and consultation are separate processes. The major difference between them is that collaborators are active participants in all phases of the change process while consultants do not participate in implementing the intervention. The use of the term *collaborative consultation* has apparently led to definitional confusion that we have tried to dispel. An attempt has also been made to differentiate consultation from other helping strategies such as teaching, supervision, and advocacy.

One topic addressed in this chapter, cultural competence, will be a continuing theme of the book. Because of the demographic changes in this country's population, it is incumbent on all helping professionals to develop a full understanding of communication preferences, cultural values, and other cultural issues that affect the dynamics of the consultation and collaboration processes.

TIPS FOR THE PRACTITIONER

1. Start the process of selecting a model of consultation that best fits your style and personality. Selecting a model of consultation and the values and assumptions that underpin it is the first step in becoming culturally competent.
2. Work hard to understand your own cultural values, beliefs, and behaviors. Are you future-oriented or do you have another time orientation? What is your reaction when someone asks you to disclose personal information? What are your beliefs about the importance of eye contact? A firm handshake? Developing cultural competence is a long journey. The quicker you get started in self-understanding the sooner you will achieve some semblance of cultural empathy.
3. Begin to consider when consultation and collaboration might be most effective.

REVIEW QUESTIONS

1. Collaboration is increasingly popular as an intervention. Why do you think that this is true?
2. What are the advantages and disadvantages of consultation and consultation?
3. In Chapter 7 we will discuss the characteristics of effective consultants and collaborators. Based on what you know now, outline what you believe to be the characteristics of effec-

tive collaborators and consultants. How do these characteristics vary?

REFERENCES

Alper, S. K., Schloss, P. J., & Schloss, C. N. (Eds.) (1994). *Families of students with disabilities: Consultation and advocacy.* Boston: Allyn & Bacon.

Altarriba, J., & Bauer, L. (1998). Counseling the Hispanic client: Cuban Americans, Mexican Americans, and Puerto Ricans. *Journal of Counseling and Development, 75,* 389–396.

ASCA. (2003). *ASCA national model: A framework for comprehensive school counseling programs.* Alexandria, VA: Author.

Anderson, W., Chitwood, S., & Hayden, D. (1997). *Negotiating the special education maze: A guide for parents and teachers.* Bethesda, MD: Woodbine House.

Bandura, A. (1977a). Self-system: Toward a unifying theory of behavior change. *Psychological Review, 84,* 191–215.

Bandura, A. (1977b). *Social learning theory.* Englewood Cliffs, NJ: Prentice-Hall.

Brack, G., Jones, E. S., Smith, R. M., White, J., & Brack, C. (1977). A primer on consultation theory. *Journal of Counseling and Development, 71,* 619–628.

Bardon, J. I. (1985). School psychology's dilemma: A proposal for its dilemma. *Professional Psychology, 13,* 955–958.

Beer, M. (1980). *Organizational change and development: A systems view.* Santa Monica, CA: Goodyear.

Bennis, W., Benne, K. D., Chin, R., & Corey, K. E. (1976). *The planning of change.* New York: Holt, Rinehart & Winston.

Bergan, J. R. (1977). *Behavioral consultation.* Columbus, OH: Merrill.

Bergan, J. R., & Kratochwill, T. R. (1990) *Behavioral consultation and therapy.* New York: Plenum.

Bertalanffy, L. V. (1962). General systems theory: A critical review. *General Systems, 7,* 1–20.

Blake, R. R., & Mouton, J. S. (1976). *Consultation.* Reading, MA: Addison-Wesley.

Bowen, D. D. (1977). Values dilemmas in organizational development. *Journal of Applied Behavioral Science, 13,* 545–558.

Bronfenbrenner, U. (1979). *The ecology of human development.* Cambridge, MA: Harvard University Press.

Brown, D. (1997). Implications of cultural values for cross-cultural consultation with families. *Journal of Counseling and Development, 76,* 29–35.

Brown, D. (2001). An eclectic, culturally sensitive approach to consultation in mental health settings. In S. Salvatore (Ed.), *Counseling and psychotherapy: A practical guidebook for trainees and new professionals* (pp. 440–471). Boston: Allyn and Bacon.

Brown, D., Schulte, A. (1987). A social learning model of consultation. *Professional Psychology: Research and Practice, 18,* 283–287.

Brown, D., Wyne, M. D., Blackburn, J., & Powell, C. (1979). *Consultation: Strategy for improving education.* Boston: Allyn and Bacon.

Caplan, G. (1970). *The theory and practice of mental health consultation.* New York: Basic Books.

Caplan. G., & Caplan, R. B. (1993). *Mental health consultation and collaboration.* Prospect Heights, IL: Waveland.

Caplan, G., & Caplan, R. B. (1999). *Mental health consultation and collaboration* (Rev. ed.). Prospect Heights, IL: Waveland.

Celano, M. P., & Kaslow, N, J. (2000). Culturally competent family interventions: Review and case illustrations. *American Journal of Family Therapy, 28,* 217–228.

Center for Effective Collaboration and Practice. (1998). Addressing student problem behavior: Conducting a functional behavior assessment [On-line]. Available: http://www.air.org/cecp/fba/problembehavior2.main2. htm.

Conoley, J. C. (1981a). Advocacy consultation: Processes and problems. In W. C. Conoley (Ed.), *Consultation in schools: Theory and research procedures* (pp. 157–178). New York: Academic Press.

Conoley, J. C. (Ed.). (1981b). *Consultation in schools: Theory and research procedures.* New York: Basic Books.

Conoley, J. C., & Conoley, W. C. (1991). *School consultation: A guide to practice and training.* New York: MacMillan.

Cross-Bazron, B., Dennis, K., & Isaacs, J. (1989). *Toward a culturally competent system of care, Volume I.* Washington, DC: Georgetown University Child Development Technical Assistance for State Mental Health Planning.

Davis, K. (1997). *Exploring the intersection between cultural competency and managed behavioral health policy: Implications for state and local men-tal health agencies.* Alexandria, VA: National Technical Assistance Center for State Mental Health Planning.

Deming, W. E. (1993). *The new economics for industry, government, and education.* Cambridge, MA: Center for Advanced Engineering Study.

Dinkmeyer, D., & Carlson, J. (1973). *Consulting: Facilitating human potential and change processes.* Columbus, OH: Merrill.

Duncan, C. F. (1995). Cross-cultural consultation. In C. Lee (Ed.), *Counseling for diversity* (pp. 129–139). Boston: Allyn & Bacon.

Duncan, C. F., & Pryzwansky, W. P. (1993). Effects of race, racial identity development, and orientation style on perceived consultant effectiveness. *Journal of Multicultural Counseling and Development, 21,* 88–96.

Dustin, D., & Ehly, S. (1992). School consultation in the 1990s. *Journal of Elementary School Guidance and Counseling, 26,* 165–175.

English, F, W., & Hill, J. C. (1994). *Total quality education.* Thousand Oaks, CA: Corwin.

Erchul, W. P. (1987). A relational communication analysis of control in consultation. *Professional School Psychology, 2,* 113–124.

Erchul, W. P. (1999). Two steps forward, one step back. *Journal of School Psychology, 37,* 191–203.

Erchul, W. P., & Chewning, T. G. (1990). Behavioral consultation from a request-centered relational communication perspective. *School Psychology Quarterly, 5,* 1–20.

Erchul, W. P., & Martens, B. K. (1997). *School consultation: Conceptual and empirical bases of practice.* New York: Plenum.

Fiedler, C. R. (2002). *Making a difference: Advocacy competencies for special education professionals.* Boston: Allyn & Bacon.

Fuqua, D. R., & Kurpius, D. J. (1993). Conceptual models of organizational development. *Journal of Counseling and Development, 71,* 607–618.

Gallessich, J. (1982). *The profession and practice of consultation: A handbook for consultants, trainers of consultants, and consumers of consultation services.* San Francisco: Jossey-Bass.

Gibbs, J. T. (1980). The interpersonal orientation in mental health consultation: Toward a model of ethnic variation in mental health consultation. *Journal of Communication Psychology, 8,* 426–435.

Glaser, E. M. (1981). Ethical issues in consultation practice with organizations. *Consultation 1*(1), 12–16.

Gutkin, T. B. (1999). The collaboration debate: Finding your way through the maze, moving forward into the future. *Journal of School Psychology, 37,* 161–190.

Gysbers, N. C., & Henderson, P. (2000). *Developing and managing your school guidance program* (3rd ed.). Alexandria, VA: American Counseling Association.

Harris, K. C. (1993). Culture and consultation: An overview. *Journal of Educational and Psychological Consultation, 4,* 237–251.

Havelock, R. G., & Zlotolow, S. (1995). *The change agent's guide* (2nd ed.). Englewood Cliffs, NJ: Educational Technology Publications.

Heller, K. (1985). Issues in consultation to community groups: Some useful distinctions between social regulations and indigenous citizen groups. *Counseling Psychologist, 15,* 403–409.

Hines, M. L. (1987). *Don't get mad, get powerful: A manual for building advocacy skills.* Lansing, MI, Protection and Advocacy Service: (ERIC Document Reproduction Service No. ED3545683.

Homan, M. S. (2004). *Promoting community change: Making it happen in the real world* (3rd ed.). Pacific Grove, CA: Brooks/Cole.

Huse, E. F. (1980). *Organizational development and change* (2nd ed.). St. Paul, MN: West.

Idol-Maestas, L. (1983). *Special educators' consultation handbook.* Rockville, MD: Aspen.

Idol, L., Paolucci-Whitcomb, P., & Nevin, A. (1986). *Collaborative consultation.* Rockville, MD: Aspen.

Katz, D., & Kahn, R. L. (1978). *The social psychology of organizations.* New York: Wiley.

Keller, H. R. (1981). Behavioral consultation. In J. C. Conoley (Ed.), *Consultation in schools: Theory and research procedures* (pp. 59–90). New York: Academic Press.

Keys, S. C., Bemak, F., Carpenter, S. L., & King-Sear, M. E. (1998). Collaborative consultation: A new role for counselors serving at-risk youth. *Journal of Counseling and Development, 76,* 123–133.

King, M. A., Sims, A., & Osher, D. (n.d.). *How is cultural competence integrated into education?* [Online]. Available: http://www.air.org/cecp/culturzl/Q_integrated.htm.

Kluckhorn, F. R., & Strodtbeck, F. L. (1961). *Variations in values orientation.* Evanston, IL: Row Paterson.

Lewin, K. (1951). *Field theory in social sciences.* New York: Harper and Row.

Lippitt, G. L. (1982). *Organizational renewal* (2nd ed.). Englewood Cliffs, NJ: Prentice-Hall.

Lippitt, G. L., & Lippitt, G. (1986). *The consulting process in action* (2nd ed.). San Diego, CA: University Associates.

Lopez, E. C. (2000). Conducting instructional consultation through an interpreter. *School Psychology Review, 28,* 378–388.

Mannino, F. V., & Shore, M. F. (1985). Understanding consultation: Some orienting dimensions. *Counseling Psychologist, 13,* 363–367.

Mannino, F. V., & Shore, M. F. (1986). Introduction. In F. V. Mannino, E. J. Trickett, M. F. Shore, M. G. Kidder, & G. Levine (Eds.), *Handbook of mental health consultation* (pp. xi–xvii). Washington, DC: U. S. Government Printing Office.

Martens, B. K. (1993). A behavioral approach to consultation. In J. Zins, T. R. Kratovwill, & S. E. Elliot (Eds.), *Handbook of consultation services for children* (pp. 78–99). San Francisco: Jossey-Bass.

Meyers, J. (1978). Training school psychologists for a consultation role. *School Psychology Digest, 7,* 26–31.

Meyers, J., Parsons, R. D., & Martin, R. (1979). *Mental health consultation in schools.* San Francisco: Jossey-Bass.

Morrill, W. H., Oetting, E. R., & Hurst, J. C. (1974). Dimensions of counselor functioning. *Personnel and Guidance Journal, 52,* 354–359.

Naumann, W. C., Gutkin, T. B., & Sandoval, S. R. (1996). The impact of consultant race and student race on perceptions of consultant effectiveness and intervention acceptability. *Journal of Educational and Psychological Consultation, 7,* 151–160.

Owens, R. (2004). *Organizational behavior in education* (8th ed.). Boston: Allyn & Bacon.

Parsons, R. D., & Myers, J. (1984). *Developing consultation skills: A guide to training, development, and assessment for human services professionals.* San Francisco: Jossey-Bass.

Pinto, R. F. (1981). Consultation style and client systems perspectives: Styles of cross-cultural consultation. In R. Lippitt & G. Lippitt (Eds.), *Systems thinking: A resource for organizational diagnosis and intervention* (pp. 231–265). Washington, DC: International Consultants Foundation.

Pryzwansky, W. P. (1974). A reconsideration of the consultation model for delivery of school-based psychological services. *American Journal of Orthopsychiatry, 44,* 579–583.

Pryzwansky, W. P. (1977). Collaboration or consultation: Is there a difference? *Journal of Special Education, 11,* 179–182.

Randolph, D. L. (1985). *Micro-consulting: Basic psychological consultation skills for helping professionals.* Johnson City, TN: Institute for Social Sciences and Arts.

Reyes, O., & Jason, L. A. (1993). Collaborating with the community. In. J. E. Zins, T. R. Kratochwill, & S. E. Elliot (Eds.), *Handbook of consultation services for children* (pp. 224–242). San Francisco: Jossey-Bass.

Reynolds, C. R., Gutkin, T. B., Elliot, S. N., & Witt, J. C. (1984). *School psychology: Essentials of theory and practice.* New York: Wiley.

Rockwood, G. F. (1993). Edgar Schein's process versus content consultation model. *Journal of Counseling and Development, 71,* 636–638.

Rowley, W. J., Sink, C. A., & MacDonald, G. (2002). An experimental, systemic approach to encourage collaboration and community building. *Professional School Counseling, 5,* 360–365.

Rubin, H. (2002). *Collaborative leadership.* Thousand Oaks, CA: Corwin.

Russell, M. L. (1978). Behavioral consultation: Theory and process. *Personnel and Guidance Journal, 56,* 346–350.

Schein, E. H. (1969). *Process consultation: Its role in organizational development.* Reading, MA: Addison-Wesley.

Schein, E. H. (1989). Process consultation as a general model of helping. *Consulting Psychology Bulletin, 41,* 3–15

Schulte, A. C., & Osborne, S. (1993). What is collaborative consultation? The eye of the beholder. In D. Fuchs (Chair), *Questioning popular beliefs about collaborative consultation.* Symposium presented at the annual meeting of the Council for Exceptional Children, San Antonio, TX.

Schulte, A. C., & Osborne, S. (2003). When assumptive worlds collide: A review of definitions of *collaboration* and *consultation. Journal of Educational and Psychological Consultation, 14*(2), 109–138.

Sheridan, S. M., & Henning-Stout, M. (1993). In J. E. Zins, T. R. Kratochwill, & S. E. Elliot. *Handbook of consultation services for children* (pp. 95–113). San Francisco: Jossey-Bass.

Smith, K. K., & Corse, S. J. (1986). The process of consultation. In F. V. Mannino, E. J. Trickett, M. F. S. Shore, & G. Levin (Eds.), *Handbook of mental health consultation* (pp. 247–278). Washington, DC: U.S. Government Printing Office.

Snapp, M., & Davidson, S. L. (1982). Systems interventions for school psychologists: A case study approach. In C. R. Reynolds & T. B. Gutkin (Eds.), *The handbook of school psychology* (pp. 858–861). New York: Wiley.

Srebalus, D. J., & Brown, D. (2001). *Introduction to the helping professions.* Boston: Allyn & Bacon.

Steele, F. (1975). *Consulting for organizational change.* Amherst, MA: University of Massachusetts Press.

Steffy, B. E., & Lindle, S. (1994). *Building coalitions: How to link TQE schools with government, business, and community.* Thousand Oaks, CA: Corwin.

Tharp, R. G., & Wetzel, R. J. (1967). *Behavior modification in the natural environment.* New York: Academic Press.

Werner, J. L., & Tyler, J. M. (1993). Organizational consultation. *Journal of Counseling and Development, 71,* 689–692.

West, J., & Idol, L. (1987). School consultation: An interdisciplinary perspective on theory, models, and research. *Journal of Learning Disabilities, 71,* 388–408.

West, J. F., & Idol, L. (1990). Collaborative consultation in the education of mildly handicapped and at-risk students. *Remedial and Special Education, 11,* 22–31.

West, J. F., & Idol, L. (1993). The counselor as a consultant in a collaborative school. *Journal of Counseling and Development, 71,* 673–683.

Whitaker, K., & Moses, M. (1994). *The restructuring handbook.* Boston: Allyn & Bacon.

CHAPTER 2

MENTAL HEALTH CONSULTATION

GOAL OF THE CHAPTER

The goal of this chapter is to present Caplan's mental health model of consultation and related work by other theorists and researchers.

CHAPTER PREVIEW

1. The historical events that precipitated the development of mental health consultation are delineated.
2. Mental health consultation is defined and the fundamental assumptions that underlie it are examined.
3. Caplan's description of the process of consultation is summarized.
4. The four types of consultation discussed by Caplan—client-centered case consultation, consultee-centered case consultation, program-centered administrative consultation, and consultee-centered administrative consultation—are described.
5. Consultee-centered consultation and the related concepts of theme interference and theme interference reduction are discussed in detail.
6. Developments and reformulations of mental health consultation since its introduction are summarized.

One of the most influential figures in the field of psychological consultation has been Gerald Caplan. A psychiatrist and a leader in the development of community psychiatry, Caplan was one of the first mental health professionals to write about consultation. His ideas still are pervasive in psychological consultation and reflect both an environmental and psychic perspective. In this chapter, Caplan's (1964, 1970, 1974, 1977, 1986, 2004; Caplan & Caplan, 1993, 1999) approach to psychological consultation, often referred to as mental health consultation or Caplanian consultation, will be described. In addition, models of con-

sultation that have been based in part on Caplan's ideas will be described (e.g., Altrocchi, 1972; Ingraham, 2000). Finally, further developments in Caplan's approach to prevention of mental health problems will be discussed.

ROOTS OF MENTAL HEALTH CONSULTATION

After World War II a new perspective on mental health and disorders emerged. Termed the *community* or *preventive* approach, this perspective emphasizes the importance of social support systems within a community in the prevention of psychological disorders (Sarason & Sarason, 1984).

From a preventive perspective, maladaptive behavior and psychological disturbance arise in part because caregivers, family, friends, and community groups within a social system do not provide sufficient direction, support, and stability when an individual is faced with a stressful life event. If the community mechanisms for supporting persons under stress are improved, the incidence of psychological disturbance that requires direct intervention by mental health professionals can be reduced and the overall mental health of a community enhanced (Albee & Fryer, 2003).

Caplan was an early leader in the development of this approach (Caplan, 1964; Rosenfeld & Caplan, 1954). He viewed consultation as a key tool for the prevention of mental disorders. By consulting with caregivers, such as teachers, police, and clergy, mental health professionals could improve the support mechanisms in a community and reduce the need for more intensive mental health services (Caplan, 1974). Caplan (1970; Caplan & Caplan, 1993, 1999) traces his interest in consultation to his work in a child guidance center in Israel after World War II. He was part of a team of psychiatrists, psychologists, and social workers who supervised the mental health of approximately 16,000 new immigrant children who were cared for in over 100 residential institutions throughout Israel. Because of the large geographic area served and the high rate of referrals, traditional mental health services involving referral, diagnosis, and treatment of individual children were not feasible. To provide services, a child guidance staff member would travel to a particular residential institution to deal with a group of referrals. Rather than provide psychotherapy, the staff member would discuss with the childcare staff alternative ways of managing the child that would resolve the child's problems while he or she remained in the residential institution.

Child guidance staff members functioning in this way made several discoveries that pointed to consultation as an important and efficient means of dealing with mental health problems (Rosenfeld &

Caplan, 1954). First, specific institutions and childcare workers seemed to have difficulties with particular groups of children. One institution might have a high rate of referrals of children with learning problems, while another institution might refer a high rate of aggressive children. This finding suggested that by improving the ability of the staff of an institution to cope with a particular problem, a large number of children's problems could be resolved without direct service to the individual children. Second, consultants noted that many times childcare workers seemed to have developed a rather narrow perspective on children and the problems they presented. A sympathetic and objective discussion with the consultant often allowed staff members to see children as persons with difficulties rather than as problem children, to develop a wider range of action alternatives for dealing with problems, and subsequently to deal with the problems more effectively (Caplan, 1970). Third, consultants found that working in the childcare institution rather than dealing with referred children at the guidance center allowed them to quickly understand the variety of factors within the institution that might be affecting a particular child and caregiving agent. These factors might have been unknown to them had the child been treated at the center. The teachers and other caregivers also seemed more comfortable in their own setting and were more likely to share their perceptions of cases freely with consultants.

Following his experiences in Israel, Caplan journeyed to Harvard to work with Erich Lindemann, another pioneer in preventive psychiatry. There, Caplan continued to develop and refine the techniques of mental health consultation through his work in the Field Training Unit of the Harvard School of Public Health and the Laboratory of Community Psychiatry at Harvard Medical School. Caplan saw consultation not as a new profession, but as an important form of mental health service delivery that had not been formally recognized and distinguished from other forms of mental health services (Caplan, 1970). In his book *The Theory and Practice of Mental Health Consultation* (Caplan, 1970), as well as in several related works (Caplan, 1964, 1974, 1977), Caplan sought to formalize and further develop consultation as part of the role of a mental health professional.

BASIC CONCEPTS IN MENTAL HEALTH CONSULTATION

Definition of *Consultation*

Caplan (1970) as well as others (Gallessich, 1982; Reschly, 1976) note that the term *consultation* is used in many ways. However, in his writing, Caplan used *consultation* in a restricted sense, referring to a process of interaction between two professionals in which one professional (the consultee) seeks the help of a specialist in a particular area (the consultant) with regard to a current work problem that the consultee has decided is within the consultant's area of specialized competence (Caplan, 1970).

Mental health consultation is a service provided to caregiving professionals such as doctors, nurses, teachers, lawyers, welfare workers, probation officers, police, and clergy to assist them in dealing with the psychological aspects of a current work problem and, most importantly to deal more effectively with similar problems in the future (Caplan, 1970). Caplan includes both individual and group consultation in his definition, although his emphasis in earlier writings (Caplan, 1970) was on individual consultation.

A fundamental aspect of Caplan's definition of consultation, and one that has had a strong influence on consultation (Gutkin & Curtis, 1990; Meyers, 1981; Meyers et al., 1993; Schulte & Osborne, 2003), is his conceptualization of the consulting relationship as non-hierarchical and coordinate. Both the consultant and consultee are viewed as experts in their own areas. The consultant has no authority over the consultee—he or she is free to accept or reject any of the consultant's suggestions and maintains sole responsibility for carrying out any interventions. Caplan views a coordinate relationship as important for ensuring that the consultee incorporates the knowledge gained in consultation into his or her own system of think-

ing. Hierarchical relationships in which one party has authority over the other are seen as an impediment to learning because the subordinate may feel coerced to accept the other's suggestions and resist acting on them to preserve his or her autonomy (Caplan, 1970).

Caplan distinguishes between four types of consultation based on two major divisions: (1) whether the content focus of consultation is difficulty with a particular client or an administrative difficulty, and (2) whether the primary goal of consultation is providing information in the consultant's area of specialty or improvement of the consultee's problem-solving capacity. Though each type of consultation is discussed in detail in subsequent sections, they are described briefly here.

In *client-centered case consultation* the focus is upon the consultee's management of a particular client or group of clients for whom he or she is responsible. The primary goal in this type of consultation is prescriptive—the consultant assesses the client and provides information to the consultee so that he or she may deal more effectively with the client. *Consultee-centered case consultation* also is concerned with the consultee's management of a particular client or group of clients, but improvement in the client is a secondary goal of this type of consultation. The primary goal is increased skills for the consultee, and the focus of consultation is on the consultee's difficulties in dealing with the client (or clients) in question. *Program-centered administrative consultation* is the administrative counterpart of client-centered case consultation. The consultant functions as an expert in mental health and social systems and provides recommendations relevant to program development and administrative concerns for a particular agency. The last type of consultation, *consultee-centered administrative consultation,* also is concerned with program development and administrative concerns, but like consultee-centered case consultation, the focus is on increasing consultee effectiveness rather than consultant-generated solutions to specific organizational concerns. In early conceptualizations of mental health consultation, it was generally assumed that the consultant was not a member of the consultee's organization and had no administrative responsibility for clients (Caplan, 1970).

Fundamental Assumptions in Mental Health Consultation

Before describing the process of mental health consultation, some of the fundamental assumptions that underlie mental health consultation and distinguish it from other types of consultation need to be delineated.

Both intrapsychic and environmental factors are important in explaining and changing behavior. More than any other model of consultation, mental health consultation focuses on intrapsychic variables, such as consultee feelings, attitudes, and beliefs, that are important in behavior change (Lambert, 2004; Meyers, 1981). However, as already noted, Caplan's work also reflects a strong environmental focus, and his conception of the environment is not incompatible with more current, multilevel systems frameworks. Problems are not viewed as residing solely within the client, but as potentially residing at several different levels within and external to an organization. Assessment in mental health consultation focuses on a wide range of factors that may be relevant to a problem, including characteristics of the client, communication between the consultee and client, consultee skill level, consultee perceptions and attitudes, organizational factors that contribute to similarities in problems across consultees and clients, and community concerns and undercurrents that may make selected issues more salient. Even Caplan's focus on intrapsychic factors within the consultee reflects an environmental focus because the consultee is seen as an important part of the client's social environment (Meyers, 1981).

More than technical expertise is important in designing effective interventions. The adoption of an intervention technique is not solely a function of its effectiveness, but is influenced by many other factors. As Alpert and Silverstein (1985) stated: "Basic to Caplan's method is the concept that each consultee is embedded in a profession with norms, roles, language, and a body of knowledge. Each consultee is also a member of a specific organizational culture.... Because of the unique aspects of these contexts, the consultant could not presume to fully understand the consultee's framework, and must assume that any recommendations for change will be adapted by the consultee" (p. 285). In other words, it is unlikely that consultants will be able to design interventions that are appropriate for consultees from other institutions and professions. Despite the consultant's expertise, intervention is left in the hands of the consultee.

Learning and generalization occur when consultees retain responsibility for action. Within Caplan's model, responsibility for action belongs to consultees. The consultant does not become involved in case management in client-centered case consultation or the implementation of organizational changes in administrative consultation. In Caplan's (1970) view, the direct involvement of consultants in problem resolution diminishes the consultees' feelings of ownership over problems and solutions generated to resolve them. Therefore, they are less likely to incorporate the concepts introduced in consultation into their working style.

Consultation concerning a single case issue also is restricted to two or three short interviews to prevent consultees from relying on the consultant for more than discussion of issues relevant to a problem. Consultants' brief involvement and lack of participation in selecting and implementing interventions or change strategies also communicates the expectation that consultees can manage work problems independently.

Consultee attitudes and affect also are assumed to be important in generalization. Even if consultees possess the skills to deal with a particular problem, they may not apply these skills if they do not perceive the situation objectively, have conflicting needs, or a particular strategy does not fit their own belief system. For example, a physician who has been trained to interact with patients in a paternalistic manner may be reluctant to allow patients to take an active role in treatment decision making even though he or she is aware that allowing patients more control may lead to greater compliance and feelings of well-being.

Mental health consultation is a supplement to other problem-solving mechanisms within an organization. Caplan (1970) assumes that there are several ways of addressing difficulties with clients within an organization and that, for many types of problems, procedures other than consultation are more appropriate. For example, under most circumstances skill deficiencies in the consultee should be handled through supervision because the consultant is unlikely to understand the skills involved in another profession and organization setting.

Consultee attitudes and affect are important in consultation, but cannot be dealt with directly. As noted earlier, Caplan's approach places considerable emphasis on the thoughts and feelings of the consultee. For example, stereotypes of particular persons or situations may interfere with consultees' understanding of their clients, or unresolved conflicts in the consultees' past or present personal lives can be brought out by similarities to current work problems.

Although consultee feelings are important, they cannot be dealt with directly. Instead, the consultant forms hypotheses about the types of personal issues that are interfering with the consultee's functioning and intervenes indirectly, by using the work problem as a metaphor for the consultee's problem. Caplan and Caplan (1993, 1999) refer to this as "using the displacement object." In Caplan's (1970; Caplan & Caplan, 1993, 1999) view, direct confrontation would impede consultation for several reasons. First, if the con-

sultant were to point out that consultee attitudes and feelings appear to be blocking effective problem solving, the coordinate relationship between the consultant and consultee would be upset. Concerns about personal autonomy would interfere with the consultee's ability to benefit from consultation and resolve the work problem. Second, making the consultee aware of his or her apparent feelings would result in loss of face and arouse anxiety and defensiveness, further reducing the consultee's capacity to deal with the problem. Third, the focus of consultation would be off the work problem. By dealing simultaneously with manifest content (the work problem) and latent content (the personal conflict), the consultant is able to assist the consultee in resolving the work problem. As a side effect, the consultee may also find some resolution of conflicts outside of work.

THE CONSULTATION PROCESS

Although the process of consultation unfolds somewhat differently within each of Caplan's types of consultation, many concerns and tasks are common to all types. Caplan's original book on consultation (1970) and its updated version (Caplan & Caplan, 1993, 1999) provide detailed descriptions of many of the issues faced by the consultant during the course of consultation and how they might be handled. This detailed and pragmatic advice about entering an organization and working with consultees is useful reading for consultants working within any model. Caplan's description of the consultation process from the first contact with an organization to follow-up and evaluation is summarized here to provide the reader with an overview of his approach, before the four types of consultation are described in detail.

Building a Relationship with a Consultee Institution

Caplan notes that establishing ties with an organization that eventually result in consultation can be a lengthy process. The consultant may gradually

---

Student Learning Activity 2.1

Caplan believes that learning and generalization are most likely to occur when the consultant does not impose his or her viewpoint and the consultee retains responsibility for the problem. List the conditions you believe are most conducive to generalization of skills to other settings. Compare your assumptions with Caplan's.

Answers to Student Learning Activities appear at the end of the chapter.

work into the role of consultant from a more limited, direct-service role. For example, a human services professional from a community mental health center may visit a school first to gather data regarding a child he or she is treating at the center. After several of these contacts, the professional may be asked to provide a workshop. As the organization becomes more familiar with the professional and finds that he or she interacts well with the staff and provides useful information, these contacts may develop into a more formal consultative relationship.

In these initial contacts the consultant works to develop cordial relations with upper-level administrators as well as staff members. A second goal is to establish a reputation as competent, trustworthy, and willing to help, but respectful of the organization's and staff members' own prerogatives (Caplan, 1970). The consultant also tries to understand the organization so that eventual consultation contacts are successful. Caplan notes that each institution has its own unique set of social norms regarding such issues as formality, ways of making appointments, and punctuality that must be understood by the consultant.

Consultation generally is initiated by negotiation of an agreement between the consultant and the consultee organization. The consultant seeks sanction from the highest-level administrator, but also informs and seeks sanction for consultation at all levels of the organization, since lack of support from any source can impede consultation. As the consultant's role changes, the initial contract or agreement is renegotiated to better describe the new role. Thus, consultation agreements are generally explicit, formalized, successive, and negotiated at the highest level of the organization (Caplan & Caplan, 1993, 1999; Kelly, 1993).

Establishing Relationships with Consultees

The nature of the consultant's relationships with consultees is a central component of all types of mental health consultation. The consultees must view themselves as active participants in consultation who educate the consultant regarding their professional role and its constraints so that the con-

sultant can make relevant contributions. As discussed earlier, the consultant works to establish a coordinate, nonhierarchical relationship with consultees where professional issues and concerns can be discussed openly. A key issue here is confidentiality. Caplan emphasizes the importance of dealing with confidentiality issues explicitly and repeatedly assuring consultees that their handling of cases will not be discussed with others, particularly their superiors (Caplan & Caplan, 1993, 1999).

The consultative relationship is important not only because consultees' feelings of ownership will affect their disposition to act, but because a major avenue of skill learning in consultation is the consultees' identification with consultants. That is, a strong, positive relationship makes it more likely that the consultant will serve as a role model to consultees. Caplan lists three general aspects of professional functioning that are modeled by the consultant: (1) empathy toward clients, (2) tolerance of feelings in others and oneself, and (3) a belief that by gathering enough information in a systematic and objective manner, human behavior can be understood.

Status issues are often a concern within consultative relationships and are discussed in detail by Caplan. Although the consultant has no administrative authority over consultees, the latter may feel threatened by the consultant or relate to the consultant as a superior rather than a colleague. Caplan advises the consultant to avoid judgmental statements regarding consultees' actions since these may reinforce the superior/subordinate relationship. Caplan also suggests that the consultant counter consultees' attempts to place him or her in a superior position by responding in kind to self-deprecating actions by the consultee. For example, the consultant who senses that the consultee is overly solicitous might devote more attention to the statements of the consultee and insist on meeting solely at the convenience of the consultee.

Assessment

The responsibility for assessment as well as the type of assessment information collected varies with the type of consultation. However, in all types of consultation the consultant privately assesses, to some extent, both the consultee and organizational factors that may have bearing on the problem and its resolution. This point will be discussed later in more detail with reference to each type of consultation.

One important aspect of assessment is the consultant's examination of the problem with consultees. This form of problem assessment is also an intervention aimed at changing consultees. Through questioning, consultees' views of their problems may be broadened, and they also may learn to approach new problems in a similar manner in the future. This technique is summarized by Caplan:

> His [sic] principal mode of communication is not by stating his assessment of the situations or by giving advice, although when appropriate he may do both, but by the questions he poses about the material. These do not take the form of an interrogation of the consultee. Instead, the consultant sits beside the consultee, as it were, and engages in a joint pondering about the complexities of the problem. His contribution mainly takes the form of widening and deepening the focus of discussion by suggesting new avenues for collecting information, new possibilities for understanding the motivations and reactions of the characters in the case history, and new ways in which the situation might be handled. (1970, p. 59)

Interventions

In all types of mental health consultation, responsibility for action concerning the presenting problem remains with consultees. However, in both types of consultee-centered consultation, the consultant formulates and carries out interventions to remedy shortcomings within the consultee without the consultee's awareness. These interventions may be relatively simple, such as altering a consultee's perception of a case by asking questions dealing with a broad range of topics related to the problem or modeling a rational, problem-solving approach by remaining calm despite a consultee's sense of urgency and anxiety about an issue. Inter-

ventions may also be complex. For example, in theme interference reduction, the consultant may decide over the course of a consultation session (or series of sessions) that a consultee anticipates a disastrous outcome for certain types of cases because of their similarity to unresolved issues in his or her personal life. The consultant then assists the consultee to successfully resolve such a case, demonstrating that the outcome is not inevitable and thereby increasing the consultee's effectiveness with similar cases in the future. Theme interference reduction and other intervention techniques targeted at consultees are described in detail in the section discussing consultee lack of objectivity.

Follow-Up and Evaluation

Although responsibility for action rests with consultees, the consultant indicates an interest in knowing the outcome of individual cases or organizational problems that have been discussed in consultation. Caplan also advises the consultant to attempt to evaluate consultation services as a means of increasing professional effectiveness, and he discusses several evaluation methods. However, he notes the difficulties involved in evaluating consultation, a complex indirect service, where effectiveness depends on successful linkages between the consultant's intervention, change in consultee perceptions and attitudes, change in consultee behavior, change in the client, and change in the organization or consultees' interactions with future clients.

Student Learning Activity 2.2

Caplan maintains that consultees' problem-solving capabilities can be influenced by the types of questions asked by the consultant. Try his questioning approach in a roleplay of a consultation problem. Do you feel comfortable avoiding direct suggestions about how the problem might be handled? Ask the person who played the consultee to discuss his or her perceptions of the consultation session.

TYPES OF MENTAL HEALTH CONSULTATION

In this section the four types of consultation delineated by Caplan (1970; Caplan & Caplan, 1993, 1999) are described in detail. Table 2.1 compares the four types of consultation on a number of dimensions.

Client-Centered Case Consultation

Caplan (1970) characterizes client-centered case consultation as the most familiar type of consultation performed by mental health professionals. In this type of consultation, the consultant functions as a specialist who assesses the client, arrives at a diagnosis, and makes recommendations concerning how the consultee might modify his or her dealings with the client. Frequently, this type of consultation is seen as a means of screening clients for more in-depth diagnosis and treatment. The consultant is to make a recommendation regarding whether referral is warranted and, regardless of that decision, provide suggestions to the consultee regarding his or her day-to-day interactions with the client.

Often, the assessment, diagnosis, and recommendations are summarized in a written report to the consultee. The consultee uses the

---

TABLE 2.1   Comparisons among Caplan's Four Types of Consultation on Several Dimensions

	MENTAL HEALTH CONSULTATION			
	CLIENT-CENTERED CASE CONSULTATION	**CONSULTEE-CENTERED CASE CONSULTATION**	**PROGRAM-CENTERED ADMINISTRATIVE CONSULTATION**	**CONSULTEE-CENTERED ADMINISTRATIVE CONSULTATION**
Focus	Focuses on developing a plan that will help a specific client.	Focuses on improvement of the consultee's professional functioning in relation to specific cases.	Focuses on improvement of programs or policies.	Focuses on improvement of consultee's professional functioning in relation to specific programs or policies.
Goal	To advise the consultee regarding client treatment.	To educate consultee using his or her problems with the client as a lever.	To help develop a new program or policy or improve an existing one.	To help consultee improve problem-solving skills in dealing with current organizational problems.
Example	School psychologist called in to diagnose a student's reading problem.	School counselor asks for help in dealing with students' drug-related problems.	Nursing home director requests help in developing staff orientation program.	Police chief asks for help in developing ongoing program to deal with interpersonal problems between veteran and new officers.
Consultant's Role and Responsibilities	Usually meets with consultee's client to help diagnose problem.	Never, or rarely, meets with consultee's client.	Meets with groups and individuals in an attempt to accurately assess problems.	Meets with groups and individuals in an attempt to help them develop their problem-solving skills.
	Is responsible for assessing problem and prescribing course of action.	Must be able to recognize source of consultee's difficulties and deal with them indirectly.	Is responsible for correctly assessing problem and providing a plan for administrative action.	Must be able to recognize source of organizational difficulty and serve as catalyst for action by administrators.

information provided in the report to develop and implement his or her own plan for dealing with the client with minimal involvement of the consultant. Examples of client-centered case consultation include a psychologist at a hospital who is asked to examine a medical patient and provide insights regarding the mental health aspects of the case or a teacher's request that a school psychologist assess a child who is having difficulty learning to read, provide insight regarding the child's difficulty, and suggest appropriate instructional approaches.

The primary goal of client-centered case consultation is to develop a plan for dealing with the client's difficulties. Education or skill development for the consultee is a secondary focus. Assessment focuses upon the nature of the client's difficulties, and much of the consultant's time is spent in direct contact with the client. The consultant also assesses the resources and constraints in the consultee's setting that will affect the type of plan that can be implemented successfully.

Direct assessment of the client often includes formal assessment techniques such as psychological or educational tests or clinical interviews, but the focus of assessment is on providing usable information to the consultee. In the example where the school psychologist is asked to consult with a teacher regarding a child's reading difficulty, the consultant would be more likely to use a criterion-referenced test, which provides information about a child's specific skill deficits, rather than a norm-referenced test, which provides information concerning the child's standing in relation to his or her classmates, but whose results do not translate easily into remedial strategies.

The emphasis on providing usable information for the consultee implies that consultants also must have an understanding of the environment in which a difficulty occurs so that their recommendations are feasible within that setting. Therefore, the resources and constraints operative in the consultee's work setting are examined, such as role expectations, norms, financial and time constraints, and individual consultee strengths and weaknesses that

will affect the type of plan that can be implemented. Of particular interest during this phase of assessment is the consultee/client relationship and how this relationship might be strengthened or altered to improve the problem situation. The consultant looks for misunderstanding and miscommunication that may be blocking problem resolution and then tries to improve communication and understanding by acting as a "communication bridge" (Caplan, 1970, p. 115) between consultee and client. An understanding of the consultee and his or her work setting also aids the consultant in deciding the manner in which information can be communicated most effectively to the consultee. As Caplan points out, this is not just a matter of avoiding technical jargon, but carefully choosing the concepts to be conveyed and the manner in which they are conveyed to suit the consultee's professional role and personal style. For instance, a psychologist making recommendations to a manager about an employee who is under severe home-related stress might discuss a recommendation about dealing with the employee in terms of maintaining his or her productivity rather than relieving the employee's discomfort and improving his or her coping skills, even though both are expected outcomes of the recommendations.

Implementation of the consultant's recommendations is the responsibility of the consultee. However, the consultant may meet with the consultee to discuss the recommendations and ensure that the consultee understands them. The consultant may also contact the consultee later to check on the progress of the client, which provides the consultant with a general idea of the accuracy of diagnosis and the usefulness of his or her recommendations.

Consultee-Centered Case Consultation

The terms *mental health consultation* and *Caplanian consultation* are sometimes used synonymously in the consultation literature for consultee-centered consultation. This type of consultation is most closely identified with Caplan and, of the four types of consultation Caplan delineates, he devotes the most attention to it. Like its counterpart, client-centered case consultation, consultee-centered case consultation is concerned with difficulties a consultee encounters with a particular client for whom he or she has responsibility in the work setting. However, the primary goal of consultation is remediation of the shortcomings in the consultee's professional functioning that are responsible for difficulties with the present case. Client improvement is viewed as a secondary goal.

Because the focus of this type of consultation is on those characteristics of the consultee that are contributing to his or her difficulty with the client, there is little or no direct assessment of the client. The consultant's primary mode of assessment is careful listening and probing while the consultee describes the case. Through inconsistencies and inaccuracies in the consultee's description of the problem, the consultant is able to identify the cognitive and affective factors that are interfering with consultee functioning.

Caplan divides the sources of consultee difficulty into four major categories that necessitate different actions on the part of the consultant. There are (1) lack of knowledge, (2) lack of skill, (3) lack of confidence, and (4) lack of objectivity. Each of these sources of consultee difficulty and consultant actions is described below.

Lack of Knowledge.   When lack of knowledge is contributing to the consultee's present difficulties with a case, he or she may be ignorant of, or fail to see the relevance of, psychological or social factors pertinent to the case. A nurse may be aware that providing a rationale or explanation for requests increases compliance, but may fail to follow this principle when giving instructions to outpatients regarding medication. Likewise, a teacher may be aware that rehearsal increases the probability that information will be remembered, but may give instructions only once to the class.

Although consultee lack of knowledge can be dealt with by supplying the information to the consultee, Caplan maintains that when the consultant encounters repeated instances of consultation falling in this category, it signals a system-level need or

inadequacy for which individual consultation with a specialist represents an expensive, inefficient alternative. In such cases the consultant should provide feedback to the organization regarding the unmet need he or she perceives and suggest alternate ways of dealing with the need such as continuing education, supervision, or group consultation. For example, a school counselor who repeatedly encounters requests for consultation regarding discipline concerns may suggest to administrators that this is an appropriate topic for an inservice presentation to all interested teachers.

Lack of Skill.   The second category, lack of skill, refers to instances in consultation where the consultee appears to understand the relevant factors in dealing with a case, but is unable to find a satisfactory solution to the problem the case presents. Within Caplan's model of consultation, lack of skill on the part of the consultee is not a problem that is ideally suited to consultation because the consultant typically is from another profession and institution and, therefore, is not likely to have complete knowledge of the methods and techniques that are part of the consultee's profession and accepted within his or her organization. Such difficulties are more appropriately handled though supervision because the supervisor is a member of both the consultee's profession and institution. Thus, the plans generated in supervision are more likely to be consonant with the consultee's professional identity and the norms within the work setting.

Caplan suggests that the consultant's role in problems involving consultee lack of skill should be to support the consultee in understanding the issues involved in the case and exploring appropriate avenues for skill development available within the work setting. In instances where means other than consultation are unavailable for dealing with a consultee's lack of skill, Caplan advises that the consultant avoid providing a single solution that may not fit the norms for the consultee's profession and institution. A more desirable procedure is to suggest a variety of alternative actions to the consultee. The difficulties inherent in designing a plan that is compatible with professional and institutional norms that are unknown to a consultant are illustrated in the following example:

> *A consultant whose previous experience had included working with adults trying to break habits or reduce undesirable behaviors (e.g., chronic worrying) by applying mild self-punishment techniques began working in a school and received a request for consultation from a teacher who wanted some of her fourth graders to stay on task. The consultant suggested a behavior control technique in which children applied mild self-punishment when they found themselves off task (snapping a rubber band on one's wrist). Despite the fact that corporal punishment was used routinely at this particular elementary school and that the recommended technique was mild in comparison, this particular technique was so foreign to the norms of the school that the implementation of the technique caused considerable uproar among teachers, administrators, and parents. Both the consultant and consultee met with much criticism and the consultant's role and credibility were considerably diminished. While the consultant's judgment in this case is questionable, this example illustrates Caplan's cautionary note about failure to fully appreciate norms operative in a setting.*

Lack of Confidence.   The third source of consultee difficulty discussed by Caplan is lack of confidence. As with the previous sources of difficulty within the consultee, Caplan does not view lack of confidence as a problem well suited to consultation. When consultants believe that problems stem from lack of confidence, they provide support and assurance to consultees temporarily, while assisting consultees to find other sources of support within their organizations. A psychiatric social worker dealing with his or her first adolescent suicide attempt may be aware of the legal and ethical obligations with regard to parental notification and also be aware of the usual procedures for dealing with suicide attempts, but may still find the case frightening and seek reassurance that the case is handled appropriately. The consultant would provide this support, but would also help the consultee find more senior members of his or her own profession to provide this support in the future.

Lack of Objectivity.   The final source of consultee difficulty is lack of objectivity. In Caplan's estimation, when supervisory and administrative mechanisms are functioning well in a human service organization, the majority of consultee-centered consultation cases will fall in this category. This type of consultee difficulty occurs when consultees lose their usual professional distance or objectivity when working with a client and cannot apply their skills to resolve a current problem with a client. In addition, the consultee's failure to resolve the problem independently may exacerbate the consultee's original difficulty. For example, a nurse who has difficulty dealing with uncooperative patients will be even less objective when several attempts to gain compliance from an uncooperative patient have failed. Assessment of consultee lack of objectivity is based primarily on the consultee's description of the case, the factors he or she chooses to emphasize, the reasoning and premises that underlie conclusions the consultee has drawn, and inconsistencies in the facts the consultee relates. Typically, the consultant asks the consultee to describe the problem and, through questioning, prompts the consultee to repeat his or her description and perceptions.

Caplan delineates five categories that comprise most instances of consultee lack of objectivity. While these will be described in more detail in the following paragraphs, the categories are (1) direct personal involvement, (2) simple identification, (3) transference, (4) characterological distortion, and (5) theme interference.

The first type of lack of objectivity, *direct personal involvement,* occurs when the consultee's professional relationship with the client changes to one of personal involvement. For example, a physician may be attracted to a patient (Caplan, 1970), a childcare worker may become so involved with a child in residential care that he or she considers adoption, or a teacher is unduly punitive with a child who possesses some characteristic that he or she finds objectionable.

Caplan (1970) suggests two interventions when the consultant suspects that direct personal involvement is clouding the consultee's judgment and blocking effective action. In both cases consultants indirectly attempt to influence consultees to resume their professional role with regard to the client. With the first technique, the client's role conflict with the consultee is used to indirectly illustrate the consultee's own role conflict, for example, by pointing out the importance of the client's learning to relate appropriately to persons in various social roles and distinguish appropriate from inappropriate behavior in varying social contexts. In our example of the childcare worker who becomes overinvolved with a child in a residential institution, the consultant might point out how the child seems to be relating to the childcare worker as a parent.

With the second technique, the consultant serves as a role model to the consultee. For example, the consultant who suspects that a consultee is responding to a client on the basis of some personal bias, such as strong feelings against homosexuality when dealing with a homosexual client, can assist the consultee to see the client and his or her problems more objectively by appraising all aspects of the client's situation during consultation rather than focusing on a single characteristic of the client.

The second category, *simple identification,* occurs when consultees identify with clients or other persons involved with their clients and lose their neutral viewpoint regarding the clients' situation. A social worker who assumed custodial care for her elderly parents and experienced considerable conflict over the disruption of her own family's routines and lifestyle may feel strongly that a client in a similar situation should seek other alternatives. As in consultation cases involving direct personal involvement, the consultant models objectivity while examining the client's situation with the consultee to assist the consultee in seeing the case more objectively.

The third category of lack of objectivity, *transference,* is derived from the psychodynamic construct of transference in psychotherapy where the client transfers feelings and attitudes from other relationships onto the psychotherapeutic relationship. In transference cases encountered in consultation, the consultee imposes a pattern of roles and expectations onto the client's situation based on his or her own past experiences. Over time, this pattern is repeated with similar clients.

Caplan relates an example of transference in which a teacher requested consultation regarding an immature child. The teacher appeared hostile toward the child and through the teacher's description of the case, the consultant surmised that she viewed the problem as an instance of a youngest child who was spoiled and expected his or her own way. There were several cues that indicated this assessment might not be realistic, such as (1) the teacher's clearly negative view of the child, (2) her difficulty providing convincing examples to support her assessment, (3) the teacher's report that the child got along well with peers and did not have a history of problems in school, which conflicted with the teacher's negative description of the child, and (4) the consultant's recollection that a similar case had been presented by the same teacher earlier. The consultant hypothesized that the teacher may have been involved in some unresolved conflicts regarding a spoiled younger sister similar to those she perceived in the present case. The consultant attempted to reduce the teacher's transference by asking her to observe the child more closely in hopes of prompting a more objective view of the child and describing the child's problem as one in which the child was seeing the teacher as an older sister and the teacher was to help the child differentiate the teacher from an older sister.

The fourth category, *characterological distortion,* is the most extreme example of consultee lack of objectivity. Here, some enduring aspect of the consultee's personality interferes with his or her professional functioning. For example, a consultee who works with delinquent boys and has not resolved issues surrounding his own relationship with authority figures may consistently overreact to normal adolescent challenges of his authority, and yet display some of the same noncompliant behavior and challenges to his supervisors.

Although the consultant probably cannot improve the long-term functioning of the consultee, Caplan maintains that the consultant can assist the consultee in keeping deep-seated personal issues from disrupting the consultee's functioning on a case-by-case basis. The consultant provides support to the consultee to relieve the anger and anxiety he or she may feel and models objectivity and understanding of the clients' behavior when dis-

cussing the case, hoping this will increase the consultee's distance and objectivity.

Theme Interference

Although theme interference is only one subcategory of consultee lack of objectivity, it is discussed here in a separate section because Caplan gives it a central place in his writing.

According to Caplan, a theme represents an unsolved problem or defeat that the consultee has

---

Student Learning Activity 2.3
Mental Health Consultation Case Example Exercise

Marcie Templeton works as a visiting nurse. She is white and in her mid-twenties, and this is her first job after receiving a nursing degree. She has requested a conference with the mental health consultant for her agency because she is concerned about one of her patients. The consulting psychiatrist, Carter Moss, is an experienced senior medical staff member who is African American.

When the two meet, Marcie explains the situation to Dr. Moss:

NURSE: I'm concerned about one of my patients that I visit weekly, Roy Johnson. He is sixty-nine years of age, African American, and has diabetes and high blood pressure. He is at considerable risk for a stroke, and I can't seem to get through to him about the importance of his taking his meds and complying with the diet we've given him. Neither his blood pressure nor his diabetes is well controlled. When I visit, he and his wife are very friendly and gracious, but they just don't seem to understand the importance of what I'm telling them.

PSYCHIATRIST: Tell me about your last visit there.

NURSE: Last week I visited on a Monday. Roy's blood pressure and blood sugar were both very high. I asked him if he had taken his meds, and he said he'd taken part of them.

PSYCHIATRIST: Just part?

NURSE: Yes, I tried to get him to explain why he'd only taken part, but he just changed the subject. When I tried to make it clear to him how important it was to follow his doctor's orders, Roy's grandson ran in the room, and, well, it just got too noisy and confusing to talk any further.

PSYCHIATRIST: Then what happened?

NURSE: Well, not much. I tried to talk to Roy's wife about diet. I'd given her a pamphlet with recipes that had low salt and sugar, and I asked her if she'd tried any of them. But she said she hadn't had time yet. She said church had kept her real busy, but she thought she'd have time this week. I just can't seem to get through to this couple about the risks they're taking with Roy's health. I was hoping you could give me some direction—this is really a compliance issue.

PSYCHIATRIST: I see.

1. What aspects of the mental health consultation approach do you see in the psychiatrist's approach to this case?
2. What hypotheses might the psychiatrist be forming about the case at this point?
3. If the consultant thought that cultural misunderstanding or insensitivity played a role here, how would he handle it?

experienced, which influences his or her expectations concerning a client. The theme often takes the form of syllogism—that is, the consultee sees an inevitable link between a situation and an undesirable outcome. In Caplan's words: "Statement A denotes a particular situation or condition that was characteristic of the original unsolved problem. Statement B denotes the unpleasant outcome. The syllogism takes the form, 'All A inevitably leads to B.' The implication is that whenever a person finds himself [sic] involved in situation or condition A, he is fated to suffer B; also that this generalization applies universally, that everyone who is involved in A inevitably suffers B" (Caplan & Caplan, 1993, 1999, pp. 122–123). For example, a consultee might believe that all boys who are raised in single-parent homes will have poor self-control and end up as school dropouts and juvenile delinquents. An eight-year-old boy from a single-parent home who is somewhat immature and overactive and encounters minor difficulties when moving to a new school might be seen by the consultee as fitting the initial situation of the theme (boys from single-parent homes), and consultation is sought to prevent the undesirable outcome (poor self-control, dropping out, and juvenile delinquency).

When a consultee experiences theme interference, he or she views the current situation as hopeless and may make a number of problem-solving attempts that are ill-conceived, hasty, and ineffectual. These actions confirm the consultee's feelings of hopelessness about the case.

In Caplan's conceptualization of theme interference, consultees manipulate the situation to fit their preconceived notions: "Unconsciously, his [sic] consolation is that this time the catastrophe will occur to a client and not to himself. At a deeper level, there may also be the reassurance that he stage-managed and directed the whole drama by manipulating the actors to conform to his theme and so achieved some measure of mastery by this vicarious experience" (1970, p. 147).

Caplan believes that theme interference is a relatively frequent, but normal, work impediment. However, themes do not always interfere with a consultee's functioning. Theme interference typi-

cally occurs when some other current circumstances make a particular theme more salient. (Again, this is an example of how Caplan links environment and intrapsychic causes of behavior.)

The consultant who encounters a case involving theme interference has two intervention options: (1) unlinking, which is only temporarily effective, or (2) theme interference reduction, which brings about a long-term improvement in the consultee. Unlinking occurs when the consultant influences the consultee to perceive the client differently, so that he or she no longer fits the initial situation of the theme. As the consultee begins to see the client more objectively, his or her usual problem-solving skills return. Caplan considers unlinking a cardinal error in consultation technique because it leaves the consultee's theme intact and theme interference may occur again. The preferred intervention for theme interference is theme interference reduction, which involves accepting the consultee's unconscious premise that the client's difficulty is a test case for his or her theme and then persuading the consultee that the outcome is not inevitable. This relieves the consultee's anxiety about the case, and he or she then is able to resolve his or her problem with the client. This successful experience also serves to invalidate the theme so that the consultee's personal conflict is reduced and future professional functioning is enhanced.

Four principal methods can be used by the consultant to accomplish theme interference reduction. In each case, the consultant tries to weaken the link between the consultee's initial situation and inevitable outcome. The four methods are (1) verbal focus on the client, (2) the parable, (3) nonverbal focus on the client, and (4) nonverbal focus on the relationship.

Verbal Focus on the Client. With this method of theme interference reduction, the consultant and consultee examine the client's case in detail and consider possible outcomes. The consultant does not deny that the inevitable outcome feared by the consultee is possible, but also brings out the possibility of less dismal outcomes. In the example of the boy from a single-parent family, the consultant would acknowledge that some males from single-parent families do encounter school difficulties, drop out, and have brushes with the law, and that there is reason to be concerned about this possibility in the present case. However, other possibilities would also be considered. For example, the client's difficulties in school are not serious at this time and the family has expressed interest in a tutor. Alternately, the child may have missed some basic skills when he moved from another school district that used a different curriculum.

The consultant's actions serve two purposes. First, the consultee is influenced to perceive the present situation more realistically through an objective examination of the facts. Second, his or her preconceived ideas about the outcome of similar situations are also questioned implicitly by their relation with this particular case. This questioning and the successful resolution of the present case then reduce the strength of the theme.

The Parable. With this technique, the consultant uses an example derived from his or her own experiences to illustrate that the inevitable outcome feared by the consultee does not always occur. The consultant relates a story that is similar in crucial details to the present situation confronting the consultee, but alters the nonessential details such as setting and age or sex of the main character. A consultant working with a welfare eligibility worker who fears that a client's decision to allow her husband to return to the home will inevitably lead to wife and child abuse might relate a story about another family in which the husband's return led to increased stability in the home.

Nonverbal Focus on the Case. The consultant also can communicate indirectly that the consultee's concerns about the client are overstated by modeling a more realistic attitude toward the case. The consultant discusses the feared outcome of the case in enough detail to reassure the consultee that he or she has not misinterpreted the case. But this discussion is done in a relaxed way, and the consultant does not respond to the consultee's urgency and call for quick action.

Nonverbal Focus on the Consultation Relationship. In theme interference the consultee's feelings and perceptions concerning a personal issue have been displaced onto a case. Caplan notes that these perceptions and feelings also may be displaced onto the consultation relationship. If so, what occurs in the consultation relationship can be used to invalidate the consultee's theme or show that the consultee's expectations are not correct. To illustrate, a teacher sought assistance for a child who was noncompliant at home and school. When the consultant suggested that the teacher might speak to the parents about parent training at a community mental health center, the teacher vehemently objected, stating that she knew about their methods and they would only chastise the parents and provide no real help. The consultant noted that throughout the consultation interviews the consultee would frequently make antagonistic remarks about mental health personnel that seemed to invite confrontation since the consultant was a member of a mental health profession. The consultant consistently ignored these remarks or dealt with them in a friendly, nondefensive manner.

Caplan states that these four techniques can be used alone or in combination to invalidate the theme that causes theme interference and improve the consultee's objectivity and problem-solving capacity with reference to the present case. When these objectives have been accomplished, the consultant leaves the consultee to deal with the client's problem independently. The consultant's exit assures that the consultee plays an active role in handling the difficulty that he or she previously saw as unsolvable, further invalidating the theme.

Program-Centered Administrative Consultation

Program-centered administrative consultation is similar to client-centered case consultation. The consultant is viewed as a specialist who is called in to study a problem and provide a set of recommendations for dealing with the problem. In client-centered case consultation, however, the consultant's assessment, diagnosis, and recommendations are concerned with the problems of a particular client; in program-centered administrative consultation, the consultant is concerned with problems surrounding the development of a new program or some aspect of organizational functioning.

Unlike consultation concerning a case, organizational factors that are important in administrative consultation may be outside of the mental health professional's usual area of expertise. Caplan cautions that, in addition to their clinical skills, administrative consultants should have an understanding of organizational theory, planning, financial and personnel management, and administration. The primary goal of program-centered administrative consultation is the development of an action plan, usually in the form of a written report, that can be implemented by the consultee and his or her associates to resolve the administrative problem that prompted consultation. As such, it is important that both the consultant's formulation of the problem and subsequent recommendations are correct. Therefore, the consultant takes an active role in data collection rather than using the perceptions of the consultee as the sole source of information.

Program-centered administrative consultation is usually rapid paced, reaching completion in a matter of days or weeks. Typically, the consultation process begins with initial contacts from the organization to explore the possibility of consultation. The consultant uses these contacts to assess the match between his or her skills and the perceived problem, as well as to identify at what level of the organization sanction will be needed for consultation, and the person or persons with the authority to implement consultative recommendations. Unlike case-centered consultation, where a single consultee usually has primary responsibility for a client, the identity of the appropriate consultee who has responsibility for an organizational problem may not be readily discernible.

Assessment procedures include understanding the organizational context by reviewing written documentation concerning the history of the organization, its goals, functions, and formal organizational structure, as well as any memos or reports concerning the specific issues to be addressed by the consultant. The consultant may contact others who are familiar with the particular organization or the type of organization with which he or she will be consulting. On-site assessment generally takes the form of interviews with individual staff members and groups of employees. Here, sanction of the top administrator as well as confidentiality are important to assure that staff members feel comfortable sharing their perceptions. By gathering multiple views on the same problem, the consultant arrives at an independent formulation of the problem. The consultant may also observe the behavior and interactions of organizational members as part of assessment.

Caplan (1970) divides problem formulation into three phases: an initial definition of the problem, a period of confusion where the consultant considers multiple viewpoints and data that may reinforce or conflict with the original conceptualization of the problem, and finally, a "gestalt closure" (p. 241) where the consultant views the problem in a more complex way that allows him or her to make sense of the data that have been gathered.

From this problem definition the consultant develops recommendations. The consultee and other members of the organization play an active role in the formulation and refinement of recommendations. Caplan describes the development of recommendations as a process of accretion. That is, the consultant seeks staff reactions to tentative recommendations and uses these to modify and refine the recommendations. This collaborative procedure not only helps assure that recommendations are workable, but reflects the basic assumption that the technical correctness of a recommendation is not the sole determinant of its adoption. Caplan states that "unless people are personally involved in collaborating with the consultant in developing a plan, they are less likely to accept it and work toward its implementation" (1970, p. 247).

As with other types of consultation, the consultant does not take an active role in the implementation of recommendations made in his or her report; the consultee is free to accept, modify, or reject the consultant's proposed plan. However, the consultant does indicate interest in what actions the organization takes.

Consultee-Centered Administrative Consultation

The goal of consultee-centered administrative consultation is to improve the professional functioning of members of an administrative staff. Although consultee-centered administrative consultation may take many forms, such as consultation with the head of a program or with a particular group of administrators, much of Caplan's (1970) description of this type of consultation is based on a more broadly conceptualized role for the consultant.

The consultant agrees to work with an organization on a long-term basis. However, the specific focus of consultation and the particular consultees are not specified. Administrators at all levels may seek consultation. In addition, the consultant is allowed to move freely throughout the levels of the organization. This freedom gives the consultant a view of the total organization that cannot be obtained by consultees who have a more prescribed role in the organization. Therefore, the consultant does not restrict consultation to problems brought to his or her attention by consultees, but takes an active role in identifying organizational problems and approaching potential consultees to discuss these issues.

Although the consultant may deal with almost any issue within the organization, consultation is still a voluntary relationship, and the consultant has no authority to determine the content of consultation or responsibility for identifying and implementing solutions. Instead, the consultant acts as a catalyst, identifying a salient issue, bringing it to the attention of consultees, and hoping they will want to discuss it and initiate their own problem-solving efforts.

Consultee-centered administrative consultation may grow out of other types of consultation, or an organization may initially request this type of consultation. In negotiating an initial agreement, the consultant seeks sanction from the highest level within the administrative unit to assure free movement through all levels of the organization, as well as freedom to contact any organizational members who might have relevant information. The consultant then works to build relationships with the staff and develop an understanding of how the organization functions.

Caplan comments that several difficulties may impair building relationships in consultee-centered administrative consultation. The consultant's unrestricted movement and freedom to inquire about all aspects of the organization may be threatening and disturbing to staff members who are used to their customary patterns of communication and operation. The consultant also may be perceived as a spy or agent of the director. The consultant works to dispel these fears and build trusting relationships with potential consultees by attending meetings, making efforts to meet consultees informally, giving consultees opportunities to determine topics and issues for consultation, and maintaining a coordinate relationship with consultees.

During this period the consultant also works to understand the consultees and their organization, looking for barriers to effective consultee functioning at many different levels. The consultant must be prepared to "appraise individual personality characteristics and problems among the key administrators, intragroup and intergroup relations in and among the various units of the enterprise, organizational patterns of role assignment and lines of communication and authority, leadership patterns and styles, vertical and horizontal communication, and traditions of participation in decision making" (Caplan, 1970, p. 280).

Over time, the consultant develops a broader network of consultees at many levels of the organization and a greater understanding of the contextual factors that affect administrators' functioning. Within this ongoing set of relationships, the consultant deals with a broad range of consultative issues on a short-term basis. For example, over the course of a year, a consultant to college campus administrators might deal with such topics as communication between admissions officers and individual departments, procedures for dealing with students caught cheating, lack of objectivity in a particular administrator in relation to a hiring decision, dealing with a depressed employee, and conducting more productive meetings.

Interventions in consultee-centered administrative consultation can be directed toward individuals, groups, or the organization as a whole. At the individual level, the consultant might try to broaden the range of factors a consultee considers when trying to understand subordinates' actions. Or, the consultant might work to increase a consultee's tolerance of negative feelings and confusion, so that he or she is less likely to avoid dealing with difficult work problems that arouse these feelings. At the group level, the consultant might work to improve communication between members of a group or between a supervisor and his or her staff members. The consultant also might work to improve the overall health of the organization. For example, the consultant could work to open up formal avenues within an organization for acknowledging and dealing with negative feelings, such as helping a high school develop a student transfer policy for dealing with student/teacher personality conflicts.

As in consultee-centered case consultation, the consultant intervenes only to increase the consultees' problem-solving capacity or to direct their attention to an organizational issue. It is assumed that the consultant does not have sufficient information about the organization to design appropriate interventions and that any action plans are the responsibility of the consultees. As in other types of mental health consultation, however, the consultant always indicates an interest in knowing the outcome of any problem-solving efforts.

Resistance in Mental Health Consultation

Consultee resistance to change is a problem that must be addressed within all consultation models. Within mental health consultation, the relationship established with the consultee plays an important role in minimizing resistance (Caplan, 1970). The consultant assumes a coordinate, nonhierarchical stance toward the consultee, who is free to accept or reject the ideas of the consultant. In Caplan's

view, the consultee is more likely to accept ideas and incorporate them into his or her work setting under these circumstances.

FURTHER DEVELOPMENTS IN THE MENTAL HEALTH CONSULTATION MODEL

In the 35 years following publication of Caplan's landmark text, *The Theory and Practice of Mental Health Consultation* (Caplan, 1970), the field of consultation has taken many directions. A limited body of research has emerged to support the use of mental health consultation (Medway & Updyke, 1985). Other writers and researchers have modified mental health consultation (Altrocchi, 1972; Ingraham, 2004; Meyers, 1981, 1989, 1995; Meyers et al., 1993; Meyers & Kundert, 1988; Meyers et al., 1979; Pryzwansky, 1974, 1977) to fit particular settings or consultees. Finally, Caplan himself (Caplan, 1981, 1982, 1986, 2004; Caplan & Caplan, 1993, 1999; Caplan, LeBow, Gavarin, & Stelzer, 1981; Erchul, 1993) has modified some of his ideas about consultation and the use of consultation as a preventive technique.

In this section, several developments in mental health consultation will be discussed. First, research related to the mental health consultation model will be summarized. Second, models that draw heavily from Caplan's model or were developed in response to Caplan's model will be described. Third, Caplan's reflections on mental health consultation and changes in the model will be summarized.

Research on the Mental Health Consultation Model

In a 1985 meta-analysis of consultation outcome studies, Medway and Updyke synthesized the results of 24 studies examining the effectiveness of mental health, behavioral, or organizational development consultation. Meta-analysis is a quantitative technique for integrating findings across studies (Glass, 1976). With this technique, the results of individual studies are converted to a common metric, effect size. Although space does not permit a detailed description of how effect sizes are calculated and interpreted, the conversion of all study results to this common metric allows a reviewer to average results across studies. The reviewer can then make general statements about the effectiveness of a treatment and compare groups of studies that differ on important dimensions. For example, the average effect size of studies using one method of treatment for a particular problem can be compared to the average effect size of studies using a second method of treatment.

Averaging effect sizes over the 24 studies which examined mental health consultation, Medway and Updyke (1985) found that mental health consultation had a positive impact on both consultees and clients, although its effects were most pronounced on consultees. Looking at the relative effectiveness of the three models of consultation across consultants, consultees, and clients, no differences were found in terms of effectiveness.

Gutkin and Curtis (1990) have questioned whether the studies classified in the Medway and Updyke meta-analysis as using the mental health model were truly examples of mental health consultation. Because little consultation efficacy research has provided data documenting how consultation was actually implemented during the study (Gresham, 1989), this issue is not easily resolved. The difficulty in verifying what consultants did and how they did it in existing consultation research points to the importance of collecting treatment integrity data in research concerning any consultation model.

In a follow-up to Medway and Updyke's (1985) meta-analysis, Sheridan, Welch, and Orme (1996) examined consultation efficacy studies that had been published after Medway and Updyke had completed their meta-analysis. They also found positive outcomes for mental health consultation, although lack of data documenting how consultation was implemented continued to be a problem with many consultation studies. They reported that studies investigating behavioral consultation were more numerous and stronger methodologically than studies investigating other models, including mental health consultation.

Modifications to Mental Health Consultation

Since Caplan proposed his mental health consultation model in 1970, a number of mental health professionals have proposed variants of the model, or modified some of the original concepts. For example, Altrocchi (1972) drew heavily from Caplan's model of consultation, but included nonprofessionals as consultees. He also explicitly included group consultation within his definition of consultation and discussed the advantages and disadvantages of consultation with groups and individuals. In his early work, Caplan (1970) had expressed concern that consultation with groups of consultees could present problems, particularly in consultee-centered consultation. With a group approach, the consultant has more difficulty controlling verbal interaction and consultees might lose face with peers should someone point out their apparent emotional involvement in a case. In addition, Caplan expressed concern that group members would not benefit from discussion of another consultee's problem.

In contrast to Caplan's (1970) position, Altrocchi argued that group consultation offers some advantages. For example, more hypotheses and perspectives are available to the consultees. Similar experiences by other consultees and their successful ways of dealing with the problem can be shared to provide support to consultees currently experiencing distress. In his later work, Caplan (1977; Caplan & Caplan, 1993, 1999) also acknowledged the importance and benefits of group consultation, commenting that his concerns about this approach had not been borne out in practice. In recent years, there have been a number of applications of consultee-centered consultation principles to work with groups of professionals (Babinski, Knotek, & Rogers, 2004; Babinski & Rogers, 1998; Ekenbark, 2004; Webster, Knotek, Babinski, Rogers, & Barnett, 2003).

In addition to the increased use of consultee-centered consultation in a group format, another innovation in consultee-centered consultation has been the introduction of a cognitive perspective. A central focus of consultee-centered consultation has always been stimulating cognitive and affective growth in the consultee. Given Caplan's background as a psychodynamically trained psychiatrist, it is not surprising that his description of the process of consultee change has focused on the consultants' actions and their role in addressing the perceptual distortions and defenses that may affect consultees' interactions with their clients (Caplan, 1970). However, several writers (e.g., Knotek, Rosenfield, Gravois, & Babinksi, 2003; Rosenfield, 2004; Sandoval, 1996, 2003, 2004) have discussed consultee change from a social constructivist (Vygotsky, 1978) and cognitive framework. From this framework, one goal of consultee-centered consultation is to change the schemas or cognitive constructions that consultees use in conceptualizing their difficulties with their clients (Sandoval, 2004). The constructivist perspective emphasizes the importance of dialogue and active participation in acquiring new learning (Knotek et al., 2003; Rosenfield, 2004). Just as in a psychodynamic perspective, the dialogue between the consultant and consultee and retention of responsibility for action by the consultee remain important levers for change within this new perspective on consultee-centered consultation. However, the rationale for the use of these two key elements is quite different from a cognitive framework.

For example, Sandoval (1996) noted that consultees often enter consultation with their own implicit theories about why the client is experiencing difficulty and that these theories may interfere with problem solving. He has proposed that theme interference be considered a process of conceptual change, in which the consultant endeavors to help consultees change incorrect assumptions about a client or group of clients. He provides examples from his consultation with teachers working with students with physical disabilities where misunderstanding of a disorder and its effects on child functioning interfered with teachers' effectiveness with particular children. Maital (1996) has proposed that from a cognitive-behavioral perspective, consultee themes can be seen as irrational beliefs that interfere with effectiveness.

Mental Health Consultation in the Schools

Meyers and his colleagues (Meyers, 1973, 1981, 1989, 1995; Meyers et al., 1979; Meyers et al., 1993; Meyers & Kundert, 1988; Parsons & Meyers, 1984) have written extensively concerning how mental health consultation constructs can be applied in a school setting. They have modified many of Caplan's constructs specifically for the school setting, as well as introduced new content and activities to consultation that were not discussed by Caplan. These changes and new content will be summarized here.

Meyers defines consultation as a problem-solving process that occurs between a help giver (consultant) and help seeker (or consultee) who has responsibility for another person as part of his or her work. The goal of consultation is to help the consultee solve a current work problem and respond more effectively to similar problems in the future (Meyers, 1989). Similar to Caplan, consultation is considered a voluntary relationship that is nonhierarchical, but the consultant is not assumed to be from an external agency.

Meyers has replaced Caplan's four types of consultation with a typology that is specific to the school setting. Within this typology, there are three levels of service that vary in terms of how directly services are provided to the student by the consultant (Meyers, 1989; Meyers et al., 1979). Level I is a focus on the child, Level II, a focus on the teacher, and Level III, a focus on the system. For example, at Level I, a consultant might work with a teacher to develop a strategy for dealing with a specific child's reading problem. At Level II, the consultant would work with the teacher to modify class grouping and instructional strategies so that all children with reading problems in that classroom receive more effective instruction. At Level III, the consultant would help develop inservice and other staff development activities to improve the entire faculty's effectiveness with children who are experiencing reading difficulties. Like Caplan, Meyers characterizes consultation as often beginning with a child-centered focus and assuming a more preventive focus as teachers and schools become more comfortable and confident with the consultant and consultation (Meyers et al., 1993).

Meyers has modified many other aspects of mental health consultation to better match the school environment and professionals' roles in that environment (Meyers, 1981, 1989; Meyers et al., 1979; Meyers & Kundert, 1988). Caplan's five types of objectivity have been reconceptualized as four common conflicts experienced by teachers:

1. *Authority conflicts*—teachers may have ambivalent feelings about their need to maintain control in the classroom versus being liked by students.
2. *Dependency*—teachers may require excessive dependence and obedience from students and relate to authority figures in the same manner.
3. *Anger and hostility*—teachers may experience feelings of anger and hostility toward students and also be disturbed by them because they believe these feelings should not occur in professionals.
4. *Identification*—teachers may identify with a student or someone else involved in a case and fail to see the situation objectively.

Meyers and his colleagues maintain that consultee affect and conflicts, such as those described above, can be assessed and dealt with in consultation in both an indirect and a direct manner. Direct approaches include asking the consultees to express their feelings, relationship-building techniques that focus on bringing out consultees' views, and confrontation (Meyers, 1981; Meyers et al., 1993). Unlike Caplan, who uses only indirect methods of dealing with consultee affect, Meyers and his colleagues maintain that indirect methods may not have an impact on consultees and do not credit consultees' ability to handle appropriate confrontation.

Meyers described how consultation and an assessment role for school psychologists can be integrated (Meyers & Kundert, 1988) by broadening school psychologists' testing role to focus on the interaction of child, task, and setting characteristics. This broadened focus would result in a more direct link between assessment, intervention, and consultation. Meyers (Meyers et al., 1993) also has written about the role of school-based mental health consultation in primary prevention and maintains that preventive efforts may be most effective when they focus on working to modify school routines to better support children and teachers (Meyers, 1988). Modifications might include the teaching of interpersonal cognitive problem-solving skills or coping skills by teachers, programs to ease common but stressful school transitions (e.g., moving from elementary to secondary school), or modifying teaching materials (e.g., reading texts) to be more relevant to children's own experiences and needs.

Meyers (1995) reflected back on the publication of his original consultation model for school psychological services in 1973, its evolution, and its applicability today. He notes the changes in his model over time and notes that consultants may operate on more than one level when consulting (e.g., using a child-centered approach for a particular case while working on a systems level to be sure that better procedures are in place for handling similar cases in the future). He expresses the concern that consultation in schools is too often focused on improving the functioning of a single child in crisis rather than examining how schools as a system can respond effectively to the large numbers of children in need, and he calls for increased attention to consultation as a primary prevention technique in light of the pressing mental health issues that now face children and schools. He notes the lack of research on mental health consultation as opposed to other models, such as behavioral consultation, and calls for an increase in consultation research that examines a broad range of consultation models using diverse research methodologies, including large group designs, single subject designs, and quantitative and qualitative approaches.

Pryzwansky (1974, 1977; Babcock & Pryzwansky, 1983; West, 1990) has also written about the use of the mental health consultation model in schools. He maintains that the internal locus of most school-based consultants' (e.g., school counselors, psychologists, and social workers) and teachers' desire for concrete solutions makes collaboration a more appropriate helping strategy in the schools than consultation.

Within a collaborative model, the consultant and consultee assume joint responsibility for all aspects of the consultation process. Consultants and consultees agree upon the objectives for consultation, define the problem together, jointly develop an intervention plan, and share responsibility for implementation and evaluation of the outcome of their plan. As noted later in this chapter, Caplan also sees consultation as an inappropriate strategy for internal consultants and has proposed that collaboration replace mental health consultation under these circumstances (Caplan, Caplan, & Erchul, 1995).

More recently, mental health consultation concepts have been used in the schools to provide group-based support for new teachers and facilitate their professional and problem-solving skill development (Babinski & Rogers, 1998). In addition, Astor and Pitner (1996) provide an intriguing model that combines ecological systems theory and mental health consultation to address youth and school violence in low-income urban communities. Potential interventions in their model include consultation to address specific problems related to lack of knowledge, skills, objectivity, and self-confidence facing teachers in urban areas, and group consultation to reduce ethnic stereotyping and negative feelings toward particular racial, ethnic, or religious groups.

A Multicultural Adaptation of Consultee-Centered Consultation

Ingraham (2000, 2004) has used Caplan's taxonomy of sources of consultee difficulty (lack of knowledge, skill, confidence, and objectivity) as a way of classifying the difficulties consultees encounter when working with clients from cultural groups that are outside their range of experience. In keeping with the cognitive focus now prevalent in consultee-centered consultation, she portrays

these as "domains for consultee learning and development" (Ingraham, 2000, p. 330). These domains are part of a model of cross-cultural consultation she has developed with Tarver Behring (Ingraham, 2002, 2004; Tarver Behring & Ingraham, 1998).

Within the knowledge domain, consultees may be unaware of aspects of a client's culture or experiences that are important in understanding the client's actions or developing a plan to address a particular problem. For example, a teacher may interpret a child's failure to make eye contact as a sign of shyness rather than deference because he is unaware of cultural differences in eye-contact patterns. Within the skill domain, consultees may not be able to adjust their professional functioning to accommodate clients who have unique needs due to different background experiences.

In terms of lack of confidence, faced with a situation where their usual way of resolving problems is ineffective, consultees may feel less confident and more anxious when working with clients from a different culture. They may be aware that their usual interventions are inappropriate, but be unsure how to proceed, resulting in "intervention paralysis" (Ingraham, 2000, p. 333).

Within the domain of consultee lack of objectivity, Ingraham has described four different types of distortions that can occur when consultees encounter difficulties working with clients from unfamiliar cultural groups: filtering perceptions through stereotypes, overemphasizing culture, taking a "color-blind" approach, and fear of being called a racist (Ingraham, 2000, 2004). In *filtering perceptions through stereotypes* and *overemphasizing culture,* consultees may use stereotypes about particular cultural groups to account for clients' actions, or consider only cultural differences as the explanation for clients' behavior, when a more nuanced analysis that also considers situational factors and individual differences is needed. In *taking a "color blind" approach,* consultees may treat all individuals the same, despite the fact that gender, ethnicity, and other differences among clients may mean that the same actions have a different meaning or effect for particular clients. *Fear of being called a racist* may cause consultees to avoid confronting problem situations or have difficulty problem solving because they are afraid their actions might be viewed as the result of prejudice.

Beyond Mental Health Consultation

As stated earlier, mental health consultation is a central component of Caplan's approach to preventive psychiatry. Over time, Caplan has broadened his theory of prevention into support systems theory (Caplan, 1982; Caplan-Moskovich, 1982). Unlike his theory of prevention, which focuses on the role mental health professionals play in preventing mental illness, support systems theory places more emphasis on the role of informal caregivers and community support in prevention.

Caplan's increased emphasis on informal caregivers grew out of his work in consultation (Caplan-Moskovich, 1982). In a project with the Episcopal church, Caplan taught senior bishops how to consult with their less experienced colleagues. The consultants began meeting with each other to provide support and later formally organized peer support programs where clergy alternated roles as consultant and consultee with each other (Richards, 1976). This development led Caplan to rethink his approach to community mental health to recognize how peers rather than mental health professionals could provide support and buffer the effects of acute or chronic stress (Caplan-Moskovich, 1982). Thus, much of today's emphasis on mutual help groups and peer support programs in community mental health can be seen as an outgrowth of consultation.

Caplan also recognized that the indirect nature of consultation presented limitations when the mental health aspects of a case were complex, or when more rapid change was desired. In Caplan's words,

> a purely enabling role has not proved optimally effective. We have found that in order to achieve our preventive goals we must also take part in dealing directly with clients in a community facility, and we must accept a commitment and responsibility inside the institution to enlarge its mission and change its organization. (1981, p. 4)

To address this limitation of consultation, Caplan proposed two additional patterns of partnership between mental health and other human services professionals that complemented consultation (Caplan et al., 1981). One of the patterns proposed was *mental health collaboration,* an alternative similar to Pryzwansky's (1974) collaborative model of services for the schools. Unlike consultation where the consultee retains sole responsibility for the client, in collaboration the mental health professional accepts responsibility for the mental health aspects of a case and works directly to improve conditions seen as counter to positive mental health goals. The second alternative to consultation is *executive partnership,* where the mental health professional accepts a leadership role within an organization or administrative unit. For example, a psychiatrist and pediatrician might co-lead a hospital unit that treats the physical and psychosocial aspects of children's illnesses simultaneously.

Caplan and his daughter, Ruth B. Caplan, have updated and expanded the ideas and concepts originally detailed in his 1970 book. This newer work, *Mental Health Consultation and Collaboration* (Caplan & Caplan, 1993, 1999), places collaboration alongside consultation as a major tool for mental health professionals to infuse psychological and preventive principles into diverse work settings. They maintain that when mental health professionals are internal to an organization (e.g., school counselors or social workers), many aspects of their functioning fit poorly with mental health consultation. The professional has an established service role, has responsibility for aspects of clients' functioning, and is governed by the institution's policies. Under these circumstances, Caplan maintains that mental health collaboration represents a better fit with the professional's existing role.

On a continuum of direct to indirect service, the Caplans place testing and therapy on one extreme, where the professional has the greatest control and responsibility; mental health consultation is at the other extreme—the professional has minimal control, and the consultee retains responsibility for the client. Collaboration falls in the middle of this continuum and combines direct and indirect roles. The professional accepts responsibility for the mental health aspects of a client (direct service) but also works to have others with whom he or she collaborates understand, and be more responsive to, the mental health aspects of their work with clients (indirect service).

In a recent chapter, Caplan (2004) discussed the evolution of mental health consultation, touching on many of the adaptations summarized in this chapter. He characterized mental health consultation as a pragmatic and pluralistic model in which practitioner success rather than theory has driven the incorporation of new techniques into the model. He attributed the many changes in mental health consultation over the years to two factors: (1) the use of mental health consultation by professionals with diverse theoretical backgrounds who have adapted the model to fit their needs and belief systems, and (2) his own use of the model in settings that posed different challenges than the ones faced when the model was developed.

In sum, mental health consultation was one of the earliest models of consultation described for human services personnel and remains an area of continuing interest and development. Both mental health consultation and the theory in which it is embedded have evolved. Consultation no longer stands alone, but has spawned a range of techniques, such as mutual help groups and collaboration, that can be used to meet the mental health needs of a community.

Implications for Practice

Caplan's work in consultation has great historical significance. However, professionals-in-training who will be internal consultants or whose future

---

Student Learning Activity 2.4

Identify the type of consultation described in each example.

1 = client-centered case consultation
2 = consultee-centered case consultation
3 = program-centered administrative consultation
4 = consultee-centered administrative consultation

A psychologist assesses a first grader with poor social skills and recommends ways of increasing positive social interaction in the classroom.   _____

A social worker visits a rest home to help the staff develop a cost-effective way of monitoring and improving residents' psychological adjustment.   _____

A psychiatrist is available to a group of visiting nurses to discuss the psychological aspects of patients' illnesses.   _____

A school counselor works with a teacher to improve his or her classroom management skills.   _____

A counseling psychologist assists the on-campus housing director in developing a plan for handling dorm residents who may be suicidal.   _____

The head of a large division meets on an ad hoc basis with a consultant to discuss personnel concerns.   _____

A psychiatrist assesses back pain patients before surgery to estimate the extent to which psychological and physical factors contribute to their discomfort.   _____

practice will not incorporate psychodynamic perspective may have difficulty seeing how Caplan's work on consultation applies to them.

The particular aspects of Caplan's work that apply to different settings and roles will vary. But enduring aspects of Caplan's work have been noted in a volume honoring Caplan's contributions to professional psychology (Erchul, 1993). Drawing from this work and others (e.g., Caplan & Caplan, 1993, 1999; Caplan et al., 1995; Kelly, 1993), as well as our own experiences, we believe that some of the important points for practice that can be attributed to Caplan are:

1. Recognition that the perceptions and feelings of consultees are important, and that they influence their interactions with clients.
2. Discussion of how a consultant can serve as a role model to consultees for systematic problem solving and broaden the consultee's view of a client and his or her problems.
3. Description of the dynamic process of entry into an organization and recognition of the importance of explicit contracting and administrative sanction for assuring lasting change in an organization.
4. Recognition of the importance of prompt, effective treatment for the mental health needs of clients, and a focus on maximizing the impact of mental health professionals rather than focusing on intensive treatment for a small number of clients.
5. Recognition of the importance of consultee involvement in problem solving for increasing the likelihood that the intervention will fit the role requirements of the consultee's profession and will be carried out.
6. Recognition that working indirectly (i.e., as a consultant) requires different skills from direct intervention and, as such, requires additional training for the professional.

As noted in Chapter One, the implications of gender, ethnicity, and culture for consultation have begun to be the topic of research and discussion (e.g., Duncan & Pryzwansky, 1993; Harris, 1993;

Ingraham, 2000; Sheridan & Henning-Stout, 1994; Tobias, 1993). Caplanian consultation differs sharply from a number of consultation models to be discussed in upcoming chapters in terms of its focus on the consultees' thoughts, feelings, and perceptions; indirect communication techniques; and focus on maintaining a nonhierarchical relationship. As such, mental health consultation and its intervention techniques can be valuable tools for consultants working with consultees from cultural groups where feelings are not discussed or direct confrontation is not used. Conoley and Welch (1988) have offered some preliminary findings suggesting that male and female consultants-in-training adopt different consultation styles. The consultee support, relationship building in the context of a nonhierarchical relationship, and nondirective communication style characteristic of Caplanian consultation may be a better fit with the interpersonal style and expectations for female consultants in our culture than more directive, instrumentally (versus interpersonally) oriented models of consultation. Mental health consultation may be inappropriate for consultees from cultural groups who are more accustomed to lineal (versus nonhierarchical) professional relationships and who expect the consultant to assume a more directive role.

SUMMARY

Mental health consultation was developed as part of a preventive approach to dealing with mental disorders and is primarily identified with Gerald Caplan. Consultation is viewed as a process of interaction between two professionals where the consultant assists the consultee in dealing with the psychological aspects of a current work problem and, most important, to deal more effectively with similar problems in the future. A fundamental aspect of mental health consultation is the coordinate, nonhierarchical relationship between the consultant and consultee.

Several assumptions that underlie mental health consultation are delineated. Among these are the importance of intrapsychic and environmental factors in explaining and changing behavior, the unique aspects of each profession that make it likely that consultees will adapt any recommendations made by consultants from another profession, and the importance of the consultee's attitudes and affect in consultation.

Caplan distinguishes between four types of consultation: client-centered case consultation, consultee-centered case consultation, program-centered administrative consultation, and consultee-centered administrative consultation. Of the four types of consultation, Caplan discusses consultee-centered case consultation in the most depth. Four major sources of consultee difficulty often encountered in consultee-centered consultation are lack of knowledge, lack of skill, lack of confidence, and lack of objectivity. Of these, Caplan believes consultee lack of objectivity is most appropriately dealt with in consultation. He delineates five categories of lack of objectivity. Intervention techniques to deal with lack of objectivity include theme interference reduction, the parable, and modeling an objective approach to problem solving.

Variations of mental health consultation have been proposed by Altrocchi, Meyers, Pryzwansky, Ingraham, and others. A recent development is the rethinking of the conceptual underpinnings of consultee-centered consultation to reflect a greater focus on understanding and modifying the cognitive constructions that consultees use to represent the problems they are facing and potential solutions. The Caplans have suggested that consultation be complemented by other support roles, such as collaboration, particularly when consultants are part of the same organization as the consultees.

TIPS FOR THE PRACTITIONER

1. As discussed in more depth in Chapter Six, it is important to seek sanction for your work as a consultant from the highest-level administrator in an organization.
2. Keep in mind that the consultant role often begins with success in a direct service role.

3. Model thoughtful deliberation and rational problem solving in your interactions with consultees.
4. Starting consultation by allowing consultees to relate the problem in their own words, with minimal interruptions, gives you an opportunity to assess how they are viewing the problem and the client, and consider how this should affect your approach to them and the problem.

REVIEW QUESTIONS

1. What are some of the factors that led to the emergence of consultation as an intervention strategy?
2. How does Caplan's definition of consultation differ from the definition presented in Chapter One?
3. Why does Caplan believe that it is important for the consultee to retain responsibility for any action taken as a result of consultation?
4. How do client-centered case consultation and consultee-centered case consultation differ?
5. How do program-centered administrative consultation and consultee-centered administrative consultation differ?
6. Describe the four sources of consultee difficulty in consultee-centered case consultation.
7. Give an example of a Caplanian theme.
8. Why is theme interference reduction preferred to unlinking when dealing with theme interference?
9. How does the consultant serve as a catalyst in consultee-centered administrative consultation?
10. Why is collaboration seen as more appropriate in some settings than consultation?
11. How might taking a "color-blind" approach be seen as a lack of objectivity in a consultee?

REFERENCES

Albee, G. W., & Fryer, D. M. (2003). Praxis: Toward a public health psychology. *Journal of Community and Applied Social Psychology, 13,* 71–75.

Alpert, J., & Silverstein, J. (1985). Mental health consultation: Historical, present, and future perspectives. In J. Bergan (Ed.), *School psychology in contemporary society* (pp. 281–315). Columbus, OH: Charles E. Merrill.

Altrocchi, J. (1972). Mental health consultation. In S. E. Golann & C. Eisdorfer (Eds.), *Handbook of community mental health* (pp. 477–508). New York: Appleton-Century-Crofts.

Astor, R. A., & Pitner, R. O. (1996). Ecological approaches to mental health consultation with teachers on issues related to youth and school violence. *Journal of Negro Education, 65,* 336–355.

Babcock, N. L., & Pryzwansky, W. B. (1983). Models of consultation: Preferences of educational professionals at five stages of service. *Journal of School Psychology, 21,* 359–366.

Babinski, L. M., Knotek, S. E., & Rogers, D. L. (2004). Facilitating conceptual change in new teacher consultation groups. In N. M. Lambert, I. Hylander, & J. H. Sandoval (Eds.), *Consultee-centered consultation: Improving the quality of professional services in schools and community organizations* (pp. 101–113). Mahwah, NJ: Erlbaum.

Babinski, L. M., & Rogers, D. L. (1998). Supporting new teachers through consultee-centered group consultation. *Journal of Educational and Psychological Consultation, 9,* 285–308.

Brown, D., Wyne, M. D., Blackburn, J. E., & Powell, W. C. (1979). *Consultation.* Boston: Allyn & Bacon.

Caplan, G. (1964). *Principles of preventive psychiatry.* New York: Basic Books.

Caplan, G. (1970). *The theory and practice of mental health consultation.* New York: Basic Books.

Caplan, G. (1974). *Support systems and community mental health.* New York: Behavioral Publications.

Caplan, G. (1977). Mental health consultation: Retrospect and prospect. In S. C. Plog & P. I. Ahmed (Eds.), *Principles and techniques of mental health consultation* (pp. 9–21). New York: Plenum.

Caplan, G. (1981). Partnerships for prevention in the human services. *Journal of Primary Prevention, 2,* 3–5.

Caplan, G. (1982). Epilogue: Personal reflections by Gerald Caplan. In H. C. Schulberg & M. Killilea (Eds.), *The modern practice of community mental health* (pp. 650–666). San Francisco: Jossey-Bass.

Caplan, G. (1986). Recent developments in crisis intervention and in the promotion of support services. In M. Kessler & S. E. Goldston (Eds.), *A decade of progress in primary prevention* (pp. 235–260). Hanover, NH: University Press of New England.

Caplan, G. (2004). Recent advances in mental health consultation and collaboration. In N. M. Lambert, I. Hylander, & J. H. Sandoval (Eds.), *Consultee-centered consultation: Improving the quality of professional services in schools and community organizations* (pp. 21–36). Mahwah, NJ: Erlbaum.

Caplan, G., & Caplan, R. B. (1999). *Mental health consultation and collaboration.* Prospect Heights, IL: Waveland. (Original work published in 1993.)

Caplan, G., Caplan, R. B., & Erchul, W. P. (1995). A contemporary view of mental health consultation: Comments on "Types of Mental Health Consultation" by Gerald Caplan. (1963). *Journal of Educational and Psychological Consultation, 6,* 23–30.

Caplan, G., LeBow, H., Gavarin, M., & Stelzer, J. (1981). Patterns of cooperation of child psychiatry with other departments in hospitals. *Journal of Primary Prevention, 4,* 96–106.

Caplan-Moskovich, R. B. (1982). Gerald Caplan: The man and his work. In H. C. Schulberg & M. Killilea (Eds.), *The modern practice of community mental health* (pp. 1–39). San Francisco: Jossey-Bass.

Conoley, J. C. (Ed.). (1981). *Consultation in schools.* New York: Academic Press.

Conoley, J. C., & Welch, K. (1988). The empowerment of women in school psychology: Paradoxes of success and failure. *Professional School Psychology, 3,* 13–19.

Duncan, C., & Pryzwansky, W. B. (1993). Effects of race, racial identity and development, and orientation style on perceived consultant effectiveness. *Journal of Multicultural Counseling and Development, 21,* 88–96.

Ekenbark, M. (2004). The consultation process in corporate groups. In N. M. Lambert, I. Hylander, & J. H. Sandoval (Eds.), *Consultee-centered consultation: Improving the quality of professional services in schools and community organizations* (pp. 221–232). Mahwah, NJ: Erlbaum.

Erchul, W. P. (1993). *Consultation in community, school, and organizational practice: Gerald Caplan's contributions to professional psychology.* Washington, DC: Taylor & Francis.

Gallessich, J. (1982). *The profession and practice of consultation.* San Francisco: Jossey-Bass.

Glass, G. V. (1976). Primary, secondary, and meta-analysis of research. *Educational Researcher, 5*(10), 3–8.

Gresham, F. M. (1989). Assessment of treatment integrity in school consultation and prereferral intervention. *School Psychology Review, 18,* 37–50.

Gresham, F. M., & Kendell, G. K. (1987). School consultation research: Methodological critique and future research directions. *School Psychology Review, 16,* 306–316.

Gutkin, T. B. (1981). Relative frequency of consultee lack of knowledge, skills, confidence, and objectivity in school settings. *Journal of School Psychology, 19,* 57–61.

Gutkin, T. B., & Curtis, M. J. (1990). School-based consultation: Theory, techniques, and research. In T. B. Gutkin & C. R. Reynolds (Eds.), *The handbook of school psychology* (2nd ed., pp. 577–611). New York: John Wiley & Sons.

Harris, K. C. (1993). Culture and consultation: An overview. *Journal of Educational and Psychological Consultation, 4,* 237–251.

Ingraham, C. L. (2000). Consultation through a multicultural lens: Multicultural and cross-cultural consultation in schools. *School Psychology Review, 29,* 320–343.

Ingraham, C. L. (2004). Multicultural consultee-centered consultation: Supporting consultees in the development of cultural competence. In N. M. Lambert, I. Hylander, & J. H. Sandoval (Eds.), *Consultee-centered consultation: Improving the quality of professional services in schools and community organizations* (pp. 135–148). Mahwah, NJ: Erlbaum.

James, B. E., Kidder, M. G., Osberg, J. W., & Hunter, W. B. (1986). Traditional mental health consultation: The psychodynamic perspective. In F. V. Mannino, E. J. Trickett, M. F. Shore, M. G. Kidder, & G. Levin (Eds.), *Handbook of mental health consultation* (pp. 159–174). Washington, DC: U.S. Department of Health and Human Services.

Kelly, J. G. (1993). Gerald Caplan's paradigm: Bridging psychotherapy and public health practice. In W. P. Erchul (Ed.), *Consultation in community, school, and organizational practice: Gerald Caplan's contributions to professional psychology* (pp. 75–85). Washington, DC: Taylor & Francis.

Knotek, S. E., Rosenfield, S. A., Gravois, T. A., Babinski, L. M. (2003). The process of fostering consultee development during instructional consultation. *Journal of Educational and Psychological Consultation, 14,* 303–328.

Lambert, N. M. (2004). Consultee-centered consultation: An international perspective on goals, process, and theory. In N. M. Lambert, I. Hylander, & J. H. Sandoval (Eds.), *Consultee-centered consultation: Improving the quality of professional services in schools and community organizations* (pp. 2–20). Mahwah, NJ: Erlbaum.

Maital, S. L. (1996). Integration of behavioral and mental health consultation as a means of overcoming resistance. *Journal of Educational and Psychological Consultation, 7,* 291–303.

Medway, F. J., & Updyke, J. F. (1985). Meta-analysis of consultation outcome studies. *American Journal of Community Psychology, 13,* 489–505.

Meyers, J. (1973). A consultation model for school psychological services. *Journal of School Psychology, 11,* 5–15.

Meyers, J. (1981). Mental health consultation. In J. C. Conoley (Ed.), *Consultation in schools* (pp. 35–58). New York: Academic Press.

Meyers, J. (1989). The practice of psychology in the schools for the primary prevention of learning and adjustment problems in children: A perspective from the field of education. In L. A. Bond & B. E. Compas (Eds.), *Primary prevention and promotion in the schools* (pp. 391–422). Newbury Park, CA: Sage.

Meyers, J. (1995). A consultation model for school psychological services: Twenty years later. *Journal of Educational and Psychological Consultation, 6,* 73–81.

Meyers, J., Brent, D., Faherty, E., & Modafferi, C. (1993). Caplan's contributions to the practice of psychology in schools. In W. P. Erchul (Ed.), *Consultation in community, school, and organizational practice: Gerald Caplan's contributions to professional psychology* (pp. 99–122). Washington, DC: Taylor & Francis.

Meyers, J., & Kundert, D. (1988). Implementing process assessment. In J. L. Graden, J. E. Zins, & M. J. Curtis (Eds.), *Alternative educational delivery systems: Enhancing instructional options for all students.* Washington, DC: National Association of School Psychologists.

Meyers, J., Parsons, R. D., & Martin, R. (1979). *Mental health consultation in the schools.* San Francisco: Jossey-Bass.

Parsons, R. D., & Meyers, J. (1984). *Developing consultation skills.* San Francisco: Jossey-Bass.

Pryzwansky, W. B. (1974). A reconsideration of the consultation model for delivery of school-based psychological services. *American Journal of Orthopsychiatry, 44,* 579–583.

Pryzwansky, W. B. (1977). Collaboration or consultation: Is there a difference? *Journal of Special Education, 11,* 179–182.

Reschly, D. J. (1976). School psychology consultation: "Frenzied, faddish, or fundamental?" *Journal of School Psychology, 14,* 105–113.

Richards, D. E. (1976). Peer consultation among clergy: A resource for professional development. In G. Caplan & M. Killilea (Eds.), *Support systems and mutual help* (pp. 261–271). New York: Grune & Stratton.

Rosenfeld, J. M., & Caplan, G. (1954). Techniques of staff consultation in an immigrant children's organization in Israel. *American Journal of Orthopsychiatry, 24,* 42–62.

Rosenfield, S. (2004). Consultation as dialogue: The right words at the right time. In N. M. Lambert, I. Hylander, & J. H. Sandoval (Eds.), *Consultee-centered consultation: Improving the quality of professional services in schools and community organizations* (pp. 337–347). Mahwah, NJ: Erlbaum.

Sandoval, J. (1996). Constructivism, consultee-centered consultation, and conceptual change. *Journal of Educational and Psychological Consultation, 7,* 89–97.

Sandoval, J. (2003). Constructing change in consultee-centered consultation. *Journal of Educational and Psychological Consultation, 14,* 251–261.

Sandoval, J. (2004). Constructivism, consultee-centered consultation, and conceptual change. In N. M. Lambert, I. Hylander, & J. H. Sandoval (Eds.), *Consultee-centered consultation: Improving the quality of professional services in schools and community organizations* (pp. 37–44). Mahwah, NJ: Erlbaum.

Sarason, I. G., & Sarason, B. R. (1984). *Abnormal psychology* (4th ed.). Englewood Cliffs, NJ: Prentice-Hall.

Schulte, A. C., & Osborne, S. S. (2003). When assumptive worlds collide. *Journal of Educational and Psychological Consultation, 14,* 109–138.

Sheridan, S. M., & Henning-Stout, M. (1994). Consulting with teachers about girls and boys. *Journal of Educational and Psychological Consultation, 5,* 93–113.

Sheridan, S. M., Welch, M., & Orme, S. F. (1996). Is consultation effective? A review of outcome research. *Remedial and Special Education, 17,* 341–354.

Tarver Behring, S., & Ingraham, C. L. (1998). Culture as a central component of consultation. A call to the field. *Journal of Educational and Psychological Consultation, 9,* 57–72.

Tobias, R. (1993). Underlying cultural issues that effect sound consultant/school collaboratives in developing multicultural programs. *Journal of Educational and Psychological Consultation, 4,* 237–251.

Vygotsky, L. V. (1978). *Mind in society: The development of higher psychological processes.* Cambridge, MA: Harvard University Press.

Webster, L., Knoteck, S. E., Babinski, L. M., Rogers, D. L., & Barnett, M. M. (2003). Mediation of consultees' conceptual development in new teacher groups: Using questions to improve coherency. *Journal of Educational and Psychological Consultation, 14,* 281–302.

West, J. F. (1990). The nature of consultation vs. collaboration: An interview with Walter B. Pryzwansky. *The Consulting Edge, 2*(1), 1–2, 3.

ANSWERS TO LEARNING EXERCISES

2.1 Caplan assumes that persons are most likely to generalize when they feel ownership of the ideas and there is no outside pressure to change. It is important that the consultee retains responsibility for action and that the consultant has no direct involvement in working with the client.

2.2 There are no answers. This exercise is meant to allow you to experiment with indirect forms of questioning.

2.3 1. The psychiatrist says very little and encourages the consultee to present the case.

2. Although the psychiatrist has too little information to determine what is limiting the nurse's effectiveness at this time, some hypotheses might be that: (a) the nurse lacks knowledge of the many potential cultural differences between the patients' family and her own background and is interacting with them in a way that may be seen as disrespectful or judgmental by the family,

(b) the nurse's difficulties with the patient are exacerbated by her anxiety about being seen as effective in her first job, (c) the family may not be able to afford the required medicine and is uncomfortable admitting this to the nurse, (d) the age difference may make the nurse uncomfortable, and (e) there may be some ethnic and age-based stereotyping on the part of the nurse, who is expecting the family to be compliant because of her "superior" background, and the family, who is dismissing her advice because of her youth and obvious inexperience. Can you generate any other hypotheses?

3. The psychiatrist would not discuss these concerns directly, particularly because the nurse might be easily threatened by his higher status and ethnic similarity to the patient. He would indirectly prompt her to gain more perspective on the family by asking questions that might help her to reframe or reconsider the family's failure to follow her instructions in a way that is less threatening to her. For example, the psychiatrist might ask the nurse to consider what may account for Roy's only taking part of the medication, or the psychiatrist might inquire about the presence of grandchildren at the house (prompting her to think about possibly limited income because the grandparents may be raising their grandchildren). The psychiatrist might also ask whether the nurse believes the patient is bothered by the age difference and the idea of taking suggestions from a younger person.

2.4 1, 3, 2, 2, 3, 4, 1

CHAPTER 3

BEHAVIORAL CONSULTATION AND COLLABORATION

GOALS OF THE CHAPTER

The goals of this chapter are to discuss behavioral consultation and collaboration and to present a model of behavioral consultation/collaboration based on classical, operant, and social learning theory.

CHAPTER PREVIEW

1. A brief discussion of the evolution of behavioral models of consultation and consultation will be presented at the outset.
2. An in-depth presentation of an eclectic model of behavioral consultation is included.
3. The differences between behavioral consultation and behavioral collaboration will be discussed.

Five behavioral models of consultation have emerged to date. The earliest of these behavioral models (Tharp & Wetzel, 1969) was rooted in operant learning theory. Bergan (1977) also drew on operant learning theory for the conceptual basis of his theory, as did Russell (1978), Keller (1981), and Piersel (1985). Because Bergan's model was so exquisitely detailed, it soon became a major force in consultation, both as a blueprint for practice and as a stimulus for research. In 1990 Bergan and Kratochwill fine-tuned and extended Bergan's model, but its original premises remained unchanged for the most part. One of Bergan's tenets, that the consultant should control the consultation process through the use of specific interview strategies and by reinforcing consultees for desired responses and behaviors, remains one of the most controversial issues in behavioral consultation.

For many years Bergan's (1977) assertion and some early research (Bergan & Tombari, 1975, 1976; Tombari & Bergan, 1978) that the consultant should control the consulting relationship was accepted without question by behaviorists. Control in the context of consultation means that the consultant tenders leads that elicit information needed to identify the problem, analyze the dimensions of the problem, and formulate solutions that meet the consultant's expectations and serve the consultee and client. This position is at odds with Caplan's (1970) proposition that the consulting relationship should be nonhierarchical (Schulte & Osborne, 2003).

In late 1987 Erchul initiated a line of research aimed at documenting that the effective consultant controls the interview with carefully selected leads and responses. Other studies followed (e.g., Erchul, 1992; Erchul & Chewning, 1990; Witt,

Erchul, McKee, Pardue, & Wickstrom, 1988; Witt, Erchul, Pardue, McKee, & Fitzmaurice, 1991). The authors concluded that effective consultants control the interview.

Not unexpectedly, other consultants questioned the conclusion reached by Erchul and his associates. For example, Gutkin (1999) argued that the logic supporting collaboration in the consulting relationship, as opposed to controlling the interview, is compelling. In order to support his case, Gutkin reviewed the research literature regarding control versus collaboration in the consulting process and concluded that the findings support the collaborative (nonhierarchical) approach. In his reply to Gutkin, Erchul (1999) also reviewed the literature that supports the collaborative point of view (e.g., Gutkin, 1996; Houk and Lewandowski, 1996; Wickstrom, Jones, LeFleur, & Witt, 1998) and suggested that, although there may be some room for reapproachment between the hierarchical and nonhierarchical points of view, the preponderance of evidence supports the point of view that consultants should structure and direct the consulting interview, as he stated earlier (Erchul & Martens, 1997).

Erchul and Gutkin are both to be commended for their efforts to clarify an important consultation issue. However, the issue remains unresolved, primarily because of the nature of the research methodology used. Many of the studies employed small sample sizes, used correlational statistics, and were analogue studies that did not involve actual consultation interviews. Moreover, the use of consultee satisfaction measures as dependent measures is particularly inappropriate (e.g., Hughes, Erchul, Yoon, Jackson, & Henington, 1997) when one considers that the objective of the research was to evaluate the effectiveness of behavioral consultation. The only appropriate measures for this type of research are those that focus on the behavior of the consultee and the client (see the discussion by Witt, Gresham, & Noell, 1996). The matter of controlling the consultation interview remains unresolved. However, behavioral consultants who believe that the only acceptable interventions are

well-conceived behavioral intervention may have no option other than controlling the interview.

One final word regarding control in collaboration is needed. We do not believe that controlling the interview is appropriate or workable in collaboration. Control by one person, either in dyadic or group collaboration, runs counter to the basic tenets of collaboration. This position by no means rules out behaviorally oriented collaboration. However, it suggests that in behavioral collaboration (1) all parties must agree at the outset that the process will be based on behavioral principles, and (2) all collaborators must either have a working knowledge of behavioral psychology principles or agree to acquire that knowledge during the collaborative process. It was suggested in Chapter One that some collaborators would join the collaborative process for short periods of time for the purpose of lending their expertise to the collaboration. Short-term collaborators could be used to inform the collaborative process and establish a type of parity among the collaborators.

A BEHAVIORAL–ECLECTIC MODEL: FOUNDATIONS

In the 1980s several authors began to develop behavioral models of consultation that were based on multiple learning theories (Brown, Pryzwansky, & Schulte, 1987; Brown & Schulte, 1987; Reynolds, Gutkin, Elliot, & Witt, 1984), which we will refer to as behavioral–eclectic models. For the most part, these models recognized the legitimacy of operant and classical learning theories as a basis for consultation, but they incorporated social learning theory (Bandura, 1971, 1976, 1977a, 1978, 1982a, 1982b) principles and modeling interventions into the repertoire of strategies that could be utilized by consultants. Bandura's theory and the reciprocal deterministic philosophy that underpins it recognize the importance of the environment in developing and maintaining behavior, but they also include a cognitive component. Bandura theorizes that change can be effected by altering a person's environment, behavior, or cognitions. His assertion that most new behavior is acquired via observational learning, that is, the observation of models represents a major departure from operand learning theory, which contends that new behavior is primarily shaped by environmental contingencies including positive and negative reinforcement, punishment, and/or the absence of reinforcement. The use of environmental contingency management is an important tool in the behavioral–eclectic model, but interventions are not limited to manipulating environmental variables. In Bandura's conceptual framework, the cognitive constructs of self-efficacy (the confidence that one can perform a task) and appraisal (the importance one attaches to completing a task or attaining a goal) are constructs that can be used to explain many aspects of human behavior. Human beings, are to a large extent, self-regulating and can self-reinforce or self-punish in the absence of external stimuli. Moreover, they construct creative solutions to issues that confront them if they have been exposed to personally relevant models solving similar problems. Models may include people in the immediate environment and vicarious models such as books and videotapes.

Two final points regarding the foundations of behavioral–eclecticism are in order. First, although the behavioral–eclectic point of view posits that human behavior is contextual, that is, a response to the immediate environment, it also recognizes that some of the antecedents to behavior may be related to cultural variables including the family, school, and neighborhood. The child who sits in the classroom worrying that his parents will carry out their threats to get a divorce may not be responding to the immediate environment. In this same vein, the American Indian child who refuses to excel because of his collateral social value, which dictates that he not elevate himself above the norms of his reference group, is responding to a cultural variable that may not be related to the immediate environment. Second, behavioral–eclectic practitioners subscribe to the principle that behavior is functional; that is, it serves a purpose. However, the function of behavior may not be as easy to discern as psychologists and others once believed. Some behaviors serve internal functions related to physiology and cognitions that are not easily observable.

A BEHAVIORAL–ECLECTIC MODEL: THE RELATIONSHIP

The debate regarding control in the consultation process was previewed earlier and will not be revisited in depth at this point. However, the equal power–equal value approach (Schulte & Osborne, 2003) has been adopted by many of the eclectic model builders (e.g., Brown & Schulte, 1987). One of the objectives of behavioral–eclectic consultation is to change the consultee's behavior and cognitions in a manner that will increase his or her self-efficacy, that is, the confidence that they can handle the problem at hand as well as similar problems that arise in the future. The self-efficacy of consultees can be continuously assessed using simple questions that ask them to rate their ability to handle the problem at hand on a 1–10 scale with a 1 indicating very little confidence and a 10 indicating a high level of confidence. Self-efficacy can be improved by modeling the behavior required to deal with the problem, expressions of confidence that the consultee can deal with the problem, observing other models who are handling the problem, and the use of authoritative books and visual aids. In the matter of improving self-efficacy, collaboration has an obvious advantage when compared to consultation. Collaborators can readily learn from each other via modeling because the collaborative dyad or group works together throughout the entire process. It therefore seems likely that the outcomes (improvements in self-efficacy and the adoption of new behaviors) for all parties involved will be superior when collaboration is used instead of consultation.

The difference between the perspective being presented here and traditional behavioral consultants (Bergan, 1977; Bergan & Kratochwill, 1990) lies in the philosophy that underpins the two approaches. Gallessich (1982) and others criticized Bergan because the process he outlined smacked of manipulation, a charge Bergan denied.

Bergan and Kratochwill (1990) stated that their approach to control is not a covert process. They believe that consultants should be forthcoming about their role, including their intent to influence the outcome of consultation. They should also communicate that their role is to provide psychological information and teach behavioral principles to the consultee once an intervention is selected. Additionally, from Bergan's perspective, the consultee's role in the process is to describe the process in observable, measurable terms, choose an intervention consistent with behavioral learning principles, implement the plan, and oversee the client's behavior during the intervention. Consultee and consultant work together during the process to evaluate progress and make changes as needed.

We have adopted the nonhierarchical, equal power–equal value conceptualization of the consulting relationship for philosophical and practical reasons. We agree with Gallessich (1982) that some manipulation of the consultee is necessary in Bergan's and Kratochwill's (1990) consultant-structured/consultee-participation approach even though they and Erchul and Chewning (1990) argue otherwise. Moreover, as stated earlier, we believe that a nonhierarchical approach would be counterproductive in collaboration.

Schulte & Osborne (2003) suggest that the equal power–equal value relationship requires that five conditions be present: the process must be voluntary; parity between or among the participants exists defined as equal value (they see themselves as equal partners), with equal input in decision making; participants must share mutual goals; participants must share their resources; and there must be shared responsibility for problem identification and decisions regarding interventions. We suggest that two additional conditions must exist before an equal power–equal value relationship exists. One of these conditions is that the communication must be characterized by honesty, respect, empathy, and trust (see Chapter 6). The other condition is that disputes must be resolved using win–win negotiation. Although it is a bit of a contradiction, in the

equal value–equal value approach to consultation, even the decision that a behavioral approach will be utilized is negotiable. The outcome of an equal value–equal power relationship should be the enrichment of all participants, not simply the improvement of the skills of the consultee and the resolution of the client's problem. The consultee should gain technical knowledge as well as enhanced ability to assess problematic behavior and deliver interventions. In the process the consultee will collect and provide information about the setting and setting events, the strategies that have been used in the past and why they failed, and preassessment information that may be useful in determining the best strategies to use in assessment. In this model the consultant assumes the stance of learner and collaborative problem solver rather than expert diagnostician and instructor. The consultant's knowledge of human functioning in complex situations will be enriched as a result of each consultation. Because of the unique characteristics of each consultee and client and their interactions, each consultation will require the consultant to reconsider his or her knowledge base in the light of the information provided by the consultee and the information gathered in the assessment process. Consultants and consultees will merge their knowledge and craft creative strategies to assist clients.

A BEHAVIORAL–ECLECTIC MODEL: IDENTIFYING THE CLIENT'S PROBLEM

Problem identification begins when a caregiver, such as a teacher, determines that a client (student) (1) has the ability to perform the behavior but declines to do so, (2) exhibits a behavior that is inappropriate for the context in which it occurs, or (3) has skills deficits that preclude him or her from behaving appropriately. Aggressive behavior such as hitting or name-calling, in almost any context, talking at inappropriate times in the classroom, self-injurious behavior of any type, lying, stealing, out-of-seat behavior, and disturbing others when they are attempting to study or attend are examples of inappropriate behavior. Conversely, students may have academic and/or social skills deficits. Inability to identify words or spell them directly, solve math problems, or write acceptable stories are typical academic deficits. Inability to make or keep friends, passive responses when assertive responses are required, and inability or unwillingness to participate in class skills are examples of social skills deficits. Failure to complete homework with regularity, too little time spent studying, inability to manage one's time are examples of behaviors that can be performed by most students, but may not be exhibited regularly, if at all. Generally speaking, the objective of behavioral consultation is to increase the occurrence of certain behavior when deficits exist or occur too infrequently or to decrease behavior that is inappropriate or that occurs too frequently. Problem identification begins when the consultee provides a general description of the problem and continues as the problem is defined in specific, observable, measurable terms. However, not all problems addressed via behavioral consultation is observable, an issue that will be discussed in greater detail later in this chapter.

The next step in the problem-identification process is to conduct a functional behavioral assessment. Functional behavior assessment, like many of the approaches in the behavioral–eclectic model, grew out of operant and social learning theory. According to Martella and his associates (2003), the simplest model that can used to explain behavior is a three-term model: antecedents, behavior, and consequences, or the ABC model. However, they suggest that a four-term model should serve as the basis for functional behavior assessment because it adds to our understanding of the behavior. The fourth term is *setting events*. A setting event is a variable that changes the dynamics of the interactions among antecedents, behaviors, and consequences. Look at the following example:

SETTING EVENT

Mother
Father

ANTECEDENT

Go do your homework
Go do your homework

BEHAVIOR

Watches television
Does homework

CONSEQUENCES

No homework; punishment
Verbal praise; good grade

The influence of the father and mother on the behavior and outcome are clearly important. Many factors may be setting events. A headache or an illness may alter the usual interactions among antecedents, behaviors, and consequences. The absence of a supervisor, the addition of a peer, and "distant' variables may be setting events. There are times when setting events do not add to our understanding of problem behavior and the ABC model is sufficient. However, behavioral consultants and collaborators should use the four-factor model in their work because it increases the likelihood that that the assessment or behavioral functional analysis will result in a fuller understanding of the behavior being assessed.

Teachers and others who are familiar with the process often conduct functional behavioral assessment informally. However, when the assessment is conducted for the purpose of informing the development of an individualized educational program (IEP) or when students or others exhibit or fail to exhibit behaviors that have serious consequences on a continuing basis, a formal, systematic process is required. Formal assessment begins when a consultant and a consultee or collaborators define the problem and estimate where it is most likely to occur. Once this is done, a student may be observed in various settings such as classrooms, informal areas such as the cafeteria and hallways, and so forth. The objective of this initial phase of the assessment is to determine where the behavior occurs (the context), how often it occurs, and when (time of day) the behavior occurs. Recall that one of the assumptions of behavioral–eclectic consultation is that behavior typically fulfills a specific function in the context in which it occurs. For example, a five-year-old who hit another student 80 percent of the time during her first thirty minutes at school was acting out of the anger generated by being told by her mother that she hated her and was glad she was going to school. The attention that she received after the violent behavior reinforced the aggressive behavior. The bored high school student who passed notes to a friend alleviated his negative physiological state (boredom) and received a reinforcer in the form of peer attention. Ultimately, the problem description will include the what (description in behavioral terms), when, where, and with whom (contextual variables), and the frequency, duration, or intensity of the behavior. It will also include examples of typical behaviors so that the behavior can be easily observed and recorded.

Direct Assessment

One common assessment strategy is the use of direct observation, using a scatterplot to record the incidence of the behavior being observed (Martella, Nelson, & Marchand-Martella, 2003). A scatterplot is simply a grid that depicts the time of the day in intervals ranging from one day to much smaller intervals on one axis (8:00–8:30, 8:30–9:00, and so forth) and the days in the week on the other axis (see Figure 3.1). The length of the interval will be lower for frequently occurring behavior and higher for less frequently occurring behavior. For example, the Center for Effective Collaboration and Practice (1998) suggests that a behavior such as fighting might be charted using an observation unit of one school day. As can be seen in Figure 3.1, the interval box is left blank when the behavior does not occur, marked with one perpendicular line (|) if the behavior occurs once, a cross (†) if the behavior occurs twice during the observation, and a perpendicular line with two horizontal lines (‡) if the behavior occurs three times; the box is blackened if the behavior occurs more than three times during the observation. Observations using scatterplots

can answer the "how often" and "when" questions. They do not provide data regarding the antecedents to or the function of the behavior.

Learning when and how often the behavior occurs is only the first phase of the formal functional behavioral assessment process. The objective of the second phase of the assessment process is to develop a hypothesis about factors such as contextual variables or physiological conditions that may help predict the occurrence of the behavior and the consequences that maintain the behavior once it is exhibited (Center for Effective Collaboration and Practice, 1998; Malott & Suarez, 2004). This portion of the assessment can be conducted using either direct or indirect assessment approaches, but a combination of the two is probably preferable. Regardless of the assessment approaches used, the objective is to determine the antecedents and consequences of the behavior. An ABC (antecedents–behaviors–consequences) chart can provide functional information, that is, information regarding the antecedents to the behavior and the function the behavior fulfills in a particular setting. Table 3.1 contains examples of antecedents, behaviors, and consequences.

An ABC Observation form can be seen in Figure 3.2. It includes a brief description of the setting variables followed by the antecedents, behaviors, and the maintaining consequences of the behavior being assessed. The results of an ABC observation might be appear as follows:

SETTING EVENT: Supervised math seatwork
ANTECEDENT
Jeremy told to begin work
BEHAVIOR
Closes book and begins to talk to other student
CONSEQUENCES
Teacher quietly reminds Jeremy to get to work; Other students smile at Jeremy

Indirect Assessment

As Touchette, MacDonald, and Langer (1985) suggest, a Functional Behavioral Assessment should

FIGURE 3.1 Scatterplot

Student's Name _____

Starting Date _____

Observation Site _____

Behavior to be observed: aggressive physical behavior including pushing, hitting, biting, scratching, and gouging

TIME	MONDAY DAY 1	TUESDAY DAY 2	WEDNESDAY DAY 3	THURSDAY DAY 4	FRIDAY DAY 5
AM					
8–9					
9–10					
10–11					
11–12					
PM					
12–1					
1–2					
2–3					
3–4					

TIME	MONDAY DAY 6	TUESDAY DAY 7	WEDNESDAY DAY 8	THURSDAY DAY 9	FRIDAY DAY 10
AM					
8–9					
9–10					
10–11					
11–12					
PM					
12–1					
1–2					
2–3					
3–4					

Blank square = nonoccurrence

Number = frequency of occurrence

reveal relationships between the occurrence of the behavior and the time of day, the individuals in the setting, the nature of the physical environment, the type of activity, the reinforcement contingencies, and a number of other factors as well. By using scatterplots and ABC observations, many of these relationships can be discerned. However, indirect approaches are needed to complete the assessment in most instances. A complete functional analysis provides cognitive, affective, and environmental/cultural information that may be antecedents of the behavior and may provide valuable information when interventions are selected. Accordingly, indirect assessment approaches such as

TABLE 3.1   Some Examples of Antecedents, Behaviors, and Consequences

I. Antecedents: Causes or contributors to the problem behavior. There are at least three categories of these that are often interrelated.

A. Physiological/Psychological Antecedents
- Health problems that sap the student's energy, require absence from school, etc.
- Sleep deprivation
- Never gets breakfast
- Low scholastic ability (e.g., WISC-R IQ = 72)
- Learning disability (e.g., dyslexia)
- Diagnosed as ADD with Hyperactivity
- Anxiety

B. Environmental/Cultural Antecedents

Home
- Cultural beliefs of parents and community
- Little or no supervision in the home
- Too much time spent watching TV and/or playing computer games
- Noisy
- Crowded
- No home or lack of stability in home
- Reinforcement of inappropriate behavior
- Lack of reinforcement of appropriate behaviors
- Aversive atmosphere that causes avoidance or that results in negative reinforcement
- Limited facility with English

School
- Classroom not well controlled
- Teacher style/techniques (e.g., pacing, giving instruction, individualization issues)
- Peer group norms

Neighborhood
- Peer group pressure (positive or negative)

Cognitive Issues
- Boredom
- Frustration
- Low self-efficacy
- Low appraisal of task
- Lack of goals
- Anxiety

II. Behavior (frequency, duration, or intensity)
- Homework completed 35% of the time
- ISSP 3 times per week
- Out of seat 4 times per silent reading period
- Cries for 15 minutes when fails a test
- Hits others with open hand with moderate force on average of once per day in cafeteria

III. Consequences: Events that maintain, increase, or decrease the behavior
- Positive reinforcement (increases or maintains behavior)
- Negative reinforcement (increases or maintains behavior)
- Self-reinforcement/punishment (increases/ maintains or decreases behavior)
- Reduction of an aversive physiological state such as boredom (increases or maintains behavior)
- Punishment/logical consequences/ withholding a reinforcer (suppresses behavior or causes avoidance)
- Ignoring (in short term increases behavior; in long term reduces incidence of behavior)

interviews with parents, teachers, and administrators should be included in the process, along with interviews with the students. An example of a Functional Behavior Assessment Interview Schedule that could be used with parents or teachers can be seen in Figure 3.3. A Student-Directed Functional Interview Schedule is shown in Figure 3.4.

Other Sources of Assessment Data

There are many other sources of data that can inform the behavioral functional assessment process. Psychological tests and achievement histories may reveal information about scholastic aptitude and mental health issues. Health records and neurolog-

FIGURE 3.2 ABC Observation Form

Student: _____   Observer: _____

Date: _____   Time: _____

Activity: _____

Context of Incident:

Antecedent:

Behavior:

Consequence:

Comments/Other Observations:

Source: Center for Effective Collaboration and Practice 1998—retrieved from: http://www.air.org/cecp/fba/problembehavior/appendixa.htm

Used by permission of the author.

ical tests may also provide valuable information and should not be overlooked. A summary of the data that might appear in a behavioral functional assessment can be seen in Table 3.2 along with sources of data.

After data collection ends it is up to the consultant and consultee or the collaborators to compile the data in a manner that will enable them to determine the origins and consequences of the behavior and begin the process of selecting an intervention. One way to accomplish this is through data triangulation, which, as the name implies, involves examining three sources of data such as an ABC chart, scatterplot data, and information

gained in the interview to interpret the student's behavior. A data triangulation chart is shown in Figure 3.5. The ABC chart information reveals that when Trish does not get her way she yells and hits, particularly when there are no adults in the immediate vicinity. The scatterplot provides additional data regarding the types of behavior Trish displays and the incidence of appropriate and inappropriate behaviors. The interpretation of the data suggests that the antecedent of the behavior is unsupervised play with other girls. The behaviors are verbal aggression, physical aggression, and inappropriate behavior, which need to be more fully described. The consequences that maintain the inappropriate behavior are that Trish gets to play with the other girls and she gets attention from her teacher. A second Data Triangulation Chart is shown in Figure 3.6. It shows how a scatterplot, a teacher interview, and an interview with a student can be used in the triangulation process.

Problem behavior pathways, such as the one shown in Figure 3.7, can also be used to organize data and to discern antecedents to the behavior, the behavior(s) itself, and the maintaining consequences. This chart begins by listing the setting events for Trish, the antecedents to her aggressive behavior, the problem behavior, and the maintaining consequences. This particular behavior pathway gives us some potentially useful information that we did not have before and some superfluous information as well. The useful information is provided in the form of the demands that Trish makes and how her success results in reinforcement. The information about Marsha is unneeded unless an intervention is planned for Marsha as well. Both Problem Behavior Pathways and Data Triangulation Charts provide useful methods of organizing the data that has been collected regarding the student of concern. They also provide the basis for generating a hypothesis about the antecedents and maintaining consequences (functions) of the behavior. The Center for Effective Collaboration and Practice (CECP; 1998) suggests that the hypothesis be formulated as a prediction that contains the context in which the behavior is likely to occur. Charles, a student with poor math skills, will drop material on the floor and talk in loud tones to other

FIGURE 3.3   Functional Behavior Assessment Interview Schedule

Student's Name _____

Age _____   Grade_____

Interviewee_____

Relationship to Student _____

Interviewer _____

Date _____   School _____

FOCUS ON PROBLEM BEHAVIOR

1. What is the specific behavior of concern in observable terms?
2. What are examples of the behavior of concern?
3. What time of day does the behavior occur?
4. How often does the behavior occur?
5. So far as you can tell, what causes the behavior to occur?
6. Describe the setting at the time the behavior occurs. For example, does it occur during a particular subject, during a particular type of instruction, or during transitions? (Teacher) Does it occur before or after school, prior to bedtime, and so forth? (Parent) Are there other events that occur prior to or at the same time as the behavior?
7. What action do you take when the behavior occurs?
8. Typically, behavior occurs to gain reinforcement, to avoid punishment, to alleviate certain internal states such as boredom, or to cover up certain cognitions/emotions such as fear, lack of confidence, and so forth. What functions does the behavior seem to serve for the student?

9. Does this behavior occur at other times and settings than the ones you have identified?

SUMMARY OF PART ONE: HYPOTHESES

A. List the antecedents/setting events that seem to cue the behavior. _____
_____

B. Identify the behavior that occurs. _____
_____

C. Identify the function of the behavior. _____
_____

SEARCH FOR POSITIVE ALTERNATIVE BEHAVIORS

1. Does the student ever exhibit positive or appropriate behaviors in the presence of the antecedents and in the setting instead of the inappropriate responses? If yes, how can these be increased?
2. Are there antecedent conditions such as frustration or boredom with the material that can be eliminated or reduced?
3. Are there setting variables that could be altered or changed completely that might help reduce or eliminate the behavior?

---

students when seatwork is involved in order to be sent to time-out because of his frustration. The hypothesis should be written to include setting events, antecedents, behaviors, and consequences. The CECP suggests that the next step is to test the hypothesis, either by simulating the conditions under which the behavior may manifest or using the natural classroom setting. Testing the hypoth-

esis may be useful if there are gaps in data collection. However, placing Charles in a frustrating situation to determine whether he will act out when there is good reason to expect that he will is ethically questionable because the student will experience negative consequences. Once goals are set the next step is to proceed with goal setting and intervention.

FIGURE 3.4 Student-Directed Functional Interview Schedule

Student's Name _____

Age _____ Grade _____

Interviewer _____

Date _____ School _____

SELF-EFFICACY

1. Rate how difficult each of the following classes is for you using a 1 to 10 scale (1–5 for young students) with a one being very easy and a 10 being very hard.

Class	Rating	Boredom/ Frustration
Reading	_____	_____
Math (specify)	_____	_____
Spelling	_____	_____
Science	_____	_____
Cursive (if appropriate)	_____	_____
Language Arts/English	_____	_____
Social Studies	_____	_____
PE	_____	_____
Music	_____	_____
Computers	_____	_____

2. Sometimes when classes are very easy we get bored with them. Do you ever get bored with any of the classes you just rated? (Repeat the list and place a B after classes that are cited as boring). Classes that are very difficult for us can be frustrating because we have trouble understanding what to do. Are any of the classes that were listed frustrating for you? (Repeat the list and place an F after classes that are cited as frustrating.)

APPRAISAL OF SCHOOL

1. Do you like school?

2. How important is it for you to do well in school?

3. Do you believe that it is important to your parents that you do well in school?

4. Does your teacher notice when you do something well?

5. Do your parents notice when you do something well in school?

BEHAVIOR

1. Your teacher(s) and others suggest that you do some things in class that perhaps you should not do? What behaviors do you think your teachers want you to stop doing?

2. Are there things that your teacher would like you to do more of? (Give examples.)

3. If you get into trouble with your teacher, when is it most likely to occur?

4. How often do you get into trouble with your teachers?

5. When are you on your best behavior in school? Why is that?

ANTECEDENTS

1. Are you bored or frustrated just before you get into trouble?

2. How many hours of sleep do you get each night?

3. Do you eat breakfast before you come to school?

4. Are you sometimes upset when you come to school?

5. Do other students get you into trouble? (if yes) How?

CONSEQUENCES

1. Do other students notice when you get into trouble? What do they do?

2. Are you sometimes happy that you got the teacher to notice you even though you are in trouble?

3. What does the teacher do when she believes that you have done something wrong?

4. Do you sometimes think that it is funny to see the teacher angry at you?

5. What types of rewards would you like when you do the things the teacher wants you to do?

HYPOTHESES

A. List the antecedents/setting events that seem to cue the behavior.

B. Identify the behavior that occurs.

C. Identify the function of the behavior.

TABLE 3.2   Behavioral Functional Assessment: Summary

ANTECEDENTS	PROBLEM BEHAVIOR	CONSEQUENCES
Environmental/Cultural	*Observable & Measurable*	*Reinforcers*
Home	What is the problem behavior?	Negative (sensory/external)
School	Who is involved?	Positive (sensory/social/tangible)
Neighborhood	When does the behavior occur?	Self (self-statements/control)
Peer group norms	Where does the behavior occur?	
	Frequency of behavior?	*Punishment*
Cognitive	Is duration an issue?	Self-imposed
Self-efficacy beliefs	Is latency of the response an issue?	Externally imposed
Appraisals	Is force of the response an issue?	
Boredom		*None (Ignored)*
Frustration		
Expectations of reinforcement		
Retardation		
Psychological reactance		
Psychological Issues		
Learning disabilities		
Mental health problems		
Physiological		
Nutrition		
Rest /sleep		
Health problems/medication		

SOURCES OF INFORMATION

1. Interviews with parents, teachers, and students
2. Observation
3. Psychological tests
4. Physical examination
5. Achievement histories
6. Health histories
7. Attendance records
8. Teachers' grade books

THE INTERVENTION PROCESS

Establishing Objectives

The intervention process begins with the establishment of a behavioral objective, a process that is greatly facilitated by scatterplot information, which provides baseline information for the behavior that needs to be increased or decreased. The first step in the objective-setting process may be to establish a terminal behavioral—that is the ultimate behavioral objective that is sought—followed by the establishment of an initial or intermediate behavioral objective. Behavioral objective establish-

ment should be conducted with the student (client) by the consultee in consultation and by the collaborators in the collaboration process. The role of the consultant in behavioral objective setting is to provide technical information and/or training in the behavioral objective setting process. Behavioral objectives should involve observable/measurable behavior that is attainable in a reasonable timeframe.

We believe that behavioral objective selection may not have received the attention it deserves in some instances. Typically, there is considerable discussion of the mechanics of establishing base-

FIGURE 3.5 Data Triangulation Chart

Student: _Trish_   Date(s) _9/26 — 10/8_

SOURCE 1	SOURCE 2	SOURCE 3
ABC Chart:	_Interview with playground supervisor (teacher)_	_Scatterplot:_
Trish yells at students when they don't do what she says. She hits students when she does not get her way.	Trish yells at and hits other girls when she doesn't get her way. This usually happens when there are no adults nearby.	Trish engages in appropriate behavior on the playground about 73% of the time; verbally aggressive behavior about 19% of the time; and physical aggression 8% of the time.

Interpretation:
1. Antecedent (includes setting events): Playground, undersupervised games involving girls.
2. Inappropriate behavior: Trish usually gets her way when she becomes verbally and/or physically aggressive. She also gets to spend time with the playground supervisor.
3. Consequences: Attention from teacher; gets to play with other girls; perhaps self-reinforcement.

Source: Center for Effective Collaboration and Practice (1998). Retrieved from: http://www.air.org/cecp/fba/ problembehavior2/appendixf.htm—March 10, 2004
Used by permission of the author.

FIGURE 3.6 Data Triangulation Chart

Student: _Dom Z._   Date(s)   _3/6/99–3/17/99_

SOURCE 1	SOURCE 2	SOURCE 3
Scatterplot Dom's comments are most frequent during board work, the end of group lectures, and, although inconsistent, during independent work. Dom's inappropriate comments drastically decrease when working in small groups.	Teacher lesson plan book Discussion w/teacher Examination of lesson plan book reveals Dom's inappropriate comments were higher during assignments that required a lot of reading.	Discussion with Dom reveals that he sometimes feels frustrated when he has to read a lot of material. He often makes distracting comments so his classmates won't find out he has problems reading.

Interpretation:
1. Antecedent: Frustration because reading materials beyond his ability.
2. Inappropriate behavior: Comments distract teacher and classmates.
3. Consequences: Avoids reading aloud, redirecting internal anxiety about frustration and embarrassment

Source: Center for Effective Collaboration and Practice (1998). Retrieved from: http://www.air.org/cecp/fba/ problembehavior2/appendixf.htm—March 10, 2004
Used by permission of the author.

FIGURE 3.7   Problem Behavior Pathway

Student: _Trish B._   Grade: _4th_   School: _Tucker Creek Elementary_   Date _10/6_

Time: _10:15–10:30 a.m._   Setting: _Recess_

Setting Events	Triggering Antecedents	Problem Behavior(s)	Maintaining Consequences
Playground free play	Trish sees Marsha with the class football and decides playing catch with her friend Rae would be fun.	Trish approaches Marsha and says, "Give me the football." Marsha says, "No," so Trish yanks the ball from Marsha and shoves her to the ground.	Trish gets the ball and finds Rae. They play catch until the bell rings to return to class. Marsha goes and sits alone on a swing, too afraid to tell the playground supervisor what happened.

Source: Center for Effective Collaboration and Practice (1998). Retrieved from: http://www.air.org/cecp/fba/ problembehavior2/appendixf.htm—March 10, 2004
Used by permission of the author.

lines and establishing appropriate intermediate and terminal objectives (see Alberto & Troutman, 2003). Malott and Suarez (2004) suggest that, in order to maintain behavior after the behavioral intervention is withdrawn, individuals need to develop personal rules that allow them to perceive that the outcomes of following the rules will produce sizable outcomes even if the behavior is not immediately reinforced. The establishment of behavioral objectives is the first step in helping individuals develop rules that will continue after the intervention. Therefore, we suggest that the following issues be considered when establishing objectives with students:

1. The attainment of the intermediate and terminal objectives should be important to the individual as indicated by his or her appraisal ratings.
2. The individual should perceive that the goal is attainable as indicated by self-efficacy ratings.

3. Contingencies used in the process of facilitating objective attainment should approximate "real" world contingencies.

Interventions

Intervention selection is a critical element in the behavioral consultation/collaboration process. Because behavioral–eclectic models draw on classical and operant learning theory as well as social learning theory, the number of interventions available to them is large. However, some of the strategies associated with behavioral approaches are so difficult to implement that they should probably be avoided unless the collaborators and/or consultees are totally committed to them. Complex interventions often become aversive because of the time and energy required to maintain them and may be abandoned as a result.

The task of consultants, consultees, and collaborators is to select the interventions that are least intrusive, least restrictive, ethical, and most effective (Martella et al., 2003). Restrictive interventions are those that limit students' freedom of movement. Parents who punish their children by grounding them are using a restrictive strategy as are teachers who send students to in-school suspension programs that take the student out of the classroom, the lunch hour, and other activities in which he or she would interact with peers.

Martella and his associates (2003) define intrusiveness as the degree to which it affects bodily or personal rights. They note that exclusionary time out that removes the student from the immediate setting (e.g., to another portion of the classroom behind a screen) is more intrusive that nonexclusionary time out in which the student must sit and watch instead of participating. We believe that there is another dimension to intrusiveness that may be more important when considering potential interventions and that is the impact the intervention makes on the overall environment in which it is being implemented. An intervention such as verbal reinforcement can be delivered without changing the nature of the environment substantially. Token economy systems require substantial environmental change.

Every team of collaborators and consultants and consultees want to select the most effective intervention. Unfortunately, this often cannot be ascertained until the intervention has been implemented. However, interventions that require the least amount of work, are the least restrictive and intrusive, and are ethical are likely to be effective if they are implemented properly.

Ethical interventions are those that do not violate the law or the consultant or collaborators codes of ethics. Some states have banned exclusionary time out and many states place substantial restrictions or the use of punishment. In all cases, interventions with exceptional children must be a part of the Individualized Education Plan (IEP). Clearly interventions that put the client or clients at risk physically or emotionally are unethical and should not be used. Psychologists, counselors, and educators have begun to classify interventions based on the expected outcome. Therefore the ob-

jective to be achieved as a result of the intervention is probably the best starting place in intervention selection after the criteria discussed in this section have been considered.

The Goal Is to Reduce the Incidence of an Inappropriate Behavior. The obvious approach to reducing the incidence of a behavior is to remove the reward that maintains the behavior and wait for extinction. There are two problems with this solution. First, after the withdrawal of a reinforcer, the incidence of the behavior often goes up. Second, behavior is rarely extinguished completely and it may take a very long time for the incidence of the behavior to decrease to the level that it is tolerable. Therefore, other strategies, such as differential reinforcement, should be considered. Differential reinforcement is simply the process of reinforcing alternatives to the problem behavior and ignoring the inappropriate behavior. This may involve reinforcing incompatible behavior (being seated is incompatible with being out of seat), reinforcing any behavior other than the problematic behavior, and/or reinforcing low levels of a response with the intent of strengthening the response, thus reducing the incidence of another response. For example, if we eliminate fighting in some neighborhoods students will not arrive at school with their lunch money. Our goal in this case should be to reduce the incidence of fighting by teaching the student to discriminate between the cues that should prompt fighting and those that require other responses.

Other strategies that decrease the incidence of inappropriate behavior are aversive strategies such as response cost approaches, nonexclusionary time-out, and restitution (Martella et al., 2003; Walker, Shea, & Bower, 2004). Aversive strategies, such as contingent exertion (give me 20 push-ups), negative practice (stay out of your seat), exclusionary and seclusionary time-out, and reprimands are not recommended for use because of the negative impact they may have on the relationship between the person administering them and the client and potential problems with supervision. A teacher who has problems with a student who blurts out answers to queries without raising his hand could establish a response cost situation in which the student is given two tokens. Each time he blurts out an answer she would remove a token from his desk each time the behavior occurs. If the student has one token left on four days of the week he will avoid being assigned to one hour of after-school detention. As noted earlier, nonexclusionary time-out limits the participation of a student without removing him or her from the group. A basketball player who fouls out is subjected to nonexclusion-ary time-out. Restitutional overcorrection is often used by the courts in lieu of fines and incarceration. One judge in Los Angeles County routinely re-quires gang members to restore areas of the city by repainting walls and sidewalks that have been spray-painted with gang signs and messages.

One last strategy that can be used to reduce the incidence of inappropriate behavior is to eliminate negative reinforcement. Take the following scenario:

> John is bored with the math lesson → He drops his books on the floor and nosily picks them up → Then he mutters, "This is dumb," under his breath, but loudly enough for the teacher to hear → He is sent to the assistant principle for punishment.

John has been sent from one aversive situation to one that the teacher supposes is more aversive. In doing so, she has increased the possibility that John will throw his books on the floor and mutter. Negative reinforcement, that is, either escaping or being sent out of aversive situations, is a powerful influence on behavior and one that is often over-looked.

If the Goal Is to Increase Behavior.   Increasing behavior requires a basic understanding of several principles including modeling, successive approx-imations and shaping, cuing, the Premack princi-ple, the response deprivation hypothesis, and behavioral momentum. These terms are defined as follows:

- Modeling: the use of live models (in vivo) or vicarious models such as books, movies, and videos to teach new behavior

- Self-Talk: subvocal speech that can be used in self-instruction, self-reinforcement, and self-punishment
- Positive Reinforcement: a desired reward fol-lows a behavior
- Successive Approximations and Shaping: the use of systematic reinforcement of approxi-mations of the desired behavior or behavioral patterns; an approximation of a behavior oc-curs when the behavior exhibited contains some of the elements of the desired behavior
- Cuing: environmental signals or cues used as prompts for appropriate and inappropriate behavior
- Premack Principle: high probability behavior (playing video games) used to reinforce low probability behavior (doing homework)
- Response Deprivation Hypothesis: low prob-ability behavior used to reinforce itself if the opportunity to participate is reduced
- Behavioral Momentum: increasing a desired behavior by reinforcing related behaviors that individuals use to respond to a class of cues (A student who does not respond to direction to do math can be reinforced for following di-rections in other areas, increasing the likeli-hood to respond to direction in math.)

Three types of interventions used to increase positive behavior will be discussed in this section, although others could be included. One of the most important of these positive strategies, self-man-agement training, will be discussed first, followed by a discussion of behavioral contracts and token economy systems. Self-management strategies fall into five categories. The first of these is self-re-cording of data. This is a relatively simple process that requires the student or adult to record informa-tion such as how many cigarettes he or she smokes, how many times he or she holds up a hand during a particular recitation, how many math problems are solved correctly, and so forth. This process be-gins by determining and operationally defining the behavior to be recorded. Typically, a rather simple recording technique, such as a blank three-by-five card or a wrist counter is used. However, students or adults can be provided with a sheet that contains hours in the day, class periods, or other ways of partitioning time relevant to the objectives of the effort. Data gathered by a high school student who has agreed to record each time he begins to study may show that studying occurs only late at night when the student is not as alert as he would be earlier. Figure 3.8 shows a typical chart for self-recorded observations. If duration of study-related behavior is added to the recorded data, a clearer picture of studying behavior may emerge.

Self-recording may be, and often is, coupled with a prompt or cue. After the behavior to be recorded has been selected and defined, the next step is to select a cue or prompt. In some instances a teacher, parent, or other caregiver will provide the prompt. In others, mechanical devices, such as the MotivAider® (Behavioral Dynamics, 2004), are used. This device, which weighs less than three ounces, is typically strapped to the arm or attached to a belt, emits a slight vibration on a more or less random basis, cuing the individual to check

FIGURE 3.8 Self-Recording Device for Homework

1. Place a check in the time box that is closest to the time you began to study in the day row.
2. When you stop studying, record the amount of time you spent studying in minutes.
3. Total the number of minutes spent for each day and compute the Grand Total of minutes for the week.

TIME	4:00	4:30	5:00	5:30	6:00	6:30	7:00	7:30	8:00	8:30	9:00	9:30	10 or after	Total Minutes
Monday														
Minutes														
Tuesday														
Minutes														
Wednesday														
Minutes														
Thursday														
Minutes														
Friday														
Minutes														
Saturday														
Minutes														
Sunday														
Minutes														
Grand Total														

whether he or she is in his or her seat, studying, attending to the teacher, daydreaming, or engaged in other appropriate or inappropriate behavior. Individuals are then taught how to use the recording device in at least one practice session to ensure that the device is appropriate and the individual understands the directions. In an informal test of the MotivAider®, two middle school boys who attended to the teacher less than 20 percent of the time immediately increased their attendance rate to over 70 percent, but their attending behavior dropped rather precipitously after two to three weeks, apparently because teachers stopped providing verbal reinforcement. Visual cues can also be used as a part of self-recording systems. We have used photographs and drawings to prompt students to hold up their hand during class discussions and to eliminate talking at inappropriate times. The process, when using photographs, is to take a picture of the student performing the desired behavior, tape it to his or her desk, model and practice the desired behavior, and have the students record whether they were engaged in appropriate behavior when the prompt was provided. Drawings may be used for the same purpose. The photograph or drawing serves as a more or less constant reminder of how the student is to behave.

Alberto and Troutman (2003) reviewed the research literature regarding self-recording and concluded that it produced positive behavior change in a number of areas, but that these changes may be short-lived. They suggest that self-recording may be most effective in maintaining behavior that has been developed through caregiver-managed strategies. They also suggest, and we concur, that self-recording should be used in concert with self-reinforcement or extrinsic motivational strategies.

Self-Reinforcement and Punishment. The use of external reinforcement and punishment strategies is based primarily on the principles of operant learning theory. Self-management procedures are rooted in social learning theory (Bandura, 1976, 1977, 1978, 1982a). The essence of the theory is that people are self-regulating beings who interact with their environment in a dynamic fashion, an idea that he called reciprocal determinism. As noted earlier, self-efficacy, appraisal, and observational learning are three key constructs in Bandura's theory. If, as Bandura suggests, people are self-directed, it follows that internal dialogues involving praising one's self (self-reinforcement) and scolding one's self (self-punishment) can be used as potent forces for change. Students should be encouraged to establish appropriate personal standards and reward or punish themselves subvocally, depending on their level of performance.

Bandura suggests that self-efficacy can be increased via symbolic modeling (e.g., using videos), in vivo modeling (using live models), covert modeling (imagining others performing the desired behavior), and performance enactments (successfully practicing the desired behavior). He also indicates that avoidance behavior (e.g., avoiding public speaking because of fear) often requires anxiety reduction techniques in addition to modeling, such as cognitive restructuring (substituting noncoping [I'm going to fail this test] with coping statements [I can pass this test if I study] and relaxation strategies. Clearly, self-reinforcement (and contingent reinforcement) should play a role in the process of teaching new skills to improve self-efficacy.

Self-reinforcement and self-punishment can be thought of in terms of the internal dialogue people have with themselves. It can also be thought of as having students and others arrange for their own contingencies, that is, their own rewards and punishments. Teachers often use the latter approach by specifying that students can choose from a menu of reinforcers generated by the class if they achieve a particular level of performance. For example, a fifth-grade teacher who was interested in having students memorize the capitals of all fifty states specified three rewards for identifying forty-eight out of fifty capitals correctly: one candy bar a day for a week, spending one hour at the end of the week with five friends in supervised play, or fifteen minutes of free time each day to play video games. Students who scored less than 75 percent were also given a variety of rather unpleasant options, ranging from retaking the quiz, writing a paper that included all fifty states and their capitals, and presenting a blank map to the class and locating the state capital along with its name on the map. The use of self-reward and self-punishment should not be limited to in-school behavior. Students can be encouraged to self-reinforce for positive behavior and self-punish for inappropriate behavior through the use of informal contracts because some of the most powerful sources of rewards and punishment lie in the environment outside of school. Intrapersonal contracts (e.g., I will not watch my favorite television show if I do not score at least 85 percent on the math test) involve students in the use of self-punishment and self-reward.

Self-Instruction. Self-instruction involves directing one's self in the procedures needed to complete tasks such as solving a mathematics problem or assembling a complex machine. Self-instruction can also be used to help students develop new approaches to interpersonal behavior by using self-talk. Teachers who want to teach students to solve mathematics using self-instruction would use the following strategy:

1. model the process of solving the problem by verbalizing the cognitive processes involved while working the math problem (in vivo modeling);
2. have students work the same problem while repeating the instructions aloud (performance enactment);
3. have students work a number of problems directing their own behavior subvocally with self-reinforcement.

A biology teacher might use this same strategy to teach the scientific method and a school counselor might use it to teach assertive behavior. Ultimately, proficiency in the performance of complex tasks is dependent on students' and adults' ability to direct their own behavior.

Behavioral/Contingency Contracts. Behavioral contracts can be used with individuals or groups. A

discussion of using contracts with groups can be found in Brown (1999). This discussion will be limited to providing an overview of using contracts with individuals. In simple terms, a behavioral contract is an *If–Then* statement. If the student attains an agreed-on academic or behavioral goal, he or she will be rewarded. Martella and associates (2003) suggest that there are three main components of behavioral contracts: accomplishing a task (*If*), the reward (*Then*), and the record. The development of a behavioral contract begins with establishing the record, that is, identifying problem behavior in observable, measurable terms and determining the rate of occurrence via some of the strategies already discussed. The duration or intensity of the behavior may also be ascertained depending on the type of problem (screaming uncontrollably on the playground). These data become the baseline in the contract. Either prior to or after the baseline is established, the student needs to be included in the process to determine his or her interest in changing the inappropriate behavior. Assuming an agreement can be reached, an initial objective that specifies the improvement will be made and the date by which it is to be accomplished, the reinforcer if the objective is achieved, the nature of the record-keeping process, and the anniversary of the contract (when it is to be reviewed). A sample behavioral contract is shown in Figure 3.9.

Contracts can be self-managed or managed by caregivers such as teachers. In self-managed contracts the client collects baseline information via self-recordings, establishes goals, and selects reinforcers form a predeveloped menu of possibilities. If the process is behavioral consultation, the consultee is more likely to be the contract manager. If the contract has been developed as a part of a collaborative effort, one or more of the collaborators will assume the role of contract manager. The manager meets with the student on the anniversary date of the contract and determines if the student has achieved his or her goal. If the goal has been achieved, the reward is provided and the next goal is established. This process is repeated until the terminal objective is attained and then the contract is gradually withdrawn (faded). Alberto and

FIGURE 3.9   Sample Generic Contingency Contract

Date _____   This contract begins _____   and ends _____

Student's Name _____

What is the target behavior? _____

What is the student's level of performance of the target behavior at this time? _____

What is the criterion for success? (rate, duration, accuracy, response time)_____

Where is the behavior to occur? _____

Who will evaluate the contract? _____

How will the student be rewarded and by whom? _____

Signatures (Signed by everyone involved)

Student _____

Teacher _____

Counselor _____

Parent_____

Other_____

Troutman (2003) suggest that the fading process is primarily a matter of withdrawing the prompts and warn against ending the contract precipitously. Prompts may be withdrawn by gradually eliminating any cuing system and substituting maintenance of behavior agreements that do not involve reinforcers, or by reducing the quantity and/or quality of the reinforcers.

It is not uncommon for contracts to work in their initial phases and then become less effective. If initial contracts fail, it is typically because the first goal was set too high. Contract objectives should be based on the principle of successive approximations, so the first objective should be fairly easily attainable. Initial success builds a foundation for future goal attainment because it increases self-efficacy. Progress toward goal attainment also falters because the behavior to be reinforced has not been carefully defined, so rewards are not pro-

vided on the basis expected by the student. Other reasons that contracts fail are that rewards are not provided immediately, contracts are viewed as unfair by students, arousing resentment, managers interpret early success as a signal the problem is solved and do not follow through, contract managers do not honor the anniversary date, encouragement and social reinforcers are not provided concurrently with other reinforcers, and/or the reinforcer has lost some or all of its reinforcing properties and must be replaced by another reinforcer.

Finally, if contracts are not designed properly they may become aversive to the contract manager and/or the students. If they are too much work they become aversive to caregivers. If objectives are unattainable and/or punishment for nonattainment of objectives is included, they may become too aversive for students. In either case the contract is likely to fail. Contracts that are not culturally appropriate may also be aversive to students and others. Behavioral interventions were originally based on Eurocentric values including a future time orientation and individualism. Some unacculturated ethnic groups, including Hispanics, Asian Americans, and some Native American tribes, do not share these values.

Token Economy Systems.   It will not be possible to provide a full discussion of token economy systems, but they are a positive means of promoting behavioral change. However, according to Martell and associates (2003), token economy systems should include a cost response component that involves taking tokens away when inappropriate behavior occurs. The development of a token economy system begins in much the same way that the design of a contract does. The behavior to be influenced, either by providing or confiscating tokens, must be identified and the worth or value of the behavior established in terms of the tokens to be provided or removed. Once behaviors to be rewarded or punished are identified and defined, and their "values " established, a record-keeping system should be designed. We suggest that this system be based on the standard record-keeping system in the school or institution insofar as possible. For example, teachers routinely track absences, tardiness, homework completion, accuracy of homework, seatwork, and quizzes, and referral for disciplinary action. In many schools, teachers also track the number of misbehaviors that occur using something like the three-strike rule. The three-strike rule involves writing a student's name after a carefully defined classroom rule is broken, circling the name after the second offense and drawing a line through the circle after the third offense. The third offense may result in referral for disciplinary action, a note home to parents requesting a disciplinary conference, or in-school suspension. Students who have no strikes after each segment of the school day could be given one token. Conversely, students who receive two or less strikes could have a token deducted for each strike. Students who have three strikes could have five tokens deducted from their tally.

The other steps in establishing a token economy system include: (1) determining a method of delivering tokens as close as possible in time to the occurrence of the behavior, (2) determining how tokens can be spent, (3) determining the cost of the backup reinforcers, (4) making sure that social reinforcers are paired with token delivery, (5) establishing a formal method of evaluating the efficacy of the system, and (6) scheduling ongoing troubleshooting session for collaborators.

Token economy systems can be very effective, but require dedication and careful monitoring. However, the teachers in one elementary school, after consultation with their school psychologists, developed a plan to increase overall academic performance using a token economy system. Students in grades 4 and 5 who completed homework assignments were given one white token for each assignment completed and a red token, equal to five white tokens, if all assignments were completed during a week. Students could also earn a white token if they (1) held up their hands to participate during class discussion, (2) completed seatwork during supervised study, (3) completed projects on time, and (4) quietly helped other students during supervised study after they completed their own work. Red tokens were given to students who (1) earned passing grades on each quiz and test, (2) earned passing grades on projects, and (3) worked cooperatively on group projects (based on peer nomination). Tokens were used to purchase school supplies and healthy snacks at the school store that was funded by the Parent Teacher Association. Teachers designed this system during a paid week in the summer with input from the school psychologist. During the school year, the teachers met weekly for the first six weeks and monthly thereafter to evaluate the efficacy of the system.

Intervention Strategies that Focus on Antecedents.   After a lengthy discussion of interventions that focused on changing behavior or the consequences of behavior, it may come as a surprise that, in some instances, functional behavioral assessment suggests that the problem behavior is functionally related to antecedents. Many teachers have noticed that students are rowdier after breaks, physical education, lunch, transitioning from class to class, and so forth. These activities stimulate many students and may overstimulate others to the point that they have difficulty regaining their composure. Students may also become bored because the pacing of the instruction process is too slow, and, once they become bored, the next step is to relieve the boredom by pestering a nearby student or engaging in some other disruptive behavior. Similarly, other students may become frustrated because pacing is too fast or the material is too difficult. In some instances, students may be sleepy because of sleep deprivation, resulting from a variety of circumstances, or angry because of treatment at home, bullying by peers, or relationships with significant others. Fear of embarrassment may preclude students from answering routine questions, working problems at the dry-erase board, or giving oral reports.

Internal antecedent conditions that are functionally related to inappropriate behavior are most likely to be identified using indirect assessment procedures with teachers, students, and parents. The interventions for these behaviors may require indirect strategies that alter the environment in which the student functions, such as consultation with parents to improve parenting skills, teacher consultation regarding pacing instruction and individualization of instruction, and/or peer group intervention. Students may also be referred to counselors to learn stress management techniques. Advocating for a hungry student's inclusion in the free and reduced breakfast and lunch programs is not a behavioral intervention and neither is referral for peer mediation. The purpose of the behavioral functional analysis is to develop a plan in which the intervention is designed to eliminate or alter the dynamics among setting events, antecedents, behaviors, and consequences so that the behavior exhibited is altered in the most positive fashion, making it appropriate to the setting in which it occurs. Moreover, the process is not merely one of fitting round pegs into square holes. In many instances the hole is refitted. Behavioral psychologists have been slow to recognize the importance of

cognitions and internal emotional states that produce inappropriate behavior (Alberto & Troutman, 2003), but they now recognize that a host of physical and psychological conditions can be antecedents (Walker, Shea, & Bauer, 2004) that must be included in the assessment and intervention plan.

MONITORING AND EVALUATION

As suggested by Bergan and Kratochwill (1990), in behavioral consultation the consultee, after being trained by the consultant, implements the intervention in consultation. In collaboration, all collaborators would be involved in the implementation process, although they would not necessarily assume the same roles. One collaborator might deliver the intervention while another would monitor progress toward the established objective by continuing the data-gathering process. The consultee would be expected to bear the brunt of the evaluation process in behavioral consultation, although the consultee would guide the process. In both processes, periodic meetings involving consultant, consultee, and client or collaborators and clients (students) would be required to discuss the progress that was being made, evaluate the appropriateness of the reinforcers or other strategies being used, and, perhaps, to set new objectives.

Evaluation is built into the behavioral consultation/collaboration process. A baseline regarding the occurrence, frequency, or duration of the behavior is established prior to goal setting and intervention implementation. Data collected during the intervention phase, whether it is observational data using a scatterplot or self-recordings, are periodically compared to the baseline to measure progress. The data being collected can also be compared to the criterion that has been included in the terminal objective.

Resistance

Resistance is a phenomenon encountered by all consultants. The sources of resistance to behavioral consultation may be related to a number of factors, including what some consultees perceive as the indeterministic, manipulative philosophy of behavior-

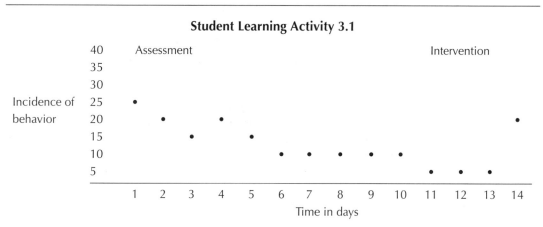

Student Learning Activity 3.1

The goal of the intervention is to reduce the incidence of a problematic behavior. Examine this chart. Is the intervention working? Why or why not?

ism. With the inclusion of Bandura's social learning theory as one of the foundations of the behavioral–eclectic approach, these beliefs are false and can quickly be dispelled. Some consultees, teachers in particular, object to what they see as bribing students for "what they should be doing anyway." Sometimes this objection to behavioral approaches can be eliminated by pointing out that most people come to work because they get paid with a token (money) that can be used to purchase food, gasoline, and other items. It may also be necessary to point out that some students are reinforced at home and at school for their behavior while others are not. Finally, resistance may arise because the process is aversive due to the time and effort involved. Overcoming this issue is more difficult, but in some instances teachers and others can be provided extra pay, time off, and other "perks" for their efforts. Consultants should also work to establish a culture in which caregivers receive formal and informal social recognition from supervisors and others for their efforts. For example, the evaluation instrument should include a statement such as "engages in successful consultation and collaboration with others." Informal recognition can be provided in evaluation conferences, newsletter notes—when an intervention has gone particularly well—and reports during staff meetings.

Cultural Limitations

The behavioral–eclectic model is rooted in the Eurocentric values of future time orientation and individual achievement and may not be appropriate for unacculturated client groups and consultees with different time orientations and a collateral social value such as some American Indian tribes and certain subgroups of Hispanics. The idea that people organize their lives around calendars and clocks to meet short- and long-term goals is alien to people who have present or circular time orientations. Similarly, the concept that the individual is more important than the group and that it is acceptable to compete with one's peer group is not readily acceptable in many cultures. People with an individual social value put themselves ahead of the group. Individuals with a collateral social value place the welfare of the group ahead of their own welfare (Sue & Sue, 1999).

When clients have a collateral social value that dictates that the individual not achieve above the level of the group, consultants, consultees, and collaborators will need to switch from an individual to a group approach to interventions. Behavioral contracts can be established for small groups or for an entire classroom. Token economy systems can be designed to reward cooperative behavior such as cooperative learning groups (Brown, 1999).

Behavioral approaches have major advantages with groups that value independence, have a future or past-future time orientation, and who value self-control. Planning and engaging in systematic approaches to problem solving are familiar concepts to people who have a Eurocentric future time orientation or a past-future time orientation that is common to many Asian subcultures. People who value self-control, as do many Asian groups, believe that it is important to avoid self-disclosing their thoughts and feelings. Because overt behavior is the primary focus of the assessment and interventions, questions regarding thoughts and feelings may not be necessary in the consultation or collaboration process. In other instances, when internal factors appear important in the assessment process, clinical decisions regarding these states can be substituted for direct questions.

Behavioral consultants should ascertain the values of consultees and clients either through direct questioning and/or observation. Adjustments in the time orientation of interventions can be made by developing anniversary dates that are not closely tied to the clock or the calendar. Scheduling appointments with collaborators and consultees can also be difficult if time orientation is not considered. For example, consultants who discover that consultees do not appear at the scheduled time for appointments have found that they must be more flexible when they make appointments by allowing for the possibility that the session will begin late.

Status of Behavioral–Eclectic Consultation and Collaboration

Behavioral consultation based primarily on operant learning theory (e.g., Bergan, 1977) has been criticized because of its indeterministic philosophy (Heller & Monahan, 1977), and what some see as manipulation of the consultee (Erchul, Hughes, Meyers, Hickman, & Braden, 1991; Gallessich, 1982; Winett & Winkler, 1972). More recently Witt, Gresham, and Noell (1996) have questioned

the wisdom of accepting the consultee's description of the problem. As suggested at the beginning of this chapter, the issue of controlling the interview remains unresolved (Erchul, 1999; Erchul & Chewning, 1990; Gutkin, 1996, 1999). The behavioral–eclectic model of consultation should eliminate some of these criticisms because it endorses the equal value–equal power concept of the relationship, includes a complex assessment approach that does not depend entirely on the consultee, and emphasizes that students and others are largely self-directed.

It is hoped that research such as that conducted by Erchul and his associates (Erchul & Chewning, 1990; Witt, Erchul, McKee, Pardue, & Wickstrom, 1988; Witt, Erchul, Pardue, McKee, & Fitzmaurice, 1991) will be continued to explore the issues surrounding behavioral approaches to consultation. This type of research will keep behavioral approaches in a prominent position in the consultation literature. Recent provisions of the 1997 amendments to IDEA will also insure that behavioral approaches to consultation and collaboration remain a major force. These amendments specify that, whenever a child with a disability has a behavioral problem that requires disciplinary action, a team should develop a behavioral functional analysis assessment that can be used as the basis for revision of an existing plan or the development of a new behavioral intervention that addresses the problematic behavior. Another objective of the functional behavioral assessment is to determine whether the behavior requiring disciplinary action is functionally related to the student's disability. If it is not related, the student can be disciplined in the same fashion as other students. Not only have these changes in IDEA reinforced the importance of behavioral approaches, they have made it mandatory that school counselors, psychologists, special education teachers, and others who deal with handicapped students understand and be able to practice the behavioral model in a collaborative fashion. The word *team* appears frequently in the wording of the 1997 amendments to IDEA, prompting many authorities (see Center for Effective Collaboration and Practice, 1998) to suggest that assessment and intervention should be collaborative processes.

CASE ILLUSTRATION: A SELF-MANAGEMENT PLUS COST-RESPONSE

The fifth-grade teacher's description of Gerrard was decidedly nonbehavioral. She said he "has ants in his pants." She was asked to clarify her statement by describing Gerrard's behavior during the time it seemed to be the worst, using the "run-it-like-a-movie strategy." Gerrard was at his worst during math instruction. At the outset of the twenty to twenty-five minutes, when the teacher was teaching math concepts, Gerrard was attentive, but as the instruction continued he became less and less attentive. He doodled on his math sheet, bothered other students around him by attempting to initiate conversations, showing them his pictures, and, from time to time, moving into their seats. By the end of the twenty to twenty-five minutes, Gerrard sometimes left his seat and wandered about the room, which distracted other students. Gerrard had been referred and assessed for ADD with hyperactivity, but the results were negative. He regularly attended school and had no apparent health problems.

The classroom aid conducted a scatterplot assessment of Gerrard's behavior during math instruction for one week. Gerrard was off-task an average of twice per five-minute observation period, but the scatterplot revealed that, as the teacher suggested, the behavior accelerated from an average of less than one time per five-minute period at the outset of math instruction to three times per five-minute period at the end of the instruction period. In this case, the antecedent to the problem seemed to be math instruction because Gerrard was off-task from time to time in other subjects, but his behavior was "tolerable" according to his teacher. A review of Gerrard's grades revealed that his grades in math were declining even though his WISC-R IQ was 128. Interviews with Gerrard and his parents revealed that: (1) Gerrard did not like to come to school because it was boring, (2) his parents seemed to have no expectations of Gerrard's

achievement so long as he passed everything, (3) the notes that the teacher had sent home were for the most part disregarded, although they had brief discussions of his nonattentive behavior in which he promised to do better and (4) parents paid little attention to Gerrard's report cards or school work. The conclusion drawn from the interview data was that the setting event in Gerrard's case was boredom.

Three interventions were selected by the teacher. Gerrard was placed in an accelerated math group. A prompt in the form of a picture of Gerrard attending to the teacher during instruction was taped to his desk along with a list of unacceptable (non-attending) behaviors. A response-cost system was implemented. Initially Gerrard received six tokens. Each time he engaged in one of the non-attending behavior listed on the sheet, one token was to be removed by either the aid or the teacher. If at least one token remained at the end of the instructional period, Gerrard received a star, which was to be placed on his star chart. If, at the end of week one, Gerrard had accumulated three stars, he was allowed to select one thirty-minute activity from a list that he and the teacher developed. It was agreed that the criterion for receiving a star and the end of the week reinforcer was to become more stringent in week two and three. The teacher and the aid agreed to verbally reinforce Gerrard's attending behavior in all of his subjects. In four weeks the incidence of Gerrard's non-attending behavior was lower than it was in his other subjects according to the teacher's estimate.

SUMMARY

Behavioral consultation has a long and distinguished history and remains as one of the dominant approaches to consultation. Recent legal developments regarding the treatment of disabled students require the use of collaborative functional behavioral analysis to develop behavioral interventions for students have provided additional impetus to the use of behavioral approaches and to the importance of collaboration. Fortunately, the methodology used in the assessing and intervening with exceptional students generalizes nicely to other students who do not have disabilities and enhances the status of behavioral consultation and collaboration.

The approaches used by behavioral consultants and collaborators are rigorous and thorough. They require the development of a behavioral definition of the problem behavior, a pre-assessment review, systematic observations using scatterplots and ABC anecdotal observations as well as indirect approaches to assessment. Behavioral consultants and collaborators may draw from a wealth of interventions, but it is suggested here that positive approaches that involve self-management are preferred in many instances. It was also suggested that behavioral approaches require modification with some ethnic groups, particularly with cultural groups that do not have a future time orientation or an independence social value.

TIPS FOR PRACTITIONERS

1. Before consulting with a person from a culture different than your own, check your knowledge of the customs, values, and traditions of that culture. If you are not familiar with them, it is probably inappropriate for you to continue.
2. You are a model in the consulting relationship whether you accept the idea or not. Building a warm, trusting relationship will enhance your characteristics as a model.
3. Assume the stance of a learner rather than an expert as you begin the consulting process.
4. Let consultees lead the consulting process. Let them tell the story in their own words, encourage them to ask questions, suggest that you are collaborative problem solvers, and share the credit for successes and failures.

REVIEW QUESTIONS

1. What are the major differences between Bergan's consultation model and the behavioral–eclectic model?

2. Bergan and Erchul believe that it is important to control the interview so that the outcome will be a well-designed behavioral intervention. What is your reaction to this idea?
3. What are the pros and cons of behavioral consultation and behavioral collaboration?
4. What are the steps in the functional behavioral analysis process?
5. The equal value–equal power concept of the relationship has been adopted to underpin the relation in the behavioral–eclectic model. Some consultants believe that maintaining this type of relationship during consulting is impossible because the consultee will automatically defer to the consultant. Is it possible to maintain an equal value–equal power relationship in consultation? Why or why not?
6. More and more emphasis is being placed on cultural competence because of the diversity in our society. What are the advantages and disadvantages of the behavioral–eclectic model as an approach with major cultural groups in the United States?
7. If you needed to increase the incidence of a behavior, what intervention would you use? Why?
8. If you needed to decrease the incidence of a behavior, what intervention would you use? Why?
9. It was suggested that interventions should approximate real-world situations if they are to lead to long-term change. Which behavioral interventions most closely approximate "the real world," and why do you think this is true?

REFERENCES

Alberto, P. A., & Troutman, A. C. (2003). *Applied Behavior Analysis for Teachers* (6th ed.). Englewood Cliffs, NJ: Merrill/Prentice-Hall.

Bandura, A. (1971). Psychotherapy based on modeling principles. In A. E. Bergin & S. L. Garfield (Eds.), *Handbook of psychotherapy and behavioral change: An empirical analysis* (pp. 653–708). New York: John Wiley & Sons.

Bandura, D. (1976). Self-reinforcement: Theoretical and methodological considerations. *Behaviorism, 4,* 135–155.

Bandura, A. (1977a). Self-efficacy: Toward a unifying theory of behavior change. *Psychological Review, 84,* 191–215.

Bandura, A. (1977b). *Social learning theory.* Englewood Cliffs, NJ: Prentice-Hall.

Bandura, A. (1978). The self system in reciprocal determinism. *American Psychologist, 33,* 344–358.

Bandura, A. (1982a). The assessment and predictive generality of self-precepts of efficacy. *Journal of Behavior Therapy and Experimental Psychiatry, 13,* 195–199.

Bandura, A. (1982b). Self-efficacy mechanism in human agency. *American Psychologist, 37,* 122–147.

Behavioral Dynamics. (2004). About the MotivAider®. Thief River Falls, MN: Author.

Bergan, J. R. (1977). *Behavioral consultation.* Columbus, OH: Charles E. Merrill.

Bergan, J. R., & Kratochwill, T. R. (1990). *Behavioral consultation and therapy.* New York: Plenum Press.

Bergan, J. R., & Tombari, M. L. (1975). The analysis of verbal interactions occurring during consultation. *Journal of School Psychology, 13,* 209–226.

Bergan, J. R., & Tombari, M. L. (1976). Consultant skill and efficiency and the implementation and outcomes of consultation. *Journal of School Psychology, 14,* 3–14.

Brofenbrenner, U. (1979). *The ecology of human development.* Cambridge, MA: Harvard University Press.

Brown, D. (1999). *Proven strategies for learning and achievement.* Greensboro, NC: CAPS.

Brown, D., Pryzwansky, W. B., & Schulte, A. (1987). *Psychological consultation: Introduction to theory and practice.* Boston: Allyn & Bacon.

Brown, D., & Schulte, A. (1987). A social learning model of consultation. *Professional Psychology: Research and Practice, 18,* 283–287.

Caplan, G. (1970). *The theory and practice of mental health consultation.* New York: Basic Books.

Center for Effective Collaboration and Practice. (1998). Addressing student problem behavior: Conducting a functional behavior assessment. [On-line.] Available: http://www.air.org/cecp/fba/problembehavior2.main2.htm.

Erchul, W. P. (1987). A relational communication analysis of control in school consultation. *Professional School Psychology, 2,* 113–124.

Erchul, W. P. (1992). On dominance, cooperation, teamwork, and collaboration in school-based consultation. *Journal of Educational and Psychological Consultation, 3,* 363–366.

Erchul, W. P. (1999). Two steps forward, one step back: Collaboration in school-based consultation. *Journal of School Psychology, 37,* 191–203.

Erchul, W. P., & Chewning, T. G. (1990). Behavioral consultation from a request-centered relational communication perspective. *School Psychology Quarterly, 5,* 1–20.

Erchul, W. P., Hughes, J. N., Meyers, J., Hickman, J. A., & Braden, J. P. (1992). Dyadic agreement concerning the consultation process in relationship to outcome. *Journal of Educational and Psychological Consultation, 3,* 119–132.

Erchul, W. P., & Martens, K. (1997). *School consultation: Conceptual and empirical bases of practice.* New York: Plenum Press.

Gallessich, J. (1982). *The profession and practice of consultation.* San Francisco: Jossey-Bass.

Goodwin, D. L., & Coates, T. J. (1977). The teacher-pupil interaction scale: An empirical method for analyzing the interaction effects of teacher and pupil behavior. *Journal of School Psychology, 15,* 51–59.

Gutkin, T. B. (1996). Patterns of consultant and consultee verbalizations: Examining communication leadership during initial consultation interviews. *Journal of School Psychology, 34,* 199–219.

Gutkin, T. B. (1999). Collaborative versus directive/prescriptive/expert school-based consultation: Reviewing and resolving a false dichotomy. *Journal of School Psychology, 37,* 161–190.

Heller, K., & Monahan, J. (1977). *Psychology and community change.* Homewood, IL: Dorsey Press.

Houk, J. L., & Lendowski, L. J. (1996). Consultant verbal control and consultee perceptions. *Journal of Educational and Psychological Consultation, 7,* 107–118.

Hughes, J. N., Erchul, W. P., Yoon, J. Jackson, T., & Henington, C. (1997). *Journal of School Psychology, 35,* 281–297.

Keller, H. R. (1981). Behavioral consultation. In J. C. Conoley (Ed.), *Consultation in schools: Theory, research, and practice* (pp. 59–99). New York: Academic Press.

Malott, R. W., & Suarez, E. A. T. (2004). *Principles of behavior* (5th ed.). Upper Saddle River, NJ. Pearson/Prentice-Hall.

Martella, R. C., Nelson, J. R., Marchand-Martella, N. E. (2003). *Managing disruptive behavior in the schools.* Boston: Allyn & Bacon.

Piersel, W. C. (1985). Behavioral consultation: An approach to problem solving in educational settings. In J. R. Bergan (Ed.), *School psychology in contemporary society* (pp. 331–364). Columbus, OH: Charles E. Merrill.

Reynolds, C. R., Gutkin, T. B., Elliot, S. N., & Witt, J. C. (1984). *School psychology: Essentials of theory and practice.* New York: John Wiley & Sons.

Russell, J. L. (1978). Behavioral consultation: Theory & process. *Personnel and Guidance Journal, 56,* 346–350.

Schulte, A., & Osborne, S. (2003). When assumptive worlds collide: A review of definitions of *collaboration* and *consultation. Journal of Educational and Psychological Consultation, 14*(2), 109–138.

Sue, D. W., & Sue, D. (1990). *Counseling the culturally different: Theory and practice.* New York: Wiley.

Sue, D. W., & Sue, D. (1999). *Counseling the culturally different: Theory and practice* (3rd ed.). New York: Wiley.

Tharp, R. G., & Wetzel, R. J. (1969). *Behavior modification in the natural environment.* New York: Academic Press.

Tombari, M. L., & Bergan, J. R. (1978). Consultant cues and teacher verbalizations, judgments, and expectations concerning children's adjustment problems. *Journal of School Psychology, 16,* 212–219.

Touchette, P., MacDonald, R., & Langer, S. (1985). A scatterplot for identifying stimulus control of problems. *Journal of Applied Behavior Analysis, 18,* 343–351.

Walker, J. E., Shea, T. M., & Bauer, A. M. (2004). *Behavior management: A practical approach for educators* (8th ed.). Englewood Cliffs, NJ: Prentice-Hall.

Wickstrom, K. F., Jones, K. M., LaFleur, L. H., & Witt, J. C. (1998). An analysis of treatment integrity in school-based behavioral consultation. *School Psychology Quarterly, 13,* 141–154.

Winett, R. A., & Winkler, R. (1972). Current behavior modification in the classroom. *Psychology, 5,* 499–504.

Witt, J. C., Erchul, W. P., McKee, W. T., Pardue, M. M., & Wickstrom, K. F. (1991). Conversational control in school-based consultation: The relationship between consultant and consultee topic determination and consultation outcome. *Journal of Educational and Psychological Consultation, 2,* 101–116.

Witt, J. C., Erchul, W. P., Pardue, M. M., Mckee, W. T., & Fitzmaurice, J. (1988). Quantification of interpretational interactions in school-based consultation: A molecular analysis. Paper presented at the meeting of the American Psychological Association, Atlanta.

Witt, J. C., Gresham, F. M., & Noell, G. H. (1996). What's behavioral about behavioral consultation? *Journal of Educational and Psychological Consultation, 7,* 327–344.

ANSWERS TO LEARNING EXERCISE

The intervention is probably succeeding, but because of the latest data, which is moving away from the baseline, it is impossible to tell. The next two observations will either confirm or disconfirm the latest data point and indicate whether the last data point is an anomaly or a trend.

CHAPTER 4

ADLERIAN CONSULTATION

GOAL OF THE CHAPTER

The goal of this chapter is to introduce the Adlerian model of consultation.

CHAPTER PREVIEW

1. A brief history of the Adlerian approach to consultation will be provided.
2. The theory underpinning Adlerian consultation will be outlined.
3. The process of Adlerian consultation will be described.
4. Empirical support for Adlerian approaches will be summarized.

BACKGROUND

Alfred Adler is often characterized as a neo-Freudian, and in fact he was a colleague of Sigmund Freud from 1902 to 1911. However, in 1911 Adler resigned from the Psychoanalytic Institute in Vienna because of his basic and long-standing disagreements with Freud about human functioning, particularly the matter of infant sexuality (Furtmuller, 1964). He had been invited to join Freud's inner circle in 1902 after he defended Freud's work, *Interpretation of Dreams,* after it was harshly criticized by a Viennese newspaper, but it was clear from the outset of their relationship that their positions on the nature of human functioning had little in common (Furtmuller, 1964).

Although Ansbacher and Ansbacher (1964) were able to link Adler to over 300 citations, he was an active practitioner and spent relatively little time writing. The result was that his theoretical positions were not widely known in this country until the middle of the twentieth century because they had never been translated from German to English or presented in a comprehensive fashion. In 1956

Ansbacher and Ansbacher translated and published excerpts from Adler's papers that clarified his theory to a significant degree. Their publications (Ansbacher & Ansbacher, 1956, 1964) contained some of Adler's important essays and made his work accessible to a wide variety of people in this country. One of Adler's disciples, Rudolph Dreikurs (1968), was also highly instrumental in disseminating information about Adler's theory. Dreikurs developed applications of Adler's ideas into approaches that can be used in the consultation process in books such as *Psychology in the Classroom* (Dreikurs, 1968) and *Children: The Challenge* (Dreikurs & Stoltz, 1967). Donald Dinkmeyer, who collaborated with Dreikurs (Dinkmeyer & Dreikurs, 1963) on a book regarding the encouragement process, coauthored the first book on consultation based on the work of Adler (Dinkmeyer & Carlson, 1973). Dinkmeyer and McKay (1989) also developed a popular parenting program, Systematic Training for Effective Parenting (STEP), which is based on Adlerian psychology. Others, such as Linda Albert (1996a, 1996b), have developed applications of Adlerian ideas that are useful to consultants. The result of Adler's work and that of his followers is a theoretical position than can be translated easily into consultation practice with teachers, parents, and others. Moreover, Adlerian theory endorses the concept of collaboration. Adler may have been the first to recommend collaborative approaches in the family, school, and other social institutions.

ADLERIAN THEORY

Adlerian theory (see Ansbacher & Ansbacher, 1956; Dreikurs, 1953), also referred to as individual psychology and socioteleoanalytic theory, has several premises regarding human functioning. These premises are (1) human beings are embedded in a social context from which they cannot be separated, (2) human beings operate on the basis of subjective reality, (3) individuals function holistically, (4) all aspects of the functioning of the personality are oriented toward a single goal, which Adler called fictional finalism, and (5) human beings have the creative power to control their own destiny. Of these assumptions, none is more important than the idea that behavior is goal-oriented. Adler referred to all life goals as guiding fictions because they are based on subjective perception, not objective reality. The specific nature of the life goal develops early in life, but the predisposition to function in a goal-oriented fashion is present at birth. Life goals guide the individual toward a single life striving: overcoming feelings of inferiority. Adler divided feelings of inferiority into two groups: normal and heightened or abnormal feelings of inferiority. Feelings of inferiority are a part of each child's cultural legacy due to the frailty of human beings when juxtaposed to the tremendous forces of nature. These innate feelings of inferiority continue to grow due to children's relatively small stature and because of their dependency on larger, more powerful adults. It is these feelings of inferiority that are the genesis of teleological or goal-oriented thinking, which is aimed at striving for superiority. As the child grows and develops, conditions within the family result in the child's turning either to the useful, so-

cially oriented goals or to heightened feelings of inferiority and guiding fictions that lead to antisocial functioning and mental health problems. The guiding fictions that are adopted become the focal point for the organization of personality. Adler contends that these guiding fictions are not fully in awareness, a point that could be interpreted to mean that Alderians accept the idea of an unconscious portion of personality. However, Dreikurs (1953) contends that the word *unadmitted* is a better descriptor than the word *unconscious* because people have access to and can "know" the goal-oriented basis for their functioning. Often individuals will not admit the nature of their goals, even to themselves. This is why Adlerians often find it necessary to disclose the essence of individuals' goals to them in their work.

Adler believes that personality, which he termed the lifestyle, develops during the first five to six years of the child's existence. Children who receive encouragement, live in a collaborative environment, are accorded a place in that environment, and are given the opportunity to develop their strengths turn to the useful side of life and have social interest, courage, and the ability to make decisions, which Adler called common sense. Adler defined social interest as being interested in contributing to the collective, the greater good. The essence of social interest lies in the individual's identification with all other human beings and the ability to empathize with them. The ability to cooperate with others is one measure of social interest. Unselfish contribution to the social good is another indicator that social interest has developed (Dreikurs, 1953). Children who are abused physically and/or emotionally, are hated and despised, are deprived of the essentials of life, are pampered by having things done for them they can do themselves, or have organ inferiorities may develop heightened feelings of inferiority, become discouraged, turn to the useless side of life, and develop mental health problems. Adler stresses that the child *may* become discouraged under the conditions described above, but the final outcome will be based on the child's perceptions of his or her environment, not the perceptions of others.

In order to illustrate the role of perception in the development of personality, consider for a moment the idea of organ inferiority, which can be something, on the one hand, as mundane as needing glasses or a much more severe physical or mental deficiency such as a restrictive physical disability, mental retardation, or a learning disability. However, it is not the presence of the disability that determines the developmental path of the child's personality; it is the child's view of the disability. If the child views himself or herself as disabled, discouragement will result, and heightened feelings of inferiority will follow. The result of heightened feelings of inferiority is the adoption of a faulty lifestyle.

The Emergence of Personality

As noted above, Adler posited that personality is formed during the first five to six years. In his writings, he seems to have subscribed to Freud's idea of a latency period, because he alludes to the emergence of the personality as occurring at about the onset of puberty. However, Rudolf Dreikurs (1953), who specialized in child psychiatry after he came to this country, extended Adler's ideas, suggesting that personality is in fact developed in an *identifiable* form by age five or six. Children who have been nurtured properly have developed social interest. Children who are discouraged turn to the useless side of life and attempt to find their place by striving for attention, power, or revenge, or by withdrawing from social interactions. Each of these goals may manifest itself in varying ways. Attention getters may want to "show off," be treated as special—often at inappropriate times, or act helpless. Their goal is to gain recognition by constantly calling attention to themselves. The child who has a power goal may be domineering or passive aggressive. This child's goal is to entice people into power struggles. The child who has a revenge goal commits antisocial, destructive acts in many instances and may respond to punishment with aggression or attempts to make others feel bad. The goal in this instance is to get even by inflicting physical or psychological pain. The child who has adopted goal four, withdrawal, focuses on his or her inadequacies, lacks self-confidence, and, in extreme cases, simply withdraws from social activities. Dreikurs (1968), who termed these the four goals of disturbing behavior, suggested that they can be observed in children to age ten. Importantly, Dreikurs believed that children do not necessarily adopt a single misguided goal, but may, in fact, operate on two or more. However, he believed that in all likelihood one of these goals is dominant.

Discouraged children try to attain status and find their place by acting on one or more of the four goals. Dreikurs (1968) believes that these four goals are also present in adolescence and adulthood, but they take on somewhat different, often more complex forms. Sweeney (1989), in agreement with Dreikurs, identified both constructive and destructive manifestations of these goals in adolescence. Striving for superiority to the point of perfectionism, conforming rigidly to adult standards, being obsequiously charming, and pursuing popularity for its own sake are constructive manifestations of what may be misguided goals. If these are manifestations of misguided goals, adolescents believe that they are worthwhile and belong only when they are superior to others, conform totally to adult standards, are the most popular persons in their class, and so forth. Destructive manifestations of misguided goals include passive and aggressive defiance, drug abuse, sexual promiscuity, perfectionism, and displays of inadequacy or hopelessness. Adolescents for whom these are misguided goals believe that they are worthwhile and belong when they are being defiant, are abusing drugs, or are sexually promiscuous. Displays of hopelessness may be signs that the individuals have given up on themselves and believe they will never be worthwhile or belong, although this can be ascertained only by tapping the internal perspective of the individual.

The four goals of misguided behavior can also be used to some degree as the basis for understanding the misguided motivation of adults, although in order to develop a complete understanding a lifestyle (personality), analysis is required. While a discussion of lifestyle analysis goes beyond the

Student Learning Activity 4.1

Please respond to the following true/false questions. Answers are at the end of the chapter.

T F 1. Adler's theory can best be described as phenomenological.

T F 2. The lifestyle of the individual develops around guiding fictions.

T F 3. Adler believed that personality is fully developed by the onset of puberty.

T F 4. Organ inferiority refers to Adler's belief that people who have serious disabilities invariably develop deep-seated feelings of inferiority.

T F 5. The most important factor in determining the child's outlook on life is the family atmosphere.

T F 6. The key to understanding human functioning is the way individuals behave in critical situations.

T F 7. Adler believes that normal people have social interest, which he defines as an unselfish interest in others.

scope of this presentation, Mosak (1979) suggests that adults who are discouraged and have turned to the useless side of life make what he terms basic mistakes. These are (1) overgeneralizations, such as believing that all people are untrustworthy because of one experience, (2) establishing impossible goals such as perfection, (3) misperceptions about life such as believing that luck is the primary variable in success, (4) denial of their worth or value, and (5) faulty values that suggest that success is necessary regardless of the cost or that justify illegal behavior.

CONSULTATION

Preventive Approaches

One of the goals of consultation is the prevention of mental health problems, a position Adler adopted about the turn of the twentieth century. He established child guidance clinics where families and individuals could receive help, consulted with and provided education to teachers so that they could deal more effectively with the children in their classrooms, and worked with other caregivers in an effort to establish a therapeutic climate within social institutions. In all aspects of his work, Adler emphasized the importance of encouragement, which he saw as the primary antidote to discouragement. Encouragement is defined as the process of expressing belief in individuals' ability and worth as opposed to rewarding them for accomplishments. Adler believed that positive reinforcement as used in behavioral systems actually leads to discouragement because people may come to believe that they are not worthwhile in their own right; it is their acts or accomplishments that people value. Teaching parents, teachers, and other caregivers to provide encouragement is viewed as the first step toward the prevention of mental health problems.

Dreikurs (1968), Sweeney (1989), Albert (1996a), and others suggest that there are several principles to follow when encouraging others.

Principles Guiding Encouragement

1. The cornerstone of encouragement is acceptance. In many instances, children with handicaps find that they are not accepted by their families, other children, teachers, and other adults. Culturally different children and adults often find that they are unaccepted and unappreciated because of their differences. The message that needs to be sent to all groups is, "You are a worthwhile person," not, "Your differences make you inferior."

2. Separate the actor from the act. A child may be told, "Hitting is bad," but should not be told, "You are a bad boy when you hit others" (communicates that acts are related to relative worth).

3. Effort is more important than outcome. An adolescent may be told, "You really dug in and worked on your subjects," but should not be told, "The A's you got were wonderful" (communicates that worth is related to performance). Albert (1996a) points out that some-

times people who try more things make more mistakes. Teachers, parents, and other caregivers want to encourage active participation and effort. To emphasize mistakes has the opposite effect.

4. Present functioning is more important than past performance. However, if the client has a history of past successes, be sure to point them out as a portion of the encouragement process. An adult might be told, "Hey, we really appreciate the job you are doing for us now," but should not be told, "You are doing much better that you were a few months ago" (communicates that judgment about worth may be temporary). A child who has failed might be told, "You didn't do very well on this exam, but you have done well in the past and I'm sure you will do well the next time if you just keep on working."

5. Emphasize intrinsic motivation, not extrinsic motivation. A person might be told, "I'll bet it makes you feel great to accomplish some of the things you have done," but should not be told, "The award you got for your achievements is terrific" (communicates that achievement should be oriented to extrinsic rewards, not personal satisfaction).

6. The importance of the individual should be recognized for her or his own sake, not in comparison to others. A child could be told, "You're a real asset in this class," but not "You do things so much better than others in the class" (communicates that person is worthwhile only when he or she is superior to others).

Democratic Principles. Adler's contemporary followers believe that another important approach to preventing psychological problems from arising is for all social institutions to operate on democratic principles. This idea stems from Adler's belief that human beings are social animals that need a place (belonging) within their social milieu whether it be the family, classroom, or workplace. Dreikurs suggested that children should be accorded a vote on all family matters as soon as they are capable of understanding the issues involved. Similarly, he believed that children and adolescents should be involved in rule and policy setting in schools. Adlerians also believe that providing "special" time for individual children is another way to show them that they have a place in the family. They also suggest that parents and other caregivers reject competitive approaches in favor of collaborative approaches.

Development of Competencies. Children and adolescents also need to develop their competencies including their intellectual, physical, and decision-making skills. Some parents take away opportunities to develop these competencies by pampering, or by doing things for the children that they can do for themselves. Showering children with material things is another form of pampering because it takes away opportunities to earn the things they want and to achieve the satisfaction that goes with the accomplishments. One way to help children develop competencies is by according them a role in the decision making, not just in family matters, but as applied to their own lives. For example, Adlerians believe that children should be allowed to choose their own clothing at a very early age. They also believe that children should be allowed to work out their own problems. When parents are too quick to intervene in the conflicts of their children, the children are robbed of opportunities to develop conflict resolution skills. Adlerian consultants often encourage parents to take a walk or to go into the bathroom and turn on some music when their children are fighting. Having a place in the family also requires that children are recognized and valued for their unique characteristics, have a physical space no matter how small, be accorded an allowance (it is their right and is not contingent on performance)—the size of which is to be based on the family's earnings, and take responsibility for the care and maintenance of the household and their own lives. Adlerians encourage parents to buy their children alarm clocks instead of waking them each morning, as well as to allow children to take full responsibility for their personal spaces and to assume chores that contribute to the welfare of the family.

This does not mean that parents provide no structure for their children. Adlerians believe that students of all ages need established bedtimes, curfews, and, so far as possible, mealtimes. These should be negotiated and then renegotiated at each stage of the child's life.

Adlerians believe that if children are valued, they will learn to value themselves. Conversely, if they are despised or pitied, they are likely to dislike themselves, or feel that they are unworthy and feel sorry for themselves. If children are accorded a place in and responsibility in the family, they will have a sense of belonging. If children make decisions, whether at home or at school, they will learn decision-making skills; if they have duties to perform, they will learn to accept responsibility. Importantly, if they do not complete their chores or live up to the rules they have negotiated, they will learn that not following through or obeying the rules has consequences.

Providing Natural and Logical Consequences. Replacing punitive approaches sometimes used by parents and teachers with natural and logical consequences is another preventive approach. Punitive approaches are characterized by making the person being punished feel inferior, embarrassed, or out of control. They are also accompanied by anger and verbal or physical abuse. Natural consequences are "administered" by the environment and require no direct intervention by another person (Sweeney, 1989). Natural consequences express the power of the social order (Dreikurs, 1968). Natural consequences may also be "imposed" by nature. A child who skips a meal will eventually become hungry, and Adlerians believe that it is better for the child to realize that it is unwise to skip meals via the consequences of the act than by being verbally or physically punished by the parent.

However, the Adlerians believe that all caregivers have a duty to protect the health and welfare of children. The natural consequence of not listening to one's parents and playing in a busy street might be death. The natural consequence of not brushing one's teeth is tooth decay. Neither of these natural consequences is acceptable within the Adlerian framework. Parents should explain the consequences of not brushing one's teeth, encourage children to brush, and establish a routine during their early years that includes brushing teeth. They should do whatever is necessary to keep their children out of extreme danger. On the other hand, short-term hunger or discomfort such as being cold on the way to school—results of a child's actions—would be acceptable as natural consequences. The natural consequence of spending all of one's lunch money on Monday is to be without lunch money for the remainder of the week. The natural consequences of being unable to purchase lunch are hunger or the loss of time to make the money necessary to pay for lunch. Allowing a child or adolescent to dress herself or himself badly (in the parent's view) may result in either negative feedback from peers (a natural consequence) or affirmation of the child's good taste. Early in life, children should be taught to dress themselves, and they should learn such common-sense ideas as they will be more comfortable on a cold day if they wear a coat. However, once these lessons are taught, the natural environment—not the caregiver—should assume the role of providing feedback.

Logical consequences result when a child or adult breaks a rule of the group (being tardy) or fails to act responsibly (doesn't take out the trash or complete a task on time). Logical consequences, which require action by someone, are consequences that are logically related to the violation of rules or the act committed. In this sense, they are similar to punishment, but they are administered without anger, abuse, or denigration of the violator. Whenever possible, logical consequences should be established in advance, with the child or adolescent given choices about what will occur if a rule is broken or agreed upon responsibilities are not fulfilled, but this will not be possible in all cases. When rules violations occur in the absence of predetermined consequences, the child or adolescent should be given options regarding the action to be taken in order to take away the arbitrariness associated with punitive approaches. Logical consequences, unlike natural consequences that are administered by the social and natural environment, require that the person using them understand the disruptive goal of the client. This idea will be discussed in detail in the next section.

Logical consequences involve many strategies, including restitution (see Table 4.1). The adolescent who spray-paints graffiti on school walls might be required to repaint the walls. The child who steals might be asked to repay the money and to apologize privately to the people from whom the money was taken. Arriving late for class or otherwise disregarding the welfare of the group may mean in-school suspension. Parents, teachers, and other caregivers who are involved in delivering or determining natural or logical consequences must learn to do so in a nonpunitive fashion—that is, refrain from verbal abuse, sarcasm, and other punitive tactics.

Beginning the Program. Launching an effective prevention program begins with an inservice program to train teachers, parents, and other caregivers in the use of encouragement, the development of democratic families and classrooms, and the use of logical and natural consequences in place of physical and verbal abuse. Follow-up activities for parents, teachers, and other caregivers involve consultation and continuing education. Consultants who are working in institutions such as a public schools, day care centers, or custodial facilities would also work with the leadership in those institutions to provide a supportive, encouraging environment based on democratic principles. They might also develop structures such as support groups that would allow staff and faculty members to help and encourage each other.

Mental health prevention programs for adults involve many of the same strategies just described. However, collaborative approaches to decision making are the heart of prevention programs, and one of the consultant's roles would be to help people such as employers develop collegial approaches

TABLE 4.1 Logical (L) and Natural (N) Consequences at Home and School

Home	
Infraction	*Consequence*
Late for dinner.	Misses dinner; no snacks (N).
Doesn't do chores.	Misses special time because someone else did chore (L).
Late; not home by curfew.	Curfew set earlier (L).
Spends clothing allowance.	No new clothes (N).
Picks out outrageous clothing.	Feedback from peers (N).
Doesn't place dirty clothes in hamper.	Clothes not washed (N).
Stereo too loud.	Stereo removed (for a period of time) (L) .
Fails to bathe.	Shunned by peers (N).
Destroys own toys.	No toys to play with (N).
School	
Homework not completed.	Noon detention (L).
Vandalism.	Restitution; repair/replace (L).
Aggressive behavior.	Apologies; conflict mediation training (L).
Talking; off-task behavior.	Relocate seat (L).
Out-of-seat.	Chair removed (L).
Not achieving to specified standards.	Failure (N).
Continuous rules infraction.	In-school suspension (L).

Student Learning Activity 4.2

Identify the activities that are important preventive strategies. Answers are at the end of the chapter.

1. Immediate feedback from parents and teachers.
2. Natural consequences.
3. Positive feedback about accomplishments.
4. Letting people know where they stand in relationship to the group.
5. Encouragement.
6. Allowing children to establish the structure of their lives.
7. Establishing an atmosphere in which children feel they belong.

---

in the workplace and to help them learn to use the encouragement process in their day-to-day work and in the performance appraisal process. Both compensation programs based on clearly defined standards of functioning and hiring and dismissal policies that are relatively unequivocal would serve as the basis of logical consequences in the workplace. Natural consequences would arise from the informal norms of the business and should reflect democratic ideals, respect for the individual, and supportiveness among fellow workers.

Remedial Strategies

Remedial interventions include consultation and therapy. In either process, a diagnosis of the client's problem is required in order to design the intervention properly. The obvious difference between therapy and consultation is that, in therapy, the mental health professional diagnoses the problem in a face-to-face interview. In consultation, the diagnosis occurs indirectly. Only diagnosis in consultation will be addressed here, although the two processes have much in common. The principles to be followed in the diagnostic process are as follows.

It is necessary to understand the internal frame of reference of the client. This frame of reference *cannot* be understood by observing behavior. One means of understanding the internal behavior of clients is by determining the impact they make on others, including consultees. If the client is mildly annoying, but does not arouse anger, the goal is likely attention getting. If the client pushes the consultee into power struggles (displays open oppositional behavior) and angers and frustrates the consultee, the goal is probably power. If the consultee feels that the client cannot be trusted (I cannot turn my back on him), sees the client as sneaky, and feels that the client acquiesces but only to "win" at another time, the goal of the client's behavior is probably revenge. If the client commits acts of physical aggression, this strengthens the hypothesis. If the client elicits feelings of pity or concern, the goal may be withdrawal.

Typically, in consultation, the feelings elicited in the consultee are sufficient to make the proper diagnosis. However, if it is deemed essential to explore the guiding fiction of the client further, other diagnostic clues can be gained by the consultee via direct questioning. If children are involved, they can be asked, "If you could be any animal, what would you be?" Importantly, the type of animal they choose is not particularly significant. Why they choose to be a particular animal is what reveals the goal of the behavior, and thus the follow-up to the "animal question" is "Why would you want to be that animal?" Children who want to be gorillas may choose that animal "because everyone laughs at them at the zoo" (attention getting), "no one could make them do anything" (power), "I could get back at the kids who tease me" (revenge), or "I could climb way up on a hill where no one could see me" (withdrawal). A variation of this approach with older children and adolescents is the "three wishes" question, "If you could have three wishes, what would they be?" Here again, the important aspect of this question is not the wish, but the reasons why the wish is being made (i.e., what would be gained as a result of having the wish granted?). Other options include asking clients what their personal mottoes are or having them complete open-ended sentences such as, "It is important for me…" or "My one goal in life is…"

Once a diagnosis is made, it should be shared with the consultee at the appropriate time. In sharing the diagnosis, three principles should be observed. These are:

1. The disclosure should be made tentatively. "Is it possible that in order for you to feel that you belong and are a worthwhile person you need to draw me into fights so you can try to beat me?" not "You try to draw me into fights so you can win and feel better about yourself."

2. The purpose of the goal (attention) and its hoped-for outcome should be disclosed. "Could it be that you would like to get attention so it will make you feel like people care about you?"

3. Acceptance of the diagnosis by the client should not be an immediate objective. In fact, when power or revenge are at the heart of the individual's mistaken goal, initial rejection of the disclosure is almost guaranteed, although the rejection is made for different purposes (defeating versus punishing).

THE CONSULTATION PROCESS

Relationship

Adlerians believe, in accord with most consultants, that the consulting relationship is essential to successful consultation. The procedures outlined in Chapter Six are in keeping with Adlerian approaches to relationship development.

Assessment

Adlerians use very structured approaches to getting information. For example, as is illustrated in Chapter Ten, parents are asked to describe a typical day in their household. They are also asked to describe their reactions to these events. The assessment process with teachers and other caregivers may involve direct observations. During the assessment process, Adlerians ascertain the fictitious goal of the client, the disciplinary strategies (e.g., nagging, physical punishment, negative compari-

sons with siblings or other students), the consistency of the use of disciplinary approaches, the extent to which democratic principles are employed, and the opportunities that are afforded for children to engage in personal decision making and to contribute to the welfare of others.

Goal Setting and Intervention

Goal setting is a far less formal process in Adlerian consultation than it is in the behavioral approaches described earlier. However, consultees are invited to select a target problem if several problems have been identified. The Adlerian consultant who has established that the client has not turned to the useless side, with faulty guiding fictions, will work from the assumption that the consultee needs to learn how to use encouragement, will establish a democratic atmosphere in which the client or clients can gain the ability to make decisions and develop their inherent potential, and will use logical and natural consequences properly.

If the consultant determines that the client has developed a maladaptive goal, the nature of the intervention process changes, although the interventions remain the same. Clients who are working from power or revenge goals will often resist any aspect of an intervention initially. For example, if children are asked what animal they would like to be, they may resist answering the question. They may also resist opportunities to negotiate rules, interfere in a classroom process designed to establish a democratic process, and otherwise act in an oppositional manner. Dreikurs (1968) warned not to become engaged in a power struggle that results in anger and frustration, because once this occurs, clients have achieved their goal: they have defeated the caregiver. For these clients, providing a great deal of encouragement (I'm confident that you can do this), establishing consequences in advance of breaches in agreements, and breaking off any negotiation if one feels as though he or she is entering a power struggle (becoming angry or frustrated) before the power struggle ensues are strategies that need to be employed. When negotiations are broken off, the consultee should express optimism about the likelihood that the client and the consultee can resolve the problem and invite the client to continue to work on it. Other approaches that the consultee may need to use when dealing with these clients include disclosing the goal of the client's behavior ("You would really like for me to get angry at you right now," or "You probably are thinking of some way to get even with me"), introducing humor into the process when it becomes tense ("I'll bet you would like to see me get angry and blow up; I would but the top of my head comes off when I do and I find this to be embarrassing"), and using reverse psychology—a term Adler coined long before it became a part of modern vernacular—("You are probably right, we don't need to negotiate these rules. Good parents don't care about their children and let them stay out all night. My problem is I love you") are all required from time to time when dealing with clients who have the mistaken goals of power. Perhaps more important, patience and kindness are required when dealing with these very discouraged clients.

Adlerians encourage consultees to use a number of specific interventions in addition to encouragement and natural and logical consequences. Noncontingent contracts can be used in addition to agreements based on logical consequences. Although the Adlerians believe that much of what is learned occurs in the natural environment of the home, school, and community, they are also in favor of direct teaching of social skills and other habits that are not developing as expected. Once the problem has been identified and strategies have been selected, Adlerians provide encouragement by expressing confidence in the consultees' ability to deal with the problem and suggesting that they both solicit input from the clients who are involved and tell clients of any changes that the consultees expect to make in their behavior. They also warn consultees that it is necessary, once a course of action has been embarked upon, to be very consistent in their behavior. They believe that clients who have been accustomed to the old approaches of the consul-

tee expect them to return to those approaches. Thus, any deviation from the new approaches is interpreted by clients to continue business as usual—that is, to continue to function as they did in the past because that is the way to achieve their goals.

As just noted, Adlerian consultants often train all caregivers (e.g., teachers and parents) in the principles of Adlerian psychology as one of the initial steps in the establishment of a program to prevent educational and mental health problems from arising. When this has been done, there is very little need for imparting to consultees, or for teaching, Adlerian techniques. Even when the consultee is unaware of the principles of Adlerian psychology, consultants provide only as much information as is needed to implement the intervention. No attempt is made to familiarize them with the premises of the theory. Instead, Adlerian consultants rely upon the common sense of consultees to grasp the significance of concepts such as engaging children in democratic procedures, understanding how the clients' goals may influence interventions, and the need to involve clients in activities that will give them a sense of belonging and allow them to develop competencies.

Follow-Up Sessions and Termination

Follow-up sessions may occur within a few days or in two or three weeks depending upon the perceptions of consultees and consultants. The purpose of these sessions is to review progress, begin to address new concerns, and provide encouragement to the consultee. Termination occurs when consultees feel they have accomplished their goals, although the consultant might terminate the session in the event a consultee seems resistant or is unmotivated.

Resistance

Adlerians accept the idea that resistance to change may result from more work or diminution in pay or status. Additionally, resistance in parent consultation may occur because of fear that sensitive (e.g., facts regarding a messy divorce) or illegal issues (e.g., child abuse) may surface. They also subscribe to the idea that resistance may occur because of lifestyle issues that result in oppositional behavior. Resistance may take an active form in which consultees attempt to draw consultants into power struggles by questioning their credentials (Where did you get your degree?) or experience (Have you ever been a teacher?) or by open confrontation regarding the best course of action for the client or other issues. Consultees may resist passively by not following through, not appearing for appointments, or by simply "yes, buting" the consultant (yes, that sounds like a good idea, but...*reasons not to try it*). Consultants are likely to become aware of the resistance when they develop a sense of anger or frustration growing out of the consultee's actions. Direct, confrontational approaches should be avoided when resistance occurs. Rather, the consultant should shift more responsibility to the consultee by requesting clarification and suggestions (Perhaps I didn't understand what you told me. Please tell me how you think this situation can best be handled based on your perceptions.) or terminating the consultation.

CULTURAL LIMITATIONS

Adlerian psychology, like all psychological systems, is rooted in a cultural values system. For example, it accepts the Eurocentric idea that insight is a prerequisite to self-understanding and growth, an idea that may not be as palatable to some Asian groups. It is also rooted in the Eurocentric idea of dominating time (things must be done *on time*), a value that may be less important to many Native Americans and Hispanics. Moreover, the Adlerian approach to consultation emphasizes collegial relationships as opposed to hierarchical relationships, which may not be acceptable to some Asian Americans, and a future-oriented approach that may not be in keeping with the past/present time orientation of some Native Americans (Sue & Sue, 1990). One departure from Eurocentric values lies in the importance attached to cooperation

rather than competition, an emphasis that is more in keeping with the values of Asian and Hispanic cultures than with those of Eurocentric culture.

Consultants with Eurocentric values systems may find that Native Americans and Hispanics do not accept the importance placed on doing schoolwork or chores in a timely fashion. They may also find that Asian Americans are less receptive to the idea of encouraging independent decision making in their children. In sum, Adlerian constructs and interventions need to be tendered with an awareness that they may be accepted or rejected by consultees and clients because they run counter to their cultural values.

EMPIRICAL SUPPORT

At the outset it should be acknowledged that empirical support for the Adlerian approach to consultation is sparse. However, Palmo and Kuzniar (1972) compared the effectiveness of Adlerian teacher–parent plus Adlerian group counseling to parent–teacher consultation alone, to Adlerian group counseling, and to a no-treatment control group on classroom behavior. They found that all treatment groups produced significant results based on teacher ratings. However, only the parent–teacher consultation treatment significantly decreased troublesome classroom behavior based on the analyses of data collected using classroom behavior observations.

Three studies have examined the efficacy of teacher-delivered encouragement. Hillman and Shields (1975) concluded that a combination of encouragement and corrective feedback was successful in improving both attending behavior and achievement in arithmetic in a seventh-grade boy. However, Abramowitz, O'Leary, and Rosen (1987) were unable to replicate Shields' findings using a larger sample. In 1990, Rathvon reported the results of a multiple baseline study designed to look solely at the impact of encouraging statements delivered at one and seven meters on off-task behavior and achievement. Rathvon concluded that delivering encouragement when students were off

A Parent Consultation: High School

S came for consultation because she had "no relationship" with her adolescent son J. She explained that whenever she tried to discipline her son, the result was an explosive reaction, and that she is becoming increasingly angry and frustrated. (This suggests that the son's goal is power.) Negative, resistive actions also result whenever J's teachers tried to impose any type of restriction on him. J had also been involved in stealing a car and some other antisocial acts. (This suggests that revenge cannot be ruled out as a possible goal.)

An exploration of a typical day in the family revealed that J is one of two children (L, a sister, is two years younger), that the father is relatively uninvolved in the family, S is primarily responsible for disciplining the children, and J is the only child perceived to be problematic. Additionally, J does not receive an allowance, has few responsibilities in the home, and is frequently involved in negative, punitive interaction with S (three or four times a day).

During the first meeting it was recommended that family meetings be undertaken to make decisions about family affairs, that J be given an allowance (a mistake made by the consultant), and that S replace her punitive approaches with logical consequences that would be written out and posted. It was also suggested that S set aside a "special" time for each of her children.

A telephone follow-up one week later revealed that nothing had changed because S had not implemented any of the suggestions, and that she had not discussed them with her husband as recommended. She was encouraged to talk to her husband about the proposed changes and to try to institute the family meetings.

One week later, a second telephone follow-up call was made. The family had met, but S was concerned that she talked too much. It was suggested that the person leading the family meeting should rotate, an idea she embraced immediately. S reported that she had initiated "special times" with her children and that these had gone relatively well. J had also been given an allowance, but the mother was concerned about this. Unfortunately, she had not given the younger sister an allowance, and this had caused problems in the form of complaints about favoritism. It was recommended that S give L an allowance as well, and she agreed to do so.

One week later, a telephone conversation revealed that J had indeed spent his money unwisely and S wanted to drop the allowance. Since she was unwilling to allow J to experience the natural consequences of his action (she gave him more money), it was agreed that the size of the allowance would be reduced, and that money for major items such as clothing would be provided on an "as needed" basis.

A face-to-face consultation session occurred one week later and a new crisis had arisen. J had locked himself out of the home and broken a window so he could unlock a door. S wanted to punish J but was not sure what to do. It was suggested that J fix the window himself (he has the skills) and pay for the materials himself. S agreed that this would be a logical consequence of his behavior. The family meetings to discuss issues seemed to be going well and G, the father, was now participating in these sessions to some degree.

The fifth and final session was conducted on the telephone. J's functioning at home had improved, and S reported that her relationship with him was not as strained as it had been. She expressed concern that J still seemed to have problems with his teachers. It was suggested that S encourage him to work on his behavior at school by expressing confidence in his ability to solve the problems he was experiencing, but to be careful not to nag or threaten him, thus returning to the punitive methods she had used in the past. She agreed to try this approach and to call again if she needed assistance.

task did improve on-task performance regardless of the distance involved but did not improve academic performance. Encouragement delivered at one meter seemed to be a bit more effective in reducing off-task behavior than encouragement delivered at seven meters, but Rathvon cautions against drawing premature conclusions in this area. None of the treatments increased academic performance.

SUMMARY

The Adlerian model of behavior provides consultants with a phenomenological alternative to the traditional behavioral model. The Adlerian model, like the behavioral model, is based upon certain Eurocentric values and thus must be modified for use with consultees who do not share these values. Specifically, concepts such as democracy in the family, sibling rivalry, and feelings of inferiority may not be palatable to minority groups that subscribe to the idea that relationships should be lineal or collateral and that it is important to maintain control over one's thoughts and emotions. Unlike the behavioral model of consultation, the Adlerian model has not been widely researched, a situation that needs to be corrected.

TIPS FOR THE PRACTITIONER

1. As a consultant, you will need to help consultees become aware of their own feelings as a way to determine how they will interact with the child. Ask teachers or others to identify several problem children. Spend 15 to 20 minutes with each of them. During this time try to identify the feelings that you develop as a result of your interactions. Are you annoyed? Do you feel frustrated or sense that you are being pushed into a power struggle? Do you feel sorry for the child? Once these feelings develop, determine the child's fictitious goal by using other strategies listed in the chapter.
2. Sit in on several parent conferences. Listen for the themes as the parents describe their children. Do they use punishment or logical and natural consequences? Encouragement or positive reinforcement? Autocratic or democratic procedures?

REVIEW QUESTIONS

1. How does Adlerian theory differ from behavioral theory?
2. In Adlerian theory, how does one determine that enhanced feelings of inferiority have developed?
3. What are the four mistaken goals that children manifest?
4. What is the lifestyle? How does it differ from the four mistaken goals of childhood?
5. What are the steps in the Adlerian consulting process? How do these vary from the other approaches you have studied?
6. What are the differences between logical and natural consequences?
7. Which, if any, cultural groups might react negatively to certain aspects of Adlerian approaches to consultation?

REFERENCES

Abramowitz, A. J., O'Leary, S. G., & Rosen, L. A. (1987). Reducing off-task behavior in the classroom: A comparison of encouragement and reprimands. *Journal of Abnormal Child Psychology, 15,* 153–163.

Albert, L. (1996a). *Cooperative discipline.* Circle Pines, MN: American Guidance Service.

Albert, L. (1996b). *Coping with kids* (2nd ed.). Circle Pines, MN: American Guidance Service.

Ansbacher, H. L., & Ansbacher, R. R. (Eds.). (1956). *The individual psychology of Alfred Adler.* New York: Basic Books.

Ansbacher, H. L., & Ansbacher, R. R. (Eds.). (1964). *Superiority and social interest.* New York: Viking Press.

Dinkmeyer, D., & Carlson, J. (1973). *Consulting: Facilitating human potential and change processes.* Columbus, OH: Charles E. Merrill.

Dinkmeyer, D., & Dreikurs, R. R. (1963). *Encouraging children to learn: The encouragement process.* Englewood Cliffs, NJ: Prentice-Hall.

Dinkmeyer, D., Sr., & McKay, G. D. (1989). *Systematic training for effective parenting: Leaders manual.* Circle Pines, MN: American Guidance Service.

Dreikurs, R. R. (1953). *Fundamentals of Adlerian Psychology.* Chicago: Alfred Adler Institute.

Dreikurs, R. R. (1968). *Psychology in the classroom* (2nd ed.). New York: Harper & Row.

Dreikurs, R. R., & Stoltz, V. (1967). *Children the challenge.* New York: Duell, Sloan, & Pearce.

Furtmuller, C. (1964). Alfred Adler: A biographical essay. In H. L. Ansbacher & R. R. Ansbacher (Eds.), *Superiority and social interest* (pp. 311–394). New York: Viking Press.

Hillman, B. W., & Shields, F. L. (1975). The encouragement process in guidance: Its effects on school achievement and attending behavior. *The School Counselor, 22,* 166–173.

Mosak, H. (1979). Adlerian psychotherapy. In R. J. Corsini and Contributors, *Current psychotherapies* (2nd ed., pp. 44–94). Itasca, IL: Peacock Publishers.

Palmo, A. J., & Kuzniar, J. (1972). Modifications of behavior through group counseling and consultation. *Elementary School Guidance and Counseling, 6,* 255–262.

Rathvon, N. W. (1990). Effects of encouragement on off-task behavior and academic productivity. *Elementary School Guidance and Counseling, 24,* 189–199.

Sue, D. W., & Sue, D. (1990). *Counseling the culturally different* (2nd ed.). New York: John Wiley & Sons.

Sweeney, T. L. (1989). *Adlerian counseling: A practical approach for a new decade* (3rd ed.). Muncie, IN: Accelerated Development Press.

ANSWERS TO LEARNING EXERCISES

4.1 1-T, 2-T, 3-F, 4-F, 5-T, 6-F, 7-T

4.2 Natural consequences; encouragement; establishing an atmosphere in which children feel they belong.

CHAPTER 5

FACILITATING SYSTEMIC
CHANGE THROUGH CONSULTATION
AND COLLABORATION

GOALS OF THE CHAPTER

The primary goals of this chapter are to (1) present an overview of systems theory, (2) present a model of organizational consultation, and to (3) outline a collaborative model of educational reform.

CHAPTER PREVIEW

1. Systems theory will be outlined at the outset of the chapter
2. A systems-based approach to organizational consultation will be presented
3. A collaborative approach to educational change, Total Quality Education (TQE), based on Deming's Total Quality Management approach, will be outlined along with recommendations for implementing educational reform using TQE.

As was noted in Chapters Two and Three, Mental Health Consultation and Behavioral Consultation have implications for reengineering various types of organizations including schools. However, much of current thinking focuses on systemic approaches to organizational change, primarily because past approaches to change have either failed or resulted in pocket change, that is, change in one or two parts of the organization rather than the total system. However, mounting criticisms of American education beginning with *A Nation at Risk: The Imperative of Educational Reform* (National Commission on Excellence in Education, 1983) have changed educators perspectives on the need for school reform even though some authorities see many of the criticism of the schooling process in this country as uninformed (see Berliner & Biddle, 1995). American business, like American education, resisted change until the late 1980s when competition from Japan and elsewhere threatened their profitability and their ability to stay in business in the long term.

The catchword in both business and education is quality. In business the aim is to produce the product with the highest quality possible. In a sense, educators have the same goal, but educational goals are usually cast in terms of student achievement. However, both business and education now use the standards of the world as their baseline because of the global economy, business competition, and the growing competition for jobs. If businesses do not produce competitive products, they will fail. If students do not receive the type of education needed by U.S. businesses, they will be unable to compete for jobs that can easily be placed offshore physically or via the Internet. Many "high tech" jobs such as programmers are now being shipped to India and elsewhere both because of cost and the unavailability of enough skilled workers in the U.S.

W. Edwards Deming (1993) took his ideas about statistical quality control to Japan during the post-WW II era after he had been rebuffed by businesses in the U.S. The Japanese, who had struggled with quality control in their businesses, embraced Deming's idea of Total Quality Management, implemented them in their businesses, and their subsequent success in developing high quality products is well documented. In 1993 Deming published a book, *The New Economics for Industry, Government and Education* that outlined how his principles could be applied to institutions such as government and education. Deming's model is rooted in systems theory, as are many of the other models of organizational change. His collaborative approach to change has caused many educators to rethink important factors such as leadership style and will be dealt with extensively later in this chapter. However, because systems theory underpins Deming's model and the other models and ideas included in this chapter, we will begin by discussing general systems theory.

PRINCIPLES OF SYSTEMS THEORY

Systems theory has its roots on the biological sciences (Bertalanffy, 1962), but the principles have been adapted by a number of authors (Beer & Spector, 1993; Katz & Kahn, 1978; Kuhn & Beam, 1982; Morasky, 1982) for use in describing organizations, communities (Homans, 2004), and families (Bonfenbrenner, 1979). Generally speaking there are two types of systems, open and closed. Moreover, open systems can be further subdivided into those that exist in the natural environment, such as the ecosystem of a pond, and human structures such as families, organizations, and communities. Closed systems have impermeable boundaries and operate without

taking in resources or producing products. The pump in a water fountain that simply circulates the water is an example of a closed system. The open systems found in nature such as an untilled meadow differ from human systems because they have no goals. Human beings form systems such as marriages, schools, business, and human services organizations as a means of accomplishing a goal or goals (Morasky, 1982). Although human systems have goals they may or may not be clearly stated and if they are, they may not be the sole influence of the functioning of the system.

The philosophy underpinning system thinking is postmodernism. All of tenets of postmodern philosophy will not be revisited here, but familiarity with several of the assumptions of postmodernism is essential to understanding systems theory. These are:

- Human behavior is non-linear
- Cause and effect relationships cannot be ascertained (although consultants and collaborators may speculate about causality)
- The foci should be on processes such as communication, not products
- The whole is greater than the sum of the parts
- We are all interconnected. Change in one aspect of the system reverberates throughout the remainder of the system (the butterfly effect)

Readers will note that many of these postmodern assumptions appear repeatedly throughout the discussion of systems theory that follows.

SYSTEMS PRINCIPLES AND ORGANIZATIONAL FUNCTIONING

Differentiation is a natural tendency of open systems. Two interacting people can make up a system (Kuhn & Beam, 1982). Even with two people (e.g., a husband and wife), there is tendency toward role differentiation. When many people are involved, this tendency toward specialization normally results in a variety of structures or subsystems. These subsystems are depicted in Figure 5.1.

The *leadership* subsystem is that group of people who are the organizational decision mak-

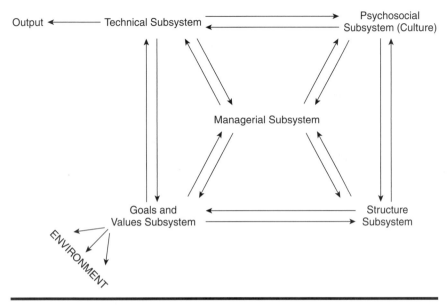

FIGURE 5.1   A Systems View of Organizational Functioning

ers. For the most part, members of this subsystem hold formal positions of authority, but as Beer (1980) and others have noted, there is also an informal power structure within any organization that influences the decision-making process. Beer uses the term *dominant coalition* to describe the leadership subsystem.

The *goals and values* subsystem has two components. One of these pertains to the products produced by an organization. Products may range from the number of clients helped by a community mental health center to the number of tons produced by a large steel mill. These productivity goals are established in terms of expected outputs to the organization environment. The second type of goal relates to meeting the needs of the people within the organization. Lippitt (1982) classifies these needs into two areas: personal life and personal fulfillment. *Personal life needs* involve food, clothing, shelter, and security, while *personal fulfillment needs* relate to affiliation, achievement, recreation, work, and social support.

Structure is the subsystem that has as its basic function the control of behavior within the organi-

zation. Reward systems, evaluation procedures, promotion policies, and formal policies aimed at regulating day-to-day behavior, such as attendance, are a part of the structure subsystem.

The *technology* subsystem is usually aimed at increasing the effectiveness and efficiency of human processes within the organization (Lippitt, 1982). It involves those processes that at times operate somewhat independently from human processes (e.g., automated assembly lines), but more typically interact with them. There is an increasing awareness that the installation of technology without considering its impact upon human factors can have disastrous effects (Golembiewski, 1993).

The *psychosocial* subsystem consists of all the people in the organization, and, as Kurpius (1984) suggests, is an interaction of the knowledge held, beliefs about the organization, behavior, motivations, and emotions of the people. The result of this interaction is the creation of an organizational culture according to Beer (1980). It is the goal of any organization to socialize people in a manner that will enhance the likelihood that organizational goals will be achieved. This is done through a variety of processes including recruitment, orientation, supervision, and rewards. However, much of the socialization process occurs through informal interaction and results in an inculcation of beliefs held widely in the organization.

The psychosocial subsystem is more typically termed the culture of a system. Schein (1990) defines organizational culture as

> *(a) a pattern of basic assumptions, (b) invented, discovered, or developed by a given group, (c) as it learns to cope with problems of external adaptation and internal integration, (d) that has worked well enough to be considered valid and, therefore, (e) is to be taught to new members as the (f) correct way to perceive, think, and feel in relation to those problems. (p. 111)*

Essential to understanding of culture is the idea of values or, as Schein termed them, *basic assumptions.* As an organization grows and develops, the people in it develop beliefs about how the organization can be successful and how they can be successful within the organization. These beliefs become institutionalized values. "Autocratic approaches are the best way to get things done" and "Consensus is the only approach to decision making" are values statements that have characterized some organizations from time to time. The question always is, "Are they appropriate today?" Unfortunately, as Beer and Spector (1993) noted, the values that undergird culture are based upon experience and may become dysfunctional. Much of the work of organizational consultants is devoted to changing culture.

The subsystems of an organization are interrelated and interdependent. The process of differentiation creates a series of distinct entities within organizations. However, these structures are bound together in a dynamic fashion. A problem in one subsystem, for example, changes in leadership, invariably causes reverberations in the other components of the organization. Beer (1980) reports that prior to systems thinking, organizational planners and consultants thought linearly—that is, in terms of a single cause for each problem, with a single solution, and a solitary outcome. The realization

that the subsystems within an organization are interrelated requires us to consider the possibility of multiple causation. A business failure may result from (1) inadequate technology, (2) poor leadership, (3) inadequate communication, (4) low worker morale, (5) foreign competition, or (6) two or more of the above.

Just as the concept of interrelatedness requires that the possibility of multiple causation be considered, so must the multiple effects of interventions be anticipated. Installing a new computer may be an apparent solution to accounting's difficulty in billing customers on time. However, it may also require retraining of staff, introducing a personal touch in communicating with customers, and/or eliminating incompetent employees.

Because of the dynamic interrelatedness of organizational subsystems, there is no single solution to a particular problem. This postulate, usually referred to as the principle of *equifinality,* defies common-sense thinking that there is one best solution for each problem. It also flies in the face of many current decision-making models that send the decision maker through a series of steps, culminating in selecting the best alternative. Because of the dynamic, interdependent nature of organizations, it is assumed that there are many paths to a particular goal. If, for example, we wish to increase productivity, we may (1) improve our technology, (2) improve staff morale, (3) allow more overtime (change a part of the structure subsystem), and/or (4) change our supervision strategy to include quality circles. Problem solvers in organizations that produce services (as opposed to goods) also have multiple solutions available. Havelock and Hubermann (1978) noted that one educator identified 20 ways to solve a particular problem. While this may not be typical, it is illustrative.

Organizations relate dynamically with their environments. As was noted earlier, organizations are open systems that interact to gain inputs and to produce outputs. Inputs come into the organization in the form of resources, such as people, raw materials, money, technology, and so forth. Outputs are marketed in the environment, and the extent to which organizations are successful is highly dependent upon this function. Public schools must market their product, public education, since increasingly private schools vie for the resources they need to operate. Even organizations such as the Salvation Army must market their programs in order to maintain a flow of donations.

The interactions that occur regarding inputs and outputs between an organization and its environment are easily identified. However, subtler forms of interactions occur that also influence how well an organization functions. One of these interactions has to do with legislation that regulates some aspect of the business. Local expenditures for education influence the quality of the workforce and thus the functioning of businesses. However, higher property taxes, which might be needed to fund better education, will also influence how a business functions. Not unexpectedly, profit and nonprofit organizations alike initiate efforts to influence any initiative that will impair or improve their operations.

Viable open systems can adapt to changing conditions within and without. Several key organizational processes and characteristics contribute to adaptability, including sensing/communication, decision making and planning, organizational flexibility, and research and development. Perhaps none of these processes is so critical as the sensing/communication mechanisms, which are of two types (Kuhn & Beam, 1982; Morasky, 1982). The first of these has to do with (external) communication with the organization's environment. An organization that cannot anticipate the current economic and social trends and thus the demands for its products will probably not survive. For example, community mental health centers are greatly concerned about the demands for their products, which include direct services in the form of counseling and therapy, indirect services, or consultation, and educational programs, since this demand will ultimately be reflected in their funding base (Backer, Shifren-Levine, & Erchul, 1983).

Sensing devices must also be established that discern (1) the impact of technology upon production and competitiveness in the marketplace and (2) shifts in societal values and legislative programs that will influence markets and production. For example, Congress currently seems determined to reduce expenditures for social programs, a trend that may reshape the delivery of various programs and services. Perhaps technologies such as the videophone and the Internet will enable mental health programs to deliver certain kinds of services more efficiently.

Adaptable organizations also have internal sensing mechanisms that identify conflicts within the organization that may adversely affect the functioning of the organization. These mechanisms include routine needs assessments, structured and unstructured feedback sessions, and surveys of various types (e.g., morale). Internal consultants are often employed to act as coordinators of these sensing mechanisms.

Sensing mechanisms are necessary, but interpretation and communication of what is seen or heard are the key to organizational adaptability. Havelock and Hubermann (1978) classified information flow into two types. Lateral communication involves communication between two equal units in an organization—for example, between research and development and production. Vertical communication involves communication between components of an organization that have differential status, such as the director of an agency and the staff. Bureaucratic organizations, such as public schools and the military, are organized primarily according to status and have notoriously poor internal communication, particularly from the bottom up. Both lateral and vertical (including top down and bottom up) information flows are necessary if organizations are to be adaptable.

Adaptable organizations avoid chaotic change and entropy. Chaotic change may destroy the basic harmony needed for organizational functioning. Entropy is a process of losing energy or momentum. Systems theory (Katz & Kahn, 1978) posits that entropy is a natural process in an open system. However, those organizations that produce products that are valued in the environment receive a constant supply of inputs from the environment in the form of raw material, workers, and technology, and they avoid entropy.

PRACTICAL ADVICE FOR CONSULTANTS AND COLLABORATORS

In the next section a model of organizational consultation will be presented. Theoretical models are suppositions about the manner in which consultants should proceed. However, theoretical models must be coupled with common-sense ideas if consultants are to be effective. Some of these ideas will be presented in this section.

Expectations about People and Organizations

Patterson (2003) advises consultants and collaborators not to hold naïve assumptions about people and organizations as they enter the change process. He suggests that the realities about people include:

- Most people act in their own best interests, not the best interests of the organization.
- Most people do not genuinely want to understand how the organization functions.
- People engage in organizational change primarily to alleviate their own pain, not to improve the organization.
- People expect to be viewed as trustworthy although they frequently mistrust the motives of the change team.
- In general, people opt to be the victims of change, not the architects of change.

Patterson makes the following observations about organizations:

- They are not rational.
- They are set up to protect the status quo.
- Most change efforts begin because of events such as criticisms rather than deeply held beliefs that change is desirable.
- Many organizations embark on long-term change efforts with leaders who can be classified as short-term.
- Organizations expect change with a minimum of conflict.

In spite of Patterson's rather pessimistic view of people and organizations, he concludes that both people and organizations can rise above their basic dispositions and participate meaningfully in change processes and that is what consultants and collaborators need to keep in mind.

Avoiding the Ouroboros Effect: Unintended Consequences

The symbol for the Ouroboros effect is a serpent devouring its own tail. According to Swenson (2002), this symbol represents how our best attempts to solve problems come back to bite us. Swenson provides a German synonym for the Ouroboros effect, *verschlimmbessern,* which, translated literally, means "to worsen by attempting to make something better." The unintended consequences of poorly conceived problem-solving efforts achieve the opposite of what is intended; they make matters worse. Swenson offers several pages of examples of problem-solving projects in business, agriculture, and elsewhere that went awry. He calls these efforts systemic backfires, which occur whenever problem solvers focus on the immediate problem and fail to consider the systemic, long-term impact of their solution. That welfare programs aimed at promoting independence have, in many instances, increased dependence, exemplifies unintended consequences.

Swenson (2002) and Swenson and Anstett (n.d.) point out that many precautions must be taken if consultants and collaborators are to avoid unintended consequences. Perhaps chief among these is defining the problem "correctly." Swenson and Anstett suggest that problem solvers avoid traditional problem-solving strategies that focus on what is wrong and its elimination. They recommend that it is far more productive to adopt a solution-focused approach to problem solving that begins by identifying what is right and how these positive aspects of the situation can be amplified. The focus in traditional problem solving is on eliminating the problem, which may not be linked to the solution. The goal in solution-focused problem solving is to increase the presence of what is right. Swenson also suggests that consultants and collaborators determine who will be impacted if the changes are made as well as their reactions to change. For example, many school counselors have concluded that one solution to the inordinate amount of time they spend on advising and scheduling is to use teacher advisors. Clearly, before implementation of this solution can occur teachers must be involved in the process.

Solution-focused problem/solution identification involves four levels of questioning:

1. Are there any times or situations when the problem does not exist? (exceptions)
2. If this problem were miraculously solved, how would our organization appear? (future)

(Typically questions 1 and 2 are sufficient to identify a solution. If not, then use 3 and 4.)

3. Why aren't things worse than they are in our organization? (How people cope with the situation and what can be learned from their behavior.)
4. If the problem is not eliminated, what will happen in the future? (scenario of non-problem solving)

The result of asking this series of questions should be the identification of strategies that can serve as the targets (vision) for the change process. Finally, Swenson and Anstett do not completely rule out the use of traditional problem-solving models. They provide the guidelines in Table 5.1 for determining when the solution-focused problem-solving model should be selected instead of traditional approaches.

It is also important to determine the "butterfly effects" of change if unintended consequences are to be avoided. Butterfly effects are accelerating effects of small, initial changes. North Carolina was one of the first states to adopt an extensive high-stakes testing program. Because no testing coordinators were funded, school counselors were forced to coordinate these programs, which resulted in a dramatic decrease in their services to students (Brown, Galassi, & Akos, in press). Although no definite link has been established between these events, the number of dropouts and discipline problems has skyrocketed.

TABLE 5.1 When to Use Solution-Focused Problem Solving versus Traditional Problem Solving

SOLUTION-FOCUSED

1. Highly complex issues (most organizational issues)
2. Recurring problems
3. Initial solution creates more problems or makes matters worse
4. No problem resolution can be agreed to by problem solvers

TRADITIONAL

1. Relatively simple problems
2. First occurrence

Problem solvers must also discern that new problems will be created by the intended solution if it is implemented. Another question that problem solvers must ask as they craft solutions is: Will the tentative solution make the problem worse? Zero-tolerance policies were adopted after the shootings in Littleton, Colorado, Paducah, Kentucky, and elsewhere. Suspended students in North Carolina missed one million school days in 2003 (Associated Press, 2004), a situation that creates a number of new problems.

One school district started an in-school suspension program in their middle schools. Because of the activities in the program and the fact that the middle school students wanted to be with their friends, the suspension rate went up.

Finally, problem solvers must identify the person or groups who will take responsibility for monitoring the solution in both the short- and long term. There are no guarantees that solutions will not produce the Ouroboros Effect, so someone needs to assume responsibility to ascertain whether the solution that was implemented is having the expected effect.

Remember Peer's Law

Peer's Law states, "A solution to the problem changes the problem" (source unknown). Whoever formulated this "law" understood systems theory and organizational change perfectly. Businesses that become successful have to determine whether to build on their success or to maintain the status quo. Successful public schools often find that their enrollment increases because parents who learn of the success want their children to go to effective schools. Organizational problem solving never stops. Recall that viable systems have sensing mechanisms, individuals or groups that monitor internal and external conditions that may influence the functioning of the organization. Consultants and collaborators have to be aware that the solutions they shape may create a number of unexpected negative consequences and open up possibilities that require continuation of the problem-solving process. Moreover, because of the dynamic relationship between the organization and its environment, new problems will arise on a continuing basis.

Work toward Cultural Change

Dooley (1995) insists that systemic change requires that the values of the organization be transformed if the change is to be lasting. The values of an organization are the collective beliefs about the way "things are" and, when combined with the rituals and behavior of people in the organization, make up the culture of the organization. Dooley suggests that people in organizations have two sets of values, espoused and hidden. In situations that involve stress and threat, such as change efforts, hidden values come to the fore and may conflict with the espoused values of the organization. Consultants and collaborators should be alert for the emergence of behavior that contradicts the espoused values of the organization, identify those values, and work to allay the fear that is more than likely present. Finally, although not couched in these exact terms, Dooley suggests that the more threatening the change, the more likely it will be that hidden values emerge.

Organizational Variables Will Affect the Process

The setting in which a consultation or collaboration takes place greatly affects the process (Ilbeck & Zins, 1993). Change efforts within organizations with little turnover, high morale, and adequate personnel and fiscal resources can expect to face very different issues than those who work with an organization with high turnover, budgetary problems, and an overworked consultee. However, no comprehensive model relating system, resources, and personnel variables has yet been set forth. The content of this section, therefore, is based largely on suppositions drawn from systems thinking, some authoritative thinking in the consultation field, and a modicum of research on this issue (Chin & Benne, 1976; Huse, 1980; Sarason, 1982). Some of the commentaries available in the literature regarding the problems of applying behavior modification techniques in natural settings, without regard to systems variables, also stimulated some of the thinking found in this section (e.g., Abidin, 1982; Reppucci & Saunders, 1974). However, none of these sources attempts to describe the intrusion of organizational variables into the consultation process per se.

Conoley (1981) and Sarason (1982) have each provided a partial listing of organizational characteristics that are intervening variables in the life of an organization and, thus, the consultation/collaboration process. These can be divided into *extrasystem variables,* such as legislatures, local governmental bodies, the political and economic climate, unions, advocacy groups, accrediting bodies, and existing laws, and *intrasystem variables.* The latter group includes the power structure, the overall characteristics of the people involved, the normative structure of the organization, role clarity, decision-making patterns, and communications systems.

Accrediting bodies influence a variety of organizations including training programs, hospitals, counseling centers, public schools, and colleges and universities. Accrediting organizations set forth regulations regarding the qualifications of staff, physical facilities, and administrative procedures. They may also influence variables such as the size and diversity of the library, the qualifications and geographic origin of students, the demographic characteristics of students (in the case of training programs), or the manner in which services are delivered (in hospitals or counseling centers). Often, consultants are told at the outset that these programs, policies, or procedures are untouchable because they are required for certification or accreditation. This inability to change existing policies or practices is often the source of problems. For example, a number of teacher-preparation institutions have attempted to ignore the accreditation standards of the National Council for the Accreditation of Teacher Education, only to find that their graduates were hampered in the certification and employment process. Unaccredited hospitals are ineligible to receive certain payments, including those from Medicare. Consultants working within institutions operating under the auspices of accrediting agencies would be well advised to determine the impact of the agency regulations on individual and organizational behavior prior to initiating consultation.

Union agreements influence an organization and the individuals in it in much the same way as accrediting bodies, although the influence is much more likely to be felt at the level of the individual worker. For example, many consultants have been frustrated in their efforts by the seniority rules included in many contracts. Tenure laws in public schools and universities have a similar impact. This is particularly problematic in situations such as public schools and civil service agencies when principals or other managers attain tenure and are virtually guaranteed a position regardless of how they perform on the job.

For the most part, accrediting standards, union rules, and tenure laws are relatively well-known influences and can, therefore, be anticipated by the consultant and consultee. However, there are more subtle external factors that are just as influential but much more difficult to anticipate. Delicate racial/ethnic relationships may suddenly present themselves during the course of a consultation, particularly when public institutions are the settings for consultation. More than one consultation has been disrupted because those in authority informed the consultant and consultee that a certain individual's approach couldn't be altered because of a real or presumed concern within an ethnic or racial group. Political power blocks provide similar problems.

Institutional norms loom as one of the most potent of the internal variables that will intervene in the consultation. Norms are implicit standards that regulate, to some degree, the behavior of the members of a particular group. An obvious indicator of norms is the manner in which employees, students, or other organizational members dress. Unfortunately, not all organizational norms are as easy to discern as the "dress code."

Norms exist in all institutions and are evident in a variety of functions including communication patterns, interaction between peers and superiors, standards of performance, and a host of other variables. Of these, normatively based perceptions regarding performance appear to pose the greatest problem for consultants. For example, if a norm has developed that Fridays after one o'clock are to be "happy hours" for the employees, productivity and quality of product will suffer. A norm that dictates that students pass whether they have learned the subject matter or not has developed in some public schools. This norm influences both teacher and student behavior. Some correctional agencies have abandoned rehabilitation programs and reverted to being custodial institutions or, to use a more popular term, *warehousing*. The internal consultant is particularly at risk in these kinds of situations because consultees may very well be acculturated, with the result that their view of the situation follows the "party line." The external consultant may be frustrated because the consultee seems unwilling or unable to deal with the problems that are presented. Finally, a client, such as a student in the aforementioned school, may not respond to the efforts of a single teacher because implicit communications within the school support the notion that effort is not needed to succeed.

Norms regarding communication patterns can also present problems for consultants and collaborators. For example, most bureaucratic organizations like schools and many businesses expect communication to flow through the formal chain of command, an expectation that is rarely realized. However, if a norm develops that significant figures such as principals or agency heads are routinely by-passed by their subordinates, these principals or agency heads are cut off from much-needed information about the working of the organization that they supposedly direct. These patterns must be altered in order to restore authentic communication.

The power structure has been identified by many as the key to change in any institution. This structure can be divided into two components: formal and informal. The formal power structure consists of those designated individuals vested with coercive/reward power. The principal, an agency head, a dean, and a plant manager are all formal power authority figures. As was stated earlier, these authority figures need to endorse and continuously reinforce change efforts if these are to be successful (Beer & Spector, 1993).

The informal power structure is, to a large degree, related to the normative structure. It is discussed here as a separate entity because it can be, and often is, as influential as the status leaders in determining the success of consultation. The informal power structure consists of an individual, or more likely a group, that has acquired the ability to influence others because of expertise, tenure in a position, control of a key process, or some external factor, such as social position in the community. Secretaries acquire power because they control, to some degree, access to status leaders. Very proficient teachers, clinicians, and other workers also acquire power because of their ability to function in the work setting. Particularly in the case of the latter group, these proficient workers become role senders, that is, they establish norms regarding organizational performance. If consultation is not viewed as an "appropriate" role for the counseling psychologist who heads the Employee Assistance Program, resistance to consultation may occur.

Lack of clarity in organizational goals has confounded consultants in many instances (Morasky, 1982; Sarason, 1982). Public schools often lack clarity of direction because goals are often ill defined and may shift as the political winds pressure schools to stress fundamentals, prepare individuals for the labor market, drop humanistic education because of its "godless nature," and so forth. However, consultants in public schools are not the only ones to run aground in the shoals of goal ambiguity. Most human resource agencies have a number of goals, some of which have not been articulated clearly, but more often the goals of the agency have not been clearly prioritized. Another problem is that resource expenditures may not follow stated goals, a problem that often exists when an agency places a high priority on prevention of crime, problem pregnancies, mental health problems, or family violence. It is a truism that primary prevention efforts are not supported to the same degree that secondary and tertiary prevention efforts are by most agencies.

Morasky (1982) recommends that the place to begin in organizational consultation is in goals clarification. This recommendation can be enlarged to include all types of consultations, whether they are aimed at individuals, groups, subsystems, or the total system. "What are the goals of the organization and how do these influence the consultant and the consultee?" is the question to be asked and answered.

Role clarity may be problematic for both the consultant and consultee. As was mentioned earlier, internal consultants and collaborators may be particularly susceptible to ambiguity regarding their roles if they have assignments other than consultation. Some managers, division heads, principals, and others in authority positions are jealous of their prerogatives in the area of leadership and change, and see themselves as the "consultant." In these situations, the consultant is viewed as usurping the role of the status leader, and consultation as a function becomes problematic. In other instances, the status leader may hold only a few areas sacred (e.g., personnel relations) but may not communicate this well. Consultants and collaborators need, insofar as is possible, to clarify these territorial problems prior to beginning the process. External consultants and collaborators who carefully define their roles may be less likely to encounter problems of role ambiguity until, as it often does, the presenting problem shifts to broader areas. At this juncture, role redefinition is required.

[Consultees and collaborators are often concerned about violating their role boundaries.] It is probably true that the greater the specialization within an agency, the greater the likelihood that this problem will arise (Sarason, 1982). Whenever a concern arises about roles, all of the individuals involved should clarify the issues prior to proceeding by seeking input from the agency head and others whose role boundaries might be violated.

The time commitment required in a particular occupational role as well as the job description will influence the extent of involvement by consultee and collaborators and may influence the model of consultation utilized when consultation is the process of choice. For example, job descriptions of personnel employed in many human services agencies allow a great deal of control over one's time. In other cases, the description specifies extensive time commitment to the job, limiting the amount of time available for consultation. Secondary school teachers are often given only one free period per day, and that is supposed to be devoted to class preparation. Understandably, consultation is difficult to initiate. In these situations, the consultant will have to consider the time required by various consultation models and roles and choose accordingly. In some instances, job descriptions limit the extent to which consultees can alter their functioning, and the focus of the consultation may have to shift to the program or organizational level prior to working with individuals. The characteristics of the consultees or collaborators also influence the nature of the process. This topic will be considered in detail in Chapter Seven.

The following lists summarize organizational variables that influence change efforts, whether they are consultation or collaboration.

External Organizational Variables

1. Accrediting bodies
2. Union agreements
3. Legislation
4. Community pressure groups
5. Community political organizations
6. Tenure laws
7. Civil service regulations

Internal Organizational Variables

1. Group norms
2. Formal power structure
3. Informal power structure
4. Clarity of organizational goals
5. Prioritization of organizational goals
6. Role clarity
7. Consultee's characteristics
8. Job description

Advice for Internal and External Consultants and Collaborators

It would seem obvious that consultants and collaborators would know whether they are internal or external to the organization. However, this may not be the case. Before the issues regarding the locus of the consultant are addressed, it should be noted that there are times when consultants may have to consciously consider whether they are functioning internally or externally or, as Alpert and Silverstein (1985) maintain, somewhere on the continuum between the two. For example, school psychologists are employed by school districts partially to provide consulting services, but they are often not assigned to a particular building. Although it would seem obvious that personnel paid by the organization are internal to it, most school psychologists/consultants realize that their status may vary as they function in various schools within the educational system because of their itinerant status. Counselors and counseling psychologists working in college counseling centers have a similar problem when they become involved as consultants with housing officials, career planning and placement workers, and other personnel within the college or university. The point here is a simple one: actual employment on a full-time basis may not be the only variable that determines whether a professional is functioning as an internal or external consultant or collaborator. The perceptions of the consultee and other collaborators may be more important determiners of the status than employment status. Perceptions of status are probably shaped by the consultant's or collaborator's identity within the situation in which the consultation or collaboration occurs, territorial issues, and the consultant's and consultee's attitude regarding who is "us" and who is "them" (Alpert & Silverstein, 1985). The school psychologist who provides services to eight schools, and has limited contact with the majority of the staff, is unlikely to be considered as an internal consultant.

Technically, "an external consultant is administratively and legally independent of the organization for which he [sic] works" (Kuhr, 1978, p. 12). Perhaps the key word in the foregoing sentence is *technically,* since external consultants, particularly those who work within an organization for a long period of time, may begin to take on some of the characteristics of the internal consultant. However, the constructs of internality and externality have real meaning within the consulting process, and it is up to consultants to identify where they are on the internal-external (I-E) continuum. A school counselor assigned to a single school is an internal consultant. A clinical psychologist who works with the police department in riot control as a part of his or her responsibilities in a mental health center is serving as an external consultant. But what of the earlier mentioned school psychologist who works out of the central administrative offices of the school district or the counseling psychologist who works out of a counseling center on a university campus? Are they internal or external consultants when they work with other parts of the organizations that employ them? Quite simply, they are both.

Lippitt and Lippitt (1986) provide an interesting and useful summary of the relative advantages of being an internal or an external consultant. How a particular consultant fares in each of these areas can be an indicator of how he or she is viewed on the I-E continuum. A summary of the advantages and disadvantages is presented in Table 5.2.

From Lippitt and Lippitt's (1986) point of view, the major advantages internal consultants have are their proximity to the problem, their access to data, both in the problem identification and evaluation stages, and their ability to make judgments about the potential for change in the system. External consultants are viewed as being accorded more status, being freer to make demands on personnel (particularly authority figures), having a broader perspective, and arousing less defensiveness generally. It is worth noting that the advantages and disadvantages of being an internal or external collaborator are probably similar, but to date no authoritative opinion or research regarding this matter has been presented.

Steele (1982) provided some support, albeit nonempirical, for the Lippitt and Lippitt position regarding internal consultants. Steele notes that internal consultants are often confronted with situations where they have no legitimate power and must rely on personal influence and power derived from expertise as the basis for their functioning. Additionally, there are few performance measures by which consultants can be judged, there are conflicting demands on their time, and, as already noted, they often have less credibility than outside consultants. To Steele's list should be added the fact that most human resource consultants provide other services such as assessment, counseling, therapy, and supervision. The result of all of these factors, according to Steele, is role conflict and ambiguity.

Internal consultants limit their own effectiveness in a number of ways. For example, Steele (1982) recommends that internal consultants begin to consciously define their functioning within an organization in order to maximize their effectiveness. When individuals' expertise is spread too thin, they may have less impact. School counselors who have no carefully defined role may find that it is difficult to move into the consulting role. Consultants may also limit their effectiveness by making it difficult to schedule meetings, being unable to communicate the time that will be required to complete the consultation process, and/or assuming inappropriate authority. These same behaviors would limit the effectiveness of collaborators. Establishing a time perspective similar to that of the consultee or collaborative team regarding the length of the consultation makes good sense, as does arranging one's schedule to coincide with those of others involved. Assuming inappropriate authority is always to be avoided.

TABLE 5.2 Advantages and Disadvantages of Being Internal and External Consultants and Collaborators

| STAGE | INTERNAL | | EXTERNAL | |
	ADVANTAGES	DISADVANTAGES	ADVANTAGES	DISADVANTAGES
Entry/Early	1. More aware of problem	1. Harder for peers to admit the need for help	1. Easier to share problem with an outsider	1. Less actual knowledge (e.g., history)
	2. Better prepared to clarify problem because of experience	2. May cause defensiveness	2. Accord more expertise	
		3. Defensiveness may hinder establishing a collaborative relationship	3. Can openly test readiness for change	
		4. May stereotype people because of experience in organization	4. Better able to determine resources available for change	
Entry/Contract Setting	1. Better able to assess feasibility of consultation	1. Individuals may be hesitant to enter into contracts because of concern about withdrawing from them	1. Brings greater perspective	
		2. Less able to make demands if immediate superior is involved		
Assessment/ Diagnosis	1. Closer to data flow		1. May be better able to get commitment for evaluation	1. Dependent on insiders for information
Goal Setting/ Intervention	No differences identified)			
	1. More aware of potential consultees	1. Less able to involve power figures	1. Better able to make demands on power figures	
	2. Better able to discern linkages to be established		2. More leverage generally regarding participation	
Evaluation	1. Better able to assess outcomes on a continuous basis	1. Consultees may "hide" data because of defensiveness		

Eliminating role ambiguity can enhance one's effectiveness as an internal consultant, but it requires a host of actions. Role definitions that legitimize consultation are one useful means of clarifying the consultant's role, although they will not solve the problem totally. Formally identifying consultants as separate from other employees and managers in organizational charts may give consultants more status and will help identify the target groups with whom they are to consult.

Although it is possible to consult with people who are higher in the organizational hierarchy, organization charts may remove the expectation that this is to occur routinely. Finally, defining workloads more realistically can reduce the demand on consultants' time and keep them from spreading their expertise so thinly they will be ineffective. School counselors, school psychologists, and school social workers may be unable to serve as consultants because of large caseloads and because they are assigned duties that limit the time they have available for consultation.

ORGANIZATIONAL DEVELOPMENT CONSULTATION

Organizational development consultation, as it currently exists, has been contributed to heavily by a number of theorists and social scientists, including Argyris (1970), Schein (1969), Bennis (1970), and Lippitt (1982). Kurt Lewin and Carl Rogers were particularly instrumental in the development of the philosophy of this approach. Lewin (1951) contributed to a field theory orientation—that is, a view that organizational problems must be solved in a manner that incorporates all individuals in the organization into the process because of the forces they bring to bear upon each other. Rogers (1951) postulated that the environment in which one works can either contribute to or detract from the self-actualization of the individual, and he set the tone for this approach to consultation.

A number of assumptions serve as the foundation for organizational development models of consultation. The first is that conflicts among individuals and groups are the basic barriers to effective and efficient organizational functioning. In this regard, Bennis (1970) states: "These chronic conflicts probably dissipate more energy and money than any other single organizational disease" (p. 57). These conflicts are presumed to arise from several sources. Poor communication is viewed as a basic reason for group and individual conflict. It stems from the fact that either the individuals in the organization do not possess the skills to communicate properly or the organization has

not established appropriate communication devices. Other causes of conflict are individuals with inadequate personalities, conflicting value systems among individuals and groups, lack of information, conflicting organizational objectives, and managers who lack decision-making skills (Baldridge, 1971; Chamley, McFarlane, & Young, 1987; Huse, 1980; Lippitt, 1982).

These models also assume that organizations benefit whenever they place the psychological needs of their staff ahead of the bureaucratic concerns of the individuals (Bennis, 1970; Huse, 1980). Baldridge (1971) refers to this assumption as the "contented cows give more milk" theory. In short, when workers are able to meet their psychological needs, an organization becomes more productive and efficient. Another assumption underlying what has been termed a human relationship approach to consultation is that democratically governed organizations are more effective than those where managers use autocratic approaches (Beer, 1980; Lippitt, 1982). This is quite closely related to the concept that psychological well-being of individuals should be considered ahead of organizational goals. More precisely, individual need attainment is a prerequisite to organizational efficiency and effectiveness.

The Entry Process

Consultation passes through a series of stages, some of which are more distinct than others. Kurpius, Fuqua, and Rozecki (1993) identify six consultation stages: (1) preentry; (2) entry, problem exploration, and contracting; (3) information gathering, problem confirmation, and goal setting; (4) solution searching and intervention selection; (5) evaluation; and (6) termination (p. 601). The preentry phase is really not a phase at all for many internal consultants, but external consultants must make a reasoned decision about whether they have the time and expertise to tackle the problem presented to them. This phase is simply a go/no-go decision-making stage (Beer, 1980; Hale, 1998).

Contract setting actually begins in the preentry and concludes in the entry phase. Contract setting consists of both formal and informal processes. The consultant must establish that the resources and commitment needed to achieve the change goals are available or consultation should be terminated. Similarly, the consultant should ascertain that there will be an adequate source of valid data to provide a basis for problem identification, or termination should occur. Finally, in the early stages the consultant must set an agenda and establish the relative roles the consultant and consultee will fill during consultation. This process is outlined in Table 5.3.

Step 4(b) in Table 5.3 indicates that part of the entry process is to establish acceptable role relationships between the consultant and the consultee. These relationships may take many forms, ranging from the consultant as expert on one hand to process consultant on the other.

In Schein's (1969, 1989, 1990) model of process consultation, which he defines as "a set of activities on the part of the consultant which helps the client to perceive, understand, and act upon process events which occur in the client's environment" (p. 9), the consultant assumes a role far different from the expert. In this model, the consultant generates data regarding the basic human processes, including communication, role interrelationships, leadership, decision making, group interaction, and normative structure of subsystems and the organization itself. These are shared with managers, and they are encouraged to draw their own conclusions. Managers are also encouraged to make their own decisions about solutions to the problem at hand.

Consultants usually fill a number of roles at various times in the consultation process. For example, consultants sometimes fill the role of experts while on other occasions they function as process consultants (Hale, 1998). Perhaps the only advice that should be tendered to the prospective consultant is that both the formal contract and the informal agreements reached during entry should reflect the breadth and depth of roles that the consultant expects to fill.

Diagnosis: Some General Considerations

Diagnosis is the process of assessing the specific problem or problems being experienced by the organization and isolating causal factors associated with those problems. Although the consultant's clinical ability plays a role in this process, organizational development consultants view themselves as scientists at work, and thus diagnosis is a process of systemic data collection and synthesis. Four major data sources are tapped during the diagnosis phase (Beer, 1980; Kuhnert & Lahey, 1993; Lippitt & Lippitt, 1986). Genetic data involve basic information such as vision statements and purposes and historical data such as minutes of meetings, year-end reports, internal memoranda, and other similar data. Current descriptive data

TABLE 5.3 The Entry Process of Organizational Consultation

STEPS	NO GO
Step 1. Generally survey the problems the organization has and the goals that the organization wishes to pursue.	a. Consultant views goals as unattainable.
Step 2. Determine commitment to change.	a. Commitment is lacking.
Step 3. Ascertain whether necessary resources (e.g., money, time, personnel) are available to complete desired change.	a. Resources are unavailable.
Step 4. Establish a contract to continue the consultation.	a. Time lines too severe. b. Acceptable role relationships to accomplish task cannot be established.

include organizational charts (how the organization is structured), personnel systems, reward structures, such as salary schedules, equipment/technology, and office arrangements. Process data depict communications systems and devices, decision-making approaches, and other problem-solving related activities. The fourth type of data, interpretive data, consist of perceptions of the current functioning of the organization, attitudes and beliefs about the organization, and descriptions and/or perceptions of the informal relationships that exist within the organization.

The consultant must be prepared to utilize a number of data collection techniques to secure needed information, including questionnaires, focus groups, brainstorming sessions, analysis of records, interviews, systematic observation, and problem-diagnosis sessions where various members of the organization focus their expertise on problem identification (Kuhnert & Lahey, 1993). Often these approaches to data collection focus on six problem areas: (1) inadequate goals have been established or goals have shifted without proper planning; (2) conflict is managed poorly within the organization; (3) the division of labor (structure) is problematic; (4) leadership deficiencies exist; (5) methods used to direct and coordinate the organization have broken down, usually because of poor communication; and (6) the reward system is problematic because of internal or external discrepancies—that is, rewards (e.g., hourly wage) within or without are not relatively equal for persons filling approximately the same roles (Weisbord, 1976).

Diagnosis: A Systems Perspective

The systems principles outlined earlier provide a basis for diagnosing organizational problems. Beer (1980) suggests that the starting points for a systems-based organizational analysis are threefold: the efficiency of operation, the organization's effectiveness, and the health of the organization. An organization is operating efficiently when a minimum expenditure of energy and resources is required to keep people happy. When an organization is inefficient, absenteeism, grievances, and turnover are high.

Organizational effectiveness is equated with environmental compatibility. Profit statements and/or general community financial support, freedom from governmental regulations and/or societal sanctions, and keeping pace with technological advancement germane to the operation of the organization are indicators of organizational effectiveness.

Finally, organizational health refers to the ability of the organization to adapt to changing internal and external conditions. Indicators of health are the presence of structures that identify difficulties and a track record of reacting appropriately to both internal difficulties and external demands, as noted earlier.

Beer's constructs of efficiency, effectiveness, and organizational health are helpful as a consultant begins to think about the complex task of analyzing the dynamic operation of an organization. Morasky (1982) was even more concrete about how a systems analysis of an organization should occur. He suggested that the first step in the diagnostic process is to get a general picture of the organization. This process begins by describing the boundaries of the organization. This should be followed by an attempt to identify the general processes utilized within the organization and its general function.

The police department in a mid-sized community might serve as a case in point. Geographically, the boundaries of the department would be restricted to those accorded it by legal statute. Functionally, its boundaries would include traditional law enforcement responsibilities. However, many police departments have extended these boundaries to include education programs in the public schools, the organization of recreation leagues as prevention measures, public relations activities such as a speakers bureau, and other outreach efforts.

The general processes utilized by the department would parallel its functions (e.g., surveillance, arrests, incarceration, monitoring, education, counseling, communication). Since the appropriate use of technology would be important in many of these processes, the analysis would also include a technology audit.

Finally, the function of the police department would include a description of its products such as number of arrests, convictions, crime rates in various categories, number of speeches, outcomes of prevention programs, and so forth. The result of this preliminary analysis should be in a who, what, where, when, and how description of the police department (Morasky, 1982). Who works in the police department? What do they do? When do they work? Where does the work occur? How does the work occur? Generally, how effective is it?

Once a general description of the organization is developed, the more specific analysis of the organization begins by determining what goals were established when the organization began (or when the last analysis occurred) and what goals are in effect at this time. Questions to be answered are: Is there a discrepancy between these two sets of goals? If a discrepancy exists, is the discrepancy the result of planned or unplanned change? Are the current goals appropriate? Organizational goals are a major subsystem in that they determine the direction and/or preferences of the organization. Without a clearly articulated set of goals, the other subsystems of the organization are likely to be in conflict.

Goal identification should be followed by the delineation of input/output boundaries (Morasky, 1982). Input boundaries for some organizations, such as schools, are easily identified. Children come from a community area set forth by school board regulations. Technology comes from a few publishing companies, and for some subgroups in the school, such as school psychologists or counselors, the source of technology is even more limited. Similarly, staff inputs are from rather specific sources—colleges and universities that prepare professionals in a given area.

Outputs in schools are also easily defined. But input and outputs are a great deal more difficult to define for our aforementioned police department, a public health department, or a department of social services. Several days may actually be required to construct this type of audit.

The next step in organizational analysis is identifying specific target groups within the environment (Morasky, 1982). In some instances, these groups are defined by law—for example, school psychologists must serve certain classes of handicapped students. In other instances, community agencies are influenced both by law (the Department of Social Services must investigate child abuse complaints) and policies that originate both within and outside the agency. For example, a community mental health agency might decide that it will target a 65 and over population, unwed mothers, or some other group that the staff considers in need of services. In the organizational analysis not only must these target groups be identified, but some determination of how they can be reached must be made as well.

The external support network of the organization must also be described (Morasky, 1982). This process involves answering a number of specific questions. Are there environmental factors such as laws or governmental regulations that impinge on the organization? Are there environmental trends such as outmigration of the population that will affect the source of personnel (inputs)? Do local factors such as a poor educational system or a high tax rate influence the recruitment process? Is the overall environment friendly or unfriendly? Basically, the consultant must generate a clear picture of the interaction of the environment with the organization.

The production process, whether it be for goods or services, is the essence of the organization. Morasky (1982) suggested that it is necessary to understand the components of this process, the subsystems, and how they relate to inputs and outputs. Consider a small counseling center at a prestigious eastern university. The production processes include (1) individual counseling, (2) group counseling, (3) assessment, (4) outreach/education, and (5) consultation. Inputs into these processes come from the student body, the faculty, and the staff of the university. Outputs are better-adjusted students.

TABLE 5.4 Conducting a Systems Analysis of an Organization

Step 1. Conduct a general review of the organization.	a. Define geographic and functional boundaries. b. Identify production processes. c. Identify products.
Step 2. Identify input–output boundaries.	a. List input–output boundaries.
Step 3. Identify the goals of the organization.	a. State goals operationally. b. Relate these to input–output boundaries.
Step 4. Identify target groups.	a. List target groups in terms of priorities.
Step 5. Describe external support.	a. List environmental factors that interact with the organization (e.g., laws, availability of personnel, etc.).
Step 6. Describe production processes.	a. Relate each aspect of the process to input–output.
Step 7. Identify feedback mechanisms.	a. List external sensing mechanisms. b. List internal feedback mechanisms.
Step 8. List organizational constraints.	a. List external constraints. b. Identify internal constraints by subsystem.

Questions to be answered regarding inputs include the following:

1. How are workers selected?
2. Are selection criteria appropriate?
3. Is the reward system appropriate for new workers?
4. What attitudes develop as workers are socialized? What norms emerge?
5. Are these at variance with the expectations held when the workers enter the organization?
6. How do management processes facilitate/retard the input processes that are involved in production?

Questions that need answers regarding the production process relate to productive use of technology, quality of product, cost/price considerations, and, in some instances, competitiveness with other agencies (counseling center versus student mental health center).

Questions regarding the relationship of production to marketing (output) must also be posed and answered. Is our program effective? Do we have the most effective form of advertising? Is our sales program having the desired impact?

The sixth set of questions has to do with feedback mechanisms (Morasky, 1982). Essentially, these sensing mechanisms are the basis for adjustments to external conditions and internal difficulties. An analysis of these mechanisms requires that we (1) describe the input–output sensing mechanisms, (2) determine how valuable the information is that comes from these sensors, and (3) evaluate the mechanics (e.g., the frequency with which data are collected) of the systems.

The final set of questions that should be answered in our organizational analysis has to do with the overall constraints on the organization. Is the personnel supply adequate? What is the morale level of the staff? What is the financial picture? What economic trends may retard development? Has the management team been forward-looking? What community and societal trends need to be countered? What internal problems pose a threat to growth? Are there geographic factors that preclude or diminish functioning in a given area or areas? The result of this series of questions should be a compilation of organizational constraints. These steps are summarized in Table 5.4.

Beer and Spector (1993), like Morasky, view data collection as the first step in the diagnosis.

Student Learning Activity 5.1
Applying Morasky's Principles

Analyze the organization of which you are currently a part by completing the following questions.

1. What are the goals of the organization?
2. Are the current goals clear? Appropriate?
3. What are the input boundaries?
4. What are the output boundaries?
5. What are the target groups of the organization?
6. What is the external support network of the organization?
7. Are the input and output processes well integrated?
8. What are the chief marketing strategies employed?
9. What are the major constraints placed on the organization at this time?

The critical step is ascertaining which of a myriad of factors are limiting the function of the organization. They label this critical step the *discovery process,* which occurs when top-level managers begin to assimilate and discuss the implications of the data that have been collected. Beer and Spector also suggest that the discovery process can be enhanced if the data are analyzed and interpreted in a systemic framework such as the one developed by Waterman, Peters, and Phillips (1980).

In this framework the 7 S's are examined. In other words, the data should be used to answer the following questions:

1. Are the management *strategies* employed appropriate, given the nature of our organizational pattern, the relationship we are trying to establish between processes and outcomes, and how we hope to have the organization interface with our environments?
2. Does our organizational *structure* allow us to accomplish our goals in an efficient manner?
3. Are the reward and communications *systems* synchronized with our goals? Does our per-

sonnel *system* produce the types of leaders we need?
4. Do our managers have the *skills* they need to facilitate the processes that have been set into place?
5. Do we have the *staff* we need to accomplish the tasks to be performed?
6. Is the management *style* appropriate?
7. Are the *shared values* appropriate given the goals of the organization, the structure, the processes, and our need to interact with our environment?

Perhaps the oldest and most useful tool for synthesizing data is the force field analysis (Lewin, 1951). The beginning of this process is to identify the major problem(s) that exists in the environment. For example, a problem that arose in an outpatient drug rehabilitation agency pertained to staff burnout and turnover. The problem, generally stated, was as follows: how can we reduce staff stress and its resultant impact upon staff attrition?

The second step in the force field analysis is to identify driving forces—that is, forces that exert pressure to, or support for, solving the problem. This is followed by listing restraining forces, or forces that retard problem resolution.

The force field analysis developed for the aforementioned drug rehabilitation program appeared as follows:

1. Driving Forces.
   a. Absenteeism due to stress.
   b. Low staff morale.
   c. Staff turnover.
   d. Lowered program effectiveness.
   e. Cost of recruiting/retraining.
2. Restraining Forces.
   a. Heavy caseload results in little time for change activities.
   b. State-level bureaucracy.
   c. State-level policies/laws/regulations.
   d. Judges that sentence all offenders to drug rehabilitation programs.
   e. Recruitment policies (e.g., don't get best-trained personnel).

Once driving and restraining forces are identified, an attempt should be made to rank order them in terms of what appears to be their degree of contribution to the problem. Turnover may be the result of recruitment and orientation mechanisms, supervisory practices, and/or compensation. However, in this case, it is clear that the primary problem is stress evolving out of the treatment program. Thus, focusing on approaches that both reduce the case load (e.g., group treatment, educating judges about use of rehabilitation services) and those that reduce stress (e.g., stress management training) received the highest priority in this situation.

After ranking forces that are related to the problem, alternate solutions to the problem should be considered. Each potential solution needs to be examined not only for its potential for solving the identified problem but for unintended negative consequences as well (Huse, 1980).

Goal Setting and Intervention

Diagnosis is followed by goal setting and intervention. At the outset, agreement regarding the nature of the problem should be established along with the hoped-for outcomes of problem resolution. Beer (1980) and Huse (1980), as well as others, indicate that goal setting and intervention begin during the diagnosis phase, since the result of this process is a heightened awareness of the problem and reposturing to cope with the difficulty. Although it can certainly be argued that intervention begins during problem identification, the formal process of intervention does not begin until after specific objectives are established and measures designed to achieve these objectives are implemented. These steps can be illustrated by returning to our hypothetical drug rehabilitation program.

In our force field analysis, six forces were identified as driving the program staff toward problem resolution including absenteeism due to stress, low staff morale, high staff turnover, lowered program effectiveness, and the added costs of recruiting and retraining new staff. Some obvious goals might be: (1) to reduce absenteeism growing out of

staff burnout by 75 percent; (2) to increase staff morale as indicated by survey instruments developed to measure that aspect of functioning; (3) to reduce staff turnover by 25 percent; and (4) to decrease the client recidivism rate by 30 percent.

The restraining forces could also be used to develop similar objectives, such as decreasing the caseload by educating judges regarding the types of clients that could most benefit from the program being offered.

Once goals are set, intervention strategies must be selected. Kurpius (1985) indicates that "Choosing an intervention is not a matter of imposing a favorite technique, but rather entails an approach that will address specific needs and concerns" (p. 373). He goes on to indicate that there are four factors that should influence the choice of an intervention: (1) the diagnosed need, (2) the context in which the intervention is to be used, (3) the target group with which it is to be employed, and (4) the consultant's match of values and skills with the interventions being selected. Beer (1980) earlier identified some additional criteria to be used in the selection of an intervention. For example, he suggests that interventions should be utilized that (1) reduce costs, including money, time, and energy, (2) speed the change, (3) minimize psychological and organizational strains, and (4) maximize the likelihood that goals will be attained.

In summary, there are three general considerations when selecting an intervention. One of these is the consultant's values and knowledge. Another is the context in which the intervention will be applied. The third is the nature of the intervention itself (e.g., amount of strain it will produce).

Organizational development consultants have generated vast numbers of intervention strategies, which have in turn been classified using a number of systems (Blake & Mouton, 1993; French & Bell, 1973; Beer, 1980; Lippitt, 1982; Kurpius, 1985). Perhaps the most parsimonious classification system has been one developed by French and Bell. Their system begins with individual or intrapersonal interventions and progresses through relatively simple interpersonal interventions (dyads) to more complex interpersonal situations, including groups, intergroup relationships, and the total organization.

Individual Interventions. This class of interventions is aimed at enhancing the functioning of organizations by improving the performance of key individuals within the organization. Coaching and counseling activities aimed at skills development or attitudinal change (Blake & Mouton, 1993; French & Bell, 1973) are examples of individual interventions, as are life and career interventions (Hale, 1998; Kurpius, 1985) aimed at having persons intensify or redirect their career-related energies.

Group Interventions. Process consultation, mediation, and conflict management strategies are utilized by organizational development consultants as means of enhancing the functioning of dyads or triads. Group goal setting and group building techniques aimed at enhancing group communication and cohesiveness are techniques often employed when groups within organizations are having difficulties (Cadence Group, 1995; French & Bell, 1973). Quality circles, which Kurpius (1985) depicts as primarily small problem-solving groups, are also increasingly used as a means of helping work groups function more effectively. Diversity training and using self-directed work groups are also being employed with groups (Hale, 1998).

Intergroup Organizations. Installing intranets and other communication devices is one way to enhance intergroup functioning. Process consultation, mediation, conflict resolution, and providing data gained from surveys regarding the problems being experienced are examples of these techniques (French & Bell, 1973; Hale, 1998; Lippitt, 1982).

Total Organization. Interventions involving the total organization include surveys and questionnaires regarding the problems being experienced, large group meetings where people are allowed to air their concerns, examining basic processes such as communications and decision making, culture building focused on developing a new normative structure, strategic planning, job enrichment and redesign, and utilizing management by objective procedures (Beer, 1980; Kurpius, 1985; Lippitt, 1982). These are perhaps the most complex of the interventions and may need some additional clarification.

All of these procedures grow out of the philosophy that by placing the welfare of the individual first, the organization will benefit. Accordingly, techniques aimed at assessing organizational functioning, such as surveys, would focus on the extent to which human needs are being met. Analysis of basic processes would be conducted to determine the degree to which open and valid communication characterizes the organization and the extent to which participatory decision-making procedures are employed. Culture development would be largely undertaken in small groups and would focus primarily on the degree to which organizational development philosophy, that is, meeting the needs of individuals, first, is being espoused and practiced. Job enrichment and redesign flow from the same philosophy, and attention would be given to whether the job is meeting the needs of the individual. Specific attention is paid to the extent to which the employee has personal responsibility for his or her own function and whether or not the task performed contains enough variety and importance to satisfy the worker's needs in this area. In job redesign an attempt is made to determine the degree to which the worker receives verbal feedback from supervisors and, if there is a deficit in this area, corrections are made in this process as well (Hackman & Oldham, 1980).

Strategic planning (Fuqua & Kurpius, 1993) and management by objectives (MBO), which came not so much out of organizational development philosophy but from scientific management, are now widely used by organizational consultants. MBO is a management scheme that attempts to establish a series of objectives that will serve as the basis for decision making in the company (see Table 5.5). Strategic planning attempts to help

TABLE 5.5   Strategic Planning in Organizations

1. What are our beliefs about ourselves? . . . . VALUES STATEMENT
   - A. What is our culture?
   - B. Are we focused on the past or the future?
2. Where do we wish to go? . . . . VISION STATEMENT
   - A. What is our overall goal?
   - B. What is our specific objective?
3. What are our internal strengths and weaknesses in relation . . . . SELF-AUDIT STATEMENT
   to our mission?
   - A. Will our culture support our new mission?
   - B. What is the nature of our staff and other resources?
4. What are the immediate opportunities and barriers in our . . . . ENVIRONMENTAL
   environment?   ASSESSMENT STATEMENT
   - A. What is the competition?
   - B. How will factors like governmental regulation influence us
     in the short term?
5. What "futures" might we encounter en route to our mission? . . . . FORECASTING STATEMENT
   - A. Where can we find information about our futures?
   - B. What scenarios do these sources suggest?
6. What policies and strategies do we need to negotiate . . . . STRATEGIC PLANNING
   alternative futures?   STATEMENT
   - A. What policies regarding management and the allocation
     of resources do we need to put into place to cope with
     alternative futures so we can adapt as change occurs?
7. Who is responsible for monitoring our progress toward . . . . MONITORING STATEMENT
   our mission?
   - A. What person or persons are responsible for monitoring
     our progress?
   - B. Who has the authority to make changes?
8. How do we revise our strategic plan? . . . . RECYCLING STATEMENT

managers develop an awareness of the relationship between their values and the choices they make and encourages creative decision making by focusing on an unknown future and the organization's functioning in that unknown future. Managers are taught to identify the knowledge bases required for making decisions; to establish procedures, such as environmental scanning, to generate that data; and to learn systematic problem-solving skills needed to utilize the data at hand (Kurpius, 1985).

The French and Bell (1973) system of classifying interventions is the most parsimonious, but Blake and Mouton's (1993) scheme is the most comprehensive. Blake and Mouton have attempted to classify interventions as they relate to the four general types of problems found in organizations:

power/authority, morale/cohesion, norms/standards, and goals and objectives. These problems may reside within individuals, groups, among groups (intergroup), in the total organization, within the larger social system of which the organization is a part, or in a number of these components simultaneously. In order to deal with these problems, the consultant may choose from among five interventions, which Blake and Mouton label acceptant, catalytic, confrontation, prescriptive, and theory or principles.

Acceptant interventions are similar in nature to Rogers' (1951) client-centered therapy in that consultants (1) rely upon listening and empathy as basic tools, (2) restate, clarify, and accept the feelings of the consultee, and (3) use encouraging leads such as "Tell me more." Consultees are also encouraged to diagnose their own problems through direct questions such as "What do you believe the problem to be?" Finally, the consultant not only expects self-growth and progress toward problem resolution but states this belief.

Catalytic interventions are most nearly related to acceptant reactions, but are designed to speed problem resolution, and thus the consultant tends to be somewhat more active. The consultant suggests processes for collecting data about the problems once consultees have defined them; once data are collected, the consultant encourages consultees to rethink and possibly redefine the problem in light of this new information. As was the case with acceptant interventions, the consultant encourages consultees to make their own decisions and avoids making specific suggestions regarding the problem. This intervention approach is analogous to Schein's (1989) process consultation.

Consultants who use confrontational interventions take nothing for granted. They assume that the consultee will rationalize about the problem at hand, and they act in a manner that will force the consultee to face the facts of the situation. Consultants employing this strategy do not hesitate to ask probing questions designed to stimulate insight into the problem and to share their thinking with the consultee, openly challenging the consultee's assumptions, values, and conclusions. The

utilization of this intervention strategy requires the consultant to interact genuinely, but not to be so abrasive as to make consultees feel attacked. If a consultee becomes defensive, the consultant should solidify the relationship before continuing.

Prescriptive interventions are based upon the assumption that the consultant is an expert or authority in the area under scrutiny. These consultants collect data needed to solve the problem, draw conclusions, provide the best solution, and turn it over to the consultee to implement. Resistance is attacked logically, and if consultees do not proceed to solve the problem along prescribed lines, the consultation is terminated. Blake and Mouton (1993) note that this approach is most effective when a consultee has exhausted all possible alternatives and is in a state of desperation.

Theory/principle interventions are based upon validated models (e.g., communication process) drawn from the social sciences. The assumption of this set of interventions is that intuition, trial-and-error learning, and common-sense approaches to problem solving are less effective than theory-based approaches because the latter are more systematic and can be easily tested. The goal of the consultant using this intervention strategy is not only to introduce theory based interventions, but to have the consultee internalize the theory that is introduced. In order to accomplish this, the consultee is asked first to describe the problem and state how he or she has attempted to solve it. Then the consultant introduces a theory, for example, one regarding job satisfaction, that pertains to the situation at hand. The consultee is then asked to redefine the problem using the theory that has been introduced, and the consultant gives feedback about the consultee's understanding of the problem. Once the theory is understood by the consultee, the consultant asks him or her to develop strategies for its application through discussions, roleplaying, and simulations. The theory-based solution is then implemented and evaluated by the consultee. The consultant monitors the process and provides feedback. Blake and Mouton (1993) believe that theory-based interventions can be used to make changes in the consultee's values, perspective, approach to communication, motivation, creativity, and autonomy.

Selecting an Approach

Given these five intervention strategies or styles, which one should a consultant use? Blake and Mouton (1993) suggest that personality style may dictate consulting style. They posit that some consultants, because of their personality, may be overly concerned about people and thus rely too heavily upon acceptant interventions. Others may focus more on products and thus become more content or prescriptive oriented.

Blake and Mouton (1993) believed that it is an error to over-rely upon a single intervention strategy, and they suggest that the approach be governed by the shifting dynamics of the consulting relationship. For example, they have observed that when power and authority issues are involved and the consultant is dealing with individuals in the organization who are not in authority positions, the acceptant intervention strategy is most useful and confrontational approaches are least useful. Catalytic interventions are the second most used strategy in this situation; theory-based interventions rank third; prescriptive interventions, fourth. Thus, in consulting situations it is incumbent upon the consultant to make decisions based not only on the focus of the intervention and the nature of the problematic situation, but upon the characteristics of the consultee as well.

Resistance

Resistance to change is an inevitable fact of life, but one that is often perceived as a negative force. Resistance allows an organization to maintain its homeostasis in the face of multiple forces for change. However, to remain viable organizations must undergo ongoing, systematic change. Change that threatens people's jobs, status in the organization, and/or workloads are most likely to encounter resistance. The first step in minimizing resistance is to communicate the nature of the change that is

---

Student Learning Activity 5.2
Consulting Case: What Would You Do?

Your agency has sent you to work with a local school that is experiencing an inordinate amount of vandalism, the source of which, they believe, is their own students. The principal describes himself as "being from the old school" and runs a tight ship. Little input is sought from teachers or pupils, and everyone in the school is expected to follow the rules as set forth in the policy manuals for teachers and students. You have made successful entry into the school and have agreed with the principal that some changes are needed. Which one of Blake and Mouton's approaches would you expect to be the most successful? Why?

---

contemplated. Moreover, planned incremental change is less likely to raise resistance than poorly planned, chaotic change. The term *reengineering* is popular in the organizational change literature, perhaps because it suggests that changes will be systematic, planned, and orderly. Involving employees in the change process, as collaborators, is one means of minimizing resistance. Another means of lessening resistance is reinforcing the efforts of employees involved in the change process.

Evaluation and Termination

These two phases often occur simultaneously, particularly if the goals that were established at the outset have been accomplished. Evaluation, then, is the process of systematically measuring the impact of the intervention that was selected when the problem was identified (Hale, 1998). If this is the case, termination is a natural culmination of the consulting process. (Approaches to evaluation will be discussed in a later chapter.) If the evaluation reveals that the established goals have not been reached, the consultant and consultee have two choices: reevaluate the intervention and perhaps modify it or select another, or terminate the consulting relationship. Often the decision is to continue the relationship. Termination can be initiated by either the consultant or the consultee independently, or they can arrive at a conclusion to terminate jointly. Kurpius, Fuqua, and Rozecki (1993) recommend that, if the intervention has failed to produce the desired result, the consultant and consultee make every attempt to understand why the failure occurred prior to termination.

A COLLABORATIVE PROBLEM SOLVING APPROACH TO EDUCATIONAL RESTRUCTURING

As noted at the outset of this chapter, the work of Dr. W. E. Deming has transformed business and educational leadership and management. Deming developed an approach to quality control labeled Total Quality Control (TQC) (1993), which is often summed up in fourteen basic propositions. English and Hill (1997) used Total Quality Education (TQE) in their discussion of the application of Deming's ideas to education in which they pointed out that his management theory and ideas about education have many implications for education, but that his fourteen principles to not apply directly to the field. Some of the more controversial beliefs advanced by Deming are that all forms of competition in schools should be eliminated except those that occur in sports, and that grading and testing as we know it should be eliminated. Competition, grading, and testing sort students into winners and losers, according to Deming, and are counterproductive. Deming (1993) also suggested that effective organizations follow the PDSA cycle (Plan, Do, Study, Act) in their self-improvement process and that they attend to profound knowledge as the act. Profound knowledge includes (1) appreciation for the school as a system, (2) differentiation between common cause variation and special cause variation, (3) the best knowledge available about the problem or organization (today's truisms), (4) not expecting today's truisms to be true tomorrow, (5) people have a need for relationships, (6) students want to take joy from their work, and (7) extensive reliance on extrinsic motivation crushes intrinsic motivation. Deming's ideas about

common cause and special cause variation warrant some clarification. Common cause variation is a naturally occurring phenomenon and results from differences in human behavior. Special cause variation, as the name suggests, is the result of special circumstances that cause variation in the functioning of a team or group that cannot be accounted for by common cause variation. Minor fluctuations in high-stakes test scores are to be expected, but dramatic decreases or increases are not. The latter is special cause variation and should be studied before taking action.

The fourteen assumptions underpinning TQE, which are based on Deming's propositions, are as follows:

- Schools must have constancy of purpose to improve the educational processes and, thereby, the "products of education" (students). This process never stops.
- Schools must drive out fear in their staff, faculty, and students by creating a supportive environment that encourages effort. Fear discourages communication, something essential in the quality improvement process.
- Schools must use collaborative approaches to leadership. Involvement in the leadership process by all concerned parties is a prerequisite to educational change, continued improvement, and pride in ownership.
- Schools must stop depending on test results as indicators of increases in achievement. Success is defined on an individual basis, not by comparing individuals to each other.
- Schools must abolish grading and the harmful effects of rating teachers and students. Tracking that sorts students into categories must also be abandoned.
- Schools must work with parents and community agencies to improve the quality of education. The community and the home are educational institutions, too.
- Schools must involve everyone in the school in continuous job training.
- Consultation should replace supervision. Consultants should work continuously with

teachers and others to help them use technology and other products to improve educational processes.

- Barriers between school district levels, school departments, and school programs should be eliminated. People and students should work in collaborative teams.
- Schools must eliminate externally set goals for teachers and students.
- Schools must eliminate quotas and work standards such as decreasing dropouts or certain new levels of achievement. Deming suggests that getting good results requires focusing on the processes of education, not the outcomes. If processes are improved, outcomes will follow.
- Schools must abolish merit raises and merit ratings for staff, teachers, and administrators.
- Schools must involve everyone in a vigorous self-improvement program.
- Cooperative learning approaches should replace classroom practices based on competition.

Deming's ideas about reforming education are in opposition to many of the aspects of educational reform including high-stakes testing, higher academic standards for graduation, rating schools based on their test scores, threats from state departments of education to take over "failing" schools, national report cards that rate schools based on a variety factors, and so forth. However, for the remainder of this section we will assume that a traditional school believes that it should restructure and move toward what English and Hill (1994) call a learning place, and seeks to do this via a collaborative change process.

Beginning the Restructuring Process

Whitaker and Moses (1994) point out that restructuring a school can occur from the top down or from the bottom up. They also note that collaborative leadership is an important precondition for the restructuring process because it empowers would-be change agents. School psychologists, school

counselors, school social workers, and human services workers are unlikely to initiate the monumental task of restructuring their schools or their agencies unless they believe that they have the support of the leadership team. Therefore, potential collaborators should ascertain the degree to which administrators will support restructuring efforts. In many instances, would-be collaborators will have to persuade members of the power structure that change is necessary and that the proposed change will move the school or district toward a desired goal. Havelock and Zlotolow (1995) call this step in the change process *arousal of concern*. In many instances this can be accomplished by identifying similar schools or districts in other parts of the state or country that have restructured themselves and achieved positive outcomes. The presentation of data to support the proposed change can also be persuasive. If the change agent is successful in raising the level of concern in the school district, the time for mobilizing the system to act has arrived.

Forming the Collaborative Team

The collaborative team should be comprised of representatives from the major stakeholders in the educational enterprise. These include teachers, administrators, student support personnel, parents, students, human resource workers from community agencies, and business leaders. People who support quality education generally should be included on the team.

Training Team Members to Be Collaborators, Role Taking, and Team Building

It was noted at the outset that some people do not have the skills needed to be collaborators. Collaborators need communication skills, respect for other members of the team, an understanding of collaboration, and decision-making strategies. Collaborators should be polled to determine whether or not they believe they need training in these areas.

Initial role taking requires that some members of the team assume leadership responsibility, which includes communication to collaborative team members, taking minutes to document the action of the team, and managing the logistics of the team (e.g., securing meeting places and scheduling appointments). Leading the actual meetings of the team may be the most important task of the team leader. Basham, Appleton, and Dykeman (2000) suggest that effective team leaders are facilitators and not directors, look for opportunities to share leadership, work to ensure that everyone is involved in the communication, monitor and protect the well-being of team members, motivate and encourage others, and work to ensure that credit for any successes are shared. Collaborators should possess many of these same characteristics.

The first task of the collaborative team is to determine whether collaboration is the best approach to solving the problem at hand (Rubin, 2002). When the issues involved are as complex as restructuring an educational system, the answer is almost invariably "yes." Basham and his colleagues (2000) suggest that, prior to the beginning of the problem-solving process, four other tasks should be accomplished: (1) having the team understand how effective teams function, (2) developing a clear understanding of the collaborative team's mission, (3) developing an expectation of commitment and high-quality work, and (4) developing assurances that the team is a safe place in which teams members are free to express their opinions. However, Patterson (2003) warns against equating a safe environment with a conflict-free environment. He suggests that conflict that involves expressing varying opinions is an essential aspect of the collaborative process.

Developing a Vision for the School

There are many clichés that speak to the importance of the vision: If you don't have a destination, it doesn't matter which route you take. Having a well-articulated vision of the program, school, or agency to be changed is essential. Therefore, the collaborative team's first task should be to develop a vision for the school embodied in the mission statement. The mission statement, once drafted and agreed to, will guide the remainder of the

team's work (Patterson, 2003; Whitaker & Moses, 1994). A mission statement should reflect the values of the school district, the fundamental reason that the school exists, and how the school or district wishes to appear in the future. It should also be short, contain no jargon, be relevant to everyone in the school, have charisma, and have integrity. Accordingly, mission statements are typically brief and to the point, although there is no single way to craft a mission statement. The team's mission statement for the school might be: Collaboration for Quality: Quality Educational Practices + Quality Involvement by the Community + Quality Leadership = Quality Students. It might also be somewhat longer, for example,

Our Mission Statement Is to Produce Quality Students in an Atmosphere That:

1. Values Inclusion Rather Than Exclusion
2. Values Collaboration Rather Than Competition
3. Teaches Students That Quality Education Is a Life-Long Process
4. Recognizes the Parents and the Community Are Educators
5. Recognizes the Uniqueness of Each Student
6. Measures Quality One Student at a Time

Once the mission statement is drafted it should be circulated to all professional and nonprofessional employees as well as students and other stakeholders. This is the beginning of what will be a consensus-building process that will set the stage for the action phase of the change process. Collaborative team members should participate in as many discussions as possible to monitor reactions to the mission statement. Ultimately, there must be agreement among the majority of the stakeholders about the nature of the mission statement.

Audit the System

The American School Counselor Association (ASCA; 2003) has developed an extensive set of guidelines for conducting a program audit that could easily be transformed and used for school-wide audits. ASCA's audit includes looking at the beliefs and philosophy, the mission statement, goals, delivery systems, leadership and management, the availability and use of data, accountability systems, and a host of other variables. The audit should also include an inventory of the fiscal, human, and physical resources available to support the educational mission, an assessment of the needs of the students who are to be served, and an accounting of the cooperative/collaborative arrangements, including those with parents and community agencies. Finally, focus group data or survey data from students, teachers, and others should be gathered to ascertain the climate of the school as well as the views of people external to the school. In keeping with the solution-focused problem-solving model, auditors should try to ascertain what is working as well as areas that people see as problematic.

Havelock and Zlotolow (1995) suggest that the collaborative team arrange the data into two categories: diagnostic data and solution-oriented information. Diagnostic data involve rank-ordering the problems that have been identified, major elements of the system that require restructuring, an estimate of the stakeholders' views of the need for change, and strengths and assets of stakeholders that can be used to facilitate change. Solution-oriented data include solutions suggested by stakeholders, research studies that outline changes, and information about people and material that might be helpful in the change effort. Finally, Havelock and Zlotolow recommend that the change team build a diagnostic inventory around five basic questions: (1) What are the school's goals? (2) Does the structure of the school facilitate attainment of its goals? (3) Do people communicate freely? (4) Does the school have the resources to attain its goals? and (5) Are goals flexible enough to change as circumstances change? Is the school living in the past?

Selecting a Strategy

In our example, we have already chosen TQE as the strategy to be used to restructure our school. However, in addition to TQE, there are other strategies that could be chosen, including those rejected by Deming (1993), such as management by objectives and incentive programs. Changing management style (authoritarian to collaborative), ad-

vocacy, and resource acquisitions are also methods that are used to reengineer schools. Space will not permit a discussion of alternatives to TQE.

Develop a Strategic Plan

A strategic plan is a series of action steps that include the action to be taken, the date by which it is to be completed, and the person or group responsible for taking the action and monitoring its change. All of these steps are important, but, given the failure rate of innovation in public education, monitoring may be the most crucial step.

Innovation in education and elsewhere is a long and sometimes painful process. Because the process is so long and painful, resistance may arise that either totally stymies or substantially limits the change process. The Concerns-Based Adoption Model (CBAM) was developed at the University of Texas Research and Development Center for Teacher Education as a systematic approach to identifying and remedying problems that arise during the innovation process (Hall & Hord, 1987). This model was developed to monitor the concerns and behaviors of individuals as they try to grasp the meaning of and implement changes in their school. Developers of the model suggest that people involved in innovations move through seven stages: (1) awareness, (2) wanting to know more about it, (3) personal (How will it affect me?), (4) wondering how they will manage the new aspects of the innovation, (5) wondering how it will affect students, (6) collaborative, (wondering how they can relate what they are doing to the work of others), and (7) identifying innovations that will work better than the one at hand. These seven levels of concern run parallel to levels of use. Educators who are developing an awareness of an innovation are nonusers. As they learn more about the innovation, they go through an orientation phase in which they learn more about the innovation. A process of reorganization that allows them to use the innovation follows this, but the innovation is used very much as it has been taught. Once the innovation is adopted for use, users refine it, coordinate their use with others, and then begin to actively seek approaches that are alternatives to the innovation.

By using CBAM monitors can determine the concerns that people have and their actions regarding them. If those involved are at a preawareness stage, the collaborative team has to question the tactics they have used to develop a consensus regarding the mission of the school and how it relates to the innovation. Similarly, if a great many people are seeking information about the innovations, dissemination efforts need to be increased. Other strategies, such as consultation, may be needed as the implementation process moves along. In sum, data from the CBAM monitoring system can be used as the basis of continuing efforts to adopt and implement innovative changes.

Implementation

English and Hill (1994) believe that the process of restructuring a traditional school to a TQE school involves making sure that the people involved understand the concepts that underpin this approach and to gain consensus that this is the path to take. That is precisely what happened at Mt. Edgecombe High School in Sitka, Alaska. The entire process began when one teacher attended a seminar regarding Deming's ideas in Arizona and brought them back to his colleagues (Cotton, n.d.). The faculty at Mt. Edgecombe High School did not adopt all of Deming's ideas, but clearly they worked to make sure that they had constancy of purpose to improve, a culture based on trust and collaborative decision making, and a focus on the customer (student). They accomplished this by involving students and teachers in bimonthly TQE meetings that keep both groups focused on improving educational achievement and involving students extensively in assessing their own learning. Students and teachers have worked collaboratively to develop competency matrices for each class. They have moved away from standardized tests and replaced them with assessment devices such as portfolios.

Whitaker and Moses (1994) suggest that if collaboration is to become the norm in the school it must be encouraged among the staff, teachers, and other professionals in the school. Rosenholtz (1989) found that, when collaboration was encour-

aged, teachers were more likely to seek help, principals more often encouraged people working together, and teachers more readily agreed to assist colleagues than was the case when people were expected to work independently. Teachers who collaborate can use multiage groups, develop quality improvement teams, provide teamwork training, and develop conflict-resolution programs with other teachers and counselors.

Current educational reform requirements will not permit TQE schools to eliminate state mandated curricula and the ubiquitous high-stakes tests as Deming (1993) suggested. However, schools could, if they chose to, develop flexible scheduling, employ cooperative learning strategies, eliminate tracking, use collaborative leadership strategies, and do away with grades if their communities agree.

Developing Collaborative Partnerships in the Home and Community

Schools are systems that function in the larger system of the community. Collaboration can align the goals of the community and the school in order to better achieve the goals of all concerned. Deming (1993) and English and Hill (1994) suggest that schools need to implement collaborative relationships that enhance the learning process. Businesses can assist schools by providing expertise that would otherwise be unavailable and by allowing students glimpses of the real world of work. Conversely, schools with business partners can design learning experiences that prepare students for the transition to adulthood. Likewise, school–university alliances, collaborative relationships with health and dental care providers, social service agencies, law enforcement agencies, recreational departments, the YMCA and YWCA, and state and federal agencies can enrich schooling and the agencies involved. Steffy and Lindle (1994) suggest that the school work to bring all agencies and professions that serve students into the school. Once the collaborative team completes an audit and gains consensus about the direction that the school is to take, the team can serve as a consultant to teachers and others who wish to develop collaborative relationships in the community by sharing the expertise about the collaboration gained in the restructuring process.

One of the themes in all school reform movements, including those using Deming's principles, is the need to involve parents in the educational process. Schools can assist parents by teaching or sponsoring educational experiences that will allow them to be more proactive in the educational lives of their children and including families in the decision-making processes. Parents can assist schools by volunteering, facilitating learning in the home, and by supporting community actions that increase support for and collaboration with schools.

Evaluation of TQE Schools

It should come as no surprise that evaluations based on traditional objectives are not acceptable in TQE schools. Qualitative evaluation approaches such as case studies, focus groups, and ethnographic studies (Patton, 1980, 1997) are much more likely to provide useful data about the critical processes in TQE schools.

SUMMARY

At the outset of this chapter, the characteristics and principles that govern open systems such as businesses and school were explored. This was followed by some practical advice for consultants and collaborators including what to expect from people and organizations engaged in a change effort, how to avoid unintended consequences, and suggestions for functioning as an internal and external consultant. An organizational development model of consultation was then presented, followed by a collaborative model of organizational change. If either collaboration or consultation is to be successful, the result must be to alter the basic values and beliefs of the organization.

TIPS FOR THE PRACTITIONER

1. Analyze your family or current living arrangement using systems principles:
   A. What roles do people play? (Differentiation)

   B. How are decisions reached? (Leadership)
   C. Are family goals well articulated? Are there conflicts in goals?
   D. What is the basic reward system in the family?
   E. What technology is used to enhance family functioning? Is any of the use of technology counterproductive?
   F. What are the values of the family? How are these communicated? Enforced?
   G. Identify problems that could be solved in several ways.
   H. How does the family adapt to changing conditions?
2. Now use these same principles to analyze a simple organization. Get permission to observe the organization for a day or two. Do not interact with the people. After you have made your observations, test them with the head of the organization to determine their accuracy.
3. Volunteer to help a consultant who works with organizations.

REVIEW QUESTIONS

1. Identify instances in which linear thinking has produced undesirable consequences in organizations.
2. How can human resources agencies make their boundaries less permeable? Take a specific agency (school, counseling center, health department, etc.) and outline a plan.
3. Identify a problem of concern to you. Using the force field analysis approach, generate a problem-solving approach to deal with the concern.
4. What are the assumptions underlying the human relations model of consultation?
5. Do you agree with Schein's recommendations on the consultant's role regarding the content of consultation? Why or why not?
6. Identify specific situations in which acceptant, catalytic, confrontational, prescriptive, and theory-based interventions could be used. Generate rules for determining what you would use.

7. What organizational factors are likely to impinge upon the change process?

8. Contrast consultation with collaboration. Why is collaboration becoming increasingly popular?

9. Discuss an approach to assembling a consultation team and preparing the team to function.

10. What are Deming's principles? What problems do you see with implementing them?

REFERENCES

Abidin, R. R. (1982). A psychosocial look at consultation and behavior modification. *Psychology in the Schools, 9,* 358–364.

Alpert, J., & Silverstein, J. (1985). Mental health consultation: Historical, present, and future perspectives. In J. R. Bergan (Ed.), *School psychology in contemporary society* (pp. 121–138). Columbus, OH: Merrill.

American School Counselor Association. (2003). *ASCA national model: A framework for comprehensive school counseling programs.* Alexandria, VA: Author.

Associated Press. (2004). Getting into more trouble: NC student suspension rates continue to increase in 2003. *Wilmington Star-News,* p. 2B.

Backer, Shifren-Levine, & Erchul (1983). *Consultation and educational activities in mental health programs.* Los Angeles: Human Interaction Research Institute.

Basham, A., Appleton, V. F., & Dykeman, C. (2000). *Team building in education.* Denver, CO: Love.

Beer, M. (1980). *Organizational change and development.* Santa Monica, CA: Goodyear.

Beer, M., & Spector, B. (1993). Organizational diagnosis: Its role in organizational learning. *Journal of Counseling and Development, 71,* 642–650.

Berliner, D. C., & Biddle, B. J. (1995). *The manufactured crisis: Myths, fraud, and the attacks on America's public schools.* Reading, MA: Addison-Wesley.

Blake, R. R., & Mouton, J. S. (1993). The consulcube: Strategies for consultation. In R. T. Golembiewki, (Ed.), *Handbook of organizational consultation* (pp. 37–42). New York: Marcel Dekker.

Bonfenbrenner, U. *Ecology of human development: Experiments by nature and design.* Cambridge, MA: Harvard University Press.

Brown, D., Galassi, J. P., & Akos, P. (in press). School counselors' perceptions of the impact of high-stakes testing on their ability to deliver services. *Professional School Counseling.*

Chin, R., & Benne, K. (1976). General strategies for effecting change in human systems. In W. G. Bennis, K. D. Benne, R. Chin, & K. D. Corey. *The Planning Change* (3rd ed.). (pp. 45–63). New York: Holt, Rinehart and Winston.

Conoley, J. C. (1981). Emergent training issues in school psychology. In J. C. Conoley (Ed.), *Consultation in schools: Theory, research and procedures* (pp. 223–263). New York: Academic Press.

Cotton, K. (n.d.). Applying total quality management principles to secondary education. [On-line.] Available: http://www.nwrel.org/scpd/sirs/9/so35.html.

Deming, W. E. (1993). *The new economics for industry, government, and education.* Cambridge, MA: Center for Advanced Engineering Study.

Dooley, J. (1995). Cultural aspects of systemic change. [On-line.] Available: http://www.well.com/user/dooley/ culture/pdf.

English, F., & Hill, J. (1994). *Total quality education.* Thousand Oaks, CA: Corwin.

Golembieski, R. T. (1993). Cuing the reader to six orientations: An interpretive introduction. In R. T. Golembieski (Ed.), *Handbook of organizational consultation* (pp. 1–26). New York: Marcel Dekker.

Hackman, J. R., & Oldman, G. R. (1980). *Work redesign.* Reading, MA: Addison-Wesley.

Hale, J. (1988). *The performance consultant's fieldbook.* San Francisco: Jossey-Bass.

Hall, G. E., & Hord, S. M. (1987). *Change in schools: Facilitating the process.* Albany, NY: State University of New York at Albany Press.

Havelock, R. G., & Huberman, A. M. (1978). *Solving educational problems: The theory and reality of innovation in developing countries.* Englewood Cliffs, NJ: Educational Technology Publications.

Havelock, R. G., & Zlotolow, S. (1995). *The change agent's guide* (2nd ed.). Englewood Cliffs, NJ: Educational Technology Publications.

Homan, M. S. (2004). *Promoting community change: Making it happen in the real world* (3rd ed.). Pacific Grove, CA: Brooks/Cole.

Huse, E. F. (1980). *Organizational development and change* (2nd ed.). St Paul, MN: West.

Ilbeck, R. J., & Zins, J. E. (1993). Organizational perspectives on child consultation. In J. E. Zins, T. R. Kratochwill, & S. N. Elliot (Eds.), *Handbook of consultation services for children* (pp. 87–109). San Francisco: Jossey-Bass.

Katz, D., & Kahn, R. L. (1978). *Social psychology of organizations.* New York: Wiley.

Kuhn, A., & Beam, R. D. (1982). *The logic of organizations.* San Francisco: Jossey-Bass.

Kuhnert, K. W., & Lahey, M. A. (1993). Approaches to organizational needs assessment. In R. T. Golembieski (Ed.), *Handbook of organizational consultation* (pp. 467–474). New York: Marcel Dekker.

Kuhr, M. (1978). *Management consulting: A guide to the profession.* Geneva, Switzerland: International Labour Offices.

Kurpius, D. J. (1984). *Quality of worklife: Preparing consultants to work with the total organization.* Paper presented at annual conference of the American Association for Counseling and Development, Houston, TX (March 18–21).

Kurpius, D. J. (1985). Consultation interventions: Successes, failures, and proposals. *Counseling Psychologist, 13,* 368–389.

Kurpius, D. J., Fuqua, D. R., & Rozecki, T. (1993). The consulting process: A multidimensional approach. *Journal of Counseling and Development, 71,* 801–606.

Lewin, K. (1951). *Field theory in the social sciences.* New York: Harper & Row.

Lippitt, G. (1982). *Organizational renewal* (2nd ed.). Englewood Cliffs, NJ: Prentice-Hall.

Lippitt, G., & Lippitt, R. (1986). *The consulting process in action* (2nd ed.). San Diego, CA: University Associates.

Morasky, R. L. (1982). *Behavioral systems.* New York: Praeger.

National Commission on Excellence in Education. (1983). *A nation at risk: The imperatives for educational reform.* Washington, DC: U.S. Department of Education.

Patterson, J. L. (2003). *Coming even cleaner about organizational change.* Lanham, MD: Scarecrow Education.

Patton, M. Q. (1980). *Qualitative evaluation methods.* Thousand Oaks, CA: Sage

Patton, M. Q. (1997). *Utilization-focused evaluation* (3rd ed.). Thousand Oaks, CA: Sage.

Reppucci, N. D., & Sanders, J. T. (1974). Social psychology of behavior modification: Problems of implementation in natural settings. *American Psychologist, 5,* 649–660.

Rogers, C. R. (1951). *Client-centered therapy.* Boston: Houghton-Mifflin.

Rosenholtz, S. J. (1989). *Teachers' workplace: The social organization of schools.* New York: Longman.

Rubin, H. (2002). *Collaborative leadership.* Thousand Oaks, CA: Corwin.

Sarason, S. B. (1982). *The culture of the school and the problem of change* (2nd ed.). Boston: Allyn & Bacon.

Schein, E. H. (1969). *Process consultation: Its role in organizational development.* Reading, MA: Addison-Wesley.

Schein, E. H. (1970). *Organizational psychology* (2nd ed.). Englewood Cliffs, NJ: Prentice-Hall.

Schein, E. H. (1989). Process consulting as a general model of helping. *Consulting Psychology Bulletin, 41,* 3–15.

Schein, E. H. (1990). Organizational culture. *American Psychologist, 45,* 109–119.

Steele, F. (1982). *The role of the internal consultant.* Boston: CBI.

Steffy, B. E., & Lindle, S. (1994). *Building coalitions: How to link TQE schools with government, business, and community.* Thousand Oaks, CA: Corwin.

Swenson, D. X. (2002). The Ouroboros Effect: The revenge effects of unintended consequences. [Online.] Available: http://www.css.edu/users/dswenson/web/REVENGE. HTM

Swenson, D. X., & Anstett, D. N. (n.d.). Solution-focused problem solving: Finding exceptions that work. [On-line.] Available: http://www.css.edu/users.dswenson/web/Solfocus.htm.

Von Bertalanffy, L. (1967). General theory of systems: Application to psychology. *Social Science Information, 6*:125–136.

Waterman, R. H., Peters, T. J., & Phillips, J. R. (1980). Structure is not organization. *Business Horizon, 23,* 14–26.

Weisbord, M. (1976). Organizational diagnosis: Six places to look for trouble without a theory. *Group and Organizational Studies, 1,* 430.

Whitaker, K., & Moses, M. (1994). *The restructuring handbook.* Boston: Allyn & Bacon.

ANSWERS TO LEARNING EXERCISES

5.1 The answers will depend on the organizations you chose.

5.2 Either a prescriptive or theory/principle intervention is called for, given the immediacy of the problem.

CONSULTATION STAGES AND PROCESSES

GOAL OF THE CHAPTER

The goal of this chapter is to provide a description of the consulting process and some illustrations of the communication skills needed by the consultant.

CHAPTER PREVIEW

1. Two views of the consultation process are provided: a description of the stages of consultation that details the activities that comprise consultation and a description of the interpersonal processes that contribute to effective problem solving in consultation.
2. Eight stages of consultation are identified and illustrated: entry, initiation of a consulting relationship, assessment, problem definition and goal setting, strategy selection, strategy implementation, evaluation, and termination.
3. An overview of the different issues faced by internal and external consultants, particularly in the early stages of consultation, is provided.
4. Carkhuff's model of helping is extended to consultation.
5. Research and concepts from the consultation literature are discussed in relation to Carkhuff's model and its application to consultation.

Traditionally the process of consultation has been conceptualized in two distinct, although not necessarily contradictory, ways. In the first of these approaches, consultation is viewed as an activity that consists of stages in which each stage involves qualitatively different activities. In the second, the relationship between the consultant and consultee is examined within an interpersonal framework (Meade, Hamilton, & Yuen, 1982). The stage approach is primarily descriptive: It details activities that occur in most instances of consultation. The process approach focuses upon the consultant–consultee dyad and how consultant behavior influences subsequent consultee behavior and attitudes. Both approaches are useful in understanding what goes on in consultation and in linking specific aspects of consultation with desired outcomes. This chapter begins with a description of consultation, dividing it into eight stages. In the second half, interaction between the consultant and consultee will be discussed in depth.

STAGES OF CONSULTATION

In broadest terms, consultation is a process by which a consultant and consultee seek to change a problem situation. Therefore, it is not surprising to find that those writing about consultation (e.g., Bergan & Kratochwill, 1990; Erchul & Martens, 2002; Hansen, Himes, & Meier, 1990; Havelock, 1973; Kurpius, 1978; Lippitt & Lippitt, 1978; Meyers, Parsons, & Martin, 1979; Sheridan, Kratochwill, & Bergan, 1996) typically portray consultation as a problem-solving process that includes the stages common to problem-solving models in many disciplines (assessment, problem definition, strategy selection, implementation, and evaluation). In the following discussion consultation has been divided into eight stages: (1) entry into the organization, (2) initiation of a consulting relationship, (3) assessment, (4) problem definition and goal setting, (5) strategy selection, (6) strategy implementation, (7) evaluation, and (8) termination.

When a complex process is described in stages, a lock-step sequence that must take place in all instances of the process is often implied (such as the stages of human development described by Piaget). The term "stages" is not used in that sense when applied to consultation. Rather, the stages described here reflect the activities that typically occur in consultation and their usual sequence. In many instances of consultation one or more stages will not be present, or activities within different stages may overlap. For example, entry into the consultee's setting, initiation of a relationship with the consultee, and assessment of factors relevant to the presenting problem are often described as separate stages in consultation, yet these activities often occur simultaneously. In other instances, consultation is initiated when a consultee approaches a consultant with a description of his or her concerns and the consultant responds with pertinent questions. Thus, assessment of the problem has begun and entry and relationship building as separate, preceding stages have been bypassed. However, as interaction between the consultant and consultee progresses, a positive working relationship must be established or consultation is likely to be aborted.

The division of consultation into stages also does not imply that consultation occurs in an invariant sequence; consultants and consultees may recycle through earlier stages of consultation if new information arises that calls for reinterpretation of information from a prior stage (Bergan, 1977; Gutkin & Curtis, 1990). For instance, if a strategy developed in consultation does not bring about problem resolution, the consultant and consultee may decide that more assessment is needed in order to develop a workable solution, and the focus of consultation would return to assessment.

The purpose of the following sections is to describe a common core of activities and issues that characterize consultation, regardless of the model of consultation that is employed or the setting in which consultation takes place. In some cases the activities of internal and external consultants will be discussed separately; particularly in the early stages of consultation the issues faced by each type differ.

Entry into the Organization

Entry refers to the consultant's crossing of organizational boundaries into a system or work setting. As such, entry issues are most relevant for consultants who are external to the organization in which consultation takes place. In this section, issues pertinent to the external consultant will be discussed first, followed by a discussion of issues pertinent to entry for internal consultants.

There are two distinct components to entry: formal entry, or sanctioning of the consultant's activities by persons in authority positions within the organization, and informal acceptance, or acceptance of the consultant by organizational members who will be consultees. Both aspects of entry are crucial in setting the stage for successful consultation.

Formal Entry.   Gallessich (1982) has delineated several substeps in formal entry. For the external consultant, entry usually begins with a preliminary exploration of the match between organizational needs and the consultant's skills. Generally, this exploration takes the form of one or more preliminary meetings where the consultant and a member (or members) of the organization exchange information. Topics included in these preliminary discussions may include basic descriptive information about the organization, perceived needs of the organization and desired outcomes, information regarding the consultant's skills and working style, and a formulation of how consultation might be implemented in that particular work setting. Fees and a time frame may be discussed. Such a meeting also provides an opportunity for both the consultant and members of the organization to assess each other and form judgments about the potential for a productive working relationship.

Prior to reaching a formal agreement, the consultant may want to consider why the organization chose to ask for consultation at this particular time and for this particular problem, as well as why he or she was approached rather than another consultant (Pipes, 1981). Several factors playing into this decision could have a profound effect on the course and outcome of consultation. For example, the choice of a consultant with a particular area of expertise, such as increasing productivity or schoolwide discipline programs, tells the consultant how the organization has conceptualized the problem. Should the consultant conceptualize the problem differently, he or she may meet with resistance. There also may be hidden agendas in the request for consultative services. A supervisor may have pressured a manager to seek help, or an organization may be looking to gather evidence to scapegoat someone for a particular problem. Also, more than one consultant has found that he or she is expected to legitimatize a decision that has already been made by the director of an agency, such as the dismissal of certain personnel or the discontinuation of a service. The consultant who carefully considers the questions "Why me?" and "Why now?" not only has begun the assessment process, but may anticipate and avoid many difficult consultative dilemmas (Pipes, 1981).

Provided the consultant and the representative(s) of the organization can reach agreement about some potential ways the consultant can be of use to the organization, they move onto the second step of formal entry, contracting. *Contracting* refers to negotiation and agreement between the consultant and the organization regarding the nature of consultation. Although contracting may not involve a formal written contract, the outcome of the activity is the same as that of negotiating a written contract—clear understanding and agreement by both parties of the other's responsibilities. Although contracting is typically carried out at several levels of an organization to assure understanding of consultation by all those involved, sanction from the highest-level administrator is especially important to assure that subordinates participate in the consultation process (Caplan, 1970; Caplan & Caplan, 1993; Kelly, 1993; Marks, 1995; Meyers et al., 1979). Without this sanction, it may be unclear to employees how participation in consulting activities will be viewed and what the potential consequences of participation might be.

Although Chapter Twelve discusses the components of a consulting contract in depth, it is relevant here to list some of the topics typically discussed in contracting:

- goals or intended outcomes of consultation
- identity of consultees
- confidentiality of service and the limits of this confidentiality
- time frame—how long will the service be provided to the organization? to the individual consultee?
- times the consultant will be available
- procedure for requesting to work with the consultant
- space for consultant
- how to contact the consultant if needed
- possibility of contract renegotiation if change is needed
- fees, if relevant
- consultant's access to different sources and types of information within the organization
- person to whom the consultant is responsible

At times, contracting may take the form of discussion between the consultant and a representative of the organization. In this case, the consultant may wish to write a letter to the administrative head of the organization, summarizing his or her understanding of their agreement and asking that the consultee organization bring any points of disagreement up for further discussion. This letter can serve as a written document to which both parties can refer should any question arise about the consultant's activities and also prevent problems where the consultant and the consultee organization have perceived the nature of their agreement differently.

The third step in formal entry is the actual physical entry of the consultant into the workplace (Gallessich, 1982). Often the external consultant's entry into the organization takes the form of a formal introduction of the consultant to consultees and other staff of the organization. It is often beneficial for the external consultant to arrange to be introduced in a staff meeting where he or she is also given a few minutes to summarize the types of services to be provided and answer any questions potential consultees may have. This procedure has several advantages. Introduction at a staff meeting is one way of communicating that the consultant's activities have been formally recognized and sanctioned and also communicates the consultant's interest in meeting with prospective consultees and answering their questions. This procedure also gives the consultant control over how his or her services are represented. When no introduction takes place, or consultation is introduced in a less formal or systematic manner, misunderstanding or distortion of the consultant's role is more likely to occur. For example, a formal meeting where confidentiality of consultation is discussed and endorsed by the administrative head of the organization may dissipate the notion that the consultant is a "spy" for the administration who will report on consultees' weaknesses and failures. Finally, such a formal introduction assures that all consultees have had a preliminary introduction to both consultation and the consultant in a non-threatening manner. Consultees are more likely to approach the consultant if their uncertainty about the consultant's role and interpersonal style has been reduced prior to individual contact.

Informal Acceptance. After formal contracting and introduction to the staff have been accom-

plished, the consultant enters the organization. Even though the consultant now may begin work with individual consultees, there is generally a transition time where the external consultant has entered the workplace, but has not been entirely accepted by staff members. During this time, consultation may be hindered by lack of trust, lack of cooperation, or consultee reluctance to share information (Gallessich, 1982). An inexperienced consultant may be frustrated by this period of what, on the surface, appears to be largely wasted time. However, this transition period should be expected, and in many ways it serves a useful function for both the consultant and consultees.

Consultees' wariness in accepting the consultant can serve as a protective mechanism: it allows consultees an opportunity to evaluate the consultant, his or her skills, operating style, cultural awareness, and potential value to the organization, and to assess the risks (e.g., loss of time, adverse organizational consequences) that may be associated with consultation, before engaging in consultation. For the consultant, this time period provides an opportunity to go beyond a surface-level understanding of the organization and gain information important in functioning successfully as a consultant. The consultant may become aware of subtle, but critical, aspects of organizational functioning, such as interpersonal schisms, formal and informal networks within the organization, and organizational taboos and norms, as he or she observes and participates in the day-to-day activities of the organization. An example follows:

> *The head of a large company hired a consultant to provide guidance regarding the selection of corporate sales staff. The sales staff needed considerable technical knowledge and many new hires stayed only a brief period on the job after they had been trained. The consultant was initially impressed by the sales division head. He was articulate, engaging, and appeared concerned about his staff. However, in the ensuing weeks of work with the organization, it became clear that the division head's manner with employees deviated considerably from his interactions with the consultant. He was sarcastic, took constructive feedback about*

his ideas personally, and was patronizing toward women and minority employees. It became clear to the consultant that improved selection methods would probably not solve the problem with turnover in the sales staff.

The consultant who acts too quickly, without gaining acceptance or taking time to fully understand the organization, may find that he or she has misdiagnosed the problem, ignored factors important in the design of successful interventions, or failed to gain the cooperation of consultees.

Although all external consultants can expect a period of time between formal entry into the organization and acceptance by organizational members, the time required for acceptance can vary as a function of several factors. Many times, characteristics of the consultant can impede or facilitate acceptance. For example, similarity to organizational members in background, training, or outside interests can sometimes aid informal acceptance. Another factor that can facilitate acceptance is a reputation based on previous consultation work or expertise in a particular field. Both may enhance the consultant's status and consultee willingness to participate in consultation.

In addition to characteristics of the consultant, such as similarity to consultees or reputation, characteristics of the organization and critical incidents that take place during the entry phase can also have an impact on informal acceptance of the consultee. With regard to characteristics of the organization, some organizations may be more open to new ideas and more readily accepting of the consultant. This attitude may grow out of an administrator's consistent rewarding of innovative subordinates or an organizational history of successful innovations. Another organizational factor that can facilitate acceptance is crisis (Caplan, 1970). As it becomes clear that some action is needed to alleviate a crisis situation, organizational resistance to change may be lowered, allowing the consultant to progress more quickly from entry to problem solving.

Often a critical incident can have a substantial impact on the consultant's acceptance, such as a successful instance of direct service that makes the consultant more credible. For example, a consultant worked in a school for several months and achieved only minimal entry, working largely with one teacher and on relatively trivial problems. One day, in passing, the teacher mentioned difficulty with several fourth graders who had failed to master their times tables. The consultant volunteered to work with them for a brief period each day and discovered that the students were overwhelmed by the task and had no idea where to begin on a task so large. The consultant brought in some index cards and taught the children to make flashcards, to break down the memorizing into small units, and how to rehearse. After a few sessions, the children had made substantial progress with their multiplication tables. Within a few weeks, the consultant experienced a dramatic leap in the number of teachers seeking her services and later learned that the fourth-grade teacher had told several teachers of the consultant's work and its effectiveness. This successful instance of direct service had provided the staff with evidence of the consultant's credibility in dealing with classroom problems. In another situation, a counseling psychologist worked with police officers on stress management and also consulted with community groups regarding the design of drug prevention programs. The success of his direct service to police officers in the stress management area resulted in numerous referrals

---

Student Learning Activity 6.1

If you are entering a new training placement, keep a journal where you record your impressions of the organization, leaders, leadership style, communication patterns, and the common concerns and issues that you observe among staff members. Also record the basis of your impressions. At the close of your placement, look back at your journal. How has your perspective changed? What misconceptions did you have? In what areas were your impressions on target? Also note how staff perceptions of you have changed over time.

from officers for consultation with community groups interested in drug prevention programs.

Consultees' apprehension about the consultant also can be decreased by interactions that provide a means for the consultant and consultee to get to know one another prior to consultation (Caplan, 1970; Scholten, 1990). For example, the consultant may give a lecture or workshop for potential consultees and, afterwards, talk informally with the group. The consultant might attend organizational social events or have lunch in the staff lounge and initiate conversation with potential consultees. These contacts can help assure consultees that the consultant is friendly and interested in the organization and its members. Also, concerns about consultation may be breached informally by consultees, and the consultant can clarify any misconceptions about himself or herself or consultation.

To summarize, entry for the external consultant is not a single step, but an ongoing process that has both formal and informal components. Successful entry is characterized by a progressively deeper understanding of the organization on the part of the consultant, increased trust and acceptance of the consultant by members of the consultee organizations, and a clear, mutual understanding of the objectives, methods, and procedural details of consultation by both parties.

Internal Consultants. Many models of consultation assume that the consultant is from outside the organization in which he or she is consulting. However, it is not unusual for a professional with specialized skills in an organization to be asked to act as an internal consultant. For example, a psychologist in a university counseling center might be asked to provide consultation to residence hall directors about student matters (Cooper, 2003), or a child psychiatrist might be asked to consult in the pediatric surgery department about children's reactions to surgery (Caplan, 2004).

In one sense the consultants described in these examples have already accomplished entry because they are members of the organization in which they consult. However, ignoring entry issues completely and moving immediately into the problem-solving aspects of consultation can lead to difficulties. Several aspects of both formal and informal entry are of special concern to the internal consultant.

With regard to formal entry, administrators may be less likely to question aspects of consultation before making a commitment because they are familiar with the consultant, although in another role. Thus, expectations on the part of the consultant and the organization may not be clearly defined, leading to misunderstandings later. Even if such detail is not called for by members of the organization, the internal consultant should delineate his or her role and clarify administrative expectations (Finc, Grantham, & Wright, 1979).

The formal introduction of the consultant to staff members also should not be ignored. Although internal consultants usually are known by their colleagues, their particular role as a consultant in a particular situation may not be understood. For example, a counseling psychologist who is assigned to the student development and counseling center may be acquainted with most of the persons in the student service organization. However, a formal explanation that this individual is to assume a consulting role with housing staff members to assist in resolving a vandalism problem may need to be made by the director of housing. This introduction provides the necessary sanction for consultation from the head of an agency, just as an announcement by the principal at a faculty meeting that a school counselor has been asked to provide consultation assistance to teachers as a part of a dropout prevention program legitimizes that activity.

Another issue to be dealt with during formal entry is the confidentiality of consultation. The internal consultant will be with an organization much longer than the external consultant and is more likely to interact with other individuals and groups within the organization (Pipes, 1981). This situation makes confidentiality concerns more acute. The internal consultant should take steps to assure that administrators understand that information remains confidential in consultation and also try to anticipate confidentiality issues that could place the consultant or consultee in uncomfortable positions or present conflicts of interest. For example, a school psychologist who has acted as a consultant to a teacher with classroom discipline problems may find that confidential information obtained while consulting is relevant to decision making about a child referred to special education services from that classroom, or the principal may ask for information to be used in evaluating that teacher. Formal entry into the consultation process is an opportunity to deal with confidentiality issues before critical situations arise.

Like formal entry, informal acceptance also is more easily achieved by the internal consultant. He or she may already know consultees or, at the least, be perceived as similar to the consultee in an important way. However, this advantage is gained at the loss of role clarity (Lippitt & Lippitt, 1978). It is important that internal consultants spend time clarifying their role as a consultant and distinguishing it from their role within the organization, particularly when the other role(s) involve direct service. For example, when a school counselor or school psychologist acts as a consultant, there may be the expectation that he or she eventually will take responsibility for the problem by providing counseling or testing the child.

Initiation of a Consulting Relationship

A central premise of consultation is that two professionals with different areas of expertise can engage in more effective problem solving than would be possible if either worked alone.

However, a productive working relationship is not a given in consultation. One of the earliest activities in working with a new consultee should be the establishment of a positive working relationship. The components of this relationship have been identified in Chapter One—an egalitarian relationship characterized by open communication between the consultant and consultee, collaboration between the consultant and consultee at each phase of consultation, and confidentiality of all communication.

The first step in initiating a productive working relationship is a discussion of the roles the consultant and consultee will take in consultation.

This procedure assures that the consultee has an opportunity to express his or her preferences and that the consultant and consultee understand and agree on the basic parameters of consultation (Parsons & Meyers, 1984). An open discussion of the working relationship, initiated by the consultant, can provide a model to the consultee of the clear, open communication that should characterize later consultative communication, and agreement about roles is associated with more positive outcomes in consultation (Erchul, Hughes, Meyers, Hickman, & Braden, 1992).

Typically, this initial role structuring aims toward establishing a coordinate, nonhierarchical relationship between the consultant and consultee. This type of relationship is viewed as critical in assuring that a consultee freely expresses his or her views to the consultant, allowing a shared view of the problem to develop, as well as a solution that works for the consultee. However, consultants also need to be aware that the expectation for a nonhierarchical relationship varies among cultures (see Chapter One) and may also vary depending on the type of problem. For example, Graham (1998) found that consultants who were directive and provided specific advice were perceived more favorably than those who were collaborative in situations where consultees came to the consultation with a clear idea of the problem and had already tried their own solutions.

A second important component of role structuring involves establishing an agreement for action. Consultation is aimed at altering a problem situation, resulting in change, which requires action on the part of *both* the consultant and consultee. As mentioned earlier, there may be the unspoken expectation that eventually the consultant will assume responsibility for the problem and its solution. Agreement regarding the extent of consultant involvement in implementation and the expectation for action on the part of the consultee should be established early.

Finally, development of the initial relationship should take place in such a way that termination is an expected result (Dougherty, Tack, Fullam, & Hammer, 1996). Although it may seem somewhat strange to talk of termination in the initial phase, it is important to immediately recognize the goal of developing a fully functioning, independent consultee.

Efforts at role structuring can prevent unspoken expectations from blocking successful consultation. For example, the consultant may assume that the consultee understands that he or she is to take an active role in problem solving, while the consultee perceives the consultant as an expert who is to solve the problem. Similarly, the consultant may assume that the consultee understands the importance of being open with the consultant, yet the consultee may be hesitant to be entirely truthful, especially when he or she believes that what is said may not be pleasing to the consultant.

Another source of misunderstanding is the consultee's experiences in working with other consultants who operate differently. The consultee may assume that all consultants operate in the same manner, and this can be a source of conflict that retards the consultation process.

Structuring role relationships also includes a discussion of ethical concerns, such as the confidentiality of communication and data collected within consultation. Consultees may have concerns that seeking consultation services is an admission of weakness, or they may feel that information divulged to the consultant will be passed on to their supervisors. Assurances that the content of consultation is confidential are seen as central to the free exchange of information and opinions that determines successful consultation. Agreements about the confidentiality of data collected through surveys, observations, and other assessment strategies also need to be reached.

Structuring role relationships and discussing confidentiality concerns are part of establishing a relationship with the consultee. So is providing an atmosphere in which the consultee feels accepted and comfortable. Because consultation involves interaction between consultant and consultee, consultants who are able to use their interpersonal skills to make such interactions rewarding for consultees will be more successful. The consultee who perceives the consultant as genuinely interested in him or her and the problem at hand is more likely to accept consultant help and ideas. Facilitative characteristics of the consultant and their role in consultation are discussed in more depth in the second half of the chapter.

Internal Consultants.   Initiation of a consulting relationship presents special concerns for the internal consultant. As with informal acceptance by staff members, the initiation of consultation with individuals may be easier for the internal consultant because of prior interactions with staff members. However, despite efforts during entry to distinguish the consulting role from other roles the human services professional plays in the organization, consultees may still fail to understand the nature of consultation. The internal consultant should not bypass a discussion of the parameters of consultation and the role-structuring steps outlined above because of familiarity with the consultee.

The following excerpts illustrate the use of role structuring by two consultants to clarify expectations about consultation. The first excerpt is part of a consultation session between a psychologist and a visiting nurse, and represents an example of role structuring by an external consultant. The second excerpt is from a consultation session between a school counselor and elementary school teacher. In this case, the consultant is internal to the consultee's organization and known to the consultee, but only in his or her role of providing counseling services to students. Both excerpts begin after the consultee has briefly described the problem.

Excerpt One, External

CONSULTANT: You're right, the population using your services has changed dramatically but the staff seem to be using the same approaches. It's time to take a look at the agency's responsiveness to Latino clients.

CONSULTEE: Most of us are very aware that we need some guidance. I'm happy to take a leadership role in implementing your suggestions.

CONSULTANT: I wish I had some magic answers for you, but it's important we develop a plan together. Lasting change is much more likely if you and your staff "own" the changes. I do have experience working with Latino clients, but keep in mind that my experience has been in an urban setting and this is a rural setting. Some issues, like language barriers, will be the same, but some issues will be different. Your staff will need to educate me.

CONSULTEE: You're right. I guess we're just anxious for simple answers to what's really a complex set of circumstances.

CONSULTANT: I can outline some of my ideas and ways that I can be helpful to you. But, I want a chance to hear what your staff has to say. It's a matter of all of us coming up with strategies that are feasible given your center's budget—whether it's updating staff skills, hiring bilingual therapists if they're available in this area, recruiting translators from the community, or some combination of strategies.

Excerpt Two

CONSULTEE: So that's my problem with Bobby. I know how to deal with his learning difficulties; it's his behavior that I have trouble handling. He sees how much further ahead all the other children are in reading and it frustrates him. He's the class clown. He'll do anything to get a reaction out of the other children.

CONSULTANT: You've really touched on an important aspect of working with students with learning disabilities. You've got to deal with the children's feelings about themselves as well as the academics. Not all teachers recognize that.

CONSULTEE: The other children avoid him. Of course, that just makes him do even sillier things to get their attention.

CONSULTANT: I think we could help Bobby learn a few more positive ways to get attention in your class. Would you be interested in working together on that?

CONSULTEE: I'd like that.

CONSULTANT: What I had in mind was two or three sessions, each lasting about 20 minutes or so, where we try to come up with some strategies for you to use to help Bobby.

CONSULTEE: That's fine, as long as the plans don't take too much of my time during teaching.

CONSULTANT: It's important that we devise some-thing that will work for you. That's why I suggested we work together. I don't know the details of how you manage your classroom, you're the expert in that area. Your input about the amount of time a plan would require and how the plan fits with your classroom is important.

CONSULTEE: Oh, I'd let you know if a plan took too much time.

CONSULTANT: Well, I'd want you to tell me. There's no point in coming up with ideas that are unworkable.

CONSULTEE: Sometimes it's easy to forget that there are twenty-five kids who need my time.

CONSULTANT: I know you take your commitment to your children seriously. Turning back to how we might work together, does that sound like a workable plan? Two or three sessions to brainstorm some ideas?

CONSULTEE: Yeah, I can use part of my planning period, if you're available during third period.

CONSULTANT: That would work out. I'm hoping that we can come up with a fairly specific plan in those sessions. There also might be some ways I can help you carry it out in the classroom. For example, cover your class if you need time to explain the plan to Bobby or meet with his parents.

CONSULTEE: Thanks, I'll keep that in mind.

CONSULTANT: One last thing about working together. I guess it goes without saying that our work together is confidential. Sometimes that aspect helps teachers feel more comfortable about having me in the class to observe or help carry out a plan.

CONSULTEE: Oh, that doesn't worry me. I've been teaching too many years to be worried about what people say about my classroom.

Assessment

The primary activity that takes place during the assessment stage is an examination of factors relevant to the problem that the consultee brings to

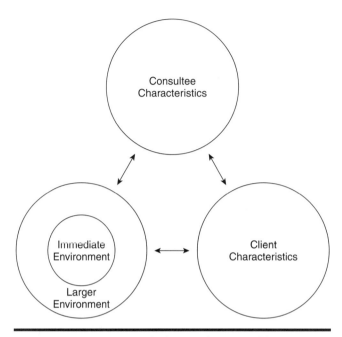

FIGURE 6.1   Domains in Which Consultation Problems
May Be Conceptualized

consultation. Another type of appraisal that can be considered part of assessment, the consultant's and consultee's assessment of each other, also plays an important role in consultation. Both aspects of assessment are discussed in this section.

With regard to assessment of the presenting problem, consultation models vary in terms of what is assessed. These differences are largely attributable to underlying assumptions within each of the models, discussed in earlier chapters, regarding the causes of human behavior and how people change. Figure 6.1 divides potential causes or maintaining factors in human behavior in terms of three major domains of assessment. These major domains are *consultee characteristics, environmental characteristics,* and *client characteristics.* Models of consultation differ in terms of the particular domain(s) assumed to be important in the change process, as well as the particular variables that are emphasized within a domain. For example, within operant learning theory, human behavior is explained largely in terms of changes in the imme-

diate environment, particularly consequences following a given behavior. Working within a consultation model that draws heavily from operant learning theory, such as Bergan (1977; Bergan & Kratochwill, 1990), the consultant would be likely to focus assessment and intervention on aspects of the immediate environment, such as schedules of reinforcement. Alternately, a consultant working with the Caplanian model would focus assessment on the attitudes, feelings, and skills of the consultee, because they are seen as the most important factors in problem resolution within this model. A consultant with a systems or ecobehavioral orientation (Gutkin, 1993; Sheridan et al., 1996) might focus on both the immediate environment and how that environment is affected by events in the larger environment.

The domains and factors within a domain that will be the focus of assessment represent a major choice in consultation. The choice of what factors are to be examined during the assessment phase has a major impact on subsequent stages of problem solving. Variables that are ignored during assessment most likely will not be considered in defining a problem and developing a solution. If a consultant and consultee assume that a problem lies in the client and design a problem solution based on that assumption, consultee actions or aspects of the environment that contribute to the problem will not be addressed, jeopardizing problem resolution. Or the consultant and consultee may ignore system-level factors important to problem resolution. To illustrate, a consultant began working with the classroom teacher in a children's psychiatric facility who had requested help in developing a social skills curriculum. Since the children in the classroom spent much of their time in the care of psychiatric nurses on the ward, the consultant and consultee planned to request assistance from the nurses to assure that skills taught in the classroom were reinforced on the ward. However, in developing the program, the consultant failed to consider the ideological differences between the teacher, who used a behavioral approach, and the nurses, who worked within a psychoanalytic framework. The program failed to gain the backing of the nurses once it was implemented, and the children's gains were minimal. Another consultant found that her efforts to assist a school district to mainstream students with behavior disorders failed because she had not considered teachers' reluctance to accept disruptive students when a district-wide teacher observation system had been implemented and linked to merit pay.

With increasing cultural diversity in the United States, it has become essential that the assessment phase include a consideration of cultural factors that may be factors in the problem situation addressed in consultation. Quinn and Jacob (1999) recommend that traditional assessment be supplemented with a cultural inquiry process that examines ways in which cultural differences contribute to problematic situations with clients. They provide examples of questions that are important in understanding student problems in a school context. Their list of questions has been broadened and adapted for more general use in consultation:

- What cultural assumptions of the consultee organization might be contributing to the problem situation?
- What perceived imbalances of power might be contributing to the problem situation?
- How might (mis)interpretation of the client's culture be contributing to the problem situation?
- Are language barriers contributing in some way to the problem?
- What conflict in styles of communication might be contributing to the problem situation?
- How might value differences between the consultee and client be contributing to the problem situation?
- To what extent are issues of transition, such as recent immigration, contributing to the problem?
- To what extent is the problem behavior considered normal within the client's culture?
- What are the cultural strengths that can be used in addressing the problem? [Some of these questions were based on the suggestions of Pinderhughes (1989) and Diller (1999).]

Because a wide range of factors may have an impact on a problem situation, the consultant and consultee should begin assessment with a broad consideration of all factors that might be important in correctly designating the problem and designing its solution. *A priori* rejection of a

---

Student Learning Activity 6.2

With a partner, formulate a problem situation that you might encounter in consultation. Tape record a five minute roleplay where one of you is a consultant and ask the consultee about various aspects of the problem situation. Listen to your session. What domains did you touch upon in your assessment?

What domains and factors within domains did you ignore? Discuss the same problem situation with others and ask what types of information they would ask for from a consultee when assessing a similar situation.

domain of assessment, or potentially important variables, on the basis of the consultant's or consultee's preconceived notion of the problem and what contributes to it will lower the probability of a correct solution. As in counseling (Ivey, 1983), one possible goal of consultation is to help the consultee view the problem in a more complex way than would be possible without the consultant (Caplan & Caplan, 1993; Sandoval, 1996, 2004). Table 6.1 provides examples of factors that might be considered in each of the three domains of assessment.

While the consultant and consultee assess factors relevant to the problem situation, another type of assessment is also taking place—the consultant and consultee are learning more about each other. As the consultee describes the problem for which he or she is seeking consultation, the consultant is assessing aspects of the consultee that will influence the consultation process. For example, does the consultee perceive a child's misbehavior as a result of poor parental control or as a result of poor classroom management? Does the agency manager seeking help in increasing employee morale view the problem as the employees' or as a result of his overcontrol of their duties? Have previous interventions the consultee describes been simplistic, or do they show a high

TABLE 6.1   Examples of Concerns within Each of the Three Domains of Assessment in Consultation

CLIENT CHARACTERISTICS

- What client behaviors are of concern?
- How are client cognitions contributing to the problem?
- If the client is a child, are there developmental issues that must be considered?
- How does the client perceive the consultee?
- What cultural factors need to be considered in developing a definition of the client's difficulties?

CONSULTEE CHARACTERISTICS

- Is the problem one of lack of knowledge, skill, objectivity, and/or confidence?
- How does the consultee view the problem?
- What are the consultee's expectations for self and client?
- What intervention skills does the consultee possess?
- What types of treatment are acceptable to the consultee?

ENVIRONMENTAL CHARACTERISTICS— IMMEDIATE ENVIRONMENT

- What aspects of the environment are reinforcing or maintaining the client's behavior?
- What resources are available that could be used in resolving the problem?
- What constraints in the immediate environment must be considered?

ENVIRONMENTAL CHARACTERISTICS— LARGER ENVIRONMENT

- Are there structural aspects of the environment that are contributing to the problem?
- Are there factors outside of the immediate environment that are affecting client behavior?
- Are the changes proposed for the client or consultee consistent with organizational norms and expectations?
- Are the proposed changes and change strategies culturally adaptive for this client and consultee?

skill level on the part of the consultee? Are cultural differences affecting the consultee/client or consultant/consultee relationship? In each case, the consultant's assessment may result in changes in his or her interactions with the consultee. In some instances, the consultant and consultee may spend additional time on problem definition and client assessment if their perceptions of the problem differ. The consultant who works with a less-skilled consultee may use more examples and explanations when outlining a proposed intervention plan or may provide more support to the consultee during implementation. The consultant who suspects that cultural differences in communication styles are affecting consultation process may adapt his or her questioning style, time in relationship building, or nonverbal behaviors to better fit the consultee (see Chapter One).

The consultee also assesses and forms judgments during this phase about the consultant, his or her style, the probability that the consultant will be able to aid in solving the problem, and what the consultant wants. These judgments can influence the process and outcome of consultation.

Tombari and Bergan (1978) found that consultant questions consistent with a medical or behavioral model of consultation elicit consultee definitions of the problem that are consistent with that viewpoint and also affect consultees' estimates of how effective they will be in resolving the problem. For example, consultant questions that focus on the client's behavior and the consultee's actions in relation to the client's behavior elicit definitions of the problem that focus on the client's behavior and lead the consultee to view the problem as more likely to be solved.

Particularly if the consultant is from a different cultural group than the consultee, the consultee's appraisal may include an assessment of the consultant's cultural sensitivity and willingness to explore the role of cultural differences, ethnicity, or racism in the problem situation. Both Gibbs (1980) and Duncan (1995) have suggested that African American consultees may appraise European American consultants' cultural awareness and ability to work with minority consultees and

clients, and then use this as a basis for deciding whether to continue or terminate consultation.

In an intriguing analogue study on this topic, Rogers (1998) examined the effect of ethnicity and consultant verbal behavior on perceptions of consultants' competence and multicultural sensitivity. Prospective teachers watched a videotape of a mock consultation session in which the ethnicity of the consultant, the ethnicity of the consultee, and the verbal behavior of the consultant varied. In one condition, the consultant followed up when the consultee expressed concerns about racism. In a second condition, the consultant responded empathetically to the consultee, but did not follow up or acknowledge the consultee's concerns about racism. Across all raters, who were either African Americans or European Americans, the race-sensitive consultant was viewed as more competent and multiculturally sensitive than the consultant who did not respond to the consultee's concerns about racism.

The following excerpt illustrates the difference between an empathetic response that responds directly to cultural concerns and one that does not:

CONSULTEE: I've brought my concerns about overprescribing of stimulant medication to African American boys to the director on several occasions, but she seems to brush my concerns aside.

CULTURE-BLIND CONSULTANT RESPONSE: You don't feel "heard" by the administration, despite bringing up important issues on several occasions.

CULTURALLY SENSITIVE CONSULTANT RESPONSE: Are you sensing there may be a lack of concern or insensitivity regarding the needs of African American clients? Perhaps a willingness to see the problem as "in" the child instead of examining whether schools and the agency currently meet the needs of African American children?

Problem Definition and Goal Setting

As the consultant and consultee examine variables that might be relevant to the presented problem, a more complex conceptualization of the problem should emerge. Both research and theoretical works characterize this stage as crucial in consultation. Bergan and Tombari (1976) found the best predictor of behavioral consultation outcome was definition of the problem as a discrepancy between desired and actual behavior in the client. Research by Curtis and Watson (1980) suggests that less skilled consultants differ from highly skilled consultants in the amount of time spent clarifying and defining the problem. Less skilled consultants appear to focus more quickly on planning a strategy to cope with what may be an ill-defined problem.

Failing to spend sufficient time in problem definition may result in a situation where the consultant and consultee misdirect their efforts because they are solving the wrong problem (Raiffia, 1968). Two examples illustrate this notion. A consultant was called in to assist a teacher in a sheltered workshop for adults with mental retardation. One of the clients had recently started to ask for soft drinks almost incessantly during the workday. The consultant and consultee developed a plan to use reinforcement and response cost to decrease the client's requests for drinks. Only later did the consultant and consultee discover the true problem—the client had recently been placed on a medication whose side effects included increased thirst. Once the client's medication was changed, the drink requests decreased dramatically. In another consultation case, a consultant assisted an organization in implementing a mandatory drug-testing policy for all employees to cut down on absences and increase productivity. Although the program identified a few substance-abusing employees, it did not achieve its intended effects on absenteeism and productivity. When another consultant reconceptualized the problem as one of low employee morale due to an authoritarian management style and the boring, repetitive nature of most employees' jobs, the organization initiated quality circles and other programs designed to allow employees more control over their work. Absenteeism decreased and productivity showed a marked increase.

How does the consultant avoid solving the wrong problem? As suggested by Dunn (1981)

and others who have studied change (e.g., Watzlawick, Weakland, & Fisch, 1974), this may be the least understood aspect of problem solving. One key factor in successful problem definition may be a broad-based assessment in which the consultant and consultee spend sufficient time on assessment to consider how a broad range of factors may be related to the problem.

A second factor, suggested by Monsen and Frederickson (2002), may be the use of "accessible reasoning" (Robinson & Halliday, 1988), making it clear to the consultee how the information he or she is sharing is being incorporated into a hypothesis about the cause of the problem and a matching plan of action. By making reasoning accessible, consultees have a chance to correct any consultant misperceptions and provide additional input so that the consultant and consultee together develop a higher-quality representation of the problem.

A clear and specific statement of the problem and objectives for resolving it should be the culmination of the problem definition stage. Such a statement can facilitate successful problem solving in several ways: (1) it assures that all parties involved have a clear understanding of what is viewed as the problem and what objectives they are working toward, (2) such specificity suggests techniques for measurement, which facilitates development of an evaluation strategy, and (3) an explicit statement of objectives assures the consultant that the consultee's expectations regarding change are realistic. Two sample statements that provide a problem definition, state the focus of interventions to resolve the problem, and give specific objectives relevant to the interventions follow. Both are statements of the problem that might be developed by a consultant and used to assure that the consultant, consultees, and other organizational members agree on the specifics of a problem and plans to resolve it. The first example refers to a situation where a consultant is asked to help determine the cause of a high turnover rate in volunteers and assist the organization in developing a program to reduce the turnover rate. In the second example, a consultant was called in to help develop a more effective in-school suspension program. However, after meetings with several administrators and teachers, the consultant and consultees redefined the problem as one of schoolwide difficulty with classroom management that resulted in a high referral rate for in-school suspension.

Problem #1

Services to adults with mental retardation have been disrupted because of a 60 percent turnover among sheltered workshop volunteers. This turnover appears to be due to:

1. Selection of volunteers who are unaware of the behavior, mannerisms, and problems of adults with mental retardation.
2. Poor communication between professional staff and volunteers.
3. Lack of a support network for volunteers, including no systematic program for providing positive feedback and recognition.

Interventions will focus on reducing volunteer turnover.

Objectives

1. To alter the volunteer orientation process so that volunteers develop an understanding of the functioning of adults with mental retardation to facilitate volunteer self-screening.
2. To develop and implement a communications skill development program for volunteers and staff members.
3. To develop a budget for providing recognition lunches, plaques, certificates, and the like to volunteers by soliciting funds from local businesses, industries, and service organizations.

Problem #2

Teacher referrals have overloaded the in-school suspension program because of:

1. Lack of understanding by staff of the changing cultural values in the community served by the school.
2. Need for different classroom management strategies that are more effective with the population now served by the school.

Interventions will focus on reducing the rate of in-school suspension referrals.

Objectives

1. Teachers will be made aware of the values of the students in their classrooms as a result of a comprehensive program including speakers, workshops, and films addressing this concern.
2. Teachers will be systematically exposed to a classroom management program that includes individualizing classroom instruction, managing learning activities to reduce disruption, and empirically based principles of classroom management.

Strategy Selection

When the problem has been defined and a goal selected, the next step is the selection of a means for reaching the goal. Just as models of consultation vary in terms of their domains of assessment, the type of strategy typically employed also represents a major point of divergence among models. However, some general comments about strategy selection can be made.

First, one of the major premises of systems theory is *equifinality* (Katz & Kahn, 1978), that is, within a system, there are multiple means of achieving the same goal. The consultant should explore several strategies with the consultee and aid him or her in making a considered choice among alternatives. Increasing the ability of the consultee to develop alternatives and choose among them leads to more adaptive functioning on the part of the consultee and is an important aspect of the preventive nature of consultation. Another important aspect of the preventive nature of consultation is helping consultees identify and use resources that exist within the system that have not been previously utilized (Riley-Tilman & Chafouleas, 2003).

Three additional important factors are: (1) evidence to support a strategy's effectiveness (Hoagwood & Johnson, 2003; Kratochwill & Stoiber, 2002; Newman & Tejeda, 1996), (2) strategy integrity (Reynolds, Gutkin, Elliott, & Witt, 1984), and (3) strategy acceptability to the consultee (Witt,

Elliott, & Martens, 1984). Prior empirical evidence to support a strategy's effectiveness has always been important, but the movement to promote more widespread use of educational and psychological treatments validated through well-designed research (Hoagwood & Johnson, 2003) has made this consideration a critical concern for consultants. Strategy integrity refers to the extent to which interventions vary in how much they can be adapted or changed without an impact on their effectiveness. It is important that the consultant consider the level of understanding and skill of the consultee, as well as the ease of implementing particular intervention strategies in the consultee's work setting, when selecting among alternatives. Some interventions may be changed so much by the consultee to fit his or her skill level and environment that the treatment is no longer effective (Fuchs, Fuchs, Bahr, Fernstrom, & Stecker, 1990). For example, an employee incentive program that rewards productivity with increases in salary might be effective in one workplace where considerable money is available for merit pay, but ineffective in a setting where the amount of money available for merit increases is so small that the raises are meaningless. Similarly, a classroom teacher who has little training or experience in behavior modification may not implement a behavioral treatment effectively because he or she does not understand the importance of providing reinforcement only when the desired behavior is displayed and providing specific rather than general praise.

Several researchers also have proposed that the acceptability of a particular intervention to the treatment agent plays an important role in whether the treatment is implemented (Kazdin, 1984; Reimers, Wacker, & Koeppl, 1987; Witt & Elliott, 1985). Based on this premise, a sizable body of research has emerged concerning the acceptability of various treatments and the factors that affect persons' judgments of treatment acceptability. Much of this research has involved teachers' judgments about the acceptability of behavioral treatments for school children (Elliott, 1988) and, therefore, has important implications for consultants working in the schools. However, a portion of the research has focused on the acceptability of various treatments to parents (Frentz & Kelley, 1986; McMahon & Forehand, 1983), children themselves (Elliott, Witt, Galvin, & Moe, 1986; Shapiro & Goldberg, 1986), or psychiatric staff (Kazdin, French, & Sherick, 1981).

Several variables have been found to affect teachers' judgments about the acceptability of a particular intervention strategy or treatment. Elliott (1988) has divided these into four categories: consultant, consultee, treatment, and client variables. *Consultant variables* include how the consultant describes the intervention and the rationale given for treatment. For example, Witt, Moe, Gutkin, and Andrews (1984) found that teachers rated an intervention more highly when it was described in pragmatic terms rather than in humanistic or behavioral terms (e.g., describing staying in from recess as a logical consequence of not doing work versus an intervention important to the child's development, or as punishment to decrease inappropriate behavior). Other researchers have found that behavioral jargon can increase the acceptability of some interventions (Hyatt & Tingstrom, 1993). In another study, Conoley, Conoley, Ivey, and Scheel (1991) found that rationales that were individually formulated to match each consultee's perspective on a referral problem and its causes increased consultee ratings of treatment acceptability. *Consultee variables* that have been found to affect judgments of treatment acceptability include the consultees' years of experience, knowledge of behavioral techniques, and feelings of self-efficacy in their jobs (DeForest & Hughes, 1992; Hughes, Barker, Kemenoff, & Hart, 1993). Cultural values may also affect consultees' perceptions of treatment acceptability. For example, a consultee who values cooperation over competition may reject an intervention that singles out a particular individual for reward or censure and be more comfortable with an intervention that is targeted toward a group. *Client variables* thought to influence treatment acceptability include types of problems, such as acting out versus withdrawn behavior, and problem severity.

Treatment variables that have been found to be related to teachers' judgments of acceptability include the time required, type of treatment, and reported effectiveness in the research literature. Of these, the time required and type of treatment seem to have the strongest effects. Teachers predictably prefer interventions that require less time, but are more willing to accept larger treatment time commitments for problems they consider severe (Elliott, 1988). Teachers also prefer treatments that involve positive rather than negative treatment procedures (Witt, Elliott, & Martens, 1984). In one large-scale study of general and special education teachers' perception of a wide range of school-based interventions (Martens, Peterson, Witt, & Cirone, 1986), two categories of treatments were rated as most effective, easiest, and most frequently used. These were redirection of the student to appropriate behavior (e.g., telling the student to get back to work) and manipulating material rewards (e.g., behavior contract).

The above discussion gives some sense of the variables that may influence the consultees' judgments of treatment acceptability. But the consultant should not depend on research to determine what interventions are acceptable to a particular consultee. As noted by Elliott (1988) and Rosenfield (1987), there is considerable individual variability in consultees' reactions to a particular treatment. Consultants should be sensitive to consultees' beliefs about the causes of a problem and how behavior changes and should try to match treatment rationales to these beliefs (Conoley et al., 1991). In addition, the early stages of strategy selection should include a discussion with consultees about the types of interventions they have found to be successful and they would be willing to implement. As the consultant and consultee begin to discuss the specifics of a particular strategy, the consultant also should specifically inquire about the consultees' comfort level with the interventions that are considered. Some examples of how the consultant might discuss treatment acceptability issues with a consultee are presented in the following dialogues.

Excerpt One

CONSULTANT: So we both agree that the major focus of our work should be to decrease the amount of time that Sally spends off task, particularly settling down to her work once you've given an assignment.

CONSULTEE: Yes. Once she starts a task, she seems to be OK, but she has difficulty getting started. Sometimes, I'm amazed. I'll check on her 10 minutes after seatwork time has started and she's just put her name on the paper.

CONSULTANT: Yes, I saw that when I observed her during math. Before we discuss any strategies to get Sally started, I want to be sure that what we decide on is comfortable for you. If I've learned one thing through the years, it's that if an idea doesn't fit with a teacher's style and classroom, it won't work. So please, be sure and tell me if any of the ideas we come up with are unrealistic, or don't fit with your classroom.

CONSULTEE: I guess the most important issue for me is time. The kids do seatwork while I'm with a reading group, so I can't be running over to Sally to check on her work every few minutes. I'd disrupt the reading groups.

CONSULTANT: OK, so an important aspect of devising a plan is that it can't involve much of your time.

Excerpt Two

CONSULTANT: If we're seeing eye to eye here, a major concern for the bank is turnover in teller positions. Training is a considerable expense and even decreasing turnover in these positions by a small amount would save a lot of money. Plus, it's good for public relations if customers see familiar faces at the counter. Also, experienced tellers make less errors, so you've got another savings factor there.

CONSULTEE: That about sums it up. Tellers have the highest turnover rate of any position at the bank.

CONSULTANT: Good. I'm glad we have agreement on the problem. Now, what to do about it? Other banks have tried a number of ideas, such as longevity pay, increased flexibility in hours, more teller involvement in decision making about their jobs, contests, and team building experiences. But I need to have some ideas about what would be acceptable here and would fit your resources and management philosophy. Can you tell me a little bit about what you've considered in trying to address this problem in the past?

CONSULTEE: We tried a contest where customers could nominate tellers who had done an exceptional job. We called it the "Teller of the Month." I didn't like the program. I didn't like the idea that only one teller could win. We weren't recognizing everyone who did a good job.

CONSULTANT: Good. That gives me some ideas about what you want. You don't want a program that only lets one person get recognition or some kind of reward. But you do feel comfortable with a reward program?

CONSULTEE: Yes, but we've really got limited funds for that kind of thing. Also, I'm not sure that a simplistic solution like that will get the results we want.

CONSULTANT: It sounds like a program that involves more than just one facet would be acceptable to you. For example, we could work on having tellers feel that their jobs are more integral to the bank and also have some kind of incentive program. But you don't have a lot of money to play with. How do you feel about allowing employees extra time at lunch or breaks?

CONSULTEE: That's an idea. Or maybe even just trying to make breaks more pleasant. Our lounge is pretty dismal.

Some Practical Guidelines for Strategy Selection. We close this section by paraphrasing the guidelines offered by Zins and Erchul (1995) for selecting and implementing interventions in consultation. Although the original guidelines were formulated for school-based consultants, these general guidelines are useful in a variety of settings:

1. In general, implement positive intervention approaches before resorting to behavior suppression or reduction techniques.
2. Choose the least complex and intrusive intervention possible. Modifying existing prac-

tices rather than learning new skills is generally easier for consultees.
3. When a new skill must be learned by the consultee, design it to fit into current organizational structure and routines as much as possible.
4. Promote interventions that require less time, are not ecologically intrusive, and are seen by consultees as effective.
5. As a long-term strategy, help consultees access existing resources or develop new ones in their own organizations.
6. Focus intervention efforts on promoting change at the highest organizational level possible.

Implementation

In many ways, plan implementation is the moment of truth in consultation. Most of the other stages of consultation involve only the consultant–consultee dyad, but this stage involves the enactment of an action plan in a complex environment. No matter how thorough strategy selection and planning have been, it is likely that the plan derived during consultation will be in need of adaptation and adjustment to meet unanticipated problems. For example, one consultant had worked for several weeks with a teacher to develop a token economy for her class. During implementation, the teacher contacted the consultant and was quite upset. Small plastic chips had been used as tokens, and one child had become quite adept at pilfering others' tokens without detection. The intervention ran smoothly after the consultant and consultee decided to switch to checks on name cards in place of tokens. In another instance, a consultant from a community mental health center had to revise a plan for collegial governance in a small religious order when the bishop vetoed the idea. Consultees should be aware that unanticipated problems may occur and that such problems are not unusual or a sign of failure.

Frequent contact between the consultee and consultant can help assure that a plan is implemented successfully. It also provides support to the consultee at a time when the extra effort and alteration in routines and habits involved in change may lead the consultee to abandon the plan (Zins & Erchul, 1995). Some consultants have found that telephone calls or e-mails can effectively replace more time-consuming face-to-face contacts at this stage. However, consultees may not accurately perceive the extent to which they are implementing the plans developed in consultation (Robbins & Gutkin, 1994).

Research on consultee implementation of the plans developed during consultation suggests that implementation may be one of the most critical issues facing consultants. For example, Wickstrom, Jones, LaFleur, and Witt (1998) monitored consultee implementation of behavioral interventions developed to decrease disruptive behavior in elementary school classrooms. With their most stringent measure of implementation, teacher use of the planned consequence when the child displayed the undesirable behavior, teachers were only observed administering the planned consequence 4 percent of the time. Similarly, Noell (Noell, Duhon, Gatti, & Connell, 2002; Noell, Witt, Gilbertson, Ranier, & Freeland, 1997) found that consultee implementation of consultation plans was high when the consultant was present providing training, but unlikely to continue when the consultee implemented the intervention independently.

Recently, Noell et al. (2002) examined the impact of consultant follow-up meetings, and follow-up meetings with performance feedback, in increasing consultee implementation of planned interventions. They found that performance feedback was associated with better implementation than follow-up meetings without performance feedback. Performance feedback consisted of graphs portraying (1) the clients' behavior across each day of the intervention, and (2) the percentage of treatment components implemented by the consultee. Consultants provided these graphs to consultees in brief meetings and discussed how to improve implementation if the consultee was not implementing the intervention. Consultees rated consultants positively, suggesting that they did not perceive

the consultants' evaluation of their work as intrusive or overcontrolling.

Evaluation

For any procedure to be self-correcting, some indication of the match between desired and actual outcomes must be obtained. Within social science, the formal mechanism for this feedback is often termed evaluation. Two types of evaluation are important in consultation: formative evaluation and summative evaluation. *Formative evaluation* takes place during plan implementation; *summative evaluation* takes place after consultation has been completed.

Formative evaluation is often less formal than summative evaluation. Information is sought regarding how well the plan is working and whether adjustments must be made to the plan. One outcome of formative evaluation might be a decision to return to an earlier stage of consultation. The consultant and consultee might decide that the plan they had developed is unworkable and return to the strategy selection phase, or a consultee might decide that the original conceptualization of the problem as a lack of motivation on the part of the client was incorrect and that the client lacks the skills necessary to complete his or her work. In this case, the consultant and consultee might return to the problem definition stage.

Summative evaluation is generally more formal. Although one purpose of summative evaluation often is to provide corrective feedback, it is frequently associated with questions of overall effectiveness. What is important in summative evaluation depends on who desires the feedback. Consultees and organizations that hire a consultant will desire different information about consultation than consultants. Consultees are likely to be interested in the effectiveness of consultation to individual consultees and the overall organization, its benefits relative to its costs, and the satisfaction of consultees and clients. Consultants will be interested in these aspects of consultation, but may also desire additional feedback to help them understand processes or aspects of consultation that are of less interest to the consultee. For instance, was the consultant effective in establishing trust, transmitting an understanding of consultation to consultees, or working with particular types of consultees?

As Gallessich (1982) comments, many organizations may be resistant to evaluation of consultation interventions because of the cost and difficulty. However, by planning for evaluation early in the consultation process, by addressing issues of interest to both the consultant and consultee, and by defining goals of consultation precisely enough to allow measurement, information valuable to the consultant and consultee can often be gained through evaluation. Specific strategies for evaluation of consultation are discussed in depth in Chapter Eleven.

Termination

Termination refers to the cessation of consultation. Although termination generally takes place when the consultee and consultant agree that the problem that prompted consultation has been resolved, earlier termination is also an option. Two major reasons for early termination are discussed in literature. Caplan (1970) discusses instances where a more direct intervention strategy may be mandated by the seriousness of the problem or the need to act quickly. For instance, a client who is threatening suicide may necessitate direct intervention by the consultant rather than consultative services. Gallessich (1982) discusses the possibility of early termination when consultation is not progressing. She comments that in some instances termination may serve as a stimulus to both the consultant and consultee to define their values and professional goals.

As discussed earlier, termination should be addressed early in consultation. Gallessich (1982) and Dougherty, Tack, Fullam, and Hammer (1996) offer several additional guidelines for consultants to prevent termination difficulties. First, consultants may gradually transfer responsibilities to the consultees. This transfer of responsibility signals the consultant's exit and also prevents an abrupt change upon departure of the consultant that can be disruptive to consultees. Second, consultants should openly discuss their impending departure, validate the consultee's success, and encourage them to continue on their own. Third, a disengagement period where the consultant reduces his or her involvement on a trial basis may give consultees a chance to see if the problem is resolved or if he or she can make needed changes without consultant input. Lastly, rituals, such as a summary conference, a request that the consultee fill out an evaluation form, or a formal review of a case, can help signal or remind consultees that the end of consultation is imminent.

INTERPERSONAL PROCESSES

To date, no comprehensive model of the interpersonal processes in consultation and their relation to different consultative stages has been proposed, although some models of consultation, such as the mental health and social learning models, have emphasized the importance of interpersonal variables in consultation. The small amount of research that has been concerned with interpersonal processes in consultation reflects a variety of approaches and perspectives and often focuses on an isolated aspect of consultation (Horton & Brown, 1990). In the present discussion, consultation is treated as a particular instance of the more general process of helping, and the model of helping developed by Carkhuff (Carkhuff, 1969a, 1969b, 1983; Carkhuff & Anthony, 1979; Carkhuff & Berenson, 1977) is extended to consultation. Although the application of this model to consultation has not been empirically validated, aspects of the model have been extended to consultation previously (Brown, Wyne, Blackburn, & Powell, 1979; Conoley & Conoley, 1982; Meyers, 1981; Meyers et al., 1979), and both the relationship and problem-solving skills emphasized in the model have been related to consultation outcome (Bergan & Tombari, 1976; Maitland, Fine, & Tracy, 1985; Schowengerdt, Fine, & Poggio, 1976).

Overview of Carkhuff's Model of Helping

Carkhuff has proposed a generic model of helping that describes phases a helpee (person seeking assistance) progresses through in resolving a problem or achieving meaningful change. Also included in the model are helper (person providing assistance) actions that facilitate the helpee's progression through these phases.

In Carkhuff's model, providing assistance or information to a person will only be effective in bringing about change when the person: (1) feels that the helper has understood the problem, (2) perceives the need for action on his or her part, and (3) receives assistance in carrying out the desired change. Therefore, the effective helper not only has expertise in the particular content area in which he or she is offering assistance, but also has the interpersonal skills to facilitate ownership and action on the part of the helpee (Carkhuff, 1983).

Two types of interpersonal skills are important: responsive skills and initiating skills. Responsive skills include empathy, warmth, respect, and concreteness. Initiating skills include advanced levels of empathy and genuineness, as well as self-disclosure, confrontation, and immediacy. The next section will define these terms and illustrate how they might be used in consultation. However, a brief overview of Carkhuff's phases of helping is provided here as an advanced organizer.

Figure 6.2 depicts helpee phases in resolving a problem and helper actions that facilitate the helpee's progression through these phases. Initially, a helpee must be willing to devote time and energy to change. He or she must recognize that an undesirable situation exists and believe that there is some possibility of resolving it. The helpee must also believe the helper is capable of providing some assistance and be willing to share his or her experiences with the helper. In this prehelping phase, the helper's role is to respond in a way that promotes involvement on the part of the helpee. The helper is polite and pleasant and listens carefully to the helpee. He or she tries to see the problem from the point of view of the helpee and withholds judgment.

These actions lead the helpee to feel "listened to" and accepted by the helper. In turn, the helpee feels free to examine the problem in depth. During this exploration phase, the helper's role is to reflect the content, feeling, and meaning of the helpee's statements, and to prompt the helpee to be specific about his or her concerns.

After the helpee has fully explored the problem, the helper uses initiating skills to assist the helpee in viewing the problem in a more objective manner (Egan, 1994) and to establish a direction for problem solving. In this stage, the helper continues to respond empathetically to the helpee, but also uses self-disclosure, confrontation, and immediacy

PHASES OF HELPING

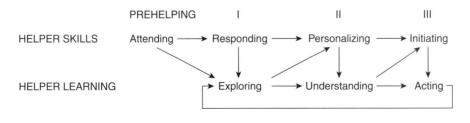

FIGURE 6.2 Carkhuff's Model of Helping
From Carkhuff, R. R., & Berenson, B. G. (1977). *Beyond counseling and therapy* (2nd ed.). New York: Holt, Rinehart & Winston. Used by permission of the authors.

to assist the helpee in personalizing the problem or understanding what aspects of the problem are within his or her control. The helper also prompts the helpee to formulate specific goals based on the personalized problem definition.

In the final stage, acting, the helpee develops and carries out plans to achieve these goals. Here, at last, the content area skills of the helper become important. The helper assures that the helpee's plans are sound and assists the helpee in implementing them. Recycling occurs once the helpee has acted. The helper and helpee evaluate the results of the helpee's actions by recycling through the exploring, understanding, and acting phases. They explore the results of the new course of action, develop new goals, or try new ways to achieve the original goals.

The preceding paragraphs provided only a brief overview of Carkhuff's model. In the following sections, Carkhuff's model is offered as a heuristic tool for understanding and discussing the role of consultant–consultee interaction in facilitating consultee problem solving. The discussion will be organized around three issues that reflect Carkhuff's model of helping: establishing the consultation relationship, facilitating consultee understanding of the problem, and facilitating action. For each of these topics, Carkhuff's model will be applied to consultation.

Before presenting Carkhuff's model, however, it is important to note that this model of helping and the description of interpersonal processes in consultation based on it reflect the concerns, values, and communication patterns that are normative within a European American perspective. As such, the model is most likely to be appropriate for consultees who share this perspective and less likely to be appropriate for consultees who hold different values and perspectives. Components of the model may be inappropriate for some cultural groups. For example, the extended eye of the SOLER model may be uncomfortable for some Latinos, Native Americans, and Asian Americans.

In the following presentation of Carkhuff's model, some brief comments about adaptation of the model for consultees from other cultures will be offered after the description of each phase. More extended discussion on adapting a consultation to fit the needs of consultees who hold different cultural values is provided in Chapter Seven. Consultants have the responsibility to match their helping skills with the needs of consultees from a range of cultural groups. Both Diller (1999) and Srebalus and Brown (2001) provide thorough discussions of culturally competent helping in the human services. These books may be useful to consultants in modifying assessment and intervention strategies for a range of non-European American consultees and clients.

Establishing the Consultation Relationship

Consultation culminates in goal-directed action on the part of the consultee. In order for goal definition, strategy selection, and action to take place, the consultee first must be willing to commit time and energy to identifying and resolving the problem. The problem situation must be explored in sufficient depth that the consultant and consultee understand the nature of the problem and reach agreement regarding the aspects of the problem that can be addressed through consultation. These preconditions for effective action are facilitated through the establishment of a good working relationship between the consultant and consultee.

The consultant's function at this point is to use the responsive skills of warmth, empathy, respect, and concreteness to facilitate the establishment of this relationship. Warmth refers to skill in communicating to the consultee that the consultant cares for and is committed to the consultee. It is conveyed by paying attention to the consultee and clearly showing interest in what he or she has to say. Empathy, or accurate understanding, is communicated primarily through restatements of the consultee's verbalizations. By restating the consultee's concerns, the consultant shows that he or she has grasped the verbal and affective content the consultee is trying to convey. It is also important for the consultant to convey respect for the consultee by suspending judgment and communicating that the consultee is valued despite any perceived self-deficits.

Warmth, personal respect, and empathetic understanding also are communicated through the consultant's nonverbal behavior. Egan (1994) uses the acronym SOLER to describe the attending behaviors that communicate concern for and interest in the consultee:

S—face the other person SQUARELY.
O—adopt an OPEN posture.
L—LEAN toward the other.
E—keep good EYE contact.
R—try to be "at home" or relatively RELAXED in the position.

Finally, nonverbal and verbal demonstrations of warmth, personal respect, and empathetic understanding must be coupled with concreteness. In the early phases of consultation, concreteness refers to skill in eliciting descriptions of specific experiences and feelings from the consultee rather than vague abstractions (Gazda, 1973).

To illustrate the foregoing ideas, let us consider a first-year junior high teacher who came to a consultant with some grave concerns about her teaching ability. Although the teacher discussed her problems very openly, it was still necessary to establish a basic relationship along the lines that Carkhuff describes. The consultant began simply by listening attentively and restating (empathic understanding), as is illustrated in the following excerpt:

T: I just became aware that you were working in a school this year as a consultant to teachers. Believe me, I could use some consultation or I'm going to need my own counselor full time.
C: Sounds like things aren't going well for you this year and you're kind of happy to have someone like me around.
T: Yeah...I'm a first-year teacher and to say the least things aren't going as planned. If they don't get better in a hurry I may go back to working in a bank.

C: At this point, things have already gone so badly you're beginning to think about getting out...going back to the bank?
T: Well, I really don't want to do that. What I want to do is teach. But I didn't know that schools could be such a zoo. The kids here are horrible.
C: You want to teach...but the kids are really getting to you.

Later in the same session:

T: There are times when I think I shouldn't be in this school. I feel so different.
C: How, specifically, do you feel different?
T: My ideas about teaching and my students seem to be different from other teachers in this school.
C: You feel a little odd because your views are different from the other teachers', but they are uniquely yours and that seems important to me.
T: Well, I'm glad to hear you say that.... I get the feeling that nobody else around here cares whether I have any opinions or not.

In the opening statements, the consultant responds empathetically to the consultee and merely listens. In response, the consultee continues talking, providing more information and bringing out another aspect of the problem, his or her disillusionment about teaching. In the later statements, the consultant uses concreteness to clarify the consultee's statements. Following the clarification, the consultant's demonstration of respect serves to increase consultee involvement and bolster the consultee's own self-respect.

At this point, the consultant's verbalizations have primarily served to establish a relationship between the consultant and consultee. By withholding judgment and reflecting the content of the consultee's verbalizations, the consultee feels "listened to" and free to discuss his or her own concerns. But in later phases of helping, movement toward problem resolution becomes important. The relationship between the consultant and consultee changes—the consultant becomes more genuine in his or her own actions and uses responsive skills to foster consultee understanding of the problem.

Adapting Responding Skills to Different Cultural Groups.

The effectiveness of the relationship-building skills outlined here can be expected to vary to the extent that the consultees' background and expectations are consistent with the Northern European cultural values that predominate in the United States. Although the consultant must approach each consultee as an individual and treat his or her guesses about a consultee's cultural background as determinations to be verified clinically (Diller, 1999), the following recommendations for adapting relationship-building skills are provided by Srebalus and Brown (2001):

- If consultees from other cultural groups avoid eye contact, be respectful of their preference. Avoid prolonged, intense eye contact with any consultee, especially Asian American and Native American consultees, who may view this as aggressive.
- If it appears that a consultee is adjusting the interpersonal space by moving his or her body forward or backward, moving a chair forward or backward, or turning to the side, do not move your own body or chair to readjust the interpersonal space.
- Be aware that cultural groups vary in the extent of hand gestures, smiles, head nods, and comfort with minimal encouragers (versus silence). You may need to modify your typical interaction style to make the consultee more comfortable.
- Tracking what the consultee is saying verbally and nonverbally is an essential skill for all helping groups.

Concepts from the Consultation Literature.

Several authors within consultation have suggested that relationship-building skills play an important part in consultation (Brown et al., 1979; Conoley & Conoley, 1982; Gutkin & Curtis,

1990; Meyers, 1981). In one of the few research studies on this topic within consultation, Schowengerdt et al. (1976) found that the facilitative characteristics of school-based consultants accounted for a major portion (44 percent) of the variance in consultee satisfaction. The consultant who exhibited warmth, understanding, and empathy when interacting with the consultee was more likely to have had a significant impact. This finding was confirmed by Maitland et al. (1985), who also found that consultant facilitativeness was related to problem resolution in consultation.

Another concept that has been discussed in the context of establishing a consultative relationship is interpersonal or social power. Generally, a nonhierarchical relationship between the consultant and consultee is seen as one of the cornerstones of the consulting relationship (e.g., Caplan, 1970; Gutkin & Curtis, 1990; Meyers et al., 1979, 1993) for several reasons. First, it assures the free exchange of ideas and opinions. When the consultee is hesitant to express his or her own views of the problem situation, is inhibited in suggesting how principles and ideas brought up by the consultant might apply in a particular situation, or does not share his or her reservations with the consultant, it is unlikely that an effective plan will be designed and carried out. Second, when the consultee takes an active role in understanding the problem and developing a solution, it is more likely that he or she will feel some ownership for the problem and its solution. By minimizing feelings of coercion through collaborative problem solving, the consultee is more likely to carry out whatever action plan is developed during consultation. Finally, active participation is seen as a means of increasing the probability that the consultee will generalize techniques used in consultation to similar situations in the future.

Despite the fact that the consultant has no supervisory or formal power over the consultee, other types of power have potential impact on the consulting relationship. The social bases of power proposed by French and Raven (1959) provide a useful framework for understanding how power and influence operate in the consulting relationship (Erchul & Raven, 1997; Martin, 1978).

French and Raven (1959) and Raven (1965) identified six forms of social power that are operative in interpersonal relationships. These are reward power, coercive power, legitimate power, expert power, referent power, and informational power. *Reward power* refers to person B's perception that person A is capable of giving him or her access to desired or needed resources contingent on some desired behavior. *Coercive power* includes and extends beyond reward power and is based on the perception that person A can reward or punish B. *Legitimate power* is exercised when person B allows person A to influence him or her because of a belief by person B that person A has a legitimate right to control his or her actions. These three sources of power, reward power, coercive power, and legitimate power, form the basis for supervisory or line authority in our society (Martin, 1978). As such, they are typically not sources of influence in consultation, since the consultant does not have line authority over the consultee.

Three other types of power that are operative in interpersonal relationships are potential sources of influence in consultation. *Expert power* is person B's perception that person A has certain knowledge or skills that are necessary for person B to accomplish his or her goals. *Referent power* is based on person B's perception that A possesses characteristics similar to B or that B would like to possess. When a consultant possesses referent power, the consultee identifies with the consultant and is more likely to internalize the consultant's beliefs, attitudes, and actions as his or her own. A final source of power that is also available to consultants is *informational power*. This source of power was added by Raven (1965) and is somewhat similar to expert power. Unlike expert power, informational power is not a characteristic of the person, but a characteristic of the information presented. When the consultant is able to offer information that is perceived as relevant by the consultee, regardless of whether or not the consultant is perceived as an expert, he or she gains additional influence.

An update and expansion of French and Raven's original typology (Raven, 1992, 1993) led Erchul and Raven (1997) to propose that other

forms of social power are also operative in consultation. Erchul and Martens (2002) have incorporated elements of Raven's revised power bases into a model of consultation and proposed that a primary task of the consultant is to lead the exchange of information in consultation such that the consultee's information about the presenting problem and the consultant's expertise both shape the conception of the problem and proposed solution that are developed during consultation.

In a series of survey-based studies, Erchul and his colleagues (Erchul, Raven, & Ray, 2001; Erchul, Raven, & Whichard, 2001; Erthul, Raven, & Wilson, in press) have investigated the forms of influence that are seen by consultants and consultees as effective in achieving this task. These studies have confirmed that expert, referent, and informational power are seen as important means by which consultants influence consultees. They characterize these as "soft power bases" because they are not coercive influence strategies, but depend on the consultee's perception that the consultant has expertise relevant to the problem at hand and the consultant's ability to establish a positive working relationship with the consutee.

Does the notion that consultants should try to lead the consultee mean that relationship-building skills are unimportant in consultation? No, the converse is true. As in counseling, consultants have only indirect sources of influence open to them and are largely dependent on their interpersonal effectiveness in encouraging consultees to engage in effective problem solving.

Facilitating Consultee Understanding

The issues discussed in the previous section were concerned with facilitating consultee involvement and exploration of the problem. But merely involving the consultee in consultation does not bring about change, as pointed out by Carkhuff and Berenson (1977):

> *Responding only to what is presented by the helpee is not enough. The helper must be able to organize the resulting helping exploration to give the*

helping process direction. More specifically, the helper must make the process goal directed. The helper's ability to appropriately initiate may be even more important than his or her ability to respond, in the sense that without initiating the helpee never gets to where he or she needs to be.... The determination of goals concerning where the helpee needs or wants to be, and getting there, wait upon helper initiatives. (p. 153)

Once a basic relationship has been established with the consultee, the nature of consultant–consultee interaction changes. The consultant's verbalizations move the consultee toward understanding his or her degree of personal control and responsibility in the problem situation. A personalized understanding or definition of the problem is necessary if the consultee is to perceive a role for himself or herself in problem resolution. This point is particularly important in consultation. Because the problem involves a client, or third party, consultees may focus on the problem as it relates to the client, rather than focusing on the aspect of the problem that they can control. When the focus of problem exploration is on aspects of the problem the consultee cannot control and no connection is drawn between the actions of the consultee and problem resolution, it is unlikely the consultee will perceive a need for action.

Within Carkhuff's model, there are a variety of strategies to assist helpers in seeing a role for themselves in the formulation of a problem and it's solution. Among these strategies are self-disclosure, advanced accurate empathy, summaries, and confrontation (Carkhuff, 1983; Egan, 1994).

Self-disclosure can be helpful by encouraging the consultee to more freely share his or her own feelings and thoughts. In the early stages of facilitating consultee understanding, it is important that the consultee feel comfortable exploring all aspects of the problem and self-disclosure may be used as one strategy to encourage the consultee. The following excerpt illustrates the use of self-disclosure to encourage further consultee reflection:

CONSULTEE: There's just a limit to what I can do with this many clients. I feel myself burning

out and I wonder if it's worth it and I made the right career choice.
CONSULTANT: I think all human services staff feel a bit overwhelmed in the beginning. I know I struggled with where to draw the line with all the needs my clients brought to me. But I found a balance and I'm confident you can too.
CONSULTEE: Sometimes it's so discouraging. Maybe it's just easier to turn your back on it all. But there are other times when I really feel I'm making a difference.

Summaries are particularly useful in moving consultees toward action. Combined with advanced accurate empathy, summary statements can express what has only been implied, tie together fragmented material, and identify themes. By making interpretations of the consultee's statements, the consultant assists him or her in adopting a more ob-

---

Student Learning Activity 6.3

Consider the following two consultant responses to a consultee verbalization occurring early in the consultative relationship:

CONSULTEE: This job is so stressful. I never imagined that managing a staff of seven could be so draining. Everyone has different agendas, no one seems to realize that I can't please everyone all the time.
CONSULTANT ONE: It sounds like you feel a lot of pressure to keep everyone happy and no one seems to realize how hard it is.
CONSULTANT TWO: You know just from talking to you for 10 minutes, I can see that you're not assertive enough and your employees have lost respect for you. I think one goal of our work together could be to help you become more assertive.

Within Carkhuff's framework, what type of response has Consultant One made? What errors has Consultant Two made? Why is Consultant One's response more likely to facilitate consultation?

jective and focused view of the problem and what action is needed.

This approach is demonstrated in the following excerpt:

C: Things haven't been going well for you this year and, in fact, they are extremely frustrating. Thus far in our session you've raised questions about your choice of a school, your skills in dealing with students, and underlying the whole thing has been your concern about your competency as a person in all areas.
T: That's right. You know it's all so overwhelming. Things just couldn't be worse. (sigh)
C: Things seem pretty bad now...hopeless.
T: Yeah, if I could just get on top of something, particularly my classroom.
C: So right now your classroom discipline seems to be the most important thing to you.

By summarizing and specifying the parameters of the situation, the consultant causes the teacher to focus upon the global nature of the problem. Then, out of this series of communications emerges a primary concern: classroom discipline. The consultee is now ready for goal setting, strategy selection, and action.

Confrontation occurs when the consultant points out discrepancies between consultee verbalizations and behavior, underlying effect and cognitive content, or consultant and consultee experiences (Carkhuff, 1969b). Confrontation is used only when the consultant feels it will lead the consultee to understand the problem more fully.

In most cases, direct confrontation is less desirable than more tentative, indirect confrontations. The following two statements contrast direct and tentative confrontations:

DIRECT: You've told me that you have a good relationship with Jamaal, but in the interactions I've observed, you seem reluctant to praise him or recognize his accomplishments.
INDIRECT: I'm wondering if in addition to your affection for Jamaal, there isn't some anger or frustration at his episodes of defiance?

Adapting Personalizing Skills to Different Cultural Groups. The use of summaries is a key skill in facilitating consultee understanding. However, consultants need to be aware that the conceptualization of the problem that facilitates action on the part of the consultee may not be the same as the consultant's. Soo-Hoo (1998) has suggested that it is important for consultants in multicultural consultation to understand the consultee's frame of reference and then reframe the problem in a way that facilitates problem solution, but is also culturally consistent. For example, Soo-Hoo describes a consultation case in which a Filipino mother was overly protective of her son and stayed with him in the classroom all day. When the mother's presence was framed as a impediment to the child's independence (a child-rearing value that was not particularly important to the mother), the mother was unresponsive to efforts to address the situation. However, when her actions were recognized as coming from a need to protect the child from the dangers of a new country, and his gradual separation from her was framed as a graduated attempt to have him learn how to protect himself, the mother became actively involved in the intervention.

Consultants should be aware that for many cultural groups, confrontation is inappropriate. Unless fully acculturated, confrontation should not be used with Asian Americans, Latino, and Native American clients (Srebalus & Brown, 2001). In addition, restatements that include content about feelings may be inappropriate for persons from cultural groups where self-control is highly valued, such as Native Americans and Asian Americans.

Concepts from the Consultation Literature. Consultant skills in assisting the consultee to see a role for himself or herself in resolving whatever problem is brought to consultation, although a critical part of consultation, have not been discussed extensively in the literature. However, the results of three studies (Bergan, Byrnes, & Kratochwill, 1979; Cleven & Gutkin, 1988; Tombari & Bergan, 1978) suggest that the content of consultant verbalizations can affect both the way that consultees conceptualize problems and their expectancies for solving problems.

Tombari and Bergan (1978) and Bergan, Byrnes, and Kratochwill (1979) found that when consultants focused on events and actions controllable by the consultee (e.g., the client's behavior and environmental variables affecting it), consultees were more likely to focus on these aspects in their definition of the problem and see the problem as more likely to be solved. Cleven and Gutkin's (1988) study suggests that this effect can be enhanced when consultants make explicit references to the process they are using in assisting the consultee to define the problem. For example, a consultant working with a teacher concerned about an inattentive student might state, "In helping Robin, it's important that we specify very precisely the types of problems you are seeing in the classroom." More recently, Gutkin (1993) has suggested that integrating explicit memory aids such as a sheet that the consultant and consultee fill out as they progress through the stages of problem solving may facilitate consultee's skills in problem analysis.

Facilitating Action

The skills emphasized in the two previous sections have focused primarily on involving the consultee and assisting him or her in "owning" the problem or seeing a need to act. Only when both of these conditions have been met is the consultee ready for action. At this time, the consultant continues to use responsive skills to maintain and deepen consultee involvement and understanding, but also uses skills in his or her particular content area to assist the consultee in developing and implementing a workable solution to the problem (Carkhuff, 1983).

This process begins with assisting the consultee in defining his or her goal in objective and measurable terms and assuring that the goal is achievable (Carkhuff & Berenson, 1977). One way this task can be accomplished is to ask questions that prompt the consultee to focus on specific aspects of his or her goal, such as who, what, where, when, and how. Next, the consultant as-

sists the consultee in exploring alternatives for reaching the goal by prompting the consultee for alternatives or suggesting alternatives when the consultee is unable to provide them. Finally, the consultant assists the consultee in choosing between alternatives on the basis of how each alternative fits with the consultee's values (Carkhuff & Anthony, 1979). This process is illustrated in the following interchange between a consultant and staff at a drug treatment center.

CONSULTANT: We have pretty much agreed that the current program of treating offenders referred to the center just isn't getting the job done; the recidivism rate is just too high.

STAFF MEMBER ONE: Yeah! And we aren't doing a thing to prevent the problem in this community either. But given our mission, I suppose that prevention programs are out of the question.

DIRECTOR: Perhaps not. But for now, let's focus on getting a more effective treatment program together.

STAFF MEMBER TWO: That would be a big step. I get tired of seeing some of these people walk through the door. It's frustrating…just makes me think we are spinning our wheels.

STAFF MEMBER THREE: We do have some successes though. I think our first job is to determine who benefits from what we're doing right now. I don't want to throw the baby out with the bath water.

CONSULTANT: That's a good point! It's a good idea to retain what you are doing right, and I agree that some people are being helped, but a lot aren't. Based upon the data we have collected, the younger offenders seem to be returning the most often. However, some of those over 21 are getting back into drug abuse and being sent here as well. Maybe the best plan of action is to work with one group or the other.

DIRECTOR: Well, I opt for the younger group at this time. I think that there are some alternatives to our current individual and group therapy programs that may be helpful to this group, such as family therapy and working with school personnel.

STAFF MEMBER TWO: I'd like to see us try to establish some support groups in the schools as well. I've found that a lot of the kids don't have many friends, and they use drugs and alcohol either to be one of the gang or to escape the reality of their loneliness.

CONSULTANT: There seems to be some consensus based upon the nodding heads that the younger group of offenders should be the target group, at least at first. That doesn't preclude focusing on the older group later, but I believe that you should take one group at a time. Now there is a matter of which path to take in reducing recidivism among the 16 to 21 year olds who come to the center. First, let's try to establish some realistic expectations about how much this problem can be reduced and then select some alternatives for pursuing that objective. Two have already been suggested.

When a particular action plan has been selected, the consultant then assists the consultee in operationalizing the goal by developing steps to meet the goal. The consultant and consultee discuss each step and the consultant monitors the consultee to see that he or she fully understands each step and has the skills needed to complete it. This monitoring and adjustment of each step are accomplished by reviewing, rehearsing, and revising each step of the program with the consultee prior to implementation. At the completion of each step, "recycling" begins as the consultant again uses responsive skills to help the consultee assess the action taken.

Adapting Initiating Skills to Different Cultural Groups.
The consultant may need to alter the interventions adopted during this phase in consultation to match the value systems of the consultee and client. For example, in cultures where cooperation is valued over competition, an intervention that rewards individual achievement would be inappropriate. Clients from some cultures may feel uncomfortable being singled out, or disclosing thoughts and feelings. As mentioned in an earlier section, consultants and consultees should also consider if the goals they select for the client are

consistent with his or her culture. For example, interventions to increase assertiveness and independence may place some clients, particularly females, in conflict with the expectations and values within their families and cultures.

Concepts from the Consultation Literature.
This last set of skills described by Carkhuff is similar to the problem-solving skills included in several models of consultations. For instance, Kurpius (1978) includes problem definition, exploration of alternatives, and planning effective behavior change programs as skills for the consultant.

Bergan's (1977; Bergan & Kratochwill, 1990) model of behavioral consultation discusses in some detail how the consultant can assist the consultee in setting measurable, objective goals and developing a plan through questions and summary statements covering specific topic areas. Bergan and Tombari (1976), working within this model, have identified several factors that are related to facilitating consultee plan implementation. Using multiple regression, they examined the contribution of three general classes of consultant variables (consultant efficiency, flexibility in applying psychological principles, and interviewing skill) to the occurrence of problem identification, plan implementation, and problem solution in school-based behavioral consultation. The authors found that consultant variables had their greatest impact on the problem-solving process at the problem identification stage. Problem identification was more likely to occur with consultants who were efficient, that is, who had a small time lag between a request for assistance and the initial interview and who were flexible in applying psychological principles. Flexibility was determined by examining the range of plans formulated by consultants over all cases. Presumably, the consultant with a narrow set of intervention techniques, who fit the case to the technique, rather than fit the intervention technique to unique variables in the case, was less likely to be successful.

One indicator of interviewing skill, message control, also contributed significantly to problem identification. Message control was defined as the proportion of elicitors (generally questions) to emitters (or statements). It appeared that effective consultants used a higher rate of elicitors, which served to direct the consultee to various topics relevant to consultation.

The extent to which consultants should direct and structure consultative problem solving has emerged as one of the more controversial topics in recent consultation research and writing. Gutkin and Curtis (1990) maintain that consultants must be experts on how to go about solving problems and that "the major responsibility of the consultant during consultation is to maintain and direct the collaborative problem solving process" (Gutkin & Curtis, 1990, p. 585). In keeping with this view, Erchul and his colleagues (1987; Erchul & Chewning, 1990; Erchul & Schulte, 1990) have found that behavioral consultants tend to structure and control verbal interaction and that higher levels of structure and control of verbal processes are associated with more positive perceptions of the consultant by consultees. Fuchs (Fuchs & Fuchs, 1989; Fuchs et al., 1990) also found that school-based behavioral consultation was more likely to lead to changes in target student behavior when prescriptive instructions were used to guide both consultant and consultee through the consultation process.

These findings seem to contradict the research pointing to the importance of interpersonal skills and support of the consultee in consultation (Hughes & DeForest, 1993; Schowengerdt et al., 1976). However, as noted in our earlier discussion of social influence and its role in consultation, this contradiction is probably more apparent than real, because it assumes that a consultant must choose between structuring consultation and establishing a positive, supportive relationship with consultee (Erchul, 1992). In fact, the research by Maitland et al. (1985) suggests the extent to which consultants use a problem-solving process that integrates behavioral problem solving *and* interpersonal facilitativeness predicts consultee satisfaction and professional growth, as well as problem resolution.

Culturally Sensitive Consultation

As noted earlier, Carkhuff's model of effective helping, and the description of interpersonal processes in consultation based on it, reflects communication patterns that are normative within a European American perspective. As such, the description is most likely to be appropriate for consultees who share this perspective. Modifications to the model may be necessary when interacting with consultees who hold different values and perspectives. Throughout our presentation, we have tried to provide examples of how the model might need to be adapted to various cultural groups that the consultant is likely to encounter in his or her work.

These examples are not meant to suggest that the consultant approach cross-cultural consultation in a "cookbook" fashion, making choices about which consultation approach and communication style to adopt solely on the basis of a consultee's apparent cultural background. As discussed in Chapter One, there are cultural value differences among the major cultural groups within the United States (Asian American, African American, European American, Hispanic American, and Native American), but there is also overlap and individual differences within each group. For example, Herring (1996) has characterized Native American families as adopting one of four cultural identities that vary in terms of their incorporation of traditional and European American cultural values.

SUMMARY

Several authors have described consultation as an activity comprised of particular stages (Meade et al., 1982). Though these descriptions of consultation vary in terms of the number and order of stages, they all conceptualize consultation within a problem-solving framework. Drawing from several descriptions of the stages of consultation, the activities of consultation include: (1) entry into an organization, (2) initiation of a consulting relationship, (3) assessment, (4) problem definition, (5) strategy selection, (6) strategy implementation, (7) evaluation, and (8) termination.

Another means of understanding the "how" of consultation is to examine the interaction of the consultant and consultee and its role in facilitating consultee action. No comprehensive model of interpersonal processes in consultation has been proposed. Therefore, Carkhuff's (1969a, 1969b, 1983) model of helping, which emphasizes the role of relationship building, initiating skills, and problem-solving skills in facilitating constructive action, was proposed as a general framework for understanding and interpreting consultant–consultee interaction and its role in consultation outcome.

TIPS FOR THE PRACTITIONER

1. Ask experienced consultants to share materials, such as letters of agreement, intervention plans, and evaluation materials with you. It is generally easier to modify materials that have been successful to fit your situation than to devise new materials on your own.
2. If you are new and inexperienced at consultation, using treatment manuals such as the ones developed in the Fuchs studies (Fuchs, Fuchs, Reeder, Gilman, Fernstrom, Bahr, & Moore, 1989) to guide consultation problem solving may increase the effectiveness of your intervention plans.
3. Ask consultees if you can record your interviews. Then transcribe them and look for examples of relationship building, facilitating action, and problem solving in your interactions.
4. Be sure to ask consultees what they have tried previously when consulting. Proposing an already tried intervention is often frustrating to the consultee.

REVIEW QUESTIONS

1. How does the concept of stages of consultation differ from the concept of stages in child development?
2. What is contracting? Why is it important in consultation?
3. How can direct service by the consultant facilitate entry?
4. What special difficulties does the internal consultant face when trying to ensure that the administrative head of an organization and staff members understand consultation?

5. What are the three major domains of assessment? Give an example of a problem that might be presented to you in consultation and list several factors within each domain that might be relevant in understanding the problem and developing a solution.
6. Distinguish between formative and summative evaluation.
7. Briefly describe the three phases of Carkhuff's model of helping.
8. Describe the nonverbal and verbal components of relationship building. Why is relationship building important to the subsequent problem-solving and action components of consultation?
9. How might you detect that your communication style is not matching a consultee's?
10. What is a personalized understanding of a consultation problem?
11. Develop an action plan for a problem you might deal with as a consultant, specifying a goal and steps to meet that goal.

REFERENCES

Bergan, J. R. (1977). *Behavioral consultation.* Columbus, OH: Charles E. Merrill.

Bergan, J. R., Byrnes, I. M., & Kratochwill, T. R. (1979). Effects of behavioral and medical models of consultation on teacher expectancies and instruction of a hypothetical child. *Journal of School Psychology, 17,* 307–316.

Bergan, J. R., & Kratochwill, T. R. (1990). *Behavioral consultation and therapy.* New York: Plenum.

Bergan, J. R., & Neumann, A. J. (1980). The identification of resources and constraints influencing plan design in consultation. *Journal of School Psychology, 18,* 317–323.

Bergan, J. R., & Tombari, M. L. (1975). The analysis of verbal interactions occurring during consultation. *Journal of School Psychology, 13,* 209–226.

Bergan, J. R., & Tombari, M. L. (1976). Consultant skill and efficiency and the implementation and outcomes of consultation. *Journal of School Psychology, 14,* 3–13.

Brown, D., Wyne, M. D., Blackburn, J. E., & Powell, W. C. (1979). *Consultation.* Boston: Allyn & Bacon.

Caplan, G. (1970). *The theory and practice of mental health consultation*. New York: Basic Books.

Caplan, G. (2004). Recent advances in mental health consultation and collaboration. In N. M. Lambert, I. Hylander, & J. H. Sandoval (Eds.), *Consultee-centered consultation: Improving the quality of professional services in schools and community organizations* (pp. 21–36). Mahwah, NJ: Erlbaum.

Caplan, G., & Caplan, R. B. (1993). *Mental health consultation and collaboration.* San Francisco: Jossey-Bass.

Carkhuff, R. R. (1969a). *Helping and human relations, Vol. 1: Selection and training.* New York: Holt, Rinehart & Winston.

Carkhuff, R. R. (1969b). *Helping and human relations, Vol. 2: Practice and research.* New York: Holt, Rinehart & Winston.

Carkhuff, R. R. (1983). *The art of helping* (5th ed.). Amherst, MA: Human Resource Development Press.

Carkhuff, R. R., & Anthony, W. A. (1979). *The skills of helping.* Amherst, MA: Human Resource Development Press.

Carkhuff, R. R., & Berenson, B. G. (1977). *Beyond counseling and therapy* (2nd ed.). New York: Holt, Rinehart & Winston.

Cleven, C. A., & Gutkin, T. B. (1988). Cognitive modeling of consultation processes: A means for improving consultees' problem definition skills. *Journal of School Psychology, 26,* 379–389.

Conoley, J. C., & Conoley, C. W. (1982). *School consultation.* New York: Pergamon.

Conoley, C. W., Conoley, J. C., Ivey, D. C., & Scheel, M. J. (1991). Enhancing consultation by matching the consultee's perspective. *Journal of Counseling and Development, 69,* 546–549.

Cooper, S. (2003). College counseling centers as internal organizational consultants to universities. *Consulting Psychology Journal: Practice and Research, 55,* 230–238.

Curtis, M. J., & Watson, K. L. (1980). Changes in consultee problem clarification skills following consultation. *Journal of School Psychology, 18,* 210–221.

DeForest, P. A., & Hughes, J. N. (1992). Effect of teacher involvement and teacher self-efficacy on ratings of consultant effectiveness and intervention acceptability. *Journal of Educational and Psychological Consultation, 3,* 301–316.

Diller, J. V. (1999). Cultural diversity: A primer for the human services. Belmont, CA: Wadsworth.

Dougherty, A. M., Tack, F. E., Fullam, C. D., & Hammer, L. M. (1996). Disengagement: A neglected aspect of the consultation process. *Journal of Education and Psychological Consultation, 7,* 259–274.

Duncan, C. F. (1995). Cross-cultural school consultation. In C. Lee (Ed.), *Counseling for diversity* (pp. 129–139). Boston: Allyn & Bacon.

Dunn, W. N. (1981). *Public policy analysis: An introduction.* Englewood Cliffs, NJ: Prentice-Hall.

Egan, G. (1994). *The skilled helper* (5th ed.). Pacific Grove, CA: Brooks/Cole.

Elliott, S. N. (1988). Acceptability of behavioral treatments: Review of variables that influence treatment selection. *Professional Psychology: Research and Practice, 19,* 68–80.

Elliott, S. N., Witt, J. C., Galvin, G. A., & Moe, G. L. (1986). Children's involvement in intervention selection: Acceptability of interventions for misbehaving peers. *Professional Psychology: Research and Practice, 17,* 235–241.

Erchul, W. P. (1987). A relational communication analysis of control in school consultation. *Professional School Psychology, 2,* 113–124.

Erchul, W. P. (1992). On dominance, cooperation, teamwork, and collaboration in school-based consultation. *Journal of Educational and Psychological Consultation, 3,* 363–366.

Erchul, W. P., & Chewning, T. G. (1990). Behavioral consultation from a request-centered relational communication perspectives. *School Psychology Quarterly, 5,* 1–20.

Erchul, W. P., Hughes, J. N., Meyers, J., Hickman, J. A., & Braden, J. P. (1992). Dyadic agreement concerning the consultation process and its relationship to outcome. *Journal of Educational and Psychological Consultation, 3,* 119–132.

Erchul, W. P., & Martens, B. (2002). *School consultation: Conceptual and empirical bases of practice* (2nd ed.). New York: Kluwer Academic/Plenum.

Erchul, W. P., & Raven, B. H. (1997). Social power in consultation: A contemporary view of French and Raven's bases of power model. *Journal of School Psychology, 35,* 137–171.

Erchul, W. P., Raven, B. H., and Ray, A. G. (2001). School psychologists' perceptions of social power bases in teacher consultation. *Journal of Educational and Psychological Consultation, 12,* 1–23.

Erchul, W. P., Raven, B. H., & Whichard, S. M. (2001). School psychologist and teacher perceptions of social power in consultation. *Journal of School Psychology, 39,* 483–497.

Erchul, W. P., Raven, B. H., & Wilson, K. E. (in press). The relationship between gender of consultant and social power perceptions within school consultation. *School Psychology Review.*

Erchul, W. P., & Schulte, A. C. (1990). The coding of consultation verbalizations: How much is enough? *School Psychology Quarterly, 5,* 256–264.

Fine, M. J., Grantham, V. L., & Wright, J. G. (1979). Personal variables that facilitate or impede consultation. *Psychology in the Schools, 16,* 533–539.

French, J. R. P., & Raven, B. H. (1959). The bases of social power. In D. Cartwright (Ed.), *Studies in social power* (pp. 150–167). Ann Arbor, MI: University of Michigan Institute of Social Research.

Frentz, C., & Kelley, M. L. (1986). Parents' acceptance of reductive treatment methods: The influence of problem severity and perception of child behavior. *Behavior Therapy, 17,* 75–81.

Fuchs, D., & Fuchs, L. (1989). Exploring effective and efficient prereferral interventions: A component analysis of behavioral consultation. *School Psychology Review, 28,* 260–283.

Fuchs, D., Fuchs, L. S., Bahr, M. W., Fernstrom, P., & Stecker, P. M. (1990). Prereferral intervention: A prescriptive approach. *Exceptional Children, 56,* 493–513.

Fuchs, D., Fuchs, L., Reeder, P., Gilman, S., Fernstrom, P., Bahr, M., & Moore, P. (1989). *Mainstream assistance teams: A handbook on prereferral intervention.* Nashville, TN: Department of Special Education, Peabody College of Vanderbilt University.

Gallessich, J. (1982). *The profession and practice of consultation.* San Francisco: Jossey-Bass.

Gaupp, P. G. (1966). Authority, influence and control in consultation. *Community Mental Health Journal, 2,* 205–210.

Gazda, G. M. (1973). *Human relations development: A manual for educators.* Boston: Allyn & Bacon.

Gibbs, J. T. (1980). The interpersonal orientation in mental health consultation: Toward a model of ethnic variations in consultation. *The Journal of Community Psychology, 8,* 303–308.

Graham, D. S. (1998). Consultant effectiveness and treatment acceptability: An examination of consultee requests and consultant responses. *School Psychology Quarterly, 13,* 155–168.

Gutkin, T. B. (1993). Moving from behavioral to ecobehavioral consultation: What's in a name? *Journal of Educational and Psychological Consultation, 4,* 95–99.

Gutkin, T. B., & Curtis, M. J. (1982). School-based consultation: Theory and techniques. In C. R. Reynolds & T. B. Gutkin (Eds.), *The handbook of school psychology* (pp. 796–828). New York: John Wiley & Sons.

Gutkin, T. B., & Curtis, M. J. (1990). School-based consultation: Theory, techniques, and research. In T. B. Gutkin & C. R. Reynolds (Eds.), *The handbook of school psychology* (pp. 577–611). New York: John Wiley & Sons.

Hansen, J. C., Himes, B. S., & Meier, S. (1990). *Consultation: Concepts and practices.* Englewood Cliffs, NJ: Prentice-Hall.

Havelock, R. G. (1973). *The change agent's guide to innovation in education.* Englewood Cliffs, NJ: Educational Technology Publications.

Herring, R. D. (1996). Synergistic counseling and Native American Indian students. *Journal of Counseling and Development, 74,* 542–547.

Hoagwood, K., & Johnson, J. (2003). School psychology: A public health framework l. From evidence-based practices to evidence-based policies. *Journal of School Psychology, 41,* 3–21.

Horton, E., & Brown, D. (1990). The importance of interpersonal skills in consultee-centered consultation: A review. *Journal of Counseling and Development, 68,* 423–426.

Hughes, J. N., Barker, D., Kemenoff, S., & Hart, M. (1993). Problem ownership, causal attributions, and self-efficacy as predictions of teachers' referral decisions. *Journal of Educational and Psychological Consultation, 4,* 369–384.

Hughes, J. N., & DeForest, P. A. (1993). Consultant directiveness and support as predictors of consultation outcomes. *Journal of School Psychology, 31,* 355–373.

Hyatt, S. P., & Tingstrom, D. H. (1993). Consultants' use of jargon during intervention presentation: An evaluation of presentation modality and type of intervention. *School Psychology Quarterly, 8,* 99–109.

Ivey, A. E. (1983). *Intentional interviewing and counseling.* Monterey, CA: Brooks/Cole.

Katz, D., & Kahn, R. L. (1978). *The social psychology of organizations.* New York: John Wiley & Sons.

Kazdin, A. E. (1984). *Behavior modification in applied settings* (3rd ed.). Homewood, IL: Dorsey.

Kazdin, A. E., French, N. H., & Sherick, R. B. (1981). Acceptability of alternative treatments for children: Evaluations by inpatient children, parents, and staff. *Journal of Consulting and Clinical Psychology, 49,* 900–907.

Kelly, J. G. (1993). Gerald Caplan's paradigm: Bridging psychotherapy and public health practice. In W. P. Erchul (Ed.), *Consultation in community school, and organizational practice: Gerald Caplan's contributions to professional psychology* (pp. 75–85). Washington, DC: Taylor & Francis.

Kratochwill, T. R., & Stoiber, K. C. (2002). Evidence-based interventions in school psychology: Conceptual foundations of the Procedural and Coding Manual of Division 16 and the Society for the Study of School Psychology Task Force. *Journal of School Psychology, 17,* 341–389.

Kurpius, D. (1978). Consultation theory and process: An integrated model. *Personnel and Guidance Journal, 56,* 18–21.

Lippitt, G. & Lippitt, R. (1978). *The consulting process in action.* San Diego, CA: University Associates.

Maitland, R. E., Fine, M. J., & Tracy, D. B. (1985). The effects of an interpersonally based problem-solving process on consultation outcomes. *Journal of School Psychology, 23,* 337–345.

Marks, E. (1995). *Entry strategies for school consultation.* New York: Guilford.

Martens, B. K., Peterson, R. L., Witt, J. C., & Cirone, S. (1986). Teacher perceptions of school-based interventions. *Exceptional Children, 53,* 213–223.

Martin, R. (1978). Expert and referent power: A framework for understanding and maximizing consultation effectiveness. *Journal of School Psychology, 16,* 49–55.

McMahon, R. J., & Forehand, R. L. (1983). Consumer satisfaction in behavioral treatment of children: Types, issues, and recommendations. *Behavior Therapy, 14,* 209–225.

Meade, C. J., Hamilton, M. K., & Yuen, R. K. (1982). Consultation research: The time has come, the walrus said. *Counseling Psychologist, 10,* 39–51.

Meyers, J. (1981). Mental health consultation. In J. C. Conoley (Ed.), *Consultation in schools* (pp. 35–58). New York: Academic Press.

Meyers, J., Brent, D., Faherty, E., & Modafferi, C. (1993). Caplan's contributions to the practice of psychology in the schools. In W. P. Erchul (Ed.), *Consultation in community, school, and organizational practice: Gerald Caplan's contributions to professional psychology* (pp. 99–122). Washington, DC: Taylor & Francis.

Meyers, J., Parsons, R. D., & Martin, R. (1979). *Mental health consultation in the school.* San Francisco: Jossey-Bass.

Monsen, J. J., & Frederickson, N. (2002). Consultant problem understanding as a function of training in interviewing to promote accessible reasoning. *Journal of School Psychology, 40,* 197–212.

Newman, F. L., & Tejeda, M. J. (1996). The need for research that is designed to support decisions in the delivery of mental health services. *American Psychologist, 51,* 1040–1049.

Noell, G. H., Duhon, G. J., Gatti, S. L., & Connell, J. E. (2002). Consultation, follow-up, and implementation of behavior management interventions in general education. *School Psychology Review, 31,* 217–234.

Noell, G. H., Witt, J. C., Gilbertson, D. N., Ranier, D. D., & Freeland, J. T. (1997). Teacher intervention implementation and performance feedback. *School Psychology Quarterly, 12,* 77–88.

Parsons, R. D., & Meyers, J. (1984). *Developing consultation skills.* San Francisco: Jossey-Bass.

Pinderhughes, E. (1989). *Understanding race, ethnicity, and power: The key to efficacy in clinical practice.* New York: Free Press.

Pipes, R. B. (1981). Consulting in organizations: The entry problem. In J. C. Conoley (Ed.), *Consultation in schools* (pp. 11–33). New York: Academic Press.

Quinn, M. T., & Jacob, E. (1999). Adding culture to the tools of school psychologists. *NASP Communique, 28.*

Raiffia, H. (1968). *Decision analysis.* Reading, MA: Addison-Wesley,

Raven, B. H. (1965). Social influence and power. In I. D. Steiner & M. Fishbein (Eds.), *Current studies in social psychology* (pp. 371–382). New York: Holt, Rinehart & Winston.

Raven, B. H. (1992). A power/interaction model of interpersonal influence: French and Raven thirty years later. *Journal of Social Behavior and Personality, 7,* 217–244.

Raven, B. H. (1993). The bases of power: Origins and recent developments. *Journal of Social Issues, 49,* 227–251.

Reimers, T. M., Wacker, D. P., & Koeppl, G. (1987). Acceptability of behavioral treatments: A review of the literature. *School Psychology Review, 16,* 212–227.

Reynolds, C. R., Gutkin, T, B., Elliott, S. N., & Witt, J. C. (1984). *School psychology: Essentials of theory and practice.* New York: John Wiley & Sons.

Riley-Tilman, T. C., & Chafouleas, S. M. (2003). Using interventions that exist in the natural environment to increase treatment integrity and social influence in consultation. *Journal of Educational and Psychological Consultation, 14,* 139–156.

Robbins, J. R., & Gutkin, T. B. (1994). Consultee and client remedial and preventive outcomes following consultation: Some mixed empirical results and directions for future researchers. *Journal of Education and Psychological Consultation, 5,* 149–168.

Robinson, V. M. J., & Halliday, J. (1988). Relationship of counsellor reasoning and data collection to problem analysis quality. *British Journal of Guidance and Counselling, 16,* 50–62.

Rogers, M. R. (1998). The influence of race and consultant verbal behavior on perceptions of consultant competence and multicultural sensitivity. *School Psychology Quarterly, 13,* 265–280.

Rosenfield, S. A. (1987). *Instructional consultation.* Hillsdale, NJ: Erlbaum.

Sandoval, J. (1996). Constructivism, consultee-centered consultation, and conceptual change. *Journal of Educational and Psychological Consultation, 7,* 89–98.

Sandoval, J. (2004). Constructivism, consultee-centered consultation, and conceptual change. In N. M. Lambert, I. Hylander, & J. H. Sandoval (Eds.), *Consultee-centered consultation: Improving the quality of professional services in schools and community organizations* (pp. 37–44). Mahwah, NJ: Erlbaum.

Scholten, P. T. (1990). What does it mean to consult? In E. Cole & J. A. Siegel (Eds.), *Effective consultation in school psychology* (pp. 33–52). Toronto: Hagrefe & Huber.

Schowengerdt, R. V., Fine, M. J., & Poggio, J. P. (1976). An examination of some bases of teacher satisfaction with school psychological services. *Psychology in the Schools, 13,* 269–275.

Shapiro, E. S. (1987). Intervention research methodology in school psychology. *School Psychology Review, 16,* 290–305.

Shapiro, E. S., & Goldberg, R. (1986). A comparison of group contingencies for increasing spelling performance among sixth grade students. *School Psychology Review, 15,* 546–557.

Sheridan, S. M., Kratochwill, T. R., & Bergan, J. R. (1996). *Conjoint behavioral consultation: A procedural manual.* New York: Plenum.

Soo-Hoo, T. (1998). Applying frame of reference and reframing techniques to improve school consultation in multicultural settings. *Journal of Education and Psychological Consultation, 9,* 325–345.

Srebalus, D. J., & Brown, D. (2001). *Becoming a skilled helper.* Boston: Allyn & Bacon.

Tombari, M. L., & Bergan, J. R. (1978). Consultant cues and teacher verbalizations, judgments, and expectancies concerning children's adjustment problems. *Journal of School Psychology, 16,* 212–219.

Watzlawick, P., Weakland, J., & Fisch, R. (1974). *Change.* New York: W. W. Norton.

Wickstrom, K. F., Jones, K. M., LaFleur, L. H., & Witt, J. C. (1998). An analysis of treatment integrity in school-based behavioral consultation. *School Psychology Quarterly, 13,* 141–154.

Witt, J. C., & Elliott, S. N. (1985). Acceptability of classroom management strategies. In T. R. Kratochwill (Ed.), *Advances in school psychology* (pp. 251–288). Hillsdale, NJ: Erlbaum.

Witt, J. C., Elliott, S. N., & Martens, B. K. (1984). Acceptability of behavioral interventions used in classrooms: The influence of amount of teacher time, severity of behavior problem, and type of intervention. *Behavioral Disorders, 9,* 95–104.

Witt, J. C., Moe, G., Gutkin, T. B., & Andrews, L. (1984). The effect of saying the same thing in different ways: The problem of language and jargon in school-based consultation. *Journal of School Psychology, 22,* 361–367.

Zins, J. E., & Erchul, W. P. (1995). Best practices in school consultation. In A. Thomas & J. Grimes (Eds.), *Best practices in school psychology-III* (pp. 609–623). Washington, DC: National Association of School Psychologists.

ANSWERS TO LEARNING EXERCISES

6.1 There are no answers. This exercise is meant to help you develop entry skills.

6.2 There are no answers. This exercise is meant to help you examine your own biases and how they influence your questioning techniques.

6.3 Consultant One is using an empathetic response to show the consultee that he or she understands the consultee's point of view. Consultant Two has moved into problem solving without establishing a relationship with the consultee or providing evidence that he or she has understood the problem.

CHAPTER 7

THE SKILLS AND CHARACTERISTICS OF CONSULTANTS AND COLLABORATORS

GOALS OF THE CHAPTER

The primary goal of this chapter is to explore the skills needed by consultants and collaborators with a primary emphasis of the skills of cross-cultural consultants and collaborators. Secondarily, the characteristics of effective collaborators and consultants will be discussed,

CHAPTER PREVIEW

1. Some skills and characteristics needed by both collaborators and consultants will be discussed with a focus on cultural competency.
2. The personal characteristics of consultants will be presented.
3. Recommendations for research regarding the skills and characteristics of consultants and collaborators will be made.

The skills needed by effective consultants have been discussed extensively by a number of authors (Brown, 1993; Idol & West, 1987; Kratochwill, Vansomeren, & Sheridan, 1993). Conversely, the personal characteristics and traits of effective collaborators have received relatively little attention. It is interesting to note that literally thousands of research studies have focused on the traits and personal attributes of counselors and therapists (Herman, 1993), while only a handful have dealt with the traits and personal characteristics of consultants (Horton & Brown, 1990). The failure to focus on the personal characteristics of consultants may be because behaviorists like Bergan (1977) have placed little emphasis on the importance of the relationship and the personal characteristics needed for effectiveness in the consulting process, although Erchul (1987) has addressed this topic empirically. Even less attention has been directed to the personal characteristics of successful collaborators and, while some discussion of the skills needed by collaborators can be found in the literature (e.g., Rubin, 2002), neither the issue of collaborators' traits nor the skills needed by effective collaborators has been addressed empirically. However, there does seem to be a growing consensus that consultants, collaborators, and others involved in the helping professions need to acquire the knowledge, attitudes, and skills that will result in cultural competence because of the increasing diversity of our society and societal institutions and because of our concerns about disabled students (King, Sims, & Osher, 1998). Accordingly, this discussion will begin with the issue of becoming culturally competent, followed by a discussion of other characteristics and skills needed by consultants and collaborators.

CULTURALLY COMPETENT CONSULTANTS AND COLLABORATORS

Becoming Culturally Competent

What is cultural competence? Culturally competent individuals have the knowledge, attitudes, and behaviors that allow them to function effectively in cross-cultural consultation and/or collaborations (Cross, Bazron, Dennis, & Isaacs, 1989). A culturally competent organization has transformed its knowledge of culture into attitudes, policies, and practices that enable it to increase the quality of its services (1997). King et al. (1998) suggest that the process of becoming culturally competent is developmental and moves from cultural destructiveness—a stage in which individuals and institutions that represent the dominant culture actively work to destroy other cultures by coercive means—and ends with valuing diversity and cultural proficiency.

Several individuals and groups (e.g., Sue & Sue, 1999) have constructed models depicting the steps or stages that individuals take or pass through on their way to cultural competence. Holcomb-McCoy (2001) summarizes these steps as developing (1) an awareness of one's own culture and the worldviews and cultural conditioning associated with it, (2) knowledge of the culture and associated worldviews of others, and (3) the skills needed to transform cultural knowledge into skills and successful practice.

Somewhat more detailed models have been developed by Arredondo and her associates (1996) and Helms (1990, 1992). As can be seen in Table 7.1, the end of the process of becoming culturally competent may have different outcomes depending on the model. Arredondo and her associates believe that culturally competent individuals can engage in culturally appropriate activities including the design of systems level interventions. Helms posits that the end result of the process of becoming culturally competent is the development of an autonomous racial identity. Professionals with an autonomous racial identity have a positive view of their own race,

are able to integrate information about the characteristics of other racial groups, including their similarities and differences, into their belief systems, and dedicate themselves to the abandonment of racism. For white consultants, developing an autonomous racial identity involves becoming aware of the ethnocentrism in our culture, the privileges that accompany being white in this country, and the oppression and injustices that have resulted.

King and associates (1998) suggest a process that organizational consultants might use in the design of systems level interventions that result in culturally competent organizations. The process begins when organizations learn to value organizational diversity and continues as the people in the organization assess the organization's cultural sensitivity, institutionalize the cultural knowledge that they as a group have acquired, become aware of the dynamics of cultural interactions that occur in the organization, and develop culturally appropriate policies and practices.

Finally, a relatively comprehensive list of indicators that an individual has become culturally competent was identified by Holcomb-McCoy and Myers (1999) and can be found in their *Multicultural Counseling Competence and Training Survey*. There are 50 of these skills, which are based on the work of Arrendondo and her associates (1996). Space will not permit listing all of the multicultural competencies that culturally competent persons develop, but these can be summarized. The critical skills of the culturally competent consultant/collaborator are: (1) Can discuss the manner in which their culture influences their thinking and how this may interfere when they are involved in cross-cultural helping situation, (2) Can identify their own stereotypes and discuss how they might interfere with their ability to engage in cross-cultural consultation, (3) Can verbally and non-verbally communicate acceptance of people from different cultures and communicate in a style that is acceptable by the consultee, and (4) Can identify how the values that underpin the various consultation models may interfere with the cross-cultural

TABLE 7.1

ARREDONDO AND ASSOCIATES (1996) STEPS	HELMS (1990, 1992) STAGES
Tell how their own culture has impacted the psychological processes and biases	Contact: All people should be treated equally. There is no acknowledgment of race and ethnicity.
Identify the limits of their cultural competency	Disintegration: Some awareness of cultural differences develops. May attribute these differences to intrapsychic or contextual variables such as poverty.
Understand their own communication style and how it may conflict with the styles of people from other cultures	Reintegration: Awareness of difference; culturally different seen as inferior.
Articulate how race and culture may influence values, development, aspiration, motivation, decision-making style, and family functioning	Pseudo-Independent: Believes that culturally different should adopt the values of the dominant culture, but has a genuine desire to help.
Understanding of overall group and within-group differences	Immersion/Emersion: Wants to learn more about other cultures and engages in activities that will improve knowledge and skill base.
Articulate how sociopolitical forces such as poverty, immigration policy, racism, and power differentials influence both the perspective and functioning of racial and ethnic groups	Autonomous: Values cultural difference and consistently uses culturally appropriate strategies. Understands that injustices have occurred and may work to correct these injustices.
Engage in culturally appropriate consulting processes and design culturally sensitive interventions	
Design systems-level interventions to increase cultural sensitivity, reduce institutional racism, and empower racial and ethnic minorities	

consultation process including the design of interventions.

Developing a Cross-Cultural Consultation Style

Individuals preparing to become cross-cultural consultants would do well to consider the complexity of the process. All cross-cultural interactions in general, and cross-cultural consultation and collaboration in particular are fraught with potential problems. Verbal and nonverbal communication, the consultation model to be used, the hierarchy in the relationship, and the nature of the intervention should all be influenced by the *current* cultural beliefs of the consultee. To make matters

even more difficult, consultants and collaborators must consider the degree to which consultees from races and ethnic groups different from their own have adopted the worldviews of the dominant culture. Judgments about one's own cultural autonomy, knowledge about cultural groups, and, to a certain extent, one's skill in cross-cultural consultation can be made prior to entering the consultation process. However, cross-cultural consultants are faced with making clinical judgments about the cultural values and worldviews of their consultees "on the fly" and altering process variables based on their conclusions.

It has been widely acknowledged that consultants should become aware of their own values (e.g.,

Caplan, 1970; Conoley & Conoley, 1991; Dough-tery, 2004). In no area is this more important than in cross-cultural consultation. Values form the core of consultants' worldview (Carter, 1991; Richardson & Molinaro, 1996), which is defined as the manner in which individuals perceive their relationship to other people, time, nature, and societal institutions (Ivey, D'Andrea, Ivey, & Simek-Morgan, 2002). Consultants, particularly those who hold a typical set of Eurocentric values and are unaware of the differences that exist in the value structures of different ethnic and racial groups, may inadvertently impose their values on their consultees and alienate them in the process. Moreover, it is unwise for consultants to assume that the value structures of consultees from their own culture is the same as theirs, based on the research of Carter (1991). He suggests that there is nearly as much variability within cultural groups as there is across cultural groups. Therefore, cross-cultural consultants must be prepared to ask questions and structure the consulting process in order to ensure that the process will proceed without alienating the consultee, for example,

- Determining the hierarchy: I'm comfortable being called by my first name, but some people prefer a more formal approach. What is your preference?
- Determining who should be involved: Given the nature of the concern, what people other than ourselves should be involved in the consulting process?
- Determining the types of leads to use: It makes some people uncomfortable to talk about their feelings. We can focus solely on behavior. What is your preference?
- Acknowledging the right not to participate: If at any time our discussion makes you uncomfortable, simply tell me that you would rather not answer the question.

OTHER CHARACTERISTICS AND SKILLS OF CONSULTANTS AND COLLABORATORS

The skills and attitudes necessary to become culturally competent have been emphasized to this point in this chapter. Now, a number of generic skills and characteristics needed by effective consultants will be discussed, starting with consultant characteristics. Unfortunately, most of this discussion is based on supposition rather than empiricism. In a few instances, there is research to support the suppositions.

Because consultation and collaboration are problem-solving processes (e.g., Caplan, 1970; Kurpius & Fuqua, 1993), consultants and collaborators must be problem solvers (Henning-Stout, 1993). Salmon and Lehrer (1989), in an analogue study, investigated the problem-solving behavior of two consultants and found that their interpretation of the problem was influenced by the beliefs held by the consultee (teacher) about the client (student), the consultee's involvement with the client, and their own beliefs about the child. Not unexpectedly, the background and experience of the consultants were also instrumental in the way they viewed both the consulting process and the manner in which problems are to be resolved.

The fact is that we know little about the characteristics of effective problem solvers in the context of consultation. Varney (1985) suggests that consultants need to have the ability to engage in high levels of moral reasoning. He also suggests, along with Hunsaker (1985), that consultants need to be able to analyze problems from many perspectives. Bushe and Gibbs (1990) termed this quality *tactical flexibility* and suggested that this trait, along with a strong self-concept, are essential to success in consultation.

Bushe and Gibbs (1990) attempted to carry their suppositions about the characteristics needed by effective consultants one step further. They tried to develop a predictive model of success in consultation as determined by trainer and peer evaluations. They found that intuition as measured by the Myers-Briggs Type Indicator (MBTI) and level of ego development (Loevinger, 1976) were in fact predictors of consultation success, with level of ego development being the better predictor. Their work supports not only their own hypotheses about the characteristics needed by consultants but also those of others already cited. With higher levels of ego development come increasing self-awareness, reliance on self-generated standards, levels of moral reasoning, ability to accept ambiguity, and ability to accept the paradoxes that occur within the consulting situation. Earlier, in a study of internal organizational development (OD) consultants, Bushe and Gibb (1989) found that only when consultants reached what Loevinger (1976) terms the *conscientious stage* did they adopt consulting styles that were in accord with OD philosophy. Also in an earlier study, Hamilton (1988) found that intuition as measured by the MBTI is related to trainers' rating of competence. However, Hamilton did not study the levels of ego development.

Another essential characteristic of consultants is that they can establish working alliances. One aspect of establishing working alliances is the proper use of skills, some of which were outlined in Chapter Six. They will be revisited briefly in the section to follow. However, there is widespread agreement that people who can establish effective working relationships possess certain key characteristics, namely, empathy, genuineness, and positive regard (Horton & Brown, 1990; Kurpius & Rozecki, 1993). Empathy is the ability to perceive the internal frame of reference of another while maintaining one's objectivity. Positive regard involves prizing others even when they are quite different from oneself. Genuineness involves understanding oneself to be capable of freely interacting with others in an honest, spontaneous manner.

The aforementioned characteristics of empathy, genuineness, and positive regard were derived from the literature on effective therapeutic alliances. This list of traits needed to establish working alliances is probably not extensive enough to cover the complexity of the consulting relationship. To the list should be added the willingness to take interpersonal risks. Consultants are often required to initiate the consulting relationship, to act as models as they help consultees acquire new skills, and to give opinions and advice based upon their expertise. These all require risk-taking behav-

Student Learning Activity 7.1

Will you be a good consultant? Rate your consultation characteristics using the following scale:

1 = not like me
2 = somewhat like me
3 = very much like me

A. Self-confident. A risk taker. _____
B. Empathic. Can see others' points of view. _____
C. Genuine. Not afraid to be myself. _____
D. Respect others even if they hold values different from mine. _____
E. A good model. Willing to use my own behavior to instruct others. _____
F. Highly motivated. Want to help consultees and clients. _____
G. An achiever. I get things done. _____

ior. Maher (1993), when discussing the characteristics of the organizational consultant, termed this risk-taking quality *entrepreneurship,* which he defined as "the ability to create value by recognizing new professional opportunities, managing risk associated with those opportunities, and following through with value-added services" (p. 319). While the human services consultant may not be entrepreneurial in the way Maher suggests, they are just as involved in risk taking.

Maher (1993) identified some additional characteristics of effective consultants that, although they have not been widely discussed as some of those already mentioned, would probably be accepted by most people. He suggests that effective consultants possess commitment, determination and persistence, desire to achieve, and a desire to continuously enhance their effectiveness through feedback about their services. He also suggests that, in addition to being risk takers, effective consultants may be risk seekers, which is consistent with his concept of the consultant as an entrepreneur. Perhaps this "package" of characteristics can be more succinctly labeled as "motivated to succeed," because without a high level of motivation a consultant will certainly be discouraged by the inevitable failures that occur in the consultation process.

Prerelationship/Preentry and Entry

Organizational consultants such as Kurpius and others (1993) emphasize the importance of the preentry phase of the consulting process. They stress that, in this phase, consultants need two essential competencies: the ability to do realistic self-estimates of their characteristics and skills and to communicate these skills to potential consultees. The human resources consultant needs the same types of skills, although entry and preentry are probably misnomers for this group because they are typically internal consultants and thus have theoretically entered the consulting arena. However, having a firm understanding of self and one's consulting skills is essential to effective, ethical practice. Being able to communicate the nature of these skills is also essential because, without some understanding of the benefits that can be derived from consultation, potential consultees will not avail themselves of the services. External consultants call this skill *marketing*. Internal consultants are in no less need of marketing skills than are external consultants, although they rarely think in terms of the need to market their services. To summarize, the essential skills required in the preentry/prerelationship phase are:

1. Capacity to analyze one's own strengths and weaknesses.
2. The ability to identify consulting skills and make estimates of how these can help consultees.
3. Marketing skills, that is, the ability to persuade others that they can benefit from consultation.

Entry is that point in the consulting relationship at which consultant and consultee make contact and begin to negotiate a working agreement. This latter aspect of consulting is called *contracting*. A contract may be a complex legal document or an informal agreement to work together to solve

a problem. The consultant needs a basic understanding of the legal aspects of developing contracts but will probably need to consult with a lawyer for verification that the contract does in fact constitute a workable document (Remley, 1993). If the contractual agreement is informal, as it often is, the consultant needs to be able to explain the nature of consultation to the consultee, to identify the roles each is to play in the process, and to reach accord on the dimensions of the process and the roles.

Consultants need to be able to ascertain, on a preliminary basis at least, whether consultation is feasible. *Feasibility* means that the consultee has the motivation and resources needed for success (Kurpius, Fuqua, & Rozecki, 1993). They also need to consider whether they have the skills needed to proceed, because to proceed without the necessary competencies to bring the consultation process to successful fruition is unethical (ACA, 1995; APA, 2002).

To reiterate, consultants need skills to:

1. Make preliminary estimates of the likelihood of success if the consultation process is joined.
2. Make accurate estimates of their own ability as consultants.
3. Draw up preliminary formal contracts and develop informal consulting contracts.
4. Explain the nature of consultation to consultees.

Relationship Skills

Research has consistently shown that consultants who have the skills (and characteristics) needed to establish good interpersonal relationships are more favorably perceived by consultees than those who do not (Hansen & Himes, 1977; Maitland, Fine, & Tracy, 1985; Weissenberg, Fine, & Poggio, 1982). Paskewicz and Clark (1984) looked at a different dimension of the consulting relationship: language structural errors. They found that, when abstract rather than concrete words were used, the child rather than the child's behavior became the topic of consulting behavior, and when words were used that suggest actions should be taken, consulting became less effective. Hansen and Himes (1977) also looked at the nonverbal dimension of the relationship and, not surprisingly, found that teachers thought that attending (e.g., eye contact) and minimizing nonverbal distractions were effective consulting behavior.

One area of controversy regarding the verbal skills needed by the consultant is in the area of controlling the counseling conversation. Bergan (1977) was the first to suggest that, to be effective, consultants needed to have the skills to control the consulting conversation. To that end he elaborated an extensive list of skills that were set forth in Chapter Three. Early research (Bergan & Tombari, 1976) generally supported Bergan's propositions, as has some additional research by Erchul (1987) and Erchul and Chewning (1990). However, as Henning-Stout (1993) reports, "there is ample evidence that consultees resist being told what to do" (p. 18). The basis of this argument is whether the consultant needs the skills to establish what have variously been termed *coordinate, collegial,* and *collaborative* relationships or the skills needed to skillfully elicit the responses needed to dominate the consulting relationship. Few would disagree that consultants should be prepared to elicit responses that will lead to problem identification and goal setting. However, with a few exceptions such as Erchul and Chewning (1990) and Witt (1990), most consultants believe that the skills needed by the consultants lie in the area of establishing coordinate, not dominant, relationships (Henning-Stout, 1993).

One caveat is necessary at this point. The research mentioned above was conducted using a Eurocentric model that may not apply equally well to all cultural groups. For example, some African Americans may not be totally comfortable with the same level of eye contact that is the norm among European Americans, and some Asians believe that smiling is a sign of weakness. For European Americans, the across-the-desk corner of 42 or so inches is a comfortable distance between people, but Latin Americans who interact at closer distances may perceive this as being aloof, particularly if the consultant moves away when the

consultee moves closer (Sue & Sue, 1999). Just as norms regarding nonverbal behavior vary across cultural groups, so do certain aspects of verbal communication. Cultural groups that value self-control, including Asian Americans, some American Indians, and some Hispanics, may be reluctant to share their thoughts and feelings and may value less direct approaches (Sue & Sue, 1990). The culturally insensitive consultant may perceive this as resistance, when in fact—with patience and understanding—the consultee will engage in self-disclosure. However, it is unlikely that an Asian American or American Indian consultee will disclose feelings in the same manner as will other consultees, something the consultant should not attribute to inability to deal with emotions.

What conclusions can be drawn from this conflicting information? Most consultants would agree that consultants need the active listening skills required to establish basic human relationships (Horton & Brown, 1990; Idol & West, 1987; Parsons & Meyers, 1984; Randolph, 1985). These basic skills would include attending (including maintaining appropriate eye contact and other nonverbal behavior) and communicating to the consultee that both the verbal message and the affective content of the message have been heard using the skill known as *reflection.* Additional active listening skills include clarifying both the content of the consultee's communication, using questions and synthesizing a series of communications in summaries, and soliciting information by asking both open-ended (What can you tell me about the client?) and closed (What grade is the student in?) questions. In building consultation relationships, consultants may also use "soft" confrontations that gently point out discrepancies in consultees' communications and leads that focus on the consulting relationships in an effort to repair problems that have developed or to flush out problems that lie beneath the surface (Kurpius & Rozecki, 1993).

Veterans will attest to the fact that consultants need to be able to avoid being drawn into therapy-like discussions with consultees. In order to avoid this possibility, consultants need to master a strategy termed *supportive refocus* (Randolph, 1985). This technique is used to return the focus of the consultation relationship to the client when consultees have inadvertently started to talk about their own problems.

However, basic attending skills will have to be altered to some degree depending upon the cultural identity of the consultee. As has already been noted, there are cultural differences regarding kinesics (bodily movements such as eye contact), proxemics (use of interpersonal space), and communication style. The ability to establish effective consulting relationships with nonacculturated clients may very well be dependent to some degree upon the clients' knowledge of these differences in approaches to communication. Even when dealing with consultees who are acculturated to a large degree, techniques such as the use of confrontation with Asian American clients may need to dropped from the consultant's repertoire to maximize the effectiveness of the relationship. In this same vein, reflection of feeling—a standard technique when consulting with European Americans—may need to give way to reflection of verbal content with American Indians and Asian Americans. Direct approaches may need to replace the relatively indirect techniques found in active listening when the consultee has poor communication skills. Moreover, active listening approaches may need to become more indirect in dealing with some Native Americans. These exceptions do not negate the effectiveness of traditional active listening approaches with many consultees. They do, however, argue that the consultant must gear his or her communication style to the cultural preferences of the consultee in order to be effective.

To summarize, consultants need the following skills:

1. Active listening skills and the ability to vary according to the racial/ethnic background as well as the degree of acculturation of the consultee.
2. Skills to discern the difference between resistance and culturally appropriate behavior; when resistance is present, the skill to determine the extent to which it might be a result of cultural background and/or other psychological or contextual variables.
3. The skill to discern when cultural background is contributing to perceptions of power inequality, and the ability to ameliorate these perceptions.
4. The skill to maintain the focus of the consulting relationship on the client.

Consultants and Collaborators as Problem Solvers: General Considerations

Consultants and collaborators are problem finders. Several writers have likened the role of the consultant to that of a detective (Kolb, 1983; Sandoval, Lambert, & Davis, 1977) probing for clues and information while gathering ideas to develop their hunches. Preliminary data indicate that experts in various fields analyze and deal with problem situations in ways that novices do not. Problem-solving studies have been in the subject matter domains of physics, geometry, art, and the social sciences. Given the fact that the social sciences typically deal with problems that do not have well-established, generally agreed upon solutions in the manner of the physical sciences, the focus of this discussion will be on the studies from the social sciences area.

In their studies Voss, Tyler, and Yengo (1983) compared the strategy used in solving social science problems (e.g., a hypothetical Russian agricultural problem) by experts in the field (faculty members whose expertise was the Soviet Union) and novices (undergraduates taking a course on Russian domestic policy). Given the similarity of problem solving in social science domains, their findings might begin to help us better understand this aspect of the consultation process. What they found was that experts spent a relatively large proportion of their time in developing a representation of the problem they encountered. That is, the expert took time to consider the "givens" of the problem and the goal. Constraints of the situation that impede solutions and knowledge of past solution attempts also contributed to the problem orientation being drawn up.

By contrast, novices spent little time in developing problem representations. In fact, any representations were included in a strategy of isolating possible causes of the problem. The causes are quite specific, and the proposed solutions are stated in relation to the specific causes. Novices began discussing possible solutions to the problem without any consideration of constraints on or orientations to the solutions proposed. In summary then, novices represented the problem only as a set of specific causes requiring solutions. Interestingly, when experts from another discipline had their problem-solving approach to this problem analyzed, they resembled the novices to a great degree.

In terms of solutions, the experts proposed one or a few proposals that were usually abstract. Much of the solution activity then went into justifying and examining what was proposed. The development of arguments may have been done for several reasons: (1) to justify a solution and in doing so show that it can be achieved; (2) to consider problems that may arise from the solutions and examine how those may be solved; (3) to evaluate the solution in terms of the problem representations; (4) to elaborate on the solution; and (5) to contribute to the possibility that new information may be retrieved that may suggest even more solutions. By contrast, novices tended to do little in the way of such argument development.

Only a few studies have applied the findings from the cognitive psychology literature to the consultation process. In the exploratory study comparing the think-aloud protocols of school psychology graduate students with practitioners in response to an audiotape of an actual consultation session, definitive and some parallel observations to the novice–expert differences noted above were reported (Pryzwansky & Vatz, 1988). Essentially three levels of problem representation were evident with the highest level characterized by a problem definition and solution reflecting abstract- and theoretically based information. In contrast to the lowest level, this group critically examined the premises and evidence used by the consultees in defining the problem. They were more global in their assessment versus the lowest group's acceptance of the problem and restricted child focus. Equally important was the observation that the highest-level group used what was labeled an "orientating mechanism" and defined as metastatements regarding the consultation process. Examples of orientating mechanisms include the consultants questioning of himself or herself, the role he or she was being asked to play, and the perceived expectations of the consultee. In this study, seven out of 32 subjects reflected this level of problem finding and six of those were from the practitioner group, although there was no relationship with years of experience and consultation coursework. In two subsequent studies (Vatz & Pryzwansky, 1987; Pryzwansky & Vatz, 1988) repeating the study with nominated expert consultants from the school psychology field (practitioners and trainers), the three levels were again reflected in the protocols with the highest group similar in approach to those in the previous study but made up primarily of trainers; problem-finding level was not related to years of experience or coursework. Also, 90 percent of the interventions proposed by the highest level were focused *within* the session, while 69 percent of the interventions proposed by the lowest level were externally based (class discussion, student interview, parent consultation). Interestingly, in all these studies the number of problems and categories of intervention strategies proposed by the different levels may not differ, but clearly the lowest level offered nearly double the number of strategies; perhaps they were more concerned with the challenge of what to do versus identifying the problem. Perhaps the biggest surprise was the finding that five out of 17 nominated experts were similar to the lowest group in the manner of representing the problem, including only a limited use of orientating mechanisms. Finally, a study of novice (graduate students in counseling) problem-solving approaches reported that, as a group, they adopted the literal givens of a presented problem whether it was appropriate or not (Pryzwansky & Schulte, 1989). Similarly, their interventions were client-focused, even if no clear-cut client problem had been identified. Also their problem solving did not differ in response to changes in the nature of the problem or the consultant's approach which was being employed.

What are the implications of these findings for consultation? For one, it suggests that consultants and consultees may go about a problem-solving activity in very different ways, such as how they perceive the problem and what may be necessary to their thinking before closure on a solution is achieved. The above description suggests that the consultant (expert) will want to spend more time on problem definition and to focus on abstract material. By contrast, the consultee may be reminded of the role of expertise differences and become either intimidated or put off by this questioning and abstract emphasis. Descriptions of consultation as a collaborative effort between equals may be seen as misrepresentations, and the potential for failure in this aspect of the consultation process is understandable. The consultant is advised to remain sensitive to the problem-solving differences and even consider utilizing techniques that promote the functioning of the consultee during the early stages of problem solving.

Consultant and consultee should agree:

1. To take stock of the situation together either as a review or refinement task.
2. That the consultant should evaluate the quality of the information provided by the consultee.
3. That the consultant needs to consider the expectations the consultee holds for the consultant.
4. That the consultant and consultee should collaboratively collect data in a systematic manner.
5. To conduct a process analysis of the problem. (Do contributing variables, identified problems, and problematic outcomes relate logically?)

6. To identify a (or several) competing hypothesis.
7. To consider the constraints affecting a problem solution.

Cultural Issues in Decision Making

Finally, Davis and Sandoval (1991) presented a framework that relies on a systems perspective for thinking about problems the consultee presents. This will then lead the consultant to consider a variety of interventions depending on the system(s) and subsystems to be influenced. Priorities are set so that a consultation plan can be developed, using the interventions most likely to succeed. Davis and Sandoval consider the dyadic subsystem as well as the family, school, consultant, and other subsystems. This multiple problem, multiple intervention way of thinking helps with continued problem solving when interventions are not successful. Flexibility in identifying multiple problems in an interacting systems perspective provides the consultant with multiple interventions that can be utilized. The authors note that a consultation plan, rather than a specific intervention, becomes a possible outcome.

Once a problem is identified, then a range of interventions is considered and one selected. Evaluation of the degree of success of the intervention leads to a consideration whether the "right" intervention was used and/or the original hypothesis as to the nature of the problem needs reconsideration. Such reflection sharpens the overall decision-making process in problem solving. Eley and Lyman (1987) described a problem-solving thinking process that they use with beginning teachers in which the problem identification and selection of a preferred solution is taught. At both of those steps a "think link" or "map" strategy is emphasized as a way to reinforce thinking about the challenge faced by the teacher. In the map a variety of *causes* and *effects* of the presenting problem should lead to a sharpened view of the problem, or even a restatement of the problem. Similarly, possible solutions are diagrammed with their advantages or disadvantages until a preferred solution is selected.

As pointed out earlier, cultural values are also variables that influence problem solving and decision making. In European American culture, decision making is an individual matter, that is, decision makers typically make decisions independently, often with little regard to the views of other people. Unacculturated Asian American and American Indian decision makers often defer to their families or groups and put their concerns first in the decision-making process (Brown & Crace, 1996). Moreover, unacculturated Asian Americans may defer to the consultant in the decision-making process because they view relationships with experts in lineal, as opposed to collateral, terms. The result may be that the consultant is expected to provide solutions to the presenting problem and forego collaborative approaches. Perhaps the most important point to be made here is that consultants need to be aware of cultural values of consultees that may influence the decision-making process.

A promising construct that takes cultural differences into account in the problem-solving process is represented by what Barnett and others (1995) call "ethnic validity." Barnett and his associates define ethnic validity as the extent to which both the problem and the approach identified to resolve the problem are in accord with the client's cultural values and beliefs. They go on to list the key ingredients for establishing ethnic validity: (1) employing problem solving within the consultation context, (2) acceptability of the intervention to the consultee, and (3) utilization of teaming strategies. In order to approach consultation from an ethnically valid perspective, the consultant must take a holistic approach that considers the cultural context of consultation as well as the purpose and expected outcomes of consultation. Perhaps it goes without saying, but ethnic validity in consultation also requires that the consultant accept and understand the cultural values of the consultee and use this knowledge

and understanding as the foundation of the problem-solving approaches used. Barnett and others (1995) also suggest that, to function from an ethnically valid point of view, consultants should be prepared to advocate for the consultee. Acceptability of consultation approaches, the second aspect of ethnic validity, refers to the consultee's perspective on the "appropriateness, fairness, reasonableness, intrusiveness, and normalcy of the intervention" (p. 221). Finally, teaming—from the perspective of Barnett and colleagues—involves "interactive and collaborative problem solving" (p. 222) that fully involves the consultee in the decision-making process and takes into consideration cultural barriers to problem solving such as language.

Problem Identification and Goal Setting

Research has shown that, when consultants' verbal skills do not aid in problem identification (Bergan & Tombari, 1975) and when the consultant is unable to quickly help the consultee identify the problem, the process is more likely to fail (Bergan & Tombari, 1976). As has already been noted, Bergan (1977) and, more recently, Bergan and Kratochwill (1990) have set forth a set of skills that, if mastered, will allow the consultant to identify the problems from a behavioral perspective.

Idol and West (1987), Parsons and Meyers (1984), and many others have suggested that consultants need a host of assessment skills that will allow them not only to assess the consultees' problems, but also will guide the process of identifying the clients' problems as well. The organizational consultant quite obviously needs the skills to diagnose a wide range of problems from maladaptive aspects of the culture to managerial style problems. The human resources manager working in the school needs to be able to assess instructional and classroom management deficiencies. Consultants working with parents must be able to determine whether parents are engaging in child-rearing techniques that are facilitating or retarding the child's psychological and educational development. Quite obviously there are many ways to assess organizational, instructional, and parenting problems, many of which are discussed in this book.

Once consultee and client problems have been identified, consultants need to—with their consultees—consider the locus of the problem (Kurpius et al., 1993). Consultants who work in schools often encounter teachers who want students to be "fixed" so that they will fit into the classroom. The likelihood of this occurring may increase when the student comes from a culture quite different from the teacher's. Research suggests that the learning and classroom interactional styles of students from various ethnic groups vary. For example, Mexican American children and some North American Indian students prefer cooperative approaches (as opposed to competitive approaches) to learning (Grigg & Dunn, 1989). Teachers may misinterpret this lack of aggressiveness as disinterest, or worse, lack of ability. Dunn, Gemake, Jalali, and Zenhausern (1990) studied the learning styles of Mexican American, African American, Chinese American, and Greek American children and found numerous differences on variables such as preferences for structure, the manner in which material is presented, whether they learned alone or in groups, and even the temperature of the classroom. Teachers who make no attempt to match instructional approaches to students' preferences may very well conclude that the problem lies with the student. Analogous problems arise in organizations when management style fails to match the preferences of the employees. The manager may very well blame the employees, when in fact many of the problems that have occurred result from her or his managerial style. It is the consultant's responsibility to point out that the consultee's assumptions are erroneous when this occurs.

Kurpius and others (1993), drawing upon the work of McClelland (1989), observed that the primary reason that interventions fail is that problems are not adequately diagnosed. The primary skills needed to properly diagnose problems and establish a course of action in consultation are:

1. Understanding theories of individual/organizational behavior and the ability to use that information to conceptualize problems.
2. Using various information-gathering strategies including the interview and questionnaires to collect valid information about the problem.
3. Communicating the nature of the problem in a manner that is readily understood by the consultee.
4. Developing ownership of the problem.
5. Establishing attainable goals.

Intervention Selection and Implementation

Kurpius and his colleagues (1993) suggested another set of reasons why consultation failures can be linked to intervention selection. As has been said repeatedly, consultation is a problem-solving process. The crux of this process is changing problematic practices in a manner that will be acceptable to the consultee and will have the desired impact on the client. Often it is the consultant's role to identify the intervention, explain it to the consultee, and then teach it to the consultee (Zins, 1993). This process presupposes that the consultant has a considerable knowledge of the duties of the consultee and the forces that impinge on those duties. Some of the interventions used by various types of consultants were listed in earlier chapters, and they will not be repeated here.

Consultants will, for the most part, use interventions that are tied to their theoretical orientation, that is, behavioral consultants will use behavioral contracts and cost-response interventions, and consultants following a social learning model will use modeling strategies in conjunction with cognitively oriented interventions. Staying within a single theoretical framework may be an error (Brown, 1985; Carlson & Tombari, 1996), particularly if the framework is incompatible with that of the consultee or does not adequately consider factors such as cross-cultural concerns.

What then are the key skills needed in the all-important intervention selection process? Some of these are:

1. Assessing consultees' values and world view to determine which types of intervention are likely to be most acceptable.
2. Having a working knowledge of numerous interventions related to the problems that the consultant is likely to encounter.
3. Being able to communicate the nature of an intervention as it relates to consultees'/clients' problems and, if necessary, teaching the intervention to the consultee.
4. With the consultee, monitoring the efficacy of the intervention and redesigning it as necessary.

Evaluation and Termination

Evaluation may not lead to termination, particularly if the data suggest that the intervention has been ineffective. However, if the evaluation is not supportive, intervention redesign (one of the techniques mentioned above) will be needed. If it is supportive, then termination should be the result.

Termination can occur under circumstances other than success and often does. If the consultant and consultee develop a disagreement about the goals that should be pursued or the strategies that should be employed, termination of the process should occur unless these differences can be resolved. Also, in human resources consultation, the process should be terminated if the consultee consistently fails to follow through or if the resistance cannot be eliminated.

The skills required at this stage of consultation are:

1. Ability to evaluate the extent to which the consultation intervention is achieving the goals that have been established.
2. Communications skills needed to explain the outcomes that are being observed.
3. Ability to identify factors in the consultation that prevent it from being untenable and terminating the relationship for cause.

4. Skills for terminating consultation processes that have been successful, that is, when goals have been attained.

NEEDED RESEARCH

In a review of the empirical foundations of consultation, Henning-Stout (1993) noted several gaps in our knowledge base about consultation. Interestingly, she did not mention the fact that we know relatively little about the characteristics of the effective consultant. As mentioned earlier, it is particularly odd that hundreds of studies have focused on the characteristics of the effective therapist, but the traits of the consultant have been ignored by researchers. Perhaps this is because much of the research on consultation has been conducted by behaviorally oriented consultants who have paid more attention to the technology employed by the consultant than they have to the characteristics of the person employing the technology. This oversight stands as a major gap in the consultation research literature, particularly when the literature suggests, but does not confirm, that certain characteristics such as warmth and empathy seem to be important to consultees (Horton & Brown, 1990) when rating consultants.

The skills of the consultant have been studied much more extensively than the characteristics, but much of this research has been conducted from a behavioral perspective. Some of this research (Erchul, 1987; Erchul & Chewning, 1990) has led to a current debate about whether the consulting relationship should be collegial/coequal or dominated by the consultant. Consultants need very different skills if they are to dominate the counseling relationship as opposed to acting as a coequal. Henning-Stout (1993) marshals support for both sides of this argument, but, nevertheless, considerable research is needed in this area. This research should focus on the goals of consultation, which are to reduce or eliminate current mental health and/or educational problems and prevent future problems from occurring by empowering the consultee with new perspectives and skills.

Student Learning Activity 7.2

Rate your consultation skills using the following scale.

1 = inadequate in this area at this time
2 = somewhat skilled but need additional work
3 = very skilled; feel totally competent

1 2 3   **1.** Analyze my personal strengths and weaknesses.

1 2 3   **2.** Identify my areas of competency as a consultant.

1 2 3   **3.** Market my consultation skills.

1 2 3   **4.** Forecast the likelihood that consultation will be successful.

1 2 3   **5.** Develop formal consulting contracts.

1 2 3   **6.** Establish informal consulting contracts.

1 2 3   **7.** Explain the consulting process in easily understood terms.

1 2 3   **8.** Listen and understand both the affective message as well as the verbal content of the consultee's communication.

1 2 3   **9.** Respond sensitively to consultees who have a cultural perspective different from my own.

1 2 3   **10.** Clarify the consultee's communication using various techniques such as open-ended questions.

1 2 3   **11.** Identify the points of conflict and resolve them before they impair the consulting relationship.

1 2 3   **12.** Have sufficient knowledge of individual behavior, including educational and psychological concerns, so that I can conceptualize problems and communicate them in easily understandable terms.

1 2 3   **13.** Have sufficient knowledge of organizational functioning so that I can conceptualize problems and communicate them in easily understandable terms.

1 2 3   **14.** Can conceptualize family problems and communicate them in a manner that is easily understood.

1 2 3   **15.** Can conduct a fact-finding interview that will yield valid data about the individual, the organization, or the family.

1 2 3   **16.** Can assist consultee in developing ownership of the problem once it is identified.

1 2 3   **17.** Can help consultee identify and prioritize attainable goals.

1 2 3   **18.** Can use supportive refocus to maintain focus on client and avoid therapy.

1 2 3   **19.** Can assess consultee's values prior to intervention selection.

1 2 3   **20.** Can design interventions based on at least two divergent theoretical perspectives and communicate these in understandable terms.

1 2 3   **21.** Establish monitoring system to determine intervention effectiveness.

1 2 3   **22.** Design evaluations that will establish efficacy of intervention.

1 2 3   **23.** Determine whether resistance is interfering with consultation progress and either terminate or ameliorate resistance.

1 2 3   **24.** Communicate the outcomes of consultation and explain reasons for success or failure.

1 2 3   **25.** Terminate successful consultations.

1 2 3   **26.** Can conduct all of the above in a culturally sensitive manner.

We also need additional research on the process of consultation as it relates to the skills of the consultant. Henning-Stout and Conoley (1987) found that counseling and consultation are procedurally divergent, which was not unexpected. But the questions of how best to establish consulting relationships in what is often a brief process, assess consultee values and skills, and deal with issues such as resistance remain unanswered.

Finally, the area of multicultural consultation has begun to be addressed by researchers. It is tempting to generalize from the counseling literature (e.g., Ponterotto & Casas, 1991) and suggest that there are a host of problems in these cross-cultural consultation interactions. However, whether there are always problems and what the nature of these problems are remain to be established. Perhaps more important, the skills needed to handle problems must be developed and validated.

SUMMARY

In this chapter the skills and characteristics of collaborators and consultants have been addressed in some detail. Admittedly, there are few answers to the questions, "What are the characteristics of the effective consultant?" and "What basic skills must a consultant have to be effective?" However, we do have some preliminary information that can guide our training. It is up to the researchers to expand our knowledge base so that our selection and training processes can be more effective.

TIPS FOR THE PRACTITIONER

1. After you have completed the checklist shown in Student Learning Activity 7.2, formulate a plan for developing the skills you need to overcome your deficiencies.
2. Follow a consultant for a day, trying to ascertain the characteristics that make them effective or ineffective. Can you identify areas that need improvement? Can you identify any personal deficits that may need remediation?

3. Interview several consultants to ascertain what traits and skills they believe are essential to success in consultation.

REVIEW QUESTIONS

1. List five traits that seem to be essential to success in consultation. Which of these has the greatest support empirically?
2. List the essential skills needed at each phase of the consulting relationship based on what we know at this time.
3. Identify areas of needed research pertaining to skills and characteristics. Which of these is most essential? Defend your choice.
4. Discuss the pros and cons of the consultant's controlling the consulting relationship. What skills would be most useful if the consultant does wish to control the consultation process?
5. What would be the essential skills if the consultant wants to establish a coequal consulting relationship?

REFERENCES

ACA. (1995). *Ethical standards.* Alexandria, VA.

APA. (2002). Ethical principles of psychologists and code of conduct.

Arrendondo, P., Toporek, R., Brown, S. P., Jones, J., Locke, D. C., Sanchez, J., & Stadler, H. (1996). Operationalization of multicultural counseling competencies. *Journal of Multicultural Counseling and Development, 24,* 42–78.

Barnett, D. W., Collins, R., Cora, C., Curtiz, M. J., Kristal, Z., Glaser, A., Reyes, C., Stoller, S., & Winston, M. (1995). Ethnic validity of school psychology: Concepts and practices associated with cross-cultural competencies. *Journal of School Psychology, 33,* 219–234.

Bergan, J. R. (1977). *Behavioral consultation.* Columbus, OH: Charles E. Merrill.

Bergan, J. R., & Kratochwill, T. R. (1990). *Behavioral consultation and therapy.* New York: Plenum.

Bergan, J. R., & Tombari, M. L. (1975). The analysis of verbal interaction occurring during consultation. *Journal of School Psychology, 13,* 209–226.

Bergan, J. R., & Tombari, M. L. (1976). Consultant skill and efficiency and the implementation of outcomes in consultation. *Journal of School Psychology, 14,* 3–14.

Brown, D. (1985). The preservice training and supervision of consultants. *The Counseling Psychologist, 13,* 410–425.

Brown, D. (1993). Training consultants: A call for action. *Journal of Counseling and Development, 72,* 139–143.

Brown, D. (1997). Implications of cultural values for cross-cultural consultation with families. *Journal of Counseling and Development, 76,* 29–35

Brown, D., & Crace, R. K. (1996). *Professional manual for the Life Values Inventory.* Chapel Hill, NC: Life Values Press.

Bushe, G. R., & Gibbs, B. W. (1989). *Ego development, role enactment, and corporate behavior: A field study.* Paper presented at the annual meeting of the Academy of Management, Washington, DC.

Bushe, G. R., & Gibbs, B. W. (1990). Predicting organizational development consulting competence from Myers-Briggs Type Indicator and stage of ego development. *Journal of Applied Behavior Science, 26,* 337–357.

Caplan, G. (1970). *The theory and practice of mental health consultation.* New York: Academic Press.

Carlson, C. I., & Tombari, M. L. (1996). Multilevel school consultation training: A preliminary analysis. *Professional School Psychology, 1,* 89–104.

Carter, R. T. (1991). Cultural values: A review of the empirical literature and implications for counseling. *Journal of Counseling and Development, 70,* 164–173.

Conoley, C. W., & Conoley, J. C. (1991). *School consultation: A guide to practice and training* (2nd ed.). New York: Macmillan.

Conoley, C. W., Conoley, J. C., Ivey, D. C., & Scheel, M. J. (1991). Enhancing consultation by matching the consultee's perspective. *Journal of Counseling and Development, 69,* 546–549.

Cross, T., Bazron, R., Dennis, K., & Isaacs, M. (1989). *Toward a culturally competent system of care, Vol 1.* Washington, DC: Georgetown University Child Development Center, CASSP Technical Assistance Center.

Davis, J. M., & Sandoval, J. (1991). A pragmatic framework for systems-oriented consultation. *Journal of Educational and Psychological Consultation, 2* (3), 201–216.

Davis, K. (1997). *Exploring the intersection between cultural competency and managed behavioral health care policy: Implications for state and county mental health agencies.* Alexandria, VA: National Technical Assistance Center for State Mental Health Planning.

Doughtery, A. M. (1990). *Consultation: Practice and perspectives* (4th ed.). Pacific Grove, CA: Brooks/Cole.

Dunn, R., Gemake, J., Jalali, L., & Zenhausern, R. (1990). Cross-cultural differences in learning styles of elementary-age students from four ethnic backgrounds. *Journal of Multicultural Counseling and Development, 18,* 68–91.

Eley, G., & Lyman, F. (1987). Problem solving and action research for beginning teachers. *Maryland Association of Teacher Education Journal, 3,* 16–19.

Erchul, W. P. (1987). A relational communications analysis of control in school consultation. *Professional School Psychology, 2,* 113–124.

Erchul, W. P., & Chewning, T. G. (1990). Behavioral consultation from a request-centered relational communication perspective. *School Psychology, Quarterly, 5,* 1–20.

Grigg, S. A., & Dunn, R. (1989). The learning styles of multicultural groups and counseling implications. *Journal of Multicultural Counseling and Development, 17,* 146–155.

Hamilton, E. (1988) The facilitation of organizational change: An empirical study of the factors predicting agents' effectiveness. *Journal of Applied Behavioral Science, 24,* 37–59.

Hansen, J., & Himes, B. (1977). Critical incidents in consultation. *Elementary School Guidance and Counseling, 22,* 291–295.

Helms, J. (1990). *Black and white racial identity: Theory, research and practice.* New York: Greenwood.

Helms, J. (1992). *A race is a nice thing to have.* Topeka, KS: Content Communications.

Henning-Stout, M. (1993). Theoretical and empirical bases of consultation. In J. E. Zins, T. R. Kratochwill, and S. W. Witt (Eds.), *Handbook of consultation services for children* (pp. 15–45). San Francisco: Jossey-Bass.

Henning-Stout, M., & Conoley, J. C. (1987). Consultation and counseling as procedurally divergent: Analysis of verbal behavior. *Professional Psychology: Research and Practice, 18,* 124–127.

Herman, K. C. (1993). Reassessing predictors of therapist competence. *Journal of Counseling and Development, 72,* 29–32.

Ho, M. K. (1987). *Family therapy with ethnic groups.* Newbury Park, CA: Sage.

Holcomb-McCoy, C. C. (2001). Exploring the self-perceived multicultural counseling competence of elementary school counselors. *Professional School Counseling, 4,* 195–201.

Holcomb-McCoy, C. C., & Myers, J. E. (1999). Multicultural competence and counselor Training: A national survey. *Journal of Counseling and Development, 77,* 291–302.

Horton, G. E., & Brown, D. (1990). The importance of interpersonal skills in consultee-centered consultation. *Journal of Counseling and Development, 68,* 423–426.

Hunsaker, P. L. (1985). Strategies for organizational change: Role of the inside change agent. In D. D. Warrick (Ed.), *Contemporary organizational development* (pp. 123–137). Glenview, IL: Scott, Foresman.

Idol, L., & West, J. F. (1987). Consultation in special education: Training and practice (Part II). *Journal of Special Education, 20,* 474–497.

Ingraham, C. L. (2000a). Consultation through a multicultural lens: Multicultural and cross-cultural consultation in school settings. *School Psychology Review, 29,* 320–343.

Ingraham, C. L. (2000b). Multicultural consultee-centered consultation: When novice consultants explore cultural hypotheses with experienced teacher consultees. *Journal of Educational and Psychological Consultation, 14,* 329–362.

Ingraham, C. L., & Meyers, J. (2000). Introduction to multicultural and cross-cultural consultation in Schools: Cultural diversity issues in school consultatiom. *School Psychology Review, 29,* 315–319.

Ivey, A., D'Andrea, M., Ivey, M. B., & Simek-Morgan, L. (2002). *Counseling and psychotherapy* (5th ed.). Boston: Allyn and Bacon.

King, M. A., Sims, A., & Osher, D. (1998). How is cultural competence integrated into education.? [On-line.] Available: http://www/air.org/ceep/cultural?Q_integrated. htm.

Kolb, D. A. (1983). Problem solving management: Learning from experience. In S. Srvasta (Ed.), *The executive mind* (pp. 109–143). San Francisco: Jossey-Bass.

Kratochwill, T. R., VanSomeren, K. R., & Sheridan, S. M. (1990). Training behavioral consultants: A competency-based model to teach interview skills. *Professional Psychology: Research and Practice, 4,* 41–58.

Kurpius, D. J., & Fuqua, D. R. (1993). Fundamental issues in defining consultation. *Journal of Counseling and Development, 71,* 607–618.

Kurpius, D. J., Fuqua, D. R., & Rozecki, T. (1993). The consulting process: A multidimensional approach. *Journal of Counseling and Development, 71,* 601–606.

Kurpius, D. J., & Rozecki, T. G. (1993). Strategies for improving interpersonal communication. In J. E. Zins, T. R. Kratochwill, and S. N. Witt (Eds.), *Handbook of consultation services for children* (pp. 137–158). San Francisco: Jossey-Bass.

Loevinger, L. (1976). *Ego development.* San Francisco: Jossey-Bass.

Maher, C. A. (1993). Providing consultation services in business settings. In J. E. Zins, T. R. Kratochwill, and S. N. Witt (Eds.), *Handbook of consultation services for children* (pp. 317–328). San Francisco: Jossey-Bass.

Maitland, R. E., Fine, M. J., & Tracy, D. B. (1985). The effects of an interpersonally-based problem-solving process on consultation outcomes. *Journal of School Psychology, 23,* 337–345.

McClelland, D. C. (1989) How do self-attributed and implicit motives differ? *Psychological Review, 96,* 201–210.

Parsons, R. D., & Meyers, J. (1984). *Developing consultation skills.* San Francisco: Jossey-Bass.

Paskewicz, C. W., & Clark, C. D. (1984). *When behavioral consultation fails.* Paper presented at the annual convention of the National Association of School Psychologists. Philadelphia, PA.

Ponterotto, J. G., & Casas, J. M. (1991). *Handbook of racial/ethnic minority counseling research.* Springfield, IL: Charles C. Thomas.

Pryzwansky, W. B. (1974). A reconsideration of the consultation model for delivery of school-based psychological services. *American Journal of Orthopsychiatry, 44,* 579–583.

Pryzwansky, W. P. (1977). Collaboration or consultation: Is there a difference? *Journal of Special Education, 11,* 179–182.

Pryzwansky, W. B., & Schulte, A. (1989). *Novices responses to two types of problems and consultation approached.* Paper presented at annual meeting of the American Psychological Association.

Pryzwansky, W. B., & Vatz, B. C. (1988). *School psychologists solutions to a consultation problem: Do experts agree?* Paper presented at annual convention of the National Association of School Psychologists, Boston, MA.

Randolph, D. L. (1985). *Microconsulting: Basic psychological consultation skills for helping professionals.* Johnson City, TN: Institute of Social Sciences and Art.

Remley, T. P., Jr. (1993). Consultation contracts. *Journal of Counseling and Development, 72,* 157–159.

Richardson, T. Q., & Molinaro, K. L. (1996). White counselor self-awareness: A prerequisite for developing multicultural competence. *Journal of Counseling and Development, 74,* 238–242.

Rubin, H. (2002). *Collaborative leadership: Developing effective partnerships in communities and schools.* Thousand Oaks, CA: Corwin.

Salmon, D., & Lehrer, R. (1989). School consultant's implicit theories of action. *Professional School Psychology, 4*(3), 173–187.

Sandoval, J., Lambert, N. M., & Davis, J. M. (1977). Consultation from the consultee's perspective. *Journal of School Psychology, 15,* 334–342.

Sue, D. W., Arredondo, P., & McDavis, R. J. (1992). Multicultural counseling competencies and standards: A call to the profession. *Journal of Multicultural Counseling and Development, 20,* 64–88.

Sue, D. W., & Sue, D. (1999). *Counseling the culturally different.* (3rd ed.). New York: John Wiley & Sons.

Varncy, G. H. (1985). OD professionals: The route to becoming a professional. In D. D. Warrick (Ed.), *Contemporary organizational development* (pp. 49–56). Glenview, IL: Scott, Foresman.

Vatz, B. C., & Pryzwansky, W. B. (1987). *The problem solving style of expert consultants in school psychology.* Paper presented at annual convention of the National Association of School Psychologists, Boston, MA.

Voss, J. F., Tyler, U., & Yengo, L. A. (1983). Individual differences in solving of social science problems. In D. F. Dillon & R. R. Snack (Eds.), *Individual differences in cognition, Vol. I* (pp. 205–223). New York: Academic Press.

Weissenberg, J., Fine, M., & Poggio, J. (1982). Factors influencing the outcomes of consultation. *Journal of School Psychology, 20,* 263–270.

Witt, S. N. (1990). Collaboration in school based consultation: Myth in need of data. *Journal of Educational and Psychological Consultation, 1,* 367–370.

Zins, J. E. (1993). Enhancing consultee problem-solving skills in consultative interactions. *Journal of Counseling and Development, 72,* 185–190.

ANSWERS TO LEARNING EXERCISES

8.1 There are no answers. This is your own estimate of your characteristics.

8.2 There are no answers. This scale provides you with an opportunity to estimate your own consulting skills.

CHAPTER 8

THE CONSULTEE
AS A VARIABLE

GOAL OF THE CHAPTER

The goal of this chapter is to present the perspective and characteristics of consultees as potential factors influencing the process and outcome of consultation.

CHAPTER PREVIEW

1. Consultee expectations and preferences for consultation services as reflected in research findings are presented.
2. Characteristics of consultees such as experience, personality, problem-solving style, ethnic background, and affect are examined in terms of their impact.
3. The preparation of consultees for this role during both preservice training programs as well as the consultation process itself are discussed.

As late as the mid-1970s, writers in the consultation area were noting with concern the lack of attention directed toward the consultee as a variable affecting the process or outcome of consultation (Bardon, 1977; Mannino & Shore, 1975). A review by Piersel (1985) suggested that the situation was changing and some progress was being made in our appreciation of the consultee's impact, although not at the pace and with the breadth of coverage one would expect. Of the 87 doctoral dissertations reported in the decade following 1978, only 10 percent dealt with this influence (Duncan & Pryzwansky, 1988). Although the emerging knowledge is still fragmentary overall, the available research should be of assistance to consultants and particularly trainees as they attempt to understand and practice consultation.

This chapter has as its primary goal the development of our awareness that the characteristics of the consultee are a major influence in the consultation process. Specifically, the characteristics of the consultee that appear to influence the consultant–consultee interaction will be discussed. Special emphasis is placed on the cultural variations that have recently been hypothesized to affect the consultation relationship and the interference they may cause in the problem-solving task. The possibility of training consultees is explored as a way of enhancing their use of consultation and contributing to the eventual outcome. Some suggested approaches for training of this type are also offered.

Initially, the discussion will be centered on what is known about consultees' expectations when they consider the consultation service. As will be pointed out, expectations are different from their stated preferences for what should take place. These two consultees' views represent the emphasis of research in the past few years, and although our information is still limited, some important glimpses into the "consumers'" priorities are emerging.

EXPECTATIONS AND PREFERENCES OF THE CONSULTEE

It is important to distinguish between what consultees *prefer* to happen when they request consultation and actually *expect* to happen in consultation. The work that has been done in the counseling field suggests that this distinction reveals differences on the part of clients that were important to take into account.

Expectations refer to those preconceived notions regarding anticipated occurrences. They can include notions about the consultant's role and degree of involvement throughout the process, the stereotypical behavior pattern that should be displayed by the consultant, the nature of the process itself, and the probability of success resulting from this professional contact. *Preferences,* on the other hand, are quite separate considerations, for they represent what consultees would like to experience rather than what they believe will be experienced. It is logical to hypothesize that a smoother, more productive consultation will result when congruence exists between the expectations and preferences of the consultee and what actually transpires, although that relationship has yet to be demonstrated empirically. At the very least, we can assume that the "set" (i.e., expectations and preferences) of the consultee serves to influence the process. Thus, conscious awareness on the part of the consultant of the influence of the consultee's preferences and expectations is as important as the data regarding the consultation problem.

Expectations

A somewhat dated study provides some tentative, but nevertheless provocative, data in this area.

Macarov (1968), in a follow-up evaluation of consultation projects involving two consultants and 40 consultees, reported that consultees questioned and even rejected the term "consultation" as a descriptor for the experience. Rather, they described the contact as an informal experience that resulted in the sharing of information. To a larger degree, consultees tended to see consultants as resource persons versus any other role. Macarov later speculated that the consultee's conceptualization of what had taken place reflected negative associations with the term "consultation" in that the term suggested that help was needed and given. Consultees apparently had trouble asking for help, taking help, or admitting they needed help. This subject is explored further in Chapter Thirteen, Issues in Consultation and Collaboration, but for now it is sufficient to recognize the reactions of one group of consultees to the term. This finding suggests that at a minimum we reconsider the intent of our service (i.e., is it to give help?) as well as the manner in which it is described.

Yet another study found significant discrepancies between the expectations for service and the service actually provided or recommended by the consultant (Noy, DeNour, & Moses, 1966). In spite of a common professional background, referring physicians and psychiatric consultants tended to be caught up in the intricacies and idiosyncrasies of their particular doctor–patient relationship. In one sense the professionals were alike in their personal motivation to become a physician and help, even cure, patients. Yet each was committed to a view of the patient and illness that tended to exclude the other's point of view, according to Noy and colleagues; psychiatrists placed considerably more emphasis on emotional factors in diagnosis and treatment than did physicians. Similar relationships can be experienced in other fields, such as education where classroom teachers and special education teachers work together, or where either of those instructional staff members interacts with other resource personnel such as the school counselor or school psychologist. One of the book's authors annually documents the existence and power of preconceptions in the consultation relationship.

For example, it has been observed over several years that when students from school counseling and school psychology programs view a mental health consultation film during their initial consultation course, they bemoan the lack of directness and intellectual assertiveness in the consultant's style: for example, "He (consultant) never told her what to do." Both groups of students are completing a first year of training in which direct service has been emphasized and have an obvious expectation about the consultant's role in consultation.

One additional study in this area has suggested that teachers' expectations for consultation are influenced by a variety of factors such as work experience and position in the system. For example, Gilmore and Chandy (1973) found that teachers with four or more contacts per year with a school psychologist are more likely than the other teachers to consider the psychologist as a consultant rather than simply as a test administrator. The less experienced teachers (four or fewer years teaching) were more likely to expect the psychologist to function in the traditional role of assessment versus consultation. However, psychologists and principals are more likely to view the psychologist as a consultant than are teachers. A related finding from this same study supports the premise that consultation is reserved for rare instances. As a group, teachers were of the opinion that problems should be of a relatively serious nature before a psychologist becomes involved. If such a criterion should influence consultation contacts, it could suggest to the consultee that a variety of interventions may be warranted including immediate, direct client intervention. Furthermore, any potential preventative benefit derived from stressing the consultation model of service delivery is defeated.

Finally, Schulte and Osborne (2003), in their examination of the different definitions of *collaboration,* express the concern that professionals trained with differing views of collaboration will enter the relationship "…with very different expectations regarding goals and processes" (p. 132). They reason that misunderstanding and resentment as well as conflicting expectations regarding each other's role and responsibility are potential outcomes due to the exposure in training to only one definition or model.

Preferences

Some limited data are available to support the preferences for consultation services, but for only one setting. In an early set of studies, Gutkin (1980), Roberts (1970), and Waters (1973) found that teachers do indeed prefer that the school psychologist place more emphasis on the consultant role, particularly versus psychometric services. In a sense, this preference is somewhat inconsistent with their expectations regarding consultation, as we have just discussed.

Generally, when we think of preferences we assume that there has been some experience with all the choices from which one is to make a selection. In the absence of any experience with consultation, then, it actually may be unreasonable to be asking consultees to state their preferences for receiving this type of service. Such a dilemma makes the Waters (1973) and Gutkin (1980) findings all the more interesting. In the Waters study, data were collected six months after the psychological services department had shifted from a psychometric model to a consultant model. While a Hawthorne effect (i.e., any change brings about initial enthusiasm for the change) could be postulated as an explanation for the results, these teachers did experience at least one other service delivery model and therefore had some comparisons on which to base their ratings. In the Gutkin study (1980) using 12 student consultants over a period of 14 weeks, 69 percent of the teachers responding to the questionnaire indicated they found consultation services to be more effective than the traditional testing role of the school psychologist. Here again, there may have been strong extenuating circumstances influencing the teachers' ratings. For example, if they felt that a positive rating would increase the likelihood of continuing university services that were somewhat helpful, they might be tempted to provide supporting feedback.

By contrast, we know much more about consultees' ideas of how they would like to be worked with, that is, their preference for consultation models or approaches. This information has been almost exclusively gained from studies that ask consultees to choose between written descriptions of two or more models. For example, there is some indication that teachers prefer collaborative problem-solving relationships with consultants. In studies by Coleman (1976) and Wenger (1979) that compared collaborative consultation with conventional or expert-oriented consultation, all but one of the teachers expressed a preference for the collaborative model. Similarly, teachers and other school staff chose the collaborative model over three other models (behavioral, expert, mental health) whether descriptions of the four models were provided to them and they were asked to rank them, or the consultant–consultee responsibilities at five stages of consultation in each model were described separately (Babcock & Pryzwansky, 1983; White & Pryzwansky, 1982). Weiler (1984) reported that the preference of parents, regardless of the setting in which they served as consultees (community or school), was for the collaborative approach over three other models. The active involvement of the consultee in the collaborative consultation approach may be a critical feature of the model that influenced the choice. Indeed, Gutkin (1983) found that teachers believe that their involvement in the development of remedial programs for students is very important. Schulte, Osborne, and Kauffman (1993) studied the preferences of regular classroom teachers over time as they received consultation from special education teachers. They found a marked preference for the collaborative model before and after receiving services that involved solely consultation or a combination of consultation and direct instruction with the child. These authors considered teacher-time as a key factor for the teachers' preference of the collaborative model. Similarly, based on survey results of teachers from a study of the status of "consultant teacher service in special education," Gold and Hollander (1992) recommended revised nomenclature and suggested "collaborating teacher" may be more palatable than "consultant." Not only did it appear to the authors that the former term

would be less likely to elicit antagonism from mainstream teachers, but it would more accurately describe the relationship.

Although there is also some evidence that teachers as a whole prefer nondirective consultants to behavioral or direct consultants (Miller, 1974), the findings are not conclusive. For example, in a study using simulated consultation videotapes, teachers rated the behavioral consultant as generally more effective on three of the six effectiveness dimensions; no preference determination was reported (Medway & Forman, 1980). Slesser, Fine, and Tracy (1990) replicated aspects of the Medway and Forman study and found that both the mental health and behavioral consultants were viewed as being about equally "facilitative" overall, although higher consultation outcome scores were given to the behavioral consultant. In addition, Clark (1979) reported that teachers in a behavior modification training program did not make differential judgments between consultants who elicited an intervention plan and those who told the teachers what to do. On the other hand, Gutkin (1980) reported that 96 percent of the teachers in his sample indicated that it was "quite" or "very" important for them to be involved in the development of remedial plans for their students who were experiencing difficulties.

Finally, Mischley (1973) had teachers express their preference between the Caplanian approaches of consultee-centered consultation (mental health) and client-centered consultation (medical/expert) and found relatively equal numbers preferring each model. Furthermore, when offered one of those consultation approaches under either a group or individual format, equal numbers of teachers chose among the four conditions. Thus, Mischley's study raises an important consideration where the consultee's preferences are involved. Not only should consultants take into account the consultee's preferences by, at the very least, acknowledging them, but some attention would be well spent on recognizing the conditions under which the consultation is offered.

Several additional points should be addressed to aid in interpreting the relevance of the studies' findings. In most of the research mentioned, the consultees were not helped to adopt any "set" toward the choices, that is, asked to identify what they would *ideally* like to experience or what is the best they can hope for. Consequently, it can be argued that the choices we have just reported might be dictated by ideal versus reality considerations. Second, preferences of individuals reflect a cognitive behavior; it is not possible to predict what the consultees' preferences will be once they experience a particular consultation approach. Third, constraints on their role in the organization may be a more important factor influencing their thinking than what they would like. For example, Sarason (1971) has effectively described the demands placed on teachers and the lack of school flexibility in accommodating anything but an instructional role. The teacher role and the organizational structure of schools do not allow for collegial input from consultants; teachers simply cannot function in that way. The time required for certain consultation relationships such as collaboration may simply not be available. Similarly, there may not be administrative sanction to support such professional interchange. Given the current emphasis directed to increasing instructional time-on-task, there may be even less inclination to disrupt the teacher's primary responsibility—instruction.

As indicated, consultee preferences and expectations can be confounding variables in the consultation relationship. Although in the truly collaborative relationship the consultant and consultee engage in a process of determining the preferences and expectations of the other, it seems likely that in most situations this responsibility will rest on the consultant's shoulders. A suggested set of techniques for accomplishing this task, therefore, is presented in Table 8.1.

There are other facets of the consultee that need to be taken into account by the consultant. Some of them are obvious, such as the amount of experience the consultee has in his or her position and, in general, the age of the consultee. The ethnic background of the consultee is another seemingly obvious factor to take into account, but surprisingly has only recently been considered, with some unexpected results. The personality of consultees and their reaction to characteristics of the consultant also play a part in the nature and amount of involvement invested in the consultation relationship. Some tentative findings of other investigations into personality variables of consultees should also be noted. Mischley (1973) reported a relationship between personality characteristics and model of consultation preferred: consultees who reflected a general authoritarianism preferred a client-centered model, while more introspective consultees preferred a consultee-centered model. Finally, some relatively new ideas regarding the problem-solving ability of consultees and the degree to which their affective state may influence consultation outcome represent other characteristics that should not be

TABLE 8.1 Consultation Techniques for Determining Consultee Preferences and Expectations

CONSULTANT TECHNIQUE	MESSAGE TO CONSULTEE
Model expected behavior by sharing one's own expectations and preferences.	I've shared my attitudes with you, now tell me yours.
Direct questions such as "What do you expect from a consultant?", or use of questionnaire (see Chapter Eleven).	I'm interested in your input regarding my functioning.
Relay stories of failed consultations due to misperceptions of consultee.	It is important that we agree.
Informal contracting: "Let's agree on what our roles will be."	Commitment to models of functioning is important to our success.

overlooked. The next section examines what is known about these characteristics and suggests ways of dealing with them.

CONSULTEE CHARACTERISTICS AFFECTING PROCESS

Experience

This variable, professional experience, has received considerable attention but only when a teacher is identified as the consultee, and even this research is somewhat contradictory. In an early study, young professionals were found to be the segment of the school staff taking advantage of consultation services (Iscoe, Pierce-Jones, Friedman, & McGehearty, 1967). It could be argued that the novice is most eager for support and reassurance and also more idealistic in terms of the anticipated outcome. But Baker (1965) and Gilmore and Chandy (1973) found a positive correlation between years of experience and use of consultants. Each of these studies isolated the experience factor. As is the case in other areas of consultation research, studying variables in isolation from one another may not lead us any further toward understanding the process but only lead to simplistic answers. Consider, for example, the multivariate study where overall experience along with years of teaching at the current school were taken into account to answer this question. It was found that the longer teachers have taught in a school, the more likely they are to use consultation; just the opposite is true when simply the number of years teaching is considered (Gutkin & Bossard, 1984). If nothing else, these studies illustrate how careful the consultant must be in making judgments about a consultee from only one bit of information.

Teachers with more teaching experience gave higher ratings to both a mental health and behavioral consultation tape they viewed than did their less experienced counterparts, when the consultation experience was viewed as educational and leading to better problem solving in the future (Slesser, Fine, & Tracy, 1990). Also, these teachers were more satisfied with the mental health approach than were the less experienced teachers. On the other hand, it has been reported that, in considering 12 vignettes describing classroom problems, experienced teachers selected referral over consultation more often than less experienced teachers; however, it was noted that 89 percent of all the teachers reported using consultation services in their schools at least once a year (Hughes, Barker, Kemenoff, & Hart, 1993).

Perceptions of Consultants' Styles

We probably know less about this factor, with the exception of the degree to which consultees want to be involved as an equal in the process. The notion of receiving help may hold some negative connotation for the person who is helped. For example, in organizations such as schools, where the ideas of teaming, mentoring relationships, and consultation are positively received, the pressure on the teacher and administrator to handle all problems in their domain is still the prevalent expectation. In the one study of this phenomenon, consultees who were professionals in community volunteer agencies were found able to accept "help" if it took place as a sharing experience or an informational exchange (Macarov, 1968). Thus, the informal context of consultation seemed to be an element that intervened to make it acceptable as a valuable experience. By contrast, these same consultees (professionals in community volunteer agencies) seemed to reject both the word "consultation" and the concept. Thus, there was a clear preference for information over advice, in that it was easier to ask for and admit having received.

On a more theoretical level, the manner in which responsibility for both a problem and its solution is assumed by the consultee could be related to a style of coping/helping (Brickman, Rabinowitz, Karuza, Coates, Cohn, & Kidder, 1982). Brickman and colleagues identified four models of coping/helping: (1) moral—people are responsible for problems and solutions, (2) compensatory—people are not responsible for problems but are responsible for solutions, (3) medical—people are not responsible for problems or solutions, and (4) enlightenment—people are not responsible for solutions but are responsible for problems. Each position has an influence on the consultees' assumptions toward any problem-solving situation. Consultees should be listened to carefully in terms of the conditions under which they can accept resources. Consultants must also be careful how they describe their services and what assumptions they make regarding the helping orientation of the consultee.

Ethnic Background

The consultee characteristic that can have the most significant impact on the consultation process is sociocultural background. This factor has potential for affecting not only the consultation and the quality of the relationship that is established, but the value placed on consultation itself. The impact of cultural background differences has been explored in a number of areas, such as counseling relationships (Sue & Sue, 1977), organizational development (Pinto, 1981), schooling activities (e.g., Brady & Schneider, 1973; Bronkowski, 1968), consultation efforts (e.g., Morrison, 1970), and therapist–patient relationships (e.g., Sager, Brayboy, & Waxenberg, 1972).

The literature has noted issues involving communication barriers, negative self-attributions and feelings engendered on the part of the recipients of the service, differences in priorities in the relationship, and the potent effect of the interaction between explicit and implicit themes of change and values. Yet little has been done to address these observations in a systemic manner that could help facilitate the consultant–consultee relationship and the efficacy of the consultation contact. For the most part, consultants rely on their own sensitivity to the impact of cultural differences in their work with consultees. In addition, their training and experience, which impact on a theory of consultation, their value orientations, and their perception of the client/systems' value orientation (Pinto, 1981), play a role.

A theoretical model that emphasizes an interpersonal orientation in mental health consultation and directly addresses the ethnic question

has been proposed by Gibbs (1980). She has formulated the following three propositions: "(a) there are ethnic (e.g., black-white) differences in the initial orientation to the consultant-consultee relationship; (b) these differences are along the dimension of interpersonal *versus* instrumental competence; and (c) these differences have significant implications for the implementation of the consultation process and its outcome" (p. 195). Using both a historical/sociological perspective and a data-based literature review, stages in the consultees' behavior during entry and themes in the relationship between the consultant and black consultees during the entry phase of consultation are then delineated. Gibbs's model, which she considers tentative but nevertheless worthy of consideration at the training and practice levels, rests on the premise that black consultees focus on the "interpersonal competence" (process rather than content) of the consultant, while whites tend to focus on the "instrumental competence" (goal/task–related aspects) of the consultant. Interpersonal competence then is defined as "a measure of the ability of the individual to evoke positive attitudes and to obtain favorable responses to his actions" (p. 199). On the other hand, instrumental competence is considered to be "a measure of the degree of effectiveness with which a goal or task is accomplished by the individual" (p. 199).

Gibbs presents a predictable sequence of five stages that the interactions between the consultants and the consultees will follow during the entry phase of a consultation, modified of course by the perceived degree of ethnic and social class similarities between consultant and consultee. Those stages include an appraisal stage, investigation stage, involvement stage, commitment stage, and an engagement stage.

During the appraisal stage, the black consultee is seen as evaluating the consultant's personal authenticity and consequently remains aloof and reserved. The consultant's genuineness is gauged. The white consultee meanwhile is judged to be evaluating the overall consultation project and the professional skills of the consultant. In the second stage, investigation, black consultees shift from sizing up the consultant to making inquiries about the consultant's personal life, background, opinions, and values. Judgments are made regarding the ways the consultant relates to people of similar and different backgrounds. White consultees, by contrast, "will inquire about the details of the consultant project, not about the consultant's personal life" (p. 199).

The third stage, involvement, is characterized by the black consultee's attempt to establish a more personal relationship through exchange of personal information, personal favors, and quasisocial interactions such as lunch or a coffee break. Thus the consultant's degree of identification with others different in background is gauged. It is interesting to note that Gibbs argues that reciprocation by the consultant is crucial if the black consultee is to accept the consultant's expertise. Yet much of the consultation literature tends to argue against such an involvement, with a few exceptions (Altrocchi, 1972). The white consultee during this stage maintains the consultation relationship on a formal professional level.

A transition from personal support to program support in terms of loyalty and personal regard for the consultant by the black consultee takes place during the fourth stage, commitment. Interest is shifted to the consultation task. During this stage, white consultees "will express their commitment in terms of the goals to be accomplished" (p. 200). The final stage has both consultee groups committed to participation (task involvement). Black consultees' commitment is "the result of their evaluation of interpersonal competence of the consultant; the white consultee's commitment is made [as a result] of the instrumental competence of the consultant through the preceding stages" (p. 200).

Gibbs reports that these stages exist for both white and black consultants. Similarly, comparisons were the same whether the consultees were black or white. She also hypothesizes that the concept of an interpersonal orientation in consultation can be generalized to other ethnic minority groups sharing similar societal experiences with blacks. However, it would seem prudent to consider the

two orienting mechanisms, interpersonal and instrumental, as operating within the general population and reflecting value systems of the consultee regardless of race. Thus, such relationship needs may be triggered whenever external consultants, such as was the case in the experiences that served as the basis for Gibbs's conceptualization, enter a system wherein consultees exhibit a high level of protectionism toward their clients and/or project (e.g., a school for handicapped children, an inner city project, a center for abused women).

Beyond such obvious conditions that indicate careful review of the consultant's style, personality factors of individuals may result in their responding in varying degrees along the interpersonal–instrumental continuum wherein consultation and/or change experiences are involved. The priorities that were hypothesized by Gibbs are likely to be expressed in less obvious ways and consequently be less apparent to the consultant. The result would be that some premature closure would take place during the entry phase only to have interpersonal issues arise later. For example, a white student consultant and a white consultee worked jointly to complete consultation preference scales. The consultant then discussed reading from the scales with the consultee pertaining to working together, along with ideas on intervention strategies. As they met to develop an intervention plan, they began to share common working experiences. The discussion precipitated a crying spell on the consultee's part and the revelation of her real reasons for requesting consultation. In another situation, a white consultant to a community was told by a black consultee after a year that he was the first white person he had ever trusted. After that revelation the flow of information changed both in terms of quantity and content. It also became possible for them to engage in more collaborative problem solving.

In an extension of Gibbs's ideas, 124 black female elementary teachers with a median 10 years of experience were asked to give their preference of black and white consultants observed on a videotape and to rate their effectiveness (Duncan & Pryzwansky, 1993). No significant preferences were noted for either a same (or opposite) race consultant, although the teachers preferred the instrumentally oriented consultant. In terms of this latter finding, it is important to recognize not only the experience level of the teachers but also the fact that they fell at the highest stage of a racial identity development scale, suggesting they felt comfortable about their own racial identity. Clearly, more attention needs to be paid to these patterns of interaction.

Meyers (2002) has proposed the use of Collins's "Black Feminist Epistemology" as a first step for a consultant learning to collaborate with diverse adults whose various cultural background, life experience, and professional training contribute to epistemological assumptions unfamiliar to her or him. Ingraham (2000) notes that there has been little research on multicultural school-based consultation but some qualitative studies done in this area have appeared in a special edition of *School Psychology Review* (Ingraham and Meyers. 2000).

Finally, Stuart (2044) defines *multicultural competence* "as the ability to understand and constructively relate to the uniqueness of each client in light of diverse cultures that influence each person's perspective" (p. 6). He notes that a fine line exists between a person's membership in a particular group and that person's individuality. In order to appreciate and understand and mitigate against stereotypes, a multicultural competence approach enhances respect for cultural identities. He identified twelve skills that improve multicultural competence if research is applied to practice: (1) develop skill in discovering each person's cultural outlook; (2) acknowledge and control personal biases by articulating your world view and evaluating its sources and validity; (3) develop sensitivity to cultural differences without overemphasizing them; (4) separate theory from culture; (5) develop a sufficiently complex set of cultural categories; (6) critically evaluate methods used to collect culturally relevant data before applying the findings in psychology services; (7) develop a means of determining a person's acceptance of relevant cultural themes; (8) develop a means of determining the salience of ethnic identity for each client; (9) match any psychological tests to client characteristics; (10) contextualize all assessments; (11) consider client's ethnic and worldviews in selecting therapists, interventions, goals, and methods; (12) respect client's beliefs, but attempt to change them when necessary (p. 6).

Consultees' Perceptions of Consultants

Every "young" consultant has experienced the consultee's implicit competence check by having to answer questions such as "How long have you been a social worker?", "Do you have any teaching experience?", or even less tactful inquiries relating to age or marital status. The importance of these variables during the entry stage of consultation, let alone later stages, is unclear. Age, gender, race, assertiveness, personality, and so forth are all consultant characteristics that may affect the consultees' perception of the consultation process and their commitment to and prognosis for the success of the activity. However, little is known about these relationships, a fact that may reflect either their perceived importance for consultants or a significant oversight. One study (Gutkin, 1983) reported that the consultee's perceptions of both the consultant's communication and content skills were consistently related to the consultee's perceptions of outcomes, that is, the utility of the programs or ideas generated as a result of consultation. Likewise, the consultee's perceptions of the consultant's interest and enthusiasm were seen as important elements related to the outcome of the consultation process. Finally, the nature of the written language used to describe an intervention has marked impact on teachers' perceptions of its acceptability. Pragmatic descriptions, for example, were judged to be more acceptable than humanistic or behavioral descriptions (Witt, Moe, Gutkin, & Andrews, 1984).

Questions about the consultant's background and training are best handled in a direct, factual manner. Subtle, nonconfrontational follow-ups concerning the consultee's reasons for asking the questions can lead to some important "baring of the soul" by the consultee. Once expressed and confronted, consultation can proceed. Similarly, asking for feedback and/or identifying the presence of indices of involvement help the consultant make judgments relevant to this area.

The Consultee as Problem Solver

As consultation is increasingly defined in terms of a problem-solving activity in which the active participation of the consultee is expected, the focus on the unique skills of the consultee required to function in this way will need to be addressed.

One basic observation about the implications of the problem-solving approaches of the consultant and consultee is warranted. The literature has emphasized the importance of the first stage of the process, problem identification. Bergan and Tombari (1976) found that when problem solving was carried through the problem-identification stage, the probability of a solution was almost always assured. Given the fact that their study involved the adoption of behaviorally oriented intervention plans, it seems logical that this first step would receive such a priority. Although other writers in the consultation field have also stressed the importance of this stage of consultation, it should be noted that what is often described in this chapter is an attempt to frame problems in ways that will lead to more productive problem solving rather than just defining the elements of the problem. Consultants are also problem finders, if you will, in that they "probe beneath the surface of a dilemma or a conflict in order to isolate the essential question, then attack it" (McPherson, Crowson, & Pitner, 1986, p. 271). Pryzwansky (1989) addressed the problem-solving abilities of novices compared with that of experts, and illustrated the dynamics of the problem-finding task. How the consultant approaches identification of the problem sets up a potential conflict with the consultee, as he or she may enter the relationship feeling this step has been completed or the consultee would not yet have requested consultation. Once again, the role of the consultee has not been considered or is deemphasized. Of course, another scenario could find the consultee resisting any problem-identification activities for ulterior motives. The potential conflict may be multiplied when the consultee is in a managerial position.

Many of these professionals (managers) see themselves as rapid problem solvers, but in many cases the problems are not clearly defined. Often, quick solutions to prevent "institutional drowning" are identified as the priority (McPherson et al., 1986, p. 272). Problem-identification time is wasted time for them.

Some tips for problem identification are presented in the following list. To emphasize again the relationship between consultant and consultee, both should agree:

1. To take stock of the situation together either as a review or refinement task.
2. That the consultant should evaluate the quality of the information provided by the consultee.
3. That the consultant needs to consider the expectations that the consultee holds for the consultant.
4. That the consultant and consultee should collaboratively collect data in a systematic manner.
5. To conduct a process analysis of the problem. (Do contributing variables, identified problems, and problematic outcomes relate logically?)
6. To identify a (or several) competing hypothesis.
7. To consider the constraints affecting a problem solution.

Personality

There have been several attempts to take into account the emotional makeup of the consultee as a factor influencing the consultation process. Modeling his study after one dealing with a department's power within a university (Mann, 1972), Hirschman (1974) examined the relationship between an individual's perceived power within an organization and his or her willingness to utilize mental health consultation. Volunteers at a mental health center were required to arrange a meeting with a consultant for client-related discussions following completion of their training. The volunteers rated the importance of their service at the facility, their influence over others, the importance of consultation in general, and the perceived help of the consultant. The consultant then noted the time that elapsed between the volunteers' first helping experience and their first request for consultation help. As in the Mann study, those who took the longest to contact the consultant held a high self-perception of their importance and influence. Some indirect evidence for the existence of this relationship can be found in earlier works that reported that individuals with limited experience and skill in an organization were more likely to be the ones to use mental health consultation (Iscoe et al., 1967).

It has been hypothesized that teachers' use of consultation *versus* referral services might also vary depending how much control they perceived they had in regard to a problem a student is presenting. For example, knowing little about how to help a client or even what the difficulty is would probably influence consultees to look to others to handle the problem. On the other hand, the more confident and in charge consultees feel with respect to a troublesome situation, the more likely their orientation would be one of seeking out new ideas and strategies that increase their effectiveness. In this latter circumstance there is no felt need to have someone else take over and work with the client; the consultee feels in charge. The degree of control teachers feel they have in resolving a variety of student problems is closely related to their use of consultation, according to Gutkin and Ajchenbaum (1984).

Mischley (1973) reported a relationship between personality characteristics and the model of consultation preferred; consultees who reflected a general authoritarianism preferred a client-centered model, while more introspective consultees preferred a consultee-centered model. In a related study, highly dogmatic subjects (teachers) rated behavioral consultants more "facilitative" than they rated mental health consultants, and they rated mental health consultants less facilitative than did less dogmatic subjects (Slesser et al., 1990).

It is interesting to note that where a simple estimate of a consultee's internality-externality orientation (locus of control) is made, there seems to be no difference in how consultees (characterized along that personality dimension) prefer the consultant to work with them. There is an indication that all consultees, regardless of LOC score, prefer the collaborative approach (Pryzwansky & White, 1983). On the other hand, it may be that simply considering a person's generalized control expectancies, or even the influence of feelings of competency on those expectancies in particular cases, may be too limiting. However, in another study a consistent pattern of interaction between the method of consultation and locus of consultation and locus of control was reported (Slesser et al., 1990). In viewing a videotape of mental health consultation, teachers with an *external* locus of control (versus the internal subjects) gave those consultants higher ratings when asked how pleased they would be with the practitioner as well as the degree to which they were now able to deal with similar problems in the future. These differences were not found for behavioral consultation. Again, in another analogue-type study, it was found that teachers with a higher self-efficacy rate the consultants' effectiveness (regardless of the directness of consultant) and quality of intervention higher than did those teachers with a low self-efficacy (DeForest & Hughes, 1992). Finally, teacher self-efficacy, perceptions of control, and attributions did not predict teachers' decisions to seek consultation or to refer a child under conditions in which the teacher is presented with vignettes describing classroom problems (Hughes, Barker, Kemenoff, & Hart, 1993).

An equally important factor involves the amount of control afforded by the consultee's role in the organization. For example, the constrained, powerless, lonely role of teachers (Lortie, 1975; Sarason, 1971) has been discussed at length in the literature. However, it has been argued that personality types compatible with the role gravitate toward the profession. Using teacher locus of control scores and their responses to a consultation problem-solving interview, Friedman (1977) identified four qualitatively different modal patterns of teacher consultation behavior termed *locus of control consultation styles*. These four styles, with a name attached to reflect the teachers' consultation behavior, are presented in Table 8.2. As evident from the table, the teachers' locus of control was considered from the perspective of their professional role as well as general self-concept, which yields four different consultee styles. From her consultation interviews, Friedman also specified both the content of consultation behaviors and the effect of each consultee style on impeding or facilitating the development of a consultation relationship.

In terms of Friedman's teacher consultation behavior patterns, internal consultation styles are referred to as *controllers* and *problem solvers,* while external consultation styles are called *strivers* and *reactors.* The different orientations toward consultation of each style are evident in the reasons given to seek out consultation, and the effect they have on the process is quite different. For example, controllers seem interested in abdicating professional responsibility for a problem; they are particularly easy to work with if the consultant supports their perceptions. Strivers seek consultation to bolster their own threatened professional self-esteem and mitigate the discomfort of ambivalent emotional conflict about assuming professional responsibility for another (Friedman, 1977). By contrast, problem solvers and reactors hold congruent views of their personal and professional control. The behavior of problem-solver consultees suggests that consultants are seen as resources who can supplement their own professional competency. They are cooperative, and continuance in the relationship reflects judgment of the merit and efficiency of the consultant's recommendations. Reactors' interest in consultation tends to be one of compliance wherein they are pacifying or reacting

to the pressures of external agents such as a principal or a parent. The most acquiescent of consultees, their cooperation is less likely to advance the problem-solving process from the standpoint of active contributions they might make. The progress of the interview is less effective and almost entirely the consultant's burden.

The framework that Friedman provides, albeit theoretical, argues for individualizing consultation behavior to fit the different professional needs, phenomenological perspectives, and dynamics of the consultee. More accurate prediction of the consultant–consultee interaction can help in facilitating effective consultation.

Consultants need to recognize the obvious—different consultees will need to be handled differently because of their personality. In particular, the way in which their own inclination toward handling problems meshes with their role at work needs to be taken into account. The reader is referred to Chapter Eleven, where the Friedman interview scale and categorical system are presented as helpful aids in evaluation.

Affect: Emotional State of the Consultee

An often overlooked condition considered critical to the outcome of consultee-centered consultation by Caplan and Caplan (1993) is the emotional set of the consultee. For example, individuals in crises are viewed as ready to take advantage of consultative input; in fact, one might argue that consultees who have voluntarily sought out consultation because of the intensity of their need for assistance will be more likely to

TABLE 8.2   Consultation Styles Based on Generalized and Situational Control Expectancies

PROFESSIONAL POWER EXPECTANCY	GENERALIZED LOCUS OF CONTROL BELIEF	
	INTERNAL	EXTERNAL
Role power	Problem solvers	Strivers
Role powerlessness	Controllers	Reactors

Adapted from L. P. Friedman (1977), p. 117.

follow through on ideas generated during the consultation. If nothing else, consultants, like therapists, need to be careful to reduce the anxiety of the consultee over working with a client to a level that he or she is no longer immobilized to take action.

Obviously, consultation is not always offered under crisis conditions. Also, the effect on the consultation process of the availability of other alternatives (e.g., "Transfer the child to another class," or "Hang on, the year is almost over") has not been empirically addressed. But it is safe to say that the psychological investment in the consultation enterprise is affected by the intensity with which the consultee approaches the consultation problem.

The feeling state of the individual has been studied in terms of social interaction and decision making. In fact, positive affect has led people to be more helpful to others (Berkowitz, 1972) and influenced their decision-making strategies (Isen, Means, Patrick, & Nowicki, 1982). While the impact of these findings on problem-solving research is in its infancy, there are tentative conclusions that need to be taken into account during the consultation experience. There is evidence that persons who are in a positive mood, while inclined to increase their helping of others generally, are protective of that good mood; if their future anticipated actions are likely to affect their feeling state in a negative way, they will be less willing to cooperate. And although they may be more optimistic when faced with complex tasks, they are likely to be more conservative and reduce their risk-taking behaviors. Paradoxically, they tend to see and use intuitive hypotheses, so they usually work with more speed and are more efficient. That response, however, can lead to solutions that are sometimes biased and incomplete or incorrect. Yet if self-correcting feedback is inherent in the task, they are very responsive to that information and function as efficient problem solvers. A consultee who feels good about herself or himself in a role is likely to focus more on the problem at hand and contribute to the solving of the problem.

As is the case in most of the consultation research, there is rarely a simple relationship between two variables that can guide the consultant's behavior. The affective state of consultees in problem-solving situations is no exception. The nature and importance of the task(s) will have a bearing on the consultee's approach as well as the feedback he or she receives in the task and his or her prior experience with affect of various kinds under situations requiring different strategies. Thus, a positive mood can facilitate or impair performance depending on the circumstances involved.

One final point to be made with regard to affective states is consideration of the effects of different mood states. Isen and colleagues (1982) point out that the *valence* of the mood (positive or negative) is only one of four dimensions to consider. The *quality* of the emotion may have quite different consequences for behavior. That is, whether the consultee is anxious about dealing with a client versus angry with the client or significant others in the client's life can play a role. Similarly, the *intensity* and *arousal* dimensions may influence behavior. Low-level, everyday feeling states, such as have been used in the research of Isen and colleagues, have been shown to interrupt and influence decision making so that relatively intense states may have differing influence. Finally, the degree of arousal, stimulating versus depressing, that consultees experience may have implications for their cognitive states.

In summary then, the consultee's mood, as well as other characteristics, cannot be overlooked as a potential factor affecting the process and outcome of consultation. The context of the problem situation and the interactional influence with other characteristics are also important. It is suggested that the consultant use a mental check-off system in which consultee characteristics and their potential impact are noted and considered when a consultation approach and specific interventions are planned. For example, the particular characteristics of consultative interventions affect what is or is not accepted by the consultee, and from an examination of this chapter's findings there is reason to expect that different consultees will respond differently to various intervention plans (Witt, Martens, & Elliott, 1984).

CONSULTEE TRAINING

Preservice training to use consultation services has received little attention in literature. Yet if employees are expected to take advantage of an organization's consultative resources, *how* to make effective use of consultants should receive some attention. For example, teachers should have specific information regarding the role and competencies of school support services staff such as the counselor, occupational therapist, resource teachers in the various areas of special education, social workers, speech and language specialists, and school psychologists. The ways in which resources could be utilized along with strategies consultees could employ to maximize their use would be important to include. Consultees should know *when* to request consultation, *methods* of presenting the problem to facilitate problem solving, *what* to expect from consultants, and *how* to make their style of working known to the consultant.

All too often, direct service providers are expected to have exhausted their repertoire of problem-solving skills before seeking any consultation or making a referral. The psychological consequence of such an orientation is to reduce the consultee to a position of incompetence, which not only makes the request for consultation difficult to make, but creates a situation in which those "weaknesses" will not only be reviewed but confirmed. Although it is not unreasonable to expect that the consultee has addressed the problem in some meaningful way, consultation is often more effective in terms of outcome and consultee growth if introduced early on in the consultee's engagement with a problem. The home base of the consultant, whether internal or external to the system, as well as the resources a system has committed to consultation services are significant considerations that affect when entry by the consultant is made. The point to be made here is that the consultees' *orientation* toward consultation can be influenced during training and can significantly affect their involvement in the consultation process.

Consultees should also be trained in *methods* of framing the problem when it is presented to the consultant as well as preparing a database that will enhance the consultation experience. For example, describing a problem through the use of specific examples not only reduces communication problems caused by professional jargon, but also provides opportunities to examine intervention attempts and the reasons for their success or failure. The consultees' attempt to share all of their observations, whether of seeming relevance or not, in addition to any hunches or guesses as to the dimensions of the problem can prove valuable to consultants. Likewise, any data, whether of a formal or informal nature, that the consultee has should also be included.

The consultant's set is also important for the consultee to understand. An appreciation of the consultant's values (e.g., problem finding is as important as problem solving) will help the consultee better understand the process itself. Similarly, knowing that a consultant emphasizes the problem-identification stage of the consultation process and uses a systems orientation approach should help consultees understand and accept the service.

Consultees should also be trained to *discriminate* among the various consultation models they might expect or request. Negotiation may be the realistic outcome, but they should expect at the least that the range of their service needs be overtly stated. The scenario is all too common wherein a consultee is critical of the consultation received from a psychologist at the local mental health clinic. The reason for the criticism (e.g., "The psychologist doesn't know what schools are about") sounds plausible enough but may, in fact, not reflect the primary source of frustration. Later observation may indicate that the consultant was perceived to have asked a lot of questions including the opinion of the consultee and to have left the problem in his or her lap. What the consultees expected, and even desired, was an expert who would tell them what to do. At the minimum, they had hoped for an "active" change agent. One consultee might legitimately opt for more of an expert approach, but they should then know what the trade-offs are.

Again consultees (and consultants) should know the characteristics of the different indirect service approaches. For example, Knotee and Sandoval (2003) have compared consultee-centered consultation with behavioral consultation, and the basic distinctions that they identified between the two approaches should be common knowledge in the field. Such knowledge reduces the likelihood of the criticism we have just presented. When consultees are given the information and power to discriminate, evaluation of the consultation is more likely to reflect those choices and the ensuing outcome than to result in a retrospective critique based on unclear parameters.

Finally, it is at the preservice level of training that any professionals who will eventually be expected to work together can most easily be trained together. Such preservice models have been described for promoting school-based multidisciplinary teams (Buktenica, 1970). It would appear that similar experiences can be arranged regarding consultation training. In fact, collaborative efforts involving resource professionals, managers, and staff would seem to have the greatest probability of success. Such training could be both didactic as well as process-orientated, serving to facilitate the training objectives of the individual professionals as well.

The objectives for consultee training then are as follows: (1) the potential consultee needs to understand consultation as a process, (2) consultees need to know when consultation should be initiated and how the timing of the request can affect the process and outcome, and (3) consultees must be able to make informed choices as to when consultation can be utilized in contrast to other available services.

Training as an Objective of Consultation

More than likely, the consultee will not have experienced any of the preservice training described in the previous section. The consultant is then faced with a decision as to whether to incorporate this ed-

ucative function into the problem-solving process and intentionally address those needs. If indeed all consultation should address consultee preferences/expectations as well as develop some skills, scales measuring consultation model preferences and objectives could be given to the consultee prior to the first consultation session (see Chapter Eleven). These scales could serve to sensitize the consultee to the critical parameters of consultation for them, function as a more natural way to begin discussion of these questions, and serve as the basis for finalizing a contract. While it is hardly reasonable to predicate consultation services on the consultees' willingness to undergo a workshop-type component of consultation, some of this emphasis seems justified. However, it may be that if the consultant takes on an educative role during the consultation process, then a hierarchical relationship ensues, which is antithetical to the consultation model of choice. Indeed, beginning in a didactic fashion might contribute to either consultees' resistance to what they see as irrelevant for the task at hand or reinforcement of a passive role throughout consultation.

Zins (1993) reviewed a number of studies in which direct training of consultation-related skills was demonstrated; among the specific objectives included were the promotion of behavior consultation through knowledge of related principles, efficacy of modeling procedures for improving problem-solving skills, enhancement of communication skills, and the improvement of parent–teacher conferences. Based on the review, he proposes that consultees be trained directly in skills in order to improve the effectiveness of consultation interactions and enhance consultation outcomes. He reasons that the benefit of the training would be to increase congruence between consultants' and consultees' expectations. Although he is concerned with a specific consultation model, there are generic skills that the consultee could use regardless of the model being employed by the consultant.

The training question will continue to confront the consultant who wants to incorporate the educative function into the consultation process. For internally based consultants a particular skill or phase of consultee development may be solely emphasized during consultation on any one case. Future requests for consultation would then present opportunities for emphasizing another consultee skill or stage of consultation. In each instance, the needs of the consultee and problem situation should dictate the choice that is made. For the external consultant, modeling or overt emphasis on the target area is recommended as the strategy of choice.

Professional Development Training

The training issue can be addressed as a staff development exercise for consultees in the field or as part of an eventual group consultation format. When there is an educational component prior to group consultation experiences, the motivation to learn may be high. If consultees will eventually serve as co-consultants with the consultant or engage in peer consultation, the degree of involvement should increase even more. However, a staff development exercise that is geared to some potential future need of short duration may be of dubious value except for the inexperienced consultee.

Lambert, Sandoval, and Yandell (1975) describe the first stage in training of school-based mental health consultants as "learning how to be a consultee." Their premise was that the consultant must be aware of the different kinds of learning facing a consultee. The categories of understanding are presented here as one example of an outline for consultee training (Sandoval, Lambert, & Davis, 1977). They include: (1) recognizing how the consultation session is different from other professional contacts, (2) presenting information so the consultant understands and responds, (3) learning about the consultant, (4) learning what kind of help to expect and how to use the consultation experience, and (5) sensitizing oneself to the consultant's style of behaving in the work setting as it affects professional functioning.

Understanding of the contract provides the consultee with the behavioral limits on what can be said or done in consultation. Most important, as Sandoval and colleagues (1977) have pointed out, differentiating the role of consultant from that of the consultant's training (e.g., mental health professional) is very important. The degree to which personal matters and peer professional relationships can or should be discussed also can be explored at this time.

The need to develop the skill of presenting information to the consultant along with any hypotheses developed by the consultees is important to the consultation process. The willingness to cooperate and jointly engage in the investigatory phase of problem finding will be invaluable to both participants, but requires acceptance on the consultee's part that risk taking will be involved. Finally, there must be recognition that some problems can lead to database-supported interventions, but other problems are at best conceptualized as hypotheses.

The remaining elements of training involve an understanding of the consultant's role and professional background. Closely related to issues involving the contract are issues of confidentiality that need to be explored. Consultees should hold realistic expectations and learn how they might maximize the strengths of their consultant. Consultees should know consultation can be pursued just as effectively when problems are seen to be developing rather than when they reach a crisis level. If consultation is to enhance the competence of the consultee, the range of opportunities throughout the consultation process must be apparent.

SOME FINAL THOUGHTS ON TRAINING

In this section on consultee training we have stressed the objectives of helping consultees *understand* the consultation/collaboration service, and of increasing *their skills as consultees*. In the next chapter, we discuss training the consultee in *both* the role of consultee and consultant within the more informal helping model entitled "peer collaboration." Within this model, roles are referred to as problem solver (consultee) and problem solver facilitator (consultant). One professional then, helps a colleague brainstorm approaches that can be taken to address a challenge, but in a structured approach designed to keep the problem solver (consultee) in charge. The differences between training a professional to be a consultee versus effective collaboration with a peer may be subtle, and seem to have much overlap at times, but the distinction should not be lost on the reader. Yet, a third type of consultee training needs recognition, content- or skill-based consultee training. Examples include the consultant asking the consultee to do reading for the next session or following an intervention plan laid out by the consultant and collecting data. When taking place within the *consultation* context, the consultant runs the risk of becoming an educator and, thereby, changing his or her role vis à vis the consultee and muddying the waters concerning which process is being offered. This educative "role switch" runs into some of the same dangers mentioned under training for consultation. In addition, the complications that ensue when the consultee does not read the materials, or misinterprets them, or is critical, certainly can change the dynamics of the relationship. Educator in this context implies expertise and a capacity to evaluate. In conclusion, the advice that a consultant understands and assesses what is happening to a service is again appropriate when "training" and education is contemplated and/or involved.

SUMMARY

This chapter has attempted to sensitize the reader to an often overlooked or little emphasized aspect of consultation—the consultee. We need to consider what the consultee brings to the sessions, in terms of training for his or her role as well as cognitive and emotional characteristics, if consultation is to truly have an impact as a service delivery model. This premise is especially reinforced where the more active models of consultation are involved, although some would say that the degree of consultee involvement determines success in all models. The literature is clear that little training of consultees is being done, and even less attention is being directed toward the expectations and preferences of consultees and their characteristics in terms of consultation model selection. When the consultee does receive attention, it usually involves the issue of resistance, and then the discussion revolves more

around resolution than cause(s). Caplan has been one of the obvious exceptions to some of these general conclusions, having somewhat tied types of consultation strategies to types of consultee problems. In short, the literature reviewed in this chapter suggests that unless the consultee is more intentionally considered in the planning of consultation, we run the risk of reducing our understanding, if not effectiveness, of the process.

The consultee is treated as a variable in consultation in this chapter, but the consultee can be examined from any number of perspectives. And, in fact, the interaction of those many facets (variables) is what needs to be considered, whether in research or practice, if consultation is to be successful. Certainly the focus on any one characteristic may have its justification, but pursuing how age, personality, problem-solving ability, and so forth combine may lead to more effective consultee approaches. Finally, the consultee must be treated as a variable within the total consultation process involving the consultant, client, and setting.

Some final observations need to be made concerning the literature written about the consultee influence on consultation. For all practical purposes, research on this important variable is in the beginning stages, so that in only a few instances do we have the semblance of data-based working hypotheses. Furthermore, as in other areas of consultation research, the consultants in the studies are in training or rather inexperienced. Also the consultees tend to have a professional background themselves. The bulk of studies are done in schools. Consequently, those features must be kept in mind as we attempt to generalize the findings to specific situations.

TIPS FOR THE PRACTITIONER

1. In the preliminary phase of consultation, determine the preconceived notions that consultees have about their roles and the process (e.g., amount of time required). Take steps to make sure that your expectations and theirs are approximately the same.

2. Similarly, try to determine the model of consultation preferred by your consultees. If possible, practice their preferred model. If you cannot, you must persuade them that the model of consultation you are practicing will be effective.
3. Be sensitive to the differences in perception that arise because of ethnic, socioeconomic, and racial differences. Alter your style to accommodate consultees' preferences.
4. As you consult, try to determine the skills that the consultee brings to consultation. When deficiencies are discovered, arrange for indirect training experiences such as observation of other direct training, such as in-service training, to remedy deficiencies that will impede progress. It is inevitable that some training will have to occur during consultation.

REVIEW QUESTIONS

1. What are the types of consultee preferences for consultation that are likely to be expressed? Identify cautions that must be kept in mind as such information is considered.
2. What advice would you give to a beginning consultant who uses the age of the consultee in determining the initial style of interaction?
3. What is likely to be one of the biggest differences in the problem-solving styles of consultees versus consultants?
4. Describe the personality attributes of the consultee that could influence outcome.
5. List some important skills that individuals should possess to enhance their role as consultees, thereby contributing to the positive outcome of the consultation process.
6. Why is it important that the consultant recognize the consultee as a crucial factor in the consultation activity?

REFERENCES

Altrocchi, J. (1972). Mental health consultation. In S. E. Golann & C. Elsdorfer (Eds.), *Handbook of community psychology* (pp. 477–508). New York: Appleton-Century-Crofts.

Babcock, N., & Pryzwansky, W. B. (1983). Models of consultation: Preferences of educational professionals at five stages of service. *Journal of School Psychology, 21* (4), 359–366.

Baker, H. L. (1965). Psychological services: From the school staff's point of view. *Journal of School Psychology, 3,* 36–42.

Bardon, J. I. (1977). *The consultee in consultation: Preparation and training.* Paper presented at the American Psychological Association Convention, San Francisco, CA.

Bergan, J. R., & Tombari, M. L. (1976). Consultant skill and efficiency and the implementation and outcomes of consultation. *Journal of School Psychology, 14,* 3–14.

Berkowitz, L. (1972). Social norms, feelings, and other factors affecting helping and altruism. In L. Berkowitz (Ed.), *Advances in experimental social psychology* (Vol. 6). New York: Academic Press.

Brady, M., & Schneider, O. (1973). The psychiatrist as classroom teacher: School consultation in the inner city. *Hospital and Community Psychiatry, 24,* 248–251.

Brickman, P., Rabinowitz, V. C., Karuza, J., Coates, D., Cohn, E., & Kidder, L. (1982). Models of helping and coping. *American Psychologist, 37*(4), 368–384.

Bronkowski, R. (1968). Mental health consultation and operation Head Start. *American Psychologist, 23,* 769–772.

Buktenica, N. A. (1970). A multidisciplinary training team in the public schools. *Journal of Psychology, 8,* 220–225.

Caplan, G., & Caplan, R. B. (1993). *Mental health consultation and collaboration.* San Francisco, CA: Jossey-Bass.

Clark, R. D. (1979). School consultants give teachers what they want—A straight answer? In *Proceedings of the eleventh annual convention, National Association of School Psychologists* (Vol. 3).

Coleman, S. (1976). *Developing collaborative-process consultation: Teacher and participant-observer perceptions and outcome.* Paper presented at the American Psychologist Association Convention, Washington, DC.

DeForest, P. A., & Hughes, J. N. (1992). Effect of teacher involvement and teacher self efficacy on ratings of consultant effectiveness and intervention acceptability. *Journal of Educational and Psychological Consultation, 3,* 301–316.

Duncan, C., & Pryzwansky, W. B. (1988). Consultation research: Trends in doctoral dissertations, 1978–1985. *Journal of School Psychology, 26,* 107–119.

Duncan, C., & Pryzwansky, W. B. (1993). Effects of race, racial identity development and orientation style on perceived consultant effectiveness. *Journal of Multicultural Counseling and Development, 21,* 88–96.

Friedman, L. P. (1977). Locus of control consultation styles: A theoretical model for increasing teacher-centered consultation effectiveness (Doctoral dissertation, University of Pennsylvania, 1976). *Dissertation Abstracts International, 37,* 2074A.

Gibbs, J. T. (1980). The interpersonal orientation in mental health consultation: Toward a model of ethnic variations in consultation. *Journal of Community Psychology, 8,* 195–207.

Gilmore, G., & Chandy, J. (1973). Teachers' perception of school psychological services. *Journal of School Psychology, 11*(2), 139–147.

Gold, R. F., & Hollander, S. K. (1992). The status of consultant teacher services in special education on Long Island New York: 1989–1990. *Journal of Educational and Psychological Consultation, 3,* 25–30.

Gutkin, T. B. (1980). Teacher perceptions of consultation services provided by school psychologists. *Professional Psychology, 11,* 637–642.

Gutkin, T. B. (1983). *Variables affecting the outcomes of consultation as perceived by consultees.* Paper presented at the American Psychological Association Convention, Anaheim, CA.

Gutkin, T. B., & Ajchenbaum, M. (1984). Teachers' perception of control and preferences for consultation services. *Professional Psychology: Research and Practice, 15*(4), 565–570.

Gutkin, T. B., & Bossard, M. D. (1984). Impact of consultant, consultee, and organizational variables in teachers attitudes toward consultation services. *Journal of School Psychology, 22*(3), 251–258.

Hilke, J. L. (1984). *An examination of the relationship between consultant variables and interpersonal problem solving skills for school psychology students, recent graduates and past graduates.* Unpublished doctoral dissertation, University of North Carolina at Chapel Hill.

Hirschman, R. (1974). Utilization of mental health consultation and self-perceptions of intraorganizational importance and influence. *Journal of Consulting and Clinical Psychology, 42*(6), 916.

Hughes, J. N., Barker, D., Kemenoff, S., & Hart, M. (1993). Problem ownership, causal attributions, and self efficacy as predictors of teachers' referral decisions. *Journal of Educational and Psychological Consultation, 4,* 369–384.

Ingraham, C. L. (2000). Consultation through a multicultural lens: Multicultural and cross-cultural consultation in schools. *School Psychology Review, 29,* 320–343.

Ingraham, C. L., & Meyers, J. (2000). Multicultural and cross-cultural consultation in school consultation [Special Issue]. *School Psychology Review, 29.*

Iscoe, I., Pierce-Jones, J., Friedman, S. T., & McGehearty, L. (1967). Some strategies in mental health consultation: A brief description of a project and some preliminary results. In E. L. Cowen, E. A. Gardner, & M. Zax (Eds.), *Emergent approaches to mental health problems* (pp. 307–330). New York: Appleton-Century-Crofts.

Isen, A. M., Means, B., Patrick, R., & Nowicki, G. (1982). Some factors influencing decision-making strategy and risk-taking. In M. S. Clark & S. T. Fiske (Eds.), *Affect and cognition* (pp. 243–261). Hillsdale, NJ: Erlbaum.

Knotek, S. E., & Sandoval, J. (2003). Current research in consultee-centered consultation. *Journal of Educational and Psychological Consultation, 14* (3/4), 243–250.

Kolb, D. A. (1983). Problem management: Learning from experience. In S. Srvasta (Ed.), *The executive mind* (pp. 109–143). San Francisco: Jossey-Bass.

Lambert, N. M., Sandoval, J. H., & Yandell, G. W. (1975). Preparation of school psychologists for school-based consultation: A training activity and a service to community schools. *Journal of School Psychology, 13,* 68–75.

Lortie, D. C. (1975). *School teacher.* Chicago: University of Chicago Press.

Macarov, D. (1968). *A study of the consultation process.* New York: State Committees and Association.

Mann, P. A. (1972). Accessibility and organizational power in the entry phase of mental health consultation. *Journal of Consulting and Clinical Psychology, 38,* 215–218.

Mannino, F. U., & Shore, M. F. (1975). The effects of consultation. *American Journal of Community Psychology, 3*(1), 1–21.

McPherson, R. B., Crowson, R. L., & Pitner, N. J. (1986). *Managing uncertainty: Administrative theory and practice in education.* Columbus, OH: Charles E. Merrill.

Medway, F. J., & Forman, S. G. (1980). Psychologists' and teachers' reactions to mental health and behavioral school consultation. *Journal of School Psychology, 18,* 338–348.

Meyers, A. B. (2002). Developing nonthreatening expertise: Thoughts on consultation training from the perspective of a new faculty member. *Journal of Educational and Psychological Consultation, 13* (1/2), 55–67.

Miller, J. N. (1974). Consumer response to theoretical role models in school psychology. *Journal of School Psychology, 12,* 310–317.

Mischley, M. (1973). Teacher preference for consultation methods and its relation to selected background personality and organization variables (Doctoral dissertation, University of Texas at Austin, 1973). *Dissertation Abstracts International, 34,* 2312B.

Morrison, A. (1970). Consultation and group process with indigenous neighborhood workers. *Community Mental Health Journal, 6,* 3–12.

Noy, P., DeNour, A., & Moses, R. (1966). Discrepancies between expectations and service in psychiatric consultation. *Archives in General Psychology, 14,* 651–657.

Piersel, W. C. (1985). Behavioral consultation: An approach to problem solving in educational settings. In J. R. Bergan (Ed.), *School psychology in contemporary society* (pp. 252–280). Columbus, OH: Charles E. Merrill.

Pinto, R. F. (1981). Consultant orientations and client system perception: Styles of cross-cultural consultation. In R. Lippitt & G. Lippitt (Eds.), *Systems thinking: A resource for organization, diagnosis and intervention* (Chapter IV, pp. 57–74). Washington, DC: International Consultants Foundations.

Platt, J. J., & Spivak, G. (1975). *Manual for the means-end problem-solving procedure (MEPS): A measure of interpersonal cognitive problem-solving skill.* Philadelphia, PA: Hahnemann Medical College and Hospital.

Pryzwansky, W. B., & Vatz, B. C. (1989). *School psychologists' solutions to a consultation problem: Do experts agree?* Paper presented at the National Association of School Psychologists Convention, Chicago, IL.

Pryzwansky, W. B., & White, G. (1983). The influence of consultee characteristics on preferences for consultation approaches. *Professional Psychology: Research and Practice, 14,* 457–461.

Roberts, R. (1970). Perceptions of actual and desired role functions of school psychologists by psychologists and teachers. *Psychology in the Schools, 7,* 1–25.

Sager, C., Brayboy, T., & Waxenberg, B. (1972). Black patient—white therapist. *American Journal of Orthopsychiatry, 42,* 415–423.

Sandoval, J., Lambert, N. M., & Davis, J. M. (1977). Consultation from the consultee's perspective. *Journal of School Psychology, 15*(4), 334–342.

Sarason, S. B. (1996). *Revisiting the culture of the school and the problem of change.* New York: Teacher's College Press.

Schulte, A. C., & Osborne, S. S. (2003). When assumptive worlds collide: A review of definitions of collaboration in consultation. *Journal of Educational and Psychological Consultation, 14* (2), 109–138.

Schulte, A. C., Osborne, S. S., & Kauffman, J. M. (1993). Teacher responses to types of consultative special education services. *Journal of Educational and Psychological Consultation, 4,* 1–27.

Slesser, R. A., Fine, M. J., & Tracy, D. B. (1990). Teacher reactions to two approaches to school-based psychological consultation. *Journal of Educational and Psychological Consultation, 1,* 243–258.

Solomon, M. H. (1984). *An approach to assessing the problem-solving skills of teachers.* Unpublished doctoral dissertation, University of North Carolina at Chapel Hill.

Stuart, R. B. (2004). Twelve practical suggestions for achieving multicultural competence. *Professional Psychology: Research and Practice, 35*(1), 3–9.

Sue, D., & Sue, E. (1977). Barriers to effective cross-cultural counseling. *Journal of Counseling Psychology, 24,* 420–429.

Vatz, B. C., & Pryzwansky, W. B. (1988). *The problem finding style of expert consultants in school psychology.* Paper presented at the National Association of School Psychologists Convention, Boston, MA.

Voss, J. F., Tyler, U., & Yengo, L. A. (1983). Individual differences in the solving of social science problems. In R. F. Dillon & R. R. Sneck (Eds.), *Individual Differences in Cognition,* Vol. 1 (pp. 205–323). New York: Academic Press.

Waters, L. (1973). School psychologists as perceived by school personnel: Support for a consultant model. *Journal of School Psychology, 11*(1), 40–45.

Weiler, M. B. (1984). *The influence of contact and setting on the ratings of parents for models of consultation.* Unpublished master's thesis, North Carolina State University, Raleigh, NC.

Wenger, R. (1979). School consultation process: Analysis, application and evaluation of a process variable—consultation. *Psychology in the Schools, 16*(1), 127–131.

White, G. W., & Pryzwansky, W. B. (1982). Consultation outcome as a result of in-service resource teacher training. *Psychology in the Schools, 19,* 495–502.

Witt, J. C., Martens, J., & Elliott, S. N. (1984). Factors affecting teachers' judgments of the acceptability of behavioral intervention: Time involvement, behavior problem severity, and type of intervention. *Behavior Therapy, 15,* 203–206.

Witt, J. C., Moe, G., Gutkin, T. B., & Andrews, L. (1984). The effect of saying the same thing in different ways: The problem of language and jargon in school-based consultation. *Journal of School Psychology, 22*(4), 361–367.

Zins, J. E. (1993). Enhancing consultee problem-solving skills in consultative interactions. *Journal of Counseling and Development, 72,* 185–190.

CHAPTER 9

TEACHER CONSULTATION— TEACHER COLLABORATION

GOAL OF THE CHAPTER

The unique characteristics of the teacher role in the school setting and the implications for establishing an indirect service are discussed in this chapter.

CHAPTER PREVIEW

1. The role expectations for the teacher are examined from the training and setting perspectives, with particular emphasis on factors affecting the utilization of services.
2. Several examples of approaches to consultation and/or collaboration with the teachers are examined.
3. Two adaptations of individual consulting models tailored to the role and demands of the setting facing teachers are presented, for example, the 15-minute consultation and group consultation.

CONSULTATION—COLLABORATION

During the past decade, the *collaboration* concept has become quite popular in the education literature, and the term has certainly caught on in the vernacular of school personnel. One can probably make a similar observation in mental health professional publications and perhaps even more broadly in the population at large.

In fact, if it is true, as often seems the case, that everyone seeks the title of "consultant," then it is likewise a given that professionals will want to "collaborate." As we noted earlier, if being a consultant has a ring of prestige about it, then collaboration seems to attribute a personal characteristic to the professional in that he or she is expected to work *with* other professionals in a positive, supportive, nonhierarchical manner. Is it

any wonder then that "models" have emerged which are described as *collaborative consultation,* or the consultant is presented as collaborating with another professional? These phrases capture the best of both approaches.

Indeed, words are important, and in interpersonal situations demanding tact or sensitivity, how one describes his or her professional role can set a tone that will affect the subsequent development of any relationship. For example, describing your work as problem solving rather than consulting may alleviate some consultees' misperceptions— that they are seen as "inadequate," "in need of help," or somehow "not expert" at what they do. Similarly, the consultant title may convey to the consultee the notion that the consultant is not going to provide any help after all. Rather, the consultee is expected to implement any action. The words consultation and collaboration are indeed part of our everyday usage (i.e., their "popular" or "daily" meaning). In a recent Sunday newspaper, a TV star noted how his wife "consulted" with him about what ties he should wear, and a U.S. government official was reported to be "consulting with our allies." So, the use of these terms is widespread and commonplace, a situation that can contribute to their definitions becoming ambiguous. However, in a *professional* context, these terms do have a specific meaning, and this fact needs to be stressed. The models of helping they represent do reflect different assumptions about how people change and the manner in which the helping professional works. If we wish to evaluate the effectiveness of our work, then we must be able to describe what it is we do. Otherwise, it is impossible to determine if our behavior, the nature of the problem, the personality of the consultee, or some other element was a factor(s) in the degree of observed success. Such precision is more readily accepted in research circles, yet even there, when the topic is consultation, little or no attention is paid to what these terms actually mean, so the reader of the literature is left to project his or her own meaning onto these terms. Aside from generalizing the findings to applications in the field, replication of a study then becomes a challenge.

Therefore, we recommend that readers use the terms *consultation* and *collaboration* with their professional definitions in mind as opposed to their popular definitions. Consultation and collaboration are different in terms of their goals, the assumptions of change made by the consultant, and the role of the consultee and consultant.

This chapter will continue to address the literature dealing with teacher support as in previous editions. The difference is that we will add a separate section on teacher collaboration not only to stress the differences between consultation and collaboration, but also to acknowledge the burgeoning literature dealing with this approach. The term *indirect service* will be used to refer to the different models of consultation as well as the collaborative approach. The terms *consultant* and *resource professional* may be employed interchangeably regardless of the indirect or direct service approach being described. Finally, when a research study is being described, the terms used by the author(s) of the study will be employed.

Consultation, and to a certain extent, collaboration, are interventions which can be best categorized as *indirect* services. Simply, rather than a professional (A) offering his/her services directly to a client the services are provided to another professional (B) (consultee) with the objective of assisting that professional (B) (consultee) in his/her work with a client. Thus, professional B (consultee) becomes professional A's "client." Examples are as follows: physician B asks a physician (A), who is a specialist, to examine B's client chart and provide consultation to B regarding treatment options. Or, another example could involve a teacher seeking the help of a school counselor or school psychologist in dealing with a student in his/her class who is obsessing about guns and death wherein the child's father had committed suicide. Gutkin and Conoley (1990) have argued that the decision to use an indirect service model clearly commits the consultant to consider the consultee as their client. Thus, the ability to work effectively with adults is paramount. They argue that the professional must understand and influence adults if clients of the system are to be positively affected. In summary, this conceptualization would fit most closely with the consultee-centered consultation models. As noted in the Caplan 1970 text, the consultee is assessed in terms of needs related to information, skills, confidence, and objectivity.

Clearly, if a consultant is *internal* to an organization then an argument legitimately can be made that all employees of the organization are responsible to the clients of that organization. One employee may have prime responsibility for a client, but others in the system who are made aware of the client can now not completely ignore any responsibility. Given that caveat, it seems legitimate and helpful to clarifying roles that an internal consultant can provide an indirect service as defined here.

On the other hand, the collaborative approach, by definition, would suggest that both professionals are "active" in the process and responsible for the client intervention; they should evaluate progress toward a goal so that modification of the intervention can be made when necessary to improve it or plan a necessary next step(s). In the purest sense, however, collaborations involving an internally "based consultant" suggest professional A is providing (or has provided) some direct service such as assessment of the client through test or interview, counseling, reinforcement schedules, modeling of communication patterns, etc. The commitment of internally based professional A is more comprehensive. Thus, the differing models of intervention vary along this dimension of involvement with the consultee's client and the consultant should be cognizant of his/her role in this regard.

Of all the types of professionals that have been targeted as potential beneficiaries of indirect services (i.e., consultation, collaboration), teachers have to rank among the most frequently mentioned group. In fact, the term *teacher consultation* seems to be gaining popularity in education literature to such a degree that we run the risk of its being incorrectly conceptualized as yet another unique model of consultation rather than simply a term used to identify the professional identity of the consultee.

It is rather obvious from a purely "impact" perspective why such a level of attention would be directed to this group of professionals. As primary caregivers who serve large numbers of students each year, as well as much larger numbers during their career, the potential impact that may ensue as a result of teachers generalizing what they learned in consultation to future students they teach becomes immediately apparent. In fact, if there is one rationale that appears to heighten the appeal of teacher consultation to school administrators, it is the long-term benefit

of consultation to both teachers and students. While the number of school-based resource professionals available to teachers will always be limited, any factor that increases a teacher's independence will be valued.

Three additional reasons would seem to support the consideration of indirect service for teachers. First, the preparation of the teachers is to a large degree focused on minimum entry-level competency. That is, until the recent renewal of interest in teacher credentials, teachers could be *permanently* certified on college graduation with an undergraduate degree. If a probationary period existed before permanent certification was granted, it was often less structured and rarely included formal supervisory reviews that focused on specific teaching skills improvement. There was no formal credentialing mechanism for becoming recognized as a *competent* teacher at any level of experience, let alone criteria for recognizing master teacher status. In spite of the acknowledged complexity of the teaching position, professional growth and development are experientially determined except in cases of continuing education activities associated with certification renewal requirements. The recent availability of a national board certification for teachers has tremendous potential for changing this situation. Thus, consultation from experts would seem to be a valued resource for a practitioner group with an evolving professional identity. The teacher's task of managing instruction for such diverse populations as today's schools enroll would seem to require continued access to a variety of professional perspectives.

A second reason stems from suggestions that while teachers appreciate the fact that they have not contributed to student problems, they nonetheless are willing to engage in a problem-solving activity leading to the remedy of those problems (Pohlman, Huffman, Dodds, & Pryzwansky, 1998). Teachers often appear to feel a certain responsibility for the solution process and exhibit a willingness to seek help. However, that search for help is largely limited to other like-minded professionals, that is, teachers rather than resource professionals available to them.

Third, the isolation of the teaching assignment (Lortie, 1975; Sarason, 1996) is yet another rationale for offering indirect services. Throughout the day, many teachers have minimum interaction with other professionals that allow for the professional exchange needed for brainstorming solutions to problems.

These three observations would seem to represent a persuasive argument for providing consultation services. However, in the absence of a database, the authors do not sense that the amount of teacher consultation taking place is overwhelming, and therefore, it does not seem to be a common service. While the advocacy for such services comes mainly from the professional groups doing the consultation, teachers, when asked, do not reject this model of service (Graden, 1989).

However, since the argument for teacher consultation originates with internal school professionals who are also expected to provide direct services (e.g., counselor, school psychologists, special educators), they must convince administrators that there be a reallocation of a proportion of their time commitment to direct services.

Administrators may be leery of providing support for that reallocation when caseloads are tied to program funding (e.g., assessment eligibility determination required for special education class placement), or the value of an indirect service is yet to be demonstrated through evaluation.

Teacher as Professional or Technician

Earlier we alluded to the observation that the teaching is at best still an emerging, evolving profession. If the teacher is a technician who follows a planned, sequenced curriculum and thus engages in little decision making as a number of state legislatures have recently seemed to structure their states schooling, then, the back-up and/or resources available to this "employee" will be structured to fit that model. However, a teacher conceptualized as a professional who utilizes a variety of curriculum options to optimize learning experiences and conditions for individual children will require a different support system. For example, the local TV broadcaster is referred to as the "talent" within their station, and all resources from the producer to the cameraperson, are organized and provided to insure the "talent" succeeds in producing an outstanding program. Thinking of the teacher in such a central role in the schooling process would automatically suggest that resources (consultants among them) would be readily available to them and the organizational structure to facilitate that support would be established. Finally, the schooling enterprise, in contrast to other service areas in our society, has not been organized in such a manner that accommodates a service delivery strategy wherein several adults come together to discuss programs for individual and groups of students. There simply is little time during the school day for conferences between the teacher and a resource professional, and the immediate period of time following the official school day is often scheduled with other responsibilities. Teachers are expected to be in charge of their class, or classes, throughout the day. For a teacher to miss a class, even with a substitute provided, is not encouraged, and with the current emphasis on the time-on-task effectiveness schooling notion, any activity that reduces instructional time is probably considered skeptically by many educators. Therefore, the time available to teachers may be the greatest impediment to indirect services becoming utilized in a fashion that allows for their promise to be realized.

A rose is a rose, and consultation is consultation regardless of the professional identity of the consultee. However, as can be appreciated from previous observations, each professional group and its setting will reflect strengths and constraints that need to be considered. In this chapter, we will concentrate on those factors unique to the teaching profession, and in turn, for the resource professional to keep in mind. In doing so, most of the information sprinkled throughout the book that arose out of consultation experiences with teachers (e.g., Gibbs's work dealing with the influence of the ethnic background of consultees on the consultation process—see Chapter Eight) will often be noted, but not repeated in any detail to avoid redundancy. Chapter Eight in general should be considered when this chapter is being read, since many of the "consultee" studies were done with teachers as subjects.

Challenges Limiting Indirect Services

In this section, we have the unpleasant task of reviewing what some have called the barriers that impede teacher consultations or collaborations. It is unpleasant in that some of what we will present is not easily overcome by either the consultant or the teacher. Rather than appreciating the reality of the circumstances, some consultants have come to interpret teacher behavior associated with these constraints as resistance. Consulting with teachers does not imply that any exceptions should be made in terms of the sound principles of practice followed with other consultees. An awareness of teachers' role demands and their work environment is required, as well as the intentional incorporation of such information when interventions are planned. The absence of this perspective, or perhaps more accurately, the minimizing of such information, may be a significant factor that has slowed the progress of introducing this service model in schools, in particular, when external consultants were involved. Indeed, it would seem that the importance of such a perspective needs greater prominence in the selection of the consultation approach used in the public schools than it has thus far received (Pryzwansky, 1974). Thus, the role in setting characteristics that are to be presented should help in shaping that perspective of the teacher role and choice of model.

Training Orientation. In spite of all that has been written promoting the professionalism of teachers, much of the preparation seems to still reflect the technician rather than independent decision-maker orientation. The concentration of most preservice teacher training is methods-oriented and emphasizes the curriculum guidelines adopted by particular states. Clearly, any consideration of the conceptualizations of the role gives way to the pragmatics of functioning in the role, and if the teacher-in-training is fortunate, some skill training that is directly applicable to the demands of the classroom. The expectation that all too often is reinforced is one in which the teacher delivers a predetermined curriculum using a prescribed set of materials to a classroom of students. Perhaps this description is a bit too extreme or harsh for some readers, but it should make the point that the independent, instructional decision making often expected of this consultee may simply not be reinforced in the teacher preparation program, let alone realized in practice. This sophistication may develop over time with experience and subsequent training.

More important, a second factor to be considered is the possibility that the match between the orientation of the teacher and the consultant may be incongruent. Teachers may expect direct suggestions to handle problems since their initial training had dealt with questions in a prescriptive manner. Furthermore, they may reason that for the consultant to expect them to function in any other manner is unfair, because it neither matches their range of competencies, nor is it realistic in light of the prescribed set of responsibilities they have been assigned.

The technician orientation to teaching then also may explain why indirect services are generally advocated by specialized personnel in the schools (e.g., special educators, counselors, school psychologists) rather than receiving the grassroots support one would expect from teachers. While teachers are receptive to the offer of such assistance, they seem inclined to promote a service delivery model that involves direct treatment of students by specialists. Often, this preference reflects an honest judgment that the student requires more specialized assistance. This hierarchical model of interaction would certainly fit within the organization that has the teacher as the front-line instructor of a group and/or subgroups of students; students who do not learn under this organizational scheme would then be shifted to other, more specialized personnel who teach in an alternative instructional environment such as a small class or individualized instruction.

Another important factor that may influence a teacher's acceptance of consultation is that there is an absence of a real understanding of the various educational specialties and school services, let alone the ways in which those services could be used *as part of the teacher's classroom program.* The availability of support services is not standardized, and the ways teachers can use those services is not part of the skills they receive. Not only do these circumstances need to be changed for a consultation service to be effective, but some minimal preparation as to how to make maximum use of the services available would seem advisable (see the consultee training section in Chapter Eight). Training in consultation and collaboration could enhance the teachers' feelings of competency as consumers of such services in that their needs have a greater chance of being addressed. It might be important to add here as an example of this point that it is rare to find a text used in educational leadership training programs that deals with a description of specialized school professionals, let alone the different ways of deploying such staff.

Time. As noted in the introduction, use of school-based professional time is a critical variable affecting any teacher and student support service program. Indeed, a number of writers in the consultation field have acknowledged availability of time as a major factor affecting the initiation and quality of consultation (Gutkin & Curtis, 1982; Idol & West, 1987; Johnson, Pugach, & Hammitte, 1988). Obviously, an organization that assigns one adult per 20+ students and requires constant teacher–student contact will experience cognitive dissonance with proposals that interrupt that relationship. Even where "planning periods" exist, teachers set priorities on that time for planning so that it becomes as sacrosanct as instructional time. Such a scenario then leaves the time

before and after school as a period for conferences along with some stolen, but brief, periods of time during the day. Thus, teachers who need and/or value consultation are going to be frustrated by organizational structures that impede implementation, and teachers whose orientation and priorities run counter to those associated with consultation will be equally frustrated. In part, the time constraint may account for the amount of time educational consultants report they actually spend in consultation. Idol-Maestas and Ritter (1985) reported that only about 5 percent of resource/consulting teachers' time was spent consulting, with similar documentation characterizing the school psychologist's role (Gutkin & Curtis, 1982).

It seems imperative then that the consultant recognize this school system characteristic and deal with all of its ramifications in a realistic fashion. For example, one may have to give up the "50-minute" timeframe for the "15-minute consultation" (see a following section of this chapter) and adapt it as the model of choice. Also, there is often a tendency for beginning consultants to think of this approach in a formal manner, and as such, frame the contact(s) in a manner that suggests to the teacher (and themselves) that much more than conference time is involved. For example, getting together to discuss a teacher's questions about a child is accepted with little hesitancy, but meeting "to consult" suggests a unique, professional encounter. The end result is that time often is not allocated for such activities.

Use of supplementary contacts such as telephone consultation and electronic and facsimile mail is a potential strategy, which when combined with "quickie" or "15-minute consultations" can provide the follow-up and continuity that may be lost otherwise. Such abbreviated consultations must stay problem-focused within a circumscribed area. These targeted consults can also be bolstered by classroom observations where appropriate. Quade (1985) recommended that learning disability resource teachers "block" a period of time in their schedules for regular classroom teacher consultation and found that it promoted an expanded use of the service. Thus, the idea of the consultants posting a before/after school "office hour" may make sense in some districts. Additional strategies for dealing with time constraints have been provided in the literature (Idol, 1988; West & Idol, 1990). Whitaker (1992) highlights four strategies for arranging time for consultation. First, enlisting administrative support is important. The approval of a percentage of time for collaboration each day, or rotated from week to week, should be explored. Also, requesting time for inservice dealing with skills in getting the most out of support services would help, along with exploring the interest in consultation groups or peer-mediated learning groups if designated time were available. A second but similar strategy involves making use of existing planning times. Forming a consultation committee is a third approach. The purposes would include work on defined projects and demonstrated effectiveness, along with the development of a plan to advocate for a system-wide consultation program. Finally, the need for the consultant to have in place a workable communication network involving such strategies as a standard form for memos and/or progress reports and electronic mail is emphasized. Planned use of telephone contacts is also another example.

Administrative Support.   The example of a superintendent of one school system who would not allow teachers to hold any type of conference during school hours underscores the rationale often heard that teachers are employed to directly serve the children. This "rule" was enforced by the superintendent's unannounced visits to the schools along with brief visits to the classrooms. Needless to say, professional contact time became a premium commodity in that system, particularly when one considers the other demands on teacher time outside the school day (including parent conferences, teacher meetings, activity supervision). Generally, administrators are receptive to the consultation model, particularly when the objective of the model involves increasing teacher competence to deal with similar problems to the one being discussed in consultation. Additionally, the fact that specialized professionals can impact more stu-

dents using the consultation service delivery model versus other models is also attractive.

However, the spoken or unspoken attitude of an administrator, for example, the principal, toward teacher autonomy or, even more specifically, a service such as consultation, is emerging as a significant factor influencing teacher behavior vis-à-vis the consultant. Teachers are not only less likely to view consultation in a positive manner, but their use of such services is less likely to occur when they work under a controlling and threatening principal (Bossard & Gutkin, 1983; Gutkin & Bossard, 1984). Similarly, the degree of acceptability of interventions arising out of consultations on the part of teachers relates to the degree of administrative support that is perceived (Broughton & Hester, 1993). Such preliminary findings lend credence to the notion that the resource professionals take into account the teacher's perception of how safe the consultation plan is as interventions are being planned.

The three common reservations expressed by administrators include the time demands on the teacher, the effect on the direct service commitments of the consultant, and accountability. Regarding the first two reservations, involvement of the administrator along with some teachers in designing a service mindful of time constraints and other perceived needs of the system will insure an initial commitment. Opportunities for such a group to serve an advisory role during the first year of the model could be further documentation of the consultant's interest in developing a relevant service, while ensuring that all perspectives are taken into account as the program goes forward. There are ways of planning evaluations so that they can alleviate the administrative concerns over the effectiveness of the services and their acceptability by the teachers. Through the use of data-based evaluations, Zins (1981) was able to expand school consultation services from one hour per week to a program in which consultation was the primary service offered. During the first year, the consultation time of the school psychologist was quite limited, but recognized. Evaluations of all consultations were conducted and reported at the end of the year. These evaluations included quantitative questionnaire data regarding the nature of consultation service itself (e.g., number and frequency of consultation contacts) and its quality (e.g., benefits of working with the consultant and consultant effectiveness).

Status. In Chapter Thirteen, we discuss the challenges inherent in asking for help. In a school system in which you are "the professional" responsible for a classroom of children, the erroneous expectation can arise (and often does) that you should know what to do, and any indication that you need "help" can only reflect negatively on the perceptions of your competencies. In an attempt to identify the factors that distinguish between teachers who seek consultation from school psychologists and those who do not seek such help, Stenger, Tollefson, and Fine (1992) found a number of such variables. First, the simple presence of a school psychologist in the building was an obvious important factor. However, consultation help needs to be offered, and there is a greater chance of its being used than when the consultant waits for it to be requested by the teacher. Interestingly, only 30 percent of the teachers in this study reported its being offered! It would seem that one reason is the continued emphasis in the consultation literature on the relationship's being a voluntary one. Also, consistent with other research studies, teachers who described themselves as good problem solvers were more likely to seek consultation. However, another study found that teachers with a high self-efficacy score, that is, rating their ability to solve a child's problem (when presented with a written description of a problem), were also likely to rate consultation as helpful in solving the problem; however, there was no relationship with a subsequent use of consultation or its outcome evaluation (Hughes, Grossman, & Barker, 1990). Finally, Stenger and colleagues (1992) reported that the teachers' perceptions of school psychologists' having training in problem solving and their training as different from that of the teachers were likely to influence their seeking consultation.

As noted above, a voluntary teacher contact is often seen as critical to the offering of consultation service. Harris and Cancelli (1991) have conceptualized a continuum on which teacher consultees' level of volunteerism would be manifested at different stages of consultation and different consultation models. In order to motivate the consultee to volunteer for consultation, they suggest that the consultant should concentrate on the needs that the consultee has produced, that the teacher should be encouraged to be an active participant in the process (i.e., avoid advice giving), that the strengths and weaknesses of the consultation discussion be evaluated by the teacher, and, finally, teacher ownership of the intervention be stressed.

Consultation as a term has that common-sense ring about it that an expert is telling you what to do. One of our colleagues recently shared an interesting insight into the power of the term. The teacher workshops offered by this colleague were once labeled "consultation," but now they are referred to as "collaborative problem solving" and are now not only well attended, but enthusiastically received. Hierarchical relationships with internally based professional peers have the potential to elicit feelings of resentment and resistance on the part of teachers (Johnson et al., 1988). However, there may be exceptions of large systems in which the consultant is centrally located and dispersed to the school upon request, or the small school system with a limited staff of resource professionals may not be threatened by the consultant. Nevertheless, an internally based consultant, with fairly regular contact with the staff, should pay particular attention to the manner in which indirect services are articulated and more important, actually delivered. The overwhelming consultee preference for collaboration noted in an earlier chapter suggests, at the very least, an expectation of being treated like a professional. The irony of that finding is that teachers expect collaborators to have expertise in another area than theirs and for that knowledge to be applied to their problem.

There have been several descriptions of consultation approaches targeted on the regular teacher as consultee and that carry a title to denote that emphasis. Obviously, any of the models presented in this text could be used effectively with teachers so that it could be argued that the "teacher consultation model" should be treated within the context of those models. Similarly, much of what is written in consultation for school psychologists has instructional staff as one of its target consultee groups. However, given the growing use of the terms *teacher consultation,* or *teacher collaboration,* and their derivatives, it seems reasonable to briefly present the basic features of those descriptions. This terminology primarily grows out of the special education field, wherein the objective is the facilitation of professional work between the special education teacher/resource consultant and the regular classroom teacher.

THE CONSULTING TEACHER MODELS

The idea of a teacher expert in content and/or instructional approaches available to assist other teachers in meeting the instructional challenges they face in the classroom is not new; in fact, this notion is embodied in the nature of educational supervision. However, as Blessing (1968) pointed out, the kind of assistance that was required changed as the training and professionalism of the teacher evolved; a dynamic, democratic supervisor was needed who facilitated growth and the fostering of meaningful change. For special education teachers, Blessing and his colleagues elected to use the term *resource consultant* to designate a new role and function for this education specialty, and envisaged this individual working not only with special education teachers, but also with the regular classroom teachers, administrators, and other supportive school personnel. By the early 70s, this consultative thrust was being embraced by special educators as one strategy that the special education teacher could use in delivering services to handicapped children, for example, working through the regular classroom teacher versus the resource teacher role or instructing in the special class. This alternative has certainly caught on recently, if the

activity dealing with this theme from the middle of the 80s until now is any indication.

In 1972, McKenzie described a consulting teacher approach, often referred to as the Vermont Consulting Teacher Model, in which "the consulting teacher assists regular classroom teachers to carry out diagnoses and to develop an intervention approach to facilitate a given child's educational development" (p. 103). He presented two considerations as a rationale for the model: (1) high cost estimates and the disruption that would result from local school system plans to bus students requiring special education to regional classes, and (2) the unfortunate byproduct of separate classes, for example, developing a reliance on special services versus services that can be provided in regular classes. Providing the special assistance as part of the regular classroom would obviate the necessity of labeling children and, thus, would decrease the need for evaluation services. The help that was envisioned to be provided by the consulting teacher would be "in the form of instruction regarding principles of the behavioral model of education and application of these principles" (McKenzie, 1972, p. 109). The consulting teacher in this model then is seen as an expert in applied behavior analysis, and it is this behavioral content that is delivered by the consulting teacher. The stages in this consulting service reflect the paradigm and priorities associated with that theoretical orientation (see Chapter Three). The consultant is viewed as an expert engaged in a trainer-of-teachers role.

By 1982, Heron and Harris were proposing a mutual problem-solving process for the *educational consultant* wherein the consultant and consultee share responsibility for an intervention outcome. They stressed that education for handicapped students should take place within the least restrictive environment and, while eclectic in their coverage of strategies to accomplish this objective, still rely heavily on behavioral theory. Their work emphasized the new concepts and ideas pervading special education at that time, such as the content of the consultation rather than the process. The major exception is when behavioral approaches are discussed so that behavior management strategies and group classroom contingencies are dealt with in detail.

Although several different consultation models are available, special education models, for which program descriptions and outcome data are available for the most part, have employed a behavioral approach within a problem-solving paradigm (Cantrell & Cantrell, 1976; Knight, Meyers, Paolucci-Whitcomb, Hasazi, & Nevin, 1981; Nelson & Stevens, 1981 [see Chapter Three also]). In each of these studies, a problem-solving strategy was used in which general education teachers requested assistance from special education teachers in dealing with a child or group of children. The special education teacher then worked with the teacher to define the problem in measurable terms, collect data, develop and implement an intervention, and evaluate its effect.

Instructional Consultation

This approach obviously is geared toward the teacher as consultee. Bergan and Schnaps (1983) used the term in referring to an elaboration of *behavioral consultation* wherein the goal was "to modify teacher behavior to enhance the learning of all students in a class." In a similar vein, Rosenfield (1987) defined the term as integrating the growing knowledge base regarding instructional practices with classroom management, and utilizing consultation techniques that emphasize the collaborative relationship. She presents a rather comprehensive description of the process and content aspects of this approach, which has as its overall goal the improvement of school psychologists and other educational consultants work with teachers. What follows is a brief description of her ideas. The evolving work of special education consultation, which also targets the classroom teacher as consultee, is presented in the next section.

The role of the instruction consultant is conceptualized "not only as an indirect service method for working with children with academic problems, but also as a potentially powerful in-service training process…" (p. 7). Working in this role, Rosenfield puts forth some definitive assumptions about children with learning problems encompassing the idea that instructional mismatches underline the referred problem. The consultation interaction concerns itself with the vulnerable learner, inadequate instruction, and a "muddied conception of the task." The interaction of those three factors becomes the focus of Rosenfield's approach versus the "defective learner" assumption that she perceives to be the emphasis of current indirect services. She views the focus as indirect service to the referred child through the teacher, following the usual stages of consultation and elaborating on some of the basic skills required for collaborative (behavioral) consultation.

Rosenfield's approach essentially uses a behavioral problem identification and analysis strategy during the initial teacher interview. This information is then coupled with a classroom observation and Curriculum-Based Assessment (CBA). The instructional interventions that are developed take place in the classroom, either under the monitorship or through direct provision of the classroom teacher. In her book, Rosenfield (1987) summarizes several types of behavioral-observational and structured observation systems. The assessment of academic learning is defined as including CBA procedures as well as a task and process analysis. Finally, planning and conducting instructional interventions are defined as involving management of the learner (e.g., time management, physical changes in the classroom, contracting, and utilization of cooperative learning techniques) and management of learning (e.g., curriculum content and format changes, learning strategies, and the sequencing of instructional procedures).

An *abbreviated* example of a segment of the diagnostic interview might be as follows:

CONSULTANT: Tell me about his trouble learning to read.
TEACHER: He hasn't learned to read any words.
CONSULTANT: What reading approaches has he had some success with?

TEACHER: None, he still can't read a word. The next day, he can't remember words that have been learned.

CONSULTANT: What have you tried?

TEACHER: Phonics, whole word approach; nothing seems to work. (Teacher gives examples.)

CONSULTANT: What words does he want to learn to read?

TEACHER: I never asked him.

CONSULTANT: Let's find out. He may be motivated to learn "his" words. He can choose any word he wants. It's important we don't put any value judgment on his choice. Then, we teach him that word, plus two others he chooses using configuration cues. (Consultant explains rationale and demonstrates.)

Specific task analysis is done on initially finding the instructional level of the student. Then, the student's approach to the academic content is reviewed, for example, a process analysis. This latter step includes an analysis of errors made by the student. Thus, the consultant might suggest that the student is reversing letters and recommend that a small card, with the letters commonly reversed, be arranged vertically (since this is an easier discrimination than when presented horizontally) and taped to the desk with a visual mnemonic in order to facilitate discrimination. Specific assessment and intervention steps are then taken.

This approach would fail to meet the criterion of a consultation model per se. Rather, it can be fairly stated that instructional consultation deals primarily with the instructional content expertise of the consultant, rather than the process of consultation itself. When the consultation process is described by Rosenfield, she mentions basic interpersonal skills, while drawing on the behavioral and collaborative models of consultation. However, the consultant's involvement in the intervention phase of consultation is not considered and, as such, is collaborative only to a point. Certainly, a special educator, who is engaged in offering some instructional intervention to the student either in the classroom or under a "pull-out" arrangement, would represent one

prototype wherein a true collaboration between consultant and consultee would be realized. Another observation that needs to be made regarding the adoption of this approach involves the rather definitive set of instructional assumptions on which it is based. The degree to which the consultant explains those educational perspectives to the teacher, and in what detail, would seem to be critical questions affecting this helping relationship. Rosenfield provides little guidance on this point, let alone the question of whether or not the teacher can choose to disagree or reject those assumptions.

Education is characterized by a variety of instructional theories and methodologies, aside from conceptualizations of the learner, that are not only diverse in the premises on which they are based, but may, in fact, be in conflict. Instructional consultation, as presented, would seem to have merit, but under the condition that the teacher's views are consistent with the consultant's. How to accomplish a knowledgeable choice on the part of the teacher when she or he enters this type of consultation needs to be developed by these consultants. What are the implications for the approach when teachers adopt a different set of assumptions? Similarly, at one point Rosenfield mentions that consultants help the teacher "shift" to a collaboration approach, but how that change should be dealt with represents another challenge for consultants using this approach. Both of these questions are dealt with in Chapter Thirteen, Issues in Consultation.

COLLABORATION WITH TEACHERS

While the collaboration model modifies some of the basic aspects of consultation to fit the needs, conditions, and consultee expectations that prevail in many organizations where consultative services are provided, it is a different indirect service approach. Collaboration is still considered *indirect service* even though the support service specialties may also provide a direct service to the student. When the support service specialties collaborate with the teacher, they "mutually" decide on a coordinated effort directed toward the student (and parents, family, etc.). While they share observations regarding each other's work, the primary focus will be the classroom given the fact that this is where the student will spend the most time with either of them. Also, the specialties themselves may provide limited direct service to the student (e.g., assessment, brief counseling). Regardless of the extent of the student involvement that specialties have, it should be assumed that the teacher will have some input in the hypothesis generated by his or her colleague (i.e., the resource professional) in that involvement, and even some say in an appropriate course of action, or at the very least, an opportunity to express input. Otherwise, a unidirectional communication/focus violates an important defining characteristic of the collaboration model.

As Pryzwansky (1977) points out, there is often a poor conceptual fit between models of consultation and the realities encountered by human services professionals who engage in consultation. For example, the mental health consultation model assumes that consultation is oriented toward broadening the range of alternatives considered by the consultee to resolve a problem, that consultants are external to the organization in which consultation takes place, and that consultees possess most of the skills they need to function effectively on the job. However, these assumptions do not fit all consultative situations. In school-based consultation the consultant is often internal, such as a school psychologist or school counselor. Teachers may frequently request consultation because they lack the knowledge or skill needed to deal with a child's difficulty (Gutkin, 1981) and may look to the consultant for concrete suggestions rather than a discussion of alternatives (Pryzwansky, 1974). The ongoing contact between the consultant and the school also may lead to expectations that the consultant will be involved in implementation and follow-up activities (Pryzwansky, 1974).

Pryzwansky (1974, 1977) has proposed an alternate model of indirect service delivery, which he terms collaboration. Within a collaborative model, the consultant and consultee assume joint responsibility for all aspects of the consultation process. Consultants and consultees agree upon the objectives for consultation, define the problem together, jointly develop an intervention plan, and share responsibility for implementation and evaluation of the outcome of their plan.

Within Caplan's consultee-centered approach, the consultee maintains complete responsibility and control over implementation. Caplan and Caplan (1993) sees this as an important aspect of consultation because consultees will resist intrusion into their professional responsibilities. In several studies, however, potential consultees have indicated a preference for shared responsibility between consultant and consultee throughout the consultative process. Pryzwansky and White (1983) surveyed teachers and found that they preferred collaboration over the mental health model of consultation, as well as over two additional models of indirect service delivery. This preference was found regardless of respondents' years of experience or locus of control. Babcock and Pryzwansky (1983) also found that regular education teachers preferred the collaborative model and extended these findings to school principals and special education teachers. Wenger (1979) found that teachers who had received consultative services where a collaborative relationship was fostered were more satisfied with consultation than those who had received client-centered case consultation. Weller (1984) found that parents indicated a preference for collaboration when seeking psychoeducational consultation concerning their children. West (1985) and Schulte, Osborne, and Kauffman (1993) also have found a preference for collaboration over consultation in school settings. Although these results have not been extended to other consultation settings, they suggest that consultants should consider expectations and preferences for direct service to clients in school settings in selecting a consultation model, particularly when consultants are internal to the organization.

It is important to note that collaboration differs sharply from traditional models of consultation in terms of the level of involvement of the specialist in assessment and intervention activities related to the client. Provision of some direct service to the client is an integral part of collaboration (Pryzwansky, 1974, 1977; West, 1990), but generally not a part of the consultant's responsibility in consultation.

Although some authors distinguish collaboration from consultation, others have discussed models of collaborative consultation (e.g., Graden, Casey, & Christenson, 1984; Graden, 1989; Idol, Paolucci-Whitcomb, & Nevin, 1986; Parsons & Meyers, 1984; Rosenfield, 1987). All of these models emphasize the importance of collaborative problem solving and a collegial relationship between the consultant and consultee. However, the models differ from collaboration in that direct service to the client by the specialist receives less emphasis. Given the wide range of meanings for the terms *collaboration* and *collaborative* in the consultation literature (Schulte & Osborne, 1993), care should be taken that important distinctions between models of service delivery, such as the presence or absence of direct service to the client, are not masked by the use of the same terms by different authors when they are discussing distinctly different aspects of the consultation process or models.

Currently, it is the field of special education where the *collaboration* notion seems to have attracted the most attention, leading to a wide range of its use in describing practice. As indicated earlier, such popularity of a concept can detract from its professional meaning, but it is left to others to decide whether this has happened and if the resulting advantages are worth such a shift. Fishbaugh (1997) notes the lack of consensus on the definition of collaboration in the educational professional literature. As a result, she defines collaboration as "working together for a common end" (p. 4) and proposes that there are three models of collaboration. The first is the *consulting* model of collaboration that is defined as an expert offering advice in a relationship characterized by inequity. "The concept of mentoring as collaboration in the form of consulting" is given as an example (p. 65). The second model is the *coaching* model defined by parity in the relationship. It is further described as basically following a clinical supervision cycle. The

third model is defined as the interaction of professionals responsible for the group's problems and their solution, and is labeled the *teaming* model of collaboration. Finally, each model addresses one of the following three purposes: technical assistance, collegial support, and challenge solution.

By contrast, Dettmer, Dyck, and Thurston (1999) have argued that their concept of a *collaborative school consultant* represents synergy (a behavior of whole systems unpredicted by the behavior of their parts taken separately) rather than an oxymoron (p. 7). Recognizing the definitions of a number of terms addressing professional services, their "collaborative school consultant is a facilitator of effective communication, cooperation, and coordination who confers, consults, and collaborates with other school personnel and families as one of a team for addressing special learning and behavioral needs of students" (p. 6). Coteaching as teams is an approach highly valued by these authors, so team work involving both consultation and collaboration is seen as a promising practice for helping students with special needs. In her book promoting collaboration between special educators and general educators, Cramer (1998) sees this role of the special educator expanding in the future. Recognizing as a number of others have the legislative, societal, and political factors that have influenced the trend for greater contact among all school professionals, she stresses the importance of intrapersonal and interpersonal characteristics of the resource professional and the context as critical components of collaboration. In her book for special education teachers-in-training, she outlines projects that can influence teachers' development in the area of professional interactions. Cramer emphasizes that teachers must become curious, self-motivated learners in achieving a collaborative role with others in the schools.

Mostert (1998) stresses the *interactive* nature of the collaborative practice, emphasizing that it implies cooperation and mutual consent throughout the process. In his broad description of collaboration, he includes nonprofessionals such as parents, other family members, and the students themselves. Thus, he stresses a *collaboration orientation* for all teachers in his presentation of this concept. He goes on to promote collaborative characteristics within groups and teams. Mostert promotes what others have more explicitly endorsed, the building of collaborative contexts (Dettmar et al., 1999; Fishbaugh, 1997; Goldstein, 1998; Nevin, Thousand, & Villa, 1993). The thrust of such objectives is to produce a climate for and approach to tasks that embrace the defining elements of collaboration. For example Fishbaugh (1997) writes about the collaborative school, an organization that "is based on norms for collegiality, the professionalization of teaching, a wide array of practices, and shared decision making among all staff with the overriding goal of educational improvement" (p. 8). Dettmar and her colleagues (1999) stress the importance of using adult differences in furthering the development of collaborative settings. A description of a school's attempt to change its culture by establishing a collaborative ethic as well as collaborative practice is presented by Nevin, Thousand, and Villa (1993). They note that inherent in such a shift is the requirement that staff "relinquish traditional roles so that they may exchange skills and roles as they collaborate to create quality educational experiences for everyone." Thus, the seemingly general attractiveness of the collaborative concept (see Babcock & Pryzwansky, 1983) has evolved from a description of a professional indirect service approach for a dyadic interaction to a set of values and procedures that permeate an organization and define its mission, as well as the interactions of those individuals within that context and their relation to individuals and other organizational entities with whom they must work to fulfill their goals. In the process of such a generous application of the concept, along with its assimilation of other helping strategies and modes of work (e.g., teams), the essential premises defining its distinctiveness can be diminished, overlooked, or diluted. The result is that any effect on its uniqueness among other approaches is minimized. Such is the challenge facing those who attempt to employ any service approach let alone apply it beyond its original intended use.

In contrast to the trend in special education consultation emphasizing the content of the consultation, Idol and West (1987; Idol, 1989) present the distinguishing conceptualization of the new role. They conceptualized consultation as an "artful science." The artful base refers to both the communicative/interactive skills, which allow rapport to be established in which information and problem-solving competencies are shared, leading not only to good problem finding but also to planning and evaluating solution strategies. The scientific base includes those technological and knowledge backgrounds that enhance the assessment demands of the role, but also contribute to substance of the solution, particularly when what is required is information based on theory and research. Idol and West reiterate the principle that one aspect without the other leads to, at best, a friendly relationship with nothing of relevance to the problem shared between the professionals. Indeed, it seems as though the emphasis in instructional/teacher consultation writings has been on the technological side, and little attention has been paid to consultation per se. In affirming a consultation service, Idol and West seem to be proposing a collaborative problem-solving model that is reflected in a preceding work (Idol, Paolucci-Whitcomb, & Nevin, 1986). Idol and colleagues (1986) defined collaborative consultation as a reciprocal arrangement "that enables people with diverse expertise to generate creative solutions to mutually defined problems" (p. 1). In terms of these special education–general education models, this approach seems to represent the only proposal that deals specifically with the question of how to provide an indirect service; the others primarily advocate that position while promoting a particular theoretical and/or methodical position.

Given-Ogle, Christ, and Idol (1991) describe a project in which school resource specialists formed a collaborative working group among themselves in addition to offering collaborative consultation to classroom teachers and building administrators. Preliminary evaluation data suggest that the project was effective in bringing selected students' reading skills to grade level and their behavior to acceptable levels.

As noted earlier, Pryzwansky (1973) and later Caplan and Caplan (1993) have proposed that collaboration in schools among professionals employed by the same school district may be a more advantageous service approach than consultation. "Insiders" like resource teachers, guidance counselors, or school psychologists may experience more effective results with this approach. As these authors have pointed out, less time needs to be spent in building relationships (they are a known quantity to a certain extent) although relationship building always remains a priority regardless of the focus of employment and never should be taken for granted. Similarly, the insider will not need to spend as much time in community/context exploration or to initiate a program of collaboration, although some teachers may still assume or desire that direct services be provided to the students even when the program has been established for some time. By contrast, Caplan and Caplan (1993) point out that the consultant must overcome two obstacles (pp. 339–340). In order to realize a relationship in which the teacher feels free to accept or reject what the consultant says, a "coordinate, nonhierarchical consultative relationship" must be established. In addition, confidentiality must be preserved. This can be done if the situation does not require the support service professional's active intervention with the student, and equally important, the administration supports this model of collegial assistance.

Collaboration is then seen as a "partnership," with the support service professional taking a relatively active role throughout the process. They, and the teacher, should coordinate their efforts with those of the other specialized professionals. In addition, their work, perhaps more so than that of a consultant, is likely to be subject to modification by an overriding authority such as a team or principal (Caplan & Caplan, 1993).

GROUP CONSULTATION

Given the time constraints faced by teachers as discussed earlier, the alternative of offering consultation in a group format would seem to have intuitive appeal. There are often groups of teachers who meet on a regular basis, such as grade level or department meetings. Scheduling some of that time on a regular basis for consultation might have some support, even if only part of the meeting or every third or fourth meeting were so designated. An even more fruitful advantage of this service strategy is that it serves as a forum for observing the problem-solving process on relevant problems and could lead to effective modeling of this skill. For example, in a study offering specific cognitive modeling exercises to undergraduates, it was found that the subsequent problem-solving behavior of observers was positively influenced (Cleven & Gutkin, 1987). Similarly, Curtis and Watson (1980) reported that teachers were more factual when they worked with colleagues who mastered a skill advancement training workshop on collaboration. Such collegial discussion, as might characterize group consultation sessions, may also serve to reduce any anxiety and self-reproving attitudes contributing to a teacher's inhibition to explore challenges being presented by a student. Finally, there is the potential for "picking up ideas" and benefitting from listening to a colleague's strategies by generalizing to similar situations. Dinkmeyer and Carlson (1973) referred to this passive type of participation as *spectator therapy,* wherein an understanding of self is facilitated by listening to others problem solve.

While the impression exists that group consultation has been increasing and may accelerate, particularly in educational settings, there continues to be a paucity of empirical research, let alone case descriptions. There is a need to develop significant research efforts in this area.

A variety of group consultation type approaches will now be briefly introduced. These include case-centered groups, issue-centered groups, and task-groups. The specific "C" group's model is then described, followed by a very promising approach, peer consultation.

Case-Centered Groups

In a review of mental health consultation to groups of school personnel, Cohen and Osterweil (1986) report that studies have reported substantive advantages such as reduction in referrals for direct service, increased knowledge of child development, and improved communication among colleagues. Cohen and Osterweil point out that one major challenge facing the consultant using this approach is prevention of the sessions evolving into meetings with a psychotherapeutic objective; a number of authors usually limit discussion to work-related problems and deal with personal material in a generic manner (e.g., as universal phenomena) to prevent this from happening. Nevertheless, in spite of these benefits, Cohen and Osterweil offer their reflections on the type of group consultation that is case-study-oriented and find that a number of disadvantages exist. The group can generate some anxiety among certain consultees, discussions can focus on limitations of consultees and in doing so reinforce an expert role for the consultant, and the experience may result in defensiveness or inhibition on the part of still other consultees.

A type of group case consultation has been described recently by Babinski and Rogers (1998). They offered new teachers a consultee-centered group consultation in which the teachers shared their issues and concerns and a problem-solving process was introduced. Led by two "consultants" (a faculty member from the school psychology program and one from the elementary education program), the emphasis of the groups was on "self as teacher" while offering a group to provide social and emotional support. This type of group can be seen as one approach to promoting new teachers' professional development (see the peer consultation section for more discussion of this option).

Task Groups

One type of group consultation that has been proposed for teachers is the *task* group, in which the objective is to learn to deal effectively with students (Brown, Wyne, Blackburn, & Powell, 1979). These groups have been found to evolve through the same stages as other groups, so that the consultant must possess the necessary leadership background for the group to be successful; consultants

must have knowledge of group dynamics and be able to facilitate group development. Thus, the consultant should be able to help the group clarify its purposes and working procedures. In addition, he or she is a group facilitator, sensitive to and promoting constructive verbal and nonverbal communication and problem resolution, while remaining a participant as well.

"C" Groups

Dinkmeyer and Carlson (1973) proposed the use of didactic-experiential groups for teachers that they called the "C" group. They reasoned that "unless there is personal involvement and opportunity to test out ideas, match them to one's style of life, internalize new concepts, and then exchange results with other professionals, little change will occur" (p. 223). Acknowledging that individual consultation can be hampered by a number of factors, working within teacher groups that were structured differently than the typical inservice education experience would be necessary if school-based consultants in the area of human behavior were to be effective. Thus, the "C" group concept was developed to assist teachers in examining their interactions with students with the objective of developing specific strategies for establishing different relationships. The specific components then of the "C" group include collaborating, consulting, clarifying, communicating, being cohesive, confronting, being concerned, caring, being confidential, being committed, and being willing to change.

Beginning with the collaboration factor, Dinkmeyer and Carlson see the group working together on mutual concerns in a mutual help situation. Thus, consultation occurs among the teachers in the group with the consultant as a member of the group. The group then helps each teacher clarify his or her belief system and feelings in order to resolve discrepancies. Confrontation is one technique that is encouraged, whether it's in the examination of one's own psychological makeup or in providing realistic and honest feedback to other group members. The objective of these factors is to show that the group is concerned and that it cares. Communication is reinforced to the point that teachers became involved with each other as individuals. Group cohesiveness enables their effectiveness to be realized. All discussions in the group are confidential to encourage open and frank discussions. Finally, members of the "C" group help each other to develop a commitment to change, and in particular, the notion that they must change their approach to problems. Part of the change also includes beliefs and attitudes; the group helps each other grow professionally and personally.

These writers form their "C" groups with teachers who either have similar concerns or work with the same children. They also make the point that in forming the group, it is important to have a heterogeneous collection of teachers wherein age, experience, and theoretical/instruction approaches are represented. Involvement in their groups is always voluntary, and group involvement is preceded by an individual interview with the consultant to clarify the goals of the group as well as to establish concrete individual objectives for each teacher as they participate in the group. They report that leaders utilize the techniques that are used in group work in general. Before the group has its first meeting, leaders supply the members with written materials of a didactic nature describing the purpose, rationale, description, and benefits of the "C" group. Additionally, since Dinkmeyer and Carlson view most problems as "interpersonal and social" in nature, an explanation is provided of the Adlerian or socioteleological approach. This approach includes the basic assumptions underlying the development of personality according to Alfred Adler—that is, (a) man is primarily a social being, (b) man is self-determined, (c) man's behavior is purposive, (d) man must be viewed subjectively, and (e) man is holistic. Finally, a chart for "making hypotheses about a child's mistaken goals" is given to the participants. The group then begins its first session by identifying a child and considering the following four questions:

1. What did the child do?
2. How did the teacher respond to his or her action?

3. How did the teacher feel when the child was misbehaving and the teacher was responding?
4. How did the child respond to the corrective efforts of the teacher?

In addition to this preliminary work, the consultant structures the group so that the purpose and focus are clear and the group is sensitive to feelings expressed in the sessions. The consultant links the ideas of group members, ensures that less verbal individuals can participate beyond the spectator therapy mode, keeps the group focused on its goals, promotes feelings of adequacy, ensures consideration of alternative ways of solving challenges, and encourages changes in the behavioral pattern of teacher interaction with students.

Issue Groups

Cohen and Osterweil (1986) argue that an "issues-focused" versus "case seminar" method would meet the professional needs of the teacher-focused group. Such teacher consultation groups provide a "safe" problem-solving environment. Rather than one teacher presenting a case in the group mental health consultation model, Cohen and Osterweil advocate the consultant as "responsible for the choice, pacing, and timing of different consultation issues…" (p. 248) and various problems encountered by teachers related to the issue we addressed. Examples of issues addressed are "social relationships in the preschool" and "classroom rules and routines." These authors stress the importance of preparing for the sessions, including individual conferences with the teacher, choosing key questions in order to meet certain objectives, and evaluation.

Group consultation, whether case-study or issue focused, seems to hold considerable promise as a school-based approach. As an alternative to the individual consultation approach, it may be appropriate to use in the school environment with many of the same advantages. Clearly, the objective(s) need to be clearly stated, and a volunteer, short-term (two to four meetings) commitment at a relatively stress-free time, such as after school or piggybacked on another meeting, is important to consider. In fact, group consultation approaches in schools may even serve as initial steps in shifting from a direct service approach.

PEER CONSULTATION

Peer-mediated support systems can be structured to promote collaborative problem solving among professionals (Zins, 1996). Simply put, peer-mediated groups are groups of individuals from the same professions who come together with the purpose of helping one another with a defined task. Typically, they hold the same position in the same system (e.g., classroom teacher, school counselor). The groups, informally or formally organized, have a specific purpose. While it is not totally documented, it appears that those groups that have an agreed upon process for how they function will be effective and/or satisfying. The purpose(s) are varied and can involve learning about specific topics such as students' learning styles, collaborating on design interventions for addressing challenges in teaching a particular student, or, for internal consultants, quasi-supervision on each other's consultation. In the case of teachers, such a group reduces feelings of isolation and reinforces the professional's inclination to seek out another teacher when confronting a challenge in the classroom. Consultants can help set up such groups (or pair of teachers) and increase the effectiveness of the group in generating specific plans to work on specific problems, although the challenge to a group of discovering the utility of collaboration can be a powerful impetus to maintaining the group.

Pugach and Johnson (1988) report on one such *peer collaboration* in which teachers were introduced to a four-step, *peer-guided dialogue* based on a series of metacognitive strategies. First, teacher pairs engage in problem clarification through guided self-questioning of each other's problem. The potential for reframing the problem is enhanced. Second, the problem is then summarized to reflect new understandings. Third, "practical" plans are then generated from bringing about change while identifying associated problems that come up during the implementation phase. Potential benefits of the plan are also identified. Finally, teachers are encouraged to be specific about how they plan to go about their intervention and to include a time line and mechanism to determine the effectiveness of the plan. The authors reason that such a public dialogue in which thinking is shared aloud and guided by a peer, as well as the goal of having teaching internalize such strategies, can facilitate commitment to an intervention and improvement in the identified problem. In addition to serving as an excellent example of how to guide teacher peer collaboration, their study is important in other ways. While Johnson and Pugach (1996) report impressive results (86 percent of the 48 teachers reported satisfaction addressing the identified problem), their report of the nature of the interventions seems to have implications for consultation practice. Often the interventions that were developed were relatively simple and did not require major changes in teacher behavior. The authors hypothesize that professionals (in this case teachers) are capable of making only small changes at any point in time—that is, changes that are close to their current level of skill. They relate Vygotsky's notion of the *zone of proximal development* as an explanatory hypothesis. The peer consultant in this case is seen as guiding the colleague to attempt a change he or she can contemplate with little anxiety. Not only may that lead to a shift in thinking about the problem, it may reinforce additional attempts at intervention. The consultant then may be well advised to proceed in a similar fashion in a dyadic consultation with a teacher, that is, encourage small step(s) as a way to attack a problem. The reader is directed to the section on problem solving in Chapter Seven.

The Johnson and Pugach (1996) peer collaboration report has several interesting implications. For example, consultants/collaborators may want to operate like the *peer guide* in that study. Clearly, the adaptation of this approach may be warranted under some conditions such as limited consultation time, relatively straightforward problems, and a teacher with a personality style suited to work with others in this manner. Second, the training model may be adapted to preserve teacher-training contexts and/or teacher-induction programs. While Johnson and Pugach (1996) used experienced teachers, introducing beginning professionals to these concepts could not hurt. Third, it is known that teachers are likely to seek out other teacher leaders to advise them regarding challenges they face in the classroom. Competencies of the type being trained in this study would only improve the outcomes of such informal professional contacts. In fact, it may reinforce that level of camaraderie and lead to a sense of teaming that often can be lacking in education. Fourth, researchers in consultation and practitioners alike need to be sensitive to the Vygotsky principle of learning that suggests giving priority to the teachers' levels of understanding students in terms of identifying immediate targets of change. The relative importance of proceeding in such a manner could have an obvious impact on initial success, as well as sustain a relationship between consultant and consultee over a long period of time. Finally, the conditions under which the study took place need to be recognized. Teachers who participated in the Johnson and Pugach study voluntarily chose to participate, and chose their partners. The teachers were experienced (x = 15.15 years). Most importantly, the teacher training consisted of a two-hour group session that involved a videotaped demonstration of the approach, followed by at least two monitored tape-recorded training sessions. The training took three to four hours, and a subsequent cycle of initial problem solving for one case takes approximately forty-five minutes to an hour to complete.

Babinski and Rodgers (1998) described a rather innovative approach that introduces peer consultation within a group context to novice teachers. Their groups were designed to promote both professional dialogue and problem solving. Group facilitators (graduate students in school psychology and teacher-education specialist programs) would guide discussions about issues and challenges the new teachers were experiencing in their classrooms as well as their general entry-level professional experiences. The facilitators utilized Caplan's model of consultation to guide their role development vis à vis the beginning teachers. The facilitators explicitly described the problem-solving process and reinforced the teachers for thinking about the group discussion content in this manner, and whether to deal with their own issues or those presented by their colleagues. One obvious strength of this type of group is that it comes at a stage in professionals' development when they are most open and eager to participate in a supportive activity. It is designed not only to promote support of their feelings in a context of understanding, but also to provide them with a sounding board and a tool for handling their present circumstances that can be generalized to future situations. Furthermore, the groups expose the new professional to resource professionals in their system who are valuable for individual consultation/collaboration support. The education enterprise typically does not promote, let alone reinforce, such helping relationships as routine instruction practice. Activities of this type can promote this objective.

CONTRACTUAL SERVICE

It has been a long-held belief in public-sector therapy clinics that clients should pay something, however minimal, for therapeutic/counseling help in order to cement their commitment to the process. Consequently, an obligation to meet a "consultant" for a fixed number of meetings of a particular length may be comparable to that idea and worth trying. Certainly, in some research projects, and even consulting services projects offered from an external resource, such commitments are often the rule, and, may, in fact, have something to do with reported successes. However, the consultation literature does not address such a possibility, perhaps because of the "voluntarism" concept that underpins so much of the earlier literature (see Chapter Thirteen). Within a school system, one could imagine a school-based resource team offering to provide assistance to a teacher with an understood minimal time commitment. Or, an individual consultant could ask for a flexible, but nonetheless binding, commitment of some sort. For example, the consultant could suggest a structured set of activities for two to three sessions (problem definitions and initial intervention in the first session, followed up by an analysis and modification session, followed by another analysis/modification session). A limited time period could be part of the understanding between the two professionals. The dyadic consultation that results from a school-based resource team could be provided within a context of "contractual expectation" endorsed and planned by a single school's faculty or even a school system.

This notion of a contract is initially received as a top-down, authoritative model alien to many assumptions about relationships inherent in the consultation and collaborative process. However, the contract "understanding" could be the result of a negotiated, give-and-take between the two professionals, with the added contingency that it could be revisited and renegotiated at any point. In any event, such an approach might alleviate disappointment as well as frustration in the relationship, and serve to clarify expectations and preferences.

BRIEF CONSULTATION/COLLABORATION

As noted earlier, the constraints of the school organization and of the teacher's role have been formidable obstacles at times to offering indirect services. Consequently, we will present modifications of indirect service that may prove meritorious in some situations. A time-limited, structured experience is explored, as is the use of teleconsultation options. But, before we move to those discussions, the notion of "contract service" (collaboration/consultation) again should be mentioned. What is meant here is simply the establishment of a culture in which resource professionals are available, but only under the expectation that a set number of resource sessions at set intervals will be held (e.g., three meetings, one per week for three weeks), with each session lasting a predetermined number of minutes. There is some informal evidence that suggests that, by structuring the availability of expertise in this way, a great commitment and involvement on the part of the consultee can be expected. In the early period of consultation in which the external consultant was involved, it was anticipated that the consultee would be driven to volunteer to seek assistance by the pressure of the work problem or challenge. Time to meet with the external consultant was limited for the system (e.g., one day per week) and all consultees' schedules were reorganized to prioritize those contacts. However, the migration of this service model to the methods that internal professionals used, if it wasn't preferred, took away what many deemed an important ingredient to a successful outcome, consultee initiative (see volunteerism in Chapter Thirteen). So, the internal consultee had somewhat ready access to consultees, but often they had no training or inclination to work in this way. It may be that service expectations were unclear. Consequently, the use of a "contract" may actually facilitate the indirect service process in these situations. Obviously, there should be an understanding of flexibility in any "contract" agreement, but the commitment feature needs to be established so the consultee can maximize the time he or she invests in the experience. Perhaps an initial contact wherein the parameters are negotiated, but nevertheless, introduced, would be a prudent approach.

Given the possibility of a "contractual" option, we will now turn to intentional consultant approaches in which the consultant unilaterally has chosen to operate within a time-limited framework.

The 15-Minute Consultation

To describe any teacher's day as "full" is truly to make an understatement. The expectations and demands competing for his or her time should seem to allow only minimal meeting time opportunities after classroom responsibilities are discharged. It should come as no surprise then that most school resource professionals observe that teachers approach them for help when "on the run," that is, in between classes, at breaks, or in the lunchroom. When they do arrange to meet with another professional regarding a "problem," it is typically for 30 minutes rather than the traditional one hour consultation time—and interruptions are not uncommon. Follow-up conferences become increasingly harder to arrange as the case progresses; this phenomenon may be due in part to the teacher's limitation on how much time can be devoted to a single child in the class. Or again, the redistribution of limited time is affected by subsequent challenges that need attention, while a certain degree of intervention has already been generated through consultation on the student in question. Without a doubt, some problems are so complex that the time required for reflection and planning will be appreciated by the consultant and consultee. However, in the case of school-based teacher consultation, particularly from internal consultants, consideration of alternative and/or modified consultation may need to be considered. In this section one such alternative, the 15-minute consultation, is discussed.

It may be inevitable that we succumb to the temptation to add a miniadaption of the service approach addressed by this book. Our entire society increasingly is moving to what appears to be a reactive rather than reflective orientation, wherein speed coupled with efficiency is reinforced. It could easily be argued that problem solving is one activity that doesn't adapt itself to this trend. Yet, whenever teacher consultation is discussed, the frequency with which time is mentioned as a factor is indicative of the importance of the problem. Given the number of times internally based consultants are approached when the teacher is on the run, or in time-limited contexts such as the lunchroom or teacher workroom, it would seem advantageous to begin to deal with these interactions systematically. Such requests will continue to arise, and it would seem that they may simply be a way of life in the schools. These time-limited contacts have the potential for developing into and/or generating the more classic type of consultation.

The primary questions that consultants need to address in terms of maximizing their input involve both the type of assistance that the consultee is asking for and the nature of interaction that will facilitate the interaction. In terms of the former demand, the Caplanian topology of problems represents a rather straightforward system to use. You may recall from the discussion in Chapter Two that consultees' difficulties can be due to a lack of knowledge, skill, confidence, or objectivity. Defin-

itive action can be taken by the consultant in terms of the recommendations made regardless of which of these difficulties are involved but the purpose of those recommendations can be quite different. Similarly, Friedman's (1976) interview categories are helpful to keep in mind in assessing the consultee's style and determining the consultee's follow-through interest (see Chapter Eleven).

As far as style is concerned, Gibbs (1980; see Chapter Eight) noted that an interpersonal/instrumental (i.e., task orientation) preference for the interaction consultant style is manifested by some consultees. Furthermore, she reasoned that failure on the part of the consultant to function in that way during the initial phase of consultation (which is how the 15-minute consultation can be viewed) could negatively affect the outcomes of consultation.

A primary objective of 15-minute meetings for the consultant is to help the consultee prioritize the problems that seem to be of concern to him or her. Once problems are presented and prioritized, selecting from that list one problem that is important and lends itself to the time constraints of the session should contribute to the success of this effort. In terms of these choice points, it would seem wiser to let the teacher make these choices, and if the quality of the choices is an issue, that issue should be introduced during a later contact. Such a strategy will tend to increase the probability of greater involvement on the part of the consultee in the future.

Interestingly, Salmon and Lehrer (1989) reported that consultants' interpretations of problems are influenced by "their perceptions of the child's behavior, the teacher's sense of involvement with the child, and the teacher's beliefs about the causes of the child's behavior" (p. 173). In their analysis of two school psychologists' responses to a variety of presented problem scenarios, one consultant highlighted the technical aspect of consultation, while the other consultant seemed to be attracted to the interpersonal concerns. Thus, in making quick analysis of the consultee's approach and style in consultation, the consultant must be sensitive to the effects of his or her own implicit theories of action influencing their interpretations of the problem.

Finally, the advantages and disadvantages of this expert-oriented model versus other models for the 15-minute consultation deserve comment during this point in the contact.

During this problem-finding/identification phase, it is extremely important to determine if the consultee has a hypothesis regarding the problem. Similarly, an iteration of the interventions that have been tried is invaluable in preventing the classic gaffe of recommending an approach that is perceived to be ineffective, determining the problem-solving attitude and capability of the consultee, and gaining more insight into the problem.

Next, recommendations made by the consultant need to be made in the context of a brief explanation of the limitation of such conferences. The fact that only a tentative hypothesis can be made about the problem reinforces the advisability of focusing the attention of the consultant and consultee on a specific problem. It is advisable for this reason that the consultant share competing hypotheses and stress the point that they could lead to different interventions.

Finally, the follow-up responsibilities of the consultant and consultee need to be agreed upon along with the next meeting date. The follow-up options involving further contact between the consultant and consultee (e.g., another brief meeting or telephone conference) should have some semblance of an agreed upon agenda and take place in the immediate future.

What follows is an example of a series of six brief consultation contacts that illustrate some of the above points; moreover, they demonstrate how a series of short contacts can form a consultation.

An Example of 15-Minute Consultation

Session One. The teacher presented himself in the school psychologist's office and made the following statements. "I just did something with John; I want you to tell me if I did it right." He then disclosed that because he was unhappy with John's attitude toward school, he had placed him in the in-school suspension program. When asked to be more specific, the teacher disclosed that John had failed to complete his homework for "weeks" and was only getting by because he was extremely bright. The teacher was told that it was impossible to assess the wisdom of the action without additional information and was asked if he wished to discuss it further. He responded affirmatively. Elapsed time: 5–7 minutes.

Session Two (later the same day). The teacher began this session by telling the psychologist that he had only 15 minutes until he had to meet with a parent. The psychologist suggested that they use the time available to describe John's problematic behavior. The teacher consulted his grade book and responded that John had handed in one homework assignment in the first four weeks of school and had completed only half of the assignment. He also reported that John seemed to be off task in class and at times closed his eyes and laid his head on his desk. However, John had passed all quizzes and a major examination. He had also attended class. The teacher, partially out of frustration, had placed John in the in-school suspension program for sleeping in class. A follow-up session was scheduled three days later. The psychologist asked the teacher to identify the goals for John and to contrast them with his own goals. Elapsed time: 15–17 minutes.

Session Three. The teacher reported at the outset that he wanted John to achieve at his potential, while John apparently was satisfied with passing his subjects. Discussion focused on factors that might increase John's aspirations and performance. The teacher also vented his feelings of frustration about underachieving students. At the end of the session, it was agreed that the consultant would design a potential intervention that would be approved by the teacher. Elapsed time: 20 minutes.

Session Four. The psychologist began the session by presenting the following intervention:

1. Teacher needed to readjust his short-term goals for student to perhaps raise his performance to average from the barely passing level, and lower his own expectations and appraisals.

2. The student needed to develop some reasonable expectations about the consequence of high and low school performance. The entire class was assigned an essay, "Evaluating My Academic Success."
3. Teacher would engage the student in some goal setting that involved raising his grades.
4. Teacher would reinforce any rise in achievement and would ask parents to do the same thing to change performance standards.

Teacher agreed that plan was doable. Elapsed time: 20 minutes.

Sessions Five and Six. These sessions were brief (5–10 minutes) and were held for the purpose of monitoring the progress. The teacher reported that he felt better and that John had made some modest, but discernible, academic progress, although he was not achieving at the class average.

Telephone and E-mail Contacts

Perhaps one of the most underused follow-up approaches involves the use of the telephone. Telephone consultations would seem to have considerable potential, provided that consultees know of the availability of the consultant on designated days and times. Consultation by telephone, when used as a supplementary interaction to face-to-face approaches, helps to provide the support and review that may be the difference between a satisfied user of the service and a frustrated professional. Particularly when an agreed upon agenda is established prior to the call, it is a way of touching base quickly and efficiently for the itinerant consultant internal to the system. Determination of the need for further scheduled face-to-face consultations can take place during these contacts, along with further assessment of the initial problem-identified hypothesis that was formulated.

In order to maximize the use of telephone consultation, the consultant should have regular hours during the day when he or she may be contacted. Nothing is more frustrating, discouraging, and perhaps disappointing in consultation

than playing "telephone tag" with someone. Of course, it may be appropriate for the consultant to call the consultee, but for teachers, the only available time they may be free is in the evenings. However, giving the consultee responsibility for the contact sets an important expectation, and the timing and nature of the call give the consultant valuable data about the effectiveness of the prior contact. It is also critical for the consultant to maintain a file so that he or she can be conversant about prior contacts to maximize the benefits of the call. Such notes should help the consultant improve the quality of future contacts of this sort.

The authors are not recommending consultation by telephone either for the first contact, unless it is for preliminary discussions, or as the sole means of subsequent contacts after an initial brief consultation. Phone consultations should be used with caution since obvious disadvantages are at the forefront of the consultant's consideration. However, even with those stipulations, it appears to be an overlooked, potentially effective means of enhancing teacher consultations. Another option, of course, is to identify other school system resources that are more readily available or relevant to the expressed needs of the consultee or characteristics of the client such as a counselor, tutor, or family school coordinator. And, of course, there is the option of the observation that can be used as an adjunct to the brief consultation service.

Observations

When the idea of a 15-minute consultation is discussed with groups, one of the more common follow-up activities that is proposed involves classroom observation. It allows first-hand observation of the student, especially when a consultee is perplexed and/or has trouble describing the behavioral/cognitive patterns especially if the consultee requests it. Sometimes the observation option is entertained for other reasons, occasionally unstated. Examples of such intents include the consultant who could provide objective validation as the teacher prepares his or her "case" against the student, or give support because once the consultant "sees how bad things are," he or she can be sympathetic and verify that the best instruction is being provided under the conditions. Observations can serve to supplement follow-up conferences, so that, even if the teacher is unavailable for further timely conferences, important information relevant to the discussions can be gained. However, the consultant should be cautious when suggesting observations since the message sent to the consultee may be a negative one and defensiveness may result.

At times, observations become the classical cop-out in the sense that when the professional feels unsure and overwhelmed, the observation provides some important delay time. Observations without an obvious purpose are questionable. They can convey a lack of trust in the consultee, in the sense that the consultant does not consider the consultee's perceptions to be accurate. Observations suggest an expert model will be employed, which may be appropriate given the 15-minute scenario being discussed. However, if the consultant fails to offer insight into the problem, along with suggested interventions, and/or shifts to another consultation model, it may create some confusion on the part of the teacher. Further, it can represent a problem-solving failure whenever the consultant errs in terms of identifying the reason the teacher has approached the consultant. The observation has the potential to shift the problem to a client or contextual focus. The consultant should have a clear rationale for suggesting this action.

There is one final question that needs to be asked in each problem-solving session, but especially in this consultation adaptation: "Is there anything else going on or any background information that would be important in understanding the situation that we haven't discussed?" It is surprising how this type of inquiry helps to "mine the memory banks." It seems that when consultees become intently focused on a problem, they often overlook its salient features as they describe the problem to others. Perhaps it is because those features have become so common

to the consultee that the obvious is not mentioned. In a conference with a teacher of a third-grade boy, the teacher presented a list of behaviors clearly indicating a lack of concentration and inattentiveness. The descriptions of restlessness and inability to organize thoughts on paper were leading the consultant to speculate on one type of disorder, commonly employed by school staff, although something, or some other information, seemed to be missing. Indeed, upon asking the previously emphasized question offhandedly at the close of the conference, a viable hypothesis presented itself in the teacher's response. "Well, the parents do not want anyone to know, because they're afraid he'll find out that he's adopted!"

Constraints and Strengths of Brief Approaches

Several cautions must be noted when considering becoming involved in a brief consultation encounter. First, the teacher may distort or misrepresent the problem—such as lack of cooperation from a senior high school student—when the problem is the teacher's insecurity resulting from the student's probing, in-class questions. Because of the brevity of the session, the consultant is unable to discern contradictions that may inevitably surface during a longer session. Second, a "quickie" diagnosis, which turns out to be incorrect, may discourage the teacher from continuing and/or negatively affect the credibility of the consultant with other teachers. Third, the complexity of the intervention(s) is limited because of the time factor. For that matter, even the time to fully explain the rationale for a particular intervention is constrained. Fourth, a brief approach may reinforce the notion that an expert model is the modus operandi of the consultant regardless of the time-frame available for problem solving.

On the other hand, the advantages of this approach would suggest continued exploration of its potential and appropriate use. As argued above, the 15-minute consultation fits the teacher's time demands and, as such, reduces or even eliminates one source of resistance. Similarly, it relieves the concern of some administrators and school boards that instructional time will be sacrificed, and in the process the good of many will be jeopardized for the sake of one student. Certainly, the use of such an approach, even if on a restricted basis, allows the consultant to provide services to a greater number of teachers, particularly when individual consultation models are the alternative. Finally, a series of short, targeted, problem-solving experiences spread out over an extended time period may be a more productive and efficient strategy to use for students than a concentrated, intense helping period. It meets the immediate needs of teacher and student, reinforces a developmental orientation to seeking and providing assistance, and gives the consultant a long-term perspective useful in providing a context for the presented problem. In summary then, both the constraints and strengths of this type of service option need to be kept in mind during such professional contacts.

SOME FINAL THOUGHTS ABOUT TEACHER CONSULTATION/COLLABORATION

It is natural to associate teacher consultation with the challenges teachers face in dealing with the learning and behavioral needs of students and to overlook the consultee's needs. However, a problem such as loss of classroom control can really mask the effect of burnout on the teacher's part, or personal problems that are intruding into dealing with his or her primary job effectively. Similarly, what initially appeared to be concern about the behavior of some middle school boys on the part of a female teacher was grounded in the fact that the teacher was propositioned in writing by them and, in part, felt flattered. The confusion caused by her search for an appropriate strategy to deal with the situation, while at the same time dealing with such ambivalent feelings, led to the teacher's seeking out a school-based resource professional who did not know her. And herein lies the problem with the term *teacher consultation*. The school-based professional offering the consultation must be adept at identifying what is most appropriate in terms of the

teacher request, along with the limits of the teacher's competencies; a referral to and/or involvement of another professional may be indicated. As noted earlier, the consultant's perspective can influence problem identification so that the special educator may be tempted to see a mismatch between teacher instruction and the learner's learning approach, the counselor as a management problem, or the school psychologist theme interference; to complicate matters further, all may be partly correct in some cases. But it is important to recognize that beginning the consultation too quickly, without considering all the possibilities, can result in wasted time and energies, not to mention the frustration it causes.

Most of the time, the teacher request involves a student learning or behavior problem, and such requests can be described as "straightforward," that is, a result of a lack of information or skill. In turn, requests deserve rather straightforward resource help, rather than the typical verbal exploration in which the consultant doesn't give answers, but brainstorms (i.e., collaborates), that seems to be so prevalent. It is indeed true that there is always greater commitment to an action by someone who is involved in developing the action plan. But, that commitment can come about also through a discussion of the rationale for a recommendation, and accountability in terms of a guarantee by the consultant to keep working on finding the workable intervention if the initial plan fails.

Finally, even with the straightforward situation, values, attitudes, and hypotheses/theories of how students learn and what constitutes good teaching will quickly arise. Teachers may be reluctant to spend too much time with an individual student because the rest of the class will suffer, yet the school-based professional is strongly committed to individualized instruction. Allowing the student to do something positive may be seen as "giving in" to the student. Similarly, student recommendations to have altered assignments raise concerns about equity and implications for grading. It seems imperative that the consultant be sensitive to such issues and deal with them directly. Meeting the needs of a student within the teacher's framework

The Case of Frankie: An Example of Teacher Consultation

Frankie had been referred because of his antics in the classroom, which consisted of verbal outbursts, pulling chairs out from under students who were in the process of sitting down, mimicking the teacher when she turned her back, and making funny faces at classmates. When reprimanded, Frankie would immediately cease whatever he was doing, but return to those actions almost as soon as the teacher focused her attention elsewhere.

Frankie was 10 years old, had no learning disabilities, and tests of intellectual functioning placed him in the high average range. His grades were consistently in the high C to B range and he typically completed both his seatwork and homework, although the level of functioning in the seatwork area was consistently below his potential level of performance.

After three sessions with his counselor, which Frankie controlled by discussing off-task events and wisecracking about his teacher and fellow students, Frankie admitted that he really did want to change his behavior. At this time, counseling was terminated and the teacher was contacted to see if she wished to pursue a consulting relationship. She agreed reluctantly, admitting that complete frustration was her source of motivation.

In the first consultation session, the counselor and the teacher agreed to collaboratively address Frankie's problem by assessing the problem and designing an intervention that could be implemented by both parties. It was also agreed that, if both parties deemed it appropriate, the counselor would involve the parents in the consultation process. The consultant also solicited the teacher's perceptions of Frankie, which she indicated centered on his need for social recognition by his peers. The teacher observed that Frankie was not an unpopular child, but seemed to maintain his place in his peer group by telling jokes, engaging in witty reparté, and at times, taking physical risks, such as walking the top girder on a bridge between the school and the play area. Frankie did not have highly developed psychomotor skills and seemed to be involved in group activities more for his wit than his ability to contribute to the team effort. These perceptions were supported by observations by the counselor in the cafeteria and on the playground, although the information growing

out of the observation suggested that Frankie seemed "nearly desperate" for peer approval in that he seemed willing to go to great lengths to get attention. Specifically, Frankie would taunt other boys to "drop dead" during games and, as reported, walk a very narrow beam on top of the bridge between the school and the play area.

Because of the consultant's and teacher's concern for Frankie's safety, he was told immediately by his teacher that if he was observed on the girder again, he would be precluded from going to the play area and would be assigned to work with the assistant principal during play periods. The focus of the consultation was to develop ways of helping Frankie attain social approval without engaging in outrageous behavior such as that observed on the playground and in the classroom. A response cost system was initially put into place along with a program of supplemental verbal praise by the teacher. The response cost system was set up so that the teacher would receive one of five chips from his desk if he (1) punched or hit anyone, (2) blurted out-of-task utterances such as jokes or put downs, or (3) made faces or gestures to other students. If Frankie had at least one chip left at the end of the day, he was permitted to dismiss the class one row at a time.

Even though Frankie consented to the response cost system, it failed, probably because Frankie lost some social approval from his peer group. After four days, he would blurt out, "There goes another one," when he lost a token and soon returned to his previous behavior.

After a bit of brainstorming, it was decided to change the reward associated with the response cost system. The teacher, Frankie, and the counselor agreed to replace one of the daily oral reading sessions with a talent show that Frankie would organize with the counselor and for which he would act as master of ceremonies. In order to earn the privilege, Frankie agreed to have at least one of three chips remaining three out of four days in one week. In the event that he did not earn the right to organize and narrate the talent show, Frankie was told that another child would be recruited to replace him. He was also told that in the future (unspecified), he would have to share the responsibility of the talent show with other children.

The responsibility of the teacher and teacher's aide was to provide social reinforcement. The counselor's responsibility was to develop an announcement regarding the talent show, to meet with Frankie to assist him in developing the skills needed to emcee the show, and to train the aide to run the project when the developmental work was done.

In five of the first six weeks of the talent show, Frankie was the emcee. At that point, the criterion was raised to having at least one chip each of four days (the talent and eventually the criterion was raised to every school day). During the eighth week, other emcees were recruited for the talent show. However, Frankie was retained by the planning group for the show and assisted in the training of emcees.

(provided it is reasonable) should be considered rather than automatically planning to convert the teacher to one's own perspective. This orientation is perhaps most challenging in education, where a range of interpretations and strategies may exist for a situation.

SUMMARY

Teacher consultation and teacher collaboration have been widely discussed in the literature. The teacher consultation process has also been widely researched. One result of the discussion and research is that we are aware that we can make an impact on students by consulting with teachers and that, as a secondary benefit, teachers will be better able to deal with similar problems in the future. However, the process is not without its problems, and successful consultants consider the constraints placed on consultation by the school environment as well as the background of the teacher, and they work to overcome the limitations so presented.

TIPS FOR THE PRACTITIONER

1. The likely success of teacher consultation will be constrained by several factors such as time, administrative support, teachers' training orientation, and so forth. Prior to beginning consultation with a teacher, consider each of these variables and answer the following questions on a preliminary basis:

A. Has this teacher been oriented to using consultants?
B. How much time will I have with this teacher?
C. Does this teacher believe that the principal supports his or her involvement in consultation?

2. There are many advantages as well as disadvantages to group consultation. Prior to beginning a group effort, assess your own ability to facilitate groups.

3. Using a tape recorder, ask as many questions as you can in 15 minutes, allowing the imaginary consultee two minutes to answer each question. You will find that only a limited number of questions (perhaps seven) can be posed. The implication is that you need to prepare for each consultation session by collecting as much information as possible through observation and by examination prior to the session, and then focus your questions on the client at hand.

REVIEW QUESTIONS

1. Identify and describe both the role and system factors influencing the teacher's use of consultation services.

2. Compare the "consultation with teachers" approach reviewed in this chapter with the models of consultation introduced earlier in the text.

3. Outline alternative methods of consultation that can be utilized when individual-oriented,

relatively time-free consultation is not practical.

4. Compare and contrast two teacher group consultation services with different focuses.

5. How should classroom observations be used in conjunction with teacher consultation services?

REFERENCES

Babcock, N. L., & Pryzwansky, W. B. (1983). Models of consultation: Preferences of educational professionals at five stages of service. *Journal of School Psychology, 21,* 359–366.

Babinski, L. M. & Rogers, D. L. (1998). Supporting new teachers through consultee-centered group consultation. *Journal of Educational and Psychological Consultation, 9*(4), 285–308.

Bergan, J. R., & Schnaps, A. (1983). A model for instructional consultation. In J. Alpert & J. Meyers (Eds.), *Training in consultation* (pp. 104–119). Springfield, IL: Charles C. Thomas.

Blessing, K. (Ed.). (1968). *The role of the resource consultant in special education.* Washington, DC: The Council for Exceptional Children.

Bossard, M. D., & Gutkin, T. B. (1983). The relationship of consultant skill and school organizational characteristics with teacher use of school-based consultation services. *School Psychology Review, 12,* 50–56.

Broughton, S. F., & Hester, J. R. (1993). Effects of administrative and community support on teacher acceptance of classroom interventions. *Journal of Educational and Psychological Consultation, 4,* 169–177.

Brown, D., Wyne, M. D., Blackburn, J. E., & Powell, W. C. (1979). *Consultation.* Boston: Allyn & Bacon.

Cantrell, R. P., & Cantrell, M. L. (1976). Preventive mainstreaming: Impact of a supportive services program on pupils. *Exceptional Children, 42,* 381–386.

Caplan, G., & Caplan, R. B. (1993). *Mental health consultation and collaboration.* San Francisco: Jossey-Bass.

Cleven, C. A., & Gutkin, T. B. (1988). Cognitive modeling of consultation processes: A means of improving consultees problem identification skills. *Journal of School Psychology, 26,* 397–389.

Cohen, E., & Osterweil, Z. (1986). An "issue-focused" model for mental health consultation with groups of teachers. *Journal of School Psychology, 24,* 243–256.

Cramer, S. F. (1998). *Collaboration: A successful strategy for special educators.* Boston: Allyn & Bacon.

Curtis, M. J., & Watson, K. L. (1980). Changes in consultee problem clarification skills following consultation. *Journal of School Psychology, 18,* 210–211.

Dettmer, P., Dyck, N., & Thurston, L. P. (1999). *Consultation, collaboration and team work for students with special needs.* Boston: Allyn & Bacon.

Dinkmeyer, D., & Carlson, J. (1973). *Consulting.* Columbus, OH: Charles E. Merrill.

Fishbaugh, M. S. (1997). *Models of collaboration.* Boston: Allyn & Bacon.

Friedman, L. P. (1976). Teacher consultation styles. Unpublished doctoral dissertation, University of Pennsylvania.

Gibbs, J. T. (1980). The interpersonal orientation in mental health consultation: Toward a model of ethnic variations in consultation. *Journal of Community Psychology, 8,* 195–207.

Given-Ogle, L., Christ, B. A., & Idol, L. (1991). Collaborative consultation: The San Juan Unified School District Project. *Journal of Educational and Psychological Consultation, 2,* 267–284.

Goldstein, B. S. C. (1998). Creating a context for collaborative consultation: Working across bicultural communities. *Journal of Educational and Psychological Consultation, 9*(4), 367–374.

Graden, J. L. (1989). Reactions to school consultation: Some considerations from a problem-solving perspective. *Professional School Psychology, 4,* 29–35.

Gutkin, T. B. (1981). Relative frequency of consultee lack of knowledge, skills, confidence, and objectivity in school settings. *Journal of School Psychology, 19,* 57–61.

Gutkin, T. B. (1993). Conducting consultation research. In J. Zins, T. R. Kratochwill, & S. N. Elliott (Eds.), *Handbook of consultation services for children* (pp. 227–248). San Francisco: Jossey-Bass.

Gutkin, T. B., & Bossard, M. D. (1984). The impact of consultant, consultee, and organizational/variables on teacher attitudes toward consultation services. *Journal of School Psychology, 22,* 251–258.

Gutkin, T. B., & Conoley, J. C. (1990). Reconceptualizing school psychology from a service delivery perspective: Implications of practice, training, and research. *Journal of School Psychology, 28,* 202–223.

Gutkin, T. B., & Curtis, M. J. (1982). School-based consultation. In C. R. Reynolds & T. B. Gutkin (Eds.),

The handbook of school psychology (pp. 796–826). New York: John Wiley & Sons.

Harris, A. M., & Cancelli, A. A. (1991). Teachers as volunteer consultees: Enthusiastic, willing or resistant participants? *Journal of Educational and Psychological Consultation, 2,* 217–238.

Heron, T. E., & Harris, K. C. (1982). *The educational consultant.* Boston: Allyn & Bacon.

Hughes, J. N., Grossman, P., & Barker, D. (1990). Teachers' expectancies participation in consultation, and perceptions of consultant helpfulness. *School Psychology Quarterly, 5,* 167–179.

Idol, L. (1988). A rationale and guidelines for establishing special education consultation programs. *Remedial and Special Education, 9*(6), 48–58.

Idol, L. (1989). Reaction to Walter Pryzwansky's presidential address to the American Psychological Association on school consultation. *Professional School Psychology, 4,* 15–19.

Idol, L., Paolucci-Whitcomb, P., & Nevin, A. (1986). *Collaborative consultation.* Rockville, MD: Aspen Systems.

Idol, L., & West, J. F. (1987). Consultation in special education (Part II): Training and practice. *Journal of Learning Disabilities, 20,* 474–494.

Idol-Maestas, L., & Ritter, S. (1985). A follow-up study of resource/consulting teachers: Factors that facilitate and inhibit teacher consultation. *Teacher Education and Special Education, 8,* 121–131.

Johnson, L. J., & Pugach, M. C. (1996). Role of collaborative dialogue in teachers' conceptions of appropriate practice for students at risk. *Journal of Educational and Psychological Consultation, 7*(1), 9–24.

Johnson, L. J., Pugach, M. C., & Hammitte, D. J. (1988). Barriers to effective special education consultation. *Remedial and Special Education, 9,* 41–47.

Knight, M. F., Meyers, H. W., Paolucci-Whitcomb, P., Hasazi, S. E., & Nevin, A. (1981). A four-year evaluation of consulting teachers service. *Behavioral Disorders, 6,* 92–100.

Lortie, D. C. (1975). *School teacher.* Chicago: University Chicago Press.

McKenzie, H. S. (1972). Special education and consulting teachers. In F. Clark, D. Evans, & L. Hammerlynk (Eds.), *Implementing behavioral programs for schools and clinics* (pp. 103–124). Champaign, IL: Research Press.

Merriam, S. B. (1988). *Case study research in education.* San Francisco: Jossey-Bass.

Mostert, M. P. (1998). *Interprofessional collaboration in schools.* Boston: Allyn & Bacon.

Nelson, C. M., & Stevens, K. B. (1981). An accountable consultation model of mainstreaming behaviorally disorder children. *Behavior Disorders, 6,* 82–91.

Nevin, A., Thousand, J. S., & Villa, R. A. (1993). Establishing collaborative ethics and practices. *Journal of Educational and Psychological Consultation, 4*(4), 293–304.

Pohlman, C., Hoffman, L. B., Dodds, A. H., & Pryzwansky, W. B. (1998). Utilization of school-based professional services: An exploratory analysis of perceptions of mentor teacher and student teachers. *Journal of Educational and Psychological Consultation, 9*(4), 347–365.

Pryzwansky, W. B. (1974). A reconsideration of the consultation model for delivery of school-based psychological services. *American Journal of Orthopsychiatry, 44,* 579–583.

Pryzwansky, W. B. (1977). Collaboration or consultation: Is there a difference? *Journal of Special Education, 11,* 179–182.

Pryzwansky, W. B., & White, G. W. (1983). The influence of consultee characteristics on preferences for consultation approaches. *Professional Psychology, 14,* 457–461.

Pryzwansky, W. B. (1989). School consultation: Some considerations from a cognitive psychology perspective. *Professional School Psychology, 4,* 1–14.

Pugach, M., & Johnson, L. J. (1988). Peer collaboration. *Teaching Exceptional Children, 20*(3), 75–77.

Quade, B. S. (1985). The effects of consultation time scheduling by elementary LD resource teachers on regular teachers' attitude and use of model. Unpublished doctoral dissertation, Southern Illinois University, Edwardsville.

Rosenfield, S. A. (1987). *Instructional consultation.* Hillsdale, NJ: Lawrence Erlbaum Associates.

Salmon, D., & Lehrer, R. (1989). School consultants' implicit theories of action. *Professional School Psychology, 4,* 173–187.

Sarason, S. B. (1996). *Revisiting the culture of the school and the problem of change.* New York: Teacher's College Press.

Schulte, A. C., & Osborne, S. S. (1993). What is collaborative consultation? The eye of the beholder. In D. Fuchs (Chair), *Questioning popular beliefs about collaborative consultative.* Symposium presented at the annual meeting of the Council for Exceptional Children, San Antonio, TX.

Schulte, A. C., Osborne, S. S., & Kauffman, J. M. (1993). Teacher responses to types of consultative special education services. *Journal of Educational and Psychological Consultation, 4,* 1–27.

Slesser, R. A., Fine, M. J., & Tracy, D. B. (1990). Teacher reactions to two approaches to school-based psychological consultation. *Journal of Educational and Psychological Consultation, 1,* 243–258.

Stenger, M. K., Tollefson, N., & Fine, M. J. (1992). Variables that distinguish elementary teachers who participate in school-based consultation from those who do not. *School Psychology Quarterly, 7,* 271–284.

Wenger, R. D. (1979). Teacher response to collaborative consultation. *Psychology in the Schools, 16,* 127–131.

Weller, M. B. (1984). *The influence of contact and setting on the ratings of parents for models of consultation.* Unpublished masters thesis, North Carolina State University, Raleigh, NC.

West, J. F. (1985). *Regular and special educators' preferences for school-based consultation models: A statewide study* (Technical Report No. 101). Austin, TX: Research and Training Institute on School Consultation, The University of Texas at Austin.

West, J. F., & Idol, L. (1990). Collaborative consultation in the education of mildly handicapped and at-risk students. *Remedial and Special Education, 11*(1), 22–31.

Whitaker, C. R. (1992). Traditional consultation strategies: Finding the time to collaborate. *Journal of Educational and Psychological Consultation, 3,* 85–88.

Zins, J. R. (1981). Using data-based evaluation in developing school consultation services. In M. J. Curtis & J. R. Zins (Eds.), *The theory and practice of school consultation* (pp. 261–268). Springfield, IL: Charles C. Thomas.

Zins, J. E. (1996). Introduction to developing peer mediated support systems for helping professionals: Are we ready to practice what we preach? *Journal of Educational and Psychological Consultation, 7*(1), 5–7.

CHAPTER 10

CONSULTATION WITH PARENTS

GOALS OF THE CHAPTER

The goals of this chapter are to provide an overview of parental consultation, including its empirical support, and to provide a model for conducting parental consultation.

CHAPTER PREVIEW

1. A brief history of parental consultation will be provided.
2. An eclectic model of parental consultation will be discussed and illustrated.
3. Consultation with parents and groups will be discussed.
4. Some of the unique problems involved in consulting with parents will be presented and some solutions offered.
5. Cross-cultural parental consultation will be explored.

Several early publications (Brown & Brown, 1975; Brown, Wyne, Blackburn, & Powell, 1979; Dinkmeyer & Carlson, 1973) pointed out the importance of consulting with parents. However, consulting with parents has received much less attention than consulting with professionals, perhaps because of the influence of Gerald Caplan (1970), who defined *consulting* as a process that occurs between professionals. Moreover, although behaviorally-oriented psychologists have long worked with parents, school psychologists, such as John Bergan, have focused much of their attention on consulting with teachers, and the school psychology literature is dominated by discussions about and research on the processes of teacher consultation. A little over a decade ago, Sheridan (1993) identified a growing interest in consultation with parents, a trend that continues to this time. For example, Sheridan, Kra-

tochwill, and Bergan (1996) extended Bergan's (1970) model of behavioral consultation to include families in what they term a *conjoint behavioral consultation*. Their model, which has stimulated a great deal of research (see Grissom, Erchul, & Sheridan, 2003), is similar in some respects to the eclectic model presented in Chapter Three.

The major goal of this chapter is to present an eclectic model of parent consultation. The rationale for drawing on a number of sources for the generation of the model presented in this chapter lies primarily in our belief that families should be viewed as dynamic systems rather than as a collection of individuals. However, many of the ideas presented in earlier chapters can be applied to consulting with parents, and we have included some of them in the consulting model presented here. Finally, before discussing family consultation, we want to note that family collaboration will not be included in this discussion. Family collaboration, as it is practiced by early childhood educators and others, is a unique process that is rarely engaged in by the target audiences of this book, human services consultants who work in schools and social agencies.

EMPIRICAL SUPPORT

Because of the history of parental consultation, it is not surprising that the research in the area has focused on either Adlerian (see Frazier & Mathes, 1975; Palmo & Kuzniar, 1971) or behavioral approaches (see Weathers & Liberman, 1975, or the review by Cobb & Medway, 1978), with the latter approach being investigated far more frequently. The literature that has been produced to date does generally support the efficacy of parental consultation (Cobb & Medway, 1978), and when consultation with parents has been compared with other types of direct intervention such as individual or group counseling, it has proven to be as effective (Perkins & Wicas, 1971) or more effective (McGowan, 1969; Palmo & Kuzniar, 1971). However, it should be pointed out that many of the early studies on consultation did not have clear definitions of consultation, and the interventions seemed more like parent education than parental consultation, a distinction that needs consideration and will be made in the next section.

Even though conclusions about the efficacy of consultation must be drawn cautiously, literature from a related area, parent education, supports the potential benefits of working with parents (Dembo, Sweitzer, & Lauritzen, 1985; Dumas, 1980). However, until specific research is conducted on the process and outcome of consulting with parents, generalizations must be made tentatively.

PARENT CONSULTATION AND OTHER PARENTAL INTERVENTIONS

While definitions of consultation have been offered throughout the book, it is important to delineate the boundaries of parental consultation by differentiating it from two other parent-oriented processes: family therapy and parent education. Family therapy is a direct service to the entire family in which parents and children participate simultaneously with a therapist to correct a problem in the family (Goldenberg & Goldenberg, 2000). Parent education is an indirect approach aimed at teaching parents specific parenting skills. It is typically conducted in a group setting, follows a set curriculum determined by the instructor, and follows a specific timetable (Brown et al., 1979). Consultation, like parent education, is an indirect intervention, since only the parents are seen by the consultant.

Parent consultation has as one of its objectives the enhancement of parenting skills of the consultees, but it follows no set agenda. The process of parental consultation is determined collaboratively with the consultant and the consultee; it is aimed at determining problems that exist in the family system that are related to one or more children's maladaptive functioning; and it is designed to assist parents to increase their understanding of the problems they are experiencing with children and to help them design and implement solutions to those problems. Parent consultation, like family therapy, assumes that an interpersonal relationship is essential to a successful outcome, an assumption that varies to some degree with parent education that is typically a more impersonal process. It should also be noted that parental consultation is typically a shorter-term intervention than is family therapy.

Family consultation is viewed as an appropriate intervention for parents who lack basic knowledge of parenting principles, lack the skill to implement a solution to the problem, or have unrealistic or dysfunctional expectations of one or more of their children growing out of stereotypical perceptions or experiences with the child. It is not deemed appropriate for families in which the pathological behavior of the parents is the source of the family's problem. Nor is parent consultation appropriate for families in which there are severe marital difficulties that are influencing the parenting process.

As in all forms of consultation, the primary goal of the process is to help the consultee help the client. The gain for the client (child) should be improvement in educational or psychological functioning. The gain for the parents' consultation should be increased ability to facilitate the development of their children. The family unit as a whole should also benefit from parent consultation in that the unit should become more adaptable because of enhanced communication and problem-solving abilities. The family unit should also become more cohesive, although they should not become so intertwined in each other's lives that autonomy is not offered by the family structure (Horne, 2000; Mullis & Edwards, 2001; Olson, Sprenkle, & Russell, 1979).

MODELS OF FAMILY CONSULTATION

Behavioral Models

As has already been noted, behavioral models of parent education and consultation have been the dominant approaches to working with families. A behavioral model of consultation (Bergan, 1977; Bergan & Kratochwill, 1990) was set forth in Chapter Three. In 1981, Bergan and Duley attempted to expand on Bergan's earlier work by looking at the family as a system. More recently, Sheridan and Kratochwill (1992) have elaborated what they term a *Conjoint Behavioral Consultation Model,* which is defined as an indirect approach to consultation in which parents and teachers join with the consultant to address the needs of the child (Sheridan, 1993). The unique feature of this model is that it emphasizes collaboration between teachers and parents, an emphasis that most would agree is badly needed. Except for this different emphasis, the Conjoint Behavioral Consultation Model follows closely Bergan's (1977; Bergan & Duley, 1981) original propositions.

As we noted in Chapter Four, Adlerians view the first five to six years as crucial in the development of the child's personality. Not surprisingly, they have developed models of parental intervention, family therapy, parent education, and family consultation (Albert, 1996; Dreikurs & Stoltz, 1967). As would be expected, family consultation

focuses on establishing a democratic atmosphere in the family in order to ensure that children feel as though they have a place, requiring children to accept responsibility commensurate with their age and developmental level, and incorporating the use of logical and natural consequences instead of punishment. Many Adlerian ideas have intrinsic appeal, particularly to parents who have traditional Eurocentric values.

Eclectic Models: General Considerations

There are probably three theoretically pure models of parent consultation—humanistic, behavioral, and Adlerian—only two of which have been addressed. However, most family consultants are eclectic and have tried to some degree to incorporate systems principles into their approaches (e.g., Bergan & Duley, 1981; Sheridan & Kratochwill, 1992). The fact is that some theoretical approaches are incompatible with systems thinking. This is particularly true of traditional behavioral explanations of human behavior (classical and operant conditioning). Behaviorists subscribe to the basic scientific principle of cause and effect; systems thinkers reject this idea. Behaviorists endorse reductionistic thinking that suggests that all behavioral and environmental variables can be quantified; systems thinkers believe that as soon as you start to analyze and quantify, you destroy the essence of what is being examined. Behaviorists believe in an objective reality; systems thinkers are phenomenological. The point here is that these two theoretical approaches are antithetical and thus cannot be merged in any meaningful sense. However, less reductionistic theories can be melded with systems thinking to form meaningful approaches to family consultation.

AN ECLECTIC APPROACH

The major goal of this chapter is to present an eclectic model of parent consultation. This model draws upon social cognitive learning theory (Bandura, 1977, 1986), mental health consultation (Caplan, 1970), systems theory (Bateson,

1972; Capra, 1982), and Adlerian theory (Albert, 1996) for its underpinning. It also draws upon the growing multicultural literature in an attempt to ensure that family consultants engage in culturally sensitive consultation.

Another goal of this chapter is to illustrate how the approach to family consultation can be applied by providing concrete suggestions for conducting family consultation sessions. These suggestions grow out of the experiences of the authors and their students rather than from empiricism. It is therefore recommended that consultants-in-training accept these suggestions in the spirit in which they are offered, that is, as tentative guides to be tested in the crucible of consulting with parents and to be retained or discarded based on the result.

THE ASSUMPTIONS OF THE APPROACH

From Social Learning Theory (Bandura, 1977, 1986)

1. Most behavior is acquired as a result of imitation of esteemed models. Since in most families parents are esteemed models, the origin of much childhood behavior is imitation of the parent or, in the case of the younger children, older siblings. When parents are either absent or not held in high esteem as models, other individuals will be imitated.
2. Cognition mediates the process of behavior acquisition. Cognitions regarding one's confidence that one can perform a task (self-efficacy), the importance attached to a task (appraisal), the outcomes associated with performing a task (expectations), and the standards one has developed with regard to performing a task are of major importance. Effective parents are confident, see child rearing as important, believe that they can make a difference, and want to do an outstanding job.
3. Self-efficacy can best be heightened by performance accomplishments. Vicarious modeling and verbal persuasion are also effective means of improving self-efficacy. Whenever

anxiety is a barrier to performance, reducing that anxiety can improve self-efficacy by engaging parents in proximal goal setting and involvement in activities that are deemed important (appraisal) and achievable (expectation); self-efficacy regarding parenting can be improved.
4. Standards of functioning as a parent are probably acquired as a result of direct observation of one's own parents and observation of others. In consultation, vicarious modeling, verbal persuasion, and parental standards of functioning (e.g., how well they want to parent) are the mechanisms available for changing the standards of parents.

From Mental Health Consultation (Caplan, 1970)

1. Consultee problems can be classified as lack of knowledge, lack of skill, lack of confidence, and lack of objectivity. In this context, lack of objectivity refers to biases that are acquired either as a result of learning prior to the birth of a child (e.g., retarded children are to be shunned) or as a result of anxiety-laden experiences after the child is born (e.g., serious illness as a result of which the child nearly dies).
2. The problems of knowledge, skill, self-confidence, and objectivity are often interrelated.

From Systems Theory (Bateson, 1972; Capra, 1982)

1. The nuclear family is a part of a broader suprasystem called the extended family. Many of the values of the nuclear family are based upon those of the suprasystem. These values, whether they be positive or negative, guide the parenting process.
2. The family interacts as a system. Healthy families are interdependent, but differentiated to the degree that individuals can have distinct identities; develop subsystems (e.g., parents and children); develop distinct mech-

anisms for regulating the behavior of their members based upon principles of supportive, open communication; and have their own values and goals.

3. Cause-and-effect is virtually impossible to ascertain in the family system. Therefore, blaming should be avoided.

From the Multicultural Literature

1. The consultee in family consultation is the caregiver, which, among European Americans, is typically the mother, father, or both. However, the concept of family has different meanings in different cultures. For example, Asian and Latin American families may include grandparents, aunts and uncles, and, in some instances, godparents. In some American Indian tribes the concept of family is extended to include cousins and members of the clan (Brown, 1997; McWhirter & Ryan, 1991; Sue & Sue, 1999), and any and all members of the "family" may assume crucial child-rearing roles. The first step in cross-cultural consultation is to carefully identify the consultee.

2. It is essential that the consultation process be aligned with the world view of the consultee. An understanding of the history of the culture from which consultees come can aid in understanding their world view, as can a thorough understanding of their cultural values (Brown, 1997; Sue & Sue, 1999). European American consultants should be aware that the history of many minorities includes exploitation and oppression by Europeans; thus heritage and race may be a barrier that must be overcome in the consultation process.

3. Important changes will necessarily have to be made in the cross-consultation process if it is to be successful.

THE PROCESS

The process of family consultation should be guided by the assumptions listed above. However, the actual process of consultation with families is little different than that of other types of consultation. As described earlier in this volume, consultation is a problem-solving process that moves through certain stages: structuring and relationship development or assessment, problem identification, goal setting, intervention, and evaluation and follow-up.

One additional stage of consultation has been added to these five for parental consultation: explanation of psychological principles. This stage has been added because it is assumed that parents need to understand the *why* as well as the *what* of the intervention to be employed. It is also worth reiterating that these stages, while described as though they occur in a linear fashion, rarely do. However, for the sake of this discussion, the stages of family consultation will be described sequentially, while making every attempt to illustrate the dynamic nature of the process.

Initiating the Contact

Consultation may be initiated by the consultant or by one or more of the family members. It is important to establish a collaborative relationship at the outset by stressing that the outcome of the process is dependent upon a joint effort, but there will be significant differences in the manner in which this is achieved, based on the cultural background of the consultee. For example, with some Asian Americans, consultants may find greater degrees of deference to their expertise than is the case with European Americans, and all efforts to equalize the power relationship will fail. Also, when dealing with some American Indians, consultants may be expected to do most of the talking without a great deal of input from the consultee or to collaborate with a tribal healer; Thomason (1995) suggests that it may be necessary to defer to the tribal healer in some situations. Consultants new to the process of consulting with American Indians would be well advised to observe how a person who is held in high regard—such as a tribal healer—functions as they fashion their consultation styles.

Initiating of family consultation requires the establishment of appointments. Consultants who believe that it is important to be punctual (i.e., to dominate time) should be prepared to cope with other world views on this matter—ranging from the perspective of some Native Americans that events should begin whenever everyone is present as opposed to a specific time (Thomason, 1995), to the present orientation (as opposed to future orientation) of some Latinos, which leads to less emphasis on being punctual.

Regardless of the cultural background, the individual who initiates family consultation must be prepared to explain why the consultation is being initiated, to make some preliminary statements about the role expected of the consultee, and to take steps to begin the process. These efforts will be more successful if the focus is upon helping children and actions are taken in a culturally sensitive manner. A statement such as the following may suffice:

I'm hoping that we can get together to develop a plan to help XYZ. He is a fine boy and is trying very hard. But those of us at (school, the agency, etc.) believe that we will be better able to help him if we work with the family.

Once a statement focusing upon the nature of consultation has been made, it is also important to set forth the goals of the process (e.g., assisting parents to deal with a child's problem more effectively).

In addition to the foregoing structuring statement, the following strategies may be useful in the establishment and maintenance of an egalitarian relationship:

1. Allow the consultee the freedom to accept or reject.
2. Encourage the consultee to contribute suggestions.
3. Emphasize the consultee's contributions.
4. Encourage consultee responsibility.
5. Require effort from the consultee. (Parsons & Meyers, 1984, pp. 38–39)

Parsons and Meyers go on to suggest that the consultant act in a nonauthoritarian manner, that

questions be phrased so that the consultee feels as though he or she is actually contributing to the consultation rather than just providing data to the consultant, and that suggestions be made quite tentatively. The following excerpt from a consultation session with a parent illustrates some of these ideas:

CONSULTANT: I'm delighted that we are going to be working together. It would be very helpful to me if you could share with me the ways in which you tried to stop the aggressive behavior and how these efforts have worked.

CONSULTEE: (Mother is consultee.) Well, the main thing I've done is punish him. I've spanked him, but that just seems to make him angry. I've tried grounding him, but he ignores me. The only other thing that has worked is that I've taken away his allowance from time to time, but I really don't like doing that.

CONSULTANT: So, you have tried a number of things with varying success. Tell me a little more about what happened when you took away his allowance and why that is not an approach that you like.

CONSULTEE: He responds pretty well when I threaten to take away his allowance, but I remember what it was like at 13 and having no money. I just feel bad about taking his allowance. So even when I threaten to take it, I often don't follow through even when he hits other people.

CONSULTANT: So, sometimes you follow through with your threats and sometimes you don't. It sounds a little like your own childhood memories get in the way.

CONSULTEE: Yeah! I suppose they do.

CONSULTANT: You've obviously thought about the problem. What types of suggestions would you make to yourself?

CONSULTEE: (Laughs.) Be consistent. Everybody says be consistent. But it's harder than it sounds. I love Jeremy, and I don't want to be too hard on him.

CONSULTANT: It's obvious that you care deeply for Jeremy. I'm wondering if your present course of action is getting you where you want to go with Jeremy.

CONSULTEE: No. I guess not. I know it isn't.

To some degree, the first few minutes of the consulting relationship set the tone for the remainder of the process. It is the consultant's responsibility to structure the relationship so that the power is equalized and then to maintain this stance throughout the consultation.

Relationship Development. Relationship building and the structure of the power relationship go hand in hand. The relationship development techniques described in Chapter Six should be applied in parental consultation. However, because the process is so immediate, it is often the case that the consultant is (1) structuring the power relationship, (2) developing an interpersonal relationship with the consultee, and (3) beginning the assessment of the problem at the same time. While there never seems to be enough time to meet with parents and the problems that the consultee's child has are often severe, the use of appropriate relationship-building techniques is still an essential ingredient of the consulting relationship. Consultation research literature confirms that the perceptions held of consultants by consultees are greatly influenced by their ability to employ relationship-building techniques appropriately (Horton & Brown, 1990). It may also be a useful reminder to indicate that if a solid consulting relationship is not formed, parents may not disclose certain types of sensitive information that are necessary for accurate assessment of the problem, or they may not develop sufficient trust in the consultant so that they will follow through with the interventions that are designed.

In addition to using the relationship-building techniques described in Chapter Six, the following few tips may be useful in building relationships with parents:

1. If the parents are coming to a clinic or a school, be ready to greet them upon arrival, since they may perceive these environments as hostile.

2. Immediately reassure parents that the purpose of their visit is to work collaboratively with you for the benefit of their child. Avoid any hint that the parents are being treated; focus on the client.

3. If others (e.g., teachers, psychologists) are to be involved, bring them into the process after parents have been made comfortable. Parents may be quite threatened initially by a group of strangers.

4. Discuss confidentiality as soon as possible. Parents may be quite defensive about what they think their child has told you or others about the home environment.

5. Establish an informal atmosphere. Offer coffee or soft drinks if possible. Have parents sit in comfortable chairs.

6. If the consultation is occurring in the consultee's home, be prompt, accept offerings of refreshment, and suggest that you have your discussion where the parents are most comfortable.

7. Always consider the cultural background of the parents when deciding how to proceed.

Assessment

Many types of information must be gained during assessment. One crucial aspect of this process is to determine the values structure of the family, because knowledge of the values structure is essential both to crafting the process of consultation and to planning acceptable interventions. Most consultants have encountered consultees who teach their children that standing up for their rights means fighting, or that education is unimportant to their success. McWhirter and Ryan (1991) noted that certain aspects of education, namely, reading, are not valued by Native Americans because of the oral tradition of the tribe, and Sue and Sue (1999) report that competitive approaches to learning are not valued by many Hispanics, Asian Americans, and American Indians who value cooperative relationships. However, in addition to cultural values regarding time, relationships, and activity, other values should also be assessed. For example, such values as loyalty to family or group, independence, achievement, and humility (Brown, 1997; Brown & Crace, 1996) have important implications for overall functioning. Children who value humility may seem unassertive or backward. Those who value loyalty to family or group may see the traditions and current wishes of their family or group as more important than their own desires. Achievement in the dominant culture focuses on independence and competition—approaches that may be rejected by children from other cultures. However, the result of this different perspective may be that these children are viewed as less able than their European American counterparts (Griggs & Dunn, 1989). It is inappropriate to judge a child to be inadequate or deficient in some manner if he or she is in fact acting on the values of family—*unless* the result is demonstrably harmful to the child's psychological well-being (Nikelly, 1992). Moreover, it is the consultant's responsibility to work with the parents to help fashion a supportive environment.

Assessment begins the moment the session begins. Consultants should be aware of the use of titles by some consultees (e.g., Mr., Dr.), which may be a sign of deference, the interaction that occurs between or among consultees if more than one is present, nonverbal behavior that indicates discomfort, and so forth. Also, in cross-cultural consultation some estimate of the extent of acculturation should be determined. Values are one indicator of acculturation. So are the language spoken in the home, the nature of the community in which the family lives, and the adherence to customs such as dress.

When more than one family member is present, the consultant should be alert to potential conflicts in values that exist in the family. These conflicts can be confusing to the child, and the resolution of the conflict may become a target of consultation. Statements such as the following may reveal conflicts in values:

CONSULTEE: This is the way I see it. Betty doesn't always agree, but…

CONSULTEE: Sometimes, I just have to put my foot down.

CONSULTEE: Then I told Darrell, just wait 'til your dad gets home.

CONSULTEE: That's not the way it happens. He's finished his homework before you get home anyway.

It is also important to focus on the nonverbalizing parent when the other is talking to determine how he or she is reacting to what is being said. Nonverbal reactions can provide clues about whether parents are in agreement or disagreement about the nature of the child's problem and what is being done about it in the home. If there are differing perceptions of the child at home and/or in the way the child is being responded to by the parents, these differences need to be reconciled.

It seems to be more typical that consultation occurs with one parent because of the number of single-parent homes, as well as work schedules. Effective consultation can occur in these situations even if the parent not living in the home is not involved *or* if the absent parent is *not* in agreement with the identified problem. These situations will be discussed in greater detail later in this chapter.

Some information comes to the consultant as a result of observations of the consultee. However, the majority of the data used in the assessment often results from the verbalization of the consultee(s). In order to make an accurate assessment of the nature of the consultees' perceptions of their child's difficulty and the factors that may be contributing to the problem, the consultant needs to be able to get answers to the following questions:

Modeling Influences

1. What types of behaviors are modeled and reinforced in the home that may contribute to the child's problem?
2. Are there *outside* influences such as grandparents that influence the child's behavior? What is the nature of these influences?

Family Functioning

1. Is the child given the opportunity to perform significant tasks in the home, and are his or

her accomplishments recognized in the form of positive feedback?

2. Are siblings treated differently? Is one favored over another? Why? (Objectivity?)
3. Are the subsystems in the family well differentiated? Do children assume parental roles, or conversely, do parents assume children's roles?
4. Who is the decision maker? Mother? Father?

Communication

1. What type of expectations do the parents hold for the child? Are these communicated clearly and consistently?
2. Generally speaking, is communication clear in the family? Is it affirming?
3. Are children given the opportunity to express their individuality? (This would not be the case if parents hold a collective social value.)

Acculturation

Consultants can assess acculturation by collecting information about a number of variables. For example, families that are relatively unacculturated speak their first language in the home; follow the rituals and traditions of their ethnic group; choose foods, music, and leisure activities that are traditionally engaged in by their group; and associate extensively with members of their cultural group (Brown, 1997). Consultants to families may find that problems have arisen because the children have become acculturated, that is, they have adopted the values and traditions of the dominant culture while their parents still adhere to their traditions.

Importance of Problem

1. Do the parents see the child's problem as significant?
2. Do they "own" the problem or blame it on others or circumstances beyond their control?
3. Is "good parenting" important to the parents, or do they have low standards of functioning as parents?
4. Do the parents believe that they can make an impact on the child?

As noted earlier, assessment begins as soon as the parents and the consultant meet. However, it is incumbent upon the consultant to identify information that will result in an accurate assessment of the influences that may be related to the child's behavior. Sonstegard (1964, pp. 74–75) suggested that the following outline be used when interviewing parents:

I. Under what conditions did the complaint or problem arise?
   A. At what age?
   B. What has been its duration?
II. What is the child's relationship to siblings?
   A. Position in sibling sequence.
      1. Distribution of males and females?
      2. How are siblings different?
      3. How are siblings similar?
   B. With whom is the child compared?
      1. Whom is the child most like?
      2. Whom is the child least like?
   C. Nature and extent of:
      1. Conflict?
      2. Rivalry?
      3. Competition? (Explain.)
      4. Submission?
      5. Rebellion?
         a. Active?
         b. Passive?
III. Environmental influences.
   A. Relatives.
      1. Grandparents.
      2. Other relatives.
   B. Other people living in the house.
   C. Neighbors.
IV. What are you doing about the problem?
   A. Relate in detail the interactions.
   B. Clarify if necessary: "What do you mean by that?"
V. In what other ways does the child stand out?
   A. Conditions under which he functions adequately?
   B. In what way is he successful?
VI. What is the nature of the daily routine?
   A. How does the child get up in the morning?
      1. Who awakens him?
      2. Is he called more than once?

3. What about dressing?
4. What about breakfast?
B. Describe the lunch hour, dinner (each mealtime).
C. How does the child get off to bed? At what time?
VII. What happens when the family goes out together?
  A. Preparation for going out and special efforts.
  B. What happens when away?
VIII. How are the child's social relationships?
  A. Ability to make friends with others.
    1. Neighborhood children.
    2. Adults.
    3. Children at school.
  B. Does he have pets, and does he take care of them?
  C. Attitude toward school.
    1. Schoolwork.
    2. Relationships with teachers.
    3. How does he deal with people in authority?
  D. What impressions has he gained from the family situation?
    1. Has there been any tragedy in the family?
    2. Who is boss?
    3. What methods of discipline have been used?
    4. What kind of punishment?
    5. What kind of supervision?
IX. What does the child think about his future?
  A. What does he want to be when he grows up?
  B. What is the occupation of other members of the family?
X. Does the child have nightmares, bad dreams?

The foregoing is a lengthy and detailed interview schedule, and Sonstegard cautions against rigid adherence to it. Nowhere is his recommendation more important than when the consultee is a family from a culture that emphasizes self-control, namely, Asian American or American Indian cultures. In these cases, the interview should be restricted to "need to know," should be less direct, and should proceed more cautiously than might be the case with European Americans or African Americans.

The consultant should also focus upon the interactions of the children, the children and parents, and the children and other significant peers and adults. Sonstegard's interview schedule could be adapted quite nicely to ascertain which behaviors are being reinforced, the means by which they are reinforced, the nature of the behavior being modeled by the parents and significant others, and the maladaptive behavior that has developed as a result.

Let us assume, for example, that the consultation was initiated because the child consistently failed to complete seatwork in school. During the course of the interview, the consultee relates that the child seems unable to complete household chores, demands a great deal of help when doing homework, and generally is unable to care for himself. One possibility is that the child's helplessness in school is simply an extension of behavior that has been learned in the home.

During the assessment process, the consultant develops hypotheses about factors that may be contributing to the child's functioning. The following may illustrate this point:

Case 1. J is an emotionally disturbed fourth grader and has engaged in a long series of violent acts, including stabbing the teacher of children with emotional handicaps with a pencil. His parents have seen a number of family therapists, but they have proved to be ineffective. The reason for this failure seems to revolve around two points made by the mother in the first consultation session. At one point she said, "He (the therapist) treated us as though we were the ones with the problem." In another disclosure, she revealed that she hated all the counting and charting that one therapist had asked her to complete. She indicated that she always forgot to follow through on these assignments.

In the initial interview, the parents disclosed the following information:

1. J has a younger brother whom he has attacked, with the result being that he and his brother are never left alone.
2. Spanking and yelling are the primary modes of punishment.
3. The father is uninvolved in the family, primarily because he works from 3 P.M. until 12:00 A.M. The result is that the mother is responsible for child rearing.
4. Both parents are very much aware of the serious short- and long-term consequences of J's behavior and are committed to helping him.
5. Since the family is relatively poor, jobs are very important so that bills can be paid.
6. There is very little interaction (e.g., outings, games, etc.) as a family, although the mother and the boys do some things together.
7. The parents estimate that 100 percent of their interaction with J is negative.
8. The younger brother has manifested none of J's aggressive behavior and in most ways is really fun.
9. J is compared openly and negatively to his younger brother.
10. The parents' goals for J are for him to grow up and be normal, get a job, and be happy.
11. School is seen as mildly important.
12. There are few, if any, outside influences on the family.

When the parents were asked to draw conclusions about J and what they might do to help him, they generated the following ideas:

1. Stop spanking him. It's not doing any good. ("One doctor told us this.")
2. Pay more attention to him. Stop leaving him with baby-sitters so much. ("We feel bad because we don't spend more time with him, but we're so busy.")

The consultant's analysis of the problem, which was not shared directly with the parents, was as follows:

Contributing Factors

1. Violence (spanking) modeled.
2. No expectations for positive behavior communicated directly.
3. No feedback when positive behavior does occur.
4. Negative comparison to sibling contributes to hostility.
5. Not enough time spent with child to influence behavior change.
6. No opportunity for child to observe normal positive human interaction since he goes to emotionally handicapped classroom.
7. Insensitive to their role in child's problem.

Goal Setting

The tentative hypotheses about factors in the family that may be contributing to the child's problem must ultimately be formulated into specific consultation goals. Just as is the case in other types of consultation, there are essentially two sets of goals to establish: client and consultee goals. Client goals are typically easily established since they are the antithesis of the behavior that led to the consultation. Goals such as getting and staying off drugs, being in less trouble at school, and getting into less trouble with the law are typical. Once the parents have verbalized how they would like the child to function, then the obvious question is, "How can you as parents help your child?" Some parents will be able to answer this question directly, while others will have few ideas regarding the changes they need to make. The consultant can and should suggest goals to parents, albeit tentatively. To return to the case of J for a moment, the consultant posed the following questions: "What would you think of establishing a more positive atmosphere for J as a beginning point?" The question was followed up with an explanation suggesting that at least a part of J's hostile behavior may be partially attributable to the fact that he receives no positive feedback. This suggestion builds on the parents' perceptions that they need to find an alternative to spanking and that they need to spend more time with him, thus validating the suggestion they have made.

The culmination of goal setting should be one or two goals that then become the focus of the consultation process.

Explaining Psychological Principles

Once goals have been agreed upon by the consultant and the parents, an explanation of the psychological principles to be utilized in designing the intervention seems necessary so that effective communication can take place (Brown & Brown, 1975).

Parents need to know some of the basic premises underlying any techniques that might be utilized in the intervention process. In addition to facilitating the communication process, an explanation of theoretical concepts seems necessary so that parents can understand the nature of their own problems with their children and begin to function independently of the consultant.

Explanations of theoretical propositions should always be made as simply as possible without losing the essence of the concepts involved. Brown and Brown (1975) point out that positive reinforcement can be explained as an event that increases the probability of a behavior occurring in the future. However, they go on to recommend that common-sense examples of positive reinforcement may be more readily understood by parents than this technical definition. Similarly, communication can be explained in terms of senders, receivers, channels of communication, nonverbal communication, and verbal communication. It can also be explained by illustrating the relationships among ways of talking, learning, and understanding. Finally, books on parenting illustrate the principles under discussion and can be given to parents.

The explanation of psychological principles should not be a one-way process. It should be conducted in a manner that allows parents to question the principles and/or to discuss ways in which the principles apply in their own family. Once it becomes apparent that parents have arrived at a high degree of understanding of the concepts to be utilized, it is time to proceed.

Once the psychological principles to be employed in the design of an intervention are fully understood by the parents, the consultant and the parents should review the existing family patterns. The consultant should encourage the parents to do this by asking them simply to analyze what is occurring in their particular situation. The process can be facilitated by pointing to specific examples. The consultant might use some of the following leads:

"You were telling me about the difficulties you were having with the siblings fighting and your role in these fights. How would you explain those now?"

"What types of behaviors are you reinforcing when you are attempting to get your children to complete their homework?"

"You were telling me that you have had a lot of trouble getting your teenagers to understand the financial situation in your family. Can you analyze what is going on in that area?"

This step is, in a sense, a check on parental understanding of the principles to be utilized. However, the focus at this time should be upon those areas that seem to be of a major concern to the family and, in that sense, is a prelude to the selection of strategies.

Selecting Intervention Strategies

Goal setting and the explanation of psychological principles are followed by the selection of strategies for goal attainment. Several guidelines should be followed in this process. First, interventions should be as simple as possible. Whether the consultees are single parents, parents from blended families, or parents from intact families, they are typically involved with a variety of activities in addition to child rearing. It is necessary, therefore, to develop a strategy that will minimize parents' workload.

Second, the parent should choose the intervention. Consultants typically present options, but even this should be delayed until parents have generated their own list of possible interventions based upon either their own experiences or those of other parents. Once parents' ideas about how to best resolve the problem are ascertained, the consultant may wish to make additional suggestions.

Third, parents must be trained to use the intervention. This training may be done through behavior rehearsal, use of assigned readings, direct modeling by the consultant, and even by involving parents who have successfully used the strategy to explain the problems they encountered in the process and how they overcame them.

Fourth, the potential consequences of the intervention, including those for the parents and siblings other than the client, must be anticipated. One consultant always warns parents that if one child begins to improve, expect another to get worse. While this may not always be the case, it is important for parents to think through the changes that may occur because the family system has been altered as a result of an intervention. Parents must also be prepared to alter their strategies if the children make valid observations about the need for change.

Fifth, plan to include the children. Although the client in most parent consultation situations is a single child, all of the children in the family should be apprised of the goals that have been set and the strategies that are to be employed. Moreover, their input should be solicited regarding the efficacy of the strategies chosen and their suggestions solicited for improving both the goal(s) and its attainment.

Sixth, the interventions should be culturally sensitive. If the worldview of the client does not include dominating time as an important dimension, strategies such as contingency contracts should probably not be used. Democratic family meetings should probably not be used with Asian families that value lineal relationships, but encouragement and support may be perfectly acceptable approaches. Unfortunately, there is no foolproof way of determining whether a particular intervention will work, but being aware of cultural values generally, assessing the cultural values of your clients, and being careful not to impose interventions based on one's own values can go a long way toward ensuring that interventions are culturally appropriate.

When the changes that are to occur are discussed with the children, the potential impact of those changes for all children, and particularly the client, should be reviewed.

Once the consultant and parents are confident that the parents are ready to implement the strategy they have selected to deal with their child's problem, they should be advised to begin the intervention. They should also be cautioned that if problems arise in the course of the intervention, they should either call the consultant or discontinue the intervention until they have had an opportunity to discuss the problems they are experiencing with the consultant.

Follow-Up and Evaluation

It is probable that the process outlined to this point will take one or two 90-minute sessions with parents. If two sessions are required to develop a relationship, set goals, design an intervention, and get the children involved, these should be scheduled relatively close together. However, it is suggested that sessions following intervention selection should be scheduled for two weeks later, so that parents will have an opportunity to fully implement the strategy that has been selected. It is also suggested that the consultant telephone the consultee between the strategy selection session and the first follow-up session in order to provide support and, if needed, technical assistance.

Follow-up consultation sessions should be opened with a review of the progress that has been made toward the goals that have been established. If goals have been attained, new goals can be established, if needed, and then the session focuses upon the selection of an intervention to attain the new goal. However, if progress has either been slower than would be expected or is nonexistent, some troubleshooting must be conducted by the consultant with the purpose of determining the cause underlying the situation.

One of the first areas that should be examined in the troubleshooting process is the parents' level of understanding of the psychological principles and strategies chosen. This can be accomplished by asking parents to relate what they did on a step-by-step basis as they implemented the intervention. At times, it is helpful to roleplay the interactions that occurred in order to attain additional insight into the difficulty that the parents have experienced. It is not uncommon to find that parents have been inconsistent in their efforts or that they did not fully understand the psychological principles involved. If the counselor ascertains that parents do not have a complete grasp of the psychological principles or the specific techniques, these should be carefully reviewed before any further action is initiated.

If the parents fully understood what actions were to be taken, the consultant should reexamine the home situation. It is possible that some vital factors were overlooked in the first interview. For example, the influence of peers, relatives, and siblings upon the client should receive special attention. So should factors such as parental disagreement about approaches to be utilized and the possibility of a family schedule that prohibits the systematic utilization of certain strategies. Typically, whenever progress has not been made, the consultant has either failed to explain the approaches to be used sufficiently or has overlooked key factors in the family. However, there is at least one other factor that may have contributed to this situation: resistance. This matter will be discussed in more detail later in this chapter.

Avoiding Therapy

When consulting with parents, there are often opportunities to lapse into therapeutic behavior, since parents will often disclose material about their personal problems. For example, a single parent may burst into tears as she discloses, "My husband is no good. He's late with the child support again, and I'm so depressed because I cannot pay the rent." A counselor or therapist might respond as follows:

THERAPIST: You're really angry because your husband's late with the child support again, but as angry as you are with him, you're still depressed because of your inability to pay the rent. Tell me more about your situation with your husband.

On the other hand, a consultant should respond in a manner that will refocus the consulting endeavor on the child (Randolph, 1985).

CONSULTANT: I can understand your anger and the fact that you are quite unhappy about not being able to pay the rent. Is it likely that this emotion is going to influence your working with Jeremy?

Obviously if the parent persists in this manner, termination of consultation is in order.

Termination

Termination of the parent consultation process should occur whenever the parents are able to understand their own problems and act on those insights. Termination may occur earlier if either or both parents are in need of some type of therapeutic assistance, with the result that the problem interferes with the consulting process. In these situations, the consultant may renegotiate the consulting contract to focus on personal counseling or make a referral.

It is suggested that approximately one month after termination, a follow-up note be sent to parents in order to determine whether progress has continued. This survey should also extend an opportunity for parents to reenter the consultation process if progress is not satisfactory. This serves to provide some evaluation of the process and to enable parents who either terminated or were terminated earlier to again consider the possibility of availing themselves of the consultant's services.

GROUP PARENTAL CONSULTATION

Dinkmeyer (1973) presented the idea of the "C" group, so labeled because it involves collaboration, consultation, and confrontation, and because it clarifies belief systems. His group consists of concerned and committed members, and is confidential. He goes on to enumerate the helping forces in the "C" group as acceptance, feedback, universalization or becoming aware that one's problems with children are not unique, altruism or stimulation through assisting others, and spectator therapy or the process of receiving help by observing others being helped.

Consultation groups, unlike parent education groups, do not have a set agenda. Typically, these groups are initiated by the consultant, usually through a mailed survey to parents. Dinkmeyer (1973) suggests that the groups be restricted to parents having children at a single grade level, that the groups meet for six to eight weeks, and that the meetings be approximately 90 minutes long.

The initial letter that is sent to parents should begin the structuring of the consultation group. Essentially, the group should be described as a place where parents share their concerns about their children and receive help with these concerns. This letter should also specify the time, place, and dates of the meetings. One additional component should be included in the first letter: the procedure for selecting participants. This is included because often more parents will volunteer for the group than can be accommodated initially. Therefore, the letter may need to contain dates for later sessions and a request that the parents list the dates in terms of priority.

The process of the consulting group is much the same as that described for individual consultation. The first session should be devoted to getting comfortable, establishing relationships, and establishing the roles of the members and the leaders. Subsequent sessions should focus on the general concerns of parents with a gradual shift to the particular concerns of individuals. Since a termination date has been established at the outset, this is generally not an issue. However, there are times when pressure will be brought to bear to continue the group. If this occurs, the consultant may encourage the group to continue independently or may meet with them, depending upon individual circumstances.

Parent groups allow consultants to use their time more effectively, and because other parents are involved, the resources available to the individuals in need of help are increased. Finally, parental consulting groups do not lend themselves well to confidentiality (Dinkmeyer, 1973). Since this is an important aspect of the consulting group, it is desirable to try to establish confidentiality as a rule in the group. As a matter of practical significance, it is not likely that confidentiality will exist and it may be wiser to acknowledge this from the outset.

SOME SPECIAL CONSIDERATIONS

Resistance

As was noted in Chapter Seven, resistance occurs in all forms of consultation. As Sheridan (1993) suggests, family consultants have drawn primarily upon the family therapy literature to explain resistance in consultation, probably because there are few explanations of this problem in the consultation literature. However, it seems likely that consultants will benefit by conceptualizing resistance in consultation as stemming from intrapsychic deficiencies (mental health problems, family systems variables, problematic marriages), broader systems concerns such as cultural norms, or normal concerns such as role overload. Approaches advocated by mental health specialists often run contrary to cultural ideas about the role of the child in the family and/or child rearing. Ideas such as children should be seen and not heard and that children should obey their authoritarian parents run deep in our culture and are constantly reinforced by the authoritarian nature of much of our societal structure. Democratic family structure and open communication are contradictory concepts to these traditional ideas and are thus either distorted or ignored by parents, in spite of the fact that they are experiencing difficulty in their relationships with their children.

Resistance can also develop because of a problematic marriage, particularly if the child (client) is a pawn in the marital dispute. For example, one parent may seek a child's favoritism by showering him or her with presents to compensate for the lack of love from the spouse. In other situations, the child may be neglected because the spouses are so engrossed in their dispute, with parenting taking on secondary importance. Whenever marital problems preclude follow-through, consultation should be terminated. Overwork may also be a source of resistance. It is not an overstatement to say that some parents are grossly overburdened by their roles as parent and worker, and as a result of child involvement with their own parents. Consultants may unwittingly exacerbate this problem by involving the parents in complicated interventions and/or pursuing too many goals at once. Resistance stemming from overwork should be avoided by anticipating the problem during strategy selection. However, if it is the problem, reducing the amount of work required may put the consultee back on track.

Fear of the unknown is also a source of resistance in parental consultation. This source of resistance can be summed up in the statement, "While things are bad now, they could get worse." In fact, consultation with parents seems to proceed best whenever parents are saying, "Things could not get worse." Fear of risk-taking appears to be at the heart of resistance when parents are afraid that things could get worse. As noted earlier, some consultants warn parents that the family situation could get worse before it gets better. This type of statement seems to be a useful approach to avoid resistance from the consultee who, at the moment he or she senses things are getting worse, stops implementing the intervention. However, warning some parents that things may get worse may heighten resistance.

When resistance is present, two approaches to dealing with the problem are suggested. First, parents need to remind themselves that they came to consultation because one or more of their children is/are not functioning well. To accomplish this "self-reminding," parents can be asked, "What do you hope to accomplish with your children?" And then, "What are you accomplishing now?" Often the discrepancy between the two answers will be sufficient to motivate parents to return to the intervention. If this does not work, confrontation regarding the discrepancy between their stated goals for their children and what they are doing to establish these goals may be necessary.

Overcoming resistance resulting from mental health problems may be difficult. However, one technique that has proven to be of some use in overcoming parental resistance growing out of stereotypical views of children and/or parenting behavior is to ask parents what children are learning as a result of child-rearing techniques. The first step in this process is to ask parents what behaviors or values they are trying to teach their children. The typical answers are honesty, loyalty, cooperation, good citizenship, independence, and so on. Then parents are asked to relate what their children are learning as a result of current parental treatment. The father who does not listen soon recognizes that one cannot teach cooperation without communication, just as the overly protective parent recognizes that sheltering children and making decisions for them results in dependence rather than independence. Parents who expect their children to assume no responsibility in the home or who make excuses for them when they do not can hardly expect those children to become highly responsible citizens.

Finally, family consultants can expect resistance when the consulting process does not take into account the cultural values of the consultee. Unfortunately, resistance can occur when cultural differences are ignored. The history of the relationships between the dominant and minority cultures in this country has often been an unfortunate one. As Teresa LaFromboise (1996), a noted researcher and descendent of the Miami tribe, reports, "Expect historical distrust and earn respect through your actions. The Indian mindset is 'What is your agenda? Are you here to prey? and How long are you going to last?'" (p. 5). An African American who wrote a letter to the editor of the local newspaper to praise a white counselor began the letter with this phrase, "I never thought I would receive help from a white counselor...." If you expect distrust and go the extra mile to prove your value as a consultant, historical barriers can be overcome.

Working with One Parent

Several situations give rise to consultation involving one parent including divorce, one parent's inability to attend the sessions because of scheduling problems, one parent's being opposed to consultation, or a situation involving a parent who does not care enough about the client to become involved. These situations or others that result in the consultee's being only one parent should not prevent consultation from occurring.

If a second parent is involved with the child by virtue of a visitation agreement or still living in the home, consultation should proceed by focusing on the child in much the same manner as described previously. The only addition to the process that may be necessary is that the consultee may need to develop skills in explaining the intervention that is to be made to the other parent and, if the possibility exists that the second parent will cooperate, skills in involving the spouse or ex-spouse as a collaborator in implementing the intervention.

SOME BRIEF CASE STUDIES

The Case of Jamie

Jamie was a kindergartner (five years old) who threw temper tantrums that were quite long (five to six minutes) and intense (kicking on the floor, breaking things, etc.). Her parents were middle-class and there was an older brother (eight years old). The parents were asked to come in to school to explore "ways that the school and the family could collaborate to help Jamie with her transition to school."

During the first session, several key facts were revealed. These included: Jamie's temper tantrums at home were very severe (she had kicked through a door); the punishment used had been spanking, but now the parents were trying to ignore the temper tantrums; the older sibling was a model child; and Jamie was the result of an unwanted pregnancy and the father resented her from the start. He also revealed that he "never showed his resentment." The father admitted that he had a terrible temper and that he had been known to throw some "fits" of his own.

An analysis of the events surrounding the temper tantrums strongly suggested that, in the home at least, whenever the father threatened Jamie, a temper tantrum resulted. As a consequence of this, he had withdrawn from involvement with her. It also appeared that this reaction had generalized, to

some degree, because the mother reported a recent incident where she had corrected Jamie in the grocery store and Jamie had fallen on the floor, kicked her feet, and in doing so, had knocked over a large display of canned goods. (Follow-up with Jamie's teacher suggested that the worst temper tantrums occurred after reprimands.)

The initial goals established by the parents were (1) eliminate temper tantrums in the home and (2) reestablish the father–child relationship. The strategies selected were to stop spanking Jamie, ignore the temper tantrums *completely* by leaving the room where the tantrum was occurring, stop modeling all violent behavior (father agreed to throw "fits" elsewhere), and provide Jamie with much more contingent and noncontingent positive feedback.

Establishing the father–daughter relationship proved to be problematic in that the parents reported in follow-up sessions that Jamie had engaged in temper tantrums whenever the father had tried to engage in several routine activities with her. After much discussion, it was learned that Jamie enjoyed swinging and often asked her mother to swing her. A strategy was adopted that required the father to be present whenever Jamie was being swung and to gradually approach her and engage in swinging her while carrying on routine conversation.

As expected, the older sibling who had received little, but always positive, feedback from his parents began to manifest some negative behavior whenever the interventions were fully implemented. An analysis of the situation revealed that he had been neglected to some degree as the parents concentrated on Jamie. This situation was corrected and the problem behavior occurred significantly less often according to parental reports.

Because Jamie was experiencing problems both at school and at home, consultation with the teacher was also initiated.

Within two months (five sessions), the temper tantrums had all but disappeared. Unexpectedly, both children accompanied their parents to the final consultation session, and all four sat on a couch with Jamie sitting by her father. The parents and the children agreed that the situation in their household

Student Learning Activity 10.1

Analyze the case of Jamie by answering the following questions:

1. What parenting factors contributed (or may have contributed) to Jamie's problem?

	YES	NO
A. Parents' self-efficacy	___	___
B. Parenting standards	___	___
C. Parents' approval of the situation	___	___
D. Parenting skills	___	___
E. Systems variables	___	___

2. What interventions can you suggest other than those adopted in this case?
3. Can you provide alternative explanations to why Jamie's sibling began to misbehave?
4. What would you do about the possibility of child abuse in this case?

---

had improved dramatically. One month later, a telephone follow-up revealed that while Jamie would still occasionally engage in a temper tantrum, they tended to be short in duration and of mild intensity.

The Case of Gerrard

Gerrard was placed in an inpatient substance abuse treatment center after repeated attempts at outpatient treatment had failed. He was 15 years old at the time he entered the center. One portion of the treatment plan called for ongoing family therapy that was to be initiated during Gerrard's eight-week stay in the facility and to be continued on an indefinite basis upon his release. Family therapy was rejected by the parents because "they were not the ones with the problem." A doctoral intern approached the parents and suggested consultation as an alternative to family therapy, indicating that the entire focus of the process would be to enhance their ability to parent Gerrard. The parents agreed to participate, although the level of their commitment seemed relatively low.

Gerrard's father was a professor at a major university and his mother was a housewife. They had three children, of which Gerrard was the youngest. According to parental reports, the other children were "quite normal" in that they had done well in high school, gone on to college, and were either advancing in their careers or in graduate school. Gerrard, who is five years younger than his youngest sibling, was quite ill as a child and on one occasion, both parents expected him to die. At the time of consultation, Gerrard was experiencing no major health problems.

Both parents admitted that Gerrard had been treated differently than his older siblings in that expectations regarding academic achievement, out-of-school activities, and even in-the-home participation had been reduced. Both agreed that these lower expectations were partially because of Gerrard's health problems, but the father volunteered that Gerrard's mother enjoyed her continuing role as mother and suggested pleasantly that Gerrard had been pampered by his mother.

When it became apparent in the middle of the elementary school years that Gerrard's health problems were virtually over, his father attempted to pressure him to do better in school and to generally raise his standard of performance. His mother, while not fully in agreement with the father's tactics, agreed with the general idea that Gerrard should be expected to function at a higher level.

Gerrard rebelled at the demands of his parents, but was usually somewhat passive in his rebellion. He declared that he was different from his siblings; he started dressing dramatically differently in clothes that he purchased with his allowance at the PTA Thrift Shop. Most important to the parents, his grades continued to be in the C–D range with an occasional F even though test results indicated that he was capable of superior performance.

Once in junior high, Gerrard's academic performance fell even lower and while he "flirted" continuously with failure, he never actually failed a subject. He also fell in with the wrong crowd and was caught with a marijuana cigarette by one of his teachers. His behavior became more erratic and, once when his parents went to pick him up from a

Student Learning Activity 10.2

Analyze the case of Gerrard by answering the following questions:

1. What is the most likely explanation for Gerrard's behavior?
2. If you had known that the father was going to mousse his hair and wear an earring to the hospital, would you have advised it?
3. How do you explain the relationship of the health problem to the presenting problem?
4. What are alternatives to the interventions that appear to have been used in this case?

---

friend's house, he fell into the car, obviously inebriated. It became clear that he was using alcohol extensively near the end of junior high school and his relationship with his parents, and particularly his father, had deteriorated to the point where they interacted only on a superficial level. He failed two subjects during his sophomore year, was picked up by the police for possession of marijuana (less than an ounce), and what conversation went on at home was strained at best.

The parents agreed that they needed to:

1. Help Gerrard set some of his own goals instead of trying to impose their own goals on him.
2. Generally rebuild their relationship with him by communicating their concerned love instead of their expectations.
3. Accept his lifestyle (hair, clothes).
4. Help Gerrard develop self-confidence in areas of interest (e.g., music) by providing support in the form of lessons and purchasing instruments.
5. Model only the most responsible use of alcohol.

When Gerrard was told of his parents' plans to be more supportive of his interests and to stop the bickering over his clothes, hair, and so on, his response was one of extreme skepticism. In a subsequent visit to the hospital, his father, who was typically quite conservative, arrived wearing one earring, a vest with a Grateful Dead sticker on it, and with his hair spiked with mousse. While Gerrard was still skeptical, the ice was broken to some degree.

Throughout the remainder of Gerrard's stay in the hospital, the parents worked on helping Gerrard set some goals for himself and laying out plans for helping him achieve those goals. Gerrard was systematically reinforced for goal-setting behavior and any verbalization that related to increasing his standards of performance. Throughout these visits, the parents continuously expressed confidence in Gerrard's ability to take control of his life and in his ability to function in a wide variety of situations, including school (no great emphasis on this area).

After release from the treatment center, Gerrard returned to his high school, where he continued to struggle academically, although he passed all subjects.

The open hostility that was present in the home prior to Gerrard's admission into the treatment center was greatly reduced, except when Gerrard's parents expressed reservations about his friends who are alcohol abusers, too. According to Gerrard's own statements, tension and conflict developed. Gerrard experienced two relapses during the three months of follow-up. Each time, his parents expressed disappointment and offered their continuing help in Gerrard's efforts to stop abusing drugs.

At the final session, the parents reported that their relationship with Gerrard had improved dramatically, that his grades had improved to a small degree, and that he "was dressing better." They attributed this to the fact that his father occasionally appeared at the dinner table in an earring and a Grateful Dead vest.

Consultant's note: The unusual behavior engaged in by the father was not the result of a direct recommendation by the consultant. However, the father was encouraged to find ways to break the communication barriers between himself and his child. Had his behavior been viewed as a "put-down" by the child, this approach would have exacerbated the situation.

Student Learning Activity 10.3

Mrs. Tron, who is Vietnamese, makes an appointment to see you because of her concerns about Kahn (age 17), her youngest child and the only one living at home. Kahn, who transferred to your school from another state, is in trouble academically and personally. It is likely that he will fail English III; he sleeps in class, cuts classes, and sometimes does not come to school at all. He is not verbally or physically aggressive, and his teachers describe him as bright and able to do high-quality work when "he puts his mind to it." He has frequently been seen with Walter who only comes to school in the morning because the three classes he needs for graduation are offered then. Walter's family is wealthy, and he drives a Lexus to school. The teachers suspect that Kahn cuts classes to be with Walter, and he has been seen leaving school with Walter. Mr. Tron is listed as deceased in the school's files.

Mrs. Tron apologizes profusely when she comes into your office. She is obviously embarrassed to be there, but she also is worried about Kahn. She reveals that her husband was killed in the Vietnam War, and she immigrated to the United States where her relatives have a very successful fishing business. She also tells you that her two other sons (both older) went to college and hold good jobs in another state. She moved so that she could be closer to her daughter who attends a nearby university. The daughter has been able to find her a job at the university, and the mother is generally pleased with her new life, with the exception of Kahn's behavior.

Kahn's problems are not new. In his former state he was arrested for possession of marijuana and placed on probation. The judge gave him permission to relocate because she felt that the family move would be best for Kahn. However, he could be incarcerated if he gets into more trouble. Mrs. Tron tells you that Kahn is the first member of her family to be arrested. She also tells you that he failed English in his previous high school and was not going to graduate on time because school policy required that he retake English. Mrs. Tron discloses that she believes Kahn would act differently if he lived closer to his sister so that she could be a good influence. She also tells you that she often reminds Kahn of the successes of his brothers and his sister.

Mrs. Tron is worried because Kahn will not listen, is disgracing the family, and is unlikely to have a successful life. She reveals that he often does not come home after school, misses meals, and refuses to do anything that she suggests (actually demands). Although Kahn is always civil verbally, his nonverbal behavior is defiant. She also shares that Kahn was a good child, and she wishes that her family members were closer. She places a lot of the blame on Kahn's friends because they get no direction from their parents.

1. What is Mrs. Tron's social relationship value?
2. Does Kahn share that value?
3. What would you say to Mrs. Tron about the fact that Kahn is an embarrassment to her?
4. How would you explain Kahn's behavior to Mrs. Tron?
5. What Eurocentric approaches to parenting might Mrs. Tron try? Why is she likely to resist these approaches?

SUMMARY

Consulting with parents is a relatively new idea, primarily because of the influence of Caplan (1970), who viewed consultation as a process that occurs between professionals. However, consultants are embracing the idea with increasing vigor because they realize that consultation provides them with a tool that will allow them to intervene in the all-important family system.

The approach to consultation outlined here drew on social learning theory, systems theory, and Caplanian ideas. Eclecticism is decried by many purists, but as was suggested earlier, current psychological theories are not comprehensive enough to provide the framework for something as complicated as family intervention. Perhaps this will change in the future, but for now the family consultant needs to draw upon a number of conceptual and practical frameworks to be effective.

TIPS FOR THE PRACTITIONER

1. Interview several parents about the concerns they have about their children's educational development. Do they have complicated or simple explanations of the problems they perceive? Do they blame themselves or others?
2. Try to identify times in your own family or in the families of people you know when positive change in one child brought about negative change in one or more other children.
3. The systems principle of equifinality holds that there are many potential solutions to each problem in a system. Identify a student of any age who is experiencing a learning problem. Identify as many possible solutions as you can to the problem. How many of them involve parents? How many solutions did you generate?
4. Either observe a family therapy session or view a videotape of a session. How do these processes differ? How are they the same? What did you learn that you can use as a consultant to families?
5. If you can, attend a parent education session. How is this process similar to consultation? Different? What did you learn that you can use as a consultant?
6. Outline the process you expect to use as a family consultant.

REVIEW QUESTIONS

1. Why are systems thinking and behaviorism incompatible?
2. What are the underlying assumptions of parent consultation?
3. Consider the impact that not caring how well you raise your children might have on the parenting process. How could that view be changed?

4. Consider the factors that need to be assessed in the consultation process. How many can you list? How will you assess the factors you have identified?
5. Discuss the pros and cons of parents' understanding the basis for the interventions which they are asked to implement. Where do you stand on the issue that parents need not understand the why of intervention, only the how?
6. What are the sources of resistance to consultation? Can you identify strategies that can be used to overcome these?

REFERENCES

Albert, L. (1996). *Coping with kids* (2nd ed.). Circle Pines, MN: American Guidance Services.

Bandura, A. (1977). *Social learning theory.* Englewood Cliffs, NJ: Prentice-Hall.

Bandura, A. (1978). The self system in reciprocal determinism. *American Psychologist, 33,* 344–358.

Bandura, A. (1986). *Social foundations of thought and action: A social cognitive theory.* Englewood Cliffs, NJ: Prentice-Hall.

Bateson, G. (1972). *Steps to an ecology of mind.* New York: Ballantine.

Bergan, J. R. (1977). *Behavioral consultation.* Columbus, OH: Charles E. Merrill.

Bergan, J. R., & Duley, S. (1981). Behavioral consultation in families. In R. W. Henderson (Ed.), *Parent-child interactions: Theory, research and prospects* (pp. 265–291). New York: Plenum.

Bergan, J. R., & Kratochwill, T. R. (1990). *Behavioral consultation and therapy.* New York: Plenum.

Brown, D. (1997). Implications of cultural values for cross-cultural consultation with families. *Journal of Counseling and Development, 76,* 29–35.

Brown, D., & Brown, S. T. (1975). Parental consultation: A behavioral approach. *Elementary School Guidance and Counseling, 10,* 95–102.

Brown, D., & Crace, R. K. (1996). *Manual and user's guide for the Life Values Inventory.* Chapel Hill, NC: Life Values Resources.

Brown, D., Wyne, M. D., Blackburn, J. E., & Powell, W. C. (1979). *Consultation: Strategy for improving education.* Boston: Allyn and Bacon.

Caplan, G. (1970). *Mental health consultation.* New York: Basic Books.

Capra, F. (1982). *The turning point: Science, society, and the rising culture.* New York: Simon & Schuster.

Cobb, D. E., & Medway, F. J. (1978). Determinants of effectiveness of parental consultation. *Journal of Community Psychology, 6,* 229–240.

Dembo, M. H., Sweitzer, M., & Lauritzen, P. (1985). An evaluation of group parent education: Behavioral, PET, and Adlerian. *Review of Educational Research, 55,* 155–200.

Dinkmeyer, D. C. (1973). The parent "C" group. *Personnel and Guidance Journal, 52,* 252–256.

Dinkmeyer, D. C., & Carlson, J. (1973). *Consulting: Facilitating human potential and change processes.* Columbus, OH: Charles E. Merrill.

Dreikurs, R. R., & Stolz, V. (1967). *Children the challenge.* New York: Duell, Sloan, & Pearce.

Dumas, J. E. (1989). Treating antisocial behavior in children: Child and family approaches. *Clinical Psychology Review, 9,* 197–222.

Frazier, F., & Matthes, W. A. (1975). Parent education: A comparison of Adlerian and behavioral approaches. *Elementary School Guidance and Counseling, 19,* 31–38.

Goldenberg, I., & Goldenberg, H. (2000). *Family therapy: An overview* (5th ed.). Belmont, CA: Wadsworth.

Griggs, S. A., & Dunn, R. (1989). The learning styles of multicultural groups and counseling interventions. *Journal of Multicultural Counseling and Development, 17,* 146–155.

Grissom, P. F., Erchul, W. P., & Sheridan, S. M. (2003). Relationships among relational communications processes and perceptions of outcomes in conjoint behavioral consultation. *Journal of Educational and Psychological Consultation, 14,* 157–180.

Horne, A. M. (2000). *Family counseling and therapy* (3rd ed.). Itasca, IL: F. E. Peacock.

Horton, E., & Brown, D. (1990). The importance of interpersonal skills in consultee-centered consultation: A review. *Journal of Counseling and Development, 68,* 423–426.

LaFromboise, T. (1996). On multicultural issues. *Microtraining and Multicultural Development Newsletter.* North Amherst, MA: Microtraining and Multicultural Development.

McGowan, R. J. (1969). Group counseling with underachievers and their parents. *School Counselor, 16,* 30–35.

McWhirter, J. J., & Ryan, C. A. (1991). Counseling the Navajo. *Journal of Multicultural Counseling and Development, 19,* 74–82.

Mullis, F., & Edwards, D. (2001). Consulting with parents: Applying systems theory and techniques. *Professional School Counseling, 5,* 116–123.

Nikelly, A. G. (1992). Can DSM III-R be used in the diagnosis of non-western patients? *International Journal of Mental Health, 21,* 3–22.

Olson, D. H., Sprenkle, D. H., & Russell, C. S. (1979). Circumplex model of marital and family systems: Cohesion and adaptability dimensions, family types, and clinical applications. *Family Process, 18,* 3–28.

Palmo, A. J., & Kuzniar, J. (1971). Modification of behavior through group counseling and consultation. *Elementary School Guidance and Counseling, 6,* 258–262.

Parsons, R. D., & Meyers, J. (1984). *Developing consultation skills.* San Francisco: Jossey-Bass.

Perkins, J. A., & Wicas, E. (1971). Group counseling with bright underachievers and their mothers. *Journal of Counseling Psychology, 18,* 273–279.

Randolph, D. L. (1985). *Microconsulting: Basic psychological consultation skills for helping professionals.* Johnson City, TN: Institute of Social Services and Arts.

Sheridan, S. M. (1993). Models for working with parents. In J. E. Zins, T. R. Kratochwill, & S. N. Elliot (Eds.), *Handbook of consultation services for children* (pp. 110–133). San Francisco: Jossey-Bass.

Sheridan, S. M., & Kratochwill, T. R. (1992). Behavioral parent-teacher consultation: A practical approach. *Journal of School Psychology, 30,* 117–139.

Sheridan, S. M., Kratochwill, T. R., & Bergan, J. R. (1996). *Conjoint behavioral consultation: A procedural manual.* New York: Plenum.

Sonstegard, M. (1964). A rationale for interviewing parents. *School Counselor, 12,* 72–76.

Sue, D. W., & Sue, D. (1999). *Counseling the culturally different* (3rd ed.). New York: John Wiley & Sons.

Thomason, T. C. (1995). *Introduction to counseling American Indians.* Flagstaff, AZ: Rehabilitation Research and Training Center.

Weathers, L. R., & Liberman, R. P. (1975). The contingency contracting exercise. *Journal of Behavior Therapy and Experimental Psychiatry, 6,* 208–214.

Winkelman, M. (1994). Culture shock and adaptation. *Journal of Counseling and Development, 73,* 121–126.

ANSWERS TO LEARNING EXERCISES

11.1

1. A = no; B = yes; C = yes (maybe); D = yes; E = yes
2. Some of the Adlerian interventions discussed in Chapter Four might apply in this situation.
3. Modeling—sister is being reinforced; Systems theory—brother had assumed a role that was no longer adaptive: from his perspective Jamie changed.
4. Determine the severity of the spankings and/or emotional abuse and act accordingly.

11.2

1. Poor communication; conflicting communication and actions from mother and father; inconsistent parenting approaches.
2. This one is up to you as a consultant.

3. Sometimes when parents have a child who nearly dies, they overprotect the child and are too willing to let such children have their own way. This is invariably a problem when the child reaches adolescence.
4. Adlerian approaches involving democratic family meetings and the use of logical and natural consequences would be one set of alternatives.

11.3

1. Collective/Collateral.
2. No. Individualism.
3. Explain that it is not her fault and why Kahn has developed this behavior.
4. Use differences in social values and peer pressure as explanation variables.
5. Natural and logical consequences. Her devotion to her son.

CHAPTER 11

DATA-BASED DECISION MAKING IN CONSULTATION

GOAL OF THE CHAPTER

This chapter is designed to introduce the major considerations that need to be taken into account in making data-based monitoring and feedback an integral component of consultation and constructing an evaluation plan.

CHAPTER PREVIEW

1. Improving the consultant's effectiveness through the use of objective assessments of the process and outcome is stressed.
2. The consultant's need to consider evaluation strategies is presented, along with his or her responsibility to contribute to the consultation research literature.
3. Evaluation purposes are presented, and steps in planning and implementing an evaluation are reviewed.

As we have seen throughout this book, consultation is an intervention technique that means many things to many people. It subsumes several theoretical orientations, techniques, and target populations. Perhaps partially because of the amorphous state of our understanding of consulting, the use of the term *consultation* seems to be growing, and the literature is becoming more cluttered with less than precise terminology. These conditions are ripe for creating myths and disillusionments among the participants in any consultation effort. Thus, if there ever was an intervention strategy that was suited to the practitioner's closely monitoring of the process and outcome—consultation is it. It could lead to both improving his or her effectiveness while advancing thinking about and research

regarding practice. Consultants still operate on what seems to be a logical approach or on limited data, so practitioners should validate the hypotheses that guide their practice and share those observations with their colleagues. Consultation research is not the easiest to conduct (see Chapter Thirteen), and scholarly contributions made by consultants are needed if the promise of this intervention is to be realized (Pryzwansky, 1986). Basically then, what some have labeled a "scientist–practitioner" (Barlow, Hayes, & Nelson, 1984; Lambert, 1993) is what professionals who offer the consultation collaboration services need to consider as a way of practice.

Data-based interventions are critical to professional functioning as we conceptualize it. Given the fact that consultation is usually time-limited and goal-directed, an accountability orientation on the part of the consultant is prudent. The importance of documenting the nature and extent of consultation services and their impact from an accountability standpoint should be self-evident. Without such "validation" of the professional's work, it is difficult (and unreasonable) for an administrator to consider supporting such a service, let along increasing its use. Add to this state of affairs the fact that individuals are likely to question any alternatives to the traditional services they received, and the prudent course for any consultant to follow would include a *proactive evaluation* plan. By this we mean that consultants should utilize an evaluation strategy during each consultation case, as well as including this component of their service if they operate as an internal consultant. Collected data will not only contribute to the evaluation of the model being used but—perhaps more important—should be extremely helpful in the continuing development of consultation, as noted earlier.

MONITORING THE CONSULTATION PROCESS

The collection of information throughout a consultation can prove helpful to the consultant in several ways. It can provide a guide in terms of how to interact with a client, in terms of both expectations or preferences, and the progress that is being made. It may also prove helpful to the consultant who is working on improving certain skills or effectiveness during a particular stage of consultation or with a particular type of consultee. It can serve to validate a hypothesis as to how to approach certain problems or deal with certain attitudes or values of a consultee—for example, "The problem has its roots in the home environment so I doubt we can do much about it here at school." Data help a professional to be objective in his or her reflections about a case and to sharpen a report to a supervisor or in maximizing the benefits of a peer consultation group (see Chapter Eight, on the consultee).

At the very least, consultants should keep case notes or a diary of their work with individual con-

sultees. This information can promote a greater understanding of the case and all of its relevant variables, identify interaction patterns of the consultee (or the consultant), and provide documentation of the type and duration of consultation an internal consultant has engaged in over a period of time. The value of such a record is generally enhanced if the same type of content is entered from case to case, while allowing for the individual aspects also to be noted. The use of a consultation log/diary is definitely recommended for at least the first and last interviews, along with a general information form. A sample outline of a diary (Pryzwansky, 1989) is shown on page 268. As with all the instruments presented in this chapter, the reader should adapt them to his or her purpose and needs. However, the consultant should stay with a form for a period of time, making only additions to the form. Otherwise, such records lose their value of providing standardized information from one consultation to the next.

In terms of the monitoring objective we are discussing, let us now address specific stages of consultation and the type of information that might be collected. In this presentation, examples of various instruments (included at the end of this chapter) will be referenced. This presentation and the instruments section can be relevant for more than one stage, as will become obvious.

Entry

During the entry stage, the concern is with needs assessment type tasks. If we define the consultee as the individual who works with the consultant (in contrast to the administrator who sanctions the consultation arrangement), several approaches could be used. For example, it seems logical to expect a consultant to take into account a consultee's *preferences* and *expectations* for the consultation services. If such information can be collected and available to the consultant before the first session, it provides a starting point in selecting the approach/model to use during an initial meeting. Such a strategy also sensitizes the consultee to the range in consultation approaches that is possible;

this educative potential needs some follow-up by the consultant to determine what selected elements of the approach are critical to the consultee. The consultant should dialogue with the consultee, pointing out the advantages and disadvantages of the consultation approaches under discussion.

The Babcock and Pryzwansky (1983) Consultation Preference Scale allows the consultee to state a *preference* for one of four models of consultation during each of five stages of the process. Table 11.1 summarizes the description of the responsibilities of the consultant and consultee during each problem-solving stage of the four consultation models. (The actual scale is presented in Appendix A, along with the code for each item.) There is no reason why the scale cannot be used as an *expectation* scale; it depends on the purpose of the consultant.

The Babcock and Pryzwansky scale can be modified in several other ways. For example, with minor editing the model stages can be combined for each model into a narrative. Consultees can be presented with the four narratives, each describing

a different model, and asked to make a choice. A further modification would involve the addition of a group versus individual format, providing that the consultant is able to offer such a choice. As pointed out in Chapter Eight, Mischley (1973) found equal numbers of consultees stating that they felt more comfortable with one of the four models.

Paul (1979) recommends that a simple intake form be maintained on consultation services, similar to that used with direct services. Data that would be recorded on this form would include the consultee's organization, the problem, recommendations concerning the type of consultation indicated, and suggested disposition. Additional data could include information about consultant and consultee characteristics, the consultee's "ideal" intervention plan at the time of the interview, and prognosis of the probability of success as a result of consultation.

Parsons and Meyers (1984) have developed a Formative Evaluation Checklist (see Appendix B),

TABLE 11.1   Differentiation of Consultant Roles and Objectives in Five Stages of Four Models of Consultation

STAGE	COLLABORATION (C)	MENTAL HEALTH (MH)	CLINICAL (CL)	EXPERT (E)
1. Consultant goal	Work with cee[1] to identify problem, plan and carry out recommendations (recs).	Increase cee's ability to deal with similar problem in future.	Identify problem and develop recs for cee to carry out.	Plan and carry out recs for problems identified by cee.
2. Problem identification	Both cee and clt[2] identify problem.	Clt helps cee identify problem by clarifying his or her perceptions of it.	Clt identifies problem.	Cee identifies problem.
3. Intervention recommendations	Cee and clt suggest intervention recs.	Cee plans intervention with clt acting as facilitator.	Clt offers recs for cee to implement.	Clt plans intervention which he or she will implement.
4. Implementation of recommendations	Cee and clt may each implement some recs.	Cee implements recs he or she developed.	Cee implements recs developed by clt.	Clt implements his or her recs.
5. Nature and extent of follow-up	Cee and clt engage in continuous follow-up to modify intervention if necessary.	Further consultation may be initiated at request of cee.	Clt may offer further advice to cee.	None.

[1]Consultee.
[2]Consultant.

which assists the consultant in summarizing issues related to the entry stage and facilitates the making of similar reviews on those same issues throughout five subsequent stages. The authors' overall objective is to provide a list of sample questions that can be asked continually throughout consultation. A form or checklist like this, with any additional relevant questions, can facilitate the process of monitoring consultation.

Setting Variables. No specific scale is presented here; nevertheless the need for a preliminary consideration of such factors is strongly encouraged. Such information can serve diagnostic and evaluative purposes. Formal assessment (use of instruments) of setting variables, particularly when it does not appear directly relevant to the consultation objective, can be a tricky process. While it might be helpful to know how much a consultee's behavior may be dictated by the atmosphere of the work setting, questions about leadership style of a supervisor can create problems. Administrator "paranoia" then is just one factor that can result to complicate matters. Except where specific consultation goals directly warrant use of such content scales, this information is best gathered informally (the organizational development literature can be useful if particular scales are needed). Halpin and Croft's (1963) Organizational Climate Scale is helpful to review in terms of identifying some of the relevant dimensions distinguishing open from closed systems. The involvement of an administrator/supervisor in the consultation case and the consultee's perceived support of those individuals (aside from their stated commitment) will also need to be gauged. Gallessich (1973) has also outlined a number of considerations to be taken into account with this perspective. For example, she recommends that the consultant gather information related to organizational phenomena in the domains of *external* and *internal* forces (pressures) on the organization, the organization's *trajectory* (i.e., history and future trends), and the staff *perceptions* of the consultant's role and service. Again, an informal, non-obtrusive assessment of these factors is recommended. The data can be helpful in planning current and future consultations.

Process

A number of authors have encouraged an ongoing evaluation plan rather than one that comes at the end of consultation. This goal can be accomplished informally or by using some type of instrument for a midpoint or "taking stock" purpose. A process summary form could call for a problem definition, description of the intervention process, documents collected as a statement of the extent of fulfillment of the working contract, and a prognosis for the future maintenance of progress effect. The consultee could also be asked to rate aspects of the consultation process (Paul, 1979), or both the consultant and consultee could fill out the same form or make the same ratings independently and then share those perceptions.

A somewhat related concept of intake involves Friedman's (1977) semistructured interview scale (see Appendix C). Her list of questions, although ultimately meant to identify a consultee style that in turn indicates a consultation approach, can again be adapted easily by the consultant for a variety of purposes Her questions were framed in the student–teacher context, but the terms client–consultee could easily be substituted. Diagnostic information collected about the student (client) was as follows: Who is (are) the client(s)? What is the actual nature and extent of the problem(s) presented? What previous information has been collected that may be of use in understanding the nature of the current problem situation? What are the client's current performance capabilities? What are the client's strengths? weaknesses? What antecedent or consequent conditions maintain the behavior? What information is available about the client's social behavior? emotional functioning? What resources available within the environment may be used as reinforcers?

Diagnostic information about the teacher (consultee) included the following: What is the teacher's perception of the problem situation? What efforts has the teacher made to cope with the problem situation? What were the outcomes of those efforts, if any? Has the teacher formulated any hypothetical explanations of the problem situation? Does the teacher analyze student–teacher dyadic interaction to determine the possibility of reciprocal responsibility for the existence of a problem situation? What are the teacher's professional strengths? weaknesses? What is the teacher's attitude toward the student? What is the teacher's motivation in seeking consultation? How involved and committed is the teacher in devising solutions to the problem situation? What is the teacher's attitude toward the consultant? toward the consultation process? How willing does the teacher seem to be to retain professional responsibility for the student?

Next the consultee's information-reporting behaviors were categorized according to the alternatives in the following discussion. The answers were judged so as to conceptually group them together to identify one of four consultee styles as indicated by Table 11.2. This interview scale serves a dual function: It lends itself nicely to use as a diagnostic instrument and it allows the consultant to assess the success of his or her reactions to the various styles or characteristics of consultees. Such a review of consultant–consultee patterns of interaction can lead to different or refined consultation techniques in future cases.

Another interview approach emphasizes the exploration of work problems from a Vygotskian perspective (Partanen & Wistrom, 2004). In particular, it is hypothesized that the Vygotsky concept of the zone of proximal development facilitates interpretation of the teacher's presentation of the student's learning and behavior and the classroom context. The teacher is requested to take notes during and between consultation sessions. Guiva (2004), however, has proposed a special interview guide to facilitate the "training process." By using select questions, the "oscillation" between an original representation of the problem on the part of the consultee and later ideas can be encouraged.

Consultee Satisfaction. Although data of this type are usually associated with the termination stage, there is no reason why such feedback cannot be collected at different stages of the consultation process. Parsons and Meyers (1984) suggest a format that considers the areas of consultant efficacy expertise, administrative ability, and interpersonal style, while soliciting more general comments from the consultee (see Appendix D). Again, this

TABLE 11.2 Four Consultee Styles

	GENERALIZED LOCUS OF CONTROL	
SITUATIONAL PROFESSIONAL EXPECTANCY	**INTERNAL ORIENTATION**	**EXTERNAL ORIENTATION**
Expectancy of professional role power	*Problem-solving[1]* *1b; 1d; 2a; 2c; 2e; 2f;* *2g; 2i; 3b; 3c; 3d; 4a; 4e;* *4g; 4i; 5b; 5e; 5h; 5i*	*Strivers[2]* *1b; 1d; 2a; 2c; 2e; 2f;* *2h; 2k; 3b; 3c; 3g; 4c;* *4d; 4f; 4h; 4i; 5c; 5e;* *5i; 5k*
Expectancy of professional role powerlessness	*Controllers[2]* *1a; 1d; 2a; 2c; 2e; 2f; 2g;* *2i; 3e; 3f; 3h; 4c; 4d; 4h; 5a;* *5d; 5g; 5h*	*Reactors[1]* *1a; 2b; 2d; 2e; 2h; 2i;* *3a; 3d; 3i; 4b; 4e; 4j;* *5b; 5f; 5j*

[1]Congruent professional and personal expectancies.
[2]Conflicting professional and personal expectancies.

scale could be easily shortened or serve as a model for developing a more relevant scale.

Consultant Style.   Some feedback regarding interaction style could be helpful in some instances of consultation. The questionnaire following each session represents a form that could be used with consultees in between sessions (see Appendix E). In a sense, the use of such a scale not only forces some reflection on the pace and progress of consultation, but also sets the stage for future contacts. For consultees who are busy and/or do not engage systematically in such exercises, the mechanism may be especially helpful and beneficial to the consultation process.

Termination

It is during this stage of consultation that we generally think of the evaluation function. However, a dilemma of sorts faces the consultant when the target of change is to be identified. Given that consultation is indirect, it could be argued that the consultant can only be held accountable for changes in the consultee. In fact, in some consultation models such as Caplan's, the consultee is given considerable freedom in terms of the intervention plan that is followed, if any, and is not accountable to the consultant. Others would argue that the consultee's client is the ultimate object of change and, therefore, the only logical focus of outcome measures. The outcome/efficacy question is not a simple one and may be tied more appropriately to the model that is used or nature of the problem when an answer to outcome measures is sought. Caplan (1970) noted the complicated evaluation design needed to demonstrate the "chain of interlocking factors—that is, consultation intervention, change in consultee perception and attitudes, change in consultee-client behavior, resulting in change in client behavior and performance" (p. 295). This may be a formidable task even for a sophisticated team of research scientists. Yet some attempts at thorough evaluation by the consultant are necessary, particularly if the service is to be respected and supported. What fol-

lows then is a discussion of a range of options that are available.

A particularly difficult challenge faces the consultant who has as one objective the improvement of the consultee's handling of future situations resembling the referral at hand. It is not unreasonable to expect several such repetitions, but in each instance with notable changes in the consultee's analysis and problem solving of the case. However, this objective is dependent on the consultee working with a relatively homogeneous population so as to ensure similarity in client population needs and a long-term consultation arrangement. One alternative assessment under such a consultation goal would be an assessment of changes in future "problem-finding" skills of the consultee, that is, identifying elements of the problem, developing alternative hypotheses for explaining the problem, and generating more relevant intervention plans.

Client Changes.   A number of authors have advocated the use of single-subject designs for measuring client outcome changes (Brown, Wyne, Blackburn, & Powell, 1979; Meyers, Parsons, & Martin, 1979; Meade, Hamilton, & Yuen, 1982). Given the difficulty of generating control groups and the one-to-one nature of some consultation, these designs need to be seriously considered by consultants. The options include the ABC design and reversal designs, multiple baseline designs, case studies, and mixed designs.

An ABC design compares the effect of one intervention (B) to a second intervention (C) and the baseline data (A). Reversal designs establish that an intervention designed as a result of the consultation process has indeed caused the behavior change. As the letters A B A suggest, this design establishes an uncontrolled baseline, then introduces an intervention, and finally returns to an uncontrolled baseline condition. Multiple baseline designs permit the evaluation of the effectiveness of the intervention strategy. They can involve: (a) two or more *behaviors* by the same individual in the same situation, (b) two or more *individuals* in the same situation, or (c) an intervention applied to the same behavior, but in different *situations*. Mixed designs combine multiple baseline and reversal designs. The case study will be explained later in this chapter.

More recently, the term *time-series methodology* has been introduced to refer to these approaches that share a number of essential characteristics (Barlow et al., 1984). The designs are "organized by the nature of their estimates of stability and the logic of their data comparisons" (p. 180). Again, these designs include the necessity of specifying an intervention, repeated measurements over a period of time, and baseline data. Barlow and colleagues (1984) note that replication of effects is expected to bolster confidence in the results. Finally, they argue for an *attitude of investigative play* on the part of the practitioner to ensure the success of these approaches; their use is seen as a "dynamic-interactive enterprise in which the design is always tentative, always ready to change as significant questions arise in the process" (p. 178).

Barlow and colleagues (1984) identify three fundamentally different kinds of single-case experimentation: (1) within-series elements, (2) between-series elements, and (3) combined-series elements. The *within-series elements* design changes are considered within a series of data points across time. A single outcome measure or set of measures could be used. The traditional AB or ABA design is an example of what is meant. There are more complex variations of this design such as A/B + C/A or interactional designs but the overall logic remains the same. The *between-series elements* organize data across time by different conditions and not by time alone. Two basic types of designs are identified here: the alternating-treatment design and the simultaneous-treatment design. The alternating-treatment designs involve simply the rapid and random alternation of two or more conditions. Simultaneous-treatment designs involve the concurrent or simultaneous applications of two or more interventions in the same case. Finally, the *combined-series elements* basically combine between-series elements and within-series elements into a logically distinct and coordinated whole. The most common example is the multiple baseline design. Barlow and colleagues (1984) suggest that the multiple baseline probably represents the best

design for practitioners: "It does not require withdrawal, it is fairly simple, and applied opportunities for its use abound once systematic measures are being taken" (p. 263). For more in-depth treatment of these designs including their strengths and weaknesses, the reader is referred to the references in this section.

It is important to take notice at this point that the client-outcome designs being discussed here are typical of what is recommended by behavioral consultants. They fit the theoretical model underlying that consultation approach. As such, they may be less palatable or relevant to other consultants and to consultees. Client-outcome measures such as the GAS or paper-and-pencil measures may be deemed more appropriate. For example, changes in consultee attitudes and knowledge of self-concept may be of more interest in other models of consultation.

Consultee Satisfaction.   Perhaps the one variable that has received the most attention in the research literature is consultee satisfaction. At the same time, consultants and the individuals to whom they are accountable may underestimate this critical variable in the accountability and evaluation arenas. For example, the objective of calming anxious consultees and/or providing support can go a long way toward creating a positive environment for problem solving. Consultees' feelings of confidence and sense of empowerment can lead to their investment in dealing with professional challenges. Conoley and Conoley (1982) suggest an open-ended evaluation approach that can be used as a paper-and-pencil instrument or serve as the core of an interview process (see Appendix F). Another approach to consultation evaluation places a good deal more emphasis on the consultant's style, as noted in the boxed consultation evaluation survey (Appendix G).

Consultee Conceptualizations. Consultee-centered consultants are most interested in changes in the consultee's cognition. They are "critical" criteria to use in determining consultation effectiveness (Sandoval, 2004, p. 392). The changes involve the consultee's understanding of the problem, or the client, or him- or herself. Sandoval (2004) proposes the use of a method called "cognitive mapping" to measure such changes. What is involved is the construction of diagrams by the consultee of the identified problem both before and after consultation. The maps are examined at the end of consultation in terms of the complexity and efficiency compared to the earlier representation of the presenting problem. While the maps can be used to reveal misconceptions in understanding on the part of the consultee and, thus, contribute toward facilitating the consultation process, Sandoval argues that they can document consultation effectiveness.

Consultant Assessment.   Many of the scales contain items that can be used by the consultant as feedback for self-improvement purposes or, in certain circumstances, as an accountability measure. One of the more well-developed scales, developed specifically for evaluation of the consultant, has been proposed by Curtis and Anderson (1975). Their scale (see Appendix H) was intended to be used in an observation context, but many of the items could be adapted for a questionnaire instrument. Again, this scale, as others, reflects the priorities of the consultant in the evaluation model.

Secondary Outcomes.   As noted earlier, some authors have recognized the purposes of consultation as including changes in the client group and the consultee. However, positive changes in the latter may be seen as a secondary benefit. A sample of items that address the benefits that may accrue to the consultee is presented in Appendix I. Again, these items can be rewritten and supplemented with others to fit the consultant's situation. Although these questions are designed for consultees, it may be useful for the consultant to complete the same questionnaire and then, with the consultee, compare perceptions of the gains made by the consultee.

Another scale is suggested by Zins (1981), who asked consultees if they had benefited as a result of consultation interactions in the following areas: understanding complexities of the problem situation in greater depth and breadth; clarifying/specifying the problem situation; seeing alternatives not thought of before; finding themselves trying out some of their own ideas; making their own decisions as to management of problems; and helping them to work more effectively with client(s). Needless to say, if the original consultation request was framed solely in terms of client need by the consultee (or the supervisor), the use of such consultee-oriented questions may contribute to defensiveness on the part of the consultee or rumors regarding the consultant's hidden agenda among the staff. The latter outcome could seriously damage the credibility of the consultant for future consultation requests.

Case Study.   Traditionally, a case study analysis usually suggests that a nonexperimental, purely anecdotal report will be made. As such, case studies have been seen by traditional research methodologists as in a separate (and lower) class than experimental works (Barlow et al., 1984). Furthermore, since their primary use is to suggest hypotheses that can be an outcome of any activity, this attitude has contributed to discouragement among practitioners when it comes to analyzing their consultation cases using the case study. Consequently, using this approach as an evaluation strategy or for advancing the knowledge base of the consultant has received little attention recently. Ironically, it is this potential as a hypothesis-generating tool that should be highly valued for an increasingly popular intervention service whose application far outstrips the available database on which to base its applications (Pryzwansky & Noblit, 1990).

Barlow and colleagues (1984) note that an openness to case analysis and case studies is a "cornerstone of applied time-series methodology" (p. 281). That methodology simply means that a series of measures are collected on the same individual over a period of time. The single-case experiment design is an example of time-series methodology, but differs from the ongoing consultation process. Intervention decisions regarding particular consultation cases can be facilitated, self- or peer critiques promoted, and accountability purposes served. Thus, its value as an aid to improve the practice of consultants is an important enough reason to consider its use aside from any research utility. Qualitative case study approaches are particularly appropriate for answering the questions of "how" and "why" and can be much more than descriptive in terms of purpose. Merriam (1988) argues that this type of case study paradigm can serve interpretive and evaluative functions as well.

As participant–observer, the consultant can use session notes, retrospective notes from a journal, audiotapes, and follow-up interviews to develop his or her "notes on notes" from which a case record can emerge. This record begins to capture thoughts and tentative theories that can be read and coded multiple times to formulate a "text." Such texts serve as the basis for satisfying reliability and validity questions, thereby increasing confidence in the case analyses made. Finally, the use of a *consultation diary* that covers at least the first and last interview as well as general information, is definitely recommended. A sample outline of a diary currently in use in some courses (Pryzwansky, 1989) follows.

The descriptive case study typically involves the collection of relevant data about the consultee and/or client (and system) along with careful description of the various stages of the consultation process. Buttressed by some initial conceptualization regarding the consultation approach that is used, the potential for a defensible qualitative analysis to take place is enhanced. One challenge, however, is deciding when enough information has been collected. The recommendation that all possible data should be included recognized that the post hoc emphasis to the case study means one never knows until termination what all of the relevant data might be. However, the result, in part, is either to reduce the appeal of the case study approach or contribute to its loss of credibility even as an evaluation tool. The best advice may be that consultants using a case study approach should collect information to the degree it is practical for them to do so and that allows them to address the questions initially posed. Some compromises will obviously need to be made in this regard until single-case experimental designs are feasible. Nevertheless, the use of case studies in providing accountability data as well as contributing to follow-up research investigations because of the hypotheses they suggest should not be overlooked by the consultant.

Accountability

We have separated accountability from evaluation in order to stress the importance of record keeping for reporting purposes and self-review separate from a pure evaluation goal. The diary option already presented can certainly be utilized for accountability purposes. In addition, the resource professional should consider two other options. The filing of a consultation report, which summarizes the hypotheses generated in each session, along with the intervention-follow-up steps to be taken along with other relevant information, is one alternative, and could be placed in the student's cumulative folder once the consultation is complete. This report would be similar to assessment reports filed by educational diagnosticians or school psychologists. Besides tracking the progress of the consultation, the reports serve to facilitate continuity of intervention from year to year. On the other hand, it may be reasonable and practical for the resource professional to keep these records or place them in the department's files. In any event, the consultee should be aware from the beginning that a record will be kept, and it may prove prudent for such a record to be a jointly developed and filed document. Anserello and Sweet (1990) recommend that a final consultation report be completed for every consultation case. At minimum they believe the report should include the specific referral questions determined jointly by the consultant and consultee, a detailed list of services provided by the consultant, and detailed information regarding the intervention(s). For these authors, the report serves as an accountability device along with other service-related data compiled on an organization schedule so as to satisfy monitoring and evaluation purposes.

Diary

INITIAL INTERVIEW

1. Nature of referral as seen by consultant and consultee.
2. Type of referral (e.g., academic, behavioral), as seen by consultant and consultee.
3. Consultee's expectation for consultant style (see Chapter Eight).
4. What action does the consultee see as being most helpful for the client with all other factors being equal (i.e., discounting factors such as money, availability of community resources)?
5. What is seen as the way(s) realistically that the consultant can be most helpful from the consultant and consultee perspective?
6. Prognosis for helping client as made by consultant and consultee.
7. Degree of cooperation the consultant estimates to experience working with this consultee.
8. Consultee analysis (e.g., see Friedman Scale in this chapter).
9. Model of consultation used by consultant.

FINAL INTERVIEW

1. Most helpful function(s) (e.g., information, support, active intervention) provided by consultant as seen by consultant and consultee.
2. From a retrospective perspective, consultant and consultee opinion if referral could have been resolved without consultation.
3. Changes consultant and consultee would make if they had it to do all over again.
4. Consultee opinion of consultation as a service.
5. Degree of success as rated by consultant and consultee.
6. Major concerns expressed by consultee during the consultation as a way to identify major issues to resolve in future consultations, for example, student's problem is really a home problem, no time to follow through on recommendations, issue of favoring one student more than others.
7. Positive statements made by the consultee during consultation, for example, "I like this client," "the parents are cooperative," "it's wonderful to have services like this available to me."
8. Actual services offered to the client by the consultant.

GENERAL INFORMATION

1. Consultee characteristics: age; sex; race; if teacher, what grade teaching and years of experience.
2. Person initiating the referral.
3. Consultees' prior attempts to get assistance with the client and the result.
4. Number of consultation conferences.
5. Type(s) of recommendations made and recommendations implemented.
6. In schools, type of classroom and organization if other than self-contained.
7. Organizational climate.

A second possibility is for a log (or chart) similar to the format used in the medical field, to be kept. A short document focusing on intervention(s) based on diagnosis would be updated following each session. Such an alternative recognizes the time constraints facing each professional, but, at the same time, serves as an important documentation of each contact, ensuring verification of the contact and decision-making process. Again, the existence and purpose of such practices should be clear within the system along with questions of accessibility, confidentiality, and caveats accompanying the use of such reports.

EVALUATION

Evaluation refers to the data-gathering activity that allows the consultant and consultee to know what progress the consultee and/or client of the consultee is making or the overall success of the intervention. Evaluation questions relate to the needs of those two constituents, and a systematic procedure is followed in gathering data to answer these types of questions. Decisions can then be made regarding continuation or change in the interaction. These data also influence which consultation strategies will be utilized in future consultations, with similar consultees or similar problems. Finally, evaluation allows the consultant to document the effectiveness of his or her consultation service as well as provides information on the utility of such a service delivery approach.

What is being stressed in this chapter is that, at minimum, the consultant has responsibility for evaluation of the intervention versus assuming a program evaluator role or a research role. Often the level of skills and expertise needed by a program evaluator is different than that mastered by professionals functioning in a consultation role. Yet, most consultants are experienced and oriented toward evaluation. Although the content of this chapter is similar to what would appear in the program evaluation literature, the perspective or set emphasized here is on the evaluation responsibility of the consultant in the individual or group situation.

The distinction drawn between evaluation and research, on the other hand, often comes down to one of intent (Meade et al., 1982). Evaluation is done for some purpose related to the decision-making process; research (at least of the basic type) is done for its own sake. The problem to be solved usually defines the questions in the evaluation model, and in that sense an atheoretical or descriptive result is expected. The opposite type of objective would be true for research efforts. The question of the practitioner's obligation to address both an evaluation and research objective, particularly with respect to his or her consultation cases, is addressed in Chapter Thirteen.

Evaluation of consultation can take many different forms depending on the purpose(s), methodology, and resources available to conduct it. As we shall see, there are many purposes for an evaluation, and they are not mutually exclusive. Hylander (2004) proposes that three questions be considered: (1) *What* kind of change is to be explored? (2) *How* will the change be explored? (3) *Why* do you want to evaluate or research the consultation? Although the purposes of any evaluation may vary, hopefully a multidimensional model will be adopted by the consultant. The consultant should pursue as many of the purposes as resources, time, and circumstances will allow. It is recognized, however, that even in the most supportive environment, routine collection of data on all consultation activities and maintenance of a database can be formidable.

Evaluation Models

In this section a number of evaluation models are presented, in part from the program evaluation literature. Evaluation efforts have been categorized in different ways, so the intention of this brief review of several different frameworks is to help in conceptualizing evaluation tasks as well as to help the individual consultant set priorities. Types of evaluations are discussed first and followed by a brief discussion of purposes of evaluation.

Formative and Summative Evaluations. Scriven's (1967) model of formative and summative types of evaluation has been drawn on heavily in the consultation literature. Essentially, two different kinds of evaluations are identified. *Formative* evaluation is concerned with the planning and implementation processes of consultation. It deals with questions of "how" and, as such, examines and/or monitors the process stages of consultation. It can be used to develop an intervention or to finetune the consultation process. The planning and decision-making needs are addressed. Often referred to as *process* evaluation, it goes beyond consideration of the consultant–consultee relationship to deal with issues at all stages that are related to consultation improvement. Questions that might be addressed are as follows: Were objectives clearly identified for the consultation? How did the consultee feel about his or her participation during the problem identification stage? Was the consultant easy to relate to? How effectively were the relevance and success of the intervention monitored? Were meetings held regularly? What was the nature of the meetings that were held? The preceding section has dealt with formative evaluation.

By contrast, *summative* evaluation deals with goal achievement concerns; questions of whether a program has been implemented and its degree of success are postulated. The impact of the consultation is then addressed in this evaluation procedure. Another term used in describing this approach is *product* evaluation. This focus is concerned with the outcome of the intervention. For example, was student achievement level positively influenced? Did the number of referrals decrease? Are the services being requested by more consultees within the organization? Was the consultation cost-effective? Did the outreach program reduce alcoholism? Was the agency able to communicate better with the community? Did fundraising activities increase? These types of evaluation data can address questions related to the efficacy of the indirect service model as well as the desirability of maintaining and/or expanding the service versus considering an alternative approach.

Evaluation Criteria

A slightly different emphasis in program evaluation is represented by Suchman's (1967) presentation of evaluation criteria. His levels of criteria represent considerations that the consultant may want to keep in mind both for individual case review as well as during an annual review of services. The evaluation criteria focus on effort, performance, adequacy, efficiency, and process. *Effort* refers to the quantity and quality of programmatic inputs such as the type

and magnitude of effort of staff, money expended, and the number and type of clients served. *Performance* refers to measurement of the consequences of effort, that is, outputs. This aspect of the evaluations requires a statement(s) of short- and long-term goals specific to consultees, clients, and programs. *Adequacy* considers the relationship between effort and performance relative to the needs that exist. *Efficiency* considers the ratio between effort and performance (output divided by input, if you will) in terms of cost factors such as money, time, personnel, and convenience. Finally, *process* criteria focus on the mechanisms by which effort is translated into outcome. The study of the means employed to produce results is involved in Suchman's view. Specifically, Suchman indicated that measurement of process should include the following four areas: (1) identification of key program components that determine its effectiveness; (2) analysis of the effectiveness of an intervention with different consultees or clients; (3) specification of organizational conditions associated with smooth functioning of the intervention; and (4) delineation of the range of effects attributable to the intervention along with the strength of those results.

Purposes of Evaluation

Another evaluation framework that can assist further in planning evaluations has been proposed by Perkins (1977) in his listing of six major purposes of evaluation. They include strategic, compliance, design logic, management, intervention effect, and program impact. *Strategic evaluation* is akin to a needs assessment and consequently takes place before the intervention. One of the goals of this data-collection activity is the identification of objectives. No comprehensive format has been proposed that can be used to assess the need for consultation (Schulberg & Jerrell, 1983), and consequently, attention should be paid to this issue when consultation services are instituted on a trial basis or if the services are scheduled for review. *Compliance* evaluation considers the "fit" or correlation between the objectives of a program and the system(s) of which it is an integral part. *Design logic* evaluations assess the degree to which assumptions are clear that link resources that are available for the intervention to outcome considerations. *Management* evaluations focus on the use of resources applied to reach the goals that have been identified. *Intervention* evaluations naturally attempt to assess the relationship of the intervention activity and the outcome, but may also consider the intervention process itself. *Program impact* evaluates the degree to which the intervention program achieved its goal(s). This last purpose is typically referred to as summative evaluation, while the other five purposes would be examples of evaluations that are formative in nature.

It should be remembered that consultants are responsible for at least two independent systems—their own and the consultee system. The individual consultant may be interested in improving his or her own skills and the eventual service, so feedback is considered to be a valuable asset in reaching that goal. Similarly, either as a means of justifying the service or extending it, data will be required. The consultee, by contrast, may have little need for information beyond the pragmatic one of "did it help." Their job performance may hinge on other demonstrated performance indices so that evaluation is seen as taking away from other important tasks and/or burdening an already overfilled schedule. Likewise, their training may have extolled the virtues of intervention while giving lip service to the idea of evaluation, let alone the notion that evaluation is an integral part of any intervention. A collaborative approach to evaluation based on principles of informed consent seems the most prudent course to follow. As Gallessich (1982) points out, when the consultant has some research purposes in mind or that become his or her primary role, these considerations need review from a collaborative perspective.

One final distinction needs to be made about evaluation approaches. The terms *cost–benefit* and *cost-effectiveness* are often thrown around when evaluations are conducted. A cost–benefit emphasis examines the relationship between input costs and outcome measures, usually in a ratio of dollars to dollars. Cost-effectiveness compares the dollar input with the results of the program. The latter then concentrates on the means of obtaining the results, while the former is outcome-oriented (Robinson, 1979).

Given the above array of evaluation options, it is advisable that the consultant first clearly identify why the evaluation is being proposed. Then a model of evaluation can be chosen that corresponds to those purposes. Priorities can be more easily established and a rationale developed for sharing data with the consultee and/or organizational management. To the extent possible within organizational, resource, and personal constraints, the consultant should plan as comprehensive an evaluation plan as can be realistically implemented.

STEPS IN CONSULTATION EVALUATION

As with any stage or step model, arbitrary demarcations are made. The model that is used here is based on the work of Paul (1979) and serves as one example of the type of formulation consultants should consider as the process of consultation unfolds. The steps include considerations of purpose, measurement, data-collection techniques, data collection, and dissemination. Again, it is advisable to introduce the notion and rationale for evaluation during contract negotiation, to resolve questions of when it will be done and who has access to the findings. The issues of anonymity and confidentiality need to be explored with the consultee.

Determine the purpose(s) of the evaluation. Determining the purpose(s) of the evaluation along the lines just discussed is important. To a large extent, this step relates to the need for process and outcome data. As was seen in the foregoing section, these purposes may be subdivided in numerous ways. In large measure this decision guides the subsequent steps of evaluation. Likewise, there may be information needs of the consultee or management that need to be taken into account. Their involvement during this time will be affected by such considerations.

Practical matters associated with evaluations must also be dealt with at this time. The extent to which consultees provide or gather the data affects their involvement at this point. The opportunity to make choices that will affect the time that needs to be devoted to evaluation as well as the types of information that are collected will contribute to ownership of the evaluation. Finally, the use of the data and access by others within the system should be an issue for the consultee as well as the consultant. Confidentiality should be addressed in a direct manner, and the consultant should be in a position personally and professionally vis-à-vis the consultee's employer to honor any commitments that are made. In the long run the cooperation that is experienced may be traced to this step.

Agree on measurements to be made. To the extent possible, process and product aspects of consultation have been addressed in the formulation of purposes or objectives. Measures that apply to both of these areas will have to be selected. These measures might also serve an educative objective for the consultant. The information that is included or required may sensitize the consultees to issues or perspectives they need to address in thinking about the problem. The bottom line in the selection of measures, however, is that they can be defended as relevant indices of the intervention objectives and other stated purposes.

Identify data-collection techniques. Paul describes this step as involving the selection of data-collection techniques appropriate to the purpose of the evaluation. "The major goal here is to place the measures in a context which allows for their interpretation" (Paul, 1979, p. 39). He presents a scheme that recommends the matching of purposes, criteria, and methodological tools of evaluation in a tabular form so that the relationship among the three considerations can be visually inspected. For Hylander (2004), the question of method is also secondary to the question of the research paradigm to be used. She points out that the three main research perspectives (methodology)—hypothetic-deductive, interpretive, and theory-generating—will yield very different information. Again, the use of different approaches, data, settings, will help address the complexity inherent in the consultation process.

Set a data-collection schedule. The actual points at which the data will be collected need to

be spelled out and agreed to by the participants. These decisions include who will be involved and whether their role will be collection of information from others, filling out forms themselves, or in some other way participating in data collection, and the summarizing/scoring of the information. Decisions about follow-up, particularly measurement of long-term effects, also need consideration.

Develop a dissemination plan. The disposition of the data that are collected needs to be decided on. That decision is dictated by the purposes of the evaluation, as well as other considerations such as confidentiality and with whom the data will remain. Data supplied to the consultee's supervisor could serve to reinforce some preconceived negative notions he or she holds or support merit review decisions. Such unintended consequences of data disseminations not only affect the eagerness and openness of the consultee toward future consultation contacts, but can also influence the attitudes of other potential consultees in the organization. Similarly, evaluation of the consultant sent directly to his or her supervisor can certainly protect the anonymity of the consultee, but leaves the consultant with no option to add information important to the interpretation of the data.

In addition to providing information on the process and outcome of consultation, dissemination can serve a number of other purposes. For example, it may be utilized to justify continuation of the consultation service. An organization or consultee may be willing to give indirect services a try, but both personal experience with consultation *and* data supporting the goals laid out for the service will be needed to convince those who have handled problems in a different way for years that change is beneficial. Data can also serve a public relations function. For example, a school-based psychological consultant may use the results (anonymously) obtained in a consultation to demonstrate some of the potential benefits of consultation.

USES OF EVALUATION DATA

We have been stressing the use of an evaluation scheme as a means of improving the service. The advantages to the consultant are immediate, and, providing the consultee expects such services to be available and utilized in the future, it should have some meaning to the consultee. A visible, tangible indication of the consultant's use of the data should contribute to the consultee's willingness to participate in and even support this aspect of the consultant's role. The most logical rationale introduced at the beginning of consultation will not overcome the need for such evidence to be supplied.

Beyond this immediate need, there is the very real need for the consultant to document the quantity and quality of consultative efforts. In addition to utilizing data from the type of instruments presented in this chapter, a follow-up schedule could be arranged for each consultation. For example, consultees are sent rating scales at two four-month intervals following the last consultation contact. Or all consultees (ongoing and terminated cases) receive an evaluation instrument at midyear and end of the year. This latter schedule permits the feedback to be collected in a way to ensure the consultee's anonymity. In one of the few reported examples of the use of data to demonstrate the utility of consultative techniques and support its gradual expansion, Zins (1981) collected information over a three-year period on time spent, usage, benefits to consultees, and ratings of consultative effectiveness. It seems reasonable to assume that until and unless consultants utilize a systematic evaluation plan, the chances for using consultation as a viable means of delivering services remain precarious.

Finally, consultants are in a position to influence the consultation knowledge base, either through a case study methodology or action research paradigm. It should be made clear that practitioners have an important role to play with regard to the use of such research approaches. It is only when they are involved in sharing their experiences with their colleagues in a systematic manner that progress will be made in this research area. In a sense, some of the very needs that support evaluation plans (e.g., impact of consultee characteristics on outcome; relation-

ship of intervention strategies) constitute basic questions for the researcher.

Goal Attainment Scaling: An Example of Outcome Evaluation

Goal attainment scaling (GAS) builds on the general tradition of goal-oriented evaluation. Although GAS has been used as an *outcome* measure, it does have the potential to be used as a monitoring device. One starts by setting a goal, then implementing a program, and finally collecting information about goal attainment. That information is then used to plan future inventions. Not only does it help organize and focus the intervention(s), but the goals also become clear to all involved and, as a result, may motivate everyone involved to reach the goals of the intervention. Originally developed to evaluate the progress of individual psychotherapy programs in mental health centers (Kiresuk & Sherman, 1968), GAS has been applied to counseling in schools (Maher & Borbrack, 1984) and educational applications with students, and it seems applicable to consultation encounters.

The uniqueness of GAS is that the target goals are placed in the center of a continuum of possible outcomes rather than posited as either attained or nonattained. Thus, the interviewers arrange their goals, or goal indicators as some have labeled them, along a discrete five-point scale continuum of "most unfavorable" and "less than expected" on the one end, the "expected outcome" in the middle, and the "more than expected" and "best anticipated" on the other end (Kiresuk & Lund, 1978). Second, GAS makes use of a quantitative score in which a weighted average of scores on each goal has been formulated (usually three to five goals are selected). Goals are then weighted in terms of importance from 1 to 99 (some authors suggest weights of 1–5). The goals are then scaled, as indicated above, by placing them along the continuum of the expected five levels of outcome, which also have been quantified by an outcome score of –2 to +2. A recent book by Kiresuk, Smith, and Cardillo (1994) is both a user-friendly manual and complete reference work on GAS.

INSTRUMENTATION

In their introduction to the special issue of *Professional Psychology,* on evaluation of psychological service delivery programs, Perloff and Perloff (1977) lament the nonexistence of a taxonomy and listing of questionnaires and instruments. They reason that such a classification would save time and money if evaluators could use already developed instruments and forms. If a number of consultants used the same instruments, then possibly reliable and valid information could be generated. More important, normative data would become available, that is, consultants would know the typical response to items or the typical answer given by certain consultee types. Such standardization would make utilization of the results generalizable. Indeed, such a list of instruments would be helpful in the consultation area because of the paucity of such information. Of course, further development of instrumentation is still to be encouraged.

An initial step has been taken here to identify existing scales that might be considered (see the appendices at the end of this chapter). Some of these instruments have been designed with specific purposes in mind. Nevertheless, with some changes and/or in combination with other scales or sections of scales, they may prove more useful to consultants. If their only use is to serve as an impetus for development of other scales, the effort has been well spent. In addition, readers of this text are encouraged to develop their own instruments to ensure relevance for their practice or their organization's service.

The scales are especially recommended to students in training as one way to systematically pursue a self-assessment of their development as consultants. Appendix B presents a feedback mechanism by stages of consultation rather than by session; the consultee is asked to review the entire consultation when providing feedback. The reader is reminded that Appendix C refers to the Friedman interview described under the "process" section of this chapter; ratings of the consultee under the five interview categories should then be compared to

Table 11.2 to ascertain the style of the consultee as perceived by the consultant. Appendix I is generally identified by students in consultation classes as very helpful in obtaining overall feedback from consultees. Finally, "consultants" have used these scales, or adaptations of these scales, as part of their self-assessment and in peer consultation situations.

Essentially, paper-and-pencil tasks such as questionnaires and surveys are presented. The use of data from observations and tapes (video and audio) are not ruled out; in fact, they are encouraged. However, these data-generating sources (types) have been used primarily in research on consultation. Observations present a challenge because they require an observer who is trained; some obvious cost in actual payment or loss in manpower time is also involved. Taping can be as expensive or more so than the use of observers, particularly if consultants must provide their own equipment. Both strategies require the permission of the consultee, and it may be argued that they serve to inhibit communication. Nevertheless, both observation and taping should be seriously considered and utilized, if not routinely in all evaluations, then at least on a periodic basis. The value to the consultant would be immeasurable as a self-evaluation device or peer review type approach.

Beyond the consideration of using an already existing instrument versus one that exists in the literature, the consultant needs to consider matching the evaluation methodology to the objectives of the plan. The idea of fitting one's instrumentation/methodology to the purpose of the evaluation seems like a rather simple one. Yet, it is one rule that is likely to cause confusion and even interfere with the consultation process if not followed. It makes little sense to employ an elaborate design and complicated methodology if rather simple, straightforward questions are being proposed. Conversely, comprehensive and specific purposes will require an array of measurement strategies. Finally, the model of consultation and theoretical orientation of the consultant may also dictate the evaluation format that is used.

What follows then, in the appendices, are examples of proposed scales arranged by stage of consultation, that is, entry, implementation, and termination. The scales could be categorized as process or outcome measures, but it seemed logical to emphasize the concept of an ongoing evaluation approach to consultation. The emphasis in this book is on dyadic consultation and, consequently, that is the focus of each instrument. Also, for consulting teachers, Dettmar, Dyck, and Thurston (1999) have presented a consultee assessment scale and checklist for evaluating collaborative consultation along with a checklist that can be used to evaluate a consultation session. For information on organizational consultation instrumentation, the reader is referred to Cooper and O'Connor (1993).

SUMMARY

Consultants who are concerned about improving their service will develop an ongoing evaluation that looks not only at outcomes but also at the process. Many criteria may be used to look at the outcomes of consultation, ranging from behavioral indicators of client and consultee change to consultee satisfaction. Formative evaluation may focus on variables such as the quality of the individual consulting relationship, the expertise of the consultant, the match between the consultant's and consultee's expectations, and so forth. Perhaps the most important point made in this chapter is that evaluation requires careful planning or it will not yield useful information. Consultants must first determine the purpose(s) of the evaluation, then devise a set of strategies for attaining those purposes.

TIPS FOR THE PRACTITIONER

1. Familiarize yourself with the various approaches and instruments in this chapter. Select a strategy to evaluate the processes and outcomes of your next consultation.

2. Audiotape consultation session(s) for playback and general review and/or to improve skills or functioning during certain stages of consultation.
3. Arrange for peer consultation on audiotapes with a colleague.
4. Ask consultees for preferred manner of providing feedback on your "consultative" services.

REVIEW QUESTIONS

1. Describe a comprehensive model of evaluation. Include the types of questions that could be addressed by a consultant.
2. What are some similarities and differences between evaluation and research?
3. Identify three guidelines that consultants should consider in planning an evaluation of their consultation.
4. Describe two different types of consultation outcome measures.
5. How does the traditional case study approach compare to a time-series methodology?

REFERENCES

Anserello, C., & Sweet, T. (1990). Integrating consultation into school psychological services. In E. Cole & J. A. Siegel (Eds.), *Effective consultation in school psychology* (pp. 173–199). Toronto: Hogrefe & Huber.

Attkisson, C. C., & Broskowski, A. (1978). Evaluation and the emerging human service concept. In C. C. Attkisson, W. A. Hargreaves, M. J. Horowitz, & J. E. Sorensen (Eds.), *Evaluation of human service programs* (pp. 3–26). New York: Academic Press.

Babcock, N. L., & Pryzwansky, W. B. (1983). Models of consultation: Preferences of educational professionals at five stages of service. *Journal of School Psychology, 21,* 359–366.

Barlow, D. H., Hayes, S. C., & Nelson, R. O. (1984). *The scientist practitioner.* New York: Pergamon Press.

Bergan, T. R., & Kratochwill, T. R. (1990). *Behavioral consultation and therapy.* New York: Plenum Press.

Brown, D., Wyne, M. D., Blackburn, J. E., & Powell, W. C. (1979). *Consultation.* Boston: Allyn & Bacon.

Caplan, G. (1970). *The Theory of Practice and Mental Health Consultation.* New York: Basic Books.

Conoley, J. C., & Conoley, C. W. (1982). *School consultation.* New York: Pergamon Press.

Cooper, S. E., & O'Connor, R. M., Jr. (1993). Standards for organizational consultation assessment and evaluation instruments. *Journal of Counseling and Development, 71,* 651–660.

Curtis, M. J., & Anderson, T. (1975). *Consultant observational assessment form.* Cincinnati, OH: University of Cincinnati, Department of Special Education and School Psychology.

Dettmar, P., Dyck, N., & Thurston, L. P. (1999). *Consultation, collaboration and team work for students with special needs.* Boston: Allyn & Bacon.

Friedman, L. P. (1977). Teacher consultation styles: A theoretical model for increasing consultation process effectiveness (Doctoral dissertation, University of Pennsylvania, 1976). *Dissertation Abstracts International, 37,* 2074A.

Gallessich, J. (1973). Organizational factors influencing consultation. *Journal of School Psychology, 11,* 57–65.

Gallessich, J. (1982). *The profession and practice of consultation.* San Francisco: Jossey-Bass.

Guiva, G. (2004). How to respond to teachers who ask for help but not consultation. In N. H. Lambert, I. Hylander, & J. H. Sandoval (Eds.), *Consultee-centered consultation* (pp. 255–264). Mahwah, NJ: Erlbaum.

Halpin, A., & Croft, D. (1963). *The organizational climate of schools.* Chicago: Midwest Administration Center, University of Chicago.

Hylander, I. (2004). Identifying change in consultee-centered consultation. In N. M. Lambert, I. Hylander, & J. H. Sandoval (Eds.). *Consultee-centered consultation* (pp. 373–389). Mahwah, NJ: Erlbaum.

Kiresuk, T. J., & Lund, S. H. (1978). Goal attainment scaling. In C. C. Attkisson, W. A. Hargreaves, M. J. Horowitz, & J. E. Sorensen (Eds.), *Evaluation of human service programs* (pp. 341–370). New York: Academic Press.

Kiresuk, T. J., & Sherman, R. E. (1968). Goal attainment scaling: A general method for evaluating community mental health programs. *Community Mental Health Journal, 4,* 443–453.

Kiresuk, T. J., Smith, A., & Cardillo, J. E. (Eds.). (1994). *Goal attainment scaling: Applications, theory and measurement.* Hillsdale, NJ: L. Erlbaum Associates.

Lambert, N. M. (1993). Historical perspective on school psychology as a scientist-practitioner specialization in school psychology. *Journal of School Psychology, 31,* 163–193.

Maher, C. A., & Borbrack, C. R. (1984). Evaluating the individual counseling of conduct problem adolescents: The goal attainment scaling method. *Journal of School Psychology, 22,* 285–297.

Meade, C. J., Hamilton, M. K., & Yuen, R. K. W. (1982). Consultation research: The time has come the walrus said. *The Counseling Psychologist, 10*(4), 39–51.

Merriam, S. B. (1988). *Case study research in education.* San Francisco: Jossey-Bass.

Meyers, J., Parsons, R. D., & Martin, R. (1979). *Mental health consultation in the schools.* San Francisco: Jossey-Bass.

Mischley, M. (1973). *Teacher preferences for consultation methods and its relationship to selected background, personality and organizational variables.* Unpublished doctoral dissertation, University of Texas at Austin.

Parsons, R. D., & Meyers, J. (1984). *Developing consultation skills.* San Francisco: Jossey-Bass.

Partanen, P., & Winstrom, C. (2004). Promoting student learning by consultee-centered consultation with a Vygotskian framework. In N. H. Lambert, I. Hylander, & J. H. Sandoval (Eds.), *Consultee-centered consultation* (pp. 313–389). Mahwah, NJ: Erlbaum.

Paul, S. C. (1979). Consultation evaluation: Turning a circus into a performance. In M. K. Hamilton & C. J. Meade (Eds.), *Consulting on campus: New directions for student services* (pp. 33–46). San Francisco: Jossey-Bass.

Perkins, N. T. (1977). Evaluating social interventions: A conceptual schema. *Evaluation Quarterly, 1,* 639–656.

Perloff, R., & Perloff, E. (1977). Evaluation of psychological service delivery programs: The state of the art. *Professional Psychology, 8*(4), 379–388.

Pryzwansky, W. B. (1989). *Consulting diary.*

Pryzwansky, W. B., & Noblit, G. W. (1990). Understanding and improving consultation practice: The qualitative case study. *Journal of Educational and Psychological Consultation, 1*(4), 293–307.

Robinson, S. E. (1979). Evaluation research: An approach for researching applied programs. *Improving Human Performance Quarterly, 8*(4), 259–267.

Sandoval, J. H. (2004). Evaluating issues and strategies in consultee-centered consultation. In N. M. Lambert, I. Hylander, & J. H. Sandoval (Eds.). *Consultee-*

centered consultation (pp. 391–400). Mahwah, NJ: Erlbaum.

Schulberg, H. C., & Jerrell, J. M. (1983). Consultation. In M. Herson, A. E. Kazdin, & A. S. Bellack (Eds.), *The clinical psychology handbook* (pp. 783–798). New York: Pergamon Press.

Scriven, M. (1967). The methodology of evaluation. In R. Tyler, R. Gagne, & M. Scriven (Eds.), *Perspectives of curriculum evaluation* (AERA Monograph Series on Curriculum Evaluation) (pp. 39–83). Chicago: Rand McNally.

Suchman, E. A. (1967). *Evaluative research: Principles and practices in public service and social action programs.* New York: Russell Sage Foundation.

Zins, J. E. (1981). Using data-based evaluation in developing school consultation services. In M. J. Curtis & J. E. Zins (Eds.), *The theory and practice of school consultation* (pp. 261–268). Springfield, IL: Charles C. Thomas.

APPENDIX A   Consultation Preference Scale
___

INSTRUCTIONS: Assume you will be consulting with a _____ concerning a _____. Below are twenty statements relating to your consultation. Please rate each statement by circling the number below it which best indicates your agreement with its content.

CODE   ITEM
___

C1   1. The goal of the consultant should be to work with me to identify the problem, to plan and to carry out recommendations.

1	2	3	4	5
strongly disagree	disagree	neutral	agree	strongly agree

C2   2. The consultant and I should both identify the problem based on information we have collected.

1	2	3	4	5
strongly disagree	disagree	neutral	agree	strongly agree

MH3   3. I should plan the recommendations with the consultant offering suggestions.

1	2	3	4	5
strongly disagree	disagree	neutral	agree	strongly agree

CL4   4. I should implement the recommendations that the consultant has developed.

1	2	3	4	5
strongly disagree	disagree	neutral	agree	strongly agree

MH5   5. Further consultation should be initiated only at my request.

1	2	3	4	5
strongly disagree	disagree	neutral	agree	strongly agree

E1   6. The goal of the consultant should be to plan and carry out recommendations after I have identified the problem.

1	2	3	4	5
strongly disagree	disagree	neutral	agree	strongly agree

CL2   7. The consultant should identify the problem based on information he or she collects.

1	2	3	4	5
strongly disagree	disagree	neutral	agree	strongly agree

E3   8. The consultant should plan the recommendations that he or she will then implement.

1	2	3	4	5
strongly disagree	disagree	neutral	agree	strongly agree

C4   9. The consultant and I may each implement some of the recommendations.

1	2	3	4	5
strongly disagree	disagree	neutral	agree	strongly agree

CL5   10. It should be the role of the consultant to offer me any further advice.

1	2	3	4	5
strongly disagree	disagree	neutral	agree	strongly agree

Continued

APPENDIX A *Continued*

CODE	ITEM
CL1	11. The goal of the consultant should be to identify the problem and develop recommendations that I will then carry out.

1	2	3	4	5
strongly disagree	disagree	neutral	agree	strongly agree

E2	12. I should be the one to identify the problem based on the information I collect.

1	2	3	4	5
strongly disagree	disagree	neutral	agree	strongly agree

C3	13. The consultant and I should both suggest recommendations that we will both then implement.

1	2	3	4	5
strongly disagree	disagree	neutral	agree	strongly agree

MH4	14. I should be the one to implement the recommendations that I develop.

1	2	3	4	5
strongly disagree	disagree	neutral	agree	strongly agree

E5	15. There should probably be no follow-up consultation after the recommendations have been implemented.

1	2	3	4	5
strongly disagree	disagree	neutral	agree	strongly agree

MH1	16. The goal of the consultant should be to increase my ability to deal with similar problems in the future.

1	2	3	4	5
strongly disagree	disagree	neutral	agree	strongly agree

MH2	17. The consultant should help me identify the problem by clarifying my perceptions of it.

1	2	3	4	5
strongly disagree	disagree	neutral	agree	strongly agree

CL3	18. The consultant should suggest recommendations that I will then implement.

1	2	3	4	5
strongly disagree	disagree	neutral	agree	strongly agree

E4	19. The consultant should implement the recommendations that he or she develops.

1	2	3	4	5
strongly disagree	disagree	neutral	agree	strongly agree

C5	20. The consultant and I should engage in continuous follow-up to modify the intervention recommendations, if necessary.

1	2	3	4	5
strongly disagree	disagree	neutral	agree	strongly agree

From "Models of Consultations" by N. Babcock and W. Pryzwansky, from the *Journal of School Psychology* (1983) *21*, 359–366.

APPENDIX B   Formative Evaluation Checklist

DIRECTIONS: For each stage of the consultation process, feedback and request for corrective feedback from
institutional representatives and consultees are both appropriate and desirable. The checklist
provides a broad framework from which to conceptualize the specific formative function to be
used within your particular consultation relationship.

Name of Institution _____ Name of Consultee _____ Date of Initial Contact _____

Formative Issue	Consultation Stage				
	Entry	Goal Identification	Goal Definition	Intervention	Assessment
1. Record of contacts (record dates, length of sessions)					
2. Special focus of contacts; concerns emerging for later consideration					
3. Provide feedback to highest relevant administrator (acceptable direction, time line, cost tone)					
4. Request feedback from consultee: Expectations met? Specific concerns? New needs? Suggestions for modification of program? Consultant style? Or administrative details (meeting times, rooms, etc.)					
5. Stage-specific concerns	All relevant personnel contacted? Collaborative atmosphere? Relationship skills?	Agreement on level of entry? Optimal entry point? Possible recontact?	Consultee's skill, cooperation; facility in data gathering-reporting? Data complete?	Feedback to consultee on joint ownership? Consultee accept? Agree? Understand? Modifications? Joint agreement?	Outcomes? Inputs? Process? Design? Decision options? Assessment as collaborative effort?
6. Counselor's perception of process to date— new paths tried					

From *Developing Consultation Skills* by R. D. Parsons and J. Meyers. Copyright © 1984 by Jossey-Bass. Reprinted by permission of the publisher.

APPENDIX C   Consultation Behavior Categories and Criteria

I. Consultee Information-Reporting Behaviors

  1. *Quantity of information reported:* This category allows the consultant to focus on the extensiveness of the teacher's available fund of observations. The following behavioral criteria are used in detailing observations:

  1a. The teacher reports a limited amount of information, narrow in range, and restricted to a few aspects of the problem.

  1b. The teacher reports a wide range of information about many different aspects of the problem.

  1c. The teacher reports an extensive amount of information about a few aspects of the problem.

  1d. The teacher has used several sources of information to collect data about the problem.

  1e. The teacher has used a few sources of information to collect data about the problem.

  2. *Quality of information reported:* This category refers to differences in the quality of information reported by teachers. The following criteria are used:

  2a. The teacher's information is specific.

  2b. The teacher's information is vague.

  2c. The teacher's information is detailed.

  2d. The teacher's information is general.

  2e. The teacher primarily reports information obtained from observation of the external environment.

  2f. The teacher primarily reports information obtained from observations of his or her own feelings, thoughts, and personal reactions to the problem situation.

  2g. The teacher's information is selective and organized according to some personal hierarchy of relative importance.

  2h. The teacher's information is unorganized and does not reflect the use of any personal hierarchy of relative importance.

  2i. In response to consultation questions or comments, the teacher voluntarily offers primarily negative information about the problem situation.

  2j. In response to consultant questions or comments, the teacher voluntarily offers primarily positive information about the problem.

  2k. In response to consultant questions or comments, the teacher voluntarily offers both negative and positive information about the problem.

  2l. In response to consultant questions or comments, the teacher does not volunteer additional positive or negative information.

II. Consultee Resistance-Cooperation Behaviors

  3. *Extent of participation in problem solving:* This category refers to the extent to which the teacher displays a willingness to cooperate as an equal status problem-solving partner during the consultation interview and the degree to which the teacher exhibits commitment to problem-solving activities.

  3a. The teacher limits responses to answering the specific question asked.

  3b. The teacher answers questions and voluntarily elaborates, broadening the range of problem solving.

  3c. The teacher asks questions or requests information about the problem.

  3d. The teacher does not actively seek clarifying information about the problem.

  3e. The teacher avoids certain problem-solving activities.

  3f. The teacher engages in all three problem-solving activities.

  3g. The teacher demonstrates receptivity toward recommendations offered.

  3h. The teacher rejects or refuses recommendations offered.

Continued

3i. The teacher restricts feedback about recommendations offered.

4. *Maintenance of the interview focus:* This category refers to those teacher verbal behaviors that either facilitate, impede, or have neutral effects on the consultant's attempts to structure the interview in an orderly sequence and maintain a problem-centered focus.

4a. Teacher responses to consultant questions or comments are relevant to the focus of the problem-solving discussion and enhance the orderly progression of the interview.

4b. Teacher responses to consultant questions or comments are relevant to the focus of the problem-solving discussion, but do not enhance the progression of the interview.

4c. Teacher responses to consultant questions or comments are irrelevant or tangential to the focus of the problem-solving discussion and impede the orderly progression of the interview.

4d. The teacher answers consultant questions, but in so doing changes the focus of the interview.

4e. The teacher answers consultant questions, but maintains the focus of the interview.

4f. The teacher interrupts problem-solving activities to discuss his or her own personal and/or professional concerns, changing the problem-centered focus of the interview.

4g. The teacher sustains problem-solving activities and introduces additional personal and/or professional concerns at appropriate intervals without changing the problem-centered focus of the interview.

4h. Consultant questions or comments elicit the teacher's negative affective involvement (in varying degrees of intensity) with the problem, which disrupts the maintenance of a problem-centered focus.

4i. Consultant questions or comments elicit the teacher's positive affective involvement (in varying degrees of intensity), which maintains the problem-centered focus.

4j. Consultant questions or comments elicit the teacher's neutral affective involvement, which maintains the problem-centered focus.

5. *Consultee influence attempts:* This category refers to those verbal behaviors that reflect the teacher's attempts to actively influence the consultant's perceptions of the problem situation in a positive or negative direction. They thus reflect the way in which teachers use information available to exert influence over the consultant's perceptions or interview behavior. It should be noted that four of the criteria presented under this category (5g; 5h; 5i; 5j) were also used to delineate certain consultant information-reporting behaviors (2i; 2j; 2k; 2l). They are included here because they also allow the consultant to observe how a specific type of information may be used by the teacher to facilitate or impede problem-solving efforts.

5a. From the outset of the problem-solving interview, the teacher offers a diagnosis and solution that limit any further exploratory problem-solving activities.

5b. The teacher suspends judgment about the diagnosis and solution and engages in exploratory problem-solving efforts.

5c. The teacher seeks confirmation of the validity of his or her perceptions of the problem situation.

5d. The teacher adheres to his or her perception of the problem situation despite the introduction of alternative explanations.

5e. The teacher is receptive to additional information or alternative explanations and considers them within the framework of his or her professional experience.

5f. The teacher does not clearly articulate his or her perceptions of the problem and both seeks and willingly accepts the consultant's "expert" interpretation.

5g. In response to consultant questions or comments, the teacher voluntarily offers negative information about the problem situation.

5h. In response to consultant questions or comments, the teacher voluntarily offers primarily positive information about the problem.

Continued

APPENDIX C   *Continued*

5i. In response to consultant questions or comments, the teacher voluntarily offers both negative and positive information about the problem.

5j. In response to consultant questions or comments, the teacher does not volunteer additional positive or negative information.

5k. In response to consultant questions, the teacher introduces additional information not sought by the consultant and irrelevant to the discussion in progress.

5l. In response to consultant questions, the teacher introduces additional information not sought by the consultant and relevant to the discussion in progress.

From Friedman, L. P. Reprinted with permission.

APPENDIX D Consultee Satisfaction Form

INSTRUCTIONS: For each statement listed, check the most appropriate response as it applies to the current consultative interaction. Your response is viewed as extremely important to the ongoing improvement and facilitation of the consultation program and to the consultant's professional growth. Thank you for your assistance.

	1	2	3	4
	Strongly Agree	Agree	Disagree	Strongly Disagree

I. Efficacy of Consultation
　1. The goal definition was accurate, complete, and sufficiently concrete.
　2. The data-gathering procedures provided the necessary data.
　3. The intervention plan makes sense for my unique situation.
　4. The intervention plan has been easy enough to implement.
　5. The intervention plan has been effective to this point.

II. Consultant Expertise
　1. The consultant knows his or her "stuff."
　2. The consultant is apparently versed in not only the subject matter, but also the process of helping others.
　3. The consultant presents information and directions clearly.

III. Consultant's Administrative Abilities
　1. The consultant makes efficient use of time.
　2. The consultant is prompt in providing feedback.
　3. The consultant has efficiently distributed work assignments.

IV. Interpersonal Style
　1. The consultant is comfortable to talk with.
　2. The consultant is a good listener.
　3. The consultant is generally pleasant.
　4. The consultant is self-expressive without being overpowering.
　5. The consultant has encouraged me to be an active participant in the consulting process.

V. General Comments (regarding your likes, dislikes, recommendations for improving this and future consultations)

From *Developing Consultation Skills* by R. D. Parsons and J. Meyers. Copyright © 1984 by Jossey-Bass. Reprinted by permission of the publisher.

APPENDIX E   Questionnaire Following Each Session

1. The consultant helped me to identify what the problems were today.

   strongly disagree   disagree   unsure   agree   strongly agree

2. The consultant helped me to understand the problems better.

   strongly disagree   disagree   unsure   agree   strongly agree

3. The consultant seemed to understand what I meant when I said something.

   strongly disagree   disagree   unsure   agree   strongly agree

4. The consultant helped me to better understand what I was feeling.

   strongly disagree   disagree   unsure   agree   strongly agree

5. If the consultant did help you to understand the problem(s), did he or she do this by (check as many as apply):

   _____ sharing a similar problem he or she had
   _____ telling you about problems other teachers have had
   _____ talking about problems children have had

6. The consultant restated the problem for me in words I could understand.

   strongly disagree   disagree   unsure   agree   strongly agree

7. How often during the meeting did you feel that the consultant let you decide what you wanted to do?

   never   rarely   occasionally   usually   always

8. How often did both you and the consultant work together to discuss the problems you brought up?

   never   rarely   occasionally   usually   always

9. I think the consultant was sensitive to the problems we talked about today.

   strongly disagree   disagree   unsure   agree   strongly agree

10. I like the consultant's style in relating to me.

    strongly disagree   disagree   unsure   agree   strongly agree

11. Did something the consultant say or do affect any of your opinions or behavior?

    not at all   not very much   somewhat   very much   drastically

    a. If it did, what was it the consultant said or did?
    b. How did you respond to what the consultant said or did?

12. Overall, I feel very satisfied with what happened in today's session with the consultant.

    strongly disagree   disagree   unsure   agree   strongly agree

13. Is there anything that you would like to discuss in your consultation meeting next week as a result of today's session?

    Yes   No   If yes, can you be more specific about what it is that you would like to talk about?

APPENDIX F Open-Ended Consultation Evaluation Form

1. Compared with other teachers at your school would you say your contacts with the consultant were:

   considerably fewer
   fewer
   average
   more
   considerably more

2. With what aspect of the consultation have you been happiest last semester? least happy?

3. What would you like to see changed this semester?

4. How might the consultant be more available to you this semester?

5. What comments or suggestions do you have specifically about the consultant's work this past semester?

6. Based on the things the consultant did this past semester, how would *you* define the role of consultant?

7. Based on your experience with mental health consultation this year, you feel that mental health consultation is:

Extremely helpful						Not at all helpful
7	6	5	4	3	2	1

From J. Conoley and C. Conoley, *School Consultation.* Copyright © 1982. All rights reserved. Reprinted by permission of Allyn & Bacon.

APPENDIX G   Consultation Evaluation Survey

Your organization _____ Date_____

Consultant's name _____

Number of years you have worked in this type of organization _____

Sex (circle one):   Male   Female

Have you had previous experience with consultants?
Yes   No

To what extent have you made use of the consultant this year?
_____ Not at all
_____ Very little, 1 or 2 times
_____ To a moderate extent, about 3 to 6 times
_____ To a considerable extent, about 6 to 10 times
_____ To a great extent, more than 10 times

In general, how helpful has the consultation been to you? (Circle the number that is most descriptive.)
Not at all   1   2   3   4   5   6   7   Very helpful

Did you work with the consultant in a group situation?
Yes   No

Did you work with the consultant on an individual basis?
Yes   No

Please respond to the following items by circling the number that best describes your perception of your consultant. Response options range from 1 (not at all descriptive) to 7 (very descriptive). If an item does not seem applicable to your consultant, circle N.A.

The consultant:

1. Offers useful information.	1	2	3	4	5	6	7	N.A.
2. Understands my working environment.	1	2	3	4	5	6	7	N.A.
3. Presses his or her ideas and solutions.	1	2	3	4	5	6	7	N.A.
4. Is skilled in forming good working relationships.	1	2	3	4	5	6	7	N.A.
5. Is a good listener.	1	2	3	4	5	6	7	N.A.
6. Helps me find alternative solutions to problems.	1	2	3	4	5	6	7	N.A.
7. Increases my self-confidence.	1	2	3	4	5	6	7	N.A.
8. Helps me identify resources to use in problem solving.	1	2	3	4	5	6	7	N.A.
9. Is not concerned with my point of view.	1	2	3	4	5	6	7	N.A.
10. Encourages me to make my own decisions.	1	2	3	4	5	6	7	N.A.
11. Helps me find ways to apply content of our discussions to specific situations.	1	2	3	4	5	6	7	N.A.
12. Respects values that are different from his or hers.	1	2	3	4	5	6	7	N.A.

Continued

13. Fits easily into our work setting.	1	2	3	4	5	6	7	N.A.
14. Stimulates me to see situations in more complex ways.	1	2	3	4	5	6	7	N.A.
15. Relies on one approach to solving problems.	1	2	3	4	5	6	7	N.A.
16. Explains his or her ideas clearly.	1	2	3	4	5	6	7	N.A.
17. Has difficulty understanding my concerns.	1	2	3	4	5	6	7	N.A.
18. Encourages me to try a variety of interventions.	1	2	3	4	5	6	7	N.A.
19. Helps me in ways consistent with my own needs.	1	2	3	4	5	6	7	N.A.
20. Encourages communication between me and others with whom I work.	1	2	3	4	5	6	7	N.A.
21. Increases my understanding of basic psychological principles.	1	2	3	4	5	6	7	N.A.
22. Makes helpful suggestions.	1	2	3	4	5	6	7	N.A.
23. Does not appreciate the pressures of my job.	1	2	3	4	5	6	7	N.A.
24. Makes me feel comfortable in discussing sensitive problems.	1	2	3	4	5	6	7	N.A.
25. Encourages our work group to cooperate.	1	2	3	4	5	6	7	N.A.
26. Supports my efforts to solve problems.	1	2	3	4	5	6	7	N.A.
27. Has knowledge relevant to my work.	1	2	3	4	5	6	7	N.A.
28. Helps me understand myself better.	1	2	3	4	5	6	7	N.A.
29. Helps me develop a wider range of problem-solving skills.	1	2	3	4	5	6	7	N.A.
30. Rushes into premature solutions.	1	2	3	4	5	6	7	N.A.
31. Is sensitive to my feelings.	1	2	3	4	5	6	7	N.A.
32. Helps me to see my situation more objectively.	1	2	3	4	5	6	7	N.A.
33. Knows how and when to ask good questions.	1	2	3	4	5	6	7	N.A.
34. Is reliable about appointments.	1	2	3	4	5	6	7	N.A.

This consultant will be consulting in the future. What suggestions do you have to help him or her improve in consultation skills? Remember, this information will NOT be used for grading: It will be extremely helpful to your consultant as feedback.

What did you like most about his or her work?
What did you like least about his or her work?
If you did not use this consultant, why not?

From *The Profession and Practice of Consultation* by J. Gallessich. Copyright © 1982 by Jossey-Bass. Reprinted by permission of the publisher.

APPENDIX H   Consultant Observational Assessment Form (COAF)

Observer's Name _____

Consultant (or Session Number) _____

Date _____

ON EACH OF THE FOLLOWING DIMENSIONS, PLEASE *CIRCLE* THE NUMBER THAT *BEST* REFLECTS YOUR ASSESSMENT OF THE CONSULTANT'S FUNCTIONING ON THAT SPECIFIC DIMENSION.

1. *Expert–Facilitator*
   How would you assess the consultant's role during the session?
   (Expert)   1   2   3   4   5   (Facilitator)

2. *Relationship*
   How would you assess the consultee's role during the session?
   (Subordinate)   1   2   3   4   5   (Colleague)

3. *Value*
   To what extent did the consultant seem to try to impose his or her values on the consultee?
   (Not at all)   1   2   3   4   5   (Great extent)

4. *Empathy*
   To what extent did the consultant seem to empathize with the consultee?
   (Not at all)   1   2   3   4   5   (Great extent)

5. *Support*
   How much moral support did the consultant seem to provide for the consultee? (Support does not connote agreement.)
   (None at all)   1   2   3   4   5   (Great deal)

6. *Interest (Nonverbal)*
   How much interest did the consultant seem to express in the concerns of the consultee (nonverbally)?
   (None at all)   1   2   3   4   5   (Great deal)

7. *Interest (Verbal)*
   How much interest did the consultant seem to express in the concerns of the consultee (verbally)?
   (None at all)   1   2   3   4   5   (Great deal)

8. *Trust*
   To what extent was the consultant able to create an atmosphere of trust and acceptance?
   (Not at all)   1   2   3   4   5   (Great extent)

9. *Ventilation*
   How would you assess the consultant's allowance of ventilation by the consultee?
   (Far too much   1   2   3   4   5   (Optimal
   or far too little)   amount)
   If rated 1, 2, or 3, was the ventilation allowed _____ too much or _____ too little?

Continued

10. *Data Generation*

How much relevant information was the consultant able to draw out?

(None at all)   1   2   3   4   5   (Great deal)

11. *Follow Through*

To what extent did the consultant seem to pursue or follow up on key comments by the consultee?

(Never)   1   2   3   4   5   (Always)

12. *Questioning*

How would you assess the overall effectiveness of the consultant's questioning techniques?

(Not at all)   1   2   3   4   5   (Very effective)

13. *Summarization*

How effectively did the consultant summarize what had transpired?

(Not at all)   1   2   3   4   5   (Very effectively)

14. *Thought Clarification*

To what extent did the consultant clarify his or her understanding of consultee statements?

(Not at all)   1   2   3   4   5   (Great extent)

15. *Problem Clarification*

How effective was the consultant in clarifying the problem?

(Not at all)   1   2   3   4   5   (Very effective)

Did the consultant attempt to develop a solution before the problem had been thoroughly clarified?

_____ Yes   _____ No

16. *Strategy Generation*

To what extent were strategies developed for solving the problem in focus?

(Not at all)   1   2   3   4   5   (Thoroughly developed)

17. *Responsibility*

To what extent did the consultant leave the responsibility for selection and pursuit of a problem-solving strategy with the consultee?

(Not at all)   1   2   3   4   5   (Totally)

_____ Not applicable

18. *Follow-Up*

To what extent did the consultant leave the responsibility for follow-up or evaluation with the consultee?

(Not at all)   1   2   3   4   5   (Totally)

_____ Not applicable

19. *Evaluator*

How evaluative did the consultant seem to be of the consultee or his or her ideas?

(Not at all)   1   2   3   4   5   (Great deal)

Continued

APPENDIX H   *Continued*

---

20. *Consultee Feelings*

To what extent did the consultant delve into the feelings of the consultee?

(Too deeply)   1   2   3   4   5   (Only so far as
(Not enough)   necessary for rapport)

If rated 1, 2, or 3, indicate

_____ too deeply

_____ not enough

21. *Threat*

How much threat did the consultant's behavior pose to the consultee?

(Very   (Not at all
threatening)   1   2   3   4   5   threatening)

Please identify any specific behaviors that you would consider to be threatening to the consultee.

What types of questions asked by the consultant, if any, would you consider to be threatening to the consultee?

22. *General Effectiveness*

How would you rate the overall effectiveness of this consultant?

(Low)   1   2   3   4   5   (High)

23. *Consultee*

As a consultee, how willing would you be to use this individual as a mental health consultant?

(Not at all)   1   2   3   4   5   (Very)

                                                            TOTAL SCORE:

ADDITIONAL COMMENTS

From *Consultant Observational Assessment Form* by M. J. Curtis and T. Anderson. (1975). University of Cincinnati. Department of Special Education and School Psychology. Reprinted by permission.

APPENDIX I   Consultee Benefits

Secondary Outcome: Objectivity

1. I am better able to understand my students.
   Yes_____No_____Unclear_____
2. I have gained a new perspective regarding student behavior.
   Yes_____No_____Unclear_____
3. My biases no longer are the determining factor in the way I deal with students.
   Yes_____No_____Unclear_____

Secondary Outcome: Problem Solving

1. I am better able to establish priorities.
   Yes_____No_____Unclear_____
2. I now use a more systematic approach to problem solving.
   Yes_____No_____Unclear_____
3. I can say with some certainty that I am a better decision maker.
   Yes_____No_____Unclear_____

Secondary Outcome: Role Competency

1. I am a better teacher (parent, administrator, etc.).
   Yes_____No_____Unclear_____
2. I feel more confident about my ability as a teacher (parent, administrator, etc.).
   Yes_____No_____Unclear_____
3. I can deal more effectively with my classroom (home, school) situation.
   Yes_____No_____Unclear_____

Secondary Outcome: Understanding Human Behavior

1. I have gained greater understanding of the principles of human functioning.
   Yes_____No_____Unclear_____
2. I feel confident that independently of the consultant I can utilize the principles that I have learned.
   Yes_____No_____Unclear_____

Secondary Outcome: Facilitating Human Development

1. I am better able to design approaches that will be helpful to my students.
   Yes_____No_____Unclear_____
2. I have developed new approaches to students that will facilitate their overall development.
   Yes_____No_____Unclear_____
3. I feel confident that I can develop interventions (may specify) for students in the future.
   Yes_____No_____Unclear_____

From *Consultation* by D. Brown et al. (1979). Boston: Allyn and Bacon. Reprinted by permission.

CHAPTER 12

ETHICAL AND LEGAL CONSIDERATIONS

GOAL OF THE CHAPTER

The goal of this chapter is to discuss the ethical and legal issues that relate to the consultation process.

CHAPTER PREVIEW

1. The purposes of codes of ethics are discussed.
2. Six major ethical principles are presented and discussed. These concern the competence of the consultant, protecting the welfare of the client, confidentiality, public statements, ethical and moral issues, and relationships to other consultants.
3. The process to be followed in enforcing ethical standards is presented.
4. Legal issues relating to consultation are addressed.

The work of psychologists, counselors, social workers, and others is governed by ethical and legal guidelines. Codes of ethics are based on the moral principles of veracity, justice, nonmaleficence, beneficence, autonomy, and fidelity. For many, the first obligation of a professional is nonmaleficence, that is, to do no harm. That is why consultants are warned not to assume responsibilities or roles that exceed their training and experience. Beneficence, or the principal of doing good, is the cornerstone of codes of ethics for all involved in the helping professions. Veracity (telling the truth) and fidelity (keeping promises) underpin several of the principles of codes of ethics such as correctly stating one's credentials and maintaining confidences. Justice (or fairness) involves the responsibility of consultants to treat all persons equally and to work to see that they are treated

fairly by people and institutions in society. Finally, *autonomy* refers to the obligations of psychologists, counselors, and others to respect and promote the independence of the people with whom they work (Glosoff & Pate, 2002). Two codes of ethics, *Code of Ethics and Standards of Practice* and the *Ethical Principles of Psychologists and Code of Conduct* will be the primary bases of the discussion in this chapter, but other codes of ethics (e.g., *Ethical Standards for School Counselors*) are based on the same principles and could have been used as well.

Legal guidelines for consultants originate in at least three ways. The most obvious of these is statutory law such as the Family Educational Rights and Privacy Act (FERPA), which was passed in 1974 and assured parents access to their children's records until they reach the age of eighteen, at which time the rights to the records pass to the student. These rights extend to all educational records, defined by FERPA as all records kept by the educational institution including testing for exceptionality and the results of reviews and assessments leading up to the establishment of Individualized Educational Programs (IEPs) (Remley & Herlihy, 2001). FERPA also denies access to records to others unless they establish that they have "a need to know" what the records contain by virtue of their relationship to the student or students. Consultants would normally have access to students' records based on this standard.

The second source of legal guidelines for consultants is case law, which is based on court rulings on critical issues. For example, in 1999 the U.S. Supreme Court ruled that schools have an obligation to protect students from sexual harassment (*Davis v. Monroe County Board of Education,* 1999, p. 650), thus obligating school officials to act when harassment is severe enough to deny students access to education. Earlier, in a related court ruling (*Nabonzy v. Podlesny,* 1996), a federal court ruled that schools had an obligation to protect gay and lesbian students from harassment because of their sexual orientation. The suit was settled by the school district when they paid the plaintiff $900,000 (McFarland & Dupius, 2001). Consultants who become aware of sexual harassment or harassment of gay or lesbian students are obligated to take appropriate action to stop the harassment as a result of these and other court decisions. Laws such as the Individuals with Disabilities Education Act Amendments of 1997 (IDEA) also provide numerous guidelines for consultants who work with the teachers of students with disabilities and the action that may be taken as a result of consultation. For example, special educators and others are required to perform a behavioral functional analysis (see Chapter Three) to determine the appropriate approach to disciplining students with disabilities. If the inappropriate behavior is related to the disability, an amendment to the Individualized Educational Plan (IEP) is required. If the behavior is unrelated to the disability, teachers and others may discipline students with disabilities in the same manner as other students.

Consultants are also constrained by the licensing laws in their states. At this juncture, all states have licensing laws for psychologists and almost all states have licensing laws for counselors and social workers. These laws establish guidelines for titles, boundaries of practice, and ethical behavior. Additionally, the boards that administer these laws are typically given rule-making authority that they use to establish additional guidelines for the credentialing and practice of consultants.

It is outside the scope of this chapter to discuss the myriad of implications of case and statutory law for consultants. However, the legal entanglements that consultants may incur if they ignore ethical and legal guidelines will be addressed briefly at the end of the chapter. Consultants, like other professionals, encounter legal risks when people with whom they consult take exception to their actions and initiate litigation against them. Some of these risks will be discussed, along with defenses against them.

PURPOSES OF ETHICAL CODES

As noted earlier, codes of ethics are developed primarily to establish guidelines for practice. No code of ethics is exhaustive in the sense that it provides direct guidance for functioning in all situations. This is particularly true in the area of consultation. For example, the American Psychological Association's *Ethical Principles of Psychologists and Code of Conduct* (APA, 2002) provides little in the way of guidance to psychologists who practice as consultants. The *Code of Ethics and Standards of Practice* developed by the American Counseling Association (ACA, 1995) is a bit better in this regard, but still falls short with regard to comprehensiveness. Does this mean that psychologists and counselors are without guidelines in the area of consultation? Not at all, but it does mean that psychologists and counselors must be aware of the general principles provided by their codes of ethics and be able to apply them in the consulting process.

Finally, codes of ethics are developed as a means of assuring the public that a professional group will practice with their best interests in mind. For example, the APA Code (2002) contains the following statements:

- Psychologists strive to benefit those with whom they work, p. 3.
- Psychologists seek to promote accuracy, honesty, and truthfulness, p. 3.
- Psychologists recognize that fairness and justice entitle all persons to access and equal quality in the process, procedure, and services being conducted by psychologists, p. 3.

Similar statements can be found in the ACA *Code* (1995). Such statements, based on the principles outlined at the outset of this chapter, are an attempt to ensure the general public of the good intentions of the group. In fact, codes of ethics become contracts with the general public because violations of their principles can result in severe penalties imposed by the profession and through civil litigation.

Codes of ethics also serve the professional groups that promulgate them in several important ways. Every occupational group aspires to professional status, and one prerequisite to acceptance as a profession by society is a well-articulated, carefully crafted code of ethics. Once the code of ethics is in place and is enforced by quasilegal bodies within the profession itself, the occupational group is ready to petition for formal recognition. Typically this occurs through lobbying efforts that, if successful, culminate in licensure laws and licensure boards that are empowered to make rules governing the functioning of the group. Central to the rules adopted by these boards is a requirement that the code of ethics be adhered to by licensed professionals. At this point the standards in the code of ethics are quite analogous to legal statutes.

Codes of ethics serve occupational groups in other ways. Over forty years ago, Greenwood (1966) set forth some of the roles codes of ethics play in regulating a profession. Ethical standards delineate the responsibilities of the professional to society, to her or his profession, specify certain types of acceptable and unacceptable practices, and set forth the values that are to guide the professionals' work in the absence of specific guidelines. Codes of ethics usually do identify some specific practices to be followed. They also identify the values that are adhered to by the profession. Since the practices identified in codes of ethics are rarely comprehensive enough to cover all of the situations in which professionals find themselves, the values contained in the documents are to be used by professionals as the basis for decision making (Pryzwansky, 1993). The introduction of the APA (2002) code of ethics specifically states, "The Ethical Standards are not exhaustive" (p. 2). It is therefore important for professionals to understand the principles as well as the underlying values of the code that governs their behavior.

Codes of ethics are complicated documents that deserve much study by consultants. Since space will not permit a detailed examination of the codes of ethics followed by consultants, the discussion to follow will be directed to the general principles that underlie the codes of ethics of the ACA (1995) and APA (2002).

ETHICAL PRINCIPLES

Principle One: Competence

All major codes of ethics contain statements admonishing practitioners to gain competence prior to practicing in an area and to retain that competence by constantly upgrading their skills. Principle Two of the APA (2002) code states in part:

2.01 BOUNDARIES OF COMPETENCE

(a) Psychologists provide services, teach, and conduct research with populations and in areas only within the boundaries of their competence, based on their education, training, supervised experience, consultation, study, or professional experience. (p. 4)

The ACA (1995; D.2.b) code also addresses the matter of competency, but in a slightly different way. It states:

Counselors are reasonably certain that they have or the organization represented has the necessary competencies and resources for giving the kind of consulting resources needed....

Although the ACA and APA standards dealing with competence seem clear, their interpretation is not (Brown, 1985; Lowman, 1985; Robinson & Gross, 1985). Unlike practitioners of assessment and psychotherapy, consultants have not established clear-cut standards of training—an oversight that is likely to be corrected in the near future. However, as was noted in an earlier chapter on the characteristics of the consultant, there is increasing consensus regarding the skills consultants need to be effective. These can be a temporary guide to the practitioners who are interested in evaluating their competency. As Newman (1993) notes in summarizing this issue, "the most basic requirement for consultants in ensuring competent practice is a thorough understanding of their own limitations" (p. 153).

Codes of ethics do provide guidelines in what are termed *emerging areas,* that is, areas for which standards of training and practice have not been fully articulated. For example, the APA (2002) code states:

In those emerging areas where recognized standards for preparation and training do not yet exist psychologists nevertheless take reasonable steps to ensure the competence of their work to protect patients, clients, students, research participants, organizational clients, and others from harm. (p. 5)

Section C.2.a of the ACA (1995) code states in part, "Counselors practice only within the boundaries of their competence, based on their education, training, and supervised experience...," which of course suggests that the counselor/consultants carefully assess their own competencies prior to engaging in various types of consultation. In making this assessment, other ethical values and legal questions must come into play. Is there potential harm to the client or the consultee if consultation is initiated and I do not have the skills to carry the process to a successful conclusion? [Welfare of the Client] If I engage in consultation and fail, will I tarnish the image

---

Student Learning Activity 12.1
Principle One

1. The consultant agrees to work with a family who has an emotionally disturbed child. The thrust of the consultation is to assist the parents in developing a behavior management system that will ameliorate the child's difficulty. The consultant, who has no training in educational consultation, is also asked to help the parents work on a study skills plan. He decides that the principles being employed in the behavior management system will generalize to the study skills areas and proceeds. Is this ethical?
2. A consultant is contacted by a hospital that is experiencing staff relationship problems. The consultant has no past training or experience in working with this type of problem, but accepts the job because he intends to gain the competence needed, although the job begins in four weeks. Are there any circumstances under which this consultant could be functioning ethically?

---

of my profession and thus the ability of other professionals like myself to help members of society? [Professional Responsibility] If I engage in consultation without the proper skills, am I likely to be charged with malpractice? [Professional Liability]

Ultimately, no one is served well by consultants who practice outside their areas of competence. If a mental health professional is uncertain about his or her competency to function in a given area, she or he probably is incompetent. However, consultation with others is an appropriate and ethical way to both determine competence to function and improve competence if skills are needed to proceed with a consultation (APA, 2002).

Principle Two: Protecting the Welfare of Clients

Protecting the welfare of clients served is the *sine qua non* of all codes of ethics, and the APA (2002) and ACA (1995) codes are no exceptions. They make it apparent that consultants are to keep up-permost in their minds both the immediate client and others who might inadvertently be affected by the result of the consultation service. As Robinson and Gross (1985) and Gallessich (1982) point out, it is anticipating the impact of consultation upon the "hidden client" that is difficult. Section D.2.c of the ACA code summarizes the position taken in both codes: "Counselors attempt to develop a clear understanding of problem definition, the goals for change, and *predicted consequences* (italics added) of interventions selected." Consultants who work in community agencies, with families, in business and industry, in schools, and in other settings need to concern themselves with the wel-fare of the consultee. However, because of the tri-adic nature of consultation, they need to anticipate the consequences of their actions on the client group who may be either the beneficiary or victim of their services.

These guidelines place tremendous burdens on consultants to pay particular attention not only to their own behavior and the impact that it might make on the welfare of the consumer, but also to the actions of the institutions that employ them. Thus, a school consultant who encounters de facto segregation during program-centered con-sultation (e.g., ability grouping) would be obli-gated to state his or her objection to the policy and to work to change the regulation. A consult-ant employed in business and industry to help es-tablish a business information management system would be obligated to help ensure that data potentially injurious to the employees not be included in the system. Constant vigilance re-garding the legal, civil, and human rights of con-sultees and clients is required of consultants.

Both the ACA and APA codes of ethics make it apparent that the welfare of consultees and cli-ents needs to be protected in the selection of as-sessment devices. Principle 9 of the APA code and Section E of the ACA code contain numerous ref-erences to the potential misuse of assessment de-vices and appropriate warnings regarding their use. Since consultants frequently use various as-sessment devices in the course of their work, reli-ability, validity, and appropriateness of norms must receive the same attention that they would in clinical settings. Since these assessment tools must often be developed by the consultant, the problems of reliability, validity, and appropriate-ness are even more acute because they must be de-veloped using limited resources. Individuals who are given assessment devices have a right to a full explanation of the intended purpose of the assess-ment, regardless of how they were developed.

In both APA and ACA codes of ethics, con-sultants are told to avoid illegal practices and to keep the welfare of their clients uppermost in their minds. Moreover, consultants are instructed that, whenever institutional and/or governmental regula-tions are contradictory to their ethical guidelines, they are to adhere to the ethical principles and work to change the contradictory regulations.

Another aspect of concerning oneself for the welfare of the client is sensitivity to cultural dif-ferences (Jackson & Hayes, 1993). Consultants must be culturally sensitive to the stereotypes they hold and must avoid these in their work (ACA, 1995; APA, 2002). Gibbs (1985) points out that training programs often neglect multicultural is-sues; thus consultants may not be equipped to deal with the complex topics that arise in cross-cultural consultation. She goes on to assert that problems such as linguistic styles, interactional styles, and power-authority perceptions may impair commu-nication in the consulting relationship. Many of the assessment instruments in current use also contain cultural biases. In order to protect the wel-fare of people from all cultures, differences must be considered actively during consultation and bi-ased assessment instruments avoided. One obvi-ous solution to this dilemma is for consultants to become sensitive to and skilled in dealing with cross-cultural differences (Gibbs, 1985).

Protecting the welfare of consultees also per-tains to fee setting. Consultants are generally ad-vised that fee setting should be done with the best interests of the consultee in mind and that some ser-vices should be performed for little or no money (ACA, 1995; APA, 2002). In an unusual aspect of a code of ethics, counselor–consultants are held

Student Learning Activity 12.2
Principle Two

The consultant working with several therapists in a correctional institution introduces aversive conditioning strategies as a historical example of "what not to do." She discovers that one of the techniques is being employed by one of the therapists. After warning the therapist that the technique is inappropriate, she learns that the technique is still being employed. The consultant reports the therapist to the supervisor of the therapy program. Is this ethical?

responsible for finding appropriate services if suitable fee arrangements cannot be reached.

Consultants are told that protection of the consultee's welfare depends in part on avoiding dependency relationships, and they are instructed to terminate the consulting relationship when it is no longer productive. In the event of termination, both the APA and ACA ethical codes suggest that there is an obligation to make alternative sources of assistance available. These guidelines provide two major sources of difficulty for consultants. The first of these is that they must make continuous assessment of the progress of consultation and must be constantly alert to the possibility that a particular consultation will be unproductive. Unfortunately, there are few guidelines except those acquired through experience to aid in making the determination that a consultation is going to be productive.

Making referrals to other consultants is the other source of difficulty. Since no training standards for consultants have yet been established (Brown, 1985), the consultant must rely on word-of-mouth information to determine the effectiveness of other consultants in many instances. One of this book's co-authors was recently reminded how risky referrals can be. After 18 months of continuous work with a school district in the Northeast aimed at revitalizing certain aspects of its educational program, it became apparent that a friendship with one of the top administrators precluded effectiveness. A referral was therefore made to another consultant who, based on his professional reputation and informal feedback from individuals in the district who had observed him, was purported to be very effective. Unfortunately, the information turned out to be erroneous, at least as it applied to this particular consultative situation.

Even though no empirical guidelines exist that provide definite answers regarding termination of consultations, the consultant is not absolved from responsibility to act. The best data available should be used to make this decision, and, above all, the welfare of the consumer must be protected. Similarly, the absence of training guidelines does not mean that the consultant has any less responsibility to make appropriate referrals (ACA, 1995; APA, 2002). It only means that the consultant may have to work harder to collect information about other consultants.

Principle Three: Maintaining Confidentiality of Disclosures

The matter of confidentiality of communication in consultation is addressed directly in both the APA and ACA codes of ethics. Consultants need to discuss the limits of confidentiality with all consultees, and it is suggested that, unless otherwise indicated, this discussion should occur at the outset of the consulting relationship. Consultants need to consult the laws in their particular states that establish the limits of confidentiality.

Student Learning Activity 12.3
Principle Three

A consultant is asked by the director of a small mental health center to tell him "what the staff really thinks of him." The consultant provides a general overview of the employees' perceptions of the director, many of which are negative. The consultant does not name names. Is this ethical?

Both the APA and ACA codes are clear on consultants' responsibilities in the area of confidentiality. They suggest that, in addition to establishing the limits of confidentiality, consultants need to discuss the "foreseeable uses of the information generated through their psychological services" (APA, p. 7). In human services consultation, there are some foreseeable uses of information that might not be disclosed routinely to consultees. For example, information gained from a parent about child rearing might ultimately have to be disclosed if the consultant is ordered to testify in a child custody hearing, but the likelihood of this happening is rare. Clearly if the consultant had known that this was a possibility, the disclosure would have to be made.

Much information gained in organizational decision making is collected to inform the decision-making process. People who complete questionnaires and engage in interviews should be told the use to which the information may be put. Both the APA and ACA codes indicate that confidential information gained from organizational clients should be discussed "only for appropriate scientific or professional purposes and only with persons clearly concerned with such matters" (APA, 2002, p. 7). This type of statement opens a virtual Pandora's box for the organizational consultant unless it is taken in the context of other principles, such as protecting the welfare of clients. The problem is that the person who hires the consultant may want to have him or her disclose the "source" of information, which is contrary to good consultation practice and to ethical practice as well.

One obligation of the consultant is to identify these and other areas of potential disagreement in the preentry phase (Kurpius, Fuqua, & Rozecki, 1993). The consultee should then be encouraged to communicate to others involved in the consultation that disclosures will be held in confidence (Robinson & Gross, 1985).

Internal consultants, and perhaps external consultants, will necessarily have to keep records that pertain to consultation. These records are also to be kept confidential according to current standards. Consultants should communicate this expectation to employers.

Principle Four: Responsibilities When Making Public Statements

Both the ACA (1995) and APA (2002) codes emphasize the importance of accuracy in all public statements. Although accuracy is indeed the watchword in issuing public statements offering consultation services, several guidelines must be followed to avoid deceptive practices. First, statements announcing the availability of consultation services should be restricted to naming highest academic degree, credentials (licensure), professional memberships, and type of service provided. Second, when listing professional membership affiliations, consultants should be careful not to imply sponsorship by a particular association or that membership in the organization is indicative of skill or credentials. Third, advertisements should not include testimonials from current clients. Fourth, consultants should not engage in direct solicitation. Currently there are no restrictions regarding the type of media that may be used for advertisements. Casual observation would lead the authors to believe that direct mail solicitations and the use of the telephone book yellow pages are the most common methods of advertising, although magazine and newspaper ads are also prevalent.

It is not unusual for consultants who have well-designed, accurate advertisements to find that their credentials have been misrepresented by consultees in brochures and other media devices aimed at publicizing their employment. Consultants should make reasonable efforts to correct these public statements (ACA, 1995; APA, 2002), just as they should correct misperceptions about their credentials when they are negotiating for consulting jobs.

Public statements by internal consultants are less likely to be problematic than those by external consultants. Nevertheless, it is still important that internal consultants accurately describe the levels of their competence, outline the goals, techniques, and expected outcomes of the consultation, and make known their intent to adhere to the ethical principles of their profession.

Principle Five: Social and Moral Responsibility

All occupational codes of ethics incorporate sections that deal with general moral standards as well as professional morality. They also include certain guidelines for regulating one's own ethical behavior and reacting to the ethical breaches of others. Of major concern in both the ACA (1995) and APA (2002) codes is that consultants be aware of personal needs and/or problems that might impair their functioning. When consultants are aware of their needs for status or esteem that may influence their functioning, they are expected to exercise appropriate restraint in meeting those needs at the expense of the consultee or the clients in the consultation. When they have personal impairments that restrict their effectiveness, consultants are expected to take action that will eliminate the impairment or avoid situations, including consultation practice, where the impairment will be a factor.

Backer and Glaser (1979) identified 19 potential ethical pitfalls for consultants, and, as Robinson and Gross (1985) note, most of these are related to potential conflicts between the consultant's needs and those of the consultee. Unethical behavior that might grow out of the consultant's personal needs include (1) becoming the decision maker rather than fostering these skills in the con-

---

Student Learning Activity 12.4
Principle Four

A well-trained, school-based consultant states in her introductory remarks to the faculty of a school the desire to become involved in consulting relationships with the teachers because she is confident that many of the learning problems encountered by children can be eliminated as a result of consultation. Is this ethical?

Student Learning Activity 12.5
Principle Five

A consultant working out of a mental health center has been assigned to work with the police department to enhance its effectiveness in working with juveniles in the community. It is obvious that the consultant enjoys this association, and it continues for two years. The evaluation of the project indicates that no progress has been made toward bettering police–juvenile relationships. Was this consultant functioning ethically?

---

sultee, (2) seeking significant favors from the consultee, (3) prolonging consultation as a means of maintaining income, (4) failing to recognize one's own limitations, (5) not taking stands against unethical/illegal behavior on the part of the consultee, (6) not considering readiness for consultation prior to initiating the consultation process, (7) failing to maintain objectivity and becoming embroiled in the politics of the setting in which the consultation occurs, (8) imposing one's own values, (9) not reporting accurately the outcomes of consultation, (10) not respecting consultants from other disciplines, and (11) resisting evaluation.

As noted earlier, it is the consultants' responsibilities to make their code of ethics known and to practice those codes even when contrary institutional policies and/or governmental regulations exist. It is also incumbent upon consultants to act to ensure that fellow colleagues act ethically as well (ACA, 1995; APA, 2002). Generally speaking, the first step in correcting unethical behavior is to remind the guilty consultant of his or her ethical responsibilities. However, if the offense is severe, or if the offense is repeated after appropriate warnings have been offered, the consultant should be reported to the appropriate ethics committee.

Sexual intimacy with and harassment of clients and others have been pinpointed by the ACA and APA for special attention, and, not surprisingly, both are prohibited. Consultants who become involved in sexual intimacies with consultees, participate in sexual harassment, or condone either practice in the context of their work are acting unethically. Consultants are also admonished that dual relationships that might result in a conflict of interest should be avoided. For example, it is probably unwise to enter into a consulting relationship with a close friend, relative, business associate, or other individual where the nature of the personal relationship might attenuate the consultant's objectivity.

General standards of ethical and moral behavior are usually left to the individual. However, consultants are expected to adhere to the moral and ethical norms of their communities and not to act in ways that would diminish their profession (APA, 1992).

Principle Six: Relationships with Other Consultants

As was noted in the introduction to this chapter, a code of ethics attempts to ensure harmony within professional groups by delineating standards for intragroup and interprofessional relationships. Several aspects of the ACA and APA codes address this issue.

Consultants are generally expected to be familiar with and respect the expertise of practitioners from other disciplines. They are also to respect the client groups of other professionals and accord them the same courtesy they would individuals from their own discipline.

Consultants who make referrals to others should generally not expect remuneration for the referral. Neither should they accept payment whenever they are performing services that grow out of arrangements between the agency that employs them and another organization or agency.

ETHICAL DECISION MAKING

It is obvious that consultants must often make decisions about ethical practice in situations without clear-cut guidance from their codes of ethics. Pryzwansky (1993) suggests that one way to enhance ethical practice in this type of situation is to adopt a decision-making strategy that is rooted in

ethical principles, concern for the dignity and free will of the individuals involved, and a concern for the norms of societies. He goes on to present the ethical decision-making model developed by Haas and Malouf (1989). According to these authors, the professional is obligated to start the ethical decision-making process by first determining whether there is an existing ethical principle that provides a course of action to deal with the situation at hand. If a principle exists and there is no reason to deviate from it, such as a legal mandate, the consultant's decision making is relatively simple. If there is no clear-cut principle governing decision making in the situation, then the consultant is obligated to look at the underlying issues, such as the welfare of the client, competence, professional responsibility, respecting the dignity of the consultee and client, and his or her social responsibility as guides to decision making. Using these broader principles, the consultant should construct a plan of action, determine whether that plan of action poses any new ethical dilemmas, and proceed if no new ethical problems are apparent.

Consider the following situations:

I. A teacher–consultee seems to have a serious mental health problem that is interfering with his ability to deal with students effectively.
   A. Is there a clear-cut principle involved?
      1. No. Generally consultants are admonished to concern themselves with the welfare of others and when the welfare of the students with whom the teacher

---

Student Learning Activity 12.6
Principle Six

A consultant openly states that he is the best trained and most effective consultant in the area. He also indicates that persons from other specialties are not as well trained or effective as he is. An examination of his vita shows that he has, in fact, received excellent training and reports show that he has been an effective consultant. Is he acting ethically?

works is at risk. However, the consulting conversation is confidential. Reporting the teacher's problem breaches confidentiality.

B. Is there a viable solution?

    1. None that is clear-cut. However, the consultant can confront the consultee with the problem and offer to assist him in getting help with the problem while managing his classroom more effectively. If this fails, the consultant's broader responsibility to the welfare of the children will have to be acted on, and the teacher's problem will have to be reported.

II. The director of a mental health center with whom you are consulting reveals that she takes cash paid by clients of the center to pay for her lunches. This information has nothing to do with the consultation, which is aimed at enhancing the outreach program.

A. Is there a clear-cut principle involved?

    1. Yes. It is the principle that information gained in the consulting relationship is confidential.

B. Are there reasons to deviate from the principle?

    1. Possibly, but given the small amount of harm that can result from not disclosing the information, the need to protect the client's privacy and adhering to a basic ethical principle seems to supersede other concerns.

III. You have been providing counseling services to a fourth-grade student. It has become clear that you need to enter into a consulting relationship with the parents to speed the process.

A. Is there a clear-cut ethical principle involved?

    1. Yes. Consultant's code of ethics warns against dual relationships.

B. Is there any reason to deviate from the principle?

    1. Yes. The child's welfare may be better served if counseling continues along with consultation.

C. Are there potential problems that need to be anticipated?

    1. Yes. Requests by the parents for confidential information; discomfort on the part of the client because parents are involved.

D. How can these problems be resolved?

    1. Explain reason for decision to the client and the limits of confidentiality to both parents and client. Get permission to disclose information from client if necessary.

To summarize and reiterate to a degree, consultants must understand the values on which their codes of ethics are based, the principles that are set forth, and must adopt decision-making strategies that will reflect those values and principles. To do less is to act unethically.

ENFORCING ETHICAL STANDARDS

All professional organizations have clear-cut guidelines for accepting and adjudicating ethical complaints (see ACA, 1995; APA, 2002). These same organizations stress that it is the individual's moral stance that is the most basic ingredient in maintaining ethical behavior. Gallessich (1982) refers to this as self-discipline.

As we stated earlier, consultants also have a responsibility for the behavior of other consultants who belong to their professional group. Whenever unethical behavior is observed, the consultant should, if the breach seems to be an oversight or poor judgment, approach the guilty party and express concern, ask for an explanation, and explore with him or her the appropriate course of action. If the ethical breach is more serious, or if the unethical consultant fails to respond to informal resolution, a complaint should be filed with the state association ethics committee. Generally speaking, the complaint should contain a specific description of the unethical behavior including documentation if possible and should identify the areas of the code of ethics that have been violated.

Once complaints are received, the ethics committee will inform the accused party of the charges and ask for his or her response to them. Noncompliance with this request is in and of itself unethical and can result in disciplinary action. The ethics committee may also engage in any other data collection procedures they deem appropriate. When all data have been collected, the ethics committee renders a judgment. If the ethics committee determines that an accused consultant is guilty of unethical behavior, they may take a variety of actions. The mildest of these is to reprimand the offender. This reprimand usually includes an educational component, for example, instruction regarding ethical behavior. Harsher actions involve (1) placing the offender on probation for a specified period of time, (2) probation plus supervision, and (3) expulsion from the association. The committee may (and usually does) inform state licensing boards and certification agencies of its action. These boards then take appropriate action including initiating delicensure or decertification.

One note of caution should be inserted for the overzealous consultant regarding the filing of complaints. The accused party in these actions has the right to know who has lodged the complaint and the exact nature of the complaint. Therefore, inaccurate complaints may result in defamation suits, which, even if they are unsuccessful, can be time-consuming and expensive. Therefore, caution is advised whenever action against a colleague is contemplated.

POTENTIAL LEGAL DIFFICULTIES

Just as consultants have not been carefully scrutinized by other professionals for unethical practice (Lowman, 1985), they appear to have escaped legal entanglements as well. And just as it can be expected that the ethical behavior of consultants will receive greater attention, the likelihood of legal difficulties is also increasing. This discussion is aimed at identifying certain areas where consultants are legally vulnerable.

Legal Actions against the Consultant

Malpractice suits have been lodged against counselors, psychiatrists, social workers, and psychologists for numerous reasons, only a few of which pertain to the consultant. Among these are negligence in rendering a service, misrepresentation, slander and libel (defamation), sexual misconduct, invasion of privacy, and breach of contract. Negligence can be charged if a plaintiff can establish that a breach of duty has occurred in the course of delivering services, if a loss or injury occurred as a result of the failure, and if a causal relationship between the two can be established, that is, the breach resulted in the damage. Defamation can either be written (libel) or spoken (slander). Generally speaking, defamation is an untrue statement about a person that diminishes his or her status or reputation. Schwitzgabel and Schwitzgabel (1980) point out that professionals are held to a higher standard, and even true statements that injure an individual may be viewed as defamatory by the courts. Misrepresentation of either credentials or the efficacy of one's services could involve either explicit or implicit communications that are essentially false. Sexual misconduct involves sexual intimacies growing out of professional relationships.

In considering the prospect of consultant negligence, the first item of concern would, of course, be to determine the nature of the consultant's duty (Anderson, 1996; Remly, & Herlihy, 2001). Often, because the specific duties of a consultant are not carefully delineated, and thus are hard to establish, some written consultation contracts delineate in detail what the responsibilities of all parties are to be during the consultation process. In this situation, the consultants are particularly vulnerable to malpractice suits if they do not fulfill their responsibilities and damage results. In other cases where the consultant is hired to assist with a specific task (e.g., improve a specific service or develop an employee assistance program), the absence of a written contract would not necessarily preclude the identification of duty. A breach of the consultant's duty might involve failure to terminate the consultation process once one's expertise is exhausted, misassessing the consultee's or client's concern, violating standards of confidentiality, or undue use of one's influence during the course of consultation.

The problem for malpractice lawyers is to establish a causal link between the breach of duty and loss (Anderson, 1996; Remly, & Herlihy, 2001). It is important to note that loss may be either tangible, such as profits, or psychological, such as stress or loss of self-esteem. It is not difficult to imagine that a liability could be established between shoddy practice by a family consultant and the psychological well-being of a child. It is even easier to see that a human service agency or business might suffer loss in effectiveness or profits as a result of the work of a consultant who has not functioned ethically or who has not used reasonable judgment in the consultation process.

Slander and libel suits can conceivably grow out of several aspects of the consultant's work. The inappropriate selection, use, and interpretation of various assessment devices might lead to suits if the scores or profiles resulted in damage to a consultee or client. So could breaches in confidentiality that injured either the consultees or clients involved in the consulting process. Reports that are not carefully prepared or that do not properly protect the persons involved from identification could also be considered defamatory in some instances if loss or embarrassment results.

Sexual misconduct is apparently a problem for a small minority of psychotherapists (Bouhoutsos, Holyroyd, Lerman, Foler, & Greenberg, 1983). While there are no data supporting the idea that a similar problem exists among consultants, the consequences of such improprieties are sufficiently severe that a warning against them seems necessary, even in the presence of ethical taboos. Sexual liaisons that result in injury to consultees or to the organizations that employ them might serve as the basis of successful malpractice suits.

The use of inappropriate assessment devices may also serve as the basis of litigation regarding wrongful invasion of privacy, which is here defined as an intentional act that invades either the psychological or personal domain of an individual (Schwitzgabel & Schwitzgabel, 1980). As was discussed in the section on ethics, consultants may be involved in situations where employees, inmates, children, and others are subtly pressured into becoming a part of the consultation process. Because of the ethical expectation that this situation will be avoided, the person who can demonstrate that privacy has been invaded may have the basis of a successful suit.

Misrepresentation of one's credentials as a consultant is unethical and legally dangerous. A consultant who lacks the stated credentials and fails to provide the expected service is at risk, both from actions that may be taken by the ethics committee of his or her professional association and by injured parties who may levy charges or fraud. Similarly, misrepresentation of the efficacy of a consultant's skills and techniques can be legally unwise.

A final area of legal concern to consultants lies in the area of breach of contract (Anderson, 1996). In the presence of a written or formal contract, consultants are expected to (1) deliver the services specified in the contract and (2) follow the standards of practice of their profession while doing so. Failure to do so can result in a lawsuit. A carefully drawn contract may be the most effective means of avoiding legal entanglements concerning contractual issues. McGonagle (1981) has provided a set of guidelines for drafting consulting contracts that, if followed, would mitigate against not only breach of contract issues but other legal and ethical problems as well.

McGonagle suggests that a standard consulting agreement would contain 12 basic paragraphs. The first of these would state the terms of the agreement and would consist of a statement or two that identify the beginning and end of the consulting period.

Paragraph two of the consulting agreement would be a bit more complicated in that it would spell out in detail the nature of the consultant's activities during the consulting period. For example, a psychologist employed to provide case consultation for a mental health center might receive the following job description:

The consultant will review case material with staff members with the explicit purpose of identifying case management strategies. Monthly reports regarding consulting activities and other observed reports will be filed with the director. Within 30 days of the termination of the contract period a summary of activities is also to be filed with the director along with the consultant's informal evaluation of the outcomes.

Remuneration for consulting and expenses would be included in paragraph three of the agreement. This paragraph would normally stipulate the rate, the payment schedules, contingencies, if any (e.g., filing reports), or the nature of allowable expenses. In some instances reimbursement for expenses follows local, state, or federal guidelines, and these may simply be alluded to instead of providing a detailed statement. McGonagle points out that it is good practice to include clauses in paragraph three of the consulting contract regarding the relationship between progress on the work and payment, as well as procedures for filing requests for payment.

Paragraph four of the consulting contract should cover work facilities. Will an office be provided? A secretary? Copying equipment? Consultant and consultees alike need not only to anticipate what facilities will be required to successfully complete a project, but to contractually stipulate which party will provide them.

Reports and work products should be addressed in paragraph five, and a clause establishing the consultant as an independent contractor should be included in paragraph six. Normally, clauses regarding reports and work products stipulate when they are due and who owns the rights to reports and products. McGonagle indicates that the consultee normally retains the rights to all work products, but in some instances the consultant may wish to retain rights to materials developed for the consultee, such as assessment devices. Stipulating that an individual is an independent contractor is merely an indicator that the consultant is not an employee and thus provides the consultant with more latitude regarding the manner in which the work is performed. McGonagle (1981) points out, however, that the establishment of the consultant as an independent contractor does not protect the consultee from legal liability incurred as a result of the consultant's action.

Paragraph seven should deal with termination of the contract. Normally this involves only a simple statement that either party may terminate the agreement after a suitable notice period, usually 30 days.

Paragraph eight should make the material gained during the consulting relationship confidential, according to McGonagle (1981). He suggests the use of the following phrase: "You agree that for the term of your appointment hereunder and for two (2) years thereafter, that you will not disclose to any person, firm, or corporation any confidential information regarding the corporation" (p. 88). Obviously this phrase is intended to protect the consultee. It is suggested here that, in addition to this type of phrase, another be added to assert the intent of the consultant to follow ethical guidelines regarding confidentiality. In this way the consultee, the consultant, and the clients are served.

The last four paragraphs of the consulting contract should deal with assignability of the contract, arbitration of disputes, integration, and closing the contract. Assignability has to do with the consultant's legal right to assign all or part of the work set forth in the contract to another party. In some instances the consultee may wish to stipulate the work as nonassignable. Arbitration deals with the matter of settling disputes that arise from the contract. The consultee and consultant may wish simply to stipulate that a mutually acceptable third party will be used to resolve disputes. Included is a statement or statements that stipulate that the contract can only be changed by written agreement by both parties and that the contractual document constitutes the entire agreement. This precludes either the contractor or the consultee from raising issues that were discussed orally. Finally, in the last paragraph the contract is closed and approved by both parties. Since the contract is typically written by the consultee, this paragraph simply states that if the consultant agrees to the terms of the contract, he or she should sign in the designated place and return a copy to the contractor.

Defenses. It is not accidental that many areas of legal concern are addressed quite directly in codes of ethics. As was noted in the introduction to the chapter, promulgators of ethical codes seek to protect the profession and its members by establishing rules of conduct that avoid legal entanglements. Therefore, following one's code of ethics is the first defense against legal action.

A second and equally important defense involves following the standards of practices set down by a professional group. Unfortunately, there are few standards of practice for consultants at this time (Lowman, 1985). Therefore, consultants should take every precaution to ensure that their practices are currently acceptable within their particular group. Two examples of techniques that might have been either suggested or utilized by consultants in the past are aversive conditioning techniques and encounter groups. Neither are supported as standard practices for dealing with consultee or client problems at this time, although encounter groups are still in use to promote personal growth in some instances.

Other Legal Concerns

Although direct suits against consultants are of concern, consultants may find themselves embroiled in other types of litigation. For example, a school psychologist or counselor might be subpoenaed to testify in a child custody suit. So might a family consultant working out of a mental health center. Also, an organizational consultant might be requested to testify in a suit against management. This type of situation automatically raises a concern about privileged communications.

Confidentiality is an ethical term that admonishes the consultant to maintain communications in confidence. Privileged communication is a legal term and refers to legislative recognition that certain communications can be held in confidence. Consultees of consultants who are licensed psychologists, counselors, or social workers have been accorded privileged communication in most instances. In many states, the consultees of school counselors, school psychologists, and others have also been accorded this right. However, Sheely and Herlihy (1984) point out that privileged communication has certain distinct limitations. The most common of these is that consultants may be compelled by a judge to disclose communications if he or she deems it in the best interest of justice. In other instances, privileged communication does not extend to children (e.g., the statute for school counselors in California). As Sheely and Herlihy (1984) suggest, each consultant should become aware of the legal aspects of privileged communication in his or her own state.

Consultants may also be called on to serve as expert witnesses in litigation related to their area of expertise. Expert witnesses may be used by lawyers for either the defendant or the plaintiff and are typically paid for their services. Once an "expert" is contacted by the lawyer, it is the lawyer's responsibility to qualify the expert to the presiding judge. Ultimately, the judge determines whether the person may act as an expert in the particular case before the court.

SUMMARY

Major codes of ethics have not yet been revised to accommodate the complexities of the consultation process. However, consultants from various disciplines are bound to abide by the ethical standards of the professional organizations to which they belong. A number of ethical principles keyed to the codes of ethics of APA and ACA were set forth in this chapter that can serve as the basis for ethical behavior in consultation. The major principles identified dealt with competence, welfare of the consumers of consultation services, confidentiality, public statements, ethical and moral responsibilities, and relationships to other consultants.

Legal entanglements have been largely avoided by consultants. However, a number of potential legal pitfalls were identified and discussed, including negligence, defamation, sexual misconduct, misrepresentation, confidentiality, invasion of privacy, and breach of contract. Guidelines for avoiding lawsuits were also presented.

TIPS FOR THE PRACTITIONER

1. Make certain that you study your code of ethics carefully. Place an asterisk beside each

portion that deals with or has potential relevance for consultation.

2. Determine the legal basis for confidentiality in your state by reading the licensing laws that regulate your profession. If you work in a public school or other agency, determine whether there are privileged communication laws that accord confidentiality to any of the consultees with whom you might work.

3. Identify laws that impinge upon the statutes that regulate confidentiality in your state. For example, all states require mental health professionals to report child abuse. In some states, mental health professionals can be required to divulge information in pretrial investigations if a court order is obtained.

4. Write the statement you will use to tell consultees about confidentiality and its limits when you consult.

5. Try to determine whether a consultant has ever been sued for malpractice in your state. If the answer is yes, determine the allegations in the suit, the outcome of the suit, and the basis for the decision.

REVIEW QUESTIONS

1. Identify at least four purposes of a code of ethics.

2. What are the problems associated with identifying competent consultants?

3. Who are the "hidden clients" in consultation?

4. Explain why the selection of assessment devices in consultation may be as problematic as it is in psychotherapy.

5. Outline an ethical public statement announcing the availability of consultation services.

6. Manipulation of consultees appears to be a major ethical problem for consultants. How can this be eliminated?

7. Ethically, how should you act, as a consultant, to avoid difficulties with other consultants?

8. Identify areas where consultants are vulnerable to legal action. How should a consultant act to reduce this threat?

9. Identify the elements of a comprehensive consulting contract.

10. Distinguish between the terms confidentiality and privileged communication.

REFERENCES

ACA (1995). *ACA code of ethics and standards of practice.* Alexandria, VA: Author.

Anderson, B. S. (1996). *The counselor and the law* (4th ed.). Alexandria, VA: American Counseling Association.

APA. (2002). Ethical principles of psychologists and code of conduct.

Backer, T. E., & Glaser, E. M. (1979). *Portraits of 17 outstanding organizational consultants.* Los Angeles: Human Interaction Research Institute.

Bouhoutsos, J., Holyroyd, J., Lerman, H., Foler, B. R., & Greenberg, M. (1983). Sexual intimacy between psychotherapists and patients. *Professional Psychology: Research and Practice, 14,* 185–196.

Brown, D. (1985). The preservice training and supervision of consultants. *The Counseling Psychologist, 13,* 410–425.

Davis v. Monroe County Board of Education, 526 U.S. 629 (1999).

Gallessich, J. (1982). *The profession and practice of consultation.* San Francisco: Jossey-Bass.

Gibbs, J. T. (1985). Consultant training and supervision: Can we continue to be color-blind and class-bound? *The Counseling Psychologist, 13,* 426–435.

Glosoff, H. L., & Pate, R. H., Jr. (2002). Privacy and confidentiality in school counseling. *Professional School Counseling, 6,* 20–27.

Greenwood, E. (1966). The elements of professionalization. In H. M. Vollmer & D. L. Mills (Eds.), *Professionalization* (pp. 2–28). Englewood Cliffs, NJ: Prentice-Hall.

Haas, L. J., & Malouf, J. L. (1989). *Keeping up good work: A practitioner's guide to mental health ethics.* Sarasota, FL: Professional Resource Exchange.

Jackson, D. N., & Hayes, D. H. (1993). Multicultural issues in consultation. *Journal of Counseling and Development, 72,* 144–147.

Kurpius, D. J., Fuqua, D. R., & Rozecki, T. (1993). The consulting process: A multidimensional approach. *Journal of Counseling and Development, 71,* 601–606.

Lowman, R. L. (1985). The ethical practice of psychological consultation: Not an impossible dream. *The Counseling Psychologist, 13,* 466–472.

Luke, J. R., & Benne, K. P. (1975). Ethical issues and dilemmas in laboratory practice. In K. D. Benne et al. (Eds.), *The laboratory method of changing and learning: Theory and applications* (pp. 360–401). Palo Alto, CA: Science and Behavior Books.

McFarland, W. P., & Dupius, M. (2001). The legal duty to protect gay and lesbian students from violence in school. *Professional School Counseling, 4,* 171–179.

McGonagle, J. J., Jr. (1981). *Managing the consultant.* Radnor, PA: Chilton Book.

Nabozny v. Podlesny, 92F.3d 446 (W. D. Wisc. 1996).

Newman, J. I.. (1993). Ethical issues in consultation. *Journal of Counseling and Development, 72,* 148–156.

Pryzwansky, W. B. (1993). Ethical consultation practice. In J. E. Zins, T. R. Kratochwill, & S. N. Elliot (Eds.), *Handbook of consultation services for children* (pp. 329–350). San Francisco: Jossey-Bass.

Remly, T. P., Jr., & Herlihy, B. (2001). *Ethical and legal issues in counseling.* Columbus, OH: Merrill/Prentice-Hall.

Robinson, S. E., & Gross, D. (1985). Ethics in consultation: The Canterville ghost revisited. *The Counseling Psychologist, 13,* 444–465.

Schwitzgabel, R. L., & Schwitzgabcl, R. K. (1980). *Law and psychological practice.* New York: John Wiley & Sons.

Sheely, V., & Herlihy, B. (1984). *Privileged communication in 50 states.* Paper presented at Southern Association of Counselor Education and Supervision Convention, Nashville, TN.

Van Hoose, W. V., & Kottler, J. A. (1977). *Ethical and legal issues in counseling and psychotherapy.* San Francisco: Jossey-Bass.

ANSWERS TO LEARNING EXERCISES

12.1

1. No.
2. Yes. He/she could act as "finder" and hire a knowledgeable consultant to take the lead in this project. However, the intention to do this should be a part of the initial negotiation. Otherwise, the consultant is acting unethically.

12.2

1. Yes.

12.3

1. No. It is likely that the director will be able to determine the source of the content. The consultant could work with the director on methods whereby he could gain feedback.

12.4

1. If the consultant overstates the efficacy of consultation, she is acting unethically. It seems likely that such is the case in this situation.

12.5

1. It depends on when the feedback was received and whether it is being used to improve the consultation process.

12.6

1. No.

CHAPTER 13

ISSUES IN CONSULTATION AND COLLABORATION

GOAL OF THE CHAPTER

This chapter will address issues related to the theoretical and applied aspects of the consultation process.

CHAPTER PREVIEW

A number of issues related to the use of consultation by human service professionals will be presented, and the available literature relevant to each issue will be discussed.

Throughout this book the critical challenges facing human service professionals have been addressed. There are few commonly held conclusions about consultation; most are rarely challenged, let alone debated. However, inasmuch as consultation is an intervention used by human service professionals, the fact that there are not more controversial issues is surprising. In fact, it could be argued that the tension arising from issues might actually be positive, resulting in a more sophisticated theoretical and empirical base. In any case, as long as professionals remain enthusiastic and maintain both an open, flexible stance and an inquiring attitude regarding consultation, we can expect continued progress.

In the organization of this chapter, you will recognize two categories of topics. First, there are the issues that cut across chapter content—that is, have relevance for several chapters but are presented jointly here so redundancy is kept to a minimum. Therefore, the reader should consider the implications of each issue for the various aspects of

consultation presented throughout the book. However, there are some instances where the issue warrants special treatment, and these also are included in this chapter. Finally, there was no intent to prioritize issues by placement within the chapter or by their order of presentation.

DIRECT OR INDIRECT SERVICES

In human service agencies such as schools, mental health facilities, university counseling centers, and departments of social welfare, the tradition has been to provide direct serves through counseling, therapy, assessment, educational programs, and other approaches in which the professional interacts directly with the client. By contrast, *consultation* is defined as an indirect service. This tradition of direct services has been examined and questioned over the years (Gutkin and Curtis, 1999; Monroe, 1979; Reynolds, Gutkin, Ellio, & Wilt, 1984), with the focus how best to identify the most useful service strategy given a particular set of circumstances.

Reynolds and others (1984) suggest that there are three criteria that may be utilized in making this selection: effectiveness, cost, and acceptability. Some research has addressed the effectiveness issue by comparing consultation with one form of direct intervention, counseling (Alpert & Kranzler, 1970; Lauver, 1974; Palmo & Kuzniar, 1972; Randolph & Hardage, 1973), and has concluded that consultation is more effective. It should be pointed out that most of these studies were conducted in school situations, however, and for the most part cannot be generalized outside that setting. Comprehensive reviews of the literature support the efficacy of consultation in other settings with a variety of consultees (Fullan, Miles, & Taylor, 1980; Mannino & Shore, 1975b; Medway, 1979), but the studies reviewed do not make a comparative analysis of consultation with direct service approaches. Future research will need to focus on the relative effectiveness of direct and indirect services as they relate to specific problem situations.

Acceptability of consultation has been studied to some degree within school psychology (Reynolds et al., 1984) with the result that few definitive conclusions can be reached at this time. Witt, Elliot, and Martens (1985) studied the criteria utilized by teachers in accepting interventions and concluded that time needed to learn and implement an intervention, the potential risk to the client, and the potential negative impact on other children were the primary considerations in deciding whether to accept or reject the intervention. Kazdin (1980) has also suggested that an overall criterion of acceptance of an approach revolves around the perception of whether the expected outcome justifies the effort needed to implement the intervention. Again, no research has looked specifically at giving potential consultees alternative approaches to dealing with a problem in the form of direct services.

Which type of service is the most efficient: direct or indirect? In an era of shrinking resources, human resource professionals must concern themselves with cost/benefit factors. Unfortunately, this issue is virtually unexplored in

the professional literature. Consultation appears to have an edge on this dimension when compared to more labor-intensive direct interventions such as counseling (Reynolds et al., 1984). However, no empirically based indicators or even guidelines have developed.

As noted earlier, the tradition among professionals working in human services agencies has been one of direct service to clients. To be sure, school psychologists have adopted consultation as a primary service delivery vehicle (Bardon, 1982; Meyers, 1973; Meyers, Parsons, & Martin, 1979) just as have special educators adopted collaboration as the intervention of choice (see Chapter Twelve). However, the issue to be faced is not whether direct interventions such as counseling are to be preferred to consultation, but which intervention will best meet the clients' needs given the criteria for success or effectiveness, efficiency, and acceptability? Given the state of research in this area, this is likely to be a long-standing issue. But, it is hard to imagine a school support services delivery model that does not include a *mix* of direct versus indirect services. To the degree that there are limited numbers of certain professionals in their various roles, the question of how to make maximum use of those professionals becomes very relevant.

CLASSIFICATION SCHEMES

Although the practice of consultation has increased among the various human service professionals, and the writings and research literature have reflected this increase, professionals are still struggling with the formulation of a working ty-

---

Student Learning Exercise 13.1

Contrast consultation and counseling with regard to efficiency (amount of time spent by the professional) and acceptability to the recipient of the service. With these criteria, which intervention has the advantage?

pology or classification scheme of consultation models. Several have been proposed (Blake & Mouton, 1976; Caplan, 1970; Gallessich, 1985; Schein, 1969), but as yet none has really taken hold. They range from relatively straightforward descriptions of different types (e.g., Schein, 1969) to complex matrices involving several dimensions on which the consultant must correctly identify the point of interaction among those dimensions to theoretically expect a successful consultation (e.g., Blake & Mouton, 1976).

Some curious mixtures have resulted in the conceptual discussions related to this topic. There is a tendency to mix individual approaches with organizational models; to concentrate on the *theoretical* underpinnings of the model (e.g., behavioral) versus the *professional identity* of the consultant (e.g., resource teacher consultation, psychiatric consultation); to highlight the *content* of the interaction (e.g., instructional consultation); and to emphasize *process* (e.g., process consultation) or collaboration versus *product* (e.g., technical consultation). And, of course, we now have "consultation" versus "collaboration" versus "collaborative consultation," titles defined as problem solving. Even the *target* of the consultation creates confusion in spite of the attempts to use the words *direct* or *indirect* as modifiers of *service*. For example, in some models a consultation service can be described as "indirect," but the target of the intervention is the consultee's client! Semantics often confuses and confounds efforts to develop a typology. What is still clearly needed is a taxonomy of consultation models based upon a well-articulated rationale.

One starting point in building such a taxonomy would be to concentrate on the purpose of consultation (change, helping), the values of the consultant, and the parameters of the consultation act itself (content, goal, targets), For example, Chin and Benne (1976) reason that any planned change must be based on current knowledge of change; likewise, technologies should be utilized based on current knowledge of change as a process. They have categorized different strategies and procedures of change that have a few impor-

tant elements in common. The first type of change strategy they label as *empirical–rational.* This group of strategies begins with the assumption that individuals are rational and will act to protect their self-interest in a rational manner. Such strategies then are information- and knowledge-based, and individuals are expected to change when confronted with data and a logical rationale. What has often been referred to as "expert consultation" is an example of this approach. Medical or clinical consultation and to a certain extent behavioral consultation also fall into this category.

The *normative–reeducative* strategy is the second type of change strategy. Although embracing to some degree the assumptions of the empirical–rational strategy, this second type assumes that sociocultural norms are equally important in human motivation. Consequently, when change occurs, it involves changes in attitudes, values, skills, and significant relationships. Social norms must be addressed by consultants then if they expect to be successful. The Caplanian consultation category of consultee-centered consultation would certainly apply here, as would a number of organizational development approaches.

The third type of strategy, *power–coercive,* is based on the application of power in some form. Economic and political pressures are common illustrations of this approach, but the use of moral power, such as playing on the emotions of guilt and shame, would also be included. Such a strategy often relies on legitimate power, such as the principal who says, "My teachers will use the materials if I tell them to!" In summary then, all change models, including consultation models, are initially conceptualized in terms of the assumptions upon which they rest. The change strategies are not differentiated in terms of the size and target of the change. Chin and Benne (1976) argue that there are similarities in the processes of changing regardless of the target of consultation. Differentiation among consultation models can, theoretically, be developed from the point at which a change strategy is identified.

An alternative classification was proposed by Gallessich (1985) and had the objective of unifying "currently scattered and heterogeneous concepts" (p. 336). Theory and practice are seen as lagging far behind the increasing range of consultation applications. Her consultation *meta-theory* proposes to identify general characteristics of four different consultation conceptions or models. She proposes that the universal *characteristics* (dyadic, triadic, external) of consultation should be identified along with the consultation *parameters* (content, goals, role, and relationship rules) and *fundamental variants* (value systems or ideologies of consultants). Gallessich reasons that theory building and research efforts will be given an important boost as a result of this higher-level conceptualization, which incorporates the three factors of characteristics, parameters, and variants in a way resembling the Blake and Mouton (1976) matrix. Bardon (1985) suggests that yet another step involving "identification of reasonably consistent patterns of interactive variability" will probably also need to be taken into account before cogent descriptions of consultation emerge (p. 359).

The challenge of formulating a consultation classification scheme may be with us for some time, but the conceptualization represented by the authors referred to above and others should be considered by consultants as they plan to work with consultees. The model approach that is chosen should be clearly understood in terms of its assumptions and characteristics, the locus of the consultant's employment and target of change identified, characteristics of the consultee and his or her setting as well as the nature of the problem delineated. Consultants should get used to thinking about intervention in this complex way in approaching their day-to-day interactions, reading the literature, and conducting evaluation or research.

CONSULTATION AS A PROFESSION

The definitions of consultation range from Webster's "to give advice" and the common-sense help we can expect from a friend to the sophisticated models described in this text. For the most part, the assumption underlying any use of the term is that the consultant, by virtue of either his or her life experience or training and experience, is respected enough to have his or her opinion solicited. The former image implies a common-sense attribute, while the latter notion clearly reflects expertise in a content area.

In his book on mental health consultation, Caplan (1970) specifically addresses this question of expertise or common sense versus a new profession. He argued that consultation was a method of communication, a special way in which professionals may operate, and not a new profession. Although consultation is often distinguished from other roles such as supervision, counseling, and testing, the distinction is not always clear in the consultee's and even the consultant's mind. The fact that there are so many definitions of *consultation* and *collaboration* used seems to be the source of this confusion.

By contrast, Gallessich (1982) argued that consultation is an emerging profession. She defended her notion of a new field by pointing out that consultation is a complex process requiring specialized training, and that consultants share a common role and purpose and as a result need a common body of knowledge and code of ethics. Levin, Trickett, and Kidder (1986) came to a similar position after reviewing the topics addressed in a handbook on mental health consultation. They concluded that "the increasing knowledge base, the assertion that ethical issues in consultation are not easily clarified by the ethical standards of other professional roles, and the clear evidence that consultation activities are proliferating across populations and settings argues that the preconditions for consultation as a primary professional identity are discernible" (p. 509).

Such diverse opinions can either contribute to the confusion that exists or serve as a unifying step. For now, a simple, straightforward definition will have to suffice. Consultants are sought out for some reason related to their expertise and not necessarily the manner in which they offer services. They have something in the way of knowledge or skills that is not possessed by the consultee. In some instances the consultant's objectivity, as a result of being external to the system, plays a role in selection, but his or her bailiwick is the prime criterion for involvement. For the present, it is most useful to think of consultation, conceptually and practically, as an intervention approach. Given the lack of discussion on the "issue," it may have become a historical item or an overlooked critical premise of what the professional is all about.

THE LIMITS OF CONSULTATION

It is important to remember that just because a consultee requests consultation and a consultation is begun, there are no reasons to continue it in the face of later information that contradicts this intervention approach. Caplan (1970) has recommended that consultants keep the possibility in mind of aborting the process, thereby reminding us of the realistic limits of this method. As an example, he notes that if the consultee's actions have the potential of endangering the client, the consultant should set aside his or her consultant role and give advice or take action from the consultant's professional frame of reference, which the consultee does not have the option to reject.

The employment base of the consultant, which is internal or external, and dual role responsibilities can be factors in such a decision. External consultants certainly should not allow poor judgment on the part of a consultee to continue; an organization can expect such a level of responsibility from the consultant. By contrast, the internal consultant has more of a dilemma in that technically he or she is as responsible for the client's welfare as his or her fellow employee, perhaps not to the degree as the consultee, but responsible nevertheless. The question of boundaries between the role of a consultant versus the professional identity of the consultant can further complicate the deliberation of when to step outside the consultant role. For example, as a counselor, the consultant may do things very differently from what he or she observes as the practice of the consultee. The important question is not whether a theoretical or stylistic difference exists between consultant and consultee, but whether in fact the consultee's behavior is

harmful or is clearly indefensible from what is known in the literature about the matter at hand (see Student Learning Activity 12.2).

CHOOSING A CONSULTATION MODEL

At times when one is reading consultation literature, it would seem that only the model under discussion is the one to use. Seldom is the question "Which model for which problem?" addressed. On the one hand, it could be argued that consultants should use the model consistent with their more general theoretical and personal biases as it would prove difficult if not impossible for the consultant to do otherwise. However, shouldn't a consultation approach be chosen based on the nature of the presented problem, the characteristics of the consultee, the setting resources and constraints, or some combination of those variables? Granted, the research is not definitive as far as this question is concerned, but given what is known, the consultant should at least consider the implications of using an alternative approach in the self-evaluations that are conducted of his or her consultation. At least two writers have explicitly considered a multimodel approach, and their ideas will be briefly reviewed.

Caplan's (1970) types of consultation (client-centered, consultee-centered, program-centered, administrative, and consultee-centered administrative) are an administrative response to a need to take into account the nature of the problem (case versus administrative) and the goal of consultation (improving the problem-solving capacity of the consultee versus the giving of specialized opinion). Caplan cautioned that while most consultants may not exactly fit one of these categories, a predominance of elements will "load up" in one of the four categories. The consultant will then be in a better position to gauge the most effective strategies to use. Caplan goes on to further categorize four types of consultee-centered case consultation, which again has implications for the responses of the consultant. Finally, Caplan notes that external consultants may go through a series of successive stages before consultee-centered consultation is requested. For example, liaison expectations may constitute the initial response of host agency/institution and its consultees. A staff educator role may follow, with subsequent requests for a client-centered case consultation.

Pursuing this stage progression idea one step further, it may be prudent to approach some individual consultations with a stage concept system of consultation in mind. That is, the consultee may not be ready to enter into a collaborative problem-solving relationship or feel comfortable with a consultee-centered focus. Similarly, consultant misconceptions about a theoretical approach may preclude problem formulations of a certain type. Also, the possibility exists that some consultees prefer differential consultant styles dependent on the consultation stage that is at hand (Babcock & Pryzwansky, 1983). For example, a consultee may expect the consultant to offer expert opinions in terms of problem identification, but expect to be very much involved in deciding what to do about the problem, or vice versa. Whether consultants *should* shift from one consultation approach to another is yet to be determined, as well as whether they *can* be trained to function in this way.

A prescriptive use of consultation models was advocated by Conoley and Conoley (1981), which led to their recommendation for the training of consultants to be as broad as possible. They recommend selecting (prescribing) a consultation model based on characteristics of the consultee and the problem. In studying the question of the consultant's discriminant use of models according to contextual variables, Conoley and Conoley analyzed the logs and audiotapes of 46 consultation trainees in 24 service sites (elementary and secondary schools as well as mental-health-oriented agen-

---

Student Learning Activity 13.2

A principal and teacher request a consultation with the psychologist assigned to their school. Their concern involves a fourth-grade girl who they suspect of stealing money from the teacher's purse. The principal is worried that a lot more objects will turn up "missing" as reported to him by the teacher, and the teacher fears the child is becoming a kleptomaniac. As the session progresses, the consultant discovers that the consultees are interested in his capability as the psychologist to test the youngster and confirm that she is the culprit. Following more discussion, it turns out that over the past two years little of any significance has been reported stolen (two quarters and a pencil box). A weak documentation of circumstantial evidence is presented by the consultees and includes an incident wherein the student broke one of the teacher's earrings, left it on her desk during the time this student and another were alone in the room to clean the blackboard. The teacher has already had the police in her classroom to investigate the incident and they talked with the student. The student's parents have approached the principal relaying their child's fear that the teacher suspected her. Both consultees have proposed that a situation be set up wherein the child would be given an opportunity to steal. This entrapment approach is thoroughly explored with all its impending consequences. Following further discussion of the student's background and other information that builds a case against the student, the session appears to be winding down with the principal and teacher seemingly still disposed to arrange a scenario wherein the student might transgress, which could lead to a confession of the precipitating incident and some rehabilitative intervention.

As a consultant, how would you proceed from this point in the consultation? What type of action might be taken that would not challenge the integrity of the consultees since the consultees are employed by the school district and will need to work in this school in the future? Should the principal have been involved in the consultation? What purpose did his presence serve? Write out your assessment of this consultation session as you understand the dynamics so far, and what you would do. If you have a chance, role play the session with another student in your class. Now read the consultant's response and consider how the consultant handled this situation. Do you agree with that approach?

cies). They found that consultee characteristics were very important in the choice of behavioral consultation; most prominent were the roles of the consultee and comparative gender. Behavioral consultation was used with teachers, parents, and residential unit staff, but seldom above the elementary level. Also, consultants tended to choose this model when the consultee was of the opposite sex.

By contrast, the consultant's preference for mental health consultee-centered consultation was the largest contributor to its use. It was also seldom used at the elementary level and seemed to be employed in work with school administrators. When client-centered consultation was used, it was not clearly separated from behavioral or mental health consultee-centered consultation, although it tended to be more closely allied with the behavioral approach. The very limited use of program-centered models or advocacy approaches was attributed to the trainee status of the "consultants" in the Conoley and Conoley study. In fact, that finding plus the lack of information regarding the nature of the prescriptive training (i.e., were only models emphasized or were selection criteria also emphasized?) underscores the preliminary status of their report.

Since this issue of choice in consultation model was proposed in our first edition, it has received little attention in the literature. First, most of the research studies on consultation (75 percent) have involved primarily one approach, the behavior paradigm (Martens, 1993). Also, unproductive criticism of the collaborative model and the behavioral consultant model (see the following section) has been the level of the discussions now found in the literature. This finding leads us to the conclusion that professionals may still be searching for the *one* consultation model. An exception to this conclusion was the Tindal, Parker, and Hasbrouck (1992) exploratory study that analyzed 10 individual consultation cases and found little orderliness to the stages and activities that were employed. Engaging two experienced teachers who were enrolled in a program wherein they were receiving special education–consultation training, the researchers trained the teachers to be responsive to the critical

variables in each case when selecting a consultation approach to employ. In addition to raising some provocative questions based on their findings—such as the continued wisdom of "demarcating the consultation process into artificial stages"—the emphasis on training professionals to apply the same skills in all cases received an empirical test. The choice of using a single consultation model routinely versus a perspective model, or tailoring the model to the situation, remains a challenging decision for consultants and trainers alike. Davis and Sandoval (1991) argue, "We are forced to practice from *models* based on pragmatic, clinical or field experience," given the absence of a validated and clearly most effective model (p. 201), and emphasize the point that consultation is a process within which interventions are generated. They conclude by advocating a broad systems-oriented framework for conceptualizing problems, cautioning that this systems perspective becomes a way to think about and organize an intervention rather than a form of intervention itself. It is hoped that the future will bring additional systematic consideration of this issue.

An even more provocative question is *who* chooses the model. We presented this section from the perspective of the consultant and the variables that could be taken into account. In Chapter Eight we considered the benefits of training the consultee to be a more informed consumer of the consultation/collaboration service. Does this mean that the consultant should provide the service model preferred or expected by the consultee? Is this the starting point of the service? Should the consultant negotiate the model to be used with the consultee? Should the consultant really decide what is best?

CONSULTATION STAGES OR TURNINGS

Much of the consultation literature, and particularly that referenced in this text, conceptualizes the process as a series of steps. Indeed, to the degree that *consultation* or *collaboration* is defined as a problem-solving activity, the typical steps are reflected in the description of the process: identify the problem, plan an intervention, and so forth. While some writers/models emphasize one step over the other, either in terms of importance or responsibility of either the consultee or consultant, the problem-solving paradigm is evident, often explicitly. One exception has been noted in the novice-expert research on problem solving (see Chapter Eight), where experts were found to spend considerable time identifying the problem ("problem representation," "orientating mechanisms"), and, having done so, move to the solution, framed within a number of considerations. Thus, while one may argue that stages are helpful to the consultee in learning about the "problem area in general" and the logic of the consultant, the expert, by virtue of his or her training and experience, may be way ahead of the consultee's thinking.

Another notion that challenges our thinking about the consultation process, provoking reconsideration of the interaction between the consultant and consultee, was reported by Hylander in her consultation study. "Instead of seeing consultation as a specific set of stages, it is seen as a process oscillating between approaching and moving away from the originally presented problem" (Hylander, 2000). Sudden changes characterize the consultation process, based on her interviews with experienced consultants and consultees. In fact, she identified three types of "sudden changes": "turnings," "turning points," and "shifts." This core variable (the turning process) reflects the consultees' shifting views of their interactions with the client and the consultant as well as both the consultant's and consultee's changes in their presentations and representations. Thus, Hylander (2004) concludes that a successful consultation is one in which the consultee comes to hold a different representation of the problem, and that change is what is called a conceptual shift or "turning."

THE CONTROVERSY OVER COLLABORATION

It is hard to imagine that when collaboration was advanced (see Pryzwansky, 1974) as an approach to be utilized by a professional in his or her work with another professional, it would eventually emerge as an "issue" for this practice. Indeed it has become a "buzz word" (Fuchs & Fuchs, 1992) in much the same way that consultation is overused and misused. However, the criticism of the collaborative model (Witt, 1990) is sometimes based on erroneous assumptions. Similarly, attributing to "collaborative enthusiasts" an inclination to deemphasize fundamental *consultation* competencies (isn't collaboration different from consultation?) or emphasizing collegiality over treatment integrity (Fuchs & Fuchs, 1992) accomplishes little. The tendency to automatically assume that only professionals with a certain theoretical orientation use a particular model, or that professionals hold a certain value, is a questionable argument at best. It also contributes to a tendency generally found in the literature to be less than precise, and when that happens, it becomes harder to develop the approach under discussion. Furthermore, Fuchs and Fuchs overlook the fact that the professional who advocates an applied behavioral analysis, a "deemphasized competency," is not immune from describing the behavioral consultant as one who "collaborates."

Sheridan (1992) also points out that "one of the largest problems in school consultation literature concerns conceptual and definitional inconsistencies" (p. 88), and she comments that Witt failed to define collaboration as part of his critique. She goes on to note that two key aspects of collaboration were "misrepresented" or "not communicated" by Witt: parity and interdependence. In her analysis, *coequal* does not mean *identical;* rather, the consultant–consultee relationship is complementary. Thus, the consultant does not suspend his or her expertise in the service of the relationship because the input, experience with the problem, and expertise of the teacher are valued. The professionals in a consultation relationship are "equal in decision-making status, not equal in content or process expertise" (p. 90). Similarly, the consultant is endorsing an *interdependent* interaction wherein understanding of the consultee's conceptualization of the problem and input—as well as commitment to the interventions—is important.

This debate has subsequently emerged in the research domain with a series of point–counterpoint articles (Erchul, 1999; Gutkin, 1999a, 1999b). The reader is advised to read this exchange, if for no other reason than it offers an excellent review of selected articles in the school psychology indirect service literature; while the focus of the debate is *collaboration,* it is interesting, and not insignificant to the later conclusions that are drawn by both authors, that the critiqued research studies involved *consultation* and a specific consultation approach, that is, behavioral consultation, rather than collaboration! That observation noted, Gutkin (1999a) took issue with some of Erchul's research findings and concluded that consultant directiveness is not harmful to the process nor is consultee leadership. He proposed portraying the interaction of the directive and collaborative dimensions to be used in future investigations with the conceptualization that consultation be represented by the resulting quadrants. Erchul (1999) argues that "we seek out operational definitions of collaboration with respect to different theoretical models, processes and levels of intervention within consultation" (p. 194). He stresses that an interpersonal (dyadic) perspective is essential to understanding the process of consultation in addition to the heuristic Gutkin proposed to direct future research. Erchul preferred that "influence" and "power" be included in our attempts to understand the collaborative approach to consultation.

Schulte and Osborne (2003) explored six views of consultation and found the differences among them as not trivial. The role of the consultant and consultee may be interpreted very differently, depending on one's view of collaboration. The notion that collaboration plays a part in consultation, held by these authors (and many of the patterns that they review), rests on the faulty premise that collaboration is a part of consultation, rather than an approach distinct from consultation. That many authors have taken the collaborative approach and worked it into their brand or model of consultation, as Schulte and Osborne document, no doubt has contributed to confusion in the literature. As long as this trend continues, and authors fail to present their as-

sumptions (or ignore them) and/or mix popular with professional definitions of terms, the outlook for progress is discouraging.

The term *collaborative consultation* may be an oxymoron; collaboration is one helping model as is consultation, although one must distinguish between the expert type and the consultee-entered type in the latter instance. Each model makes different assumptions about how one professional works with another professional who is experiencing a challenge for which he or she has sought assistance. It is not unusual today for the consultees' expectations of how the consultant will work with them (i.e., the helping model) to be ignored. The theoretical perspective of the consultant/collaborator tends to be the primary factor influencing how the interaction takes place. To describe the helping approach by the theoretical perspective, e.g., behavioral consultant, ignores the fact that consultants with several different perspectives can "collaborate" or "consult," and therefore, is as misleading a term as collaborative consultation. The Chin and Benne (1976) types of change strategies presented earlier in this chapter, along with the model of Brickman and colleagues (1982), are important to keep in mind as we think about the consultation–collaboration continuum.

THE CONTROVERSY OVER BEHAVIORAL CONSULTATION

A recent critique of behavioral consultation (BC) as defined by Bergan and Kratochwill (1990) has led to a concern that the linking of changes in teacher behavior to changes in child behavior is not supported by conclusive evidence over the past 20 years (Witt, Gresham, & Noell, 1996a). These authors could find no efficacy studies demonstrating teacher behavior change. The BC under scrutiny relies primarily on indirect methods of assessment and is seen as minimally qualifying as behavioral; its reliance on "talk" is considered particularly troublesome as it utilizes consultee verbal descriptions of behavior, versus the consultant's being directly involved in the data collection process. The authors are particularly critical of this manner of collecting information in the BC problem identification approach, versus a behavioral analytic model in which functional assessment or a functional analysis is employed. The functional analysis approach attempts to determine the variables controlling behavior and, in doing so, identifies aspects of treatments that work. Furthermore, the use of teacher reports of treatment outcomes causes equal concern when that becomes the source of data used in judging efficacy (Witt, Gresham, & Noell, 1996b). Finally, the criticism of BC by Witt and others (1996b) is judged as even more damning of the *collaborative consultation* approach(es).

Erchul and Schulte (1996) argue that outcome data supports the efficacy of BC, so that while the BC approach may have weaknesses, it warrants continued use as an intervention. Also, the authors point out the compromise that consultants make in focusing on the consultee versus the client, so that one consultant can impact larger numbers of clients, must be taken into account in comparing an indirect service to a direct service. Furthermore they cite research suggesting that greater consultant involvement and control lead to greater student improvement. The recommendation that Witt and others (1996a) have made to use functional analysis over problem analysis also raised efficacy/efficiency issues for Erchul and Schulte (1996).

The foregoing debate about behavioral consultation will continue to be very important, not only in terms of the implications for the BC model, but also because it attacks a critical rationale for using consultation (i.e., indirect service) regardless of the theoretical background of the consultant. It frames the question as one of cost effectiveness—that is, whether a direct service approach with a client by an expert is not only more effective but more efficient than the indirect service approaches of consultation or collaboration. Furthermore, it has an unfortunate fallout for helping professions because it casts the debate in an "either–or" framework and thereby ignores the premise that a range of intervention approaches exists and that their appropriateness may be tied to the nature of the problem, characteristics of the "consultee," and the context in which the intervention takes place.

VOLUNTEERISM

One of the earliest parameters associated with discussions of consultation is that it is a voluntary process. That is, the consultation services are made known to the consultee, but the decision as to whether the consultee requests that service is his or hers alone. Typically, early descriptions of consultation involved an external consultant who was contracted to work within an organization, but consultees were not assigned with the understanding that they would contact the consultant. Thus, consultants at that time considered ways of "creating proximity" to the consultee (see Caplan, 1970). Even where the consultant was providing services to a group, such as school counselors in a school system, the consultee participants were not obligated to present cases. While not explicitly part of the definition of *consultation*, the principle of "take it or leave it" or accepting or rejecting the consultant's "ideas"— was sacrosanct as far as the consultee's independence was concerned. Similarly, there is an understanding that the consultee can terminate at any time. Subsequent models often do not address this premise or, in fact, proceed with a different premise critical to their change strategy.

The increasing emphasis on consultation offered by professionals *internal* to the system, those who are employees of the system, raises some interesting questions and dilemmas when the volunteerism principle is considered. Often the consultation evolves out of a service offered by the consultant (a school psychologist's assessment of a teacher's pupil) or is recommended by a supervisor or team. Since both the consultant and consultee are employees of the same organization, it can be argued that the consultant assumes some responsibility for the client by virtue of being an employee. The ambiguity of the relationship vis à vis client outcome, or even obligatory interventions, is something that can be a factor contributing to the flow or outcome of the consultation.

Harris and Cancelli (1991) examined the role of teacher volunteerism at each stage in the consultation process as well as the ramifications of other consultant–consultee contacts leading to a problem-solving situation, and made suggestions for maximizing the efforts of nonvoluntary consultation. For example, they emphasize the need to ensure greater opportunity for consultees to assess their willingness to enter the process itself, balancing the amount of effort required to participate in the process (e.g., data collection), presenting social influence strategies, and fostering ownership of the problem during the consultation process. They contend that consultees who understand the process and the expectations involved are expected to be more committed to the consequences of the service. An informed choice is a critical element in the results.

The research on what appears to be a critical variable is still scant, and our knowledge of how to work with the professionals who are quasivolunteers or have no desire to volunteer is even scanter. Who are the consultees that are least likely to seek help? Should they be a target of the consultant's service, particularly if they are internal to the system?

ASKING FOR HELP

For some consultation models it is important that the consultee ask or request the service. The motivation to seek assistance is considered an important element in the success of the consultation. In other models this question does not seem to be of much concern; it could be that the impetus for change is assumed, or the nature of the change process or its target relies less on the "felt need" of the consultee in order that some degree of consultation success be realized. Yet we know little about the dynamics of asking for help, particularly consultation assistance. It could be a powerful variable determining who does and does not seek consultation, how involved they become, and the nature of the intervention planning and implementation.

It has been proposed that one's views of who is to blame for a problem as well as who should be responsible for its solution can lead to different ways of behaving (Brickman et al., 1982). These orientations of whether or not individuals are responsible for causing their problems and solving them were further linked to models of helping and coping in the minds of helpers and recipients of the help. Brickman and colleagues (1982) proposed four such models: (1) people are responsible for problems and solutions; (2) people are not responsible for problems but are responsible for solutions; (3) people are not responsible for problems or solutions; (4) people are not responsible for solutions but are responsible for problems. In many instances, the help giver and help recipient are applying models that are out of sync with one another. Brickman and colleagues then go on to identify the *dilemma of helping.* It derives from the notion of help itself, because help would imply that recipients are not responsible for solving a problem.

Ironically, Brickman and colleagues present evidence showing that help givers benefit from helping even when recipients of the help do not. Assumptions of helping may benefit the helper more than the recipient of help. As a result of such findings, they present a number of research questions that require follow-up, such as: Are some models uniformly better than others or are different models best for different clients? Are models that tend to be discrepant from the client's initial assumptions more or less effective? Should models be applied consistently or change as consultees change their attributions? Do help givers burn out less using one model(s) versus another?

Based on the data in his study of consultation outcome, Macarov (1968) examined the psychological constraints associated with help. He noted the difficulty of asking for and taking help that some consultees experience. Consultees might present problems that were not real, or were not the ones most important to them, or were not the one problem they faced. For example, in one situation a consultant was distracted from developing a classroom management plan with a teacher by the consultant's own frustrations with a similar situation many years earlier when she was a teacher. The present consultee (a young teacher) broke down and cried, explaining she was really afraid and felt totally overwhelmed, which was the real reason she asked for classroom management consultation. Consultants must recognize that it is not easy to ask for help in a society that idolizes a "take charge," "on top of it" facade. In fact, seeking out help may be seen as a sign of weakness or at least may suggest that one's work needs to be monitored for other signs of shortcomings.

Macarov (1968) even detected problems on the part of consultees in accepting the word *consultation* because of its association with the act of receiving help. For example, the consultees in his study could accept help if it was described as occurring on a sharing or informational level or in some other way that suggested an informal context. By contrast, the label *consultation* seemed to imply a formal activity involving high-level expert help. Consultees clearly were uncomfortable in describing the service they received as consultation. As further support for this impression that help seems to be sought out in an informal context, Owen (1982) has suggested that the overwhelming bulk of society's interpersonal help-seeking and help-

giving commerce involves nonmental health professionals. Finally, Macarov (1968) found a clear preference among consultees in his study for information over advice. Information seemed to be easier to ask for and to have admitted receiving than other assistance.

Consultants, at minimum, should keep in mind these characteristics related to the process of helping, in terms of not only how terminology may affect the consultee but also what it means to the consultee. Consequently, it may be advantageous to emphasize the nature of the service rather than what it's called. As noted in Chapter Nine, a "collaborative problem-solving resource" may be a mouthful, but tastier than "consultant."

DEALING WITH CONSULTEE FEELINGS

In any problem situation there are likely to be feelings experienced by the consultee related to his or her self-concept, the client, or significant others in the organization. The issue of whether the consultant should deal directly with those personal feelings or choose an approach that deals with them only as they relate to the work problem was clearly more prominent in the early consultation writings (Caplan, 1970). At that time, the mental health consultation model was popular, and consultants were

---

The Consultant's Response to Student Learning Activity 13.3

The consultant became very direct with the principal and teacher in terms of describing the negative consequences of any attempt to "trap" this student in a stealing episode. In doing so, many of the consultees' observations of the disadvantages of such a solution to the problem that they mentioned in response to indirect probing by the consultant earlier in the session were reiterated. The consultant directly withdrew support for such a plan and advised against it. In order to positively redirect the teacher's apparent need to do something more and to ostensibly deal with her concern for the student (and save face), the consultant recommended the

following: (1) the teacher keep a list of reported missing items, (2) follow-up be made to determine if the items showed up, (3) the principal request similar information from other teachers who also had this student in class, (4) a follow-up conference be planned in two weeks, if none seemed to be necessary before then. At the second session no stealing or other incidents involving the student were reported nor were there reports of other thefts. The teacher reported that a more positive relationship did develop between her and the student. In fact, no changes were reported for the rest of the school year.

influenced by their therapeutic experiences and possibly psychodynamic training. Also, the nature of the presented problems in mental health consultation (i.e., involving emotional needs of clients) was such that it could be argued the needs of clients was likely to influence the emotional state of the consultee. As consultation methods evolved out of behavioral theories and consultation was offered under less "crisis" conditions, the consultee affect received less emphasis. Consequently, the priority of consultee affect may be related partly to the theoretical orientation of the consultant.

For Caplan (1970), recognition of personal feelings is important, but the explicit content of the consultation session is the work-related problem and ways of dealing with that problem. Although the technique of theme interference reduction is one exception to this rule, even that strategy is one in which relevant aspects of the problem remain the focus. Finally, mental health workers may by virtue of their stereotypic role in society and even style of interpersonal interaction suggest a degree of sanction for personal problems to be expressed by the consultee (Caplan, 1970).

Within the mental health consultation model Altrocchi (1972) identifies two variables that can be related to the choice of dealing directly or indirectly with consultee feelings: the personality of the consultant and group versus individual consultation. Some consultants are more comfortable in discussing emotions while being relatively open and communicative individuals. There are some advantages in such a focus, but it can unnecessarily complicate the consultation effort and even shift the emphasis more in the direction of counseling or therapy.

Altrocchi finds support for a direct approach when mental health consultation takes place with groups. He argues that groups stimulate affect and support its expression, but at the same time naturally tend to control such expression by setting limits. Providing the affect is shared by the group and does not reflect pathological qualities and is directed to the work problem, he recommends discussing such reactions under general rules set up and sanctioned by the group.

The consultee's personality and the nature of the problem are two additional considerations that need to be assessed in making this decision. In general, however, it seems best to acknowledge affect and its immediate influence on the consultation; to do otherwise would be insensitive. Consultants should be supportive resources for identifying appropriate professionals that can help consultees with personal problems.

THE INVOLVEMENT OF THE CONSULTANT

The degree to which consultants should take some active intervention on behalf of consultees should be one of the questions addressed by consultants as they engage in the consultation process. For example, should consultants participate in acquiring information for consultees, contact individuals on their behalf, advocate in their interests, and in general help turn the planning of consultation into action?

Decisions regarding the consultant's behavior of "doing for" the consultee are attributed to tactical and ethical viewpoints (Macarov, 1968). In the tactical view such behavior preempts the growth of the consultee. It clearly may result in a quicker and more efficient resolution of a problem. However, the long-term objectives of fostering better problem solving and increasing the degree to which consultees handle such matters in the future may be diminished. From the tactical perspective, the preferences, needs, and competencies of the consultee will play a role in determining involvement, but so will the model of choice, an issue addressed in earlier chapters. It seems reasonable then that the involvement decision be built into an evaluation mechanism to determine the extent to which consultees learn to function without involvement of the consultant, or the extent to which consultees see such activities on the part of the consultant as acceptable and helpful. Another tactical consideration for consultants when deciding on the degree of consultee learning to promote is the amount of turnover in the organization. If the board member receiving the consultation is in his or her last term or last year, or the consultee-teacher's husband is soon to graduate from the local university with a Ph.D., the advisability of active consultation versus a growth-centered variety of consultation takes on other dimensions. Growth-centered consultation goals might be more defensible economically when used with consultees who will remain with their organization.

The second consideration influencing involvement is of a more ethical nature. It involves the "right" of the consultant to encourage a consultee to intervene or take action of a certain type. Should the consultant influence those with whom she or he is working to consider and/or adopt goals or activities particularly when they do not coincide with those originally requested by the consultee? Under what constraints, if any, should the consultant operate? Such questions need to be explored by the consultant prior to any consultation and perhaps discussed with the consultees under each contract. Certainly, taking action on behalf of the consultee should be addressed. As this review is conducted, the consultant needs to take note that consultees may wish them to be directive and action oriented, particularly as the consultee's anxiety and/or lack of confidence increases and the client problem looms prominently in their mind. "Yet, the questions of self-determination, the right to participate in decisions affecting one, the knowledge that one is responsible for the success or failure of an effort, remain" (Macarov, 1968, p. 126).

The ethical consideration also has its more practical component. The reinforcement of a dependent relationship is one outcome that the consultant must be aware of and guard against. Stringer's (1961) observation from the early consultation era still seems to be true. "No one, apparently, will object to being called a consultant. The term has prestige value, the quietly unassailable dignity of a hallmark" (p. 85). Appreciative feedback from the consultee who relies on an assertive consultant can be very seductive.

The limits on the consultant stem from his or her personal philosophy, training, consultation model(s), and experience. As mentioned earlier, there are limits to the model that is practiced, the

ethics of the consultant's profession, and the expectations of the organization. Other roles filled by the consultant in the organization may also come into play. Finally, the nature of the request as well as the preference and experience of the consultee will also need to be assessed when considering involvement. Consultation does not need to be confined to the communication between the consultant and consultee, but the consultant should carefully consider the implication of his or her actions on behalf of the consultee.

TO MANIPULATE OR NOT TO MANIPULATE

The term manipulation generally has such a negative connotation that consultants sometimes overreact when asked about its role in their professional practice. To some, it permeates all interpersonal interactions; to others, manipulation represents, the intentional act of one person to influence another in a secretive manner. Still others may take a more positive view of manipulative acts when they are conceptualized as a professional technique. This issue has an obvious relationship to the one just presented—the involvement of the consultant—and should be read with the former discussion in mind.

It has been argued that consultation involves change and, as such, the professional change agent is a potential manipulator (Lippitt, 1973). Lippitt argues that consultants should be proactive in demonstrating their values and beliefs about how consultees learn and change. The question is not whether the consultant has a right to change others, but rather, "What right have I to withhold myself and skills from helping change to take place in a direction consistent with my convictions?" However, Lippitt also stresses that an *ethical methodology* based on those values and beliefs about the change process should guide the process of deciding what changes are needed and evaluating the changes that take place. Using such an ethical methodology, the consultant considers his or her task-oriented motivation, level of collaboration, experimental problem solving, approach toward coping, and accountability. Briefly, the consultant should be task-oriented rather than prestige-oriented, meaning that the resulting change is better than what existed before, and the matter of who gets credit for it is not important. In addition, all individuals affected by the change should be involved in the planning and development. The methods of problem solving are seen as experimental; from this position, all plans have the potential of being tried. Next, Lippitt argues that the method of change in addition to being democratic and scientific should leave those involved in a better position to solve future problems. Finally, consultants are accountable to themselves and others affected by their efforts.

Kelman (1965) has taken a slightly different tact in dealing with the question of manipulation. He acknowledges that the practitioner (consultant) is faced with a basic dilemma, that is, if that consultant believes in the fundamental value of a human being's freedom of choice, then manipulation of others' behavior constitutes a violation of that right. Kelman does recognize, however, that behavioral change will inevitably involve some degree of manipulation, and since consultants constantly are involved in change activities, they are faced with an ethical problem. The two horns of the dilemma are: (1) manipulation of others violates a fundamental value; and (2) there is no system or formula for arranging conditions wherein manipulation is totally absent. Kelman argues that the practitioner must remain conscious of the potential for imposing values on the consultee. Otherwise, the consultant may become totally insensitive to this phenomenon and/or get carried away with good intentions so that no controls will be considered.

Kelman recommends three steps to deal with this challenge. First, as was already hinted at, the consultant should increase awareness of the manipulative characteristics of the consultation intervention. The consultant must be able to recognize and label the values that permeate his or her approach to consultation and change and communicate those orientations to the consultee. In a sense, this notion of sharing introduces a sense of mutuality between the consultant and consultee that serves as a control

on the manipulative aspects of the relationship; in Kelman's notion, the consultee is able to "talk back" to the consultant. Second, he encourages building "into the change process itself procedures that will provide protection and resistance against manipulation" (p. 42). Thus, he would minimize the consultant's values while maximizing the consultee's values as the dominant criterion for change. Kelman strongly advises the practitioner to minimize the direct and indirect constraints he places on the consultee. Finally, he recommends that the consultants use their professional skill as well as their relationship with consultees to increase the consultees' range of choices and ability to choose. This latter point involves the value of enhancing the freedom and creativity of consultees.

Caplan and Caplan (1993) point out that both the "consultant" and the "manipulator" attempt to identify the weakness of the consultee. However, while the consultant's objective is to help the consultee overcome and deal with those shortcomings, the manipulator uses such information to diminish any resistance on the part of the consultee toward being influenced. While manipulation is seen as a "covert method of influence," Caplan and Caplan correctly point out it can be used in a positive or negative way. Thus, the more critical questions for them is how the consultee would react to a professional who espouses a helping orientation, but keeps hidden "the details of his thinking about them during the encounter and the mechanism he is using to influence them"(p. 353). The notion, on the part of the consultee, of tacit consent is critical for them, as is the recognition that not everyone is a candidate for consultee-centered techniques. The onus of the decision of

---

Student Learning Activity 13.4

Take the three steps recommended by Kelman (described in the "manipulation" section of this chapter) and identify specific ways they could be implemented during an initial consultation session. Role-play specific strategies if possible.

whether to use manipulation is up to the consultant according to Caplan and Caplan (1993), but "we can be confident that since we have developed an institutional framework for consultation that allows most consultees voluntary choice about invoking our help, we can safely leave it to them to keep away from us if they so desire" (p. 355).

The above discussion presents some ideas regarding a characteristic of consultation that has had less attention than it deserves—the abuse of the consultation service. The issue perhaps is not that consultants are or have become unscrupulous in their practice, but rather the need to recognize the role of their values in the process. Given such awareness they are less likely, in Kelman's terms, "to make full use—either unwittingly or by design—of the potential for manipulation that they possess" (p. 43).

Another variation on this manipulation theme has become more prominent since the first edition of this book. It involves the growing research on the acceptability of interventions by the teacher, which was presented in an earlier chapter. That research has grown out of a concern that interventions may be underutilized or improperly implemented (see Witt & Elliott, 1985). Skinner and Hales (1992) found that teachers in their study operated from a different theoretical perspective than the behavioral consultant. Therefore, they suggested that such consultants should foster an atmosphere in which teachers feel free to adapt ABP procedures to fit with their particular teaching style. They also encourage behavioral consultants to be aware of the differences between themselves and the consultees, and modify their own language.

One study examined the hypothesis that a consultee's failure to implement an intervention can be due to the intervention's lack of acceptability. It was found that the use of individualized intervention rationales that matched consultees' perceptions about themselves, the target problem, and their theory resulted in a greater acceptance of the implementation (Conoley, Conoley, Ivey, & Scheel, 1991). Conoley and colleagues suggest that searching for one rationale is futile; rather, the "consultants should be able to explain a wide array of interventions from many different perspectives" (p. 69). It appears that be-

havioral consultation intervention plans were the focus of concern of this study.

In another twist on this matter it was reported that in *behavioral* consultation the consultants with higher dominance scores (i.e., an interpersonal relationship in which one person frequently accepts the other's conversational direction) were judged to be more effective by consultees (Erchul, 1987). It has been argued that consultant dominance involves *cooperation,* in that "cooperation suggests there is a leader and a follower," and *teamwork,* in that "teamwork subsumes and implies further that who leads and who follows may change over the course of the consulting relationship" (Erchul, 1992, p. 365). Indeed, the use of interventions by the consultee is a concern worthy of serious attention by consultants. If perceived time to implement interventions is a critical factor influencing the consultee's receptivity to those ideas, then it is also a critical variable to understand. However, as it may be discerned that lukewarm acceptance or even failure to cooperate may be due to differences in the theoretical orientation of each of the participants, some thorny questions arise. What are the implications of making the language describing an intervention more palatable so that the consultee does not recognize the theoretical orientation of the consultant? This approach of "making the medicine go down" raises questions about the consultant's attitudes toward the consultee and values in the consultation process. If nothing else, such motivation to practice in this manner suggests that the consultant embraces an expert model of consultation, which is not negative in itself, except if the consultee is led to believe the consultation is collaborative. Thus, the motivation and use of this strand of research findings need careful reflection by the consultant.

CONSULTANT AS SCHOLAR PRACTITIONER

The scholar practitioner is seen as a professional who has training in both research and practice, and who, despite the differences (see Table 11.1) in procedural and philosophical differences between these areas, utilizes both in the service of clients. The professional (practitioner) who is trained in this way is a *consumer* of research findings that influence how he or she practices, an *evaluator* of his or her interventions which produces data not only for accountability purposes but as further feedback on the intervention, and a *scholar* in terms of sharing data with colleagues informally and/or formally (Barlow, Hayes, & Nelson, 1984). This type of background for the consultant has the advantage of improving his or her practice while advancing the input from the field regarding the current wisdom used to guide training activities and the actual consultation practice. The latter objective is viewed by Lambert (1993) as representing the upper rung on a developmental continuum defining the scholar practitioner. Her four stages are "(1) having knowledge of and keeping up with the development in the fields related to practice; (2) being able to select an appropriate theory or theories for framing or conceptualizing practice problems; (3) being able to test an application and weigh the value of competing theories or to devise an explanation that is the merger of perspectives; and (4) being able to communicate successful problem solving to others" (p. 184).

The consultant's role as practitioner must have first priority in the resolution of the presented problem. The most appropriate intervention applied in the least time-restricted manner is expected by the consultee and the organizational leadership. Anything less than an all-out effort to achieve the goals of the consultation is very questionable. At the same time, we argued in Chapter Eleven for the importance of accountability and the need for a data-based approach to consultation. But what of the responsibility of the consultant to contribute to the knowledge base regarding consultation from the perspective of the practitioner? Should the consultant's research expertise be in the area of consuming empirical findings and/or applying those findings, or should the consultant be expected to advance the state of the art via more research?

Lewin (1946) was the first to advocate for an *action research* approach for social scientists as a means to help solve practical problems in specific social situations. Thus, research was undertaken, but often with the objective of addressing a specific problem. As Rapoport (1970) stated, this type of research "aims to contribute both to the practical concerns of people in an immediate problematic situation and to the goals of social science by point collaboration within a mutually acceptable ethical framework" (p. 499). This position clearly attempts to capitalize on both the evaluation and research potential in any data-collection strategy. However, Meade, Hamilton, and Yuen (1982) note that those working from an action research model seem prone to subordinate research to action and those working from the evaluation paradigm tend to subordinate raising questions to providing answers.

But the blurring of the intent of the activity, that is, research versus evaluation, can lead to some serious ethical problems. Consultants should never do research in the name of evaluation. The consultant needs to face up squarely to the reasons for asking certain questions or using certain measures. Similarly, if the data-collection techniques result in higher costs or delayed services, the practices may be questionable additions to the consultation service. Finally, there may be a "review of research with human subjects" committee that may need to be contacted in the organization to review the consultant's plans as well as the need to consider written consent from the consultees to collect certain data. Again, this committee can be helpful in making these determinations as can reference by the consultant to his or her professional ethical codes of conduct. For further discussion of these points, the reader may want to consult Barlow et al. (1984). In addition, Table 13.1 provides a summary of the distinctions between purely evaluative or research effort in consultation versus a data-collection approach that emphasizes both to varying degrees.

RESEARCH DIRECTIONS

The consultation area is not suffering from a dearth of research studies. From 1978 to 1985 approximately 173 data-based studies in consultation were referenced in *Psychological Abstracts* and 81 doctoral dissertations reported in *Doctoral Dissertations International* (Pryzwansky, 1986). Also, the research seems to be relatively evenly distributed among the training as well as process and outcome dimensions of

TABLE 13.1 The Distinction between Evaluation, Consultation Evaluation, Consultation Research, and Research

OBJECTIVE	PURE EVALUATION	CONSULTATION EVALUATION/ RESEARCH	CONSULTATION RESEARCH/EVALUATION	PURE RESEARCH
Contribution to scientific knowledge	None	Secondary	Primary	Primary
Problem solving for consultee/ client benefit	Primary	Primary	Secondary	None

From D. Barlow, S. Hayes, and R. Nelson, *The Scientist-Practitioner.* Copyright © 1984. All rights reserved. Reprinted by permission of Allyn & Bacon.

consultation. Although reviews of that research period are not currently available, at least two reviews have found similar outcome effectiveness results in mental health consultation and school consultation. It has been reported that 76 to 78 percent of the reviewed studies reported a partial success rate (Mannino & Shore, 1975b; Medway, 1979). However, the interpretation of those findings remains highly qualified due to the nature of the research. The interest in this area has continued and certainly has not peaked for school psychologists (Gutkin & Curtis, 1999), special educators (see Chapter Nine), and school counselors. Several review articles are available that address the continuing challenges of research in this area along with suggestions for methodology and content (Gresham & Noell, 1993; Gutkin, 1993; Pryzwansky, 1986).

Methodological difficulties and fragmented studies often characterize research in this area. The problem most often associated with consultation research is the lack of control groups or inadequate comparison groups. It is understandably difficult to find an appropriate control as it is questionable for the practitioner to withhold a service that can be of immediate assistance to a consultee because of a research objective. It is for that reason that time series designs are recommended for research considerations (Medway,

1979; Meyers et al., 1979; Meade et al., 1982). Outcome-type studies are badly needed, particularly outcome research that measures multiple outcomes and is based on actual consultation efforts. Gresham and Noell (1993) present a number of research alternatives to the traditional methods of reporting research outcomes. They encourage a functional outcome analysis with benefits considered from both an objective standard (e.g., decreased aggression) as well as subjective (phenomenological) consideration. Also, it has been observed that all too often consultants in training serve as the "consultant" in the study without much thought given to this factor as an influence on the results. The need seems to be for more illustrations of cases on which data have been collected in a systematic manner. In their review of directions in consultation research, Froehle and Rominger (1993) echo the call of earlier authors for an operationalizing of the scientist–practitioner orientation for the consultant.

The available research also seems to be plagued with the definitional problems discussed in this book. Meade et al. (1982) have recommended that process studies of consultation be operationally based on the actual model of consultation being investigated. The theoretical propositions of the model should be spelled out to avoid the atheoretical (and thus unreproducible) studies that often typify the research studies. Specifically, Meade et al. (1982) point out that little has been done in the way of investigating different consultant behaviors at the various stages of consultation. The authors go on to identify a second implication for doing research in this area: the advantage of defining explicitly what is taking place in the consultation process. It has been suggested that all researchers provide a minimum set of information data for their studies. In addition to describing the consultation model and descriptions of the problem dimensions, consultation goals and evaluation should be delineated (Pryzwansky, 1986). Such standardization of information would help others in generalizing the findings and provide a structure for future applications. There has been an agreement in the literature that case study designs are badly needed and do not have to be subjective; designs can be of the quantitative type (Kratochwill, 1985) or the qualitative type (Pryzwansky & Noblit, 1990). The hypothesis-generating value of the latter type of investigations can be extremely helpful to this still-new service delivery approach. Similarly, Gutkin (1993) has stressed the importance of analogue research to the literature. Similarly, Henning-Stout (1994) proposes a "connected approach" to consultation research that relies on engaging the consultation participants in the description of the process. This perspective encourages going beyond the methodological choice and argues that simultaneous emphasis should be given to the social context and the "social-philosophical-political context out of which the research questions are generated" (p. 17).

Finally, it seems that consultation research will need to mirror the complexity of the process itself. Thus, multiple measures of process and outcome dimensions of consultation involving consultee and client variables should be employed in an attempt to establish interrelated interactional relationships among independent and dependent variables. At the same time, greater collaboration between consultants, trainers, and researchers will need to occur, especially during this time of limited resources. It seems that only when we shift to this more complex plane of investigation and conceptualization will we be able to realize the full potential of consultation.

SUMMARY

It is important to recall that consultation is an evolving strategy and, as a result, there are many unresolved issues. Should the consultant control the process? What is the best way to establish the limits of consultation? Which is better: direct or indirect services? Perhaps the major implication of these unresolved issues is that consultants who are trained today need to keep abreast of tomorrow's developments, in both the theoretical and the empirical domains.

TIPS FOR THE PRACTITIONER

1. Make a list of the issues identified in this chapter. What is your opinion about the "rightness or wrongness" of the opposing points of view surrounding these issues? Write about how your opinions on these issues are likely to influence your practice.

REVIEW QUESTIONS

1. Identify an additional issue that belongs in this chapter and present the current position that exists with respect to that issue.
2. Make a list of the positions you would take with respect to each of the issues presented in this chapter.
3. After reading this chapter, make a list of the issues that have been raised in Chapters 1–12 that were not covered in this chapter.
4. What will be the strategy you use in selecting a consultation approach?
5. Should consultants do research? Present a rationale for your answer.

REFERENCES

Alpert, G., & Kranzler, G. D. (1970). A comparison of the effectiveness of behavioral and client centered approaches for behavioral problems of elementary school children. *Elementary School Guidance and Counseling, 5,* 35–43.

Altrocchi, J. (1972). Mental health consultation. In S. E. Golann & C. Eisdorfer (Eds.), *Handbook of community mental health.* New York: Appleton-Century-Crofts.

Babcock, N. L., & Pryzwansky, W. B. (1983). Models of consultation: Preferences of educational professionals at five stages of service. *Journal of School Psychology, 21,* 359–366.

Bardon, J. I. (1982). School psychology's dilemma: A proposal for its resolution. *Professional Psychology, 13,* 955–968.

Bardon, J. I. (1985). On the verge of a breakthrough. *The Counseling Psychologist, 13*(3), 353–362.

Barlow, D. H., Hayes, S. C., & Nelson, R. O. (1984). *The scientist practitioner.* New York: Pergamon Press.

Bergan, J. R., and Kratochwill, T. R. (1990). *Behavioral consultation and therapy.* New York: Plenum.

Blake, R. R., & Mouton, J. S. (1976). *Consultation.* Reading, MA: Addison-Wesley.

Brickman, P., Rabinowitz, V. C., Karuza, J., Coates, D., Cohn, E., & Kidder, L. (1982). Models of helping and coping. *American Psychologist, 37*(4), 368–384.

Caplan, G. (1970). *The theory and practice of mental health consultation.* New York: Basic Books.

Caplan, G., & Caplan, R. B. (1993). *Mental health consultation and collaboration.* San Francisco, CA: Jossey-Bass.

Chin, R., & Benne, R. D. (1976). General strategies for effecting changes in human systems. In W. G. Bennis, R. D. Benne, R. Chin, and K. E. Corey (Eds.), *The planning of change* (pp. 22–45). New York: Holt, Rinehart and Winston.

Conoley, J. C., & Conoley, C. W. (1981). Toward prescriptive consultation. In J. C. Conoley (Ed.), *Consultation in schools* (pp. 265–293). New York: Academic Press.

Conoley, C. W., Conoley, J. C., Ivey, D. C., & Scheel, M. J. (1991). Enhancing consultation by matching the consultee's perspectives. *Journal of Counseling and Development, 69,* 546–549.

Cowen, E. L. (1982). Help is where you find it. *American Psychologist, 37,* 385–395.

Davis, J. M., & Sandoval, J. (1991). A pragmatic framework for systems-oriented consultation. *Journal of Educational and Psychological Consultation, 2*(3), 201–216.

Erchul, W. P. (1987). A relational communication analysis of control in school consultation. *Professional School Psychology, 2,* 113–124.

Erchul, W. P. (1992). On dominance, cooperation, teamwork, and collaboration in school based consultation. *Journal of Educational and Psychological Consultation, 3,* 363–366.

Erchul, W. P. (1999). Two steps forward, one step back: Collaboration in school-based consultation. *Journal of School Psychology, 37*(2), 191–203.

Erchul, W., & Schulte, A. C. (1996). Behavioral consultation as a work in progress: A reply to Witt, Gresham, & Noell. *Journal of Educational and Psychological Consultation, 7*(4), 345–354.

Froehle, T. C., & Rominger III, R. L. (1993). Directions in consultation research: Bridging the gap between science and practice. *Journal of Counseling and Development, 71,* 693–699.

Fuchs, D., & Fuchs, L. S. (1992). Limitations of a feel-good approach to consultation. *Journal of Education and Psychological Consultation, 3,* 93–97.

Fullan, M., Miles, M. D., & Taylor, G. (1980). Organizational development in the schools: The state of the art. *Review of Educational Research, 50,* 121–183.

Gallessich, J. (1982). *The profession and practice of consultation.* San Francisco: Jossey-Bass.

Gallessich, J. (1985). Towards a meta-theory of consultation. *The Counseling Psychologist, 13*(3), 336–354.

Gresham, F. M., & Noell, G. H. (1993). Documenting the effectiveness of consultation outcomes. In J. E. Zins, T. R. Kratochwill, & S. N. Elliott (Eds.), *Handbook of consultation services for children* (pp. 249–273). San Francisco: Jossey-Bass.

Gutkin, T. B. (1993). Conducting consultation research. In J. E. Zins, T. R. Kratochwill, & S. N. Elliott (Eds.), *Handbook of consultation for children: Applications in educational and clinical settings* (pp. 227–248). San Francisco: Jossey-Bass.

Gutkin, T. B. (1999a). Collaborative versus directive/prescriptive/expert school-based consultation: Reviewing and resolving a false dichotomy. *Journal of School Psychology, 37*(2), 161–190.

Gutkin, T. B. (1999b). The collaboration debate: Finding our way through the maze. Moving forward into the future; A response to Erchul (1999). *Journal of School Psychology, 37*(3), 229–241.

Gutkin, T. B., & Curtis, C. R. (1999). School-based consultation theory and practice: The art and science of indirect service delivery. In C. R. Reynolds & T. B. Gutkin (Eds.), *The handbook of school psychology,* 3rd ed. (pp. 598–637). New York: John Wiley & Sons.

Harris, A. H., & Cancelli, A. A. (1991). Teachers as volunteer consultees: Enthusiastic, willing or resistant participants? *Journal of Educational Psychological Consultation, 2*(3), 217–238.

Henning-Stout, M. (1994). Consultation and connected knowing: What we know is determined by the questions we ask. *Journal of Educational and Psychological Consultation, 5*(1), 5–21.

Hylander, I. (2000). *Turning processes: The change of representations in consultee-centered case consultation* (Linkoping Studies in Education and Psychology No. 74). Linkoping, Sweden: Linkoping University.

Hylander, I. (2004). Analysis of conceptual change in consultee-centered consultation. In N. M. Lambert, I. Hylander, & J. H. Sandoval. *Consultee-centered consultation* (pp. 45–61). Mahwah, NJ: Erlbaum.

Kazdin, A. E. (1980). Acceptability of alternative treatments for deviant child behavior. *Journal of Applied Behavior Analysis, 13,* 259–273.

Kelman, H. C. (1965). Manipulation of human behavior. *Journal of Social Issues, 21*(2), 31–46.

Kratochwill, T. R. (1985). Case study research in school psychology. *School Psychology Review, 14,* 204–215.

Lambert, N. M. (1993). Historical perspective on school psychology as a scientist-practitioner specialization in school psychology. *Journal of School Psychology, 31,* 163–193.

Lauver, P. J. (1974). Consulting with teachers: A systematic approach. *Personnel and Guidance Journal, 52,* 535–540.

Levine, G., Trickett, E. J., & Kidder, M. G. (1986). The Hemes promise, and challenge of mental health consultation. In E. V. Mannino, E. J. Trickett, M. F. Shore, M. G. Kidder, & G. Levine (Eds.), *Handbook of mental health consultation* (DHHS Publication No. ADM 86-1446, pp. 505–520). Washington, DC: US Government Printing Office.

Lewin, K. (1946). Action research and minority problems. *Journal of Social Issues, 2,* 34–46.

Lippitt, G. L. (1973). *Visualizing change.* Fairfax, VA: NTL Learning Responses Corp.

Macarov, D. (1968). *A study of the consultation process.* New York: State Communities Aid Association.

Mannino, F. V., & Shore, M. F. (1975a). Effecting change through consultation. In F. V. Mannino, B. W. MacLennon, & M. F. Shore (Eds.), *The practice of mental health consultation* (pp. 478–499). New York: Gardner Press.

Mannino, F. V., & Shore, M. F. (1975b). The effects of consultation: A review of empirical studies. *American Journal of Community Psychology, 3,* 1–21.

Martens, B. K. (1993). A behavioral approach to consultation. In J. E. Zins, T. R. Kratochwill, & S. N. Elliott (Eds.), *Handbook of consultation services for children* (pp. 65–86). San Francisco: Jossey-Bass.

Meade, C. J., Hamilton, M. K., & Yuen, R. (1982). Consultation research: The time has come, the walrus said. *The Counseling Psychologist, 10*(4), 39–51.

Medway, F. J. (1979). How effective is school consultation?: A review of recent research. *Journal of School Psychology, 17,* 275–282.

Meyers, J. (1973). A consultation model for school psychological services. *School Psychology Review, 11,* 5–15.

Meyers, J., Parsons, R. D., & Martin, R. (1979). *Mental health consultation in the schools.* San Francisco: Jossey-Bass.

Monroe, R. (1979). Roles and status of school psychology. In G. D. Phye & D. J. Rechly (Eds.), *School psychology: Perspectives and issues* (pp. 39–65). New York: Academic Press.

Palmo, A. J., & Kuzniar, J. (1972). Modifications of behavior through group counseling and consultation. *Elementary School Guidance and Counseling, 6,* 258–262.

Pryzwansky, W. B. (1974). A reconsideration of the consultation model or delivery of school-based psychological services. *American Journal of Orthopsychiatry, 44,* 579–583.

Pryzwansky, W. B. (1986). Indirect service delivery: Considerations for future research in consultation. *School Psychology Review, 15,* 479–488.

Pryzwansky, W. B., & Noblit, G. W. (1990). Understanding and improving consultation practice: The qualitative case study approach. *Journal of Educational and Psychological Consultation, 1,* 293–307.

Randolph, D. L., & Hardage, N. C. (1973). A comparison of behavioral consultation and consultation with model-reinforcement group counseling for children who are consistently off task. *Journal of Educational Research, 67,* 103–107.

Rapoport, R. N. (1970). Three dilemmas in action research. *Human Relations, 23,* 499–513.

Reynolds, C. R., Gutkin, T. B., Elliott, S. N., & Witt, J. C. (1994). *School psychology: Essentials of theory and practice.* New York: John Wiley & Sons.

Schein, E. H. (1969). *Process consultation.* Reading, MA: Addison-Wesley.

Schulte, A. C., & Osborne, S. S. (2003). Why assumptive worlds collide: A Review of Definitions of Collaboration in Consultation. *Journal of Educational and Psychological Consultation, 14*(2), 109–138.

Sheridan, S. M. (1992). What do we mean when we say "collaboration?" *Journal of Educational and Psychological Consultation, 3*(1), 89–92.

Skinner, M. E., & Hales, M. R. (1992). Classroom teachers' "explanations" of student behavior: One possible barrier to the acceptance and use of applied behavioral analysis procedures in the schools. *Journal of Educational and Psychological Consultation, 3,* 219–232.

Stringer, L. (1961). Consultation: Some expectations, principles, and skills. *Social Work, 6*(3), 85–90.

Tindal, G., Parker, R., & Hasbrouck, J. E. (1992). The construct validity of stages and activities in the consultation process. *Journal of Educational and Psychological Consultation, 3,* 99–118.

Witt, J. C. (1990). Collaboration in school-based consultation: Myth in need of data. *Journal of Educational and Psychological Consultation, 1,* 367–370.

Witt, J. C., & Elliott, S. N. (1985). Acceptability of classroom intervention strategies. In T. Kratochwill (Ed.), *Advances in school psychology, Vol. 4* (pp. 251–288). Hillsdale, NJ: Lawrence Erlbaum Associates.

Witt, J. C., Elliott, S. N., & Martens, B. K. (1985). The influence of teacher time, severity of behavior problem, and type of intervention on teacher judgments of intervention acceptability. *Behavior Disorders, 17,* 31–39.

Witt, J. C., Gresham, F. M., & Noell, G. H. (1996a). What's behavioral about behavioral consultation? *Journal of Educational and Psychological Consultation, 7*(4), 327–244.

Witt, J. C., Gresham, F. M., & Noell, G. H. (1996b). The effectiveness and efficiency of behavioral consultation: Differing perspectives about epistemology and what we know. *Journal of Educational & Psychological Consultation, 7*(4), 355–360.

Name Index

SUBJECT INDEX